Daughters of Hecate

Daughters of Hecate

Women and Magic in the Ancient World

edited by

KIMBERLY B. STRATTON

with

DAYNA S. KALLERES

OXFORD
UNIVERSITY PRESS

Oxford University Press is a department of the University of Oxford.
It furthers the University's objective of excellence in research, scholarship,
and education by publishing worldwide.

Oxford New York
Auckland Cape Town Dar es Salaam Hong Kong Karachi
Kuala Lumpur Madrid Melbourne Mexico City Nairobi
New Delhi Shanghai Taipei Toronto

With offices in
Argentina Austria Brazil Chile Czech Republic France Greece
Guatemala Hungary Italy Japan Poland Portugal Singapore
South Korea Switzerland Thailand Turkey Ukraine Vietnam

Published in the United States of America by
Oxford University Press
198 Madison Avenue, New York, NY 10016

Library of Congress Cataloging-in-Publication Data
Daughters of Hecate : women and magic in the ancient world /
edited by Kimberly B. Stratton with Dayna S. Kalleres.
p. cm.
Includes bibliographical references and index.
ISBN 978-0-19-534271-0 (pbk. : alk. paper) — ISBN 978-0-19-534270-3 (hardcover : alk. paper) —
1. Magic—History. 2. Women—History. 3. Witchcraft—History. I. Stratton, Kimberly B., editor.
BF1621.D37 2014
133.4'3093—dc23
2014001799

1 3 5 7 9 8 6 4 2

Printed in the United States of America on acid-free paper

To all the children of Hecate born during the production of this volume

Asher Levi and Jonah Read Copeland
Alexander Reed Fleming
Thea Brooklyn Kelleher
Amelia and Jack Kirkegaard
Isobel Claire Lewis
Rosemarie Geertje and Annabel Catharina Luijendijk
Nicholas and Alex Osadchuk
Arthur Barlow Stratton

Contents

Preface

Kimberly B. Stratton and Dayna S. Kalleres

DAUGHTERS OF HECATE presents a collection of chapters on the topic of women and magic in the Mediterranean world during the ancient and late antique periods. This volume gathers together pointed investigations by leading scholars from the fields of Classics, Judaic Studies, and early Christianity, which illuminate as well as interrogate the persistent associations of women with magic. Since Homer's depiction of Circe's pernicious brew in the Odyssey, which turned Odysseus's sailors into swine (*Od.* 10.210–213), women have been typecast as experts in dangerous supernatural arts. In Greco-Roman tradition the allegation that women engage in nefarious magic practices operated in a variety of contexts and appears in a broad range of texts from different genres, including tragedy, erotic verse, philosophical discussion, and invective. This image of female sorcery passed into Christian discourse where, in moralizing homilies, it served to denigrate women, justifying their subjugation to male control. Eventually, it contributed potent ideological ammunition to the witch-hunts of the early Modern period. This book investigates the basis of this inveterate, gendered stereotype by combining critical theoretical methods with research into literary and material evidence from across the ancient Mediterranean: a diverse array of materials including Christian homily, Latin love elegy, and Jewish Aramaic incantation bowls.

Daughters of Hecate is divided into three sections, each of which challenges presumed associations of women and magic by probing the foundation of, the processes underlying, and the motivations behind the stereotypes. The result is a thorough and more nuanced consideration of the problem than that accomplished in previous studies. In light of this volume's stated commitments, the first chapter, "Interrogating the Magic–Gender Connection," surveys the history of scholarship on women and magic in order to situate the contributions of this volume in that theoretical conversation. The following sections engage the subject of women and magic in antiquity from three angles: 1) Fiction and Fantasy:

Gendering Magic in Ancient Literature, 2) Gender and Magic Discourse in Practice, and 3) Gender, Magic, and the Material Record. This interdisciplinary approach illuminates the reality as well as the ideology and fantasy behind ancient constructions of the "witch." It avoids, as well as deliberately questions, simplistic readings that accept literary depictions at face value, consequently seeking to unearth the elements constituting such stereotypes. Furthermore, by juxtaposing the components of this portrayal with contradictory historical materials, *Daughters of Hecate* offers fresh and pertinent insights into the construction of both gender and magic in the ancient world.

This book's unique strength derives from the diverse critical methodologies scholars working in related ancient fields have used to explore the theme of women and magic in a wide array of ancient cultures and contexts. The cumulative result provides a more nuanced and critical exploration of the topic, while avoiding reductive approaches that generalize from one cultural pattern or tradition. In fact, the chapters in this volume uncover complexities and counter-discourses that challenge, rather than reaffirm, many gendered stereotypes taken for granted and reified by most modern scholarship. Due to its theoretical vigor, furthermore, *Daughters of Hecate* holds relevance in contemporary culture as well. The category of the witch continues to operate today, informing vilifying portraits of powerful women. Popular cinematic presentations of jealous girls dabbling in occult practices, for instance, demonstrate one of the many residual effects of this denigrating stereotype as do Photoshopped pictures of Hillary Clinton in a witch's hat that circulate the Internet. For this reason, understanding the historical and cultural origins of women's association with magic is as relevant as ever.

The editors would like to extend their generous appreciation to the following people without whom this volume would never see the light of day: Cynthia Read at Oxford University Press, who agreed to take on the volume when it lost its original home. She has also exhibited stalwart patience beyond even that of Job, waiting for us to finish the volume. Wendy Lochner at Columbia University Press encouraged us in our initial pursuit of this project and valiantly fought for its publication at Columbia; when that fell through, she graciously allowed us to reuse strong reviews and recommendations that she requisitioned. The contributors to the volume have been extraordinarily patient throughout the long process that brought this book to fruition and deserve their own applause. Three contributors to this volume in particular have shared their editorial expertise at various stages of the project, which has improved certain chapters in the volume: David Frankfurter, Annette Yoshiko Reed, and Nicola Denzey Lewis. Five undergraduate and graduate research assistants helped with formatting the chapters and compiling the unified bibliography: Simon Gurofsky, Véronique Émond-Sioufi,

Ian Hartlen, Lauren Tansley, and Yevgeniya Kramchenkova. We would like to thank each of them for their contribution as well.

Most of all, I would like to thank Dayna S. Kalleres for agreeing to co-edit this volume with me. Her editorial insights improved many papers, especially mine. As importantly, her enthusiasm and support for the project bolstered my flagging spirits at critical junctures. Thank you Dayna!

Abbreviations follow the *SBL Manual of Style: For Ancient Near Eastern, Biblical, and Early Christian Studies* (biblical, Jewish, and Christian texts) and *The Oxford Classical Dictionary* (Greek and Roman literature). Additional abbreviations, when used, are provided by the authors.

Contributors

Kirsti Barrett Copeland is Associate Dean in Undergraduate Advising and Research and Lecturer in the Religious Studies Department at Stanford University. Her research focuses on mining otherworldly visions for socio-cultural data. Her recent publications include "The Earthly Monastery and the Transformation of the Heavenly city in Late Antique Egypt" in *Heavenly Realms and Earthly Realities in Late Antique Religions*, ed. Ra'anan S. Boustan and Annette Y. Reed.

Nicola Denzey Lewis is Visiting Associate Professor of Religions of the Ancient Mediterranean at Brown University. With research interests in both Gnosticism and intellectual history and the social history of late antique Rome, she is the author of three books: *The Bone Gatherers* (2007); *Introduction to "Gnosticism": Ancient Voices, Christian Worlds* (2012); and *Cosmology and Fate in Gnosticism and Graeco-Roman Antiquity: Under Pitiless Skies* (2013).

Yaakov Elman is Herbert S. and Naomi Denenberg Professor of Talmudic Studies at Yeshiva University, and an associate of the Harvard Center for Jewish Studies. He has recently completed a monograph on changing elite cognitive styles in Ancient Near Eastern thought (Babylonian, biblical, Zoroastrian, rabbinic and Sasanian) from 2000 BCE to 1000 CE.

David Frankfurter is Professor of Religion and Aurelio Chair in the Appreciation of Scripture at Boston University. His publications have covered topics of magic, demonology, popular religion, apocalypticism, and Christianization in Roman and late antiquity and include *Religion in Roman Egypt: Assimilation and Resistance* (1998) and *Evil Incarnate: Rumors of Demonic Conspiracy and Satanic Abuse in History* (2006).

Fritz Graf is Distinguished University Professor of Classics at the Ohio State University and director of its Epigraphy Center. He specializes in Greek and Roman religions and mythologies, Greek and Roman literature and its reception, and ancient epigraphy. He is the author of numerous books and articles on the topic of Greek religion, literature, and magic, including *Magic in the Ancient World* (1997), *Apollo* (2008), and with Sarah Iles Johnston *Ritual Texts for the Afterlife* (2nd edition 2013).

Dayna S. Kalleres is an Associate Professor at University of California, San Diego. Her publications delve into the issues of ritual theory, Christian demonology and the relationship between magic and religion in late antiquity with a particular interest in the urban sphere and include *City of Demons: Violence, Ritual, and Christian Power in Late Antiquity* (2014).

Rebecca Lesses is Associate Professor of Jewish Studies at Ithaca College. Her research focus is on texts of ritual power and mysticism from Judaism in late antiquity, a topic covered in her 1998 publication, *Ritual Practices to Gain Power: Angels, Incantations, and Revelation in Early Jewish Mysticism* and in a 2001 article, "Exe(o)rcising Power: Women as Sorceresses, Exorcists, and Demonesses in Late Antique Judaism," in the *Journal of the American Academy of Religion* 69 (June 2001), 343–375. She is currently working on a book on Jewish women and ritual power in late antiquity, titled *Angels' Tongues and Witches' Curses: Jewish Women and Ritual Power in Late Antiquity*.

AnneMarie Luijendijk is Professor of Religion at Princeton University. As a historian of early Christianity, a scholar of the New Testament, and a papyrologist, she brings new voices, often marginal or obscure, to the fore and into conversation with the more dominant voices of history. She is the author of *Greetings in the Lord. Early Christians and the Oxyrhynchus Papyri* (2008) and of the forthcoming *Forbidden Oracles. The Gospel of the Lots of Mary* (2014).

Elizabeth Ann Pollard is Associate Professor of History at San Diego State University, where she teaches courses in Greco-Roman history, historiography of witchcraft, women in antiquity, and world history. She has published articles exploring images of witches in Roman art, Roman-Indian trade, and the impact of world historical models on traditional Greek and Roman history, the most recent of which is "Indian Spices and Roman 'Magic' in Imperial and Late Antique Indomediterranea," in the *Journal of World History* 24 (March 2013), 1–23. She is currently working on a book entitled *Women and Witchcraft Accusation in the Roman World*, which investigates the relationship between the representations and accusations of women's use of magic and the actual rituals that women conducted.

Annette Yoshiko Reed is Associate Professor of Religious Studies at the University of Pennsylvania. She is the author of *Fallen Angels and the History of Judaism and Christianity* (2005), and the co-editor of four volumes, most recently *Jews, Christians, and the Roman Empire: The Poetics of Power in Late Antiquity* (2013).

Pauline Ripat is an Associate Professor of Classics at the University of Winnipeg. She is the author of several articles and book chapters dealing with magic, divination, status, and communication in the Roman world, and is co-editor of *Themes in Roman Society and Culture* (2013).

Barbette Stanley Spaeth is Associate Professor of Classical Studies and Co-Director of the Institute for Pilgrimage Studies at the College of William and Mary. Her specialty is Roman religion, and she is the editor of *The Cambridge Companion to Ancient Mediterranean Religions* (2013) and author of *The Roman Goddess* (1996) and of recent articles in *Rome and Religion: A Cross-Disciplinary Dialogue on the Imperial Cult* (2011), and *Sub Imagine Somni: Nighttime Phenomena in Greco-Roman Culture* (2010). She is co-founder and past president of the Society for Ancient Mediterranean Religions, as well as past president of the Alumni/ae Association of the American School of Classical Studies at Athens.

Kimberly B. Stratton is an Associate Professor in the College of the Humanities at Carleton University, in Ottawa. Her research covers the fields of early Christianity, Rabbinic Judaism, as well as Greco-Roman culture and religion. Her book, *Naming the Witch: Magic, Ideology, and Stereotype in the Ancient World,* won the Frank W. Beare Award from the Canadian Society of Biblical Studies (2008). Recent articles on magic or other aspects of ancient religion appear in *Biblical Interpretation*, *The Cambridge Companion to Ancient Mediterranean Religions,* and *the Cambridge History of Magic and Witchcraft in the West.*

Ayşe Tuzlak earned her PhD from Syracuse University and is currently teaching at Bow Valley College in Calgary, Alberta. Her academic interests include ancient constructions of masculinity, the relationship between magic and the economy, and theological debates about *ex opere operato.*

Daughters of Hecate

I

Interrogating the Magic–Gender Connection

Kimberly B. Stratton

The more women, the more witchcraft.
HILLEL, *Mishnah Avot*

All [witchcraft] comes from carnal lust, which is in women insatiable.
Malleus Maleficarum

THIS BOOK INTERROGATES the association of women and magic, which as these two epigraphs suggest, has culturally endured since antiquity.[1] One historian of the Early Modern Period tellingly remarked that "witch hunting is tantamount to women hunting."[2] Yet, closer analysis of historical records reveals that, in fact, the association of women with magic does not appear as monolithic and one-dimensional as people often assume. Men, in many cases, constitute a fair share of those accused of working magic in both antiquity and the Early Modern Period;[3] where a gender bias appears in the accusations and representations, a closer look at the specific details and patterns that emerge reveal large variation, depending on culture and context.[4] Yet, despite this ambiguous history, stereotypes of women's sorcery persist to the present day, shaping not only representations of magic and witchcraft in popular culture, but scholarly analysis of historical data as well.[5]

In full disclosure, this volume began with the same preconception: namely, the expectation that women were more often represented and accused of magic than men were in ancient writings, and I sought an explanation for this bias. In addition to drawing together leading scholars who work on the topic of magic and gender in antiquity, I looked to the vast amount of scholarship on Early

Modern witch-hunts to find a sophisticated and satisfying explanation for the gendering of magic, which could be utilized to frame the ancient material in this volume. Instead I discovered a plethora of competing explanations, each one contingent upon particular historical data and limited largely to that context. When a scholar did formulate a general explanation for the preponderance of female victims of witch-hunts, a scholar working in another time period or locale quickly contradicted it. My quest to understand why women are associated with magic thus grew more frustratingly inconclusive as my research progressed.

As the chapters for this volume started to arrive, Dayna and I began to realize that they also undercut the original intention of the volume: many of the contributions revealed texts that do not identify women with magic. Or, as Annette Reed persuasively demonstrates in chapter 4, scholars themselves push a gendered interpretation, enamored, as many of us are, by revealing and critiquing ancient misogyny. This volume, thus, evolved into a much more complex and nuanced view on the topic of women and ancient magic than Dayna and I had anticipated; as we read through the contributions, we began to realize how the scholarship, which stood between antiquity and our place as moderns, contributed in some degree to the gendered stereotyping. The chapters in this volume, then, reveal instances where women are stereotyped or accused of practicing magic as well as surprising examples where they are not, although we would expect them to be.

This chapter surveys scholarship on women and magic, including theoretical explanations for the Early Modern witch-hunts. It explores how the powerful women-magic stereotype contributed not only to demonological treatises and trials of accused witches, but shaped contemporary scholarship on them as well. Interrogating this conception, thus, promises to cast some light on our fascination with this stereotype. It also serves to situate the chapters in this volume within the larger body of scholarship on the topic of women and magic. Furthermore, I hope that this volume's interdisciplinary examination of literary stereotypes, actual accusations of magic (or their absence), and material evidence for magic (or accusations of it) provides a rich and complicated view of women and magic that may be useful for scholars working in other historical periods or disciplines.

With the advent of second-wave feminism in the 1970s and 1980s, scholars examined women's history more critically, interrogating the misogyny of Early Modern witch-hunts. In the 1990s and early 2000s, classicists and scholars of ancient religion extended this investigation to the gendered portraits of magic from ancient literature, proposing different explanations for the gendered stereotyping of magic, and sometimes reinscribing that very bias. Contributions to this volume take the next step in that inquiry individually and collectively by interrogating and denaturalizing the women-magic association. This volume contributes to contemporary debates about gender construction, women's history, and magic, by offering fourteen original studies on the intersection of gender and magic in the ancient world from three different perspectives: fictional imaginaries, the discourse of magic in social practice, and material evidence for women's use of magic.

In order to situate the contribution of individual chapters in this volume, I will analyze previous approaches to understanding the frequent gendering of magic from antiquity to the Early Modern witch-hunts. Although the witch stereotype was only just emerging in the ancient world and operated under a variety of different vocabulary (*saga*, *pharmakeutria*, *striga*, *mekhashefa*), I will use the terms "witch" and "sorceress" interchangeably to refer to stereotypes of women's magic in this chapter, indicating my sense of the continuity between early and late representations. Similarly "magic" and "witchcraft" both appear throughout this chapter to refer to the ritual practices of witches/sorceresses; the language reflects the language and conceptualization of the historical period under discussion. In other words, I use the form of magic discourse appropriate for each context. Contributors to this volume provide their own definitions of magic when necessary and as appropriate for their studies.

Stalking the Women–Magic Connection

Innumerable theories and approaches to the study of women and magic appear during the course of the last four decades. These include attributing witch-hunts to the misogyny of demonological treatises, denying the importance of gender altogether in favor of other heuristic factors, such as economics or social change, or proposing psychological explanations on the grounds that the fantastic rites attributed to witches escape rationalization and can only reflect deeply subconscious fears and drives. I divide the approaches into five discernible categories, which is somewhat artificial since certain studies combine different approaches and strategies that cross the boundaries of my classification scheme. Nonetheless, this rubric provides a useful way to organize the broad array of studies on magic and women, the sheer number of which exceeds my ability to discuss them all here. This analysis is intended to present a general overview of the history of scholarship on women and magic, focusing on important studies that have shaped it; no doubt, I miss many significant contributions as well.

Guilty as Charged

Many scholars accept accusations, representations, and confessions as more or less accurate, arguing either that women did engage in the magical activities attributed to them, or engaged in (ritual) practices that were misrepresented as magic, or believed themselves to be in league with the Devil for various social and psychological reasons. The first group of scholars includes some classicists, for whom literature constitutes a primary source for reconstructing the political, religious, and social history of the ancient world; it is no surprise therefore that they rely substantially, although not entirely, on literary portraits to reconstruct women's magic practices in antiquity. While there is a large amount of material evidence for magic employed in antiquity, the extant spells pose a problem for understanding women's use of magic since the overwhelming majority are commissioned by men and were most likely produced by literate male ritual specialists.[6] Different approaches to solving this conundrum have surfaced in recent years. For example, Matthew Dickie compares material evidence for erotic magic (both men's and women's) with literary depictions and concludes that the majority of magic practiced by women stems from prostitutes seeking to protect their financial interests; they either sought to remove rivals or to attract and keep clients.[7] He postulates a demimonde populated by sexually available young women and wealthy young men looking for love affairs and, possibly, concubinage.[8] Elsewhere he draws on stereotypes in Roman satire and Old, Middle, and New Comedy to argue that aging prostitutes are responsible for the majority of women's magic.[9] By triangulating from stereotype to stereotype—that of drunken old women (who, therefore, must be prostitutes), to drunken sorceresses (even though this itself may be part of an invective charge)—he argues that most sorceresses were drunk old whores, who relied upon magic to stay in the game despite diminishing natural charms. (By contrast, see the treatment of the same material in the chapters by Frankfurter and Kalleres in this volume.) This reconstruction entirely recapitulates invective satire, and reveals more about the activity of gendered stereotypes in Roman literature than about women's actual practice of erotic magic.[10]

Christopher Faraone proposes a different theory to explain the discrepancy between material evidence for ancient Greek love magic (in which men predominate) and literary depictions of magic (in which women predominate). Based on these two types of evidence, Faraone argues that men used aggressive attraction spells (*agōgai*) to draw women for sexual gratification while women used love potions (*phitres*) to protect existing relationships that were in danger. Prostitutes, however, who played the "male" role as sexual aggressors, also used *agōgai* to draw and keep clients.[11] As in the case of Dickie, Faraone's reconstruction of women's magic relies on literary portraits, which he accepts at face value, although they are fictionalized products of a male author's imagination and likely reveal very little if anything about the private rituals of ancient women.[12]

In the context of the Salem witch trials, most scholars reject the entire proceedings as fraudulent and politically motivated. Chadwick Hansen bucks this trend by arguing that Puritan New Englanders commonly practiced forms of white magic for healing and protection, and that other more nefarious sorts of magic, such as the use of poppets to harm an enemy, also appear to have been widely used.[13] Based on trial records and eyewitness accounts, Hansen suggests that at least three of the women accused at Salem very likely practiced both types of magic, and illicit forms of divination, practiced by the young accusers, opened the door for hysterical seizures and finger-pointing. In other words, while the vast majority of accused witches at Salem were entirely innocent, he does not dismiss the likelihood that some of them may have practiced some form of magic either to heal, protect, or harm. The accusing girls' own anxiety about dabbling in magic provoked their hysteria and symptoms of possession.

In these three studies, scholars accept the representation of women's magic at face value and use it to reconstruct women's actual ritual practices along lines that follow the official record and reaffirm the stereotypes. Not all scholars accept the literary depictions or accusations so easily. Instead they discern behind the charges innocuous practices that male authors seek to denigrate by labeling them magic. Tal Ilan, for example, attributes the identification of women with magic in rabbinic literature to women's cooking, healing, and caring for the sick. Similar activities practiced by men do not attract this pejorative label; the gender of the actor constitutes the single difference between women's magic and men's medicine or religion.[14] Most rabbinic writings portray women's practices as magic and a threat to the community. In the case of Abaye's foster mother, however, Rebecca Lesses points out that rabbis rely upon and preserve her expert knowledge of medicinal and apotropaic remedies.[15] Similarly, incantation bowls from late antique Syria and Mesopotamia indicate that men as well as women used bowls for protection from demons, who were believed to cause sickness, death, and infertility (see Elman's contribution to this volume).[16] Thus, both Lesses and Ilan attempt to reconstruct the actual nature of women's ritual practices upon which accusations of magic rested and do so with nuanced awareness of the ideology of gender at work in these male-authored texts.

Many historians of Early Modern witch-hunts also accept the accusations and confessions as true to some degree, but try to discover why a woman would choose to become a witch or come to see herself as one even if she did not engage in harmful magic. One theory suggests that she despaired of salvation, having been told throughout her life that women are morally and spiritually inferior to men and naturally inclined toward evil and Satan. She may have sought, in desperation, to improve her social and financial situation through an alliance with the Devil because she believed God had abandoned her to an intolerable fate.[17] Some accused women could have been hysterical or mentally ill and imagined themselves to be witches with supernatural powers.[18] Another explanation posits that women in vulnerable situations deliberately cultivated the reputation of being a witch to protect themselves from abuse by social superiors. Or they cultivated this reputation to self-aggrandize for its own sake.[19] Scholars have also plausibly proposed that when aged female beggars were turned away without a donation they left muttering, which was regarded as a curse or request for divine vengeance. This righteous anger could easily be interpreted as witchcraft if a sudden illness or badluck befell the stingy household.[20]

All of these explanations make sense of accusations and confessions without dismissing them as fraudulent or entirely coerced. In fact, it seems that while most accused witches (male and female) had to be tortured to produce an acceptable confession, others offered a confession fairly easily and even seem to have reveled in their identity as a witch. Lyndal Roper applies psychoanalytic theory to interpret these confessions and argues that confessing women did, in fact, come to regard themselves as witches and understood themselves to be in opposition to the church and society.[21] Roper discerns in the confessions extreme anger, hatred, and a sense of being marginalized and abandoned by society, the church, and God; she understands the confessions to reflect an act of splitting and denial. These women projected their hostile emotions onto the Devil: *he* gave them the poisonous powder, *he* told them to harm the infants, etc.[22] This psychological splitting allows them to accept their negative emotions and actions by attributing them to Satan.

I include Roper's study in this section, "Guilty as Charged," rather than in "Psychological Projection" because she accepts the confessions as more or less true: some accused women did perform acts of harmful magic (*maleficia*) attributed to them and saw themselves as servants of the devil. Alarmingly, Roper regards their confessions under torture and the subsequent retractions when torture has stopped to be games of "cat and mouse" between the witch and her interrogator, driven by sado-masochistic fantasies in which the roles of sadist and masochist are sometimes reversed as the witch gains the upper hand: "in this sadistic game of showing and concealing, the witch forced her persecutors to apply and reapply pain, prising her body apart to find her secret. Once it was found, she might herself identify with the aggressor."[23] While this approach treats accused witches as subjects and not merely passive objects of trial judges' misogyny—"mere consumers of male discourse"[24]—it too readily accepts the confessions at face value and posits the feelings of hostility and Otherness to the women *prior* to being accused and as a *motivation* for their witchcraft rather than as an emotional response to being accused and tortured to confess with no hope of ever being acquitted.[25]

These studies all discern at least a basis of reality in literary depictions, accusations, or confessions of women's magic; Ilan and Lesses more skeptically interrogate the pejorative literary portraits than other scholars do; they understand it to reflect a gender ideology that maligns women's apotropaic rituals and traditional roles as cooks and healers.

Gender Is Irrelevant

In response to early feminist historiography that denounced Early Modern witch-hunts as misogyny and an attempt to wrest control over female reproduction from the hands of wise women and midwives, new theories emerged that dismissed gender as meaningful at all and looked instead to social factors such as economic difficulties and social change. Keith Thomas's *Religion and the Decline of Magic* chronicles the many hardships faced by England's population during the late Renaissance and Early Modern Period, when urban fires, poor nutrition, and lack of reliable medical care made death and disease intimate acquaintances for even aristocratic families. He provides this social-historical background to substantiate his understanding that accusations of magic occur in response to misfortune, not misogyny.[26] Based on English trial records, he argues that most accusations of witchcraft stem from interpersonal conflict and tension following a sudden misfortune.[27] Irascible neighbors garnered the most suspicion when illluck occurred as did anyone displaying aggressive or odd behavior.[28] An extension of this theory argues that since women are more likely to resort to aggressive language and cursing than physical assault in situations of conflict, their bad language—identified as a curse—becomes the basis for a witchcraft accusation.[29] Thus, structural inequalities, not ideology or gender bias, determines the sex of the accused witch in many contexts.

Other scholars identify economic instability and social dislocation to be the primary triggers of witchcraft accusations. Ian MacFarlane, for example, identifies economic changes in the sixteenth and seventeenth centuries—which put pressure on rural peasant communities and their traditional social fabric—as a key contributing factor to the rise of witchcraft accusations and fears at that time. He posits that those who breached expected and traditional neighborly conduct, by refusing to make a loan or give to a needy widow, experienced guilt and a fear of divine reprisal, resulting in psychosomatic manifestations that were then blamed on the real victim in the encounter—the person turned away without assistance.[30] An accusation of witchcraft thus justified this maltreatment of the needy poor and assuaged any guilty feelings by extirpating the evil from society.[31] Paul Boyer and Stephen Nissenbaum discover similar factors at play in the Salem witch trials, where not only the destitute but the parvenu garnered negative attention: a swift rise in economic status could be seen as a sign of discontent as much as bitter muttering, and "testified to the power of unfamiliar economic forces to alter and shape a life."[32]

These scholars regard the origins of witch-hunting to be local, arising from conflicts generated in small rural communities strained by economic hardship and new individualistic impulses that tore at the fabric of traditional peasant societies and their communally based social networks. They argue that witch-hunts did not represent an ideological war against women but were driven by individual neighbors dealing with their personal conflicts, fears, and guilt.[33] Women constituted the majority of accused witches because they were poorer and more vulnerable to social and economic disruptions. This approach had a significant influence on subsequent studies of witchcraft persecutions, sidelining gender as an explanatory factor.

While Thomas, MacFarlane, and others who adopt the social approach identify local tension and economic hardship as the primary causes of witchcraft persecutions, Walter Stephens attributes witch-hunts to intellectual debates of the day.[34] Like social theorists, however, Stephens disregards gender as a significant contributing factor; instead he attributes witch persecutions to theological and scientific questions pertaining to the reality of demons. At a time when debates over the nature and capacity of demons intensified, witches offered proof that demons had physical bodies, which could interact in meaningful ways with human bodies. Thus, the obsession with obtaining minute details about sexual congress with demons, demonstrated by so many witch tribunals, reflects a desire to prove the corporal reality of demons rather than prurient fascination with sex.[35] Witches' confessions to copulating with demons offered positive proof for the reality not only of demons but, by extension, of the Devil and God; their testimony "confirm[ed] the reality of the world of spirit" at a time when scientific method and materialism were undermining confidence in religion.[36] Despite the near exclusive focus on women's delectation of demonic sex, however, Stephens dismisses misogyny as a contributing factor. On this point, he appears to protest too much.[37] If demonologists merely sought to prove the existence of demons, why did witch commissions torture women into implicating others in their testimony, expanding the network of violence? Furthermore, why execute these women in the pursuit of scientific inquiry if not for terror and social control? It would seem that belief in women's moral weakness and proclivity toward sin forms the basis of such an inquiry and reflects gender bias and misogyny with origins in the ancient material covered in this volume.

Gender Matters

A number of scholars point to the fact that women constituted the majority of prosecuted witches, in most times and places, to argue that gender *is* relevant: the crime of witchcraft may not have been "sex specific" but it was "sex related."[38] These scholars find that in certain locales the elite directed witch-hunts according to demonological treatises that identify witches as women, and used witch tribunals to enforce a moral agenda focused on controlling the behavior of women. Based on her research of Scottish witch-hunts, for example, Christina Larner argues that the elite controlled the demand for and supply of witches in a "conspicuous and unequivocal way."[39] According to Larner, the stereotype of the witch emerges from a combination of Aristotelian theory, which conceives women to be flawed men resulting from faulty conception, and Christian interpretations of the Genesis story that identify Eve as the mother of all sin.[40] Primarily, she regards a refusal to show deference or be submissive as the reason certain women were accused of witchcraft while others were not.[41] Thus witch-hunting constituted the hunting of women who refused to conform to societal expectations about proper (submissive) female behavior.[42] Witchcraft accusations enforced moral and theological conformity in response to women's new sense of independence and equality in Protestant Scotland.[43]

Joseph Klaits links Early Modern witch-hunts with zealous religious reform and the imposition of scholastic definitions of witchcraft as heresy and Satanic allegiance onto peasant communities (which previously saw witchcraft as individual acts of maleficence without any element of diabolism).[44] In accord with Larner, Klaits regards witch-hunts to be techniques of social control allied with rigid moral reforms. Both Catholic and Protestant reformers associated anything that did not match their standards of behavior with Satan, leading them to express suspicion, especially, of carnal pleasure.[45] This created a situation, according to Klaits, in which no outlet existed for men's sexual guilt except to project it onto women, who continued to be regarded as morally weaker and liable to Satan's seductions.[46] According to Klaits, therefore, the impetus from elite reformers and their particular obsession with sexual immorality—identified both with women and Satan—determined the gender bias of the witch-hunts.

A more recent study provides an especially rich view of the role of elite ideology on witchcraft prosecutions. Jonathan Durrant examines trial records from Eichstätt, Germany, which highlight the instrumental role played by the clerical establishment and their use of demonological interrogatories to direct trial proceedings and manipulate the testimony of accused witches.[47] Durrant reveals that accusations of witchcraft in Eichstätt emerged overwhelmingly from confessions extracted under torture, which compelled accused witches to name accomplices. Thus they did not name men and women out of malice, fear, or guilt, as other scholars have argued, but because they fit into the confession narrative constructed at the direction of the interrogators.[48] The commission interrogated the accused until their confession confirmed participation in a wide Satanic cult, details of which needed to conform to ideological preconceptions about witchcraft, including sexual subordination to the devil and his demons, attendance at nighttime sabbaths, and committing acts of maleficence, although this was of less interest to the commission than the prior two elements.[49] In fact the commission rarely sought witness testimony to verify harmful magical attacks and often ignored testimony that contradicted confessions of causing harm because it cast doubt on the veracity of the confessions themselves.[50]

Durrant concludes that women constituted the vast majority of convicted witches (85 percent in Eichstätt), not because they were poorer, more cantankerous, or more likely to rebel against authority, as other scholars suggest, but because of the stereotype perpetuated by demonologists, who identified women as weak-minded and more liable to demonic seduction, and by the use of suspect lists acquired through torture.[51] Durrant concludes that in Eichstätt the ecclesiastical elite directed witch-hunts in conformity with conceptions of witchcraft shaped by scholastic demonology, which believed women's concupiscence led to sexual relations with and allegiance to the devil. By situating sexual relations with Satan at the center of witchcraft proceedings, the Eichstätt witch commission reinforced efforts to impose stricter Catholic morality on the population. Thus, the definition of witchcraft employed by the trial commission determined the gender of witchcraft suspects in a conspicuous way.[52]

In New England, witch trials similarly functioned to enforce Puritan ideals of female conduct. Carol Karlsen's study of trial records and land deeds indicates that women accused of witchcraft often refused to accept a submissive role, whether by acting bitter and angry toward social superiors, including especially their husbands, or by inheriting property and acting as heads of households.[53] She argues that women who acted independently aroused suspicion or animosity; they violated their divinely appointed subordination according to Puritan ideology. This finding resonates with other scholars investigating New England witch trials, who point out that brash behavior and contentiousness constituted signs of witchcraft in women, but not in men.[54] As in Eichstätt, the link between witchcraft and women in New England reflected gender ideology: according to Puritan thought, God created woman to serve man and obey him. Any challenge to male authority constituted rebellion, which was the origin of witchcraft.[55] Thus, any sign of self-assertion in a woman drew comparisons to Eve and her mortal alliance with Satan.[56] For Karlsen and Durrant, therefore, religious ideology drove witch trials and supported harsh strategies of social control, which goaded women into being docile and cooperative by punishing those who chafed against authority.[57]

Further evidence for the link between gender ideology and witchtrials stems from England, where ironically, the witch-hunts were least virulent and did not rely on torture.[58] Two scholars identify the comparatively light witchcraze experienced in England with the improved social standing of women in that country, suggesting that gender ideology supported witchcraft persecutions in most other countries.[59] Alan Anderson and Raymond Gordon consider factors for women such as literacy rates, marriage laws, the right to own and control property, and the right to run a business as indicators that English women of the sixteenth century enjoyed a higher social status and more freedom and respect than their peers on the continent.[60] They also suggest that having a successful and long-reigning female monarch during a period of military success, colonial expansion, and increased peace and prosperity contributed to a higher opinion of the female sex than elsewhere in Europe or prior English history. They correctly point out that stereotypes must be credible to be effective at targeting certain groups for persecution;[61] the traditional view of women as morally weak and inclined toward concupiscence and sin faced disconfirmation in England where actual women demonstrated themselves to be rational, self-controlled, and capable—Queen Elizabeth represents the most outstanding example among these women but she was not unique.[62] The findings of Anderson and Gordon reinforce the troubling link between gender ideology, female subordination, and witch persecutions that scholars working on communities outside England identified.

Shifting the line of inquiry from ideology of the trial commission and judges to the self-understanding of accused women alters the way we understand the gendered performance of witchcraft confessions. Elizabeth Reis investigates how many women internalized Puritan conceptions of personal sin and guilt, which contributed to their self-identity as sinners and their consequent public confessions to witchcraft. Puritan thinking so firmly identified women with Satan, Reis argues, that women accused of witchcraft had already come to see themselves as deeply and inherently wicked prior to their trial and examination.[63] These women understood that any moral failing, no matter how trivial, amounted to a pact with the devil and, consequently, were willing to confess to being witches.[64] Women, on the other hand, who rejected the accusation of witchcraft needed to prove that they had never sinned.[65] No middle ground existed for women; they were either witches or saints. Any woman who attempted to defend herself appeared to be an insolent liar for even suggesting she was sinless. Men, on the other hand, Reis agues, did not defer to the members of the court but either boldly confessed to outrageous crimes, or denied them completely.[66] Men were not compelled to admit their inherent sinfulness and enter into the "drama of Puritan confession and forgiveness," which Reis regards as central to New England witch trials.[67] The court proceedings thus reinforced Puritan conceptions of proper gender roles; women admitted to their sinful, weak nature and demonstrated deference to male authority, while men did not.[68]

These approaches to understanding the Early Modern witch-hunts all identify gender ideology to be behind the willingness of both men and women to accuse female members of their community of malevolent acts of witchcraft. The belief that women formed an antediluvian association with Satan, compounded by the conviction of their moral and rational inferiority, enabled women and men to regard ordinary women as witches; even women accused of magic may have come to see their individual mistakes and moral failings in this light and confessed to being under Satan's control. Confessions to sex with demons or Satan and attendance at unholy midnight masses indicate the influence of elite theories of witchcraft that have their origin in classical and biblical stereotypes, except in England, where these ideas gained little ground, possibly reflecting the relatively higher social standing of women in that country.[69]

Psychological Projection

A number of scholars look to psychology for explanations of what appears to be an irrational fear of witches. Yet others point out that belief in witchcraft seemed entirely logical in its day and commensurate with high science; even the founders of modern rationalism (Bacon, Locke, Boyle) accepted it as part of a dualistic universe, according to Hansen.[70] If psychology does not explain why people believed in witchcraft, some scholars use it to illuminate why people believed witches were usually women.

Among classicists, John Winkler first drew attention to the divergence between evidence for the actual practice of magic in ancient Greece and literary representations of it.[71] He interprets the preponderance of aggressive (even violent) attraction spells enlisted by men to attract women as forms of psychological projection. Drawing on evidence for ancient magic from the *Papyri Graecae Magicae* (*PGM*), Winkler proposes a nighttime scenario in which a love-struck young man, suffering from the afflictions of *erōs*, directs a love spell against an unsuspecting young maiden, who sleeps peacefully in her own bed. The attraction spell (*agōgē*)—which can also be classified as a binding spell (*katadesmos*)—invokes chthonic powers to inflict suffering on the woman, causing her to experience the very same sleeplessness and tortured desire that, Winkler surmises, the magician does until she unites with him carnally. Winkler proposes that, by ritually projecting his suffering onto the victim and imagining his mastery over her, the magician gains mastery over his own affliction; the violent language thus reflects this process of splitting and projection. A similar projection, Winkler argues, accounts for the literary stereotypes of women's predatory sorcery. Portraits of women's magic project undesirable male behavior onto women: "both contrasts make sense as part of a cultural habit on the part of men to deal with threats of *erôs* by fictitious denial and transfer."[72]

Other classicists adopt Winkler's explanation with additions or emendations. Fritz Graf, for example, concurs that the literary depictions of women's predatory magic represent a form of denial and projection: "these stories remove erotic magic still further away from the world of men; they are thus a means for getting rid of what should not exist."[73] To this explanation he further proposes that such stories reveal a perceived threat posed by women's love to male autonomy and provide a way to explain and justify the mad love of a man for a woman. In sum, these scholars argue that representations of women's magic in ancient literature reflect men's collective efforts to explain away their own helplessness and bad behavior in the face of love's overwhelming power.

Returning to studies of Early Modern witch-hunts and gender stereotyping, several scholars draw inspiration from Melanie Klein's work on infantile persecution fantasies to explain the surge in witch persecutions during the sixteenth and seventeenth centuries. According to Klein, infants do not yet perceive their mothers as separate individuals but merely as an extension of their own needs and desires. They identify the mother solely with her breast and the sustenance and satisfaction that it provides, which is emotional as well as nutritive.[74] When the breast fails to present itself upon demand, the child resents and wishes to hurt the offending breast, which is also the mother.[75] As the child develops and begins to register that the sustaining breast, the "good" breast, is one and the same as the "bad" breast that withholds itself, the child fears retaliation for its violent fantasies and believes that its thoughts have really harmed the mother. Klein terms this early fear "persecutory anxiety."[76] A healthy child will overcome this persecutory fear associated with the mother through reassurance that the good breast will reappear; her anger does not harm the mother and the mother does not seek revenge.[77]

Klein's work helps explain the image of the witch as an inverted mother figure.[78] Mothers nurture and give life to human children. Witches' withered bodies, in contrast, nurture demonic imps, who bring death and destruction, on secret nipples hidden often in their sexual anatomy;[79] they are monstrous mothers gone bad.[80] Deborah Willis documents changes in Early Modern childrearing practices that sent infants to wet nurses and, later, to other homes to labor or apprentice.[81] This created a social atmosphere in which children did not develop past their infantile persecution anxiety but carried it into adulthood, where it readily projected onto mother figures who resembled but were not their actual mothers or nurses, thereby preserving the ideal image of and love for one's own mother.[82] Building on the socio-economic theory of witchcraft accusations proposed by Thomas and MacFarlane, Willis speculates that old women, especially if they seemed bitter or overly demanding, provoked these primal fears from childhood as the younger person feared retaliation from an elderly beggar to whom they refused assistance.[83]

According to Evelyn Heinemann, based on trial records, the accused witch usually began as the injured party: someone had refused to repay a loan or pay for eggs purchased on credit, or give alms to poor beggars.[84] The guilty party then began to interpret every strange incident or accident as magical revenge. Their guilty conscience may even have led to psychosomatic symptoms, understood to be magical attack.[85] She argues that the witch constitutes an imago—an internal image, containing feelings of aggression and fear of persecution projected onto another person. The court could not execute a witch unless she confessed;

she had to accept the projection and go along with it. Only her execution could destroy the guilty feelings, according to Heinemann.[86] The dualistic thinking of witch beliefs reflects psychoanalytic splitting: it divides the universe between absolute good and absolute evil, God and Satan, the Virgin Mary and her antithesis the witch.[87] Heinemann links this process to the child's earliest images and impressions, split between good breast and bad breast, satisfaction and hunger. Some children fail to integrate these two images during the stage of separation and individuation that follows the prenatal symbiosis with the mother.[88] If this process of integrating good and bad experiences does not succeed, Heinemann states, fears of persecution by images of absolute evil develop.[89] Because mothers are always female, the predominant projection of the witch image falls onto women.[90]

Lyndal Roper also draws on psychoanalytic theory to explain Early Modern witchcraft in her book, *Oedipus and the Devil: Witchcraft, Sexuality, and Religion in Early Modern Europe*. Like the scholars just cited, Roper finds Melanie Klein's work on infantile experience of attachment and envy to be significant for understanding both accusations and confessions of witchcraft. She expresses surprise at the disjunction between demonological treatises, the leading questions and concerns of the trial commission in Augsburg, where her research is based, and the preoccupations of women involved in the drama as both accusers and accused. Based on accounts of witches' sabbaths, cavorting with the Devil, flying on broomsticks, and illicit connubial contacts with Satan, she anticipated that sexual guilt would be the primary underlying psychic drive for witch beliefs. Instead, she found a preoccupation with parturition and the bodily needs of infants and mothers in the early days and weeks following birth.[91] Accusations of witchcraft centered on this period, when the lives of newborns are most vulnerable.

These scholars combine socio-economic explanations with psychoanalytic theory. Most notably, they draw on the theory of infant persecution fantasies proposed by Melanie Klein to explain both the preponderance of women accused as witches and the temporal concentration of witch-hunts in the sixteenth and seventeenth centuries. This was a period when changes in social structure and early education dramatically altered the experiences of childhood, fostering persecution complexes directed at inverted mother figures.

Binary Thinking

The final approach I examine regards the gendering of malevolent magic as the result of a purely intellectual process: binary thinking. Simone de Beauvoir first articulated the idea that women represent the primal Other in her groundbreaking book, *The Second Sex*: "[woman] is defined and differentiated with reference to man and not he with reference to her; she is the incidental, the inessential as opposed to the essential. He is the Subject, he is the Absolute—she is the

Other."[92] In order to understand why societies traditionally relegate women to this state of alterity, de Beauvoir begins with an analysis of human and animal biology to determine what, from a strictly scientific point of view, differentiates male members of the human species from female members. She discovers that the human female devotes more of her biological resources to reproduction—what de Beauvoir calls being "enslaved to the species"—than other mammals, whose physiology is encumbered with the processes of ovulation, conception, parturition, and lactation less time out of every year than human women.[93] The demands of these processes on the human female distract her from outward pursuits that express the human spirit and will toward transcendence, binding her to a limited world of immanent concerns.[94] Thus, men have the leisure and physical resources to develop tools, which allow them to conquer nature and each other, creating slaves to till the subdued land.[95] Women's bodies become another object to be subdued and harnessed for their reproductive capacities as men's desire for offspring increases with the development of private property that can be passed to heirs.[96] De Beauvoir locates the origin of women's Otherness not in biology alone, but rather in the effects that those biological limitations have on women's ability to shape their world and express mastery over it.

Having discerned the origins of women's social inferiority and subjugation, she turns to mythology for an understanding of the semiotic value of women's Otherness. She notes that from the moment the idea of the Other emerges in the process of man's assertion of Self as subject and free being, the Other poses a threat, a danger. Greek philosophy identifies Otherness, alterity, as negation, and therefore Evil.[97] This is the reason, de Beauvoir argues, that laws treat women with such hostility; by keeping women down they control the chaotic forces of nature that are identified with evil: "The Other—she is passivity confronting activity, diversity that destroys unity, matter as opposed to form, disorder against order. Woman is thus dedicated to Evil."[98]

In a similar line of thinking, Stuart Clark argues that demonologists did not primarily seek to persecute witches; they concentrated on other intellectual and scientific disputes of their day bearing on such questions as the workings of nature, processes of history, maintenance of religious purity, and what constitutes legitimate political authority. Regarding them as primarily misogynists bent on persecuting women misses the point of their endeavor; demonologists drew on commonly held attitudes toward women in their day to think about larger scientific and theological problems. He consequently criticizes attempts to explain the gendering of witch-hunts in terms of women's marginality, pointing out that such explanations do not clarify why witchcraft should be the accusation chosen to persecute women when any other crime would do.[99] Clark reverses the question to ask what it was about *witchcraft* that made it most commonly associated with women.[100] Belief in witchcraft survived three hundred years because it made sense in the worldview of the time; the association of witchcraft with women similarly emerged from centuries of accepted beliefs about women's nature, biology, and moral inferiority.[101]

The logic of binary thinking, Clark demonstrates, identified witches as female. Witchcraft functioned as the classic example of a Sassurian sign; it had no referent in the real world and thus signified purely through contrast to what it was not.[102] According to this approach, witchcraft constituted a parody of social order. It was anarchic, overturning proper social roles; its rituals parodied those of the church and secular society, inverting them in a topsy-turvy manner with celebrants of the black mass walking backward or on their hands.[103] Women, likewise, represented the opposite of men, and came to be identified with everything contrary in early European thought: women were intellectually and morally inferior, they were "imperfect creatures from whom depravity and evil were expected."[104] Clark thus draws the conclusion that witchcraft, which represents an inversion and opposition to civilized society and God's rule, naturally paired with women because women were conceived to be the opposite of men according to binary logic. Men conceptually belong on the side of God, the good, and social order—women on the side of Satan, evil, and chaos.

While Clark overly diminishes the influence that these demonological tracts had on shaping people's perceptions of witchcraft and the proceedings of witch trials, especially the contents of confessions extracted through torture, as others have demonstrated,[105] his identification of binary logic as the key to understanding the common link between women and witchcraft provides one of the clearest explanations of the phenomenon. As Clark notes and we have seen, most other explanations limit themselves to local contexts and do not apply universally. The notion of binary thinking—that women are the essential Other in male discourse—in contrast, offers a useful heuristic for understanding the ubiquitous gendering of nefarious magic.

It is important to keep in mind that even with intellectually satisfying explanations such as Clark's and de Beauvoir's, accusations of magic in much of Western history have not been gendered to the extent that the binary explanation would have us believe. Men also have been targets of witchcraft accusations.

Ubiquitous but Not Universal

Despite the common association of women and magic in occidental thinking, from antiquity to modernity the gendering of magic does not occur unanimously or universally. Christian literature from the first two centuries, for example, portrays magicians as male rather than female. In the contest over legitimacy and authority, accusations of magic functioned as powerful invective in the hands of certain Christian writers, who sought to derogate competing forms of Christianity by besmirching leaders of other churches.[106] In this ideological warfare, magic discourse targeted male religious leaders, maligning them as charlatans who use magic to seduce women in their flock. The lack of accusations against women stands out given the potency of the "witch" stereotype at that time and the apparent prominence of women in many heterodox churches. Why did heresiologists miss the opportunity to accuse these women of magic and to employ powerful denigrating stereotypes of female sorcery from Greek and Roman literature to marginalize them? Only in the mid-third-century CE, when the church began to be more established, do we see magic discourse used to marginalize a female prophetess (see Tuzlak's contribution to this volume). In previous research I propose that the gendering of magic in this and other cases reflects women's *relative* position as Other vis-à-vis male writers and thinkers, who control the public discourse: "where men define their cultures' discourses and configure their identities vis-à-vis women, gender and magic will naturally be combined as discourses of alterity. Where men or a community of men see themselves as marginal vis-à-vis other larger powers, *women* will operate as a mirror for Self rather than a foil for conceptualizing the Other."[107]

As de Beauvoir and Clark both argue, according to common binary systems of thought, women most often constitute the discursive Other to men. Stereotyping patterns in early Christianity, however, reveal that this position as Other is relative; when a community perceives itself to be threatened or marginalized, as early Christianity did, the outsider or opponent replaces women in the role of symbolic and psychological Other. Women, specifically Christian women, in this case, come to signify the vulnerability of the community, represented in early Christian writings as a violated virgin.[108] In both scenarios women are being used to think with; representations of women's magical victimage do not reflect a more straightforward view of women's lives than those that depict their nefarious magical activities.

In the Middle Ages, also, accusations of magic did not target women in any special way; men were accused of being witches or sorcerers in almost equal number to women.[109] According to Joseph Klaits, prior to 1400, women comprised only a slight majority of accused witches, which suggests "that originally witchcraft was not viewed specifically as a woman's crime. . . . As the crime was redefined in the fifteenth century to stress servitude to the devil, however, witchcraft became a gender-linked offense."[110]

Norman Cohn traces this transition from men to women and attributes it to three factors: fear of secret societies, peasant beliefs, and the rise of ceremonial magic in the Renaissance. First he identifies fear of secret societies meeting under cover of night, committing infanticide, cannibalism, and incest in an effort to overthrow civilized society. Such fears appear in antiquity; Christianity itself was persecuted for being a society of misanthropes, dedicated to incest and cannibalism, before Constantine's Edict of Toleration legalized the religion in 313 CE.

These fears resurfaced during the Middle Ages against dissident Christian groups, such as Bogomils, Cathars, and Waldensians, who were accused of similar crimes and of worshiping demons and Satan. By the twelfth century, heresy became explicitly identified as allegiance to Satan—the ultimate opposition to God, Christ, and civilized society—although this alliance is insinuated already in many early Christian apologies (Justin 1 *Apol.* 9, 14; 2 *Apol.* 5.5; Tertullian, *Apol.* 22).[111]

Peasant beliefs constitute the second contributing factor to the great witch-hunts. According to Cohn, peasants widely believed in women who traveled about at night either to cause harm or to bless homes. Some women themselves claimed to fly at night, commit infanticide, cause storms, and kill neighbors. Other women were welcomed as beneficial by peasants who observed a traditional practice of leaving goodies for these "ladies" who followed the goddess Diana at night and blessed well-kept homes that welcomed them. The educated cleric and secular authorities dismissed these traditions as impossible fantasies and folk superstition until the late fourteenth century.[112] Cohn argues that the shift toward believing in these night journeys made possible the witch persecutions a century later; attendance at giant sabbaths, where witches were purported to cavort with demons and swear allegiance to Satan, required that ordinary women have a way to leave their beds and travel great distances in a single night.[113]

Finally, Cohn identifies the rising popularity of ritual magic during the Renaissance as the third contributing factor. These magicians, highly literate (male) members of the clerical and secular intelligentsia, created demonic familiars whom they controlled through magical use of divine names. While these magicians apparently regarded this practice as commensurate with Christianity, because they used names of God and divine power to *control* the demons, the practice was outlawed by the church and prosecuted. In the fifteenth century, according to trial records, roles began to shift: magicians emerge as servants of the demons they originally controlled, bowing to them, kissing their hinder parts, and signing contracts with them at the price of their own souls. Consequently, women increasingly became associated with this type of magic; it was believed that women sealed pacts with the Devil through sexual congress with Satan or one of his demons, which left a mark on their bodies signifying the Devil's ownership.[114] Long-standing belief in women's moral weakness, passivity, and proclivity to seduction contributed to this shift from men to women as demons came to be seen as dominant to the human agents they previously served.[115] Thus, changes in demonological beliefs contributed to the progressive conflation of the feminine and demonic in the Early Modern Period, but this association did not prevail during the Middle Ages despite common assumptions.

Even in the Early Modern Period, at the height of the witch panics in much of Europe, men constituted a greater percentage of accused witches in certain places like Iceland, Normandy, and Estonia.[116] In Iceland, men outnumbered women both in accusations of witchcraft (120 to 10) and executions (22 to 1).[117] Kirsten Hastrup links these figures to traditional Icelandic beliefs in magic, which shaped stereotypes of the witch despite an influx of European ideas that associated witchcraft primarily with women.[118] In Icelandic tradition, magic and sorcery were associated with knowledge, specifically with words, charms, and poems as well as with the written word in the form of runes, believed to possess esoteric power.[119] Since this type of knowledge traditionally belonged to men, the introduction of learned European ideas about sorcery and witchcraft (*maleficium*) merged with the Icelandic conception of magic (*galdur*), producing a masculine stereotype of the witch. The first person to be tried and executed for witchcraft in Iceland, for example, was arrested for possessing runes in his home.[120] Hastrup further surmises that because the generic term for "witch" in Icelandic (*galdramaður*) was masculine, women went largely unnoticed in witch-hunts: they "were less 'visible' than men, when seen through the cultural filter of 'witchcraft' and 'knowledge'."[121] This is a key observation; Laura Apps and Andrew Gow demonstrate that, for the most part, in other parts of Europe, witchcraft terminology was gender-inclusive, using either the masculine form of a word to include both male and female witches, as well as to refer to witches in the abstract, or employing gendered terminology to refer to specific persons according to their sex. This demonstrates that semantically witches could be masculine or feminine without any linguistic bias toward either gender.[122]

Susanna Burghartz's comparative study of witch-hunts in Lucerne and Lausanne during the fifteenth and sixteenth centuries raises many interesting challenges for theories about witch-hunts and gender. While Lucerne's judges were secular and apparently uninfluenced by demonological treaties in their conceptualization of witchcraft, they nonetheless targeted women.[123] In Lausanne, on the other hand, ecclesiastical inquisitors directed witchtrials on behalf of the bishop, yet men surprisingly constitute 62 percent of those prosecuted despite the patently misogynistic ideology of the Catholic church at the time and the powerful influence of demonological treatises that identify witchcraft with female concupiscence.[124] Burghartz concludes: "the traditional hostility of the medieval church towards women, though it has been repeatedly adduced in the general context of witchcraft persecution, can only be accredited with a part in the creation of the classic, stereotypical image of the witch as a female being: it is certainly not enough to explain the realities of the persecutions themselves."[125]

As these studies demonstrate, the identification of women with magic and witchcraft did not occur universally. The cultural expectation that magic is gendered, however, sometimes skews scholarship and ends up reinforcing the very stereotypes scholars seek to interrogate and critique.

Gendered Preconceptions

Despite the cases that challenge an identification of witchcraft with women, cultural expectations shape not only popular witch stereotypes but, more significantly, bias scholarship on magic and witchcraft. Apps's and Gow's insightful monograph, *Male Witches in Early Modern Europe*, highlights the degree to which scholars working to explain Early Modern witch-hunts and demonological treatises skew their findings in favor of gendered stereotypes of witchcraft. Their study does not deny that witchcraft was predominantly associated with women in demonological treatises or that in most times and places women constituted a large majority of those accused and executed for witchcraft. Apps and Gow point out instances where preconceptions about the gendering of Early Modern conceptions of witchcraft cause scholars to overlook evidence for male witches, skewing the data even more. For example, in his study of the binary logic behind demonology's association of women with witchcraft, Stuart Clark asserts that the binary scheme was so fundamental to witchcraft beliefs that male witches could not be conceived.[126] In fact, Apps and Gow demonstrate that the most influential treatises on magic use the masculine term for witch when discussing witches abstractly, demonstrating that male witches could be entertained and that the language for witchcraft did not predetermine the gender of the accused, as Clark argues. Furthermore, woodcut illustrations depicting witches' atrocities also feature male as well as female witches.[127] So one question to ask is why has the association between women and witchcraft become so compelling in recent decades that it interferes with our ability to perceive or conceive of male witches when even the perpetrators of horrible witch trials, forced confessions, and brutal executions were less biased?

The industry of scholarship on witchcraft has thus contributed to essentializing the gendered conception of witchcraft in the Early Modern Period, imposing our own knowledge construct onto Early Modern thinkers and actors, for whom it is not entirely representative. In so doing, Apps and Gow argue, we erase the many male victims of European and North American witch-hunts who suffered and died as individuals just as their female peers did.[128] We furthermore reify a powerful gender stereotype, even while distancing ourselves from it and projecting it onto male demonologists, judges, and executioners.

The Contribution of This Collection

The chapters in this volume reveal that the gendering of magic in antiquity was as complex and multifaceted as it was in the Early Modern Period; as scholars of antiquity, we need to be sensitive to this complexity when interpreting data in order to avoid reductionist interpretations that project contemporary witch stereotypes onto ancient writers and actors. The chapters are organized into sections that consider the topic of women and magic in the ancient world from three different angles. Part I, "Fiction and Fantasy: Gendering Magic in Ancient Literature," examines literary portraits of women engaging in *artes magicae* and seeks to reveal the gendered stereotypes at work in these portraits as well as to interrogate facile interpretations of such portrayals. Part II, "Gender and Magic Discourse in Practice," considers how the discourse of magic operated in certain specific contexts and illustrates that magic was not always gendered where and how we would expect it to be. Part III, "Gender, Magic, and the Material Record," investigates material evidence for women's magic, unearthing the genuine concerns and needs that prompted women to use magic and, consequently, provides a more realistic picture of women's magic than the stereotyped characters of literary fantasy. As a collection, this volume challenges the essentialized conception of magic and gender that has pervaded both academic discourse and popular culture.

The chapters in Part I, "Fiction and Fantasy: Gendering Magic in Ancient Literature," emphasize the diversity and complexity of literary representations of women's magic. By eschewing simplistic and universalizing charges of misogyny in favor of more nuanced approaches, these chapters enable us to understand the social and contextual dynamics that shaped these portraits and contributed to the formation of enduring stereotypes of women and magic in Western thought. In chapter 2, Barbette Stanley Spaeth opens the discussion of fiction and fantasy by tracing images of the witch in Greek and Roman literature. By delineating differences between witches in the two cultures and situating the portraits in their historical contexts, she illuminates the ideological work that ideas of witches perform. Roman literature, for example, depicts sorceresses with more detail and verisimilitude than Greek literature does, situating them firmly in the real world. Roman witches are not characters from mythology removed from reality by time and divine parentage, but are portrayed as women one might encounter in the market on any day. The witch serves various roles in Greek and Roman imagination: she represents popular fears and fantasies either as a magical helpmate to the male hero in Greek mythology, or as a destructive, emasculating force in Roman literature, where she functions as a negative model for proper female comportment.

Biblical, post-biblical, and rabbinic literature also portray women as sorcerers, but as Rebecca Lesses demonstrates in chapter 3, the traditions vary substantially depending on the rhetorical and ideological context of the texts in which they appear. For example, Deuteronomy prohibits certain ritual practitioners and practices because they belong to the nations that surround Israel and threaten monotheistic devotion to YHWH. The bible employs the masculine form to name these practitioners indicating that they were at least as likely to be male as female. Exodus 22:17, in contrast, explicitly states that one should not allow a witch to live (using the feminine form of the word for magician, *mekhashefa*), decisively identifying magic (*khishuf*) with women rather than men. The bible, thus, presents an ambivalent position on the sex of magic practitioners in pre-Exilic Israel. Rebecca Lesses traces this ambivalence through second temple and rabbinic writings to show that while some texts do seem to identify women (or nations personified as women) with sorcery, other texts do not, concluding that the relationship between women and sorcery as presented in early Jewish sources resists reduction to a single charge of misogyny.

Continuing this line of argument, in chapter 4 Annette Yoshiko Reed traces the tradition of the Fallen Angels through the manuscript tradition of 1 Enoch and its later interpreters. She discovers that great variability in the transmission of this story reveals changing interpretations of it over time and in different geographic and socio-religious settings. Earliest versions do not appear to blame women for the fall, nor to identify the knowledge passed to them by their angelic paramours as "magic." Later traditions, especially those influenced by the developing Greek discourse of magic, however, do identify women with magic (*pharmakeia*). Reed examines how modern concerns with gender and preconceptions about ancient misogyny predetermine our readings of these texts in circular ways:if you begin with the assumption that any knowledge possessed by women must be negative and related somehow to magic, that interpretation reinforces the perception that women are universally tarred as witches. On the other hand, if scholars resist imposing anachronistic interpretations onto ancient texts, they are better able to perceive other questions and concerns that these texts may pose. Reed considers, for example, how the story of the fallen angels in *Testament of Reuben* may have more to say about ancient optics and the power of being seen than it does about gender relations between male angels and human women. Gendered interpretations of the text in terms of active and passive subject and object are complicated or even inverted when we read the same story through a different paradigm.

Kimberly B. Stratton's reading of Roman depictions of women's sorcery, in chapter 5, revisits many of the texts discussed previously by Spaeth, but through a different theoretical paradigm. Situating those portraits of magic in the context of ancient conceptions of the body and concerns over the instability and mutability of bodies and society, Stratton enlists the concept of abjection as developed by Julia Kristeva to illuminate certain features of these portraits—namely, their consistent identification of magic with unstable bodies, identities, and threats to social order. Kristeva's notion of abjection explains not only the association of magic with the macabre in these portraits, but also helps to understand the frequent association of women with certain types of destabilizing magic in Roman texts. While the gendering of magic is by no means consistent or universal in the ancient Mediterranean, this way of reading depictions of women's magic permits us to see how ideas about magic reflected and were embedded in other social concerns and ideological systems.

Part II, "Gender and Magic Discourse in Practice," explores the ambivalent ways that gender and magic discourse intersected in a broad array of ancient literature, including historical accounts, biographies, homilies, and letters. Was the identification of women and magic as powerful and pervasive as much scholarship would have us think? The chapters in this section demonstrate that while literary stereotypes could be utilized for ideological and rhetorical purposes in actual accusations or sermons directed at women, other evidence suggests that women were not always associated with the magic arts. Thus, ancient tours of hell describe both sorcerers and sorceresses suffering punishment for the use of magic, indicating that this sin was not considered at that time to be the special province of women.

In chapter 6, Elizabeth Ann Pollard opens this section with her analysis of magic accusations against aristocratic women during the early Roman Empire. In the *Annals*, Tacitus recounts the trials of nine aristocratic women accused of magic in combination with either sexual misconduct or treason during the reigns of Tiberius, Claudius, and Nero. While other scholars have analyzed Tacitus's account in terms of literary tropes and Tacitus's own social commentary, Pollard draws on Mary Douglas's theory that magic accusations serve to regulate ambiguous competitive relationships, or to realign factional hierarchies between competing groups, to explain the political dynamics of these accusations. In the context of the early Principate, following the death of Augustus, whose shrewd leadership secured his authority, the claim to imperial power was easily threatened by the prestige and influence of venerable patrician families. Magic accusations against women of these families served as attacks against the families themselves and participated in the negotiation of authority and legitimacy during this period of political change. Magic accusations were also used to negotiate the unregulated power of aristocratic women and their personal rivalries. Pollard's study demonstrates how stereotypes of women's subversive magic reinforced and gave credibility to these political attacks. Charges of enlisting *artes magicae*, combined with trumped-up charges of adultery or of falsely presenting an illegitimate child, resonated with images of women's lustful magic circulating in literature at the time.

Dayna S. Kalleres explores the perpetuation of these stereotypes in Christian rhetoric in the Post Constantinian period, in chapter 7. As Christianity emerged from secrecy into the public sphere, following the Council of Nicea (325 CE), church leaders such as John Chrysostom expressed concern over patrolling Christian identity in the secret recesses of private homes. By drawing on literary tropes of the drunken hag who dispenses amulets and healing potions or the prostitute who casts love spells to captivate Christian husbands, Chrysostom constructs a rhetorical opposition in his sermons between magical dangers lurking in the pagan city and the vulnerable Christian home and family. In his endeavor to forge a new Christian empire, Chrysostom tries to force his flock to break from traditional pagan practices; in the process, even seemingly inoffensive *remedia* such as amulets or spells recited in the name of God and Jesus are forbidden as idolatry. Kalleres demonstrates the role magic discourse played in this rhetorical war on pagan customs and highlights the continuity between Greek and Roman literary stereotypes of women's magic and Christian rhetoric; Chrysostom gave new life to enduring images of women's magical proclivities by identifying them with demonic threats to Christian salvation.

In a fascinating study of magic discourse and internecine conflict, in chapter 8, Ayşe Tuzlak considers a polemical story about a third-century prophetess who is said to be possessed by a demon. In a letter to Cyprian, Bishop of Carthage, another lesser-known bishop by the name of Firmilian describes a female prophet who arose in the region of Cappodocia about twenty years earlier during a period of natural disasters followed by persecutions of Christians. This woman, according to Firmilian, was possessed by a demon, and under its sway attracted a large following through preternatural feats and fabulous predictions. The real source of his concern, however, is that she assumed ecclesiastical powers and baptized many of her followers. While Firmilian never enlists the specific terminology for magic or sorcery (*mageia, goēteia*) to discredit this woman, he does draw on the discourse of magic to denounce her as demon possessed, enlisting a common trope of magic accusations that served to distinguish divinely wrought miracles from demonic magic in antiquity. Tuzlak demonstrates how Firmilian enlists this story about one woman's illegitimate accessing of ritual power in support of rebaptism during highly charged ecclesiastical debates over the nature of authority and sacramental efficacy in the third century. Tuzlak's analysis highlights similarities between this accusation of demonic possession and similar uses of witchcraft accusations in conflicts over sacramental power and ecclesiastic authority during the Early Modern Period.

In chapter 9, Nicola Denzey Lewis examines the biography of a fourth-century Neo-Platonic sage or Holy Woman, Sosipatra, to see how the discourse of magic operates in the context of paganism's waning influence in late antique Roman society. The account of Sosipatra's life appears as an addendum to a biography of her philosopher husband, Eustathius, in the *Lives of the Philosophers and Sophists* by Eunapius of Sardis (ca. 405CE). Denzey Lewis's study reveals the careful avoidance of anything that might resemble magic in a context where the ban of Theodosius (391–392CE) outlawed traditional pagan practices, including oracles, sacrifices, and even philosophy, driving them underground. In this context, Christians frequently denounced theurgy as a form of degraded magic, forcing Neo-Platonist philosophers to pass on the secret knowledge discretely within families, often through daughters or wives. Drawing on folk traditions and the characteristics of the late antique Holy Man, first identified by Peter Brown, Eunapius paints a picture of Sosipatra as a powerful figure, possessed of great learning and hieratic powers such as prophecy and remote viewing. Magic plays a role in this narrative as a foil for the divine grace and spontaneous power wielded by Sosipatra, and it lurks in the background as a threat and danger in the anti-pagan climate of late fourth- and early fifth-century Rome. Denzey Lewis reveals the complex ways that gender and magic intersected in late ancient society, where women's association with magic could be a liability in the promotion of theurgy as a sacred science.

Kirsti Barrett Copeland's investigation of late ancient tours of hell in chapter 10 reveals that in their imaginings of the tortures that await sinners in the afterlife, authors of these early Christian texts did not regard magic as a specifically female sin, or at least they did not frame it that way as a method of social control. Rather, sorcery is either described with explicitly inclusive language—men and women (*andres kai gunaikes*), sorcerers and sorceresses (*pharmakoi kai pharmakides*)—or with "gender-inclusive" masculine terms (*veneficii* or *pharmakoi*). By the Medieval period tours of hell, such as Dante's *Inferno* or the thirteenth-century *Vision of Thurkill*, deliberately diverge from their late antique antecedents by limiting the crime of sorcery exclusively to female sinners. This deliberate emendation to the otherwise largely static textual tradition indicates changing ideas of magic among Christians and the growing influence of gendered witch stereotypes such as those explored in Part I by Spaeth and Stratton. Copeland's careful study of the textual transmission and manuscript tradition of early Christian and Jewish tours of hell complicates facile assumptions that later ideas about magic and gender, women and sin, can be assumed for all periods in Jewish or Christian history.

Part III, Gender, Magic, and the Material Record, considers the material evidence of women's magical practices or their effects as a counterpoint to the imagined magic of literary fantasy or the trumped-up charges of political intrigue and religious competition. The first two chapters in this section contextualize evidence for women's magic by reconstructing the social structures and power dynamics that constrained women's lives and may have contributed to the production of these surviving artifacts of magical intervention. David Frankfurter opens this section with an analysis of women's love magic. In chapter 11, he begins with a critique of two recent interpretations of women's love magic that both overly rely on literary caricature and stereotype. Frankfurter, instead, allows women to speak for themselves through the spells they left behind in the material record in order to understand the hopes, fears, and desires that motivated their use of magic. Through close readings of extant spells from a variety of locations and time periods, Frankfurter surmises that women most often used love magic to protect their social and financial position in precarious relationships with men.

He focuses on magic as an expression of agency on the part of these women, who may have otherwise felt powerless and vulnerable in their dependency on male partners. In the final section of his paper, Frankfurter enlists anthropological studies of women and magic from Latin America to analogize the situation of ancient spell-casters. Frankfurter concludes that love magic empowered ancient women to exercise agency in situations where they lacked power or control; he provides a more sympathetic and realistic picture of women's erotic magic than those of previous scholars who replicate ancient stereotypes of overwrought feminine desire and manipulative wives.

Pauline Ripat, in chapter 12, reaches similar conclusions by extrapolating from a handful of curses that target female slaves or freedwomen. She hypothesizes that Roman wives may be behind these curses, and are seeking to remove a servile rival from posing a threat to her position in the household. Ripat's study highlights the fragile social status of wives; their privileged position and honor in the household depended on a husband's preferential treatment and respect. By examining Roman social customs and connubial ideals, Ripat reveals how the difference in status between a wife and slave was relative since both were supposed to obey the paterfamilias, who was master of the house. An ideal wife resembled in many ways a good slave and vice versa, especially if the slave also played the role of lover and confidant to her master. Ripat's interpretation of this category of spells, while speculative, relies on a careful and thoughtful study of Roman social hierarchy and the substantive evidence for fraught relations between matrons and female slaves. While we will never know who authored these curses against particular women, or what motivated them, Ripat's reconstruction of the context in which such spells could have been executed stands in sharp relief with the caricatured portraits of lusty hags from literature of the time. Like Frankfurter, Ripat seeks to understand the social reality of women's magic and eschew fantastic stereotypes bred on fear and fantasy, some of which get replicated in contemporary scholarship.

Yaakov Elman, in chapter 13, investigates evidence for women's involvement in the production of Aramaic magic bowls from ancient Syria and Mesopotamia. Looking first at technical skills required for the production of the bowls—requisite literacy, knowledge of the Babylonian Talmud, or just familiarity with rabbinic culture—Elman concludes that there is no reason to exclude the possibility that women may have produced these apotropaic bowls and served as exorcists in the rituals that accompanied their production or deposition. In the second section of his chapter, he concentrates on a handful of bowls that mention women specifically as clients or exorcists. While the sample size is extraordinarily small, women appear in more than 30 percent of the total number of bowls in which exorcists are named. Elman's study thus suggests that women could be respected exorcists, manufacturing apotropaic bowls and dispensing incantations and amulets, which were valued by their clients and communities.

In this capacity, female ritual specialists operated as a type of colleague to rabbis, such as Amemar, who is the tradent of numerous protective spells in the Talmud, including one he attributes to the chief sorceress (*reishteinhi denashim keshfaniot*, b. pesahim 110a). Intriguingly, Elman identifies a version of this same incantation on one of the bowls, suggesting that Amemar's spell may in fact derive from a female exorcist as claimed. At the very least it presents a fascinating case where text and material culture intersect and offers an additional clue to women's likely participation in the Sasanian context of magic, demons, and protective exorcisms.

Fritz Graf's study, in chapter 14, of ancient tomb inscriptions that curse suspected sorcerers and sorceresses presents a different angle from which to view women's magic. He examines a class of tomb inscriptions that respond to the untimely death of a loved one by invoking divine vengeance upon an unknown magical assailant. This type of grave inscription appears infrequently given the large number of inscriptions for those who died young, indicating that suspicion of magical foulplay was not the most common way to understand an untimely death. Drawing on anthropological theory, Graf proposes that magic accusations arise most often in situations where social roles and boundaries remain ambiguous and undefined. Thus, cases involving immigrants, freed slaves, or (as Pollard also proposes) competition among aristocratic families provided contexts in which suspicion of magic flourished. Even so, Graf remarks that vague insinuations and calls for divine vengeance on epitaphs could release tension without creating worse social ruptures in tight-knit ancient communities. Actual accusations of magic, and consequently "real" witches, Graf concludes, were very rare despite the abundant depictions in ancient literature. Furthermore, the evidence for actual accusations of magic (both epigraphic and textual) indicate that accusations finger men in only slightly fewer cases than women, indicating that, despite strong tendencies toward gender-stereotyping of magic in Greek and, especially, Roman literature, magic accusations in reality were much more complex.

AnneMarie Luijendijk closes the volume with her study of a healing amulet from fifth-century Oxyrynchus, Egypt. Her careful analysis of that artifact upends common assumptions about women and magic, and recapitulates in a single example much of what the previous studies of this collection find. By reconstructing the social and historical context of an ancient amulet, Luijendijk illuminates not only the personal difficulties of a single female patient, but more significantly, the likely role of the clergy in the production of this and similar amulets. Despite denigrating attacks on the use of amulets by Christian orators such as Athanasius and John Chrysostom, who both link the production and use of these amulets to foolish old (sometimes drunk) women, who are leading unwary Christians into Satan's snare (see Kalleres in this volume), Luijendijk's close analysis of the amulet's use of scribal practices such as *nomina sacra*, invocation of local saints, and resemblance to Christian liturgy indicates that it was most likely produced by clergy at a local shrine. The orthopraxy of the amulet suggests that the owner found nothing incongruent with it and her Christian beliefs despite the rancorous censorship of amulets by certain bishops. In sermons against amulets such as this one, church fathers employed the rhetoric of foolish old women and the dangers of Satan to denigrate healing practices of devout Christians and protective amulets provided for them by fellow clergy. They thus enlist a tried and true form of magic discourse to control the boundaries of Christian practice and identity according to their own predilection.

Luijendijk's study provides a fitting conclusion to this volume, which has demonstrated throughout both the tenacity of certain powerful stereotypes of women's proclivity to practice magic as well as ample evidence that this stereotype was not universal nor univocal. While the tendency to use the trope of women's magic was persistent, many texts reveal more complex attitudes toward magic. Thus Kirsti Copeland discovers no gendering of magic in early Christian tours of hell and Fritz Graf detects only slightly more accusations of magic against women than men in ancient Greece and Rome. Nicola Denzey Lewis suggests that Eunapius studiously avoided any hints of magic in his depiction of Sosipatra as a great sage and Holy Woman precisely because he was afraid of such denigration. Yaakov Elman discovers evidence that women were likely exorcists and possibly magicians in ancient Babylonia, but they certainly did not have a monopoly on these practices, and Annette Reed proposes that the story of the Fallen Angels in Genesis 6 does not tell a univocal story about the evil temptations of women; rather reading this story without the expectation that it shares the same presumptions about women, magic, and sin that we do allows one to discover different questions and concerns than those imposed on it by many modern scholars. The evidence marshalled by the contributions to this volume takes us far beyond facile misogynistic stereotypes to consider relationships between women and magic in a variety of complex social contexts that also reveal the fragility of health, the insecurity of human relationships, and occasional resistance to gender stereotyping in struggles over power, authority, and identity.

Notes

1. I would like to thank David Frankfurter and Dayna S. Kalleres, who both read through early and unwieldy drafts of this chapter, and offered helpful editing suggestions. Both encouraged me to keep the material on Early Modern witch-hunts as theoretical context for the studies in this volume. Dayna, in particular, coached me through various versions of this chapter with sound advice at each turn.
2. Christina Larner, *Enemies of God: The Witch-Hunt in Scotland* (London: Chattoand Windus, 1981), 100. See also Clarke Garret, "Women and Witches: Patterns

of Analysis," *Signs: Journal of Women in Culture and Society* 3, no. 2 (1977): 461; Marianne Hester, *Lewd Women and Wicked Witches: A Study of the Dynamics of Male Domination* (London and New York: Routledge, 1992); Anne Llewellyn Barstow, *Witchcraze: A New History of the European Witch Hunts* (San Francisco, CA: Pandora, 1994); John Putnam Demos, *Entertaining Satan: Witchcraft and the Culture of Early New England* (New York: Oxford University Press, 1982), 63.

3. Suzanna Burghartz, "The Equation of Women and Witches: A Case Study of Witchcraft Trials in Lucerne and Lausanne in the Fifteenth and Sixteenth Centuries," in *Witchcraft, Women, and Society*, edited with introduction by Brian P. Levack, Articles on Witchcraft, Magic, and Demonology, vol. 10 (New York: Garland Pub., 1992), 69, presents the statistics chronologically and geographically.
4. See Kimberly B. Stratton, *Naming the Witch: Magic, Ideology, and Stereotype in the Ancient World* (New York: Columbia University Press, 2007) and discussion below.
5. See, for example, Lara Apps and Andrew Gow, *Male Witches in Early Modern Europe* (Manchester: Manchester University Press, 2003), and Annette Reed's contribution in this volume.
6. See John G. Gager, *Curse Tablets and Binding Spells from the Ancient World* (Oxford: Oxford University Press, 1992), 80–81; John J. Winkler, "The Constraints of Desire: Erotic Magical Spells," in *The Constraints of Desire: The Anthropology of Sex and Gender in Ancient Greece*, ed. John J. Winkler (London and New York: Routledge, 1990), 72; Christopher Faraone, *Ancient Greek Love Magic* (Cambridge, MA: Harvard University Press, 1999), 43, n. 9; and Fritz Graf, *Magic in the Ancient World*, trans. Franklin Philip (Cambridge, MA: Harvard University Press, 1997), 185.
7. Matthew W. Dickie, "Who Practised Love-Magic in Classical Antiquity and in the Late Roman World?" *The Classical Quarterly* (New Series), 50, no. 2 (2000): 581–82.
8. Ibid., 571, 573.
9. Matthew W. Dickie, *Magic and Magicians in the Greco-Roman World* (London and New York: Routledge, 2001), 89–90, 178–81.
10. This argument relies to a large degree on Horace's vitriolic invective against a particular woman, Canidia (*Satire* 1.8, *Epodes* 5, 17), which combines highly charged sexual slander with accusations of magic to denigrate and humiliate a woman who may have been a former lover. Canidia's real identity is a matter of speculation. See Ellen Oliensis, "Canidia, Canicula, and the Decorum of Horace's *Epodes*," *Arethusa* 24, no. 1 (1991): 107–35; and Stratton, *Naming the Witch*, 82–84. Similar to pictures circulating on the Internet of Hillary Clinton in a witch's hat, Horace's satires are meant to denigrate and not actually represent Canidia. http://www.cuttingedge.org/News/n1224.cfm (accessed May 24, 2013) claims Hillary Clinton is a "practicing witch" and member of the Illuminati. See also http://starkravingviking.blogspot.ca/2011/10/entrapment-usa.html (accessed May 24, 2013); http://www.loriferber.com/

the-wicked-witch-of-the-west-wing-button.html (accessed May 24, 2013); and http://www.therightperspective.org/2008/08/25/hillary-clinton-sick-and-tired-of-frank-and-john/#sthash.Z8ugU6Xy.dpbs (accessed May 24, 2013) for denigrating portraits of Clinton in witch's garb.

11. Faraone, *Ancient Greek Love Magic*, 150.
12. Richard Gordon, "Aelian's Peony: The Location of Magic in Graeco-Roman Tradition," *Comparative Criticism* 9 (1987): 64–65, also accepts that ancient women practiced magic, and proposes that the dearth of material evidence for women's magic stems from the fact that most women used common household ingredients rather than the literate professional magic employed by men.
13. Chadwick Hansen, *Witchcraft at Salem* (New York: G. Braziller, 1969), 22, 65.
14. The term *khishuf* applies to women over 50 percent of the time. Tal Ilan, "Cooks/Poisoners; Healers/Killers; Religion/Witchcraft: Jewish Women's Religious Life at Home," in *Haushalt, Hauskult, Hauskirche. Zur Arbeitsteilung der Geschlechter in Wirtschaft und Religion*, E. Klinger et al. (Würzburg Echter Verlag, 2004), 121.
15. Rebecca Lesses, "Exe(o)Rcising Power: Women as Sorceresses, Exorcists, and Demonesses in Babylonian Jewish Society of Late Antiquity," *Journal of the American Academy of Religion* 69, no. 2 (2001): 363–64.
16. Lesses, "Exe(o)Rcising Power," 362.
17. Keith Thomas, *Religion and the Decline of Magic* (New York: Scribner's, 1971), 521–22.
18. Hansen, *Witchcraft*, 15, 21–23.
19. Christina Larner, *Enemies of God: The Witch-Hunt in Scotland* (London: Chatto and Windus, 1981), 94–95.
20. Thomas, *Religion and the Decline of Magic*, 503–6, 511. Evelyn Heinemann, *Witches: A Psychoanalytic Exploration of the Killing of Women*, trans. Donald Kiraly (London and New York: Free Association Books, 2000), 34, supposes that guilt created psychosomatic symptoms in the accuser.
21. Lyndal Roper, *Oedipus and the Devil: Witchcraft, Sexuality, and Religion in Early Modern Europe* (London and New York: Routledge, 1994), 202.
22. Roper, *Oedipus*, 216.
23. Ibid., 204–6.
24. Ibid., 19.
25. The execution rate in one town was 98 percent. Jonathan B. Durrant, *Witchcraft, Gender, and Society in Early Modern Germany*, Studies in Medieval and Reformation Traditions, vol. 124 (Leiden and Boston: Brill, 2007), 21. By reading the torture scenes as a sado-masochist game of "cat and mouse," Roper ignores the absolute power the torturer wields to efface the identity and voice of the tortured woman, whose confession reveals not *her* voice and *her* "truth" but the torturer's. In the physical pain she endures, her voice, her identity, and her truth disappear, replaced by the one which the interrogator puts into her mouth through inscribing it into her flesh. On the power of torture, see Elaine Scarry, *The Body*

in Pain: The Making and Unmaking of the World (New York: Oxford University Press, 1985), 35–36. Lara Apps and Andrew Gow, *Male Witches in Early Modern Europe* (Manchester: Manchester University Press, 2003), 86, insightfully argue that the frequent recantations from confessing witches reflect attempts to salvage their Christian identity and salvation in moments when the torture has ceased, revealing not a sadistic game of cat and mouse, but their determined resistance to the narrative that was being imposed on them. One letter, by a male witch, for example, was smuggled out of prison during the Bamburg witch-hunt in 1628 and relates in detail the torture to which he was subjected and the confession he was eventually forced to give on the advice of the executioner. No one, he said, not even a lord could escape the inevitable conclusion of the witch tribunal (published in its entirety in Apps and Gow, *Male Witches in Early Modern Europe*, 159–64).

26. Thomas, *Religion and the Decline of Magic*, 5.
27. Ibid., 437.
28. Larner, *Enemies*, 97.
29. Ibid., 96.
30. Alan Macfarlane, *Witchcraft in Tudor and Stuart England: A Regional and Comparative Study* (London: Routledge & Kegan Paul, 1970), 174.
31. Macfarlane, *Witchcraft*, 174, furthermore argues that identifying a witch as the source of misfortune avoided facing the unpleasant task of analyzing one's own behavior for clues to the calamity in a world where misfortune was attributed to divine punishment for sin. The hysteria of the witch craze ended, not with the rise of medicine and better health care, but with scientific *explanations* for diseases, which replaced personalized views of causation, 205.
32. Paul Boyer and Stephen Nissenbaum, *Salem Possessed; the Social Origins of Witchcraft* (Cambridge, MA: Harvard University Press, 1974), 199, 208.
33. Robin Briggs, *Witches and Neighbours: The Social and Cultural Context of European Witchcraft*, 2nd ed. (Malden, MA: Blackwell Publishing, 2002), 344, similarly argues that persecutions arise from hostilities between neighbors in face-to-face communities rather than from political directives or religious conflicts managed by "cynical ruling groups." Ronald Hutton, "The Global Context of the Scottish Witch-Hunt," in *The Scottish Witch-Hunt in Context*, ed. Julian Goodare (Manchester, UK, and New York: Manchester University Press, 2002), 23, concludes that most accusations derive from non-elite and disempowered individuals, who gained respect and attention by accusing witches. In this regard, his findings resemble those of David Frankfurter, "Dynamics of Ritual Expertise in Antiquity and Beyond: Towards a New Taxonomy of 'Magicians,'" in *Ancient Magic and Ritual Power*, ed. Marvin Meyer and Paul Mirecki (Leiden: E.J. Brill, 1995), 174; and Louise Yeoman, "Hunting the Rich Witch in Scotland: High-Status Witchcraft Suspects and Their Persecutors, 1590–1650," in *The Scottish Witch-Hunt in Context*, ed. Julian Goodare (Manchester and New York: Manchester University Press, 2002), 114–15.

34. This argument resembles that of Stuart Clark, *Thinking with Demons: The Idea of Witchcraft in Early Modern Europe* (Oxford and New York: Oxford University Press, 1997), which is discussed below.
35. Walter Stephens, *Demon Lovers: Witchcraft, Sex, and the Crisis of Belief* (Chicago: University of Chicago Press, 2002), 16.
36. Stephens, *Demon Lovers*, 17, 25. Hansen, *Witchcraft*, 24, claims that Cotton Mather was motivated to publish his account of the witch trials for similar reasons.
37. For example, Stephens, *Demon Lovers*, 37, argues that the *Malleus Maleficarum* is not a tirade against women's sexual power but a tirade for it; Kramer (one of the treatise's authors) "did not fear that women were associating with demons; he *hoped* that they were" (italics original).
38. Larner, *Enemies*, 92.
39. Ibid., 23.
40. Larner, *Enemies*, 92. See also Clark, *Thinking with Demons*, 114; and Joseph Klaits, *Servants of Satan: The Age of the Witch Hunts* (Bloomington: Indiana University Press, 1985), 50.
41. Larner, *Enemies*, 98. Demos, *Entertaining Satan*, 86, reinforces this point when he argues that the majority of accused witches were perceived to be in conflict with peers and neighbors, with local institutions, and with generally accepted values and precepts. While Demos does not acknowledge the feminist implications of "being in conflict," his data suggests that women perceived to be "headstrong" were more likely to attract accusations than those who "knew their place."
42. Larner, *Enemies*, 100; Hutton, "Global Context," 25. See also Julian Goodare, "Women and the Witch-Hunt in Scotland," *Social History* 23 (1998): 288–308 for a similar conclusion. Demos, *Entertaining Satan*, 86, in contrast, argues that the lives of accused witches were characterized by conflict with their peers; they were regarded as unacceptably quarrelsome and aggressive. In the context of Puritan New England, where such emotions and behavior were rejected, Demos interprets witchcraft accusations as psychological projections of repressed anger and conflict onto an external figure, 196. John Demos, "Underlying Themes in the Witchcraft of Seventeenth-Century New England," *The American Historical Review* 75, no. 5 (1970): 1318, draws on demographic data to argue that accusations were at least partly generated by "structural conflict" between generations. Young women felt excessively controlled and stifled by older women; episodes of possession enabled these girls to act out and challenge authority, while projecting the aggressive behavior onto older women, whom they accused of attacking them with witchcraft. Garret, "Women and Witches," 468, similarly argues that the hostility of the accuser was, in fact, directed toward their mothers, who controlled them.
43. Larner, *Enemies*, 102.
44. Klaits, *Servants of Satan*, 50.

45. Klaits, *Servants of Satan*, 49, 59. This was as true for Protestants as Catholics; even though Protestants advocated marriage and procreation, they continued to express guilt over sexual pleasure.
46. Ibid., 61.
47. Durrant, *Witchcraft*, 42. See also Lauren Martin, "The Devil and the Domestic: Witchcraft, Quarrels and Women's Work in Scotland," in *The Scottish Witch-Hunt in Context*, ed. Julian Goodare (Manchester and New York: Manchester University Press, 2002), 77, who discovers a similar shaping of both confessions and accusations in Scottish witchtrials. In trial records from the last big witch-hunt in Scotland (1661–1662), confessions of sex with the devil were standardized and formulaic, 79.
48. Durrant, *Witchcraft*, 63.
49. Ibid., 59.
50. Durrant, *Witchcraft*, 59; Burghartz, "The Equation of Women and Witches," 73, similarly finds a lack of corresponding interest between witnesses and judges in Lucerne. However, she also does not detect substantial influence from demonological treatises, such as the *Malleus Maleficarum*, on the judges' conception of witchcraft as a predominantly female crime in Lucerne.
51. Since women tended to socialize more with other women, their "accomplices" tended to be women they knew and with whom they spent time rather than women with whom they feuded or experienced conflict. Thus, Durrant challenges the conviction that witchcraft accusations always stem from prior conflict or social tension, 126.
52. Signicantly, Durrant, *Witchcraft*, 64, points out that the commission did not pursue or bring to trial men named as attendees at midnight sabbaths, especially members of the clergy, confirming the commission's suspected gender bias.
53. Carol F. Karlsen, *The Devil in the Shape of a Woman: Witchcraft in Colonial New England* (London, 1987), 120.
54. Jane Kamensky, "Female Speech and Other Demons: Witchcraft and Wordcraft in Early New England," in *Spellbound: Women and Witchcraft in America*, ed. Elizabeth Reis, *Worlds of Women* (Wilmington, DE: Scholarly Resources, 1998), 35, 39. Interestingly, Martin, "Devil and the Domestic," 114–15, shifts her focus from the accused to the accuser and finds that witch-hunters tended to be in debt and had something to gain from conviction of the accused witch.
55. According to the influential preacher, Cotton Mather, "rebellion is as the sin of witchcraft" (quoting 1 Sam 15:23). Boyer and Nissenbaum, *Salem Possessed*, 209.
56. Karlsen, *The Devil*, 162.
57. Garret, "Women and Witches," 466, points out that women's social subordination is often most rigorously enforced by other women, who play the role of moral guardians and protectors of tradition.
58. Thomas, *Religion and the Decline of Magic*, 440.

59. Alan Anderson and Raymond Gordon, "Witchcraft and the Status of Women—the Case of England," in *Witchcraft, Women, and Society*, edited with introduction by Brian P. Levack, Articles on Witchcraft, Magic, and Demonology, vol. 10 (New York: Garland Pub., 1992), 177.
60. Anderson and Gordon, "Witchcraft and the Status of Women," 178.
61. Ibid., 172.
62. Anderson and Gordon, "Witchcraft and the Status of Women," 181. See also J.K. Swales and Hugh McLachlan, "Witchcraft and the Status of Women: A Comment," in *Witchcraft, Women, and Society*, edited with introduction by Brian P. Levack, Articles on Witchcraft, Magic, and Demonology, vol. 10 (New York: Garland Pub., 1992), 41–49, for a critique of this theory.
63. Elizabeth Reis, "Gender and the Meanings of Confessions in Early New England," in *Spellbound: Women and Witchcraft in America*, ed. Elizabeth Reis, Worlds of Women (Wilmington, DE: Scholarly Resources, 1998), 53.
64. Reis, "Gender," 56.
65. Ibid., 60.
66. Ibid., 64–65.
67. Reis, "Gender," 65. Boyer and Nissenbaum, *Salem Possessed*, 215, regard the public confession of the accused witch to be an integral part of this drama; it allowed the entire community, especially accusers, to recognize negative impulses within themselves and, by bringing them into the open, "gain mastery over them." It also staged the public reaffirmation of social values which, although sometimes failing, accusers wanted to uphold. Thus, the accused women, by confessing to pacts with Satan and crimes against humanity, allowed an important public catharsis to occur. Boyer and Nissenbaum point out that no confessing witches in Salem were executed. Only the ones who denied the accusation and refused to play their role in this social drama met a violent end at the hands of their neighbors and community.
68. Reis, "Gender," 68.
69. Anderson and Gordon, "Witchcraft and the Status of Women," 175.
70. Hansen, *Witchcraft*, 7–8.
71. Winkler, "Constraints," 90.
72. Winkler, "Constraints," 90. Dickie, *Magic*, 10–11, ridicules this approach: "There is very little, if anything, in such explanations that is not questionable. They tell us more about the preoccupations of their authors than they do about the past. . . . The Freudian notion of denial and transfer is particularly suspect."
73. Graf, *Magic*, 189.
74. Paula Heimann, "Certain Functions of Introjection and Projection in Early Infancy," in *Developments in Psycho-Analysis*, ed. Joan Riviere, with a preface by Ernest Jones, *Psychoanalysis Examined and Re-Examined* (London: Hogarth Press, 1952), 135.
75. Melanie Klein, "Some Theoretical Conclusions Regarding the Emotional Life of the Infant," in *Developments in Psycho-Analysis*, ed. Joan Riviere, with a preface

by Ernest Jones, *Psychoanalysis Examined and Re-Examined* (London: Hogarth Press, 1952), 199–200.

76. Melanie Klein, "On the Theory of Anxiety and Guilt," in *Developments in Psycho-Analysis*, ed. Joan Riviere, with a preface by Ernest Jones, *Psychoanalysis Examined and Re-Examined* (London: Hogarth Press, 1952), 278; Deborah Willis, *Malevolent Nurture: Witch-Hunting and Maternal Power in Early Modern England* (Ithaca, NY: Cornell University Press, 1995), 45.
77. Willis, *Malevolent Nurture*, 46.
78. Ibid., 14.
79. Ibid., 33.
80. Ibid., 33–35.
81. Ibid., 21.
82. Ibid., 29, 47.
83. Willis, *Malevolent Nurture*, 48. In addition to changing childrearing practices, which saw children spending more time in the homes of strangers where they were subject to harsh discipline, Willis identifies the emergence of an idealized vision of the mother as a contributing factor to witch trials; motherhood, she argues, becomes a "special vocation" at this time. Willis, *Malevolent Nurture*, 66, points out that infanticide was criminalized around the same time and prosecuted in roughly similar numbers. Carolyn Matalene, "Women as Witches," in *Witchcraft, Women, and Society*, edited with introduction by Brian P. Levack, Articles on Witchcraft, Magic, and Demonology, vol. 10 (New York: Garland Pub., 1992), 63, argues that the image of witchcraft emphasized and defined by inversion the acceptable role for women.
84. Heinemann, *Witches*, 31–32.
85. Ibid., 34.
86. Ibid., 36–37.
87. Ibid., 43–44.
88. Ibid., 45.
89. Ibid., 46.
90. Heinemann, *Witches*, 47. Aspects of the Oedipal complex also contribute to the idea of the witch's sexual consorting with Satan. According to Heinemann, Oedipal aggression toward the father is projected onto the Devil, who is the image of the evil father; the Devil is a figure upon which are projected repressed impulses that have been repudiated, 48. Klein also discusses the relation between the figures of the father and the devil in Melanie Klein, "On Identification," in *New Directions in Psycho-Analysis: The Significance of Infant Conflict in the Pattern of Adult Behaviour*, ed. Melanie Klein, Paula Heimann, and R.E. Money-Kyrle (New York: Basic Books, 1955), 322.
91. Roper, *Oedipus*, 203, 207.
92. Simone de Beauvoir, *The Second Sex*, trans. and ed. H. M. Parshley (New York: Vintage Books, 1989), xxii.

93. de Beauvoir, *The Second Sex*, 32.
94. Ibid., 25, 63, 73–74.
95. Ibid., 78–79.
96. Ibid., 79.
97. Ibid., 79.
98. Ibid., 80.
99. Clark, *Thinking with Demons*, 108.
100. Ibid., 110.
101. Ibid., viii.
102. Ibid., 9.
103. Ibid., 13–14.
104. Ibid., 113.
105. Norman Cohn, *Europe's Inner Demons: An Enquiry Inspired by the Great Witch-Hunt* (New York: New American Library, 1975), 252–53; Durrant, *Witchcraft*, 22; Stephens, *Demon Lovers*, 15, 54. In contrast, Briggs, "Women," 228, 247–48, draws on Clark to acquit demonologists of any responsibility. He blames female rivalry and separation of the sexes for the gender bias in witchcraft accusations.
106. For example, Simon "Magus" (Acts 8: 9-11; Justin 1 *Apol.* 26) and Marcus (Irenaeus *Haer.* 13.1); and my discussion in Stratton, *Naming the Witch*, 125–35.
107. Stratton, *Naming the Witch*, 179.
108. Ibid., 140.
109. Cohn, *Europe's Inner Demons*, 251; Burghartz, "Equation of Women and Witches," 69, presents the data chronologically and by geographic region in useful tables.
110. Klaits, *Servants of Satan*, 59.
111. Cohn, *Europe's Inner Demons*, 18–21.
112. Ibid., 224.
113. Ibid., 228.
114. Cohn *Europe's Inner Demons*, 233. Stephens, *Demon Lovers*, 53, notes that sexuality was presumed to be the only attribute illiterate women possessed that would attract demons.
115. Klaits, *Servants of Satan*, 59.
116. See table of statistics in Apps and Gow, *Male Witches in Early Modern Europe*, 45.
117. Kirsten Hastrup, "Iceland: Sorcerers and Paganism," in *Early Modern European Witchcraft: Centres and Peripheries*, ed. Bengt Ankarloo and Gustav Henningsen (Oxford: Clarendon Press, 1990), 385.
118. See also Antero Heikkinen and Timo Kervinen, "Finland: The Male Domination," in *Early Modern European Witchcraft: Centres and Peripheries*, ed. Bengt Ankarloo and Gustav Henningsen (Oxford: Clarendon Press, 1990), 319–38, for similar conclusions regarding the gendering of magic in Finland, although there men accounted for closer to 50 percent of accused witches.

119. Hastrup, "Iceland: Sorcerers and Paganism," 388.
120. Ibid., 392.
121. Ibid., 399.
122. Apps and Gow, *Male Witches in Early Modern Europe*, 104–8.
123. Burghartz, "Equation of Women and Witches," 73.
124. Ibid., 74.
125. Ibid., 75.
126. Clark, *Thinking with Demons*, 130.
127. Apps and Gow, *Male Witches in Early Modern Europe*, 108–11.
128. Ibid., 31–32.

PART I

Fiction and Fantasy: Gendering Magic in Ancient Literature

2

From Goddess to Hag: The Greek and the Roman Witch in Classical Literature

Barbette Stanley Spaeth

THE "WITCH" OF classical literature is a fascinating figure: sometimes beautiful, sometimes horrible, but always compelling.[1] In this article, I shall show that an analysis of the classical literary representations of witches reveals interesting similarities and important differences between the Greek and Roman sources, and I shall suggest some possible interpretations of these correspondences and contrasts. For the purposes of this article, I am employing the commonly accepted usage of the term "witch" in contemporary English, that is, "a woman claiming or popularly believed to possess magical powers and practice sorcery."[2] This broad etic definition of the term allows me to consider under the category "witch" a variety of female magical practitioners from classical literature, although the ancient terms for these practitioners divide them into different emic categories.[3] Thus, some of these women are distinguished by their methods, for example, those who used magical potions (*pharmakis* or *pharmakeutria* in Greek; *venefica* or *trivenefica* in Latin) or incantations (*kēlēteira* in Greek, *cantatrix* or *praecantrix* in Latin). Some are defined by other characteristics, such as their habit of lurking around graveyards (*tumbas* in Greek), or their ability to fly (*volaticus* in Latin). Others, particularly Roman witches, may be identified with animals (*striga* or *strix* in Latin, a term for a type of bird) or monsters (*lamia* in Latin, a mythological female monster who devoured children). Roman witches also may be identified with pejorative terms, such as *malefica*, "evil-doer," or *lupula*, "whore," or they may be called by more euphemistic terms: *saga*, "wise-woman," *veteratrix*, "well-practiced, seasoned," or *anus*, "old woman." Finally, some ancient sources classify witches by their association with certain types of magic (*perimaktria*: one who purifies with magic; *telesphoros*: one who initiates with magic), while others employ feminine versions of words designating practitioners of magic in general:

so the Greek term, *goēteia*, leads to the use of *goēteutria* for a witch (cf. *goētēs* for a male magician), while the Latin term *magia* leads to the use of *maga* for the female magical practitioner (cf. *magus* for the male practitioner).

These latter terms emphasize the association of the witch with the general concept "magic" in antiquity, itself a highly contested term.[4] For the purposes of this discussion of the witch in classical literature, I define magic as the socially unsanctioned use of supernatural powers and tools to control nature and compel both humans and superhuman beings to do one's will.[5] This definition helps to distinguish the witch from the Olympian goddess or female monster, who has no need of magical tools to carry out her will, and also from the priestess, whose contacts with the supernatural are socially sanctioned. Greek literary portraits of witches include Homer's Circe; the Medea of Pindar, Euripides, and Apollonius Rhodius; and Theocritus's Simaetha.[6] Roman examples include Virgil's Simaetha (or Amaryllis, if that is indeed her name); Horace's Canidia and Sagana; the Latin elegists' old women who sell love charms, Ovid's Medea and Circe; Petronius's Oenothea; Seneca's Medea; Lucan's Erictho; and Apuleius's Meroe, Pamphile, and Photis.[7] Now, to be sure, some of these figures overlap the distinction that I made above among witches, goddesses, priestesses, and female monsters. Medea and Circe, for example, are both of divine lineage, and Circe is called a "dread goddess" (*deinē theos*) (e.g., Hom. *Od.* 10.136), while Medea is a priestess (*arēteira*) of Hekate (e.g., Ap. Rhod. *Argon.* 3.252). It may be that in the earliest stages of their mythic life these figures were not thought to be witches, that is, magical practitioners, for the concept of magic was not fully formed until the fifth century BCE.[8] As Richard Gordon suggests, however, these figures of myth are emblematic of "magic before magic."[9] They fit the characteristics of the later witch, and so, I would argue, still fall under the etic category that I have defined as "witch." For example, they make use of tools that are later interpreted as magical; Circe has her potion and wand that she uses to turn Odysseus's men to swine (Hom. *Od.* 10.233–42), and Medea has potions that she gives to Jason to protect him from the fire-breathing bulls (Pind. *Pyth.* 4.220–29). Certainly, in later literature, Circe and Medea become paradigms of the "arch-witch" and are cited in a variety of contexts; so, for example, Theocritus has his Simaetha ask Hekate to make her drugs as potent as those of Circe or Medea (Theocr. *Id.* 2.5–16).[10] The female monster also can overlap the witch figure, as with the so-called "night-hag" type, like the Roman *strix/striga*, who can be seen either as wholly animalistic (e.g., Ov. *Fast.* 6.131–69) or as more human in nature (e.g., Petron. *Sat.* 63).[11] These anomalous instances, however, I would argue, do not vitiate the basic definition of the witch as a woman who practices magic, and this definition allows us to recognize the variety of representations of such figures in classical literature.

These representations come from a variety of genres, including epic and lyric poetry, tragedy, satire, and the ancient novel.[12] Although genre conventions certainly influenced the way in which these literary portraits of witches were constructed, nevertheless an in-depth examination of these portraits reveals certain important characteristics that transcend literary genre to show much about how the ancient Greeks and Romans thought about witches.[13] It is important to recognize that these representations do not necessarily reflect reality; they probably do not tell us much about actual witches, that is, the real women in antiquity who believed they were practicing magic or were believed by others to do so.[14] In other words, we should not read these literary portraits naively, as pointing toward the reality of the practice of magic. As Fritz Graf has recognized, "it is tempting to use [these literary representations] in order to fill the gap in the epigraphical documentation, and too many scholars have uncritically yielded to this temptation. But this procedure is dangerous. Works of literature have their own laws, and it is always risky to disregard laws."[15] Nevertheless, the analysis of literary representations is a powerful tool that can reveal much about how the societies of classical antiquity thought about and with the cognitive category of "witch." For example, when the literary sources represent witches carrying out certain procedures, but do not show their male counterparts, magicians or wizards, carrying out these practices, it may well say something about cultural concepts of the relationship between gender and magic. Indeed, I shall argue that Greek and Roman cultural conceptions inform the category of "witch" as female magical practitioner, in many ways.

Let us begin by examining the basic similarities in Greek and Roman literary representations of witches. These figures all share two important characteristics: a connection with nature and a focus on the human body.[16] The witch herself may be located in the natural world. Homer's Circe, for example, dwells in a forest glen (*Od.* 10.210), and Medea, according to Apollonius Rhodius, serves Hekate in a temple located in the woods far from the city (*Argon.* 4.47–53).[17] The tools of the witch, particularly the ingredients she needs for her magic potions, come from nature; indeed their location in the natural world is consistently emphasized in the literary sources.[18] Witches' potions contain potent herbs, which must be gathered on mountaintops at the dead of night. A fragment from Sophocles' *Rhizotomoi* shows Medea cutting the roots (*rhizōn . . . tomas*) of these herbs in the wild with a bronze sickle (Macrob. *Sat.* 5.19.9 = Pearson fr. 534). Witches' potions also contain the parts of wild animals, apparently the more exotic the better. Lucan's Erictho uses the froth of rabid dogs, the entrails of a lynx, the hump of a hyena, the marrow of a stag fed on snakes, the marine monster *echenais*, the eyes of a dragon, and the ashes of the Phoenix (6.667–84). Ovid's Medea uses the wings and flesh of screech owls, the entrails of a werewolf, the scaly skin of a snake, the liver of a stag, and the eggs and head of a crow (*Met.* 7.262–75). Witches are closely associated with animals in other ways as well. According to Homer (*Od.* 10.212) and Ovid (*Met.* 14. 255), Circe's house is guarded by wolves, lions, and bears. Witches commonly transform themselves or other humans into animals:[19] Circe transforms Odysseus's men into pigs (Hom. *Od.* 10.234–39), and Thessalian witches are said to be able to transform themselves into birds, dogs, mice, and even flies, according to Apuleius (*Met.* 2.22). Witches are frequently compared to savage animals or animal-like monsters, as Euripides (*Med.* 92, 187–89, 1342–43, 1407) and Seneca (*Med.* 407–8, 863–65) compare Medea in her wrath to a bull, lioness, tigress, and the monsters Scylla and Charybdis. Some witches look or sound like wild animals: Horace's Canidia wears serpents in her hair (*Epod.* 5.15–16), while his Sagana has hair like a sea-urchin or a raging boar (*Epod.* 5.25–28); Lucan's Erictho has a voice that sounds like a dog, wolf, owl, and serpent combined (6.685–93). Finally, some witches even behave like savage animals: Canidia and Sagana dig at the earth with their nails and tear a lamb to pieces with their bare teeth (Hor. *Sat.* 1.8.26–27); Erictho eats human corpses and tears into living flesh with her teeth and nails (Luc. 6.533–68).

This close connection between witches and the natural world may reflect a widespread cultural equation of women with nature. In a seminal article, Sherry Ortner argued that cross-culturally, women are symbolically associated with nature, as opposed to men, who are associated with culture.[20] Although Ortner has been criticized for being too reductionist in her interpretations and too universalizing in their application, I believe that her formulation of "female is to male as nature is to culture" remains an idea that is "good to think with" for understanding the role of the witch in classical literature.[21] Ortner proposed that the connection of women and nature derives in part from a woman's body and its functions, which, being more involved with "species life" seem to place her closer to nature, in contrast to man's bodily functions, which free him more completely to take up the projects of culture.[22] Women, she contended, are more commonly connected with the things of the body through their physiology, which involves menstruation, parturition, and lactation.

Witches in classical literature also exhibit this emphasis on the body, to an even greater degree than "normal women." Ancient witches, in fact, seem obsessed with the things of the body. They are driven largely by bodily lust: Homer's Circe desires Odysseus for her bed (*Od.* 10.333–35); Apollonius Rhodius's Medea lusts for Jason (*Argon.* 3.286–98); Theocritus's Simaetha craves her Delphis (*Id.* 2. 82–90); Horace's Folia has a "masculine libido" (*Epod.* 5.41: *masculae libidinis*); and Apuleius's Meroe (*Met.* 1.7), Pamphile (*Met.* 2.5), and Photis (*Met.* 2.6) are all driven by their sexual desires. Witches' lust is considered so overpowering that it can cause male impotence.[23] In Homer, Hermes warns Odysseus that having sex with the witch Circe might make him "weakly and unmanned" (*kakon kai anēnora*: *Od.* 10.301).[24] In Petronius, the woman Circe causes Encolpius to become impotent (*Sat.* 128). Although he tries to heal his impotence with the help of the witches Proselenos and Oenothea, their own lust also proves more than he can handle (*Sat.* 138). The lustful actions of these witches are a form of inversion of the "natural" order, for according to ancient conceptions, it was the male who was supposed to be the active sexual partner. In assuming the active role, witches call into question the normative sexual roles of men and women in classical culture, threatening the culturally constructed boundaries of male and female. [25] Witches are also connected with the things of the body through their spells, which, the sources emphasize, make frequent use of bodily parts and fluids. Human bones, organs, flesh, appendages, blood, spit, gore, gall, and urine are all ingredients in magical spells.[26] Thus, according to Apuleius, Pamphile's workshop contains a variety of items from the human body for use in her spells, including noses, fingers, and blood (*Met.* 3.17).

I suggest that witches' connection with nature represents an intensification of the cultural association of women with the natural world and the human body. Witches are not merely *associated* with nature, they are *identified* with it.[27] As we have seen, witches can be found out in the wild, and they can even be described as savage animals themselves. Their connection with nature, however, extends even beyond this identification with nature to actual control of natural phenomena. So, for example, Ovid's Medea addresses the gods and spirits of nature with these words (*Met.* 7.199–209):[28]

> With your help when I have willed it, the streams have run back to their fountain-heads, while the banks wondered; I lay the swollen, and stir up the calm seas by my spell (*cantu*); I drive the storms and bring on the clouds; the winds I dispel and summon; I break the jaws of serpents with my incantations (*verbis et carmine*); living rocks and oaks I root up from their own soil; I move the forests, I bid the mountains shake, the earth to rumble, and the ghosts to come forth from their tombs. You also, Luna, do I draw (*traho*) from the sky, though the changing bronze of Temesa strives to aid your throes; even the chariot of the Sun, my grandsire, pales at my song (*carmine*); Aurora pales at my poisons (*venenis*).

The image of the witch causing streams to run backward and "drawing down the moon" is found throughout the literary depictions of witches from Apollonius Rhodius to Lucan.[29] The witch's control of the natural world is an inversion of the "natural" order of things, whereby men through their association with culture have control of the world.[30] The ancient authors presented this inversion as profoundly threatening.[31] They suggested that it led to the dissolution of all law and the destruction not only of culture but also of the entire world. In Seneca's *Hercules Oetaeus* (463), Deianira's nurse notes that "naught holds to law against my incantations" (*nihilque leges ad meos cantus tenet*).[32] And in Apuleius (*Met.* 2.5), Photis warns Lucius that as a witch of the first order (*maga primi nominis*),

Pamphile knows how to "drown all the light of the starry heavens in the depths of hell and plunge it into primeval Chaos" (*omnem istam lucem mundi sideralis imis Tartari et in vetustum Chaos summergere novit*).[33] Witches, then, represent the ultimate fear of the loss of all human, or more specifically male, control over the world and of the chaos that will result from that loss of control.

Although witches' connection with nature is an important common characteristic in their representations in both Greek and Latin literature, many other aspects of these portrayals are quite dissimilar. In general, Roman witches are represented far more negatively than Greek witches are. This description is applicable particularly to the witch figures invented by the Romans, like Canidia and Erictho, rather than witches like Circe and Medea, whose portrayals were borrowed from Greek literature. Even the borrowed witch figures, however, show the influence of more negative ideas about witches than the original Greek sources.[34] The climax of this negative portrayal of the witch is found in Latin literature of the Golden and Silver Ages, that is, from the late first century BCE to the mid-first century CE. We can see the distinctions between the Greek and Roman witches by examining the representations of their physical descriptions, motives, methods, and powers.

Greek witches are generally depicted as young and beautiful, while the Roman witches are old and ugly.[35] Homer describes Circe as "fair-tressed" (*euplokamos*: *Od.* 10.136; cf. *kalliplokamoio*: *Od.* 10. 220, 310: and as having a "sweet voice" (*Od.* 10.221: *opi kalēi*).[36] Simaetha, Theocritus tells us, has a "fair body" (*Id.* 2.110: *kalon chroa*) and "beautiful lips" (*Id.* 2.126: *kalon stoma*).[37] These women dress in lovely clothes to complement their beauty: Circe wears "a long white robe, finely woven and beautiful" (*argupheon pharos mega . . . lepton kai charien*) and around her waist a "fair girdle of gold" (*zōnēn . . . kalēn chruseiēn*) (*Od.* 10.543–45),[38] and Simaetha has a "fair long linen dress" (*bussoio kalon . . .chitōna*) and a "fine wrap" (*xustida*) (*Id.* 2.73–74).[39] Similarly, Apollonius of Rhodes gives a charming picture of the beautiful witch Medea in the following lines from the Argonautica: (*Argon.* 3.828–35):[40]

> Now soon as ever the maiden saw the light of dawn, with her hands she gathered up her golden tresses which were floating round her shoulders in careless disarray, and bathed her tear-stained cheeks, and made her skin shine with ointment sweet as nectar (*aloiphēi nektareēi*); and she donned a beautiful robe (*peplon kalon*), fitted with well-bent clasps (*eugnamptoisin . . . peronēisin*), and above her head, divinely fair (*ambrosiōi*), she threw a veil gleaming like silver (*kaluptrēn argupheēn*).

In contrast, the Roman witches are old, ugly, and frightening, and they wear frightful clothing to match their evil dispositions. Horace's Canidia is one of the "filthy old hags" (*Epod.* 5.98: *obscenas anus*), and her "locks and disheveled head (are) entwined with short vipers" (*Epod.* 5.15–16: *brevibus implicata viperis crines et incomptum caput*).[41] She has uncut nails (*inresectum . . . pollicem*) and discolored teeth (*dente livido*) (*Epod.* 5.47–48); her pallid complexion makes her and her sister witch horrible to look at (*Sat.* 1.8.25–26: *pallor utrasque fecerat horrendas*). She does not wear the bright, shining garments like the Greek witches do, but instead a black robe (*Sat.* 1.8.23: *nigra . . . palla*). Ovid's Dipsas is depicted as an old woman (*Am.* 1.8.2: *anus*) who has the double pupil (*Am.* 1.8.15: *pupula duplex*) characteristic of the evil eye.[42] Petronius's Oenothea is described as an old woman (*anus*), ugly in her black clothes (*nigraque veste deformis*) (*Sat.* 134). Lucan's Erictho is most horrible of all (6.515–18): "Haggard and loathly with age is the face of the [witch]; her awful countenance, overcast with a hellish pallor and weighed down by uncombed locks is never seen by the clear sky" (: . . . *tenet ora profanae/foeda situ macies, caeloque ignota sereno/terribilis Stygio facies pallore gravatur/inpexis onerata comis* . . .).[43] Her clothes and hair are also quite ghastly (6.654–56): "She put on motley raiment, whose multi-colored wool was fit for a fiend to wear; she threw back her hair and revealed her face; and she looped up her bristling locks with festoons of vipers" (*discolor et vario furialis cultus amictu/ induitur, voltusque aperitur crine remoto,/et coma viperis substringitur horrida sertis*).[44] Moreover, it is the Roman witches, like Horace's Canidia and Lucan's Erictho, who are represented as looking and behaving like animals, while the Greek ones are only associated with or compared to animals, as Homer's Circe and Euripides's Medea.

The motives of these two groups of witches are also quite different. The Greek witches are often driven to perform their magic by their sexual attraction for a man, whom they subsequently protect. In Homer, Odysseus says that Circe is "yearning for me to be her husband" (*Od.* 9.32: *lilaiomenē posin einai*).[45] Although she turned his men into pigs, when she cannot do so to Odysseus, she tries seduction to gain control of him. He refuses to sleep with her, however, until she swears an oath that she will do him no harm (*Od.* 10.343–44), and thereafter Circe keeps her bargain, offering him food and wine for his journey and sending fair winds to speed him on his way (*Od.* 11.7–8; 12.16–19 and 148–51), as well as offering him advice on his journey (*Od.* 12.36–141). Medea also is driven by sexual attraction to help Jason. According to Euripides (*Med.* 7–8), it was erotic love (*erōti*) for Jason that drove Medea to help him obtain the fleece and slay his uncle Pelias.[46] In Apollonius Rhodius (*Argon.* 4.360–68), Medea chastises Jason for trying to leave her when everything she did, she did for him:[47]

> I have left my country, the glories of my home and even my parents—things that were dearest to me; and far away all alone I am borne over the sea with the plaintive kingfishers because of your trouble, in order that I

> might save your life in fulfilling the contests with the oxen and the earth-born men. Last of all the fleece—when the matter became known, it was by my folly you won it; and a foul reproach have I poured on womankind.

Now, to be sure, the Greek witch when crossed can turn against her man, as Euripides's Medea wreaks her vengeance on Jason after he has betrayed her by making plans to marry the Corinthian princess. However, her initial motive at least was to help rather than harm. So in general we can say that the Greek witch may cast her spells on behalf of another, or at least to attract another, and she is portrayed as morally neutral or as mixed, good and evil together. Roman witches, on the other hand, perform their magical arts for far more selfish and even evil purposes, and they are seen as morally repugnant. So, the witches in the Roman elegists Tibullus, Propertius, and Ovid cast their spells for money, seeking to bring a lover to a client, or to remove uncomfortable passion from a client whose love is now unattainable.[48] Horace's Canidia, Sagana, and Folia act out of lust alone, as do Apuleius's Meroe, Pamphile, and Photis, with no concern for their victims.[49] Erictho, on the other hand, acts purely out of an evil desire for power; according to Lucan (6.578–85):[50]

> She feared that the war might stray away to some other region, and that the land of Thessaly might miss so great a carnage; and therefore the witch (*venefica*) forbade Philippi, defiled by her spells (*cantu*) and sprinkled with her noxious drugs (*diris . . . sucis*), to allow the warfare to change its place. Then all those dead would be hers, and the blood of the whole world would be at her disposal. She hopes to mutilate the corpses of slaughtered kings, to plunder the ashes of the Roman nation and the bones of nobles, and to master the ghosts of the mighty.

The methods that the Greek and Roman witches use are also quite different, as are the divinities upon whom they call to help them in their spells. The Greek witches generally use relatively simple methods, and little time is spent on their description by the ancient authors.[51] The classic example is Homer's Circe, who works her magic rapidly and easily on Odysseus's men (*Od.* 10.233–39):[52]

> She brought them in and made them sit on chairs and seats, and made for them [a potion of] cheese and barley meal and yellow honey with Pramnian wine, but in the food she mixed baneful drugs (*pharmaka lugr* [a]), that they might utterly forget their native land. Now when she had given them [the potion], and they had drunk it off, then she presently smote

> them with her wand (*rhabdōi*), and penned them in the sties. And they had the heads, and voice, and bristles, and shape of swine, but their minds remained unchanged even as before.

Similarly, in Pindar and Euripides, Medea uses drugs to carry out her will, but no description is given of their source or method of preparation, nor of any incantations employed during their preparation.[53] Among these authors, Euripides alone mentions Medea calling upon the gods, and most of the divinities she names are familiar celestial divinities, including Themis, Artemis, Zeus, Dike, and Helios, although as she becomes more angry and desperate she also calls on the witches' own goddess Hekate and the avenging demons, the Alastores.[54]

As we reach the Hellenistic period, the Greek authors pay more attention to the methods of witchcraft and to the divinities invoked in conjunction with magical spells.[55] In Theocritus's *Idyll* 2, Simaetha's methods are carefully described, including the use of drugs and magical tools like the *iunx* and *rhombus*, although their effect seems relatively mild. In her incantations, Simaetha calls for the most part on benevolent celestial gods, primarily Selene, the Moon, but also Artemis, Aphrodite, Hekate, and the Moirai.[56] In Apollonius Rhodius, Medea uses a variety of drugs and spells to help Jason, and in two instances more information is given about her magical methods. First, when she prepares the drug (*pharmakon*) that is to protect Jason from the fire-breathing oxen and the sown men, the gathering and preparation of the appropriate plant is elaborately described, as is the necessary incantation to Brimo, queen of the underworld, identified with Hekate (*Argon.* 3.844–68). Then, when she prepares to neutralize Talos, the bronze giant who guarded the island of Crete, her incantations (*aoidais*) to the death-spirits, the Keres, are described, as is the evil eye (*echthodopoisin ommasi*) that she uses to carry out her will (*Argon.* 4.1631–77).

Although the authors of this period give more information about the methods of witchcraft and the divinities involved in magic than their predecessors, the overall impression given of the spells these witches produce is relatively benign. In contrast, the methods of the Roman witches are elaborate and frightening; the gods they call upon are the terrifying divinities of the underworld; and the overall effect of the description of their spells is horror. In one of Horace's poems (*Epod.* 5.51), the witches Canidia, Sagana, and Folia bury a living boy in the ground and starve him to death to obtain his liver for a love spell. They call upon Diana (Artmis), as did the Greek witches, but they add the more fearful Nox, the personification of Night, to their incantations. In his satire on the witches (*Sat.* 1.8.34–35), Horace has Priapus observe them tearing a lamb to pieces with their bare teeth and pouring its blood into a trench to draw forth the spirits of the underworld, as they call upon Hecate and the dread Fury Tisiphone to aid their spells. In the *Metamorphoses* (7.179–293), Ovid describes in great detail the complex preparation of the spell that Medea casts to rejuvenate Jason's father Aeson, including a long list of ingredients and an elaborate series of incantations to Night, Hecate, Earth, Moon, and Youth. At the very opening of Seneca's *Medea* (1–18), the witch casts a curse on Jason with a litany of divinities, beginning with the gods of wedlock (*di coniugales*), Lucina, Minerva, Neptune, and Titan, but ending with a long list of infernal gods, including Hecate, the "chaos of eternal Night" (*noctis aeternae chaos*), the "realms remote from heaven" (*aversa superis regna*), the "impious spirits of the dead" (*manesque impios*), the "lord of the realm of gloom" (*dominumque regni tristis* = Pluto) and his queen (*dominam* = Proserpina), and finally the "goddesses who avenge crime" (*sceleris ultrices deae* = Furies).[57] Later in the play, Medea's ritual to prepare the poisoned gifts for the Corinthian princess is elaborately described (675–843), and she herself makes a long incantation to a variety of denizens of the underworld (740–51):[58]

> I supplicate the throng of the silent and you, funereal gods, murky Chaos, and shadowy Dis' dark dwelling-place, the abysses of dismal Death, girt by the banks of Tartarus. Leaving your punishments, ye ghosts, haste to the new nuptials; let the wheel stop that is whirling his body, and Ixion stand on earth; let Tantalus in peace drink his fill of the Pierian spring. You, too, whom a fruitless toil mocks with urns full of holes, ye Danaids, come hither: this day needs your hands. On one alone, my lord's new father, let a penalty rest heavier—let the slippery stone roll Sisyphus backward o'er the rocks. Now, summoned by my sacred rites (*meis sacris*), do thou, orb of the night, put on thy most evil face and come, threatening in all thy forms.

Lucan's Erictho also calls upon the denizens of the underworld: the Eumenides, Poenae, Chaos, Hades, Styx, Elysium, Persephone, Hecate, the Fates, and Charon (6.695–705), and she uses all sorts of human body parts in her rituals, which she collects in a particularly gruesome way (6.538–49):[59]

> But when the dead are coffined in stone, which drains off the internal moisture, absorbs the corruption of the marrow, and makes the corpse rigid, then [the witch] eagerly vents her rage on all the limbs, thrusting her fingers into the eyes, scooping out gleefully the stiffened eyeballs, and gnawing the yellow nails on the withered hand. She breaks with her teeth the fatal noose, and mangles the carcass that dangles on the gallows, and scrapes the cross of the criminal; she tears away the rain-beaten flesh and the bones calcined by exposure to the sun. She purloins the nails that pierced the hands, the clotted filth, and the black humor of corruption that oozes over all the limbs; and when a muscle resists her teeth, she hangs her weight upon it.

How far have we come from the beautiful Circe and her magic wand!

Finally, the powers exhibited by Greek and Roman witches are quite disparate. The Greek witches have the power to change humans into animals, prophesy, cure childlessness, cast the evil eye, bewitch a lover, and poison an enemy. Dangerous they are, to be sure, but hardly horrific. Moreover, the powers that they exhibit are exercised largely in a mythical context. Until Theocritus's Simaetha in the Hellenistic period, the Greek witches, such as Circe and Medea, are mythological figures, rather than people in the real contemporary or historical world. By placing these figures in a mythological past, the Greek authors make their witches less "real" to their audience, and hence do not stimulate the same kind of fear among them. In contrast, Roman authors generally place their witches firmly in the real world. Except for the witches borrowed from Greek mythology, like Ovid's Circe and Seneca's Medea, Roman witches are represented as contemporary or historical figures, such as the witches from whom Propertius, Tibullus, and Ovid seek spells to beguile their lovers, or Lucan's Erictho, whom the Roman general Sextus Pompeius consults to learn his future. In addition to being more "real," the power of Roman witches is far greater than that of Greek witches. They can do all the things that Greek witches can, plus control the spirits of the dead, animate corpses, and even control the gods. Lucan's Erictho again provides the best example (6.523–28):[60]

> She addresses no prayer to Heaven, invokes no divine aid with suppliant hymn, and knows nothing of the organs of victims offered in sacrifice; she rejoices to lay on the altar funeral fires and incense snatched from the kindled pyre. At the first sound of her petition the gods grant every horror, dreading to hear a second spell (*carmen*). She buries in the grave the living whose souls still direct their bodies: while years are still due to them from destiny, death comes upon them unwillingly; or she brings back the funeral from the tomb with procession reversed, and the dead escape from death.

Erictho's powers thus break all the boundaries of natural law: the boundaries between sacred and profane, mortal and immortal and even between the living and the dead. It is this frightening power that threatens to bring primordial Chaos back to the world.[61]

How, then, can these significant differences in the literary representation of Greek and Roman witches be interpreted? A variety of explanations can be proposed, and indeed the reasons may be over-determined; that is, more than one may apply. One possible explanation is that the portraits of Greek witches that we have examined come from a period in which the concept of magic was not yet fully defined, and so its negative characteristics were not yet completely developed.

Richard Gordon notes that there are two different faces of magic in classical literature: "one face is that of religious power used illegitimately, the other the dream of power to effect marvelous changes in the real world."[62] Gordon suggests that the negative marking of supernatural power does not appear until at least the fifth century, and it is fully developed only during the Hellenistic period.[63] The literary portraits that we have of Roman witches all come from a later period, and so were influenced by the development of the concept of magic in general.[64] This explanation, however, does not address why the Roman portraits are so much more negative than the Greek. In the Hellenistic period, when the concept of magic was full blown, the portraits of Greek witches, such as Theocritus's Simaetha and Apollonius Rhodius's Medea, are not nearly as frightening as Horace's Canidia or Lucan's Erictho. There seems to be a basic cultural difference here that this explanation does not sufficiently address.

Another possible explanation for the difference in the portraits of Greek and Roman witches is that magic in general was viewed more negatively in Roman than in Greek society. To some extent, this seems to be true. The Romans seem much more concerned about the negative effects of magic on society as a whole.[65] This concern goes back to the Twelve Tables, the Roman law code traditionally dated to the Early Republic, which lists attempting to enchant another's crops as a serious crime.[66] In the time period from which most of our literary portraits of Roman witches come, the Late Republic and Early Empire, concern over the practice of harmful magic seems to have been quite high. Special legislation was passed to stamp out the practice of such magic,[67] and magical practitioners, including magicians and astrologers, were periodically expelled from Rome and Italy.[68] Negative attitudes toward magic among the Romans may then explain at least partially the negative representations of the witch in Latin literature.

On the other hand, this explanation does not address the highly problematic representations of gender and magic. Literary portraits of male practitioners of magic in Latin literature and also in Greek literature from the Empire are in general far more positive than those of female ones.[69] These men are represented as learned magicians, or even philosophers, whose interest in magic is part of their search for knowledge.[70] So, according to Varro, the ancient Roman king Numa Pompilius used magic to obtain knowledge of the rites and practices he should establish for Roman religion (Varro, cited in August. *De civ. D.* 7.35). A similar motive is attributed to the magical dabbling of Nigidius Figulus, a polymath of the Late Republic, who is described as a "keen and diligent investigator of those things which seem to be hidden by nature." (Cic. *Tim.* 1: *acer investigator et diligens earum rerum, quae a natura involuate videntur*).[71] Moreover, authors portray these male magicians as using their magic for good rather than evil. So Apollonius of Tyana, the great philosopher/miracle-worker of the Early Empire, supposedly performed exorcisms, cured the sick, averted a plague, and raised the dead

(Philostr. *V.A.* 3.38–39, 4.10, 4.45). A Palestinian miracle-worker of this period, Simon Magus, reportedly made cripples whole, the blind see, and the dead live again (Justin, *Apol.* 26.1–2). Even when these literary portraits are not quite so positive, the objection to male practitioners of magic seems to be that they are charlatans, performing conjuring tricks rather than real magic. So, Anaxilaus of Larissa, a Pythagorean and magus of the Augustan Age, had a collection of amusing spells to entertain guests at a drinking party, including one in which cuttlefish ink was put on a lamp wick to make all present look like Ethiopians (Plin. *HN* 19.19). The most famous of these supposed charlatans, Alexander of Abonuteichos, is reputed to have deluded the masses by using a fake talking serpent to give out his prophecies (Lucian, *Alex.* 26). This is not to say that men in the Roman period were not in reality accused of the practice of harmful magic, as the trial of Apuleius certainly shows (Apul. *Apol.*). My point is that the Roman literary representation of the male magician tends to be far more positive than that of the female witch. There are no portraits of evil male sorcerers in Latin literature comparable to the horrific images of the female witches Canidia and Erictho. Negative attitudes toward magic in general among the Romans thus cannot fully explain why it is specifically the women who are demonized in Roman literary portraits of magical practitioners.

We must therefore seek another explanation for the differences in the literary representations of Greek and Roman witches. One possibility is that these differences are related to the cultural constructions of the female in Greek and Roman society,[72] in particular to the divergent concepts that these peoples had of the appropriate relationship between women and power, and between women and the divine. In Greek society, at least until the Hellenistic period, the evidence suggests that women had little societal power, with the exception of religion, where as priestesses of official state cults they regularly mediated the divine alongside male priests for society as a whole.[73] If we follow Gordon's proposal that magic can be viewed as "religious power used illegitimately,"[74] we might hypothesize that since Greek women commonly had legitimate religious power, the notion that they might also have had illegitimate religious power, that is, magical power, would have seemed less threatening. Moreover, since Greek women's societal power was largely restricted to the religious sphere, the possibility that they might obtain power that would threaten male control of society as a whole would seem unlikely. The representations of Greek women with magical power thus would in general then be more positive, expressing more the positive fantasies of the men who created them rather than their negative fears. In Roman society, on the other hand, from the Late Republic on, women had considerable economic and political power, although this power was unofficial and highly contested, whereas their role in state religion was highly restricted.[75] We might hypothesize that the idea that Roman women might wield illegitimate religious power would be seen as highly threatening, both since they were generally restricted from access to religious power in general, and because the possibility seemed more likely that they could in fact threaten male control of society. Such fears might lead to the highly negative portraits of witches in the Roman sources, producing the image of the witch whose power threatened to destroy natural law and lead the universe back into chaos.[76]

If we consider in detail the cultural context in which the most negative representations of witches were produced, another possible interpretation also emerges. As I have noted, negative portrayals climax in Latin literature of the late first century BCE and the early to mid-first century CE with such frightening witch figures as Canidia and Erictho. This period from the end of the Republic through the Early Empire was characterized by political, social, and cultural turbulence. One area that was singled out for concern was a perceived decline in socio-moral standards, particularly as they affected traditional gender roles.[77] There was a high degree of anxiety expressed in contemporary literature over the ways in which women were perceived as behaving, especially at the highest levels of society.[78] The reality may not have been that women were in fact changing their behavior; however, the literary representations of that behavior indicate a perception of such a change. According to these reports, upper-class women, such as Augustus's wife Livia, were meddling in affairs of state, contrary to social norms that proscribed women's interference in such matters.[79] Examples of female moral turpitude were held up for particular societal opprobrium, such as the notorious Messalina, the third wife of the emperor Claudius, who reportedly turned the imperial palace into a brothel and serviced its customers herself (Juv. *Sat.* 6.115–32). Moreover, the laws the emperor Augustus passed that attempted to encourage marriage and to discourage abortion and adultery indicate that considerable anxiety was being expressed over women's sexual behavior in this period, whether or not there was any real change in such behavior.[80] The early imperial poet Juvenal's vituperative Sixth Satire on women showcases the highly negative reactions to these reported changes in women's traditional roles and behaviors, attacking their inappropriate desires for sex and power. Perhaps the similarly negative witch portraits that belong to this period are another way of representing anxieties regarding women "out of control," that is, behaving in ways that threatened traditional gender roles and thus social stability. Kimberly Stratton has suggested that these negative portraits are tied to an ongoing discourse in Roman literature on women's dangerous independence.[81] This discourse, which dates back to the third century BCE, was tied to magic in the Augustan period, heightening the demonizing power of the representation of the "wicked" independent and powerful woman. As we have seen, the witch represented the polar opposite of all that the "proper" Roman matron was supposed to be:[82] the witch was ugly, lustful, castrating, power-mad, and evil rather than beautiful, chaste, fertile, submissive, and good. The loathsome figure of the Roman witch therefore could serve to reassert traditional social mores through reaffirming by contrast the traditional roles held by women in Roman society.

This explanation assumes that the Roman stories regarding witches are being told as cautionary tales regarding women's behavior. We should recognize, however, that they also address issues concerning men's behavior, and that since they are tales written by men for a largely male audience, this may in fact be their primary focus.[83] These stories fit into an ongoing discourse in the late Republican and early imperial period regarding the Roman definition of masculinity and the challenge represented to that definition by *mollitia*, "effeminacy."[84] In an article on the tales regarding the Roman "night hag," the most frightening of the witch figures, I have argued that these stories focus on male concerns over their appropriate sexual and social roles and on their fears of emasculation/ feminization and its concomitant loss of social status.[85] According to the traditional Roman view of gender roles, "real" men were dominant both sexually and socially. In fact, the two areas of dominance were closely linked, for those of high social status were supposed to be sexually dominant as well, able to penetrate others readily and to defend their own bodies from any type of penetrative assault, making them, in Jonathan Walters's terms, the "impenetrable penetrator."[86] The sexually dominant male, however, was only one of four sexual roles that people could hold, according to the Roman formulation of human sexuality, as Holt Parker explains:[87]

> The Romans divided sexual categories for people and acts on the axis of "active" and "passive." Active has, in their scheme, a single precise meaning. The one normative action is the penetration of a bodily orifice by a penis . . . Thus active is *by definition* "male" and passive is *by definition* "female." Accordingly, Roman society creates exactly four sexual categories for people. There is the normal/active male (*vir*) and the normal/passive female (*femina/puella*). Each then has its antitype: the passive/abnormal man (*cinaedus*) and the active/abnormal woman (*virago/tribas/moecha*).

I propose that the Roman night hag represents the antitype of the active/ abnormal woman, while her male victim is the antitype of the passive/abnormal man. As I have noted earlier, the witch is generally driven by lust, and in the night hag stories, she acts upon that lust in a particularly violent way. Parker says of the sexually active woman, "she will desire to penetrate, but cannot be truly (phallically) active."[88] The female witches in these stories, however, actually do penetrate their male victims, and they do so not through the normal openings in the male body (anus or mouth),[89] but through monstrous orifices that they deliberately open in that body. They also penetrate their victims symbolically, by breaking through the boundaries of their household, the space that a Roman male was traditionally supposed to control. Thus, in the night hag tales, penetration is expressed on two levels that are symbolically equivalent: the corporeal and the domestic.[90] The Roman witches repeatedly violate the margins of both the dwelling and the male body.[91] By submitting to these abnormal acts, their male victims are made into weak feminized creatures and hence become objects of pity and/or derision. It is interesting that the night hag stories often end with the audience to the story laughing at the victim in the story. Such laughter may signal underlying anxiety as well as reinforcing social mores through ridicule of those who are represented as violating them.[92] These stories may well express the fears of men that they could fail in their sexual role as the "impenetrable penetrator" and thus would no longer be a "real" man, a *vir*.[93] The threats of castration frequently expressed in these tales would then illustrate the fear of emasculation/feminization through falling into the role of the passively penetrated male. Indeed, the standard expression in Latin for assuming this role is *muliebria pati*, "to have a woman's experience."[94] The man who assumes this role to a certain extent *becomes* a woman, and the stories suggest that the ultimate result of this gender bending is humiliation and a drastic loss of social stature. I propose that one significant purpose of the night hag tales is to express the anxiety surrounding the active/passive sexual dichotomy and to reinforce strictures regarding appropriate male sexual and social roles.

One example of this type of story is Aristomenes's tale from Apuleius's *Metamorphoses* (1.5–19).[95] In this tale, Aristomenes meets his old friend Socrates, who has been reduced to a sorry state by his encounter with Meroe, a witch (*Met.* 1.8: *saga*). According Socrates, Meroe had forced him to submit to her lust (*Met.* 1.7: *urigine*), taken away his clothing, and confiscated his wages. She had clearly assumed here the dominant male role, while Socrates was feminized/emasculated by his contact with the witch. Aristomenes does not sympathize with his friend, but instead castigates him for abandoning his ancestral gods and his family (*Met.* 1.8: *lari et liberis*), that is, his social status, for the witch's sexual charms. Socrates defends himself by proclaiming Meroe's power and relating a series of tales illustrating her dominance over her other lovers. These stories all emphasize the degradation that these men experience as a result of their sexual encounter with the witch, and one explicitly indicates that her goal is emasculation, for she turns one of her lovers into a beaver in the hope that like that animal, he might castrate himself in order to escape.[96] At the climax of his description of Meroe's powers, Socrates shows her control of both corporeal and domestic boundaries by relating how she had blocked up the womb of her lover's wife, so that the baby could not be born,[97] and how she had shut the population of an entire village up in their houses, preventing them from opening their doors or breaking through their walls.[98] The themes of domestic/corporeal boundary control/ violation and emasculation echo throughout the remainder of the tale. Aristomenes and

Socrates hide from Meroe in a room at an inn, but in the middle of the night, Meroe and her companions spectacularly violate the domestic boundary, causing the bolts to be run back, breaking and tearing out the pivots, and throwing the doors to the ground.[99] They then threaten to rip all the limbs off Aristomenes and castrate him.[100] Instead, however, they turn to a violation of Socrates's corporeal boundary: Meroe plunges a sword into his neck, collects his blood, and rips out his heart through his throat.[101] They staunch his wound with a sponge and some magical words, and then they turn back to Aristomenes, humiliating him by straddling his face and urinating on him.[102] This act again points to the witches assuming the dominant male role, since urination and ejaculation are closely connected in Latin terminology.[103] Moreover, Aristomenes notes that by this act they had left him naked, cold and wet, like a baby just emerged from its mother's womb.[104] This statement shows that the witches have emasculated Aristomenes, simultaneously infantilizing and feminizing him, for coldness and wetness are precisely the characteristics attributed to women according to classical medical theory.[105] The retreat of the witches again signals their control of the domestic boundary, for the minute they depart, the doors, pivots, bars, and bolts are magically restored to their prior state.[106] Aristomenes, whose very name seems to reflect his manliness ("best in strength"),[107] then imagines someone casting doubt on his manhood for his behavior in this incident by saying "You could at least have called out for help, if a big man like you could not withstand a woman by yourself."[108] When in fear and shame he then tries to commit suicide, Aristomenes falls on Socrates, who awakens, apparently restored to his former self. Socrates and Aristomenes flee the inn, but later, Socrates collapses and dies, and Aristomenes flees the country in fear and trembling, abandoning his previous life and family, and thus being deprived of all his social status.[109] When Aristomenes finishes the tale, his travel companion ridicules him, saying that his story is both fabulous and ridiculous.[110] The tale of Aristomenes is clearly a cautionary one, pointing to male fears of emasculation and loss of social status through the assumption of a passive pseudo-female role. The tale thus reinforces traditional Roman male gender roles, both social and sexual, and fits well with contemporary discourse on issues of masculinity and effeminacy.

In conclusion, then, we may note that the witch in classical literature can serve a variety of functions. First, she can represent male fantasies and fears of what it would be like to be associated with a woman of supernatural power. Like Medea in the *Argonautica* of Apollonius Rhodius, the witch can help a man to overcome impossible odds to win the object of his greatest desire; or like Meroe in Apuleius's *Metamorphoses*, the witch can utterly destroy a man, taking away his social position, his manhood, and even his life. Secondly, the witch can illustrate the consequences of inverting the "natural" order. When the female witch inverts the laws of Nature, all the boundaries that order the world are dissolved, and chaos results. The clear message is that the natural order must be preserved, in which men through their association with culture are dominant over women and nature. Third, the witch can represent a highly negative model for female behavior and thus help to reassert traditional female roles within that society. The powerful and sex-crazed witch serves as the antithesis of the traditional submissive and chaste Roman matron, and thus encourages women and the men who are supposed to be in control of them to make sure that women remain faithful to their traditional roles. Finally, the witch can also express men's fears of what might happen if they do not maintain their own traditional male role of dominance, but rather sink to effeminate submissiveness. Such a shift would make them not only powerless but also ridiculous. Interpretations of the witch figure can clearly be multiplied beyond those I have suggested here.[111] She is clearly a prime example of the Other, against whom a wide variety of anxieties and desires can be projected. However we choose to interpret her in her manifold forms, it is clear that the witch was an extremely powerful archetype in classical literature. From the divine Circe to the demonic Erictho, the witch looms threateningly in these ancient tales, alternately seducing and terrifying the reader with her magical powers.

Notes

1. This article was submitted in its final edited form in 2008, and I was not able to change the text in any substantive way or incorporate into the argument more recent bibliography after that date. I would like to thank the Loeb Classical Library Foundation, the College of William and Mary, the Reves Center for International Studies, the Newcomb Foundation, and the Center for Hellenic Studies for their financial support of my research on the witch in classical antiquity. For their helpful suggestions, criticisms, and comments on the content of this article, I would also like to thank Debbie Felton, Mary Gelfand, Fritz Graf, Sarah Iles Johnston, Dayna Kalleres, Paul Mirecki, Eric Midelfort, Kathleen Perkins, Oliver Phillips, Linda Reilly, Kimberly Stratton, and Ayse Tuzlak.
2. *American Heritage Dictionary of the English Language* (4th ed.; Boston: Houghton Mifflin Company, 2000), s.v. "witch," first definition. I do not make the distinction, common to anthropological usage between witches and sorcerers, since this distinction is largely inoperative in ancient texts. On the anthropological usage, see, e.g., Max G. Marwick, ed., *Witchcraft and Sorcery: Selected Readings* (Magnolia, MA: Peter Smith, 1971), 11–19.
3. This discussion of the terminology for "witch" in antiquity is based on a search through the English to Greek (http://www.perseus.tufts.edu/cgi-bin/enggreek?lang=greek) and English to Latin dictionaries (http://www.perseus.tufts.edu/cgi-bin/enggreek?lang=la) in the online Perseus database for the terms "witch," "sorceress," and "enchantress," and a review of the terms under the

category of "magic." For a general discussion of the terminology applied to magical practitioners in antiquity, see Matthew W. Dickie, *Magic and Magicians in the Greco-Roman World* (New York: Routledge, 2001), 12–16; Fritz Graf, *Magic in the Ancient World*, trans. Franklin Philip (Cambridge, MA: Harvard University Press, 1997), 20–60; and E. E. Burriss, "The Terminology of Witchcraft," *CPh* 31(1936): 137–45.

4. On this issue, see, e.g., Kimberly Stratton, *Naming the Witch: Magic, Ideology, and Stereotype in the Ancient World* (New York: Columbia University Press, 2007), 4–18; Jacob Neusner, Ernest S. Frerichs, and Paul V.M. Flesher, eds., *Religion, Science, and Magic: In Concert and in Conflict* (Oxford: Oxford University Press, 1989); and Dickie, *Magic*, 18–46. For more bibliography on this issue, see Daniel Ogden, *Magic, Witchcraft, and Ghosts in the Greek and Roman Worlds* (Oxford: Oxford University Press, 2002), 305.
5. For the approach that I am taking to the definition of magic as a form of socially unsanctioned religious activity, see, e.g., C. R. Phillips, "Nullum Crimen Sine Lege: Socioreligious Sanctions on Magic," in *Magika Hiera*, ed. Christopher Faraone and Dirk Obbink (New York: Oxford University Press, 1991), 260–76.
6. Hom., *Od.* 10–12; Pind., *Pyth.* 4; Eur., *Med.*; Ap. Rhod., *Argon.* 3–4; Theoc., *Id.* 2.
7. Verg., *Ecl.* 8; Hor., *Epod.* 3, 5, 17, *Sat.* 1.8; Tib. 1.2, 5, 7, 8; Prop. 1.1, 2.28, 3.6, 4.5; Ov., *Am.* 1.8, 3.7, *Her.* 6, 12, *Met.* 7, 14; Petron., *Sat.* 131–5; Sen., *Med.*; Luc. 6.413–830; Apul., *Met.* 1–3.
8. On the formation of the concept of magic, see Graf, *Magic in the Ancient World*, 20–36 and Dickie, *Magic and Magicians*, 18–46.
9. Richard Gordon, "Imagining Greek and Roman Magic," in *Witchcraft and Magic in Europe: Ancient Greece and Rome*, ed. Bengt Ankarloo and Stuart Clark (London: The Athlone Press, 1999), 178.
10. For more on the literary and artistic tradition surrounding the figures of Circe and Medea, see Judith Yarnall, *Transformations of Circe: The History of an Enchantress* (Urbana: University of Illinois Press, 1994) and James J. Clauss and Sarah Iles Johnston, eds., *Medea: Essays on Medea in Myth, Literature, Philosophy, and Art* (Princeton, NJ: Princeton University Press, 1997).
11. For the female monster, see Sarah Iles Johnston, "Defining the Dreadful: Remarks on the Greek Child-Killing Demon," in *Ancient Magic and Ritual Power*, ed. Marvin Meyer and Paul Mirecki (Leiden: Brill, 1995), 361–90. For the night-hag, see Barbette Stanley Spaeth, "The Terror That Comes in the Night: The Night Hag and Supernatural Assault in Latin Literature," in *Sub Imagine Somni: Nighttime Phenomena in Greco-Roman Culture*, ed. Emma Scioli and Christine Walde (Pisa, Italy: Edizioni ETS, 2010), 231–58.
12. For a collection of texts in translation on Greek and Roman witches, see Georg Luck, *Arcana Mundi: Magic and the Occult in the Greek and Roman Worlds. A Collection of Texts* (2nd ed.; Baltimore: The Johns Hopkins University Press, 2006), 93–96, 102–27, 53–57, 246–56, 66–71, 77–80, and Ogden, *Magic, Witchcraft, and*

Ghosts, 78–145. For further commentary, see Georg Luck, "Witches and Sorcerers in Classical Literature," in *Witchcraft and Magic in Europe: Ancient Greece and Rome*, ed. Bengt Ankarloo and Stuart Clark (London: The Athlone Press, 1999).

13. So, too, Melissa Jane Schons, Horror and the Characterization of the Witch from Horace to Lucan (PhD diss., University of California at Los Angeles, 1998), 216–20: "The complexity and flexibility of the witch's character make it possible for poets to design her to appear successfully in satire, iambics, elegy, tragedy or epic and still maintain the conventions of the genre . . . In defining the witch's character in each of these generic environments, the poet creates a figure who is immediately recognizable as a witch by drawing upon the aspects of the stereotype which suit his purposes . . . [The witch] defies the boundaries of genre, for her stereotypical character traits persist no matter what genre she inhabits . . ."
14. A lack of recognition of the difference between reality and representation can lead to such highly problematic statements as the following: "Canidia, therefore, is probably a typical witch painted from life . . . All that Horace says of her agrees with what we know of other witches. She was, like them, an old woman of haggard features and ashen complexion. Her social position at Rome was the lowest . . . As the other witches whom we have studied were either procuresses or keepers of low wine shops, it is likely that Canidia met her friends and customers through the same convenient avenue of trade . . . They are all libidinous far beyond what would expect from their years. Indeed, if we ask why any Roman woman should wish to become a witch, the answer seems to be—*libido*": Eugene Tavenner, "Canidia and Other Witches," in *Witchcraft in the Ancient World and the Middle Ages* (vol. 2 of *Articles on Witchcraft, Magic, and Demonology*; ed. Brian Levack; New York: Garland, 1992), 38–39.
15. Graf, *Magic in the Ancient World*, 175–6. Dickie, *Magic and Magicians*, 11, takes a rather different approach to the issue of representation, or as he calls it literary "stereotype": "To return to the more general question of getting behind the stereotype in ancient literature to the reality it conceals or distorts, we can either renounce the attempt as hopeless and confine ourselves to the not very demanding task of recording ancient representations or tackle the problem." Dickie uses literary portraits to try to reconstruct actual practice of witchcraft in antiquity, with somewhat mixed results. See David Frankfurter, review of *Magic and Magicians in the Greco-Roman World*, by Matthew Dickie, *BMCR* (27.02.2002; online http://bmcr.brynmawr.edu/2002/2002-02-26.html; cited May 19, 2007) on Dickie's overly credulous use of literary sources.
16. These associations are commonplace in many representations of witches. On the witch and nature, see, e.g., Sylvia Bovenschen, "The Contemporary Witch, the Historical Witch, and the Witch Myth," *NGC* 15 (1978): 83–119; on the witch and the body, see, e.g., Diane Purkiss, *The Witch in History: Early Modern and Twentieth-Century Representations* (New York: Routledge, 1996), 91–144. For a collection of tales from around the world that illustrate the figure of the witch,

see Shahrukh Husain, ed., *Daughters of the Moon: Witch Tales from around the World* (Boston: Faber & Faber, 1994). For the witch in folklore and fairytale, see, e.g., Venetia Newall, ed., *The Witch Figure: Folklore Essays by a Group of Scholars in England Honoring the 75th Birthday of Katharine M. Briggs* (London: Routledge, 1973) and Sarah Miller, "Evil and Fairy Tales: The Witch as Symbol of Evil in Fairy Tales" (PhD diss., California Institute of Integral Studies, 1984).

17. Debbie Felton has suggested to me that the description of Circe's dwelling in the forest glen, with smoke rising from her house, may be an early standard description of witches' dwellings as seen in the folktales of the Brothers Grimm, for example, Hansel and Gretel.
18. This is not to say, of course, that male magical practitioners did not use natural ingredients in their potions, as the *PGM* certainly shows. However, the issue here is one of representation: the witches are often shown in the wild gathering their natural ingredients; the same is rarely true of the male practitioners in classical literature. On the representation of male practitioners, see below.
19. The ability of witches to transform themselves into animals is connected with their hybrid nature, a characteristic of the demonic in antiquity. See Johnston, "Defining the Dreadful," 363.
20. Sherry B. Ortner, "Is Female to Male as Nature Is to Culture?," in *Women, Culture, and Society,* ed. Michelle Zimbalist Rosaldo and Louise Lamphere (Stanford, CA: Stanford University Press, 1974), 67–87; repr., Joan B. Landes, ed., *Feminism, the Public and the Private* (Oxford: Oxford University Press, 1998), 21–44.
21. For criticism of Ortner's views, see, e.g., Carol MacCormack and Marilyn Strathern, eds., *Nature, Culture and Gender* (Cambridge: Cambridge University Press, 1980). For Ortner's answers to these criticisms, see Sherry B. Ortner, *Making Gender: The Politics and Erotics of Culture* (Boston: Beacon Press 1996), 173–80. She argues as follows: "Gender difference, along with nature/culture is a powerful question. And the gender relationship is always at least in part situated on one nature/culture border–the body. What I think tends to happen in most if not all cultures is that the two oppositions easily move into a relationship of mutual metaphorization: gender becomes a powerful language for talking about the great existential questions of nature and culture, while a language of nature and culture, when and if it is articulated, can become a powerful language for talking about gender, sexuality, and reproduction, not to mention power and helplessness, activity and passivity, and so forth. The particular articulations of the relationship will vary across cultures, with surprising and unexpected shifts and alignments. But the chances that the two sets of issues will be interconnected in specific cultural and historical contexts still seem to me fairly high."
22. I find Ortner's arguments about the significance of women's physiology more persuasive than her interpretation of women's social roles and psychology in this context. It is the latter, in fact, that has led to much of the criticism of Ortner's

formulations, as well as her emphasis on the universality of the cultural devaluation of both nature and women.

23. Witches could also cause male impotence through the administration of potions; see Ov., *Am.* 3.20–36.
24. Homer, *The Odyssey*, trans. A.T. Murray, vol. 1, LCL (Cambridge, MA: Harvard University Press, 1984), 367.
25. For more on witches and normative sexual roles in classical culture, see below and Spaeth, "Terror that Comes in the Night."
26. Men's magic, as revealed by ritual recipe-books such as the *PGM* and archaeological evidence, also employed body parts, but this is a representation versus reality issue. Men's magic may have really involved these ingredients, but they aren't commonly represented using them.
27. Cf. Ortner, "Is Female to Male," in Landes, *Feminism, the Public and the Private*, 27: "Returning now to the issue of women, their pan-cultural second-class status could be accounted for, quite simply, by postulating that women are being identified or symbolically associated with nature, as opposed to men, who are identified with culture. Since it is always culture's project to subsume and transcend nature, if women were considered part of nature, then culture would find it 'natural' to subordinate, not to say oppress, them. Yet although this argument can be shown to have considerable force, it seems to oversimplify the case. The formulation I would like to defend and elaborate on . . . then, is that women are seen 'merely' as being closer to nature than men. That is, culture (still equated relatively unambiguously with men) recognizes that women are active participants in its special processes, but at the same time sees them as being more rooted in, or having more direct affinity with, nature."
28. Ovid, *Metamorphoses*, trans. Frank Justus Miller and G.P. Gould, 3rd ed., vol. 1, LCL (Cambridge, MA: Harvard University Press, 1984), 367.
29. E.g., Ap. Rhod., *Argon.* 3.528–33; Verg., *Ecl.* 8.69–67; Hor., *Epod.* 5.45–47; Tib. 1.8.17–27; Prop. 1.1, 2.28, 4.5; Ov., *Her.* 6.81–96, *Met.* 14.365–71; Petron., *Sat.* 129, 134–35; Sen., *Med.* 752–70; Luc. 6.461–506. For more on the ritual of "drawing down the moon," see Oliver Phillips, "The Witches' Thessaly," in *Magic and Ritual in the Ancient World,* ed. Paul Mirecki and Marvin Meyer; vol. 141 of *Religions in the Greco-Roman World* (Leiden: Brill, 2002), 378–85.
30. In this formulation, women are seen as intermediate between nature and culture, while men are seen as in control of the production of culture. I view this as a hierarchy, with men on top, in control of culture, then women, who are above nature, but still associated with it. Ortner points toward this hierarchy in the following passage ("Is Female to Male," in Landes, *Feminism, the Public and the Private*, 39): "I argued that the universal devaluation of women could be explained by postulating that women are seen as closer to nature than men, men being seen more unequivocally occupying the high ground of culture . . . At the same time, however, [woman's] 'membership' and fully necessary participation in culture are

recognized by culture and cannot be denied. Thus she is seen to occupy an intermediate position between culture and nature . . . (E)ven if she is not seen as nature pure and simple, she is still seen as achieving less transcendence of nature than man. Here 'intermediate' simply means 'middle status' on a hierarchy of being from culture to nature."

31. Such inversions are characteristic of demonic figures in the Hellenistic and Roman periods. See Jonathan Z. Smith, "Towards Interpreting Demonic Powers in Hellenistic and Roman Antiquity," *ANRW* II 16.1:425–39.
32. Seneca, *Tragedies*, trans. Frank Justus Miller, vol. 3, LCL (Cambridge, MA: Harvard University Press, 1987), 223.
33. Apuleius, *Metamorphoses (The Golden Ass),* trans. J. Arthur Hanston, vol. 1, LCL (Cambridge, MA: Harvard University Press, 1989), 69.
34. See, for example, Carole E. Newlands, "Medea: Essays on Medea in Myth, Literature, Philosophy, and Art," in *Medea: Essays on Medea in Myth, Literature, Philosophy, and Art,* ed. James J. Clauss and Sarah Iles Johnston (Princeton, NJ: Princeton University Press, 1997), 186–92; and Yarnall, *Transformations of Circe,* 79–98.
35. Apuleius's witches span both categories: Pamphile and Photis are of the Greek type, while Meroe and her friends are of the Roman type. This mixture of categories seems appropriate, given the mixture of sources Apuleius used to create his work. On the sources for Apuleius's *Metamorphoses*, see James Tatum, "The Tales in Apuleius' Metamorphoses," in *Oxford Readings in the Roman Novel*, ed. S. J. Harrison (Oxford: Oxford University Press, 1999), 157–94, and H. J. Mason, "Fabula Graecanica: Apuleius and His Greek Sources," in Harrison, ed., *Oxford*, 217–36.
36. Homer, *Odyssey*, 383.
37. A. S. F. Gow, ed., *Theocritus*, 2nd ed., vol. 1 (Cambridge: Cambridge University Press, 1952), 25.
38. Homer, *Odyssey*, 383.
39. Gow, ed., *Theocritus*, 23.
40. Apollonius Rhodius, *Argonautica*, trans. R.C. Seaton, LCL (Cambridge, MA: Harvard University Press, 1980), 251.
41. Horace, *Odes and Epodes*, trans. C.E. Bennett, LCL (Cambridge, MA: Harvard University Press, 1988), 315.
42. On the double pupil and the evil eye, see Ogden, *Magic, Witchcraft and Ghosts*, 224.
43. Lucan, *Civil War*, trans. J.D. Duff, LCL (Cambridge, MA: Harvard University Press, 1977), 343. The term "witch" does not appear in the Latin, so square brackets are used to indicate its absence. Erictho is referred to here instead as an impious woman (*profanae*).
44. Ibid., 353.
45. Homer, *Odyssey*, 305.

46. It is worth noting that in Pind., *Pyth.* 4.217, Jason uses magic on Medea first, getting her to fall in love with him, which is probably what he refers to in Eur., *Med.* 526–8 when he dismisses Medea's assistance, attributing all his help to Aphrodite.
47. Apollonius Rhodius, *Argonautica*, 319.
48. Tib. 1.2, 1.5, 1.8; Prop. 1.1, 3.6, 4.5; Ov., *Am.* 1.8, 3.7.
49. Hor., *Epod.* 5, *Sat.* 1.8; Apul., *Met.* 1–3, passim.
50. Lucan, *The Civil War*, 347.
51. On the simplicity of their methods, see below.
52. Homer, *Odyssey*, 36–12.
53. Pind., *Pyth.* 4.220–3; Eur., *Med.* 384–5, 717–8, 784–9.
54. Eur., *Med.* 160 (Themis and Artemis); 332, 516 (Zeus); 397 (Hekate); 764 (Zeus, Dike, Helios), 1059 (Alastores).
55. Kimberly Stratton has raised the possibility that this change in representation could reflect developments in ritual technology in this period, but concludes that ideological reasons are more likely to account for the shift: Stratton, *Naming the Witch*, 72. See also the discussion of changing ritual technologies in Gager, *Curse Tablets*, 7.
56. Theocr., *Id.* 2. 10, 69, 75, 81, 87, 99, 105, 111, 117, 123, 129, 135, 165 (Selene); 12, 14 (Hekate); 33 (Artemis); 30, 130 (Aphrodite); 160 (Moirai). Note that Simaetha calls upon the dread Moirai only at the very end of the poem, when she despairs of retrieving her lover.
57. Seneca, *Tragedies*, trans. Frank Justus Miller, vol. 1, LCL (Cambridge, MA: Harvard University Press, 1978), 229.
58. Ibid., 291–3.
59. Lucan, *Civil War*, 34–35.
60. Ibid., 343.
61. Cf. also Pamphile's description in Apul., *Met.* 2.5, cited earlier: she knows how to "drown all the light of the starry heavens in the depths of hell and plunge it into primeval Chaos": Apuleius, *Metamorphoses*, 69. Cf. on the Babylonian type of the demonic witch: Tzvi Abusch, "The Demonic Image of the Witch in Standard Babylonian Literature: The Reworking of Popular Conceptions by Learned Exorcists," in *Religion, Science, and Magic: In Concert and in Conflict*, ed. Jacob Neusner, Ernest S. Frerichs, and Paul V. M. Flesher (Oxford: Oxford University Press, 1989), 38: "The witch is transformed into a powerful human figure who introduces chaos into the social order and even intrudes on the divine world. She can compete with and even overpower the gods."
62. Gordon, "Imagining Greek and Roman Magic," 178.
63. Ibid., 178–91. For the development of the concept of magic, see also Graf, *Magic in the Ancient World*, 20–36 and Dickie, *Magic and Magician*, 18–46.
64. The earliest Roman literary portrait of a witch seems to be Vergil's and he is clearly influenced by that of Theocritus's Simaetha: so Anne-Marie Tupet, *La magie dans la poésie latine I: Des origines à la fin du règne d'Auguste* (Paris: Société d'édition

"Les Belles Lettres", 1976), 223–4. Tupet suggests that there may have been earlier such portraits, but we have little evidence for them.

65. See Graf, *Magic in the Ancient World*, 36: "The situation in Rome [regarding the nature of the concept of magic] seems comparable to what has just been described for Greece—yet, at the same time, it is rather different . . . The divergences resulted first from the fact that in Rome the practices of sorcery had always been fought by the civil authorities and, therefore, the accusation of magic was much more serious than in Greece . . . "
66. The relevant primary sources are Sen., *Q Nat.* 4.7.2 and Plin., *HN* 28.17. On magic in the Laws of the Twelve Tables, see Graf, *Magic in the Ancient World*, 41–43 and Dickie, *Magic and Magicians*, 142–5.
67. This legislation may be traced back to the Sullan law of 81 BCE, the *Lex Cornelia de sicariis et veneficiis*, although this law was probably not originally used to prosecute accusations of black magic. On the Sullan legislation and its later applications, see Dickie, *Magic and Magicians*, 145–51.
68. On these "police actions" against magicians, see Ibid., 152–7.
69. For a collection of primary texts in translation of male magicians in this period, see Ogden, *Magic, Witchcraft, and Ghosts*, 41–77 and Luck, *Arcana Mundi.*, 142–53, 57–61, 89–90, 271–2, 335–53. For further commentary, see also Luck, "Witches and Sorcerers". For an old, but still interesting, study of the male magician in classical antiquity, see E. M. Butler, *The Myth of the Magus* (Cambridge: Cambridge University Press, 1948), 44–83.
70. On the learned magicians of the Late Republic and Early Empire, see Dickie, *Magic and Magicians*, 168–75 and 202–19.
71. My translation.
72. For a basic overview of the cultural construction of gender and the recent scholarship on this topic, see D. Boyarin, "Gender," in *Critical Terms for Religious Studies*, ed. M.C. Taylor (Chicago: University of Chicago Press, 1998), 117–35.
73. On women in Greece from the Dark Age to the Classical period, see, e.g., Sarah B. Pomeroy, *Goddesses, Whores, Wives, and Slaves: Women in Classical Antiquity* (New York: Schocken Books, 1975), 32–119; Eva Cantarella, *Pandora's Daughters: The Role and Status of Women in Greek and Roman Antiquity* (Baltimore: The Johns Hopkins University Press, 1987), 38–76; Elaine Fantham et al., eds., *Women in the Classical World: Image and Text* (New York: Oxford University Press, 1994), 10–127; Sue Blundell, *Women in Ancient Greece* (Cambridge, MA: Harvard University Press, 1995), 63–196. For the role of women in Greek religion, see Ross Shepard Kraemer, *Her Share of the Blessings: Women's Religions among Pagans, Jews, and Christians in the Greco-Roman World* (New York: Oxford University Press, 1992), 22–49, 80–92; Matthew Dillon, *Girls and Women in Classical Greek Religion* (London: Routledge, 2002); Barbara Goff, *Citizen Bacchae: Women's Ritual Practice in Ancient Greece* (Berkeley: University of California Press, 2004); and Joan Breton Connelly, *Portrait of a Priestess: Women and Ritual in Ancient Greece* (Princeton, NJ: Princeton University Press, 2007).

74. Gordon, "Imagining Greek and Roman Magic," 178.
75. For Roman women in the Late Republic and Early Empire, see, e.g., Pomeroy, *Goddesses*, 149–80; Jane Gardner, *Women in Roman Law and Society* (Bloomington: Indiana University Press, 1986), 257–66; Eva Cantarella, *Pandora's Daughters: The Role & Status of Women in Greek & Roman Antiquity,* trans. Maureen B. Fant (Baltimore: The Johns Hopkins University Press, 1987), 135–70; Fantham et al., eds., *Women in the Classical World*, 260–329. The importance of the role of women in Roman religion is contested in contemporary scholarship. John Scheid, "The Religious Roles of Roman Women," in *A History of Women in the West I: From Ancient Goddesses to Christian Saints,* ed. Pauline Schmitt Pantel (Cambridge, MA: Harvard University Press, 1992), 377–408 argues that women never filled leading roles in Roman state religion. This view is clearly contradicted by such priestesses as the Vestal Virgins and the priestesses of the Bona Dea and Ceres/Proserpina, who administered public cults on behalf of the Roman state; these priesthoods, however, are the exception to the rule that in general men held official religious power and authority in Roman religion. For the Vestal Virgins, see Robin Lorsch Wildfang, *Rome's Vestal Priestesses in the Late Republic and Early Empire* (London and New York: Routledge, 2006); for the other priestesses, see Ariadne Staples, *From Good Goddess to Vestal Virgins: Sex and Category in Roman Religion* (London: Routledge, 1998) and Barbette Stanley Spaeth, *The Roman Goddess Ceres* (Austin: University of Texas Press, 1996), 102–13. Celia E. Schultz, *Women's Religious Activity in the Roman Republic* (Chapel Hill: University of North Carolina Press, 2006) also argues for the importance of women's roles in a variety of aspects of Roman religion.
76. Cf., e.g., Sen., *Herc. Oet.* 463 and Apul., *Met.* 2.5, as discussed above.
77. This argument is derived from anthropological and sociological theory on witchcraft, which suggests that at times when a society is under stresses that threaten socio-moral boundaries and the stability of gender roles, a more negative view of the witch becomes prevalent, resulting often in an increase in witchcraft accusations. The classic anthropological text for this theory is E. E. Evans-Pritchard, *Witchcraft, Oracles, and Magic among the Azande* (Oxford: Clarendon Press, 1937). For a discussion of the further development of Evans-Pritchard's ideas, see Mary Douglas, ed., *Witchcraft: Confessions and Accusations* (London: Tavistock, 1970). For the sociological adaptation of this theory, see Nachman Ben-Yehuda, *Deviance and Moral Boundaries: Witchcraft, the Occult, Science, Fiction, Deviant Sciences and Scientists* (Chicago: University of Chicago Press, 1985) and "Witchcraft and the Occult as Boundary Maintenance Devices," in *Religion, Science, and Magic in Concert and in Conflict*, ed. Joseph Neusner, Ernest S. Frerichs, and Paul V.M. Flesher (Oxford: Oxford University Press, 1989), 229–61.
78. For a discussion of the ideological reasons that such literary representations may have been promoted in the Augustan period, see Kristina Milnor, *Gender, Domesticity, and the Age of Augustus: Inventing Private Life* (Oxford: Oxford University

Press, 2005), 140–85 and Catharine Edwards, *The Politics of Immorality in Ancient Rome* (Cambridge: Cambridge University Press, 1993), 34–62.

79. For example, see Suet., *Tib.* 50.2–3 for Tiberius's concern regarding Livia's meddling: "Vexed at his mother Livia, alleging that she claimed an equal share in the rule, he shunned frequent meetings with her and long and confidential conversations, to avoid the appearance of being guided by her advice; though in point of fact he was wont every now and then to need and to follow it. He was greatly offended too by a decree of the senate, providing that 'son of Livia,' as well as 'son of Augustus' should be written in his honorary inscriptions. For this reason he would not suffer her to be named 'Parent of her Country,' nor to receive any conspicuous public honour. More than that, he often warned her not to meddle with affairs of importance and unbecoming a woman . . . " Suetonius, *Lives of the Caesars*, trans. J.C. Rolfe, vol. 1, LCL (Cambridge, MA: Harvard University Press, 1998), 381. On Livia, see, e.g., Anthony A. Barrett, *Livia: First Lady of Imperial Rome* (New Haven, CT: Yale University Press, 2002) and Elizabeth Bartman, *Portraits of Livia: Imaging the Imperial Woman in Augustan Rome* (Cambridge: Cambridge University Press, 1998).

80. On changing sexual mores in the Augustan period and the attempts to control them through legislation, see Fantham et al., eds., *Women in the Classical World*, 294–329. For a skeptical view of the reality of such changes, see Milnor, *Gender, Domesticity, and the Age of Augustus*, 140–85 and Edwards, *Politics of Immorality*, 34–62.

81. Stratton, *Naming the Witch*, 96–105. I wish to thank Dr Stratton for allowing me to read an early draft of Chapter 3 of her manuscript.

82. So, too, Schons, "Horror," 815, who argues that the representation of the witch deliberately inverts the role of the ideal Roman matron in order to provide a negative model for female behavior in Roman society. See also Stratton, *Naming the Witch*, 99: "I suggest that while Augustus was promoting domesticity and an idealized and politicized vision of female behavior as part of his imperial ideology, the image of the witch emerged as the antithesis. Her uncontrolled libido, masculine behavior, and independence signified chaos, a reversal of natural order, and social evils such as murder and infanticide. The witch thus functions as a foil for the symbol of imperial order, peace, and domestic harmony embodied in the chaste women of the imperial house, who were prominent icons of Augustus's civic renewal." For further discussion of the figure antithetical to the witch, see my work on the Roman goddess Ceres, whose image was promoted as a model for the female virtues of chastity and fertility from the Middle Republic through the Empire: Spaeth, *Roman Goddess Ceres*, 113–23.

83. Cf. Kate Cooper's argument that ". . . many ancient accounts of female behavior are shaped rhetorically to suit a judgment of male character . . ." in *The Virgin and the Bride: Idealized Womanhood in Late Antiquity* (Cambridge, MA: Harvard University Press, 1996), 13. Cooper (45–67) applies this theory to the Christian

romances in the Apocryphal Acts. These tales, she argues, although ostensibly about women and their sexual behavior, in fact are about men and their authority and status: "The challenge by the apostle to the householder is the urgent message of these narratives, and it is essentially about a conflict *between men*. The challenge posed here by Christianity is not really about women, or even about sexual continence, but about authority and the social order." See also Stratton, *Naming the Witch*, 78: "Insinuations and accusations about women's sexual misconduct and luxury thus often concealed political and social contests between men and should not be accepted as a straightforward portrayal of women's behavior."

84. This discourse is treated in detail by a number of modern scholars, including Edwards, *Politics of Immorality*, 63–98; Maud W. Gleason, *Making Men: Sophists and Self-Presentation in Ancient Rome* (Princeton, NJ: Princeton University Press, 1995); Anthony Corbeill, *Controlling Laughter: Political Humor in the Late Roman Republic* (Princeton, NJ: Princeton University Press, 1996), 128–73; Erik Gunderson, *Staging Masculinity: The Rhetoric of Performance in the Roman World* (Ann Arbor: University of Michigan Press, 2000).

85. See Spaeth, "Terror that Comes in the Night." In this article, I analyze four such tales: Ov., *Fast.* 6.131–69, Petron., *Sat.* 63, and Apul., *Met.* 1.5–19 and 2.21–30.

86. Jonathan Walters, "Invading the Roman Body: Manliness and Impenetrability in Roman Thought," in Judith P. Hallett and Marilyn B. Skinner, eds., *Roman Sexualities* (Princeton, NJ: Princeton University Press, 1997), 30.

87. Holt Parker, "The Teratogenic Grid," in Hallett and Skinner, eds., *Roman Sexualities*, 48.

88. Parker, "Teratogenic Grid," 58.

89. Parker, "Teratogenic Grid," 48–49. For the female body, the normal openings include, of course, the vagina.

90. As C. M. McDonough notes, "(t)he penetration of boundaries marking the household's outer limits is recapitulated in the penetration of the victim's bodily margins." See C. M. McDonough, "Carna, Proca and the Strix on the Kalends of June," *TAPA* 127 (1997): 332. McDonough cites Artemidorus (4.30) on how in dreams a man can be symbolized by his house, Plautus on this same theme in the *Mostellaria* (84–157), and Lucretius (3.58–8) on how the affliction of the body can be expressed through the metaphor of architecture.

91. In this violation of boundaries, the witches show that they are liminal creatures, those who straddle boundaries. Liminality is another characteristic of the demonic in antiquity. See Johnston, "Defining the Dreadful," 363.

92. Cf. Corbeill, *Controlling Laughter*, 5–6 on Roman humorous invective: " . . . Roman humorous abuse creates social norms by exposing the violators of those norms. Rome's humor of aggression caters to, in Cicero's words, 'the interests of each individual and of the community as a whole' by simultaneously creating and enforcing the community's ethical values. Jokes become a means of ordering social realities . . . At Rome, deviant behavior is behavior that public speakers so define in their invective. As they label deviance through political humor, the positive values

of society—the 'proper' way to look and behave—become reinforced by contrast. In creating and maintaining the ideal society envisioned in *On Moral Duties*, Cicero's Rome does have access to a disciplinary mechanism: laughter." Corbeill identifies accusations of effeminacy as one of the primary forms of Roman humorous invective. See Corbeill, *Controlling Laughter*, 11: "The orator had access to a specific set of external indicators that he could exploit to demonstrate his adversary's lapse from proper male behavior." On the social and psychological function of sexual humor, cf. also Abner Ziv, *Personality and Sense of Humor* (New York: Springer Publishing Company, 1984), 65–68: "Sexual humor functions as a regulator of our thoughts on the subject of sexual intercourse. By the term regulator, I mean a force that contributes to a normative organization of the system of sexual relations. Humor that ridicules 'unacceptable' forms of sexual intercourses acts as such a normative force. Sexual humor enables us to approach subjects in the area of sex that arouse anxiety: homosexuality, frigidity, sexual indifference, impotence, and so on. Mention of these subjects is apparently deeply embedded with taboos, even more so than general sexual subjects. And once again, humor allows us to approach these subjects without anxiety—or, at least, with less anxiety. By making the frightening elements of sexuality seem ridiculous, the intensity of the anxiety is lessened." For the classic work on this topic, see Sigmund Freud, *Jokes and Their Relationship to the Unconscious* (New York: Moffat Ward, 1916).

93. For the significance of the term *vir*, see Gunderson, *Staging Masculinity*, 7: "In Latin, a *vir* is an adult male. But the same word also signifies a man who is a husband or a soldier. Thus, in 'pregnant' uses, a man in Latin is a real man, a manly man. The term also designates a position of authority and responsibility: the adult is enfranchised, while the child (or slave) is not; the man rules his wife in the household: the soldier is the defender of the safety of the state. In short, the term evokes more than mere gender."

94. Walters, "Invading the Roman Body," 30–31.

95. Direct quotations from this tale in the discussion below are taken from Apuleius, *Metamorphoses* (LCL).

96. *Met.* 1.9: *amatorem suum, quod in aliam temerasset, unico verbo mutavit in feram castorem, quod ea bestia captivitati metuens ab insequentibus se praecisione genitalium liberat, ut illi quoque simile [, quod Venerem habuit in aliam,] proveniret.*

97. *Met.* 1.9: *eadem amatoris sui uxorem . . . iam in sarcina praegnationis obsaepto utero et repigrato fetu perpetua praegnatione damnavit . . .*

98. *Met.* 1.10: *. . . cunctos in suis sibi domibus tacita numinum violentia clausit, ut toto biduo non claustra perfringi, non fores evelli, non denique parietes ipsi quiverint perforari.*

99. *Met.* 1.11: *. . . repente impulsu maiore quam ut latrones crederes ianuae reserantur, immo vero fractis et evulsis funditus cardinibus prosternuntur.*

100. *Met.* 1.13: *quin igitur, . . . hunc primum bacchatim discerpimus vel membris eius destinatis virilia descamus?*

101. *Met.* 1.13: *et capite Socratis in alterum dimoto latus, per iugulum sinistrum capulo tenus gladium totum ei demergit, et sanguinis eruptionem utriculo admoto excipit diligenter . . . immissa dextera per vulnus illud ad viscera penitus cor miseri contubernalis mei Meroe bona scrutata protulit . . .*
102. *Met.* 1.13: . . . *varicus super faciem meam residentes vesicam exonerant, quoad me unrinae spurcissimae madore perluerent.*
103. Amy Richlin, *The Gardens of Priapus: Sexuality and Aggression in Roman Humor*, rev. ed. (Oxford: Oxford University Press, 1992), 251, note 8.
104. *Met.* 1.14: . . . *nudus et frigidus et lotio perlitus, quasi recens utero matris editus . . .*
105. For the theory, dating back to the works of Empedocles, see Corbeill, *Controlling Laughter*, 144–5.
106. *Met.* 1.14: *commodum limen evaserant et fores ad pristinum statum integrae resurgunt: cardines ad foramina resident, ad postes repagula redeunt, ad claustra pessuli recurrunt.* Cf. later, when Aristomenes himself is unable to open the doors, presumably because the witches still have them in their control: *Met.* 1.14: . . . *subdita clavi pessulos reduco; at illae probae et fideles ianuae, quae sua sponte reseratae nocte fuerant, vix tandem et aegerrime tunc clavis suae crebra immissione patefiunt.*
107. The name may be derived from the Greek *aristos* (best) + *menos* (strength); cf. B. L. Hijmans Jr., "Significant Names and Their Functions in Apuleius' *Metamorphoses*," in B. L. Hijmans Jr. and R. Th. Van Paardt, eds., *Aspects of Apuleius' Golden Ass* (Groningen: Bouma's Boekhuis, 1978), 116–7, who interprets it as "good councilor."
108. *Met.* 1.14: *proclamares saltem suppetiatum, si resistere vir tantus mulieri nequibas.*
109. *Met.* 1.19: *ipse trepidus et eximie metuens mihi per diversas et avias solitudines aufugi . . . relicta patria et lare ultroneum exilium amplexus . . .*
110. *Met.* 1.20: *Nihil . . . haec fabula fabulosius, nihil isto mendacio absurdius.* Cf. also *Met.* 1.2, where the companion laughs at Aristomenes after he first tells his tale, calling it an absurd and monstrous lie: *alter exserto cachinno: "Parce" inquit "in verba ista haec tam absurda tamque immania mentiendo."*
111. For example, Dayna Kalleres has suggested to me that anxieties regarding the witch's violation of boundaries may point not only to the strict divide between gender roles within the Empire, but also ethnic boundaries outside of (or more recently incorporated within) it.

3

"The Most Worthy of Women is a Mistress of Magic": Women as Witches and Ritual Practitioners in 1 Enoch and Rabbinic Sources

Rebecca Lesses

Introduction

NARRATIVES, LAWS, AND legal interpretations connect women with sorcery in three major Jewish corpora of antiquity and late antiquity: the Bible, the Enoch literature, in particular the Book of the Watchers (*1 Enoch* 1–36), and rabbinic literature.[1] When the first-century Jewish sage Hillel is quoted as saying, "the more women, the more sorcery,"[2] or the second-century rabbi Shimon bar Yohai as saying, "the most worthy of women is a mistress of sorcery,"[3] it might be possible to dismiss these statements as isolated opinions. However, when ideological statements in both the Palestinian and the Babylonian Talmuds interpret the biblical command "You shall not permit a sorceress to live,"[4] to mean "most women are sorceresses,"[5] whether Jewish or gentile, and a number of stories about women using incantations or various rituals in a malevolent fashion against men in general and rabbis in particular appear in both Talmuds, it is time to ask what these statements mean.[6] Do they represent the normative position in the rabbinic tradition? What relation, if any, do they have to earlier traditions in the Bible? Is there a connection to the earlier Enoch literature, in particular the Book of Watchers of 1 Enoch, which says that one type of forbidden knowledge that the fallen angels passed on to their human wives was sorcery? How do women figure into the various discourses of magic as a forbidden art in biblical, Enochic, and rabbinic sources? What do we learn about these sources' discourses of women from the way that they refer to them as witches? Do these discourses bear any relation to women's actual use of amulets, spells, and healing practices?

I argue in this article that these sources must not be read as presenting one monolithic view on the relation of women to forbidden ritual practices. It is necessary to read them in a nuanced fashion, especially when dealing with the question of the relationship between the theory of forbidden magic that the texts present and the particular practices that they ascribe to women or men. *1 Enoch* and some rabbinic sources create mythologies that identify women with witchcraft, but other rabbinic sources in particular undermine this very same mythology in their accounts of particular permitted or prohibited ritual practices to gain power.

Legal and Prophetic Discussions in the Bible

Exodus 22:17 commands, explicitly using the feminine form, "You shall not permit a sorceress to live."[7] At various historical points this commandment was taken very seriously, as we know from witchcraft accusations in early modern England, France, Germany, and the Massachusetts town of Salem. Is this, however, the last word on the biblical view of witchcraft? It is instructive to examine what the biblical laws of forbidden ritual activities include, and whether they specify women. Deuteronomy 18: 10–11 provide a comprehensive list of forbidden ritual practitioners and practices as follows:

> Let no one be found among you one who consigns his son or daughter to the fire, or who is an auger (*qosem qesamim*), a soothsayer (*me'onen*), a diviner (*menahesh*), a sorcerer (*mekhashef*), one who casts spells (*hover haver*), or one who consults ghosts or familiar spirits (*shoel' ob we-yid'oni*), or one who inquires of the dead (*doresh el-ha-metim*).

This passage is concerned with the ritual practitioners that the people of Israel should not consult (because that would make them like the nations previously resident in Canaan); rather, they should depend upon God to give them a prophet like Moses, and he will tell them God's will.[8] This section of Deuteronomy makes an explicit opposition between these forbidden practitioners and the prophet. None of those mentioned in this list are female, although the terms appear in the feminine in several other places. As mentioned above, Exodus 22:17 commands, "You shall not permit a sorceress to live." Leviticus 20:27, however, decrees death for *both* men and women who "have in them" a ghost (*'ob*) or a familiar spirit (*yid'oni*).[9] According to the account in 1 Samuel, after expelling those who act as mediums for ghosts and familiar spirits from the land, King Saul resorts to an *eshet ba'alat 'ob* (a woman who is a ghost-medium) to bring up the prophet Samuel from the dead and reveal Saul's fate in the war (1 Samuel 28:3–28).[10] Most of the legal and narrative discussions refer only to males or explicitly refer to both.[11] An interesting perspective on the biblical sources is provided by Yitschak Sefati and Jacob Klein, who argue that "in biblical times it was a common belief that women were engaged in the practice of sorcery more than men. The same belief is reflected in the relevant cuneiform sources from Mesopotamia."[12] Perhaps the singling out of women as witches in Exodus 22:17 can be traced back to this cuneiform tradition, but examining the biblical tradition as a whole does not lead to the conclusion that it is mostly women who engage in sorcery.

Several prophetic passages, however, make a connection between evil women (or cities symbolically represented as evil women) and witchcraft or sorcery. The prophetic passages also often connect sorcery and sexual sins, and denounce foreign women (Jezebel) or cities (Nineveh and Babylon) as witches. Jezebel is accused of performing "countless harlotries (*zenunim*) and sorceries (*keshafim*)" (2 Kings 9:22). Ezekiel attacks the Israelite women "who prophesy out of their own imagination" (Ezek. 13:17), using techniques of divination they learned in exile in Babylon.[13] Nahum 3:4 denounces Nineveh as a prostitute and sorceress: "Because of the countless harlotries of the harlot, the winsome mistress of sorcery (*ba'alat keshafim*), who ensnared nations with her harlotries, and peoples with her sorcery." Verse 5 goes on to describe her punishment in language reminiscent of the humiliation of Jerusalem in Ezekiel 16 and 23: "I am going to deal with you—declares the Lord of hosts. I will lift up your skirts over your face; and display your nakedness to the nations and your shame to kingdoms."[14] In these two cases, the harlot (Jerusalem or Nineveh) is punished through public nakedness and shaming. Isaiah 47:9 and 11–13 denounce Babylon as a sorceress, an enchanter, and one who resorts to those who predict the future by examining the skies. None of these skills can save her.

> These two things shall come upon you, suddenly, in one day: loss of children and widowhood shall come upon you in full measure, despite your many enchantments, and all your countless spells (*havarim*) . . . Evil is coming upon you, which you will not know how to charm away; disaster is falling upon you, which you will not be able to appease; coming upon you suddenly is ruin of which you know nothing. Stand up, with your spells (*havarim*) and your many enchantments (*keshafim*), with which you labored since youth! Perhaps you'll be able to profit, perhaps you will find strength. You are helpless, despite all your art. Let them stand up and help you now, the scanners of heaven (*hovrei shamayim*), the star-gazers (*hozim bakokhavim*), who announce, month by month whatever will come upon you.[15]

Babylon, like Nineveh and Jerusalem, is stripped naked as a mark of humiliation. Although the sins of Babylon do not include (in this passage) sexual sins, she still receives the same punishment:

> Get down, sit in the dust, Fair Maiden Babylon; Sit, dethroned, on the ground, O Fair Chaldea; nevermore shall they call you the tender and dainty one. Grasp the handmill and grind meal. Remove your veil, strip off your train, bare your leg, wade through the rivers. Your nakedness shall be uncovered, and your shame shall be exposed.[16]

The denunciations of Jezebel, Nineveh, and Babylon as sorceresses and harlots create a composite image that is more detailed than that found in legal and narrative biblical passages. They link sexual seductiveness with sorcery and the evil nature of foreign women (=nations) who oppress Israel and lure them to evil ways, building upon the already established prophetic sexual image of Israel's unfaithfulness to God through liaisons with foreign nations and the figure of the "strange woman" in Proverbs.[17] While 1 Samuel 28 portrays the medium of Endor in a sympathetic manner, as a woman who assists Saul when all others have failed him, these prophetic passages link female figures to the evil of witchcraft and divination. The prophetic image of the seductive foreign witch may provide some of the ideological background for the connection between women and sorcery in *1 Enoch* and in rabbinic texts.

The Book of the Watchers

The third-century BCE Book of the Watchers, comprising chapters 1–36 of *1 Enoch*, is in part an elaboration on the biblical story of the "sons of God" who descended to earth and mated with the "daughters of men."[18] Chapters 1–5 are an introduction to the book, while chapters 6–16 treat the story of the fallen angels. The figure of Enoch does not appear in the Book of the Watchers until chapter 12. He is not part of the introduction (chs. 1–5) or part of the original story of the sinning Watchers (chs. 6–11). Chapters 17–36 describe Enoch's tour of heaven, guided by angels. Chapters 6–16 interpret the events described in Genesis 6:1–4:

> When men began to increase on earth, and daughters were born to them, the sons of God (*b'nai ha-elohim*) saw how beautiful the daughters of men were; and took wives from among those that pleased them. The Lord said, "My breath shall not abide in man forever, since he too is flesh; let the days allowed him be one hundred and twenty years." It was then, and later too, that the Nephilim appeared on earth, when the sons of God cohabited with the daughters of men, who bore them offspring. They were the heroes of old, the men of renown.[19]

According to *1 Enoch* 6–11, the "sons of God" were angels, the "Watchers" (*'irin*) of heaven. They lusted after the "beautiful and comely" daughters of men. Their leader, Shemihazah, persuaded them to swear an oath together to descend to earth and take human women as wives and beget children. Chapters 6–11 are composed of several separate traditions of the angels' descent that a later author has combined, but it is still possible to discern what some of these separate traditions were.[20] Chapters 12–16 seem to assume the existence of 6–11 in its present form, building upon the earlier section but introducing the figure of Enoch and presenting details about the angels that are in some cases quite different from chapters 6–11.[21]

Enoch is introduced rather abruptly at the beginning of chapter 12: "And before these things Enoch was taken up, and none of the children of men knew where he had been taken up, or where he was or what had happened to him. But his dealings were with the Watchers, with the holy ones, in his days."[22] When Enoch was "taken up" (Gen. 5:24), he did not die, but instead dwelled with the angels in heaven, the "Watchers" and "holy ones." His task was to rebuke the fallen Watchers for their sins; he also served as their intermediary before God, and thus he is called "the scribe of righteousness."

1 Enoch 6–11

The tradition in chapters 6–11, in which Shemihazah is the leader of the sinning angels, concentrates on the sin of the Watchers—their descent from heaven, their defilement by intercourse with women, and the sins of their children, the giants, who destroy the earth. In this tradition, "there is no hint of the view that the women themselves are impure because of their human nature," and human beings do not share any guilt with the angels or the giants.[23] The flood comes upon them because of the sins of others.

A second tradition describes how the Watchers led human beings to sin by teaching them the secrets of heaven.[24] In this tradition, human beings are not the purely innocent victims of the angels. They make use of the skills that the angels teach them—the angels' sins cause humans to sin.[25] This tradition occurs in two forms; in the first one, the angels, led by Shemihazah, teach women magical arts and heavenly secrets.[26] According to the Shemihazah version:[27]

> These (leaders) and all the rest took for themselves wives from all whom they chose; and they began to cohabit with them and to defile themselves with them, and they taught them sorcery and spells and showed them the cutting of roots and herbs.[28]

The text goes on to give more details about which angels taught what skills:

> Shemihazah taught spell-binding and the cutting of roots; Hermoni taught the releasing of spells, magic, sorcery, and sophistry. Baraqel taught

> the auguries of the lightning; Kokabiel taught the auguries of the stars; Zikiel taught the auguries of fire-balls; Arteqif taught the auguries of earth; Simsel taught the auguries of the sun; Sahrel taught the auguries of the moon. And they all began to reveal secrets (*razin*) to their wives.[29]

If we look back to the sins that Isaiah ascribed to Babylon, figured as a woman, several of them also occur here: casting spells (*havarim*), sorcery (*keshafim*), studying the skies (*hovrei shamayim*), gazing at the stars (*hozim bakokhavim*), and predicting by the moon.[30] According to Leviticus, Deuteronomy, Nahum, Isaiah, and Ezekiel, the mantic and magical arts that they denounce belong to the practices of foreign nations—the nations of Canaan, Babylonia, and Assyria, the latter two identified as female personifications of the cities of Babylon and Nineveh. Given the Babylonian antecedents of the figure of Enoch, and the connections that James VanderKam has demonstrated between Jewish apocalyptic and Babylonian divination, it is interesting to note that it is just those arts that the Babylonian wise men, astrologers, and diviners practiced that the angels teach their human wives.[31]

In the second version of the teaching tradition, another rebel angel, Asael, teaches metallurgy, weapons, and cosmetics to human beings—the arts of civilization that lead people into sin. Dimant argues that these arts are reminiscent of the skills that the descendants of Cain learned, especially Tubal-cain, "who formed all implements of copper and iron."[32]

> Asael taught men to make swords of iron and breast-plates of bronze and every weapon for war; and he showed them the metals of the earth, how to work gold, to fashion [adornments] and about silver, to make bracelets for women; and he instructed them about antinomy, and eye-shadow, and all manner of precious stones and about dyes and varieties of adornments; and the children of men fashioned for themselves and for their daughters and transgressed. And there arose much impiety on the earth and they committed fornication and went astray and corrupted their ways.[33]

The Greek translation of Syncellus, which presents a slightly different version of this passage, implies that the women who learned the arts of beautification from Asael then turned around and seduced the other angels: "And the sons of men made for themselves and for their daughters, and they transgressed and they led astray the holy ones."[34] In this case, when the women learned to adorn themselves with jewelry, precious stones, colored clothing, and makeup, they tempted the angels to sin with them. They are not innocent, as in the Shemihazah version, but share guilt with the angels for the downfall of humanity.[35] The prophetic image of the foreign seductive woman who engages in witchcraft may have been a factor in the creation of this version. The idea that women were not innocent victims, but instead purposely lured the angels by their beauty is found in several sources dependent upon *1 Enoch* and in rabbinic sources that incorporate earlier traditions.

The Testament of Reuben, a pre-rabbinic text that is part of the *Testaments of the Twelve Patriarchs*,[36] explicitly refers to women lusting for the angels during sexual intercourse with their husbands:

> For it was thus that they charmed the Watchers, who were before the Flood. As they continued looking at the women, they were filled with desire for them and perpetrated the act in their minds. Then they were transformed into human males, and while the women were cohabiting with their husbands they appeared to them. Since the women's minds were filled with lust for these apparitions, they gave birth to giants.[37]

When chapters 9 and 10 of *1 Enoch* describe the punishment of the angels, the theme of secrets unjustly revealed, including the secrets of sorcery, is prominent among the reasons for their punishment. The four archangels, guardians of humanity, condemn Asael as a teacher of "the eternal mysteries prepared in heaven [who] made them known to men," presumably the arts of war and beauty that he taught to men and women, and Shemihazah as a teacher of "spell-binding," which probably includes the sorcery and divination mentioned earlier.[38] To counter the destruction that the revelation of these secrets caused, the angel Raphael (whose name means "God heals") is told to:

> Heal the earth which the watchers have ruined, and announce the healing of the earth, that I shall heal its wounds and that the children of men shall not altogether perish on account of the mysteries which the watchers have disclosed and taught the children of men. The whole earth has been devastated by the works of the teaching of Asael; record against him all sins.[39]

In the version of the story in *Jubilees*, Noah himself was given the remedies for the "illnesses" and "seductions" brought by the evil spirits who came out of the bodies of the giants.[40] These remedies consisted of "herbs of the earth," presumably beneficial in contrast to the maleficent "roots of plants" and "herbs" about which the Watchers told their wives in 1 Enoch.

1 Enoch 12–16

Chapters 12–16 of *1 Enoch* transform the combined traditions of chapters 6–11 in several ways.[41] One of the most interesting differences between them is that the miscegenation between angels and women is now described in terms of a dichotomy between spiritual and fleshly. The text sharply distinguishes between spiritual angels, eternally dwelling in heaven, and human women (and men), who are mortal, fleshly, and dwell on earth. The angels, who are clearly male in 1 Enoch, belong in heaven, but they have sought human women, who symbolize the passing, perishing nature of earth and flesh. In addition, the angels, as immortal beings, do not need to procreate, unlike men (therefore, there are no female angels).[42] *1 Enoch* 15 explicitly opposes the angels, as they used to dwell in "high heaven, the eternal sanctuary," "spirits, living forever," and their present condition, after they have defiled themselves with women on the earth and have begotten flesh and blood children, "who die and perish."[43] They have defiled themselves through sexual intercourse with women, and what is more, with the blood of women's menstruation.[44] The angels are spiritual and immortal beings who have now entered the fleshly realm. Philo makes a similar point in his remarks on this verse: "But the substance (*ousia*) of angels is spiritual (*pneumatike*); however, it often happens that they imitate the forms of men and for immediate purposes, as in respect of knowing women for the sake of begetting [giants]."[45]

Women may be the dupes of the angels, and thus not responsible for the evil of their giant children, but they are responsible for propagating the teachings the angels gave them and causing further evil on earth. Enoch denounces the fallen angels with these words: "You were in heaven, and there was no secret that was not revealed to you; and unspeakable secrets you know, and these you made known to women in your hardness of heart; and by these secrets females and mankind multiplied evils upon the earth."[46] It is significant that women are named before men in this sentence—the primary emphasis is on what *they* learned and how they multiplied evils on earth. The text in *1 Enoch* 16 does not spell out what the "unspeakable" or "rejected" mysteries are, but since chapters 12–16 were written with chapters 6–11 in mind, it is probable that the "rejected mysteries" that the angels taught women were the aforementioned cosmetics, sorcery, incantations, the loosing of spells and cutting of roots, as well as the signs of the stars, lightning flashes, the earth, the sun, and the moon.[47] They are the opposite of the secrets of heaven that Enoch learns from God and the angels.

Chapters 6–16 of the Book of Watchers thus create an antinomy between the righteous knowledge that Enoch gains by ascent to heaven and the polluting knowledge that women and men gain from the descent of the Watchers to earth.[48] Enoch is the special one who can ascend to God's throne, speak with God, tour the heavens, and learn divine mysteries.[49] The women whom the angels take as wives, on the other hand, learn sorcery and other "rejected mysteries."

The Fallen Angels in Rabbinic Texts

Does the rabbinic tradition know the story of the fallen angels, their seduction of women, and their destructive teachings? Did the Enochic tradition that associates women with witchcraft have any impact upon rabbinic exegesis of Genesis 6:1–4, and upon the strand in rabbinic tradition that identifies witchcraft with women? There is evidence, both explicit and implicit, that the Enochic traditions were known in some rabbinic circles, but were rejected or drastically rewritten from the second century CE on.[50] It was only after the close of the Babylonian Talmud and into the Geonic era that Enoch traditions were taken up by some authors and incorporated into midrashic retellings of the Bible, late Targumim, and mystical texts, in particular *Sefer Hekhalot* (also known as 3 Enoch).[51]

The fifth-century CE rabbinic commentary on Genesis, *Genesis Rabbah*[52] and the early Aramaic translation (second- to third-century CE Palestine),[53] *Targum Onqelos*, do not interpret the "sons of God" as angels. Instead, in *Genesis Rabbah*, R. Shimon b. Yohai (second century) understands them to be the *b'nai dayyana* (sons of the judges)[54]; while *Targum Onqelos* refers to them as the *b'nai ravravaya* (sons of the chiefs). In fact, R. Shimon b. Yohai "cursed everyone who called them the sons of God," which seems to indicate that he knew of the angelic interpretation and deliberately rejected it.[55] Annette Reed argues that R. Shimon's condemnation was directed at specific enemies: Christians and other *minim* who still valued the books of Enoch and the angelic interpretation of Gen. 6:2.[56] It is possible, nonetheless, to find traces of the Enochic interpretations even in these rabbinic traditions.[57] In Genesis Rabbah, after R. Shimon b. Yohai's curse, the text asks,

> Why did it call them the "sons of God"? R. Hanina and Resh Lakish: because their days were lengthened with no trouble and no suffering. R. Huna said in the name of R. Yose: in order to know the seasons and the calculations [of the heavenly bodies]. The rabbis said: in order that their [punishment] and that of future generations would be placed upon them. [58]

These three interpretations give reasons for use of the term "sons of God" that echo the attributes of the fallen angels in the Book of the Watchers.[59] The interpretation of R. Yose says that they lived for a long time in order to calculate the seasons and the paths of the heavenly bodies. The Astronomical Book, also part of *1 Enoch* (*1 Enoch* 72–80, 82), says that this knowledge was given to Enoch, and it may also have been part of the knowledge the fallen angels gave to humanity (*1 Enoch* 8:3).

In Genesis Rabbah, the "sons of the judges" or the "sons of the chiefs" commit acts that in *1 Enoch* are attributed to the Watchers or to their giant children, including their sexual transgressions.[60] One sage, Yudan, interprets the verse, "That they were fair" as: "When they were beautifying her for her husband, a great one (*gadol*) would enter and would have intercourse with her first"—so that the "great ones" were guilty of adultery.[61] Individual clauses in Genesis 6:2 are interpreted to refer to specific categories of forbidden unions: "'For they were fair'—these are the virgins; 'and they took for themselves women'—these are the married; 'from all that they chose'—these are males and animals."[62] This interpretation agrees with the Shemihazah strain of *1 Enoch* that the women themselves were innocent, and that the great men were responsible for the illicit miscegenation. The generation of the flood was suspected of greater sexual transgressions even than those mentioned above: "R. Huna in the name of R. Joseph said that the generation of the flood was not destroyed until they wrote marriages for males and for animals."[63] Homosexuality and bestiality are not mentioned in 1 Enoch, but the text does mention one other way in which the angels transgressed the proper boundaries: they had intercourse with women during their menstrual periods.[64]

An adaptation of the view that the women themselves deliberately allured the angels also appears in Genesis Rabbah: "R. Berakiah said, a woman would go out to the market and see a youth, and conceive a passion for him; she would go and have sex with him and would raise up another youth like him."[65] A later Aramaic translation, Targum Pseudo-Jonathan, contains a very similar interpretation:[66]

> When the children of men began to multiply on the face of the earth, and beautiful daughters were born to them, the sons of the great ones (*b'nai ravravaya*) saw that the daughters of men were beautiful, that they painted their eyes (*kehalan*),[67] and put on rouge (*peqasan*),[68] and walked about with naked flesh. They conceived lustful thoughts, and they took wives to themselves from among all who pleased them.

Sages quoted in Genesis Rabbah attribute many of the sins ascribed to the giants in *1 Enoch* to the Nephilim, whom they equate with the primeval inhabitants of Canaan, the "Nephilim, Eimim, Rephaim, Giborim, Zamzumim, Anaqim, and Avim."[69] They were given these titles for the following reasons:

> "Eimim" because the fear (*eimah*) of them fell on all; "Repha'im" because all who see them are melted (*nirpah*) like wax; "Giborim" (mighty ones)—R. Aba in the name of R. Johanan, the marrow of the thigh-bone one of them was 18 cubits; "Zamzumim"—R . Yose in the name of R. Hanina said they were great ones (*megistoi*) of war; "'Anaqim," the rabbis said because they would heap necklaces (*'anaqim*) on necklaces; R. Aha said because they seized (*'onqim*) the globe of the sun and demanded "bring

> rain down for us"; . . . "Nephilim" because they caused the world to fall (*hipilu*), they fell (*naphlu*) from the world, and they filled the world with abortions (*nephalim*) from their whoring. [70]

They terrified human beings, were giant warriors, destroyed the world, and filled it with licentiousness. As the editor of the critical edition of Genesis Rabbah remarks, the interpretation that understood *'anaqim* to mean that they heaped necklaces (*'anaqim*) upon necklaces may refer to the tradition that Asael taught men to make jewelry and precious stones as ornaments for women.[71]

The tradition that the angels taught (or used) the mantic and magical arts may not be present in Genesis Rabbah, but traces of this tradition occur in later mystical and midrashic texts. For example *Sefer Hekhalot* (3 Enoch), a sixth-century CE text that belongs to the Hekhalot literature, the family of Jewish mystical texts that treat the divine chariot (*merkavah*) and the journey to the heavenly palaces (*hekhalot*), contains the motif that the leaders of the fallen angels, Uzzah, Azzah, and Azael, taught the generation of Enosh magic (*keshafim*). Following a widespread rabbinic tradition that accounted the beginning of idolatry to the time of Enosh,[72] 3 Enoch 5:7–9 says that the men of Enosh's generation "roamed the world from end to end, and each of them amassed silver, gold, precious stones, and pearls in mountainous heaps and piles. In the four quarters of the world they fashioned them into idols, and in each quarter they set up idols about 1,000 parasangs in height." They then decided they wanted to bring down the sun, moon, and stars to worship these idols. "How was it that they had the strength to bring them down? It was only because Uzzah, Azzah, and Azael taught them sorceries (*keshafim*) that they brought them down and employed them, for otherwise they would not have been able to bring them down."[73]

Reed argues that this section of 3 Enoch "represents a later addition to the Enoch-Metatron material in 3 Enoch (3–16 [§§4–20]) and reflects direct literary dependence on the extracts of the Book of Watchers preserved in the Christian chronographical tradition."[74] She believes that it is "best explained with references to the distinctive traditions in 1 En. 6–11."[75] What is interesting, if Reed's argument is accepted, is that 3 Enoch 5 did not mention the angels' descent to mate with women or their teaching sorcery to their wives, despite the fact that both elements are part of the Syncellus translation (belonging to the Christian chronographical tradition).[76] *Sefer Hekhalot* thus continues the process of reinterpretation begun in the later booklets of 1 Enoch, which do not cite women specifically as recipients of angelic knowledge.

Midrash Tanhuma, a Palestinian collection of homilies that has been dated from the fourth to the eighth or ninth century CE,[77] also includes the tradition that the fallen angels or their giant sons themselves engaged in magic. Commenting on the verse, "The Nephilim were on the earth in those days . . . these were the mighty men (*giborim*) that were of old, the men of renown (*anshe shem*)," it says, "This teaches that they would see the sun and the moon and engage in magic (*keshafim*). About them it says, 'They are rebels against the light.'[78] They are the mighty men, who are strong, rebel, and perform magic (*mekhashefim*)."[79] These two passages associate the fallen angels with magic, but make no mention of women.

Unlike 1 Enoch, the tradents quoted in Genesis Rabbah do not understand the "sons of God" to be angels, but rather to be powerful men, rulers or judges. Nonetheless, they do have some of the qualities that the angels possess in 1 Enoch: they are long-lived, they have knowledge of the seasons and the stars, and they commit sexual transgressions like the angels: fornication, adultery, bestiality, and homosexuality. The Nephilim, like the giants in 1 Enoch, strike fear into the hearts of human beings: they are great warriors, and they destroy the world. The view that the women themselves acted in a sexually aggressive manner also appears in Genesis Rabbah, in this case toward "youths" in the market. The motif of the women's seduction of the "great men" or the angels is consistent throughout the interpretation of Gen. 6:1–4, both in rabbinic (Genesis Rabbah, Targum Pseudo-Jonathan, Pirke de-Rabbi Eliezer) and non-rabbinic sources (Book of Watchers, Testament of Reuben). The idea that the angels were somehow involved in teaching or using mantic and magical arts is found, however, only in 1 Enoch, 3 Enoch, and *Tanhuma*.[80] It seems unlikely, therefore, that this idea led to the rabbinic ideology that viewed most women as witches. It is more likely, given the connections between 1 and 3 Enoch, that such a negative evaluation of the angels' involvement in magic and sexuality is important in establishing the opposition between the evil angels and the pure Enoch, who is carried up to heaven and is a paradigmatic model for heavenly ascent in 3 Enoch and other works of the Hekhalot literature. It is important, nonetheless, to try to understand why the prophetic literature, 1 Enoch, and one tendency in rabbinic thinking so strongly emphasize women's connection with witchcraft.

"Most Women Are Witches"

I now turn to consider how rabbinic literature represents women as sorceresses or as engaging in other forbidden practices in legal and narrative (halakhic and aggadic) contexts, moving beyond the question of whether the Book of the Watchers' ascription of sorcery to the wives of the fallen angels is also attested in rabbinic interpretation of Genesis 6:1–4. I examine passages in rabbinic literature that explicitly target women as witches and view women as more likely to engage in witchcraft than men (mostly centering on exegesis of Exodus 22:17, but including many aggadic passages as well). A primary example of this targeting is the only witch-hunt recounted in rabbinic literature—the story of the eighty women who were crucified as witches by Shimon ben Shetah.[81]

The next section of this paper begins by citing examples from the "Chapters of the Amorites" (*t. Shab.* chs. 6–7) which demonstrate a distinctly gendered understanding of forbidden practices, without at the same time associating women in particular with sorcery or divination. It then turns to stories from the Babylonian Talmud about a woman referred to by the fourth century sage Abaye as "Em" (mother). These stories provide an additional contrast to the rabbinic stereotype of women as witches by portraying a woman whose ritual and medical expertise is relied upon by the rabbis, rather than excoriated as "witchcraft." The comparison is intended to highlight the ideological motivation of passages that target women as witches and demonstrate that they should not be taken as statements of fact, but as participating in a rabbinic discourse that identifies women specifically as the central practitioners of illicit rituals, which the rabbis name as sorcery or witchcraft (*kishuf*).

The legal discussions on the nature of sorcery and divination in rabbinic literature generally depend on the list of forbidden activities of Deuteronomy 18, and therefore do not relate specifically to the question of women's involvement in witchcraft, since Deut 18:10 refers to the sorcerer (*mekhashef*) and not to the sorceress (*mekhashefah*). *M. Sanh* 7:4, 7, and 11 deal with those who consult a ghost or a familiar spirit (*ba'al ob ve-yid'oni*) and the sorcerer (*mekhashef*), who are liable to death by stoning. About the sorcerer it says, "the one who does the act (*ha-'oseh ma'aseh*) is liable, but not one who creates illusions (*ha-'ohez et ha'eynayim*)."[82] *Sifre Deuteronomy* (a late third-century CE legal commentary on Deuteronomy)[83] defines each of the terms found in the biblical passage; for example, the one who inquires of a ghost is referred to as "a necromancer (*pitom*) who (makes the dead) speak out of his armpit."[84] The one who inquires of the dead raises them by divining (*zekuru*) or by consulting the skull of the dead person.[85] While the Mishnah deals with only a few of the categories found in Deuteronomy 18, the Palestinian and especially the Babylonian Talmuds import more of these categories and give varying definitions for them.[86] The one who casts spells (*hover haver*) is defined, as are the soothsayer (*me'onen*) and the diviner (*menahesh*).[87] There is an extended discussion of the nature of the *ba'al ob ve-yid'oni*, with several opinions given in addition to those of the Mishnah and *Sifre Deuteronomy*.[88] The question is raised whether the one who inquires of a ghost (*'ob*) is the same as he who "consults the dead" (*doresh el ha-metim*), and the answer is given: "This means one who starves himself and spends the night in a cemetery, so that an unclean spirit may rest upon him."[89]

The question of women's involvement in sorcery only arises when the Palestinian and Babylonian Talmuds bring up the *mekhashefah* (sorceress) of Exodus 22:17 in relation to the *mekhashef* (sorcerer) of Deuteronomy 18:10.[90] Both begin with a tannaitic comment cited in the Mekhilta (an early legal commentary on Exodus from the second half of the third century CE)[91]: "'You shall not permit a sorceress to live,' whether it be a man or a woman."[92] They both then ask, why does the biblical text nonetheless specify "a sorceress" in the feminine? The Palestinian Talmud says: "Rather, the Torah is teaching you the ordinary way of the world, because most women are sorceresses."[93] The Babylonian Talmud frames the earlier tradition and its objection as a *baraita*, an early tradition excluded from the Mishnah, by saying: "Our rabbis taught: The law refers to both man and woman. If that is so, then why does Scripture say 'a sorceress'? Because most women are involved in sorcery."[94] Given that previous discussions in the Mishnah, Sifre, and the two Talmuds depend ultimately upon Deuteronomy 18, which does not mention the sorceress, and that the Mekhilta's discussion of Exodus 22:17 insists that while the text says "sorceress," the same punishment is incumbent upon both men and women, it is rather surprising suddenly to come upon the claim that *most* women are witches, but it is not unprecedented.

The insistence in both Talmuds that most women are tarred with the brush of sorcery, which is after all punishable by death, is consistent with other rabbinic statements that accuse women of illegitimate ritual acts.[95] Statements that associate women with witchcraft begin with the Mishnah, and continue up through later Babylonian authorities quoted in the Babylonian Talmud. There are no significant differences between early Palestinian sources and late Babylonian sources. Hillel, the earliest tradent in the sources, who is quoted at the beginning of this article, asserts that "the more women, the more sorcery."[96] Two *baraitot* quote R. Shimon b. Yohai (second-century Palestinian) on the ubiquity of magic among women.[97] One of these passages teaches that "edibles may not be passed by"—in other words, that food left on the road must be picked up—and then goes on to say: "Rabbi Yohanan said, in the name of Rabbi Shimon ben Yohai, this was not taught except about the earlier generations, when the daughters of Israel did not indulge freely in witchcraft, but in the latter generations, now that the daughters of Israel indulge freely in witchcraft, we should pass [edibles] by" because they might have used the food for sorcery.[98] R. Yosi, another Palestinian tradent, asserts in the following *baraita*: "Our rabbis taught: if one was walking outside a city and he smelled an odor [of spices]; if the majority are idol-worshippers, one does not say a blessing; if the majority are Jews, one says a blessing. Rabbi Yosi says, even if the majority are Jews one does not say a blessing, because the daughters of Israel burn incense for purposes of magic."[99] Babylonian amoraic statements refer to specific magical acts that women perform[100] and provide a curse that one can use against witches.[101] Tannaitic traditions, therefore, firmly established the idea of women's ubiquity in magical enterprises, and Babylonian amoraim accepted this idea and further developed it.[102]

Despite the many condemnations of women as witches, there is only one rabbinic account of the execution of women for sorcery: the story in the Palestinian Talmud about eighty witches who were crucified by Shimon ben Shetah in

Ashkelon in the first century BCE.[103] Scholars differ on whether the story reflects an actual historical event or not.[104] Tal Ilan applies a "feminist hermeneutic of suspicion" to this question.[105] She writes:

> Is it historically plausible that such an event ever took place? Here the *Yerushalmi* can serve as our guide. When its editors had to confront the bizarre *mishnaic* text recounting the mass execution of women in Ashkelon, they labeled the women "witches." This suggests that according to the *talmudic* editors a mass execution of women is legitimate only when the culprits are witches. They understand Shimeon ben Shetah's action as a witch-hunt. I think we can safely follow their example.[106]

Ilan believes that there is some historical reality to the tale, argues for the veracity of the events occurring in Ashkelon, and suggests one possible historical reconstruction:

> Perhaps Jewish women, who were accused of witchcraft (or some other similar crime) and understood that they were doomed, escaped to the independent city of Ashkelon, seeking legal and political asylum. From the days of Alexander Yannai we hear of political opponents who escaped his wrath by fleeing beyond the borders of the country . . . However, the Ashkelon authorities, deeming their independence vital, did not want to appear to collaborate with the enemies of Queen Shelamzion Alexandra's government . . . Thus Shimeon ben Shatah was able to reach those women and execute them in independent Ashkelon with the collaboration of the city's civil authorities.[107]

Whether or not this is the correct historical explanation for the story is not my focus here. Instead, I use the "hermeneutic of suspicion" mentioned by Ilan to read the story against itself. The story presents Shimon ben Shetah as the Nasi (prince or ruler), slaying the dangerous witches of his day in the city of Ashkelon. My reading will point to ways in which the text both constructs a portrait of Shimon himself as using his knowledge of sorcery to fight against his female rivals and as using trickery to fool them into thinking he has engaged in sorcery. In so doing, my goal is to demonstrate that despite the rabbinic opposition to sorcery practiced by women, they had no objection to employing their knowledge of it in what they considered a good cause.

The story is told twice in the Yerushalmi, each time in a different context. In Sanhedrin, which was probably the original setting of the story, the story is told to explain the mishnaic statement about Shimon ben Shetah's hanging eighty women, which occurs in the context of laws about hanging an executed criminal:

> All of those who are executed by stoning are hanged—the words of R. Eliezer. The sages say, only the blasphemer and the idolater are hanged. A man is hanged with his face towards the people and a woman is hanged with her face towards the stake, the words of R. Eliezer. The sages say, the man is hanged, but the woman is not hanged. R. Eliezer said to them, "But didn't Shimon ben Shetah hang eighty women in Ashkelon?" They said to him, "He hanged eighty women? But we do not judge two people in the same day."[108]

The mishnaic text says nothing about witchcraft—we do not know why the women were executed and then hanged. It is only the Palestinian Talmud that gives an answer to why they were killed. The context in Hagigah is quite different, and has to do with disputes between pairs of early Pharisaic leaders on a halakhic question, with the first one in the pair being identified as the Nasi, and the second one as the head of the court. Shimon ben Shetah is mentioned because of a question of whether or not he was the Nasi, and the entire story is recounted to support the claim that he was the Nasi.[109]

In both Sanhedrin and Hagigah the story about Shimon ben Shetah and the witches is introduced after a fantastical tale about two pious men in Ashkelon, one of whom dies and then appears to his friend in a dream. The dead man is described as taking a stroll in Gehinnom and seeing the punishments of the sinners there, one of whom mentions Shimon. That is the point at which the story about the eighty witches in a cave in Ashkelon begins.[110]

> Immediately Shimon ben Shetah stood up, and it was a rainy day. He took eighty young men, and he put in their hands eighty clean garments. He put them in eighty new pots with lids on their tops.[111] He said to them, "When I whistle the first time, put on your clothes. When I whistle again, come in. When you enter, each of you should embrace one of them and hold her off the earth, because the performance of this kind of sorcery (*harsha*), while she is held above the earth cannot work at all."
>
> He went and stood at the entrance of the cave. He said to them, "*Oyim Oyim*, open for me, I am from among you."[112]
>
> They said to him, "How did you come to us on this day?"
>
> He said to them, "I walked between the raindrops."
>
> They said to him, "What have you come here to do?"

> He said, "To learn and to teach. Each one should come and do what he is skilled in."

This passage tells a great deal about the literary portrait of Shimon ben Shetah himself. His instructions to the young men, which include the phrase, "because the performance of this kind of sorcery (*harsha*), while she is held above the earth, cannot work at all," reveal that he has knowledge of different kinds of sorcery. He is not just a Pharisaic leader from the time of the Hasmonaeans, learned in the Torah—he himself knows about sorcery and how it works and uses this knowledge against the women whom he accuses of sorcery.[113] This knowledge is not unique to Shimon ben Shetah: it was attributed to later rabbinic figures as well in both the Yerushalmi and the Bavli.[114] For example, in the Yerushalmi, Rabbi Joshua foils the spell of a *min* by use of his own spell: "As this *min* was going out, R. Joshua said what he said (*amar mah d-mar*) and the door seized him [the *min*]."[115]

When Shimon ben Shetah greets the woman, his first statement is that he is one of them. While this statement is deceitful (he says this to hide his murderous intentions from them), we discover in the story that he indeed is like them in his knowledge of sorcery. His claim that he "walked between the raindrops" demonstrates special knowledge that might also be part of sorcery (or at least special knowledge about rain; compare the figure of Honi the Circle Drawer, who was able to bring rain).[116] In his dialogue with the women, in addition to his deceitfulness, we also see his claim to magical knowledge at work. He knows something and claims that he is prepared to teach it, in exchange for learning something from the women. He presents himself as an equal in magical knowledge.[117] The story continues:

> One of them said what she said (*amra mah d-hi amra*) and she brought bread (*pita*). And one said what she said and brought meat (*qupad*). And one said what she said and brought cooked dishes. And one said what she said and brought wine.

The circumlocution "she said what she said" indicates that she recited an incantation.[118] Each woman's incantation produced one of the constituents of a good meal: bread, meat, a cooked dish, and wine. Notice that their magic is for the sake of a stereotypically female action—producing food upon the arrival of a guest. For a similar action, see what the medium of Endor does for King Saul after he has been rebuffed by the spirit of Samuel, whom she had brought up from Sheol (1 Sam. 28). She sees how weak Saul is and offers him food, and despite his refusal, she feeds him.[119] From what we can see in the story, the women engage in no dangerous or malevolent actions—all their magic is toward domestic ends.

When we first hear about the women in this *sugya*, however, they are accused of destroying the world. The women are first mentioned in the Palestinian Talmud in the context of a vow that Shimon ben Shetah had uttered before he became Nasi, but did not fulfill when he actually became the Nasi: "What was the sin of Shimon ben Shetah? Because he vowed that when he became Nasi, he would kill all of the witches (*harshayya*), and when he became Nasi, he did not kill them. And there are eighty women in the cave of Ashkelon who are destroying the world."[120] We do not know how they destroy the world. In this story, however, the women present Shimon ben Shetah with food, and in return, they are destroyed in a particularly cruel manner—by crucifixion.

Shimon ben Shetah sets the women up for their destruction by tempting them with the eighty young men he has brought with him.

> They said to him, "What can you do?"
>
> He said to them, "I can whistle two times and bring you eighty young men to be with you and you can enjoy each other."
>
> They said to him, "We would like that."

The fact that the women are taken in by this offer is a sign of their evil, lustful ways—and as we have already seen in prophetic sources and the Enoch literature, women, sorcery, and illicit sexual desire are linked together. The story ends with Shimon ben Shetah's scheme to deprive the women of their power, which allows him to destroy them.[121]

> When he whistled they [the eighty young men] put on their clean clothes, when he whistled again they came in together. He signaled to them, "Each one of you should take one of them and pick her up from the earth, and what she does will not succeed."
>
> He said to the one who had brought bread, "Bring bread," and she did not bring it. He said, "Take her to be crucified." [To the one who had brought a cooked dish, he said,] "Bring a cooked dish," and she did not bring. He said, "Take her to be crucified." [To the one who had brought wine, he said,] "Bring wine," and she did not bring. And he said, "Take her to be crucified." Thus he did to all of them.[122]

Shimon ben Shetah begins with an action that appears to the women to be sorcery (whistling the young men into the cave) but that is not—he is deceiving them, not summoning the young men through sorcery. Furthermore, the action that Shimon ben Shetah tells his young men to do is not in itself sorcery—picking someone up is a physical action which does not require anything other than strength. It is, however, based upon his knowledge of how sorcery works, and it is efficacious. It is also a sexually charged act—the story may portray the women as lusting for the men, but it is the men who actually engage in the overtly sexual act of embracing the women, presumably (the women might think) the first step toward sexual intimacy. Because they are lifted off the earth, the women are unable to reproduce their feat of bringing a whole meal into existence through incantations.[123] Deprived of their power, they are then taken to be executed. Shimon ben Shetah's knowledge of sorcery does not lead to his death, of course—instead, he uses it against them, as is his right as Nasi.

This story raises the question of whether more women might have been executed for practicing witchcraft than we know of—if both the Palestinian and Babylonian Talmuds thought that most women were witches, then why were there not more executions, or at least attempts to do so? Why do we not read stories about witchcraft trials? One answer may be that the incident in Ashkelon was so singular that it could not serve as a precedent for future killings of women as witches. Beth Berkowitz suggests that the mishnaic account of Shimon ben Shetah's action (which, remember, does not refer to the women as witches) serves to discredit sages who are overly enthusiastic in exercising their right to execute transgressors. "Shimon ben Shetah's hanging cannot be used as a legal precedent, since he hanged eighty women at once, while the law limits executions to one a day."[124] Both the *Sifre Deuteronomy* and the discussion in the Yerushalmi after the story suggest that this was an extraordinary circumstance, and only in such a case, "when the times demanded it," could such an action be taken.[125] Another possibility has to do with the Talmudic characterization of *most* women as witches. This implies that "most women" included the rabbis' sisters, mothers, daughters, and wives (and in some of the stories about witches they are members of rabbis' families). Given that the rabbis did not want to destroy their own families, much less the Jewish people, this characterization must be understood as something other than incitement to mass accusations of women. It is telling us something about the rabbinic attitude to women, or the rabbinic understanding of women—that women, including a man's closest relatives, are strange to men and possess powers that they do not know about, powers which may endanger them.

Are Most Women Really Witches?

Given this rabbinic ideology that connects women to witchcraft, it is appropriate to investigate whether rabbinic passages that specify particular cases of approved or forbidden actions single out women as practitioners of incantations, divination, and sorcery. The "Chapters of the Amorites" and traditions about

Abaye's mother/foster-mother/colleague, Em, refer to women's ritual expertise but do not accuse them of forbidden sorcery. The "Chapters of the Amorites" list a number of actions and rule on whether they are permitted or forbidden by excluding or including them in the category of the "ways of the Amorites."[126] The "ways of the Amorites" are, as Giuseppe Veltri has said, "a conglomeration of different magical genres, superstitions, and medical-magical recipes which can be compared with Greco-Roman magical literature."[127] They are associated with the "laws of the gentiles" (Lev. 18:3) that Jews should not follow and are also associated with forbidden forms of divination (Deut. 18:10).[128] Both the Palestinian and Babylonian Talmudic discussions on the "ways of the Amorites" distinguish forbidden foreign customs from those practices that are permitted for the purpose of healing. In the Palestinian Talmud, it says, "R. Shmuel and R. Abbahu in the name of R. Yohanan: everything which heals is not of the ways of the Amorites,"[129] while in the Babylonian Talmud, Abbaye and Raba maintain, "Whatever is used as a remedy is not [forbidden] on account of the ways of the Amorite."[130] As Veltri says, "The contextualization of the customs of the Amorite indicate two characteristics of the category: it is synonymous with 'foreign customs'; at the same time, it is an anti-category calling attention to what deserves to be considered 'healing' versus 'quackery' or even dangerous cures."[131] Furthermore, he notes, "The Amorite is a pseudo-physician, and the context of the *darkhe ha-emori* [ways of the Amorites] as opposed to *refua*, the principle of healing, is the clearest evidence. Amorite practices are contrasted to true healing."[132] However, as soon as something can be defined as healing, it leaves the category of Amorite practices.[133] What is interesting, however, is that Amorite practices are *not* particularly associated with women, nor are Amorite practices that women follow called witchcraft (*keshafim*).

The references to women in the "chapters of the Amorites" are not very extensive. The actions that women are forbidden to do, or that should not be done for them, are gendered—that is, they relate to their roles as mothers or household managers. When the text gives examples of actions that a person of either gender could perform (e.g., if a piece of bread falls from one's hand and one says, "give it back to me so that my blessing may not be lost"),[134] the examples are always gendered masculine. Women appear in passages about birth, healing a sick child, cooking and baking, and taking care of domestic fowl.[135] If a woman "leads her son between the dead," she is guilty of following the ways of the Amorites.[136] If various things are done to help her during childbirth, some are the "ways of the Amorites" and some are not:

> He who stops up the window with thorns, who ties iron to the legs of the bed of a woman in childbirth, and he who arranges a table before her—these are the ways of the Amorites. But if they block the window with a

> pillow or an ear of grain and if they place a cup of water before her and tie up a hen for her, so that it will be a companion for her—these are not the ways of the Amorites.[137]

Blocking the window with thorns or something else, tying iron to the legs of the bed and tying up a hen for the woman in childbirth were thought to defend against demons who might threaten the woman or her child.[138] Another passage deals with baking bread, boiling something in a pot, and cooking rice and lentils.[139] The two last sections of Chapter 6 deal with raising chicks. For example, if she "sets chicks in a sieve, [or] puts iron between the chicks—these are the ways of the Amorites. If it is because of thunder and lightning—this is permitted."[140] As is generally true in these chapters, none of these are malevolent actions of sorcery targeted at other people; instead, they concentrate on health (of mother, child, and chickens), and on success in cooking. When two categories of forbidden practice known from the Bible are discussed, both examples are in the masculine: the soothsayer (*me'onen*), and the diviner (*menahesh*).[141] All of the forbidden actions that women might practice are domestic in nature, and none are malevolent. There does not appear to be any overlap between the category of *kishuf* and the "ways of the Amorites," especially when considering women's actions.

A positive rabbinic example of a woman connected to ritual and medical practices is a woman called Em who is related in some way to the fourth-century Babylonian Amora Abaye.[142] She concentrated on remedies, as well as on midwifery and the health of newborn children. She was also knowledgeable about knots and the proper way to recite incantations. Abaye quotes her as saying, "all (incantations) which are (repeated) several times should be in the name of the mother, and all knots on the left side."[143] Her advice is never described as the "ways of the Amorites," nor is she denounced as a witch. In fact, one of the statements she makes, about the healing properties of madder, a plant used for dyeing, refers to it as a remedy *against* sorcery.[144] In order to learn what some women may have actually done in Sassanian Babylonia, it is also instructive to examine the Aramaic incantation bowls, which often name women as the beneficiaries, and sometimes as practitioners who act against demons.[145] They furnish additional evidence against the blanket rabbinic condemnation of women as witches.

The actions condemned (or permitted) in the "Chapters of the Amorites" were in many cases common recommendations (also cited, for example, in Pliny's *Natural History*) for what to do in case of threats to health and well-being.[146] Em's teachings also conduce to health and protection, and in her case, she also makes a distinction between sorcery and healing. For an interesting comparison, the Cairo Geniza fragments present many instructions for amulets that should be tied onto the arm or the bed of a woman who wishes to have a successful childbirth, comparable to the iron that should be tied to the bed of the woman in the "Chapters of the Amorites."[147] Both Pliny and Calumella discuss what to do to keep newborn chicks healthy, including putting them into a sieve after they have hatched.[148] In contrast to the ideological rabbinic statements or stories about women as witches, it is much more probable that the actions prohibited or permitted in the "Chapters of the Amorites" were actually done by real people, women and men. The more realistic relating to people's actual lives may account for the fact that these chapters do not single out women as witches, but rather discuss their actions in the realms of life they were most likely to be involved in—childbirth, childrearing, taking care of animals, and cooking—rather than recounting the spells they used to kill former husbands, attempts to use witchcraft against various rabbis, or the malevolent stares they would give to men who passed between two of them at a crossroads.

Conclusions

The presentation in the early Jewish sources of the relationship between women and sorcery is complex and cannot be reduced to a simple statement that women are always associated with malevolent sorcery. In both the Bible and the rabbinic literature the situation is more nuanced—both men and women, it is assumed by texts like Deuteronomy 18, could practice sorcery and other forbidden ritual practices, but Exodus 22:17 singles out women. This emphasis on women may be inherited from earlier cuneiform literature from Babylonia, which refers far more to women than to men as sorcerers. The situation is different with prophetic literature, however, which emphasizes the feminine in passages that denounce foreign women and cities (figured as feminine) as guilty of a linked series of sexual and ritual sins. The connection of the feminine with sorcery is attached to the sexualized understanding of the relationships between Israel and other nations and Israel and God. The prophets represent women as witches as part of their gendered symbolism of Israel's relation to others, both divine and human.

Rabbinic literature, despite the statement that "most women are sorceresses," also presents a more varied and nuanced picture than the statements of Hillel or Shimon bar Yohai would indicate. The punishments incumbent on sorcerers and diviners outlined in the mishnaic and talmudic tractate Sanhedrin applied to both men and women. The "Ways of the Amorites" refer to women's forbidden actions within the context of their usual familial and household duties—just as they do men. And in both cases, the prohibitions can be mitigated if they are for the sake of healing. The ritual expertise of certain women, like Em, is a resource for rabbinic figures like Abaye (and those who redacted the Babylonian Talmud).

It is only in the Book of the Watchers that we find an unequivocally negative portrayal of women's connection to sorcery (see also Reed's contribution to this volume for a different interpretation). Women learn sorcery and divination from the fallen angels and pass this forbidden knowledge on to their descendants. In chapters 6–11 of 1 Enoch, the illicit intercourse between angels and women—"knowing" in the biblical sense—leads to illicit knowledge of sorcery, roots, and omens. This motif may depend on an already existing prophetic connection between women's sexuality and the sorcery and prognostication that are part of the rejected arts of the Babylonians. Chapters 12–16 of *1 Enoch* give a "spiritualizing" or even "Platonizing" reading of the story of the fallen angels, seeing women as the primary representatives of mortality and matter with whom the spiritual angels get entangled. Women learn the rejected mysteries that belong to the earth, while Enoch learns the authentic ones in heaven. The Enoch literature represents women as witches to express the idea that particular evils come to earth through women, who cannot be trusted to guard the boundaries between heaven and earth.[149] Women should be marrying men and having children with them, but instead they bear giant sons for fallen angels.

What is the relationship among these sources? Those who composed the Book of the Watchers would have known the Pentateuch and the prophetic writings. The whole range of biblical texts were known by rabbinic authors, and they would have been cognizant of the legal, narrative, and prophetic passages that make a link between women and sorcery. It is unlikely, however, that the myth of the fallen angels who taught women sorcery influenced the strain of rabbinic thinking that refers to women as witches. While adapted forms of this myth appear in midrashic texts, demonstrating that knowledge of it was not lost in rabbinic circles, it seems clear that the more fantastic elements were rejected by those whom the redactors of Genesis Rabbah chose to quote. Interest in the form of the myth found in *1 Enoch* and other second temple literature only occurs in more esoteric mystical works, late midrashim, and Targum Pseudo-Jonathan.

Despite the rabbinic rejection of the Enochic idea that women learned sorcery from the fallen angels, one strain of rabbinic thought seems to have shared the conviction that women were in some way inherently connected to witchcraft. We see this throughout several centuries of rabbinic literature. The rabbis, in particular, were aware of the possible disjunction between Exodus 22:17 and Deuteronomy 18, and give an explanation of why the Exodus passage focuses on women in a way that implicates "most women" in sorcery. They could have chosen not to make that comment, and have merely pointed out that the law applies to both men and women—but they did not do so. Instead, they made an interpretation that accords well with other rabbinic statements that connect women with sorcery. Women challenge rabbis through witchcraft and must be fought off—even the women of a man's own household may be threatening, such as the daughters of R. Nahman who "stir the [hot] pot" with their bare hands through sorcery.[150] Some of the rabbinic passages also link women's involvement in sorcery with illicit sexual conduct. The best example again is the daughters of R. Nahman, whom R. Ilish alleges to be sorceresses because they committed adultery.

The account of the eighty witches in Ashkelon who are executed by Shimon ben Shetah, among other stories, demonstrates that it was not only women (foreign or Israelite) who knew about sorcery—rabbis themselves, including their leaders, possessed this knowledge, and some even practiced sorcery. For example, R. Joshua uttered a spell in retaliation against a *min* who had uttered a spell against him and two other rabbis. The crucial difference between rabbis and women seems to have been that rabbis regarded themselves as legitimate leaders, with a legitimate claim to such knowledge, such that their acts of sorcery actually were not acts of sorcery, but something else. Women, on the other hand, could not legitimately use the power of sorcery.

For the rabbis, the idea of women as witches expresses the hidden (and threatening) side of women's activities toward men, presenting women as the "internal other." As in the Enoch literature, women cannot be trusted to remain within the boundaries of the rabbinic Jewish community if they are "burning incense for witchcraft," throwing away on the road the food they used for sorcery, or stirring the hot pot through sorcery. The rabbinic (and Enochic) statements and stories about women as witches reflect their fears about women's supposed mysterious powers of fascination and control over men, while the "Chapters of the Amorites" and Abaye's citations of Em reflect much more closely women's (and men's) actual attempts to control the unpredictable and dangerous world in which they lived.

Notes

1. Earlier versions of the paper on which this chapter is based were presented at the Society of Biblical Literature in 1998 and 2006, and at the Orion Center for the Study of the Dead Sea Scrolls in 1999. For research support, I thank the Raymond and Janine Ballag Fund Fellowship of the Hebrew University and the Center for Faculty Research and Development of Ithaca College. Biblical translations, unless otherwise specified, are according to the New Jewish Publication Society translation.
2. *m. Avot* 2.7. This phrase could also be translated, "The more wives, the more witchcraft." Immediately after this phrase, he goes on to say, "the more female slaves, the more licentiousness; the more male slaves, the more theft," as if to imply that a man with more than one wife, and several female and male slaves, brings upon himself the misfortunes of witchcraft, licentiousness, and theft.
3. *y. Kid.* 48a.
4. Exod. 22:17 (my translation).
5. *y. Sanh.* 7.19, 25d.
6. Simcha Fishbane, "'Most Women Engage in Sorcery': An Analysis of Sorceresses in the Babylonian Talmud," *JH* 7 (1993): 27–42, says (p. 33), "An examination of the Babylonian Talmud has not revealed any explicit illustrations of male sorcerers who

deal with black magic"; Meir Bar-Ilan, "Witches in the Bible and in the Talmud," in *Approaches to Ancient Judaism*, vol. 5, ed. Herbert Basser and Simcha Fishbane (Atlanta: Scholars Press, 1993), 7–32. See also discussion in Rebecca Lesses, "Exe(o)-rcising Power: Women as Sorceresses, Exorcists, and Demonesses in Late Antique Judaism," *JAAR* 69 (2001): 343–75.

7. My translation.
8. James C. VanderKam, *Enoch and the Growth of an Apocalyptic Tradition* (Washington: Catholic Biblical Association of America, 1984) 71–73.
9. See also Lev. 19:31: "Do not turn to ghosts and do not inquire of familiar spirits, to be defiled by them; I am the Lord your God"; and Lev. 20:6: "And if any person turns to ghosts and familiar spirits and goes astray after them, I will set my face against that person and cut him off from among his people."
10. Ann Jeffers, "Magic From Before the Dawn of Time: Understanding Magic in the Old Testament: A Shift in Paradigm (Deut. 18:9–14 and beyond)," in Michael Labahn and Bert Jan Lietaert Peerbolte, eds., *A Kind of Magic: Understanding Magic in the New Testament and its Religious Environment* (London: T. & T. Clark, 2007), 123–32.
11. Male-only passages: Exod. 7:11; Deut. 18:9–18; Dan. 2:2; 2 Kgs 21:6; 2 Chr 33:6; Isa. 8:19–20, 44:24–25; Jer. 27:9, 50:35–36; Ezek. 21:26–28; Mic. 5:11; Mal. 3:5. Male and female passages: Lev. 20:27. King Menasseh of Judah, in particular, is accused of passing his son through the fire and other sins: "He consigned his son to the fire; he practiced soothsaying (עונן) and divination (נחש), and consulted ghosts and familiar spirits" (2 Kgs 21:6; cf. 2 Chr 33:6).
12. Yitschak Sefati and Jacob Klein, "The Law of the Sorceress (Exod. 22:17[18]) in the Light of Biblical and Mesopotamian Parallels," in *Sefer Moshe: The Moshe Weinfeld Jubilee Volume*, ed. Chaim Cohen, Avi Hurvitz, and Shalom Paul (Winona Lake, IN: Eisenbrauns, 2004), 171–90, esp. 178. The article cites ample evidence from a variety of Mesopotamian sources that refer to women as witches far more than men. One question left unanswered in their article is whether the witchcraft reputation of women is borne out by evidence of women's actual practices.
13. This same passage also denounces the male prophets who have "prophesied falsehood and lying divination" (Ezek. 13:6). Moshe Greenberg, *Ezekiel 1–20* (AB 22; Garden City, NY: Doubleday, 1983), 240, argues that the description of the women's divinatory methods can be explicated by reference to Babylonian techniques. Nancy R. Bowen, "The Daughters of Your People: Female Prophets in Ezekiel 13:17–23," *JBL* 118 (1999): 417–33 argues that (pp. 421–22) Ezekiel's elaborate condemnation of these women "looks very much like a Mesopotamian magical ceremony. On the basis of both a structural and functional comparison with *Maqlû*, Ezekiel's oracle is as much an act of magic or divination as what the female prophets are engaged in."
14. J. M. Powis Smith, *A Critical and Exegetical Commentary on Nahum* (ICC; 1911; repr., Edinburgh: T. & T. Clark, 1985), 338–39 comments on this

punishment: "This seems to have been part of the punishment for fornication and adultery; . . . The figure of the harlot is still maintained. This is probably the way in which such unfortunate women were treated by the bystanders. . . . Nineveh is a captive woman exposed to shame, pelted with filth and made a spectacle for all beholders." Cf. Hos 2:11–12: "I will snatch away My wool and My linen that serve to cover her nakedness. Now I will uncover her (=Israel's) shame in the very sight of her lovers."

15. In Isa. 44:24–25, the prophet also denounces the diviners and wise men: "It is I, the Lord, who made everything, who alone stretched out the heavens and unaided spread out the earth; who annul the omens of diviners (בדים), and make fools of the augurers (קוסמים); who turn sages back and make nonsense of their knowledge." According to VanderKam, *Enoch*, 72, in Isa. 44:25 the word בדים should be emended to ברים, referring to a certain kind of Babylonian diviner. John McKenzie, *Second Isaiah* (AB 20; Garden City, NY: Doubleday, 1968), 73 comments: "The *baru* priest is known from Akkadian literature, and the text is restored from this word. The sage was the professional wise man, a counselor and a spokesman of traditional wisdom."
16. Isa. 47:1–3; translation according to NJPS. Claus Westermann, *Isaiah 40–66: A Commentary* (London: SCM, 1969), 190 comments: "[S]he (as often, Babylon is designated as 'she') is no longer 'the tender, the delicate one'—the terms conjure up the idea of luxury, the refinements of the court, the elegant life of carefree enjoyment—she is now a slave, brusquely ordered about and forced to do the most menial tasks. Her humiliation extends even to her dress: veil and train, the apparel denoting high rank, are torn off her; she works with her clothes tucked up, like a servant girl." McKenzie, *Second Isaiah*, 89 translates Isa. 47:3 in more explicit terms: "Let your nudity be displayed—yes, let your sex appear." His translation makes explicit the element of sexual humiliation that Westermann glosses over. As McKenzie comments (p. 91), "In Egyptian paintings women slaves at work are sometimes represented as very scantily clad. The image also suggests the harsh fact that women prisoners were at the pleasure of their captors." He also says (p. 92), "Babylon is addressed in terms similar to those prophets and poets used in addressing Jerusalem when it was threatened; they personify her as the young woman, the most helpless of the captives of ancient warfare. She is enslaved, put to hard labor, or forced to submit to sexual abuse."
17. Hos 2:4–15, 9:1; Prov 5; 6:24–35; 7; 10:13–18.
18. For the dating, see George W. E. Nickelsburg, *1 Enoch 1: A Commentary on the Book of 1 Enoch, Chapters 1–36; 81–108* (Minneapolis, MN: Fortress, 2001), 7 and Annette Yoshiko Reed, *Fallen Angels and the History of Judaism and Christianity* (Cambridge: Cambridge University Press, 2005), 17.
19. Translation based on NJPS.
20. Devorah Dimant, *The "Fallen Angels" in the Dead Sea Scrolls and in the Apocryphal and Pseudepigraphic Books Related to them* (PhD diss., Hebrew University of Jerusalem, 1974), 54.

21. Ibid., 22; VanderKam, *Enoch*, 129–30; David Suter, "Fallen Angel, Fallen Priest: The Problem of Family Purity in 1 Enoch 6–16," *HUCA* 50 (1979): 119, sees chapters 12–16 as a "commentary of sorts" on chapters 6–11. Annette Yoshiko Reed has demonstrated that chapters 12–16 were written as a transition from chapters 6–11 to chapters 17–36 of the Book of the Watchers, and that they resolve some of the contradictory traditions found in chapters 6–11. Annette Yoshiko Reed, "Heavenly Ascent, Angelic Descent, and the Transmission of Knowledge in 1 Enoch 6–16," in *Heavenly Realms and Earthly Realities in Late Antique Religions*, ed. Ra'anan S. Boustan and Annette Yoshiko Reed (Cambridge: Cambridge University Press, 2004), 47–66, esp. 53–56 and 58–65.
22. Matthew Black, *The Book of Enoch, or 1 Enoch* (SVTP; Leiden: Brill, 1985) 31 (1 Enoch 12:1–2). In his translation, Black takes into account the Greek and Aramaic fragments, as well as the Ethiopic manuscripts.
23. Dimant, *Fallen Angels*, 44 (my translation).
24. Ibid., 53.
25. Ibid., 58; Reed, *Fallen Angels*, 37–41.
26. Nickelsburg, *1 Enoch*, 197: "The point of the passage is that various kinds of magical and divinatory practice have their source in an angelic rebellion."
27. *1 En.*7:1 (Ethiopic). Translation is by Black, *Book of Enoch*, 28. Matthew Black edited the Greek manuscripts of 1 Enoch in *Apocalypsis Henochi Graece* (PVTG; Leiden: Brill, 1970). They are (pp. 7–9): 1) the Gizeh fragment (Codex Panopolitanus), a sixth-century papyrus from Akhmin in Egypt, which covers *1 En.* 1–32:6; 2) The Chester Beatty papyrus, from the fourth century, covers *1 En.* 97:6-104 and 106–7; 3) Substantial parts of *1 En.* are also preserved in the works of Georgius Syncellus. The Aramaic texts were found at Qumran and subsequently published by J. T. Milik—*The Books of Enoch: Aramaic Fragments of Qumran Cave 4* (in collaboration with Matthew Black; Oxford: Clarendon, 1976). The Aramaic is from 4QEn[a] 1 iii and 4QEn[b] 1ii (Milik, *Books of Enoch*, 150–51 and 166), which contains 7:1.
28. Tal Ilan, *Silencing the Queen: The Literary Histories of Shelamzion and Other Jewish Women* (Tübingen: Mohr/Siebeck, 2006), 229, remarks that "The verse from Enoch indicates that at least for the author of that composition, witchcraft and sorcery were closely associated with the intimate knowledge of plants and roots. The association with plants and roots is universal, and this is true in Jewish tradition as well." Ilan argues (p. 231) that the verse from 1 Enoch meant that women were professional healers. See also her discussion in *Jewish Women in Greco-Roman Palestine* (Tübingen: Mohr/Siebeck, 1995), 221–25.
29. *1 En.* 8:3; Black, *Book of Enoch*, 29. The Aramaic is from 4QEn[a] 1 iv and 4QEn[b] 1 iii (Milik, *Books of Enoch*, 157–58 and 170); see Nickelsburg, *1 Enoch*, 197–201, for a discussion of the exact meaning of these terms.
30. Isa 47:9, 11–13.
31. VanderKam, *Enoch*, 8, 52–75. See also Michael E. Stone, "Enoch, Aramaic Levi, and Sectarian Origins," *JSJ* 19 (1988): 159–70 and Nickelsburg, *1 Enoch*, 200, on the Babylonian antecedents of much of the learning in 1 Enoch.

32. Gen 4:22; Dimant, *Fallen Angels*, 54–55. See Paul Hanson, "Rebellion in Heaven, Azazel, and Euhemeristic Heroes in 1 Enoch 6–11," *JBL* 96 (1977), 195–233, esp. 226–32, Nickelsburg (*1 Enoch*, 191–93) and Reed (*Fallen Angels*, 38–40) on the question of whether this tradition stems from Semitic or Hellenistic sources.
33. *1 En*. 8:1–2; Black, *Book of Enoch*, 28–29; Milik, *Books of Enoch*, 166–70.
34. Syncellus of *1 En*. 8:1: *καὶ ἐποίησαν ἑαυτοῖς οἱ υἱοὶ τῶν ἀνθρώπων καὶ ταῖς θυγατράσιν αὐτῶν, καὶ παρέβησαν καὶ ἐπλάνησαν τοὺς ἁγίους*. George W. E. Nickelsburg, "Apocalyptic and Myth in 1 Enoch 6–11," *JBL* 96(1977): 398, accepts Syncellus's longer reading; see also Nickelsburg, *1 Enoch*, 195, which argues that "this reading is ancient and is not an accidental variant of the reading in" the Ethiopic and the Akhmim Greek manuscript. See also Dimant, *Fallen Angels*, 56–57.
35. Dimant, *Fallen Angels*, 56.
36. Reed, *Fallen Angels*, 127–28 argues that the *Testaments* give evidence both for early Christianity and early Judaism—they could have stemmed from a Jewish group that ultimately became Christian and retained earlier traditions. See also David Frankfurter, "Beyond 'Jewish Christianity': Continuing Religious Subcultures of the Second and Third Centuries and Their Documents," in *The Ways that Never Parted: Jews and Christians in Late Antiquity and the Early Middle Ages*, ed. Adam H. Becker and Annette Yoshiko Reed (Minneapolis, MN: Fortress, 2007), 131–43 and Torleif Elgvin, "Jewish Christian Editing of the Old Testament Pseudepigrapha," in *Jewish Believers in Jesus*, ed. Oskar Skarsaune and Reidar Hvalvik (Peabody, MA: Hendrickson, 2007), 286–92.
37. Howard Clark Kee, trans., "Testaments of the Twelve Patriarchs," in *The Old Testament Pseudepigrapha*, 2 vols., ed. James Charlesworth (Garden City, NY: Doubleday, 1983–85), 1.784. Ra'anan Abusch explains this according to the theory of "visual conception" common in late antiquity, by which seeing or thinking of someone during intercourse can lead the offspring to look like that person when born. Ra'anan Abusch, "Rabbi Ishmael's Miraculous Conception: Jewish Redemption History in Anti-Christian Polemic," in *The Ways That Never Parted*, ed. Becker and Reed (Minneapolis, MN: Fortress, 2007), 307–43, esp. 316.
38. P. Gizeh, *1 En*. 9:6–8: "And all that you see Asael has done, who taught all injustice on the earth and showed the mysteries of eternity that are in heaven . . . And Semiazas, to whom was given authority to rule those who cast spells (*τῶν σὺν αὐτῷ ἅμα ὄντωὺ*). And they went into the daughters of men of the earth and lay with them and they were defiled, and they showed them all sins." Black, *Book of Enoch*, 131, explains the Greek of *1 En*. 9:7 as a mistranslation: "The Greek version *τῶν σὺν αὐτῷ ἅμα ὄντων* (common to Sync. and G and behind Eth.) is an obvious mistranslation of *havurin*, 'spell-binders', (e.g., Tg. Neoph. Dt. 18.1) which has here been confused with *haverin* = Heb. *haverim*, 'companions, associates'. Semhazah, who taught mankind spell-binding (8.3) is the fallen watcher put in charge of those who cast spells, i.e. magicians and sorcerers." Nickelsburg, "Apocalyptic and Myth," 398, argues that the mysteries that Asael taught were "more than metallurgy and

mining," and also included other mantic and magical arts that the angels taught. Compare Syncellus; he says that Asael "(6) taught the mysteries and revealed (ἀπεκάλυψε) the eternal things in the heaven... (8) ... and they (the angels) taught them (the women) to do hate-charms (μίσητρα)."

39. *1 En.* 10:7–8; Black, *Book of Enoch*, p. 30.
40. *Jub.* 10:12–14 (O. S. Wintermute, trans., "Jubilees," in Charlesworth, ed., *Old Testament Pseudepigrapha*, 2:76).
41. VanderKam, *Enoch*, 129. See also Dimant, *Fallen Angels*, 72–79, and Carol Newsom, "The Development of *1 Enoch* 6–19: Cosmology and Judgement," *CBQ* 42(1980): 310–29, esp. 316–19; Reed, "Heavenly Ascent," 53–65, and Reed, *Fallen Angels*, 44–49.
42. As Nickelsburg writes (*1 Enoch I*, 272), "The view of woman, marriage, and sex expressed here is decidedly male oriented. Sex is for the purpose of procreating the man's line; woman was created for him to this end." Compare the Pandora myth in Hesiod's *Theogony*, lines 570–612, where only men exist at first, and women are then created for purposes of procreation (Apostolos N. Athanassakis, *Hesiod: Theogony; Works and Days; Shield* [Baltimore: Johns Hopkins University Press 1983], 9); a similar story may be told in the second creation story in Genesis. See *Theog.*, lines 590–91, 600–1: "From her comes the fair sex; yes, wicked womenfolk are her descendants . . . So, too, Zeus who roars on high made women to be an evil for mortal men, helpmates in deeds of harshness" (Athanassakis, *Hesiod*, 28). In *Works and Days*, 60–105, Pandora is created to be a "scourge for toiling men" (Athanassakis, *Hesiod*, 69, line 83), and when she opens the jar given to her by the gods, all evils fly out to afflict men (69, lines 95–96).
43. *1 En.* 15.4 (translation from Nickelsburg, *1 Enoch I*, 267). Nickelsburg (p. 271) argues that the angelic defilement is even greater because they had been functionaries in the heavenly sanctuary.
44. Ibid., 269, 271; Suter, "Fallen Angel," 119.
45. Philo, *Supplement I: Questions and Answers on Genesis*, trans. Ralph Marcus, LCL (London and Cambridge, MA: Harvard University Press, 1953), 61.
46. *1 En.* 16.3. Translation according to Black, *Book of Enoch*, 35. Ephraim Isaac refers to the "rejected secrets" in his translation,"1 (Ethiopic Apocalypse of) Enoch," in *Old Testament Pseudepigrapha,* ed. Charlesworth, 1.22. The Greek (Codex Panopolitanus; Black, *Apocalypsis Henochi Graece*, 30) reads, for the last sentence: καὶ ἐν τῷ μυστηρίῳ τούτῳ πληθύνουσιν αἱ θήλειαι καὶ οἱ ἄνθρωποι τὰ κακὰ ἐπὶ τῆς γῆς.
47. Nickelsburg, "Apocalyptic and Myth," 398.
48. Reed, *Fallen Angels*, 48–49.
49. VanderKam, *Enoch and Apocalyptic*, 131–33; Newsom, "Development," 316; and Dimant, *"Fallen Angels,"* 74–77.
50. For examples, see *Gen. Rab.* 26. 4–7, discussed below, and *Tg. Onq.* Gen. 6:2; for the text of *Gen. Rab.* see *Midrash Bereshit Rabba,* 2nd ed., 3 vols., ed. Judah Theodor and Chanoch Albeck; (Jerusalem: Wahrmann, 1965), 1.247–49, and *The Geniza Fragments*

of Bereshit Rabba, ed. Michael Sokoloff (Jerusalem: Israel Academy of Sciences and Humanities, 1982), 117. See discussion of Reed, *Fallen Angels*, 137–47 and 207.

51. For example, *Pirke de-Rabbi Eliezer* ch. 22; *Targum Pseudo-Jonathan* Gen. 6:1–2, 4; and *3 Enoch*, in *Synopse zur Hekhalot-Literatur*, ed. Peter Schäfer (Tübingen: Mohr/Siebeck, 1981), paras. §5–8.
52. The final redaction of this midrash is dated to the first half of the fifth century CE by H. L. Strack and G. Stemberger, *Introduction to the Talmud and Midrash*, trans. Markus Bockmuehl (Edinburgh: T. & T. Clark, 1991), 304.
53. Bernard Grossfeld, "Bible, Translations," *Encyclopedia Judaica*, 16 vols. (Jerusalem: Keter, 1972), 4.844 writes that Targum Onqelos was originally a Palestinian Targum, committed to writing in the second or third century, and subsequently brought to Babylonia.
54. *Gen. Rab.* 26.5.
55. Ibid. Devorah Dimant (*Fallen Angels*, 31–32) argues that his objection is to the interpretation that views the בני אלהים as one of the terms for angels. For a contrary rabbinic view see *Sifre* Deut. Ha'azinu Piska 1 (end) and *b. Hul.* 91b, which does not, however, seem to have affected the dominant rabbinic interpretation of Genesis 6. See also Theodor-Albeck, *Bereshit Rabba*, 1.247.
56. Reed, *Fallen Angels*, 138. She also (pp. 137–47) points to mishnaic passages (*m. Hag.* 2.1 and *m. Sanh.* 10.1) that militated against delving into the mysteries that interested the writers of the apocalypses, as well as reading the "outside books" (like 1 Enoch) that the rabbis ultimately did not include in the canon of the Tanakh. She demonstrates (pp. 207–8) that, unlike some of the other categorical prohibitions of the rabbis (for example, against using magic, also found in *m. Sanh.* 10.1), the second-century rabbinic rejection of the angelic interpretation of Gen. 6:2 succeeded in suppressing references to the fallen angels until after the completion of the Babylonian Talmud. "It is striking that these Rabbinic approaches to Enoch and the 'sons of God' both function to undermine the Enochic literary tradition at its very roots. By reading Enoch's death into Gen. 5:24 and reading the fallen angels out of Gen. 6:1–4, they effectively sever the exegetical threads that tie the Enochic pseudepigrapha to the Torah" (pp. 210).
57. Ibid., 210.
58. *Gen. Rab.* 26.5.
59. See Gen. 3:22, where God says that "the man has become like one of us, knowing good and evil; now, lest he reach out his hand and take also from the tree of life, and eat, and live forever." Living forever is a divine quality not given to human beings, so the long life of the "sons of God" justifies their divine title. See Theodor-Albeck, *Bereshit Rabba*, 1.248 (my translation): "therefore the days lengthened without trouble or sufferings, because if they had suffered, they would have sought atonement, but the Holy One, blessed be He, increased their measure because in the future they would receive punishment and the punishment of the later generations, for they were punished on account of all of the generations after them."

60. Reed, *Fallen Angels*, 211.
61. Gen. 6:2; *Gen. Rab.* 26.5. Cf. *Sifre, Be-ha'alotcha* 86: "'And the sons of God saw the daughters of men.' Just as the sons of the judges used to seize women from the market and force them."
62. *Gen. Rab.* 26.5.
63. Ibid. Cf. the parallel version in *Lev. Rab.* 23.9.
64. *1 En.* 15:4. *ἐν τῷ αἷματι τῶν γυναικῶν ἐμιάνθητε*, "You defiled yourselves with the blood of women."
65. *Gen. Rab.*26:7; Theodor-Albeck, *Bereshit Rabba*, 1.254.
66. *Tg. Ps.-J.* of Gen. 6:2. *Targumic Pseudo-Jonathan* is a Palestinian Targum redacted in the seventh or eighth century, but containing much earlier material (Grossfeld, *Encyclopedia Judaica*, 4.845). Aramaic according to E. G. Clarke, *Targum Pseudo-Jonathan of the Pentateuch*, with collaboration by W. E. Aufrecht, J. C. Hurd, and F. Spitzer (Hoboken, NJ: Ktav, 1984), 7, according to MS. British Museum Add. 27031. English translation according to Michael Maher, ed. and trans., *Targum Pseudo-Jonathan: Genesis* (ArBib 1B; Edinburgh: T. & T. Clark, 1992), 38.
67. The manuscript reads וכסלן, which makes no sense, and is corrected to כחלן according to the emendation of the *editio princeps* (Maher, *Pseudo-Jonathan*, 38, note 4). Compare the Aramaic of *1 En.* 8:2: "He [Asael] showed to women concerning antimony (*kohla*) and concerning eye-shadow (*shedida*)" (Milik, *Books of Enoch*, 167, 4QEn[b] 1 ii). On p. 170 Milik explains the meaning of *shedida* as eyeshadow, according to the Syriac.
68. Maher, *Pseudo-Jonathan*, 38, note 3 suggests that another possible translation is "curled (or combed) their hair." For the translation "rouge" he follows Marcus Jastrow, *A Dictionary of the Targumim, the Talmud Babli and Yerushalmi, and the Midrashic Literature* (New York: Pardes, 1950), 1210. Jastrow relates the Aramaic to the Hebrew verb פקס, which he believes (p. 1169) comes from the word *pikes*, meaning "sea-weed or rock-lichen used as a dye; red color, rouge."
69. *Gen. Rab.* 26.7.
70. Theodor-Albeck, *Bereshit Rabba*, 1.253–54. Reed, *Fallen Angels*, 214–15 comments that this kind of exegesis is distinctively rabbinic, because unlike the Second Temple Jewish literature, it identifies the giants with the Nephilim.
71. Theodor-Albeck, *Bereshit Rabba*, 1.253.
72. See, for example, Mekhilta Ba-Hodesh 6 (Jacob Z. Lauterbach, ed., *Mekilta de-Rabbi Ishmael,* 3 vols. [Philadelphia: Jewish Publication Society of America, 1935], 2.239). *Tg. Ps.-J.*on Gen 4:26 reads: "And to Seth also a son was born and he called his name Enosh. That was the generation in which they began to go astray, making idols for themselves and calling their idols by the name of the Memra of the Lord" (English translation: Maher, *Pseudo-Jonathan,* 35; Aramaic: Clarke, *Targum Pseudo-Jonathan*, 6).
73. *3 En.* 5:7–9 (Philip Alexander, trans., "3 [Hebrew Apocalypse of] Enoch," in Charlesworth, *Old Testament Pseudepigrapha*, 1. 260).

74. Reed, *Fallen Angels,* 239.
75. Ibid., 256.
76. Black, *Apocalypsis Henochi Graece*, 22.
77. Strack and Stemberger, *Introduction*, 332–33.
78. Job 24:13.
79. *Tanhuma* Bereshit 12.
80. See discussion in Reed, *Fallen Angels*, 258–70 of other later rabbinic works that cite the idea that the angels taught humans sorcery.
81. *y. Sanh.* 6.8, 23c and *y. Hag.* 2.2, 77d.
82. *m. Sanh.* 7:11.
83. Strack and Stemberger, *Introduction*, 297.
84. Chaim Saul Horovitz and Louis Finkelstein, eds., *Sifre Deuteronomy* (Berlin: Gesellschaft zur Forderung der Wissenschaft des Judentums, 1939; repr., New York: Jewish Theological Seminary of America, 1969), Piska 172, p. 219. English translation from Reuven Hammer, trans. and ed., *Sifre: A Tannaitic Commentary on the Book of Deuteronomy* (New Haven, CT: Yale University Press, 1986), 200. This is the definition of the Mishnah—see *m. Sanh.* 7:7; and compare *t. Sanh.* 10:6; *t. Mak.* 4:4 (on the חובר חבר); *Sifra Parashat Kedoshim*, Parsheta 3, Perek 7, 10 (on Lev. 19:31); *b. Sanh.* 65b. The word *pitom* is from the Greek *πύθων*, python, referring to a ventriloquist or necromancer (Hammer, *Sifre,* 456).
85. Ibid.
86. *y. Sanh.* 7.10, end. Cf. *t. Sanh.* 10:3.
87. *b. Sanh.* 65a-b.
88. *b. Sanh.* 65b.
89. Ibid.
90. Their discussion springs from *m. Sanh.* 7:11.
91. Strack and Stemberger, *Introduction*, 278–79.
92. Nezikin 17 (on Ex 22:17) in Jacob Z. Lauterbach, *Mekilta de-Rabbi Ishmael*, 3 vols. (Philadelphia: Jewish Publication Society of America, 1935), 133: אחד איש ואחד אישה. See also H. S. Horovitz and I. A. Rabin, *Mekhilta de-Rabbi Ishmae*l, 2d ed. (Jerusalem: Bamberger and Wahrman, 1960), 309.
93. *y. San.* 7:19, 25d: לא תחיה אחד האיש ואחד האישה אלא שלימדתיך התורה דרך ארץ מפני שרוב הנשים כשפניות.
94. *b. San.* 67a: תנו רבנן מכשפה אחד האיש ואחד האישה אם כן מה תלמוד לומר מכשפה מפני שרוב נשים מצויות בכשפים.

    Given that there is no other record of this statement as a baraita, and also that the Palestinian Talmud makes an almost identical statement without framing it as a baraita, I question the reliability of the tannaitic attribution.
95. Giuseppe Veltri, *Magie und Halakha* (Tübingen: Mohr/Siebeck, 1997), 65–69.
96. *m. Avot* 2:7. He is dated to late first century BCE to first century CE.
97. The first one is quoted at the beginning of this article: “Rabbi Shimon ben Yohai taught: . . . the most worthy among women is a mistress of sorcery” (*y. Kid.* 48a, paralleled in Sofrim ch. 15).

98. *b. Erub.* 64b. In several other versions of this same passage, there is no reference to the "daughters of Israel" doing magic; see *t. Pes.* 2:27–28, *Lev. Rab.* 37:3, *y. AZ* 1:9, 7b, *y. Dem.* 3:3, 13b; it seems that the fear that the "daughters of Israel" might do magic with food found on the road is original to the version of the Babylonian Talmud.
99. *b. Ber.* 53a.
100. For example (*b. Pes.* 111a): "Our rabbis taught: . . . (If) there are two women who are sitting at a crossroads one on this side of the road and the other on the other side, and they turn their faces to each other, it is certain that they are engaging in magic (*keshafim*)."
101. *b. Pes.*110a, in a statement by Amemar, fourth-century CE Babylonian amora.
102. For further references, see the story about the woman who prevented a man from begetting a child (*y. San.* 7.19, 25d); the woman who went to take dust from beneath the feet of Rabbi Hanina, in order to do some kind of incantation against him (*b. San.* 67b; *b. Hul.* 7b); the woman whom Yannai transforms into a donkey (*b. San.* 67b) or the woman who cursed her ex-husband when he had too much to drink (in pairs of cups, which is dangerous and leaves a man open to witchcraft; *b. Pes.* 110b), or the daughters of Rabbi Nahman, who "stirred the hot pot with their hands," by means of sorcery (*ba-keshafim*; *b. Git.* 45a; R. Ilish proved that they did this by sorcery by showing that they were unfaithful to their husbands when they were taken captive); the encounter between a matron and two rabbis on a boat, in which she was unable to use an incantation against the boat because of their presence (*b. Shab.* 81b); and in *b. Yoma* 83b, Rav says that the "witches playing with him" cause the symptoms of a rabid dog. See also Naomi Janowitz, *Magic in the Roman World: Pagans, Jews, and Christians* (London: Routledge, 2001), 86–87.
103. *y. Sanh.* 6.8, 23c, with parallel text in *y. Hag.* 2.2, 77d.
104. The stories about Shimon ben Shetah place him during the reigns of King Alexander Yannai and Queen Shlomzion Alexandra. According to Josephus, the Pharisees were prominent during the reign of the queen, so if there is a historical kernel to this story, it would have occurred during her reign, 76–67 BCE. Also according to Josephus, the Pharisees executed many of their political opponents (Ilan, *Silencing*, 214–20). This information makes placing the story during Shlomzion's rule plausible, but does not, of course, prove that it occurred then or at any other time. Jacob Neusner, *The Rabbinic Traditions about the Pharisees before 70*, 3 vols. (Leiden: Brill, 1971), 1.103, dates the composition of the story to third-century CE Palestine. He also says (p. 133) that the story in the Palestinian Talmud is not likely "to date before Amoraic times. The Babylonian Talmud contains no equivalent materials, and we may perhaps assign the magical accounts to third or fourth-century Palestinian schools."

    Joshua Efron, "The Deed of Shimeon ben Shatah in Ascalon," in *Jewish and Hellenistic Cities in Eretz Israel*, ed. A. Kasher (Tübingen: Mohr/Siebeck, 1990), 318–41, argued that the story was true; Martin Hengel, *Rabbinische Legende und frühpharisäische Geschichte: Schimeon ben Shatach und die achtzig Hexen von Askalon* (Heidelberg: Winter, 1984) argued that the story was an allegory.

105. Ilan, *Silencing*, 222.
106. Ibid., 223.
107. Ibid. Ashkelon was not under Hasmonaean rule, therefore one might flee there from the Hasmonaeans.
108. *m. Sanh.* 6.4. "Hanging" here is not a method of execution, but rather the practice of displaying the corpse of the deceased criminal by hanging it on a tree, in accordance with Deut. 22:22. Compare *Sifre Deuteronomy* 221 (ed. Friedman, p. 114b, Finkelstein, p. 253, as translated in Neusner, *Rabbinic Traditions about the Pharisees*, 1.90): "'And if a man has committed a crime punishable by death and he is put to death, and you hang him on a tree' (Deut. 22:22). A man is to be hung, but a woman is not to be hung. R. Eliezer says, 'Even a woman is to be hung.' R. Eliezer said to them, 'Did not Simeon b. Shetah hang women in Ashqelon?' They said to him, 'He hung eighty woman, and yet [the law is] one does not judge [even] two [capital] cases on one day, but the times necessitated teaching through exemplary punishment [and also regards to hanging women].'' The version of *Sifre* is simpler, and thus probably earlier than that of the Mishnah (on this, see Neusner, *Rabbinic Traditions about the Pharisees*, 93), but it also includes one element not found in the Mishnah—the mention that the times demanded such a punishment, which is an element found also in both the Yerushalmi and the Bavli (*b. Sanh.* 46b).
109. *m. Sanh.* 6.4.
110. The text of *y. Hag.* 2.2, 77d is translated, because it is a fuller account, but two paragraphs from the text of *y. Sanh.* 6.8, 23c are inserted when they provide more detail.
111. The German translation: "Er gab in ihre Hände achtzig reine Gewänder, tat sie in neue Helme, und sie drehten sie um (und setzen sie) auf ihre Köpfe." Gerd Wewers, trans., *Hagiga: Festopfer* (UTY II/11; Tübingen: Mohr/Siebeck, 1983), 54, comments that the word *qidrin* usually means "pots," but that in connection with this tradition he thinks that the translation "Helme" ("helmet") is appropriate, and that this may be an apotropaic head-covering.
112. Tal Ilan, *Silencing*, 216, note 8, argues that, "This is a well known Greek invocation, associated with the mysteries of Dionysus."
113. Neusner, *Rabbinic Traditions about the Pharisees*, 102, comments that this story represents Shimon "as a master of witchcraft, which illustrates R. Yohanan ben Nappaha's rule that one could not be appointed to the Sanhedrin unless he was a master of magic."
114. Kimberly Stratton, *Naming the Witch: Magic, Ideology, and Stereotype in the Ancient World* (New York: Columbia University Press, 2007), 145–50.
115. *y. Sanh.* 7.19, 25d. In *b. Sanh.* 68a, R. Eliezer teaches R. Akiba about the planting and the plucking up of cucumbers by the utterance of a "word" (דבר). The question is then raised how this was permissible—did it not transgress the prohibition on the performance of magic? The answer is given: "you may not learn in order to do, but you may learn to understand and to teach."

116. *m. Ta'anit* 3.8—Shimon ben Shetah here rebukes Honi because he importunes God. For a discussion of gender in stories of rainmakers, see Ilan, *Silencing*, 200–8.
117. Cf. *b. Sanh.* 68a, quoted above.
118. Daniel Sperber, *Magic and Folklore in Rabbinic Literature* (Ramat Gan: Bar Ilan University Press, 1994), 61.
119. On women, food, and magic, see Ilan, *Silencing*, 229–31, and Stratton, *Naming the Witch*, 169–74.
120. *y. Sanh.* 6.8, 23c.
121. These two paragraphs are from *y. Sanh.* 6.8, 23c, which gives more details.
122. Compare *y. Hag.* 2.2, 77d: "He whistled one time and they put on their garments. He whistled again and they came in together. He said, 'Each one of you who comes should recognize his partner.' They took them and they went and crucified them."
123. Janowitz, *Magic*, 93, compares this to another rabbinic story (recounted in *y. Sanh.* 7.19, 25d) where a woman is held up by her hair to diminish her power, "pointing to some kind of belief in the chthonic power of women."
124. Beth A. Berkowitz, *Execution and Invention: Death Penalty Discourse in Early Rabbinic and Christian Cultures* (New York: Oxford University Press, 2006), 146. My thanks to Kimberly Stratton for referring me to this book.
125. Compare *b. Sanh.* 46b, which discusses *m. Sanh.* 6.4, but never refers explicitly to the story of Shimon ben Shetah in Ashkelon. The *sugya* ends with a discussion of the same issue raised in the Yerushalmi—are there times when punishments may be inflicted by the court even though the Torah does not demand it?
126. They are found most extensively in *t. Shab.* chs. 6–7, but also in *y. Shab.* 6.9, and *b. Shab.* 67a–b. For text and commentary, see Saul Lieberman, ed., *The Tosefta: The Order of Mo'ed* (New York: Jewish Theological Seminary of America, 1962), 22–29; Saul Lieberman, *Order Mo'ed* (vol. 3 of *Tosefta Ki-Fshutah: A Comprehensive Commentary on the Tosefta*; 2nd edition; Jerusalem: Jewish Theological Seminary of America, 1992), 79–105; and Giuseppe Veltri, *Magie und Halakha* (TSAJ 62; Tübingen: Mohr/Siebeck, 1997), 93–220.
127. Giuseppe Veltri, "The 'Other' Physicians: The Amorites of the Rabbis and the Magi of Pliny," *Korot: The Israel Journal of the History of Medicine and Science* 13 (1998–99), 39.
128. Lieberman, *Order Mo'ed, Tosefta Ki-Fshutah*, 80.
129. *y. Shab.* 6.10, 8c.
130. *b. Shab.* 67a.
131. Veltri, "The 'Other' Physicians," 39.
132. Ibid., 49.
133. Ilan, *Silencing*, 232–33.
134. *t. Shab.* 6.2.
135. *t. Shab.* 6.1 (leading a child through the cemetery), 6.4 (to protect the woman in childbirth), 6.14–15 (cooking), 6.17–19 (taking care of chicks); and *b. Shab.* 67b (some of the same practices as found in the Tosefta).

136. *t. Shab.* 6.1. Veltri, *Magie und Halakha*, 104–5, comments that (my translation), "The act may lie in the performance of the transferring of the sickness. This explanation is also confirmed by widespread medical-magical practices in antiquity. For corpses were related to prophylactic and healing goals. Among the Romans the contact with a part of the corpse's body was reckoned as healthy; they believed that the sickness was transferred to it" (Plin., *HN*, 28.11.45).
137. *t. Shab.* 6.4.
138. Veltri, *Magie und Halakha*, 113, 117; Lieberman, *Order Mo'ed, Tosefta Ki-Fshutah*, 83.
139. *t. Shab.* 6.14–15.
140. *t. Shab.* 6.19. As Lieberman comments (*Order Mo'ed, Tosefta Ki-Fshutah*, 91), these are practices known from Pliny (*HN*, 10.75.152) and from Columella, *On Agriculture* (*De Re Rustica*), 8.5.11–12, and 16. At 8.5.16, Columella (Lucius Junius Moderatus Columella, *On Agriculture* [*De Re Rustica*] [trans. E. S. Forster and Edward H. Heffner (3 vols.; Cambridge, Mass.: Harvard University Press, 1941–55) 2.351]) recommends putting the newly hatched chicks into a sieve for their health: "The chickens should be placed in a sieve made of vetch or darnel, which has already been in use, and they should then be fumigated with sprigs of pennyroyal; this seems to prevent the pip, which very quickly kills them when they are young."
141. Deut. 18:10; *t. Shab.* 7.13–14.
142. References to her can be found in *b. Kid.* 31b, *b. Shab.* 66b, 133b, 134a, *b. Yoma* 78b, *b. Erub.* 29b, *b. Moed Katan* 12a, 18b, *b. Yeb.* 25a, *b. Ket.* 10b, 39a, 50a, *b. Git.* 67b, 70a, and *b. Avod. Zar.* 28b. On her, see Lesses, "Exe(o)rcising Power," 362–64; Veltri, *Magie und Halakha*, 230–38; Charlotte Fonrobert, *Women's Bodies, Women's Blood: The Politics of Gender in Rabbinic Literature* (PhD diss., Graduate Theological Union, 1995), 230–43, and Fonrobert, *Menstrual Purity: Rabbinic and Christian Reconstructions of Biblical Gender* (Stanford, CA: Stanford University Press, 2000), 151–59; Shulamit Valler, *Women in Jewish Society in the Talmudic Period* [Hebrew] (Tel Aviv: Ha-Kibuts Ha-Meuhad, 2000), 161–72. The word *em* is usually taken to mean "mother" or "foster-mother." Ilan, *Silencing*, 27, 234 argues that *Em* is her name and that she was a physician and a friend of Abaye's.
143. *b. Shab.* 66b. For a discussion of the very common phenomenon that incantations and amulets specifically name a person and his or her mother (and not father), see Ilan, *Silencing*, 239–40, and Veltri, *Magie und Halakhah,* 68.
144. *b. Shab.* 66b.
145. See Lesses, "Exe(o)rcising Power."
146. Lieberman, *Order Mo'ed, Tosefta Ki-Fshutah*, 80–91; Veltri, *Magie und Halakha*, 97–167.
147. *t. Shab.* 6.4; for Geniza amulets see for example, T.-S. K 1.19, page 3, lines 13–16; T.-S. K 1.143, page 18, lines 12–14, page 19, lines 1–2, in Joseph Naveh and Shaul

Shaked, *Magic Spells and Formulae: Aramaic Incantations of Late Antiquity* (Jerusalem: Magnes, 1993), 159, 196.

148. Plin., *HN*, III, 10.75.152; Columella, *On Agriculture*, VIII, 11–12, 16.

149. Compare the story of the woman who seduced Enkidu into civilization in the Epic of Gilgamesh, or of Pandora in Greek mythology.

150. *b. Git.* 45a.

4

Gendering Heavenly Secrets?

Women, Angels, and the Problem of Misogyny and "Magic"

Annette Yoshiko Reed

AT FIRST SIGHT, gender might seem to play an altogether unremarkable role in Jewish and Christian traditions about the fallen angels, unfolding according to well-worn patterns of ancient misogyny and long-standing stereotypes associating women with "magic," demons, and the dangers of the flesh. The terse account of "sons of God" and "daughters of men" in Genesis 6 might strike us as pregnant with such possibilities, with the male associated with the heavenly and the female with the earthly, and "daughters" figured simultaneously, if tacitly, as temptresses and victims of sexual violation. Their presumed violation, moreover, might seem to invite interpretation as the violation of earth by heaven, with sexual violence foreshadowing the diluvian chaos subsequently unleashed by the crossing of cosmic lines of difference. Seen from this perspective, it might seem unsurprising that later versions of the myth might make explicit, not just the identity of the "sons of God" as angels, but also the culpability of women in tempting them down to earth. Nor might it seem so strange that the sexual temptation and transgression of angels, their pollution by female blood and flesh, and their siring of monstrous hybrids might be joined with accusations about the fallen angels' revelation of corrupting skills and secrets to their wives. After all, the association of women and "magic" now seems as natural as the image of the witch.[1]

To be sure, some traditions about fallen angels do indeed seem to follow such patterns. The *Testament of Reuben*, for instance, is explicit in interpreting the myth of the fallen angels as a warning to men about the dangers of temptation by womanly wiles.[2] It seems to take for granted that angels can be likened to men, rather than women, and it argues that women are to blame for the lust of men and angels alike. To do so, it proposes that the "daughters of men" caused the angelic Watchers to come down from heaven, citing their example as a lesson in the dangers of *porneia* [cf. Hebrew *zenut*] and using the rhetoric of "magic" to condemn them as temptresses:

> Evil [*ponêrai*] are women, my children, because, having no power or strength over man, they use wiles trying to draw him to them by gestures; and whom she cannot overcome by strength, him she overcomes by craft. For also concerning them the angel of the Lord told me (i.e., Reuben), and he taught me that women are overcome by the spirit of *porneia* more than man, and in their heart they plot against men, and by their adornment they lead astray first their minds, and by their gaze they sow the poison, and then they take them captive by the act. For a woman cannot force a man. Flee, therefore, *porneia*, my children, and command your wives and your daughters that they do not adorn their heads and their faces, because every woman who uses these wiles has been reserved for everlasting punishment. For thus they bewitched [*ethelksan*][3] the Watchers before the Flood: as these looked at them continually, they lusted after one another, and they conceived the act in their mind, and they changed themselves into the shape of men, and they appeared to them when they were together with their husbands. And they, lusting in their minds after their appearances, bore giants. For the Watchers appeared to them as reaching unto heaven. Beware, therefore, of *porneia*, and if you wish to be pure in mind, guard your senses from every woman. (*T. Reuben* 5:1–6:1)[4]

In addition, here as elsewhere, scholars who wish to scour the past for statements to judge as misogynous can find much to denounce in the writings of Tertullian. In *De cultu feminarum*—the same treatise where Tertullian infamously calls women "the devil's gateway" (1.1)—he discusses "those angels who rushed from heaven on the daughters of men" (1.2), and he demonizes feminine vanity by associating cosmetics with the teachings that the fallen angels revealed to their wives (see also *On Veiling* 8).[5]

The perspectives preserved in these second- and third-century Christian sources have precedents as well as afterlives.[6] The *Damascus Document*, for instance, contains an early attestation of the appeal to the fallen angels to warn men not to "follow after . . . eyes of *zenut*" (CD 2.14–18). Much the same argument is later made by Christian authors like Clement of Alexandria (*Paedagogus* 3.2; *Stromata* 3.7.59) and Commodian (*Instructiones* 3). Such arguments, of course, bear some exegetical connection to Genesis' suggestion that all the problems began when the "sons of God *saw* that the daughters of men were beautiful" (6:2). Yet they also—and perhaps especially—draw on the more extensive traditions about the fallen angels first attested in the Enochic *Book of the Watchers*, a Jewish apocalypse from around the third century BCE (1 Enoch 1–36, esp. 6–16). Tertullian, for instance, explicitly cites this "scripture of Enoch" as his source for the inclusion of cosmetics among the teachings of the fallen angels.[7]

Just as Tertullian's treatises serve, in turn, as a source for Cyprian (*On the Dress of Virgins* 13–14), so the wide circulation of the *Book of the Watchers* and *Testament of Reuben* seems to have spurred Christian appeals to the myth of the fallen angels to decry all women as witches and temptresses.[8] Cosmetics and women's wiles became so closely associated with the myth of the fallen angels that they remain part of the complex of interpretative motifs surrounding Genesis 6, even when and where Jewish and Christian exegetes re-read the "sons of God" as human men: the image of the "daughters of men" as actively luring down "sons of God" from the heights of their spiritual purity becomes readily transferred onto Cainites and Sethites.[9] Just as Ephrem describes the Cainite "daughters of men" as women who "adorned themselves and became a snare" to the Sethian "sons of God" (*Commentary on Genesis* 6:3), so the Armenian *Sermon concerning the Flood* recounts how the "daughters of Cain made sinful inventions, braids, coiffures, antimony, and rouge" to tempt the ascetic Sethians, and the *Descendants of Adam* credits these "daughters of men" with using "potions of love and potions of hate" toward the same aims.[10]

In what follows, however, I would like to propose that the place of women and "magic" in Jewish and Christian discussions of the fallen angels is not quite as straightforward as these traditions might lead us to presume; the trajectory outlined above is just one of many. Just as a modern notion of "magic" might lead us to retroject later taxonomies of knowledge and values onto the past, so a modern temptation to self-congratulatory denunciations of pre-modern misogyny may cause us to miss much that is interesting about the rest of the ancient discussion surrounding women, fallen angels, earthly power, and heavenly knowledge. To explore these possibilities, this chapter considers four moments in the development of the discussion: the formation of the *Book of the Watchers* in the third century BCE, its translation into Greek and interpretation in the *Testament of Reuben* in the centuries around the turn of the Common Era, Christian interpretations of the work and Greek witnesses to it from late antique Egypt, and the reemergence of Jewish interest in the fallen angels in the early Middle Ages.

In the process, I shall reflect upon some of what has been assumed and effaced in past research on these materials by virtue of the modern habit of judging ancient writings as more or less misogynous, as if such judgments had some universal, normativizing force that exempts from the dangers of anachronism. In this habit, there may hide something of the very assumptions about gender and difference that earlier feminist historiography sought to expose or uproot through re-encounters with the Jewish and Christian past. Yet, as Homi Bhabha, Judith Butler, and others have reminded us, the power of stereotypes is not as much in the negative or positive images they promote, as in the totalizing systems of knowing that they naturalize, wherein such binary choices (female/male, magic/religion, nature/culture, negative/positive, passive/active) can appear to be our only options[11]—those systems of knowing that efface their own constructedness precisely by their power to direct our attention elsewhere, such as to the anxiously repeated task of judging this or that past representation of women.[12] If so, then we may further wonder whether the scholarly temptation to subject ancient traditions to a glaringly modern gaze might be less of a cure for gender stereotyping than a symptom of its present prevalence.[13] Insofar as much of the discussion surrounding the fallen angels concerns the power and limits of the human capacity to see and know,[14] I suggest that it might provide us with an interesting focus for considering the power and limits of the gendering of sight and knowledge as well—as here projected up and across the cosmic boundaries that separate earth from heaven.

Seeking Misogyny and "Magic" in Ancient Judaism

In the *Book of the Watchers,* two hundred of the angelic class of Watchers are said to have descended to earth in the days before the Flood, after the sight of human women sparked their desire to partake in the sexual and procreative prerogatives of human men. Whereas Genesis 6 provides some precedent for the notion of the sexual transgression and pollution of these "sons of God," the *Book of the Watchers* adds a potent new element: they are depicted as crossing the divinely established divide between heaven and earth, not just through physical descent and sexual mingling, but also through the dissemination of heavenly secrets to the inhabitants of earth.

The trope of illicit angelic instruction here helps to explain both the origins of human civilization and the antediluvian proliferation of earthly evils that necessitated the Flood (cf. Genesis 6:5). The teachings of the fallen angel Asael, for instance, are placed at the origins of the human arts of mining, metal-working, weaponry, shield-craft, cosmetics, dyes, and jewelry (1 Enoch 8:1). Exiled from their heavenly homes, other Watchers are said to show humankind how to wrest knowledge from the skies, by divining auguries from celestial and meteorological phenomena (8:3). Other teachings, associated particularly with the angelic leader Shemiḥazah and with the skills revealed to the Watchers' wives, evoke an association with "magic": sorcery, charms, the cutting of roots, and plant lore (7:1; 8:3).

The primary contrast explored in the *Book of the Watchers* is between heaven and earth, and the text reflects upon the proper relationship between these realms through the descent of the Watchers, on the one hand, and the ascent of Enoch, on the other.[15] That some passages associate the Watchers' revelation of knowledge specifically with their wives, however, seems to signal some subtext or secondary narrative, exploiting the charged intersection of sex and knowledge in a manner akin to that in the alternate etiology of evil in Genesis 2–3. Not only does the text's initial description of the Watchers' sexual misdeeds include a statement about how they taught sorcery and charms to their new wives (7:1b), but reference is made to the sins and secrets that the Watchers revealed to these women (9:8; 16:3; cf. 8:3i).

These passages from the *Book of the Watchers* (i.e., 1 Enoch 7:1b; 8:3i; 9:8, 16:3) have attracted much scholarly attention and have been widely adduced as early evidence for the association of women and "magic." Tal Ilan, for instance, describes the development as follows:

> In the biblical account women are also involved in the second fall story [i.e., Genesis 6], but they could be construed as the victims of rape at the hands of the sons of God. In Enoch's version they play a more active role, and are also allotted a more central position in the cosmic order. We are told that the fallen angels taught the daughters of man a number of useful skills: the wearing of jewelry and make-up (1 Enoch 8:1), *obviously* in order to allure men; the properties of roots and plants, for medicinal purposes, but *obviously* also for poisoning and witchcraft (7.1).... Thus, the description in 1 Enoch is probably the earliest wholesale association of magic with women in Jewish literature. In rabbinic literature this association is endorsed and justified. In answer to the question of why the biblical text [of Exod. 22:17] singles out witches and not wizards, the rabbis answer with resounding clarity that the law refers to both males and females, but "witchcraft was named after women ... because most women engage in witchcraft" (*y. San.* 7.19, 25d; *b. San.* 67b).... The development from the Bible to rabbinic literature, and the middle position evident in the post-biblical *1 Enoch* is, in this case, clear.[16]

Elsewhere, Ilan goes even further, suggesting that the association of certain types of knowledge and practice (e.g., plant lore) with women is ultimately what caused their association with "magic" as well.[17]

Ilan is not alone is interpreting ancient Jewish traditions about the teachings of the fallen angels as pivotal for the very gendering of "magic" as female knowledge and power.[18] William Loader, for instance, similarly reads the material about angelic teaching in the *Book of the Watchers* through the lens of the passages pertaining to women, and he thus interprets other references to the Watchers' teachings as denoting what angels revealed specifically to women;[19] by his reading, the text is "concerned with dangerous knowledge and sees women as its source."[20] Consequently, he argues that "we see the association of women with sorcery" and that "[s]orcery is in that sense gendered."[21] Likewise, Rebecca Lesses asserts that the *Book of the Watchers* "sets up a gendered dichotomy between the Watchers' human wives and Enoch; women are recipients only of rejected mysteries, while Enoch learns the true secrets of heaven from the revealing angels when he ascends to heaven alive."[22]

Such interpretations are surely alluring, but they may not be quite as self-evident as they first might seem. The skills said to be taught by the Watchers, as we shall see, are not unambiguously "magical," nor are they solely associated with women; the "sons of men" are also among the Watchers' students, and it is not always clear which teachings were for women and/or men. Furthermore, to arrive at an assessment of their representation in the *Book of the Watchers*, one must make choices about how best to reconstruct the original text, and one must do so for passages in the *Book of the Watchers* for which the manuscript evidence is perhaps the most divided. Not only is the textual situation for the *Book of the Watchers* notoriously complex, but the passages pertaining to women also seem to have been a nexus for textual variation during the course of the work's translation and transmission. This is certainly the case—as Kelley Coblentz Bautch has shown—for the passages pertaining to the possible culpability of women for angelic descent (8:1; 16:3) and to the ultimate fate of the Watchers' wives (19:2).[23]

Our earliest surviving witnesses to the text of the *Book of the Watchers* are the Aramaic fragments from Qumran (4QEn[a,b,c,d,e]), which date from the second and first centuries BCE.[24] These fragments, however, cover less than 25 percent of the book. The *Book of the Watchers* is preserved in whole only as part of an Ethiopian collection of Enochic books (*Maṣḥafa Henok Nabiy* = "1 Enoch"); this version likely reflects the Ge'ez translation of Greek version(s) under Axumite patronage between the fourth and sixth centuries CE but now survives only in manuscripts from the fifteenth century and following. Although it is likely that the *Book of the Watchers* was translated from Aramaic into Greek as early as the first century BCE, our earliest extended evidence for this translation dates from centuries later. Most of the text is preserved, with some duplications (1 Enoch 1:1–32:6 + 19:3–21:9), in Codex Panopolitanus, a fifth- or sixth-century manuscript from Egypt. Passages from the work are also extant in Greek in the form of excerpts adduced by the ninth-century Byzantine chronographer Syncellus in *Eclogae Chronographica* (1 Enoch 6:1–9:4; 8:4–10:14; 15:8–16:1).[25]

The degree of potential variation in these textual witnesses can be illustrated by the juxtaposition of the two Greek witnesses to 1 Enoch 7:1–2—the passage most widely cited as the basis for the tradition about Watchers teaching "magic" to their wives:

1 Enoch 7:1–2 in Codex Panopolitanus	Syncellus 12[26]
And they *took for themselves wives*; each of them chose wives for themselves, *And they began* to go into them (cf. Gen 6:2) and *to defile themselves with them*	These and the rest, in AM 1170, *took for themselves wives. And they began to defile themselves with them* up to the Flood.
	And they bore for them three races. First, the *great giants*. Then the giants begot the Napheleim, and to the Napheleim were born Elioud. And they were increasing in accordance with their greatness.
And they taught them (f. pl.) *sorcery and spells* [*pharmakeias kai epaoidas*], and they revealed to them (f. pl.) root-cutting and plants [*rizotomias kai tas botanas*].	*And they taught* themselves and their wives *sorcery and charms* [*pharmakeias kai epaoidas*].
Those pregnant gave birth to *great giants*, of 3000 cubits.	

Codex Panopolitanus is here closer to the Ethiopic manuscript tradition.[27] It is intriguing, nevertheless, that verbatim overlaps in the two Greek versions are so slim for this key passage concerning the Watchers' wives. Even those points of agreement that seem to speak most strongly to issues of gender in this passage—such as the claim that intercourse with women was defiling for the Watchers—are less firm than one might like: where the two Greek versions refer to the Watchers as beginning "to defile themselves" [Gr. *miainesthai*] with women, for instance, the Ethiopic versions render the more neutral "to unite" or "to mingle" [Eth. *tadammaru*].[28]

Codex Panopolitanus and Syncellus also diverge for 1 Enoch 8:3, the other passage from the *Book of the Watchers* most often cited in scholarly treatments of women and "magic":

1 Enoch 8:3 in Codex Panopolitanus	Syncellus 12
Semiazas taught spells and root-cutting [*epaoidas kai rizotomias*];	And their chief Semiazas taught them to be objects of wrath against reason [*einai orgas kata tou noos*], and the roots of plants of the earth [*kai rizas botanôn tês gês*]. The eleventh, Pharmaros, taught sorcery, spells, lore, and the loosening of spells [*pharmakeias, epaoidas, sophias, kai epaoidôn lutêria*].
Armaros the loosening of spells [*epaoidôn lutêrion*];	

continued

1 Enoch 8:3 in Codex Panopolitanus	Syncellus 12
Barakiêl the study of the stars [*astrologias*]; Chôchiêl the observation of signs [*sêmeiôtika*]; Sathiêl the observation of the stars [*asteroskopian*];	The ninth taught the observation of the stars [*astroskopian*]. The fourth taught the study of the stars [*astrologias*]. The eighth taught the observation of the heavens [*aeroskopian*]. The third taught the signs of the earth [*ta sêmeia tês gês*]. The seventh taught the signs of the sun [*ta sêmeia tou hêliou*]. The twentieth taught the signs of the moon [*ta sêmeia tês selênês*]. All of them began to reveal mysteries to their wives and their offspring [*pantes houtoi êrksanto anakaluptein ta mustêria tais gunaiksin autôn kai tois teknois autôn*].
Seriêl the course of the moon [*selênagôgias*]	

In this case, fragmentary Aramaic is extant. From the evidence of 4QEn[a] (1 iv 1–5) and 4QEn[b] (1 iii 1–5), it is possible to reconstruct the Aramaic text for this key passage; Michael Knibb, for instance, does so as follows:

> Shemihazah taught the casting of spells [and the cutting of roots;
> Hermoni taught the loosing of spells,] magic, sorcery, and skill;
> [Baraq'el taught the signs of the lightning flashes;
> Kokab'el taught] the signs of the stars;
> Zeq'el [taught the signs of the shooting stars;
> Ar'taqoph taught the signs of the earth;]
> Shamshi'el taught the signs of the sun;
> [Sahriel taught the signs of] the moon.
> [And they all began to reveal] secrets to their wives. . . .[29]

Comparison makes clear that both Greek versions have been shaped by the translation of categories of skill and knowledge into Hellenistic idioms; where the Aramaic lists a series of auguries related to discrete celestial and meteorological phenomena (i.e., lightning flashes, stars, shooting stars, earth, sun, moon), for instance, the Greek versions make references to *technai* more familiar in later times, with various types of astral sciences thus over-represented.[30]

Yet the Aramaic also appears to attest the antiquity of the final line in Syncellus's version—a line often cited in arguments about the place of gender in the *Book of the Watchers'* account of illicit angelic instruction. Here, as elsewhere, readings in Codex Panopolitanus are closer to the Ethiopic tradition. Yet such examples suggest that, when Syncellus's excerpts diverge from them, it is sometimes by virtue of preserving older traditions.[31] Inasmuch as the Aramaic is extant for so little of the text and Syncellus's version also bears quite obvious marks of having been reshaped to fit for later chronographical concerns, the task of trying to reconstruct the oldest recoverable version of the text proves all the more challenging.

By virtue of such text-critical complexities, it is problematic to base interpretations of women and "magic" in the *Book of the Watchers* on the selected citation of isolated verses.[32] Not only is it necessary to consult all of the extant witnesses, but one must also weigh them with reference to their place in the rhetoric and structure of the work as a redacted whole. When we approach the *Book of the Watchers* in this fashion, however, the task of seeking misogyny and "magic"—already fraught on both sides with the dangers of anachronism—becomes even trickier. What I shall suggest, in what follows, is that such difficulties are also often telling, signaling something of the impact of emergent discourses about "magic" and misogyny on the transmission, translation, and interpretation of this Second Temple Jewish text into Late Antiquity and beyond.

The Daughters of Men and the Dangers of Civilization

As we have seen, the first reference to angelic instruction in the *Book of the Watchers* (i.e., 1 Enoch 7:1; Greek versions of which are quoted above) is a passing comment in the course of the description of the angels' dalliances with women. Accordingly, it focuses on women, suggesting that the Watchers taught their wives "sorcery and charms" [Gr. *pharmakeias kai epaoidas*].[33] Codex Panopolitanus and the Ethiopic versions add that they revealed to them the cutting of roots and herbs as well. When the topic is picked up again in the next chapter, the recipients of the teachings are male or unspecified. In 1 Enoch 8:1, the Watcher Asael is credited with teaching about metals, including extracting them from the earth through mining, working iron and/or bronze to make weaponry, working gold and/or silver to make jewelry, and about precious stones and cosmetics; in some versions, he teaches these skills to men, who in turn make weapons, cosmetics, jewelry, etc., for themselves and their daughters.

The extensive list of teachings of other named Watchers that follows in 1 Enoch 8:3 (quoted above) initially includes no specifications as to their students' identity or gender; one could thus assume that they are male, or both male and female, depending on one's sense of 1 Enoch 8:1–2. The first two lines of the list evoke skills already associated with the Watchers' wives in 1 Enoch 7:1, while the next six are associated with the auguries of their eponymous celestial and other natural phenomena.[34] After the list, an association with women is again cited in Syncellus's version, this time with reference to "mysteries," and Aramaic is here extant to confirm the antiquity of his line; even there, however, it is unclear whether or not these "mysteries" are meant to be understood as the auguries, etc., in the preceding list.

At first sight, the revelation of "mysteries" [Gr. *mustêria,* Eth. *mešṭira,* for Aram. *razin*] might seem to be the topic most consistently associated with women, inasmuch as the same accusation is made in 1 Enoch 16:3 (see below). In 1 Enoch 9:6, however, "mysteries" are said to have been revealed by Asael to the "skillful among the sons of men," and in 1 Enoch 10:7, by the other Watchers to their children.[35] The Watchers' teachings—in other words—are not limited to women, nor is it easy to determine which teachings were for women and which for men. Even if we proceed with much caution in limiting our conclusions to what the textual evidence allows us cautiously to reconstruct, the *Book of the Watchers* does not readily give up answers to the questions that modern scholars interested in women and "magic" wish to ask of it.

Furthermore, to focus on whether the *Book of the Watchers* reflects positive or negative images of women is perhaps to miss some of the point of the work's own argument. The governing contrast throughout the work is between earth and heaven, rather than women and men. This contrast is explored through its structure as well as content.[36] In the voice of God Himself, moreover, is placed the assertion that the angels transgress in taking wives, not because taking wives is sinful, but rather because marriage, sex, and children are the domain of humankind (1 Enoch 15:4–7); their sin, as here conceived, lies in the transgression of divinely established distinctions. Likewise, if it is so difficult to determine whether women or men received this or that angelic teaching, or are most condemned through association with secrets or skills revealed by the Watchers, it is perhaps partly because the text itself, in all its versions, remains insistent on depicting *both* as involved in the spread of earthly sins catalyzed by illicit angelic instruction—with the involvement of women and men serving to telegraph the involvement of the totality of humankind, and hence a shared culpability in bringing about the Flood by which both were equally destroyed.

In this, the comparison with Genesis is telling. There, the origins of human civilization are also depicted in ambivalent terms, as resultant from Cain's sin and exile, with his progeny inventing cities (4:17), tent-dwelling and cattle-breeding (4:20), music (4:21), and bronze- and iron-working (4:22). Women are mentioned there too. Yet it is only as wives and mothers; they serve solely as links in the genealogies that connect male culture-creators to one another.

In the *Book of the Watchers*, by contrast, we find women implicated, alongside men, in the ambivalent origins of civilization. Women too traffic in the dangerous wisdom that here emblematizes the earthly reception of heavenly secrets. Inasmuch as the origins of civilization are here depicted in highly ambivalent terms, so women and men together partake in knowledge, power, sin, culpability, and punishment.[37] Accordingly, to read the inclusion of women as empowering is no less misleading than to judge it as misogynous. Considered in context, rather, their inclusion mirrors their subsequent destruction, alongside men, in the Flood—and hence serves as a defense of divine justice both for the Flood and for the eschatological judgment it is here held to prefigure.[38]

This context, moreover, draws our attention to the specific skills and knowledge here taught to women and men. A number of scholars have been perplexed by the inclusion of metalworking, alongside arts that better fit our modern notion of "magic" (and particularly women's magic). Loader, for instance, judges its inclusion "problematic and rather extreme," in contrast to other categories that he apparently feels are more of a natural fit as "forbidden knowledge."[39] Such judgments, however, may speak mostly to the gap between modern categories of knowledge and their ancient counterparts. After all, the connection of divination, pharmacology, and metallurgy is well attested in the literature of the ancient Mediterranean world. These *technai* are treated as one complex of powerful yet ambivalent arts in *Prometheus Bound* (484–500 BCE), for instance, and the fourth-century BCE historian Ephorus of Cyme similarly credits the Idaean Dactyls—whom he describes as "sorcerers [*goêtas*], who practiced charms [*epôdas*] and initiatory rites and mysteries [*mustêria*]"—with teaching humankind about the "use of fire and what the metals copper and iron are, as well as the means of working them" (Diodorus 5.64.4–5).[40] As Fritz Graf has shown, metallurgy's association with ambivalent power in the *Book of the Watchers* reflects its participation in "the eastern Mediterranean literary *Koine*."[41]

If such cases caution against the sanguine imposition of modern values and categories of knowledge upon ancient ones, they may also prompt us to be more cautious about inferring that ambivalent ritual knowledge is "magic" whenever associated with women. We may wish to be more careful, in other words, about the temptation to read the relevant ancient sources through the lens of the assumption that any association of women with knowledge must imply the condemnation of that knowledge as witchcraft, and the circular reasoning whereby sources read in this fashion are then used to support arguments about the seemingly universal idea of women as witches.[42] In the case of root-cutting and plant lore, for instance, the potentially positive medicinal connotations are clear from the alternate etiology in the *Book of the Jubilees*, a Hebrew work from the second century BCE closely aligned with early Enochic traditions; there, it is Noah who receives such knowledge from angels to protect against demons and illness (10:10–14). Yet, we may not wish to be so quick to conclude that such knowledge is simply negative ("magic") when associated with women and simply positive ("medicine") when associated with men; as in the case of ambivalence toward metallurgy here and elsewhere (e.g., Job 28),[43] the very point—in both cases—may be its power and danger as a mode of human control over the natural world.

Nevertheless, in the Greek translations of the *Book of the Watchers*, the association of these skills with women's magic does appear to have been enhanced. The image of the Watchers' wives learning *pharmakeia*, for instance, echoes the trope of the dangerous women in Athenian drama.[44] The appeal to teachings of *rizotomia* and *botanê* in Codex Panopolitanus, moreover, resonates with domains of expertise associated with dangerous women in Greek literature[45]—although even in the Greek evidence, as Lucia Nixon notes, one finds "Demeter's positive connection with plant lore" alongside "the more common, negative associations of women and 'root-cutting' represented by Medea and Circe."[46]

In light of the *Book of the Watchers'* association of such *technai* with women, it might be tempting to conclude, with Ilan, that its references to knowledge about "the properties of roots and plants" are meant not just "for medicinal purposes, but obviously also for poisoning and witchcraft."[47] To stop at what is apparently so obvious, however, is perhaps to miss something—both about the ancient traditions and about the modern assumptions that we bring to them. If we set aside the assumption that any domains of technical expertise associated with women (e.g., roots, plants) are implied to be tainted with "magical" or other negative associations in some manner that those domains associated with men (e.g., metals) are not, we are faced with a more poignant and ambivalent account of the power and danger of civilization, as perhaps emblematized by the plant lore of women no less than the metallurgy of men.[48]

Such concerns make sense, notably, in the context of the ancient discourse about the origins of civilization in both Jewish and Hellenistic cultures—including but not limited to Genesis and the traditions surrounding Prometheus. Yet a modern gendering of knowledge has often been imposed, as if universal, due perhaps to two common habits. First is the practice of reading references to women as always and everywhere meant to communicate something about gender, with the tacit implication that an author would have only included reference to men if he had wished to communicate human totality or universality, whereby the invisibility of masculinity is affirmed and the assumption of the male as model of the human re-inscribed. Second is the tendency to interpret the association of any form of knowledge or practice with women as a sign that this knowledge is being devalued or judged as negative, after which one applies the circular logic that its lesser valuation speaks to the correspondingly negative view of women.

In both cases, common modern reading practices can result in a homogenization of ancient misogyny that forecloses further inquiry into what is distinctive in specific times and sources.[49]

The Wiles of the Watchers' Wives

In the modern West, the association of women and witchcraft has arguably become so naturalized that it can be difficult to interpret pre-modern texts without imposing our own views of "magic" and misogyny as if these were stable or self-evident categories. With regard to "magic," Kimberly Stratton has stressed that "while certain types of ritual practices have been prohibited as either foreign or harmful throughout history, the formulation of a broad, polythetic discourse *magic* to classify and censure people and practices under one heading has a specific history."[50] Similarly, Ishay Rosen-Zvi has noted that "the main methodological problem with the common scholarly use of misogyny as an explanatory tool is that it tends to isolate only one component of a broader discourse";[51] he cites "the supposed triviality of the issue" as a possible reason that modern scholars have sometimes treated its identification and denunciation in ancient texts like the *Testament of Reuben* as an end in itself, rather than the beginning for further inquiry.[52] He further notes how studies that aim to unmask the misogyny of ancient literature often limit themselves largely to this task, even when the result is merely the repetition of "what is already quite well known: that ancient cultures are androcentric, chauvinistic, and, to some extent, misogynic."[53] "Misogyny is a well-known element in Hellenistic culture, and its existence in Jewish Hellenistic as well as Jewish wisdom writers, such as Philo and Ben Sira, is well documented," he notes, but thus points to all the more pressing need to recall that "misogyny is not a uniform phenomenon."[54]

Just as Stratton challenges us to historicize the association of women and "magic," so Rosen-Zvi pushes us to ask when, where, and how this association has (and has not) been tied to (what kinds of) misogyny. For Stratton, Hellenistic traditions are crucial for shaping the cross-cultural Mediterranean discourse "magic" that underlies modern notions of witchcraft, and for Rosen-Zvi, the interiorization of lust in Hellenistic Jewish transmutations of *zenut* and *porneia* is part of what produces a new "economy of gender" that shapes modern Western understandings of gender and sexuality.[55] If they are correct, it is perhaps not coincidental that the notion of women as temptresses and the association of women with "magic" in the *Book of the Watchers* are both attested most strongly in the Greek versions.

Above, for instance, we noted the use of the term *pharmakeia* in both Greek versions of 1 Enoch 7:1. In addition, the Greek of Codex Panopolitanus at 1 Enoch 19:2 asserts that the Watchers' wives will become Sirens, whereas the Ethiopic translation states that they will be peaceful. A statement unique to the version of

1 Enoch 9:8 preserved by the ninth-century chronographer Syncellus, moreover, associates the Watchers' wives with knowledge of "hate-charms" [*misêtra*].

Also unique to Syncellus's version of 1 Enoch 8:1 is the attribution of blame to women for the temptation of angels to earth. With the extant other versions, Syncellus's version first notes how the angel Asael taught humankind about metalworking, cosmetology, and related skills (see above). To this, however, Syncellus adds that "the sons of men did this for themselves and their daughters, and they transgressed and led astray the holy ones" [*kai epoiêsan heautois hoi huioi tôn anthrôpôn kai tais thugatrasin autôn, kai parebêsan kai eplanêsan tous hagious*].[56] This version asserts, in other words, that women were the cause for angelic descent, not just its victims.

As noted above, Syncellus's excerpts often diverge quite dramatically from the other witnesses. In many cases, the differences are readily explained with reference to chronological concerns, or to the context of the excerpts vis-à-vis the specific argument at hand, but there are also some cases in which they fall closest to the Aramaic fragments from Qumran. For passages like this, for which no Aramaic is extant, it can be difficult to determine whether Syncellus's unique readings reflect traditions more original than those preserved in Codex Panopolitanus and the Ethiopic versions, or much later additions.

In the case of 1 Enoch 8:1, R. H. Charles follows the Ethiopic and the other Greek witness in omitting this line, and Matthew Black dismisses it as a later "moralizing addition."[57] George Nickelsburg, however, posits that Syncellus's reading is closer to the original.[58] To support this choice, he points to the allusion to a double angelic descent in the second-century BCE "Animal Apocalypse" (1 Enoch 86:1–4), and he posits that it presupposes a complex of traditions wherein "the angels were seduced by the women"—or, more specifically, wherein Asael's teachings of cosmetics lead to the artificial beautification of human women, which in turn empowered the women to tempt Shemiḥazah and the other Watchers also to descend.[59] For Nickelsburg, then, the view of women as temptresses of angels, which we cited at the outset of this chapter from the *Testament of Reuben*, is already present in the *Book of the Watchers*.

Nickelsburg's arguments for the originality of Syncellus's longer readings concerning women are followed by Loader, for instance—with substantial implications for his assessment of the representation of women and "magic" in the *Book of the Watchers* as a whole.[60] More recently, however, Siam Bhayro has questioned whether it is wise to follow Syncellus in this case, particularly in the absence of corroborating evidence from other witnesses to the text of the *Book of the Watchers*; the supporting evidence cited by Nickelsburg is itself speculative and open to interpretation.[61] Using the same array of evidence, in fact, Bhayro can convincingly mount the opposite argument for opposite aims, insisting that "the misogynistic element, popular with the later retellings of this narrative, is not a true Enochic feature."[62]

Although I find Bhayro's argument about the textual history of this verse ultimately convincing, the concern to exempt the *Book of the Watchers* from charges of misogyny may distract from the interesting possibilities that it opens up. Indeed, what the studies of Ilan, Loader, Lesses, and Bhayro all share is an interest in whether and why the *Book of the Watchers* is misogynistic—and, hence, an approach to the extant Greek and Geʿez witnesses as sources for reconstructing its original Aramaic form. That our sources resist any easy application to these questions, however, may be significant in itself. It is perhaps telling that we find so much textual variation in the manuscript traditions surrounding the passages pertaining to women. It may also be telling that scholars who seek "magic" and misogyny most often find it in the Greek versions of the text. If modern interpreters find the place of women in the *Book of the Watchers* puzzling and bring questions to the text that might not fit its original sense, we are perhaps not alone: the text's late antique translators and tradents also seem to have struggled to make sense of how its statements about women might be made to speak their own questions too, as perhaps shaped by emergent views of "magic" and its gendering.

What I would like to suggest, then, is that we may miss an interesting story when we approach the textual witnesses to the *Book of the Watchers* only as data for the text-critical reconstruction of the original form of the work. The Greek translations and textual variants may reward re-reading, *not only* as witnesses to be weighed in the recovery of the Aramaic of this ancient Jewish text, *but also* as part of the rich evidence for the interpretations and transformations of the myth of the fallen angels. It is not clear whether the authors/redactors of the *Book of the Watchers* in the third century BCE were even concerned with women and "magic" in something of the same sense of the stereotypes later developed and now naturalized. What is clear, however, is that its transmission-history and reception-history tells us much about the later spread (and limits) of this association, particularly in relation to shifting views of the gendering of power and knowledge in Late Antiquity.[63]

When approached from this perspective, the traditions unique to Syncellus's quotations from the *Book of the Watchers* prove particularly rich—whether his is the only one of our extant witnesses that selectively preserves earlier material, as Nickelsburg suggests, and/or his version reflects later interpretation, as Bhayro suggests. Syncellus's excerpts seem to be taken from the works of earlier chronographers and thus reflect the late antique Egyptian monastic settings in which these ancient Jewish traditions entered the chronographical tradition with Panodorus and Annianus.[64] It is perhaps not coincidental, then, that the materials unique to Syncellus are also the ones most marked by a concern with the dangers of women, on the one hand, and a preoccupation with "magic," on the other.[65]

As noted above, there is also an interesting addition in Syncellus's version of the archangelic summary of the sins of Shemihazah and the Watchers who followed him in 1 Enoch 9. Here, most versions generally concur in recording the accusation that "they have gone in to the daughters of the men of the earth, and they have lain with them, and have defiled themselves with the women, and they have revealed to them (f. pl) all sins." To this, Syncellus adds: "and they have taught them to make hate-charms [*misêtra*]" (25.1). What is here made explicit is the association of women and "magic."

The statement in 1 Enoch 9:8, notably, departs from the rhetoric of the rest of 1 Enoch 9, which summarizes the earlier narrative in more abstract and synthetic terms. The introduction of a new detail about a topic of teaching, moreover, does not fit well within the structure of its immediate context, wherein the deeds of the two major Watchers are otherwise mirrored and matched. In 1 Enoch 9:6–8, Asael is first associated with teaching "all iniquity upon the earth" and revealing "mysteries in heaven, which the sons of men were striving to learn," after which Shemihazah and his followers go into "the daughters of the men of the earth" and revealed to them "all sins." Whereas this two-fold summary of angelic transgression is otherwise consistent with the use of gender specification elsewhere in the *Book of the Watchers* to express totality, the passing reference to "hate-charms" seems to reflect an interpretation that explicates the association of women and knowledge with reference to "magic."

The possibility that this detail is a later addition is also suggested by the reception-history of the *Book of the Watchers'* traditions about illicit angelic instruction in the centuries between its formation in Hellenistic Palestine in the third century BCE and the integration of excerpts from it into the Christian chronographical tradition among Egyptian monks in the early fifth century CE. Strikingly, the association of women and "magic" is simply not found in the early tradition surrounding the fallen angels. Lesses confirms, for instance, that women are not associated with "magic" in the rest of the early Enochic literature, nor are they deemed distinctively culpable for the corruption caused by the Watchers' teachings.[66]

At the outset, we noted how *Testament of Reuben* uses the rhetoric of "magic" to denounce the Watchers' wives as evil temptresses. In doing so, it may reflect some of the same Hellenistic Jewish concerns that shaped the initial Greek translation of the *Book of the Watchers* around the first century BCE; it may even draw from a version of the text that includes Syncellus's longer reading of 1 Enoch 8:1 as well as Codex Panopolitanus' association of the Watchers' wives with Sirens.[67] By the time of its integration in its present form into the second-century CE Christian *Testaments of the 12 Patriarchs*, however, such concerns seem surprisingly rare.

In the second century CE, a number of Christians were re-reading the *Book of the Watchers'* traditions about the fallen angels through the lens of Hellenistic and Roman ideas about *magoi* and *mageia*. One is hard-pressed, however, to find any explicit appeals to this association in relation to women. Where we find "magical writings" associated with the fallen angels, for instance, it is in connection to "pagan" polytheism, idolatry, and animal sacrifice, with no concern to specify the gender of the worshipers (so, e.g., Justin, *2 Apology* 5.4),[68] and when fallen angels are placed at the origins of "magical arts," it is with reference to male "heretics" (so, e.g., Irenaeus, *Against Heresies* 1.15.6; cf. *Proof* 18), consistent with what Stratton has shown for the early Christian gendering of "magic" as male.[69] In the third century, Julius Africanus mentions traditions about the fallen angels as teaching their wives "concerning magic and sorcery [*peri mageias kai goêteias*], as well as the numbers of the motion of astronomical phenomena," but he does so only in passing and in the context of dismissing these traditions as unbelievable; in fact, the implausibility of the whole complex of traditions is pivotal for the logic of the passage in question, which is the first known Christian source to promote the euhemeristic interpretation of the "sons of God" as human Sethians.[70]

One wonders whether the full articulation of the association of women, secrets, fallen angels, and hate-charms in the excerpts of the *Book of the Watchers* preserved via Syncellus might make most sense when read against the background of the Egyptian milieu of the early fifth-century monks Panodorus and Annianus. If the unparalleled density of Greco-Egyptian evidence for "magic" reflects something of its prevalence and diffusion, then this setting may also help us to understand why Codex Panopolitanus—also created in Egypt, roughly contemporaneous to Panodorus and Annianus—might reflect some intensification of earlier concerns within the Hellenistic Jewish reception and translation of the *Book of the Watchers*, even if the redeployment of the angelic descent myth as an etiology of Sirens (see below) is relatively early.

Although any conclusions must await further investigation, it is interesting to speculate as to whether a heightened interest in the pairing of women and "magic" might be rooted in the anxieties of monastic epistemology and expertise in a cultural milieu marked—as David Frankfurter notes—by "a much more fluid range of ritual experts both within and without the monastic fold. A monk was certainly as likely to provide one with an erotic binding spell as was an Egyptian priest, a rabbi, or an 'intellectual pagan,' and each could supply the counterspell as well."[71] If so, then it is also intriguing that the figure of the Egyptian monastic expert in "magic" finds a parallel in modern Ethiopian Christianity, wherein "the *däbtära,* a literate but itinerant ecclesiastical functionary, draws up elaborate protective and healing amulets for clients and is commonly viewed as a master of the demonic world . . . 'the master of spells, the paragon of ingenuousness, ruse, and deceitfulness, and, in the eyes of the more rigid priests, a fallen and impure being.'"[72] When considering the fluidity of the textual tradition of the *Book of the Watchers* on matters of "magic," it might be important to keep in mind its reading, transmission, and translation in local settings in which—again, in Frankfurter's words—a "popular religion, in which spells, talismans, and incantations, priests, monks, saints, and relics, parchment, magical figures, and sacred oil offered a panoply of resolutions for misfortune and competition in village life" and in which male ritual experts perhaps figured female power as ambivalent, not least because "the negotiation of sexuality—desire, fulfillment, fantasy, and all the social disruptions incumbent in desire—made up an essential part of this world."[73]

Women and the Secrets of the Cosmos

So far, we have focused mostly on passages in the *Book of the Watchers* attested both in Codex Panopolitanus and the excerpts in Syncellus, wherein the Ethiopic has agreed with the former. Passages relevant for investigations of women and "magic," however, also include some cases in which where Codex Panopolitanus and the Ethiopic diverge, with neither Aramaic nor Syncellus extant.

We have already made note of the example of the former's association of the Watchers' wives with Sirens:[74]

1 Enoch 19:2, Codex Panopolitanus	**1 Enoch 19:2, Ethiopic**
. . . and the wives of the transgressing angels will become Sirens [*kai hai gunaikes autôn tôn parabantôn angelôn eis seirênas ganêsontai*]	. . . and their wives, those whom the angels led astray, will become as peaceful [*wa-ʾanestiyāhomu-ni ʾasḥiton malāʾekta kama salāmāweyāt yekawwenā*]

Also interesting is a passage that has been central for determining the epistemological ramifications of the Watchers' revelations to their wives in the *Book of the Watchers,* namely, the account of God's accusation of the Watchers in 1 Enoch 16:3:

1 Enoch 16:3, Codex Panopolitanus	**1 Enoch 16:3, Ethiopic**
You were in heaven. And every secret that was not revealed to you [*kai pan mustêrion ho ouk anekalupsthê humin*] and a secret from God [*mustêrion to ek tou theo gegenêmenon*] you knew. And this you informed [*emênusate*] the women/your wives, in your hard-heartedness. And by this secret, females and mankind multiplied evils upon the earth.	You were in heaven. And hidden things still were not revealed to you [*wa-xebuḥāt ʾādi ʾi-takaštu lakemu*], and rejected/worthless secrets [*mennuna mešḥira*] you knew. And these you informed [*zēnawa*] women/your wives, in the hardness of your heart. And by this secret, women—and mankind—multiplied (f. pl.) evils upon the earth.

The Ethiopic version of the verse differs notably in sense and implications from the Greek version preserved in Codex Panopolitanus, thus puzzling many modern interpreters.[75] The contrasting readings of the verse suggest that late antique translators and tradents of the *Book of the Watchers* may have faced similar challenges when seeking to understand its statements about women and knowledge in a world in which their association was becoming a matter of danger, "magic," and witchcraft.

Where the extant Greek and Ethiopic versions diverge is on the question of what exactly the Watchers knew—and, hence, on the question what precisely they taught to their wives. The Greek suggests that these angels knew and revealed heavenly secrets, while the Ethiopic asserts that the fallen angels possessed no real heavenly knowledge but only rejected or worthless knowledge; it is the latter variant, for instance, that thus undergirds Lesses's claim that women are here depicted as knowing only rejected secrets, in contrast to Enoch, and that "magic" is thus gendered as female.[76]

Notably, the assertion of the Watchers' wrongful and corrupting use of true knowledge in the Greek fits better with the literary context, structure, and argumentative logic of 1 Enoch 12–16, which concern the transgression of cosmological and epistemological boundaries.[77] Moreover, if the Watchers are here accused of wrongfully revealing heavenly knowledge on earth, their transgression would seem to be blunted, if not altogether negated, by the assertion that the revealed knowledge was actually not heavenly or true. This, in turn, would detract from the explanatory power of the trope vis-à-vis the necessity for God to destroy the entire world by Flood.[78] It seems more likely, too, that a later scribe might feel uncomfortable with the notion of sinfulness as paired with true knowledge—as also, for instance, in the strikingly parallel case of the treatment of the knowledge of the King of Tyre in LXX Ezekiel 28.[79]

For our present purposes, however, the originality of the reading in Codex Panopolitanus proves less pressing than the late antique Egyptian context of its cultivation. Although the notion of true knowledge wrongly revealed strikes some modern scholars as so illogical as to be nonsensical, we do find this concept attested in late antique sources that seem shaped by awareness of the *Book of the Watchers*, or traditions therein, in a form similar to Codex Panopolitanus. As Charles and others have noted,[80] the reading of 1 Enoch 16:3 preserved in this Egyptian manuscript seems to be presupposed by Clement of Alexandria. For Clement, it serves as ammunition in a debate over whether or not there are hidden truths in Hellenistic philosophy:

> We showed in the first *stromateus* that the philosophers of the Greeks are called thieves, in as much as they have taken without acknowledgment their principal dogmas from Moses and the prophets. To which also we

> shall add that the angels who had obtained the superior rank, after having sunk into pleasures, told to the women the secrets that had come to their knowledge [*hoi angeloi ekeinoi hoi ton anô klêron heilêchotes katolisthêsantes eis hêdonas ekseipon ta aporrêta tais gunaiksin, hosa ge gnôsin autôn aphikto*], whereas the rest of the angels concealed them, or rather, kept them until the coming of the Lord. From there emanated the doctrine of Providence and the revelation of high things [*hê tês pronoias didaskalia erruê kai hê tôn meteôrôn apokalupsis*]. Since prophecy had already been imparted to the philosophers of the Greeks, the treatment of dogma arose among the philosophers—sometimes true, when they hit the mark, and sometimes erroneous, when they did not comprehend the secret of the prophetic allegory. (Clement, *Strom.* 5.1.10.2)

Clement's familiarity with the *Book of the Watchers* and its account of angelic teachings is well known; elsewhere, for instance, he appeals to its traditions about illicit angelic instruction to posit that "all the demons knew that it was the Lord who arose after the passion, for Enoch already said that the angels who sinned taught humankind astronomy, divination, and the other arts" (*Selections from the Prophet* 53.4).[81] Given his date and setting, moreover, it is perhaps not surprising that he might be familiar with the work in some form similar to the version preserved in Codex Panopolitanus. And, whatever the original sense of 1 Enoch 16:3, this familiarity seems to enable his assertion that women stand at the earthly origins of philosophical teachings such as "the doctrine of Providence and the revelation of high things," by which Greeks had some access to Christian truths even prior to Christ—and because of which, according to Clement, Christians can profitably draw upon such writings.[82]

A similar point is made by the fourth-century Egyptian alchemist, Zosimus of Panopolis, to posit the heavenly origins of alchemy. Again, the connection between the fallen angels and their wives is exploited as a channel for the transmission of true and powerful knowledge—transgressively yet still efficaciously—down to earth. The relevant passage, as preserved by Syncellus, reads as follows:

> . . . the ancient and divine scriptures said this, that certain angels lusted after women and, after descending, taught them (f. pl) all the works of nature [*edidaksan autas panta ta tês phuseôs erga*]. Having stumbled because of these women, he says, they remained outside of heaven, because they taught men everything wicked and nothing benefiting the soul [*panta ta ponêra kai mêden ôpselounta tên psuchên edidaksan tous anthrôpous*]. The same scriptures say that from them the giants were born. So theirs is the first teaching concerning these arts handed down by Chemeu.

> He called this the book of Chemeu, when also the art is called Alchemy, and so forth. (Sync. 14.6–14)

Here again, women are associated with heavenly knowledge that fell to earth in ancient times, thus shaping human civilization and the history of knowledge. If this knowledge is otherwise gendered, moreover, it is not made explicit. Just as Clement places women at the ambivalent origins of Greek philosophy, so too Zosimus with Greco-Egyptian alchemy.

Modern scholars have been puzzled by 1 Enoch 16:3, perhaps also because of the temptation to conflate the illicit angelic teaching of knowledge with angelic teachings of illicit knowledge. The above-cited passages from Clement and Zosimus, however, suggest that the idea of true knowledge wrongly revealed was a trope that made sense in a late antique Egyptian context, where it could prove a power strategy for legitimating types of knowledge both problematized and enhanced by their potential danger. Zosimus even notes the corrupting effects of this transmission, further echoing 1 Enoch 16:3, in a manner that also enables reflections upon the power and limits of alchemy to purify the soul.[83] These examples also suggest that the association of women with heavenly secrets was not necessarily as odd or abhorrent to all ancient men as we might expect from modern broad-brush characterizations of pre-modern misogyny.

Interestingly, neither Clement nor Zosimus seem to be the first to make their respective arguments. In the case of philosophy, Clement may be answering other Egyptian Christians who do assume that the origins of knowledge with Watchers and/or women might suffice to prove its problematic character.[84] In the case of alchemy, Zosimus may also be responding to the earlier use of the myth of the fallen angels as part of an etiology of alchemy, albeit in positive terms.

The possibility that some Enochic traditions were integrated into Greco-Egyptian Hermeticism is raised by the *Letter of Isis the Priestess to Horus*, which includes the following tradition:

> . . . it came to pass that a certain one of the angels who dwell in the first firmament [*tina tôn en tô prôtô stereômati diatribonta ton hena tôn angelôn*], having seen me (i.e., Isis) from above, was filled with the desire to unite with me in intercourse [*anôthen epitheôrêsanta me boulêthênai tês pros eme mikseôs*]. He was quickly on the verge of attaining his end, but I did not yield, wishing to inquire of him as to the preparation of gold and silver. When I asked this of him, he said that he was not permitted to disclose it, on account of the exalted character of the mysteries [*dia tên tôn mustêriôn huperbolên*], but that on the following day a superior angel, Amnael, would come . . . The next day, when the sun reached the middle of its course, the superior angel, Amnael, appeared and descended. Taken

> with the same passion for me he did not delay, but hastened to where I was. But I was no less anxious to inquire after these matters. When he delayed incessantly, I did not give myself over to him, but mastered his passion until he showed the sign on his head, and revealed the mysteries I sought, truthfully and without reservation [*kai tên tôn zêtoumenôn mustêriôn paradosin aphthonôs kai alêthôs poiêsêtai*]. [85]

If there is indeed some connection with Jewish traditions about the Watchers,[86] the link between sexual desire and secret knowledge has been taken even further. The incrimination of angels for lasciviousness, moreover, has been paired with seeming delight in female trickery, control, and resistance in the service of learning secrets from heaven.[87] If this text thus challenges our modern expectations that the pairing of women and "magic" must always be a matter of misogyny, it also attests the continued fluidity in the gendering of knowledge and power in the discussion surrounding the fallen angels.

This fluidity, moreover, seems to flow across what we might wish, from a modern perspective, to try to distinguish as "religion," "science," and "magic." Not only are similar tales attested in "gnostic," Jewish, and Islamic versions (see below), but some echo of the association of the fallen angels and alchemy may find its way into one version of the Ethiopic translation of the *Book of the Watchers*: just as the Greco-Egyptian reinterpretation of their teachings in terms of alchemy can be readily understood as an extension of the pairing of metallurgy with "magic" in the *Book of the Watchers* and its broader cultural context (see above), so some manuscripts conclude the account of Asael's teachings in 1 Enoch 8:1 with the statement that "the world was changed."[88]

Angelic Lust and Heavenly Ascent

To when and whom, then, do we owe the association of women and "magic" in the tradition surrounding the fallen angels? Although I have so far resisted the temptation to subject the dynamism of the tradition to a quest for some single moment of "origin" or "invention," it should be clear by now that I find the insights of Bhayro, Stratton, and Rosen-Zvi most insightful for understanding the full array of the extant evidence. In my view, it is only with some violence that one reads a misogyny of a later sort back into the *Book of the Watchers*, and it is only with some anachronism that one can press its notions of knowledge and power to fit the Hellenistic discourse of "magic" that has come to shape our own understandings of "magic," "religion," and "science."

Rosen-Zvi brings a sophisticated and theoretically inflected understanding of gender to bear on the *Testament of Reuben* and illumines much about the text. Rather puzzlingly, however, he asserts that it is "unparalleled in any other known source" in its claim that it was "the daughters of men themselves who tempt the Watchers."[89] Apparently unaware of the traditions noted above, he asserts several times that "[t]his is the *only known* version which presents the events as a result of the women's own initiative; in *all other* versions it is the Watchers who plot to seduce or capture the women," and this claimed originality proves central to his reading of the text as highly innovative, reflecting a moment of Hellenistic Jewish invention that ushers in a "new economy of gender" akin to that which Michel Foucault locates in Christianity toward the "birth of sexuality."[90]

Below, we will return to consider its use of the rhetoric of bewitchment to describe how the "daughters of men" tempted angels down from heaven. For now, it suffices to note that it does seem to assume some prior association between women and "magic." The statement that "they bewitched [*ethelksan*] the Watchers before the Flood," for instance, resonates so poignantly with the notion that the Sirens began their lives as the Watchers' wives that one wonders whether it is merely coincidence.[91] The language here used to describe their role in tempting the Watchers, moreover, is readily understood in terms of the exegesis of a version of 1 Enoch 8:1 similar to that preserved in Syncellus: the statement that "by adornment [*dia tês kosmêseôs*] they lead astray first their minds [*planôsin prôton tas dianoias*]" (*T. Reub.* 5.3) answers the question of how these women "led astray the holy ones [*eplanêsan tous hagious*]" with reference to the inclusion of "ornamentation for women [*kosmia tais gunaiksi*]" among the teachings of Azael, as made by men for themselves and their daughters (*1 Enoch* 8:1, Syn.).

Persuasive, nonetheless, is Rosen-Zvi's argument that the articulation of this trope within the *Testament of Reuben* is best understood within its literary and argumentative context, and appreciated for what might be innovative. Even if he is incorrect that its shifting of culpability from the "sons of God" to "daughters of men" is "a unique inversion," he is right to note that it is "the link that connects the story to the rest of the testament."[92] "Man's inclinations and female temptations appear here, just as in the case of Reuben and Bilhah, as two sides of the same coin," he suggests; inasmuch as the "shift of the narrative focus from the male figures' external action to their internal lust parallels the transformation of the daughters of men from victims to temptresses," he argues that "*T. Reuben* preserves traditional motifs, while at the same time integrating them through a series of relatively small changes into a new economy of gender."[93]

This notion of a "new economy of gender" created from "traditional motifs" may prove useful for understanding Tertullian as well. As noted above, Tertullian similarly uses the myth of the fallen angels to argue for the sinfulness of all women. In his case, the small change that makes a major difference is the attribution of teaching of cosmetics and jewelry-making directly and distinctively to women. Although Tertullian is clearly familiar with the *Book of the Watchers* and elsewhere defends its antiquity and authority, he deviates from all known versions of it in this one detail—with notable effects. Rather than a matter of cosmic renewal necessitated by universal corruption, involving men and women, the Flood thus becomes yet another example of female culpability for sin and suffering, for which Eve is the model, and the women of Tertullian's own time no less liable. Even here, however, it is not "magic" that the women learn, but rather cosmetology. What is dangerous about women, for Tertullian, is not that they know or use "magic" per se, but that they are imagined not to need it: female beauty and its artifices hold enough power to move even angels from their homes in heaven.

Whether the notion that women tempted the Watchers to earth is attested already in the *Book of the Watchers* in the third century BCE, or first in the "Animal Apocalypse," the Greek translation of the *Book of the Watchers*, or the *Testaments of the 12 Patriarchs* shortly afterward, it remains that this trope is most richly extended in late antique and medieval sources—eventually coming to be intertwined with a discourse on "magic," albeit perhaps particularly in cases where the "daughters of men" are imagined as temptresses of human "sons of God," with ancient Sethians encoding late antique monks and ascetics.[94] Similar traditions can be found at the medieval reemergence of interest in the fallen angels within Jewish literary cultures, beginning with the gaonic midrash *Pirqe de Rabbi Eliezer* and the closely aligned and contemporaneous *Targum Pseudo-Jonathan*.[95]

What proves perhaps more interesting, for our present purposes, is that medieval Jewish literature also offers examples of positions more similar to those of Clement and Zosimus, whereby women are positively associated with powerful knowledge. Even if Ilan is correct that it is possible to draw a straight line from biblical misogyny to rabbinic misogyny with the *Book of the Watchers'* reference to "magic" in the middle,[96] this is clearly not the only trajectory.

It shall suffice, for our purposes, briefly to note one complex of midrashim on Genesis 6 that exemplifies the fluid place of women and "magic" in the discussion surrounding the fallen angels—namely, what A. Jellinek, J. T. Milik, and others have called the "Midrash on Šemḥazai and Azael."[97] This complex is found in various versions, with varying degrees of narrativization, in Rabbi Moshe ha-Darshan's *Bereshit Rabbati* (11th c.), in the copy of the anthological chronicle of Yeraḥmeel ben Solomon (c. 1150) preserved in Eleazar ben Asher Ha-Levi's collection *Sefer ha-Zikhronot* (c. 1325), and in Simeon ha-Darshan's midrashic anthology *Yalqut Shimoni* (13th c.)[98] Here, we re-encounter the two main Watchers of the *Book of the Watchers,* Shemiḥaza and Asael, as Shemḥazai and Azael, and the tale of their descent to earth is retold in the style of classic rabbinic tales about human/angelic rivalry: descent is here framed as a "test" of the angels' ability to resist the evil inclination, as rooted in their jealous desires to expose the shortcomings of humankind, but they fail immediately upon taking on flesh and seeing and/or cavorting with "daughters of men."[99]

Among the subsequent traditions about their time on earth is a version of the above-cited story about Isis, retold as a tale about Shemḥazai's encounter with one of the "daughters of men," often given the name Asterah.[100] The fallen angel sees her and tries to seduce her, but she resists. Refusing to listen to his request, she demands that he teach her "the Name by which you are able to ascend to the Raqia" (i.e., the first firmament in heaven). As in the early Enochic and related traditions, as well as the Hermetic *Letter of Isis to Horus*, the angel thus teaches a heavenly secret to a woman that he desires. Here, however, the woman uses this teaching, not to spread sin upon the earth, but rather to ascend to heaven to escape his sexual advances. As a reward, God places her among the stars in the Pleaides.[101] Although Shemḥazai and Azael are said to have found other wives, the first reference to their teachings thus concerns a woman who resisted and to whom secrets were taught, albeit as a result of trickery and compulsion.

Here, we find what might be described as an inversion of the inversion in the *Testament of Reuben*: it is not the lustful woman who brings the angels down from heaven, but rather the lustful angel that sends the woman upward. Although Asterah is reminiscent of Isis in Hermetic literature and Naamah in "gnostic" literature, and her tale has Islamic parallels as well,[102] it is here told in language that resonates with rabbinic and para-rabbinic traditions. Most intriguing are the resonances with traditions about angelic adjuration and heavenly ascent in the Hekhalot literature. Whereas that literature limits such mystical and magical power to men who are pure of any defilement from woman, this tale proposes a playful reversal—with the wise and chaste woman uniquely able to learn the divine Name from an angel, ascend upward to heaven, and even gain God-given immortality as a star. In effect, Asterah thus takes on the role that had been given to Enoch in the *Book of the Watchers*, namely, as the human being who reverses angelic descent in heavenly ascent. These multiple twists are enabled, moreover, precisely by the association of women and "magic"—albeit with women now on the side of purity and "magic" now understood in terms of adjuration and ascent, even as traditional motifs are yet again redeployed in new configurations.

Gender and Other Ways of Seeing

What, then, might we conclude about the place of women and "magic" in the *Book of the Watchers* and its *Nachleben*? Above, I have tried to resist pinpointing any single moment of "origins" or "invention," or tracing any single drama of devolution or development, attempting instead to follow the evidence along the multiple lines of its richly polyvalent spread. Such lines lead us not just to encounters of Hellenism and Judaism, but also to the local cultures of late antique Egypt. We can see Greek ideas combined with biblical and Jewish ideas already in the *Book of the Watchers* and *Testament of Reuben*, and so too, even more dramatically, in Codex Panopolitanus and the writings of Clement of Alexandria. Yet the latter, as we have seen, cannot be wholly understood apart from their Egyptian contexts, as illumined by Zosimus and the *Letter of Isis to Horus*—and the same might be said with respect to Syncellus's excerpts as well, due to their Egyptian monastic mediators. Even the "Midrash of Shemhazai and Azael" might owe something to this context. This is certainly the case with the Ethiopian compilation *1 Enoch*, created in neighboring Axum in the fifth or sixth century.

Inasmuch as the present inquiry remains preliminary, I would like to conclude by reflecting on some of the challenges involved in moving ahead in a manner that takes seriously the contemporary conversations about gender, stereotype, and identity invoked at the outset, while also bringing our ancient sources to bear on the question of the universality of their insights. If Butler is correct that gender is essentially unstable—requiring embodied, social performance to maintain the fiction of natural and immutable distinction[103]—what do we as modern scholars perform when we choose to focus inquiries upon it? Does our projection of such theories and questions into the past belie our claims as to their ultimate contingency? What is effaced and naturalized by our own acts of scholarly selection, and what are the blind spots produced by our own ways of seeing and knowing, as embedded in our own practices of reading and interpreting ancient sources (whether source-critical, philological, historical, theoretically inflected, etc.)?

By means of conclusion, I would like to reflect briefly on these questions by returning yet again to the passage from the *Testament of the Reuben* quoted at the outset of this chapter and there presented as one of the "parade examples" of ancient misogyny in relation to traditions concerning the fallen angels. Looking again, however, we might wonder whether this passage also speaks—perhaps even more poignantly—to ways of seeing, ways of knowing, and the fraught potency of the interface between them. When we re-read the passage in light of ancient understandings of optics, for instance, the possibility arises that both its "magic" and its misogyny might be understood, at least in part, as expressions of a broader concern in the first centuries of the Common Era with the power of seeing to shape the soul.[104]

Contemporary discourse on gender has long taken it as axiomatic that the male gaze is active and hegemonic, whereas women are those who are seen and objectified, and thus passive. Although first developed in film theory and with reference to contemporary contexts, the trope of the active "male gaze" has become a common reading strategy in scholarship on the representation of women and gender in pre-modern contexts as well.[105] Even in cases where feminist theorists stress that gender is socially performed by both women and men, the description of sight and surveillance often remains gendered, with the "male gaze" and "imperial gaze" answered in a binary framework by a "reversal of the gaze." In a recent article on eighteenth-century literature, Rivka Swenson diagnoses the problem as follows:

> . . . inheritors of what we might call the Mulveyan meme, we have naturalized the theory of the dominant/male gaze. Laura Mulvey's significant work on filmic pornography describes gazing as the province of male spectators whose experiences are marked by uncomplicated agency. Mulvey writes, "in a world ordered by sexual imbalance, pleasure in looking has been split between active/male and passive/female"; her important thesis, implemented and adapted by other film theorists, makes spectating and agency into synonymous, as well as masculinized, conditions. Potential problems are that the theory stabilizes subject/object binaries and threatens to offer a monolithic view of sexual difference and gendered experience. [106]

With regard to the eighteenth century, Swenson points to the scientific discourses on optics and their popular reception to suggest that "the dialectics of the visual field, attended by the empirically generated nexus of seeing, knowing, and being, exceed modern equations between sight and agency," partly by virtue of the prominence of theories of intromission—theories that explain sight with appeal to the emission of particles [Gr. *eidola*, Lat. *simulacra*] from that which is seen into the eyes of those who see.[107] In such cases, the one who is seen is figured as active, whereas the one who sees is passive—the opposite of what is assumed in the case of the gaze today, particularly in discussions of its gendered and gendering power. Accordingly, she wonders whether "the [Mulveyan] meme reinforces a perceived connection between masculinity, gazing, and agency that is anachronistic."[108]

Inasmuch as the concern of the present essay is with periods even more distant from our own, it may prove all the more pressing to historicize our optics and erotics, lest we impose anachronistic assumptions about the gender, agency, and the gaze. Such caution may prove particularly apt due to the prominence of sight in the discussion surrounding the fallen angels. For the *Book of the Watchers*, as perhaps already for Genesis, the problems began when "the sons of God *saw*," and this moment of seeing also becomes a major preoccupation of later exegetes.[109] From a modern perspective, it does indeed seem all too natural to read this act of seeing as an act that marks the angelic gaze as a male one, thrust upon passive female beauty, and one finds such language widespread within scholarly treatments of these traditions. Such assumptions, arguably, are as deep as they have been invisible in scholarly treatments of the issue of the agency of Watchers and women in the *Book of the Watchers* and related writings. With regard to the *Testament of Reuben*, for instance, even Rosen-Zvi dwells on what he reads as the paradox of the passively seen women framed as temptresses of the actively seeing angels and men:

> This structure mirrors . . . *T. Reuben*'s narration of the Bilhah episode. Both passages point to women as responsible for bringing about sin. More specifically, both texts portray women as bringing upon themselves the male gaze that opens each story, thus re-interpreting the gaze and its consequences as the women's own fault. Just as T. Reuben presents Bilhah as a temptress, "drunk and naked," in the very midst of her sleep, so too the women in the Watchers tale "bewitched" the angels to lust after them. Although in both cases the male figures ultimately act on their desires (the women remain relatively passive), both texts serve as illustrations of the power of female temptation. Men are victims even in their active plots. Thus, these texts do not make a specific judgment about the particular female figures of Bilhah or the daughters of men. Rather, they make a general statement about women *qua* women . . . "Evil are women, my children." (*T. Reu.* 5.1) [110]

This, in turn, is what undergirds his broader argument that "the *Testaments* tend to expand the female characters' responsibility for causing the forbidden acts . . . as part of a much broader transformation in which internal thoughts and inclinations rather than actions become the focus of the religious struggle," such that "[t]he misogyny of the *Testaments*, . . . rather than merely a commonplace to be noted, represents the institution of a whole new era of sexual discourse, one which carries with it a new economy of gender."[111]

A closer look at the relevant passage about the Watchers may reveal, however, that its preoccupation with sight may depend on an understanding of optics that differs from modern notions of the gaze as an emblem of male agency and hegemony, and—perhaps more basically—even from modern notions of sight as abstract and internalized.[112] In the *Testament of Reuben*, the process of temptation is broken up into its constituent components: "in their heart they plot against men," "by adornment [*dia tês kosmêseôs*] they lead astray first their minds [*planôsin prôton tas dianoias*]," "by sight they implant the poison [*dia tou blemmatos ton ion enspeirousi*]" and "by the act they take them captive" (5.3); the first resonates with biblical and related tropes about women and deception, while the second recalls traditions linking cosmetics with the teachings of Asael (i.e., *1 Enoch* 8:3). In the third, a concern for tracing views of women and "magic" might lead us to focus on the appeal to poison, as elsewhere associated so closely with potion. A concern with questions of sight, however, leads us to notice the active role here granted to those being seen.

If this seems strange to modern sentiments or necessarily a matter of misogyny, it may not have been so paradoxical in the eras and contexts in which the *Testament of Reuben* took form. In the centuries surrounding the turn of the Common Era, the mechanics of vision remained debated, with the range of positions including what might be heuristically contrasted as intromissionism, as described above, and extramissionism, with beams emitted from the eye to the object seen, as well as various permutation and combinations.[113] In contrast to modern ideas about seeing, moreover, ancient optics tended to conceive of sight as a tactile phenomenon, rather than distant, disconnected, or neutral; even explanations of vision with appeal to extramission were not wholly internalized in quite the later sense of the inner self as housed in the impermeable fortress of the soul. A. Mark Smith, for instance, notes that "[w]hatever their differences of detail, ancient theories of vision all found common ground in the assumption that sight cannot occur without some *physical* mediation between the eye and visible objects . . . action at a distance is impossible."[114]

Furthermore, even though the passive eye of intromissionism was countered by extramissionist and other theories, it remained viable, and had literary and cultural effects; Shadi Bartsch has shown, for instance, how "the notion of the erotic penetration of the body by corpuscular bodies entering in through the eyes proves a remarkably consistent ancient paradigm for the workings of the gaze upon the soul" before and during the second century CE.[115] Most significant, for our purposes, is the place of such ideas of passive seeing in the interpenetration of optics and erotics in novelistic and other literary reflections on desire from the early Roman Empire.[116]

Something of the ancient scientific debate over the passivity or activity of the eye, for instance, can be glimpsed in following comments on vision and desire by the first-century Roman author Plutarch:

> Vision provides access to the first impulse to love, that most powerful and violent experience of the soul, and causes the lover to melt and be dissolved when he looks at those who are beautiful, as if he were pouring forth his whole being toward them. For this reason, we are entitled, I think, to be most surprised at anyone who believes that, while men are passively influenced and suffer harm through the eyes, they yet should not be able to influence others and inflict injury in the same way. The answering glances of the young and beautiful and the stream of influence from their eyes, whether it be light or a current of particles, melts the loves and destroys them. . . . Neither by touch nor by hearing do they suffer so deep a wound as by seeing and being seen. (Plutarch, *Table Talk* 68.1a–c) [117]

The continued place of intromission in the optics of erotics, and the erotics of optics, are evoked in the second century by Achilles Tatius of Alexandria—there with further reference to the power of sight to shape the soul. Helen Morales, for instance, draws our attention to several key passages in *Clitophon and Leucippe*, where "[v]ision is coextensive with the lover's body":

> Beauty pricks sharper than darts, and floods down through the eyes to the soul, for the eye is the channel of the wounds of desire. (1.4.4–5)
>
> The effluxion of beauty floods down through the eyes to the soul, and effects a kind of union without contact; it is a bodily union in miniature, a new kind of bodily fusion. (1.9.4–5)
>
> The pleasure of sight, flowing in through the eyes, settles in the chest. Drawing in constantly the image of the beloved, it impresses this image upon the mirror of the soul and moulds its shape. For the emanation given off by beauty, pulled via invisible rays to the lover's heart, imprints upon it its shadow-image. (5.13.4) [118]

None of these passages, notably, makes immediate sense from the perspective of modern notions of visuality, and one might be tempted to dismiss their imagery as solely metaphorical. They resonate, however, with ancient theories about seeing as tactile and potentially invasive.

I suggest that something similar might be said for the *Testament of Reuben*'s description of the mechanics of desire that led to the temptation and transformation of the Watchers. To focus on the text's misogyny is to illumine the trope of woman as temptresses, but it is also to miss the assumptions possibly shaped by ancient optics. Being seen is here figured as active, rather than passive, and thus, what we would figure as the female reception of a gaze is here likened to insemination by a glance [*blemma*].[119] What we might read as the hegemonic gaze of heaven is here an act perpetrated upon angels by women in a manner not merely reduced to the trope of the temptress: "for thus they bewitched the Watchers before the Flood: as these looked at them continually."

What enables the rhetoric of "magic" here, moreover, is that the women's act of being seen acts upon the Watchers in transformative ways: it has the power to make angels "change into the shape of men." Seeing women, in other words, is what causes heavenly beings to take on gender.[120] Furthermore, the passage implies that it is only by virtue of this gendering that the Watchers can exert transformative power upon women as well; the sight of them in this form causes the women—at a distance, with only the touch of the eyes—to bear Giant children from intercourse with their own husbands. The warning to men to "guard your senses from every woman" (*T. Reub.* 6:1), thus, is not merely a misogynistic or moralistic metaphor. It is also a warning about the transformative power of vision in a world where seeing and being seen were conceived as tactile and physical experiences, and where opened eyes were also orifices by which souls were made vulnerable to penetration by transformative powers.[121]

At first sight, the world evoked by the *Book of the Watchers* might seem akin to a perfect panopticon, with the aptly named Watchers of the first firmament peering down at the earth and its inhabitants invisibly from above, and their higher counterparts reporting human deeds to God to mete out punishments. At least for the authors of the *Testament of Reuben*, however, this surveillance also means that Watchers are vulnerable to the power of sight as a physical connection with earth: their watching as witnesses opens a conduit between earth and heaven, and intromission enables the inhabitants of the former to touch the inhabitants of the latter, through the eyes, with transformative effects.

Just as angels are thus made men by the sight of women, so the power of sight is later figured as a sort of "magic" in its own right, akin to angelic adjuration: Isis needs only to have Amnael close enough to see her, to bind the high angel to her for the knowledge of alchemy's powers to transform Nature, and perhaps so too with Asterah's empowerment by the sight of Shemihazah, whereby she gains the knowledge of heavenly ascent, transforming from woman to star. Inasmuch as the *Book of the Watchers* claims sight as the basis for Enoch's totality of understanding of cosmic realities in his tours of heaven and earth, we might also wonder whether seeing also bears some danger in its power even there. In this ancient apocalypse—where Genesis' statement that "the sons of God saw" (6:2) has slipped, so seemingly naturally, into the assertion that "the sons of God saw and desired" in 1 Enoch 6:2—the power and danger of knowing might be paired already with the power and danger of seeing, with the latter as potent yet ambivalent as true heavenly secrets revealed wrongly on earth, at the origins of civilization and "magic" among women and men alike. Read from this perspective, moreover, it is perhaps understandable that Syncellus or his sources might see these events as a story about women who "lead astray the holy ones," and no less understandable that some Ethiopian translators and tradents might conclude that "the world was changed." Nor might it be surprising that modern readers have assumed it so natural that a tale about the temptations of sight so readily slips into misogyny and "magic."

Notes

1. On the need to historicize this association, see K. Stratton, *Naming the Witch: Magic, Ideology, and Stereotype in the Ancient World* (New York: Columbia University Press, 2007).

2. For a treatment of the passage concerning the Watchers, rightly and richly understood in the literary context of the work as a whole, see I. Rosen-Zvi, "Bilhah the Temptress: The *Testament of Reuben* and the Making of Rabbinic Anthropology," *Jewish Quarterly Review* 96 (2006), 65–94 at 74–77.
3. The verb is associated with Circe in *Odyssey* 10.213, 291, 318, 326, for instance, and with the Sirens in 12.44. On the place of *thelgein* and related terms in the Greek discourse on "magic"—including but not limited to Circe and the Sirens—see, e.g., M. Carastro, *La cité des mages: Penser la magie en Grèce ancienne* (Grenoble, France: Editions Jérôme Millon, 2006). The word-choice here is especially poignant in light of the equation of the Watchers' wives with Sirens in one Greek version of the *Book of the Watchers*, on which see further below.
4. M. de Jonge, *Testamenta xii patriarcharum*, 2nd ed. (Pseudepigrapha veteris testamenti Graece 1; Leiden: Brill, 1970); translation follows H. W. Hollander and M. de Jonge, *The Testaments of the Twelve Patriarchs: A Commentary* (Leiden: Brill, 1985), 101–2. As Rosen-Zvi notes ("Bilhah the Temptress," 69 n. 15), their rendering of *porneia* as "impurity" loses something of the sense of the term, as well as its close connections with biblical and Second Temple Jewish discussions of *zenut*.
5. R. H. Bloch, *Medieval Misogyny and the Invention of Western Romantic Love* (Chicago: University of Chicago Press, 1991), 39–47. Bloch, for instance, credits Tertullian with having "articulated the link between the derivative nature of the female . . . and that of figural representation in a way that has continued to dominate thought on gender well into our own age" (p. 39).
6. Like many so-called "pseudepigrapha," the *Testament of Reuben* is often read as a pre-Christian Jewish source and/or assumed to have a Jewish "core." It is, however, clearly Christian in its present form, as preserved within the *Testaments of the 12 Patriarchs*, a second-century compilation that integrates some Second Temple Jewish testamentary materials. See, e.g., M. de Jonge, *Pseudepigrapha of the Old Testament as Part of Christian Literature: The Case of the Testaments of the Twelve Patriarchs and the Greek Life of Adam and Eve* (Leiden: Brill, 2003), and references there, as well as the broader methodological discussion in R. A. Kraft, "The Pseudepigrapha in Christianity," in *Tracing the Threads: Studies in the Vitality of Jewish Pseudepigrapha*, ed. J. Reeves (Atlanta: Scholars Press, 1994), 55–86; J. Davila, *The Provenance of the Pseudepigrapha: Jewish, Christian, or Other?* (Leiden: Brill, 2005). Of course, the question of whether it is "Christian" or "Jewish" is itself problematic, as a significant over-simplification of identity-formations in a second-century context. That said, to treat its ethics as *only* "Hellenistic Jewish" still misses as much as to treat the text as *only* "Christian"; cf. Rosen-Zvi, "Bilhah the Temptress," 94 n. 109.
7. See further A. Y. Reed, *Fallen Angels and the History of Judaism and Christianity* (Cambridge: Cambridge University Press, 2005), 24–57, 178–80.

8. On the reception of the *Book of the Watchers*, see Reed, *Fallen Angels*; H. L. Lawlor, "Early Citations from the Book of Enoch," *Journal of Philology* 25 (1897), 164–225; J. C. VanderKam, "1 Enoch, Enochic Motifs, and Enoch in Early Christian Literature," in *The Jewish Apocalyptic Heritage in Early Christianity*, ed. J. C. VanderKam and W. A. Adler (Minneapolis: Fortress, 1996), 33–101; and sources cited below. That the *Testament of Reuben* could be influential on ideas about the "sons of God," even apart from the *Book of the Watchers*, etc., is suggested by Armenian Christian treatments of primeval history. On the Armenian version of the *Testaments of the 12 Patriarchs* see M. de Jonge, "The Greek Testaments of the Twelve Patriarchs and the Armenian Version," in *Studies on the Testaments of the Twelve Patriarchs: Text and Interpretation* (Leiden: Brill, 1975), 120–39; M. E. Stone, "New Evidence for the Armenian Version of the Testaments of the Twelve Patriarchs" and "The Epitome of the Testaments of the Twelve Patriarchs," repr. in *Selected Studies in Pseudepigrapha and Apocrypha with Special Reference to the Armenian Tradition* (Leiden: Brill, 1991), 131–83. Although a book "of Enoch" is listed among those "which the Jews hold secretly" in the canon list of the thirteenth-century Mxit'ar of Ayrivank', it does not seem to correspond to any work that circulated in Armenian; Stone, "Armenian Canon Lists III: The Lists of Mechitar of Ayrivank'," *Harvard Theological Review* 69 (1976), 290–92.
9. See further A. F. J. Klijn, *Seth in Jewish, Christian and Gnostic literature* (Leiden: Brill, 1977), 65–67; Reed, *Fallen Angels*, esp. 222–26; Reed, "Enoch in Armenia," in *The Armenian Apocalyptic Tradition: A Comparative Perspective*, ed. K. Bardakjian and S. La Porta (Leiden: Brill, 2014), 149–87. I am puzzled by Kelley Coblentz Bautch's claim that "the *Testament of Reuben*, in its retelling of the story of the angels, states that it is the daughters of the Cainites who seduce the sons of heaven" ("Decoration, Destruction, and Debauchery: Reflections on 1 Enoch 8 in Light of 4QEn[b]," *Dead Sea Discoveries* 15 (2008), 79–95 at 93), particularly insofar as the scholarly study that she cites in support of this claim is concerned instead with issues in *Pirqe de Rabbi Eliezer* (p. 93 n. 38, citing Guy Stroumsa, *Another Seed: Studies in Gnostic Mythology* (Leiden: Brill, 1984), 27). Perhaps needless to say, it makes much difference for the plausibility of her speculation that "an interpretative tradition . . . that implicated the Cainites in leading astray the angels" may lie behind Syncellus's version of 1 Enoch 8:1 (p. 94) if the association of Cainites with tempting the angels found first attestation in an early parabiblical work like the *Testaments of the 12 Patriarchs* (ca. second century CE) as opposed to a post-Islamic midrashic compilation like *Pirqe de Rabbi Eliezer* (ca. eighth or ninth century CE).
10. M. E. Stone, ed. and trans., *Armenian Apocrypha Relating to Adam and Eve* (Leiden: Brill, 1996), 176–78; Stone, *Armenian Apocrypha Relating to the Patriarchs and Prophets* (Jerusalem: Israel Academy of Arts and Sciences, 1982), 85–87. See also the reference to the "paint and antinomy" of Cainite women in T'ulkuranc'i, *On the Creation of the World* §133; Stone, "Selections from On the

Creation of the World by Yovhannēs T'ulkuranc'i: Translation and Commentary," repr. in *Apocrypha, Pseudepigrapha, and Armenian Studies: Collected Papers*, 2 vols. (Leuven: Peeters, 2006), 1.187–88.

11. Still helpful, in my view, are Judith Butler's insights into the totalizing function of gender and other binaries, and their naturalization through repeated performance, e.g., most famously in *Gender Trouble: Feminism and the Subversion of Identity* (London: Routledge, 1990), where she shows how "power . . . operates in the *production* of that very binary frame for thinking about gender" ("Preface 1999," *Gender Trouble*, xxviii; italics mine). I am grateful to Phil Webster for conversations concerning the relevance of this insight for exposing governing assumptions within modern historiography on gender representations in ancient literature.
12. I am here understanding the stereotype, with Homi Bhabha, as "a form of knowledge and identification that vacillates between what is always 'in place,' already known, and something that must be anxiously repeated" ("The Other Question," repr. in *Location of Culture* (London: Routledge, 1994), 94–95).
13. That is, unintentionally re-inscribing precisely the systems of knowing that it purports to counter, perhaps with a repetitiveness akin to that diagnosed by Bhabha and Butler (nn. 11–12). This is similar to what Ishay Rosen-Zvi diagnoses as a puzzling scholarly tendency to repeat "what is already quite well known" about misogyny in ancient Judaism; "Misogyny and its Discontents," *Prooftexts* 25.1–2 (2005), 217–27 at 227. He there, however, heralds the replacement of such "old" approaches (i.e., which he presents as largely reflecting apologetic concerns internal to Jewish Studies) with "new" ones since the 1990s (i.e., as engaging with theoretical insights outside of such specialist circles). I concur with him about the pressing need for such a shift, but I am wary lest such teleological rhetoric tempts us to triumphalism and distracts from a task of conceptual reorientation that is, to my mind, much more thoroughgoing and still quite incomplete.
14. A. Y. Reed, "Heavenly Ascent, Angelic Descent, and the Transmission of Knowledge in 1 Enoch 6–16," in *Heavenly Realms and Earthly Realities in Late Antique Religions*, ed. R. S. Boustan and A. Y. Reed (Cambridge: Cambridge University Press, 2004); Reed, "Beyond Revealed Wisdom and Apocalyptic Epistemology: Early Christian Transformations of Enochic Traditions about Knowledge," in *Early Christian Literature and Intertextuality*, ed. C. A. Evans and H. D. Zacharias (London: T&T Clark, 2009), 138–64.
15. See further Reed, "Heavenly Ascent, Angelic Descent."
16. T. Ilan, "Woman in the Apocrypha and the Pseudepigrapha," in *A Question of Sex? Gender and Difference in the Hebrew Bible and Beyond*, ed. D. W. Rooke (Sheffield, UK: Sheffield Phoenix, 2007), 126–44 at 133; italics mine. See also Ilan, *Jewish Women in Greco-Roman Palestine* (Tübingen: Mohr-Siebeck, 1995), 221–25.
17. Ilan, *Jewish Women in Greco-Roman Palestine*, 223; see also Ilan, *Silencing the Queen: The Literary Histories of Shelamzion and Other Jewish Women* (Tübingen: Mohr-Siebeck, 2006), 229–31.

18. For a similar appeal to 1 Enoch in relation to Christian trajectories, see Bloch, *Medieval Misogyny*, 72; B. P. Prusak, "Woman: Seductive Siren and Source of Sin? Pseudepigraphal Myth and Christian Origins," in *Religion and Sexism: Images of Woman in the Jewish and Christian Traditions*, ed. R. Radford Ruether (New York, 1974), 89–116 at 90–91; V. Flint, "The Demonisation of Magic and Sorcery in Late Antiquity: Christian Redefinitions of Pagan Religions," in *Witchcraft and Magic in Europe: Ancient Greece and Rome*, ed. B. Ankarloo and S. Clark (Philadelphia: University of Pennsylvania Press, 1999), 277–348 at 293–95. The temptation of this view is evident in the ease with which even an otherwise careful close textual analysis can slip into its rhetoric—as we see in a recent article on 1 Enoch 8 by Kelley Coblentz Bautch, which describes how "angels descend and teach *women* various forbidden crafts and knowledge—specifically the *occult* arts—which, in turn, corrupt the earth (cf. 1 Enoch 7:1; 8:3; 16:3)" ("Decoration, Destruction, and Debauchery, 82; italics mine).
19. W. R. G. Loader, *Enoch, Levi and Jubilees on Sexuality* (Grand Rapids, MI: Eerdmans, 2007), 15–16.
20. Loader, *Enoch, Levi and Jubilees on Sexuality*, 46.
21. Loader, *Enoch, Levi and Jubilees on Sexuality*, 15–16.
22. R. Lesses, "They Revealed Secrets to Their Wives: The Transmission of Magical Knowledge in 1 Enoch," in *With Letters of Light—Otiyot Shel Or: Studies in Early Jewish Apocalypticism and Mysticism in Honour of Rachel Elior*, ed. D. Arbel and A. Orlov, Berlin: De Gruyter, 2010), 196–222 at 196; Lesses here alludes to one specific version of 1 Enoch 16:3, on which see below. Whether or not she perhaps overstates the gendering of "magic" here, Lesses's insights about the *Book of the Watchers'* distinctive resonances with prophetic, sapiential, and scribal stereotypes of women (pp. 211–21), remain persuasive.
23. Coblentz Bautch, "Decoration, Destruction, and Debauchery"; Coblentz Bautch, "What Becomes of the Angels' Wives? A Text-Critical Study of 1 Enoch 19:2," *Journal of Biblical Literature* 125.2 (2006), 766–80.
24. J. T. Milik, *The Books of Enoch: Aramaic Fragments of Qumran Cave 4* (Oxford: Clarendon, 1976); S. J. Pfann et al., eds., *Qumran cave 4, XXVI, Cryptic Texts and Miscellanea*, Part 1 (DJD 36; Oxford: Clarendon, 2000), 3–7.
25. See M. Black with A.M. Denis, *Apocalypsis Henochi graece: Fragmenta pseudepigraphorum quae supersunt graeca una cum historicorum et auctorum Iudaeorum hellenistarum fragmentis* (Leiden: Brill, 1970). On the relationship between the Aramaic, Greek, and Geʿez witnesses, also M. A. Knibb, *The Ethiopic Book of Enoch: A New Edition in Light of Aramaic Dead Sea Fragments*, 2 vols. (Oxford: Clarendon, 1978), 2.1–46; Knibb, "The Book of Enoch or Books of Enoch? The Textual Evidence for 1 Enoch," in *The Early Enoch Literature*, ed. G. Boccaccini and J. J. Collins (Leiden: Brill, 2007), 21–40; G. W. E. Nickelsburg, *1 Enoch I: A Commentary on the Book of 1 Enoch, Chapters 1–36; 81–108* (Minneapolis: Fortress, 2001), 9–17; E. Larson, "The Relation between the Greek and Aramaic Texts of Enoch," in *The Dead Sea Scrolls: Fifty Years after Their Discovery*, ed. L. H.

Schiffman, E. Tov, and J. C. VanderKam (Jerusalem: Israel Exploration Society, 2000), 434–44. For a concise and updated assessment of the Ethiopic evidence see D. Olson, *Enoch: A New Translation* (North Richland Hills, TX: BIBAL, 2004), 22 and passim.

26. Translations and citations of Syncellus here and below follow William Adler and Paul Tuffin, *The Chronography of George Synkellos* (Oxford: Oxford University Press, 2002), here at 17.
27. Nickelsburg's translation of 1 Enoch 7:1–2 integrates a number of the more expansive elements of both (*1 Enoch I*, 182). Siam Bhayro, however, stresses that Syncellus's version is "almost unrecognizable" in relation to the others, and he makes a good case that its additions reflect the later integration of traditions from the *Book of Jubilees* ("The Use of *Jubilees* in Medieval Chronicles to Supplement Enoch: The Case for the 'Shorter' Reading," *Henoch* 31.1 (2009), 10–17, esp. 14–15).
28. Nickelsburg notes that the latter likely renders Greek *meignesthai* (*1 Enoch I*, 182). For the sense of defilement, compare 1 Enoch 12:4 and 15:3, and see discussion in Martha Himmelfarb, *A Kingdom of Priests: Ancestry and Merit in Ancient Judaism* (Philadelphia: University of Pennsylvania Press, 2011), 21–28.
29. Knibb, "Book of Enoch or Books of Enoch," 23, generally following Milik, *Books of Enoch*, 158.
30. Similarly, some Christian sources largely limit the association of fallen angels' teaching to astrology, e.g., Tatian, *Oratio* 8–9; Clement, *Selections from the Prophets* 53.4.
31. Note especially the comments in Nickelsburg, *1 Enoch I*, 12–13, 18; Knibb, "Book of Enoch or Books of Enoch," 36. The most recent evidence concerns 1 Enoch 8:4–9:3 in XQpapEnoch, on which see E. and H. Eshel, "New Fragments from Qumran: 4QGen[f], 4QIsa[b], 4Q226, 8QGen, and XQpapEnoch," *DSD* 12 (2005), 134–57 at 146–57.
32. By virtue of the preservation of the *Book of the Watchers* in full form only in Ge'ez, non-specialists have tended to depend too heavily on English translations, speculative reconstructions of the Aramaic, and the Greek versions when interpreting with this work and locating it within Second Temple Judaism. Part of my purpose in focusing here on the Greek versions is thus to caution against accepting one or another translation as if a direct reflection of the original.
33. See 4QEn[a] III 15.
34. On the names of these Watchers, see M. Black, "The Twenty Angel Dekadarchs at 1 Enoch 6:7 and 69:2," *Journal of Jewish Studies* 33 (1982), 227–35.
35. One finds a similar pattern in references to "sins" [Gr. *hamartia*, *adikia*], which are said to have been taught by Asael "upon the earth" in 1 Enoch 9:6, and by the rest of the Watchers to their wives in 1 Enoch 9:8.
36. See further Reed, "Heavenly Ascent, Angelic Descent," esp. 61–66.
37. Compare *Sib.Or.* 1.88–103, where such Enochic ideas about the origins of civilization are combined with Hesiodic traditions.

38. We might also wonder whether the *Book of the Watchers* thus exhibits an expansive impulse to insert women into biblical history, similar to what Betsy Halpern-Amaru has shown for the *Book of Jubilees* in *The Empowerment of Women in the Book of Jubilees* (Leiden: Brill, 1999)—even if articulated in quite different terms; cf. K. Coblentz Bautch, "Amplified Roles, Idealized Depictions: Women in the Book of the Jubilees," in *Enoch and the Mosaic Torah: The Evidence of Jubilees*, ed. G. Boccaccini and G. Ibba (Grand Rapids, MI: Eerdmans, 2009), 338–52 at 351.
39. Loader, *Enoch, Levi, and Jubilees on Sexuality*, 38; see also Newsom, "Development of 1 Enoch 6–19," 314, 320–21. Notably, Loader brings such a normativizing lens to this material that he conflates its association of knowledge with the fallen angels with the prohibition of the practice and products thereof (a logic whose limits become clear in the case of metallurgy; p. 38), and he even expresses quite some surprise that the myth of the fallen angels is not used by ancient authors to condemn homosexuality and bestiality (p. 80).
40. See also Pliny, *Natural History* 7.61. For a comparison with early Enochic traditions, see F. Graf, "Mythical Production: Aspects of Myth and Technology in Antiquity," in *From Myth to Reason? Studies in the Development of Greek Thought*, ed. R. Buxton (New York: Oxford University Press, 1999), 322–28.
41. Graf, "Mythical Production," 322.
42. So, e.g., Ilan, who asserts without argumentation when discussing this tradition that "[w]omen's knowledge of the plant world is *what led* to the identification of the concoction of drugs and remedies from plants with sorcery" (*Jewish Women in Greco-Roman Palestine,* 223; italics mine), as well as elsewhere explaining this tradition by noting that the "association of women with plants and roots is universal" (Ilan, *Silencing the Queen*, 229, see also 231).
43. See also S. Blakely, *Myth, Ritual and Metallurgy in Ancient Greece and Recent Africa* (Cambridge: Cambridge University Press, 2006).
44. Stratton, *Naming the Witch*, 46, 50–68. On women, *pharmaka*, and Hekate, see Johnston, *Restless Dead*, 113. For the continued association in late antique Christian circles, it is interesting to note Basil of Caesaria's comment on *pharmaka* that "this is the sort of thing that women frequently do, who endeavor to attract a love to themselves by means of spells and tablets, and who give to them charms that make their thinking cloudy" (*Ep*. 188.8, translation cited after J. G. Gager, *Curse Tablets and Binding Spells* (Oxford: Oxford University Press, 1999) 260).
45. See references and discussion in L. Nixon, "The Cults of Demeter and Kore," in *Women in Antiquity: New Assessments*, ed. R. Hawley and B. Levick (London: Routledge, 1995), 75–96 at 85–88.
46. Nixon, "The Cults of Demeter and Kore," 86; see also Stratton, *Naming the Witch*, 46, 50–68. If Nixon is correct to point us to the pharmacological control and management of fertility as a major nexus for the development and transmission of this knowledge, then it is also possible that the reference to these teachings in 1 Enoch 7:1 carries some of this connotation, at least in the Greek versions;

whereas Nickelsburg and others (*1 Enoch I*, 184) have suggested that the reference "intrudes between action and result, that is, intercourse and conception" in the narrative of 1 Enoch 7, we might speculate that it may be meant to communicate, not the association of "magic" and women per se, but rather some failed attempts at contraception.

47. Ilan, "Woman in the Apocrypha and the Pseudepigrapha," 133.
48. That is, like almost all literature from antiquity, the work is clearly androcentric; whether it can be called misogynistic, however, remains an open question.
49. See further, e.g., Rosen-Zvi, "Bilhah the Temptress," 66–67; Rosen-Zvi, "Misogyny and its Discontents."
50. Stratton, *Naming the Witch*, 37. The importance of remembering this well-established but often forgotten point with respect to Judaism, in particular, is stressed in the review by G. Bohak in *Journal for the Study of Judaism* 39 (2008), 445–46.
51. Rosen-Zvi, "Bilhah the Temptress," 67 n. 6.
52. Rosen-Zvi, "Bilhah the Temptress," 66.
53. Rosen-Zvi, "Misogyny and its Discontents," 27.
54. Rosen-Zvi, "Bilhah the Temptress," 66.
55. Stratton, *Naming the Witch*, 26–69; Rosen-Zvi, "Bilhah the Temptress," 92–94.
56. Coblentz Bautch ("What Becomes of the Watchers' Wives," 769 n. 15) has recently drawn attention to the same concern within the Ethiopic tradition surrounding 1 Enoch 19:3, with variation surrounding the depiction of the Watchers' wives as "those whom the angels led astray" [*'asḥiton malā'ekta*] or "those who led astray the angels" [*'asḥitomu malā'ekta*]. She posits the former as more original; see also Charles, *Book of Enoch*, 43.
57. Charles, *Book of Enoch*, 19; Black, *Book of Enoch*, 29, 127. When discussing the related claim in 1 Enoch 19:2, Daniel Olson notes its implausibility as well, citing also the lack of reference to the punishment of these women in 1 Enoch 6–16 (*Enoch*, 54, 268–69). See also Coblentz Bautch, "Decoration, Destruction, and Debauchery," 83–89, for a fresh reconsideration of 4QEn[b] in relation to the Greek versions of 1 Enoch 8:1–2—stressing that "neither Synkellos nor the Akhmim manuscript accords perfectly with the Aramaic" (p. 86).
58. Nickelsburg, "Apocalyptic and Myth," 397. This line is thus included in his influential translation; see Nickelsburg, *1 Enoch I*, 188: "Asael taught men to make swords of iron and weapons and shields and breastplates and every instrument of war. He showed them metals of the earth and how they should work gold to fashion it suitably, and concerning silver, to fashion it for bracelets and ornaments for women. And he showed them concerning antinomy and eye paint and all manner of precious stones and dyes. *And the sons of men made them for themselves and their daughters and they transgressed and lead astray the holy ones.*" Olson, by contrast, follows the Ethiopic variant "And the world was changed" (*Enoch*, 35).
59. That is, its reference to a single star descending, only later followed by many; see further Nickelsburg, *1 Enoch I*, 195–96, and he also reads traditions about the

Watchers as sent to earth for a positive purpose before becoming tempted (e.g., *Jubilees* 4:15; 5:1–3) as reflecting this same complex of traditions. He also appeals to much later sources, such as the medieval *Targum Pseudo-Jonathan*. Coblentz Bautch cautiously accepts his conclusion ("Decoration, Destruction, and Debauchery," 95), although stressing that "one need not interpret 8:1 so as to conclude that the daughters alone are deviant in this account; indeed women are not solely implicated" (p. 91).

60. Loader, *Enoch, Levi and Jubilees on Sexuality*, 10, 17–18.
61. Bhayro, "Use of *Jubilees*," 10–17.
62. Bhayro, "Use of *Jubilees*," 15.
63. The value of Codex Panopolitanus for shedding light on the late antique Egyptian context of its production, for instance, has been demonstrated by G. W. E. Nickelsburg, "Two Enochic Manuscripts: Unstudied Evidence for Egyptian Christianity," in *Of Scribes and Scrolls: Studies on the Hebrew Bible, Intertestamental Judaism, and Christian Origins Presented to John Strugnell on the Occasion of his Sixtieth Birthday*, ed. H. Attridge, J. Collins, and T. Tobin (Lanham: University Press of America, 1990), 251–60. Note also Flint's suggestion that "[t]he textual transmission of the Book of Enoch, and its context, have much to tell about the later demonising of magic and enchantment" ("Demonisation of Magic and Sorcery in Late Antiquity," 294).
64. W. A. Adler, *Time Immemorial: Archaic History and its Sources in Christian Chronography from Julius Africanus to George Syncellus* (Washington DC: Dumbarton Oaks, 1989), 151–57. The importance of Egypt as a locus for the circulation and cultivation of Enochic texts and traditions was noted already by Lawlor, "Early Citations from the Book of Enoch"; Lawlor, "The Book of Enoch in the Egyptian Church," *Hermathena* 30 (1904), 178–83.
65. On monks and "magic" in late antique Egypt, see below.
66. Lesses, "They Revealed Secrets to Their Wives," 204–10.
67. See discussion below.
68. Justin here argues that the fallen angels enslaved humankind "by magical writings [*dia magikôn graphôn*]" as well as "by teaching them to offer sacrifices and incense and libations, which they needed after they were enslaved by lustful passions." On Justin's redeployment of early Enochic traditions see further A. Y. Reed, "The Trickery of the Fallen Angels and the Demonic Mimesis of the Divine: Aetiology and Polemics in the Writings of Justin Martyr," *Journal of Early Christian Studies* 12.2 (2004), 141–71.
69. Stratton, *Naming the Witch*, 107–41. The relevant passage is attributed to a presbyter and possibly preserves an oral tradition connected in some fashion to early Enochic traditions about illicit angelic instruction: "Marcus, you maker of idols and inspector of portents, experienced in astrology [*astrologikês*] and the magical art [*magikês technês*]. Through these, you confirm the doctrines of error. You show signs to those lead astray by you, undertakings of apostate power—which your father Satan always orchestrates for you to do through the angelic power Azazel."

70. Syncellus quotes Africanus's statements about the matter as follows: "When humankind became numerous on the earth, angels of heaven had intercourse with daughters of men. In some copies [of LXX Genesis], I found 'the sons of God.' In my opinion, it is recounted that the sons of God are called sons of Seth by the Spirit.... But let us understand them as 'angels.' Then it was they who transmitted knowledge about magic and sorcery, as well as the numbers of the motion of astronomical phenomena, to their wives, from whom they produced the giants as their children; and when depravity came into being because of them, God resolved to destroy every class of living things in a flood—this would be unbelievable!" (Sync. 19.24–20.4).
71. D. Frankfurter, "The Perils of Love: Magic and Countermagic in Coptic Egypt," *Journal of the History of Sexuality* 10.3–4 (2001), 480–500 at 499. See also D. Brakke, *Demons and the Making of the Monk: Spiritual Combat in Early Christianity* (Cambridge, Mass: Harvard University Press, 2006).
72. Frankfurter, "Perils of Love," 498–99, citing A. Young, "Magic as a 'Quasi-Profession': The Organization of Magic and Magical Healing among Amhara," *Ethnology* 14 (1975), 245–65. For ethnographical and related work on women and "magic" in Ethiopia, see R. Pankrust, "Historical Reflections on the Traditional Ethiopian Pharmacopoeia," *Journal of Ethiopian Pharmaceutical Association* 2 (1976), 29–33; T. Gedif and H. Jürgen Hahn, "The use of Medicinal Plants in Self-Care in Rural Central Ethiopia," *Journal of Ethnopharmacology* 87.2–3 (2003), 155–61.
73. Frankfurter, "Perils of Love," 499. See also Frankfurter, "The Legacy of Jewish Apocalypses in Early Christianity: Regional Trajectories," in *Jewish Apocalyptic Heritage*, ed. J. C. VanderKam and W. Adler (Minneapolis: Fortress Press, 1996), 129–200 at 142–200.
74. Translation here follows Coblentz Bautch, "What Becomes of the Angels' Wives?," 769. She there provides a detailed discussion of the textual evidence and history of discussion, suggesting an Aramaic *Vorlage* that featured a peil participle or peal passive participle of *šlm*, in the sense of "will be destroyed," as misinterpreted in terms of other sense of the root *šlm* in the Greek underlying the Ethiopic and as reinterpreted in terms of Hellenistic mythology in tradition of Codex Panopolitanus (pp. 778–80). By contrast, Bhayro argues for the originality of the Ethiopic ("Use of *Jubilees*," 16–17), as does Olson (*Enoch*, 54, 268–69).
75. Compare, e.g., the translations in Black, *Book of Enoch*, 155 and Nickelsburg, *1 Enoch I*, 267.
76. Lesses, "They Revealed Secrets to Their Wives," 196.
77. See further Reed, "Heavenly Ascent."
78. Indeed, some exegetes even speculate about the sins of animals, so to explain why they too were destroyed in the Flood. On this concern in the tradition surrounding Genesis 6, see J. Kugel, *The Bible as It Was* (Cambridge: Harvard University Press, 1999), 117–18.

79. That is, MT Ezek 28:4 attributes great wisdom to the King of Tyre before his fall, but the Greek translations invert the verse so as to assert his lack of knowledge—albeit, in the process, detracting from the sense and point of the passage.
80. See further Charles, *Book of Enoch*, 37–38; Black, *Apocalypsis*, 30; Black, *Book of Enoch*, 155; Vanderkam, "1 Enoch, Enochic Motifs, and Enoch," 47.
81. See further Vanderkam, "1 Enoch, Enochic Motifs, and Enoch," 47; Reed, "Beyond Revealed Wisdom," 159–62.
82. R. J. Bauckham, "The Fall of the Angels as the Source of Philosophy in Hermias and Clement of Alexandria," *Vigiliae Christianae* 39 (1985), 319–30.
83. K. A. Fraser, "Zosimus of Panopolis and the Book of Enoch: Alchemy as Forbidden Knowledge," *Aries* 4.2 (2004), 125–47.
84. Bauckham, "Fall of the Angels," 319–20.
85. M. Berthelot and C. É. Ruelle, *Collection des anciens alchimistes grecs*, 2 vols. (Paris: Steinheil, 1888), 2.28–33 at 29. Translation follows Fraser, "Zosimus of Panopolis," 132–33; A.-J. Festugière, *La révélation d'Hermès Trismégiste* (repr. Paris: Les Belles Lettres, 2006), 1.256–60.
86. Festugière, *La révélation d'Hermès Trismégiste*, 1.255–56.
87. That is, in this case with Isis stealing secrets from heaven to pass on to her son, Horus.
88. Black, *Book of Enoch*, 127. See E. Isaac, trans., "1 (Ethiopic Apocalypse of) Enoch," in *The Old Testament Pseudepigrapha*, ed. J. H. Charlesworth, 2 vols. (Garden City, NY: Doubleday, 1983), 1:5–89 at 16 for an interpretation of "alchemy" here. For a more recent argument for the originality of this reading, based on fresh Ethiopic evidence and comparing 1 Enoch 98:2, see Olson, *Enoch*, 34.
89. Rosen-Zvi, "Bilhah the Temptress," 75.
90. Rosen-Zvi, "Bilhah the Temptress," 76; italics mine.
91. See n. 3. On the use of the verb *thelgein* to describe "verbal and sexual seduction . . . often intertwined," see S. Goldhill, *The Poet's Voice: Essays on Poetics and Greek Literature* (Cambridge: Cambridge University Press, 1991), 60–66; also L. E. Doherty, "Sirens, Muses, and Female Narrators in the *Odyssey*," in *The Distaff Side: Representing the Female in Homer's Odyssey*, ed. B. Cohen (Oxford: Oxford University Press, 1995), 81–92.
92. Rosen-Zvi, "Bilhah the Temptress," 75.
93. Rosen-Zvi, "Bilhah the Temptress," 77.
94. See nn. 9–10.
95. The tradition to this effect in *Pirqe de R. Eliezer* §22 finds a parallel in the closely aligned Targum Pseudo-Jonathan *ad* Gen 6:2, which seems to reflect the same gaonic context; see references and discussion in Reed, *Fallen Angels*, 222–26.
96. That is, Ilan, "Woman in the Apocrypha and the Pseudepigrapha," 133, as quoted above.
97. A. Jellinek, *Bet ha-midrash* (Jerusalem: Sifre Vahrmann, 1967), 4:127–28; Milik, *Books of Enoch*, 329–39.

98. For further parallels, see L. Ginzberg, *The Legends of the Jews,* trans. H. Szold, 7 vols. (repr. ed. Baltimore: Johns Hopkins University Press, 1998), 5:169–71.
99. For rivalry see P. Schäfer, *Rivalität zwischen Engeln und Menschen: Untersuchungen zur rabbinischen Engelvorstellung* (Berlin: de Gruyter, 1975), and with reference to fallen angels also A. Y. Reed, "From Asael and Šemihazah to Uzzah, Azzah, and Azael: 3 Enoch 5 (§§7–8) and the Jewish Reception-History of 1 Enoch," *Jewish Studies Quarterly* 8 (2001): 1–32. In *Pesikta Rabbati* 34.2, for instance, humans complain to God about the angels, citing Azza and Azael in much the same way that the accusing angels cite the Generation of Enosh and the Generation of the Flood: "Master of the Universe, you gave us a heart of stone, and it led us astray; if Azza and Azael, whose bodies were fire, sinned when they came down to earth, would not we of flesh and blood sin all the more?" This tradition is also paralleled in the preface to *Aggadat Bereshit*, where the angels let themselves down without God's consent but also to prove humankind's wrong, as in the version of the angelic descent myth in Pseudo-Clementine *Homilies* 8:7–8.
100. In *Bereshit Rabbati*, this tradition is presented as an exposition of "the sons of God *saw*" (Gen 6:2). A variation of this aggadah is found twice in *Seder Hadar Zeqenim*, with reference to Gen 6:2 and to Gen 28:12 (see BHM 5:156); here, the woman becomes the constellation Virgo. For Islamic parallels, see B. J. Bamberger, *Fallen Angels* (Philadelphia: JPS, 1952), 113–16; B. Heller, "La chute des anges: Schemhazai, Ouza et Azaël," *REJ* 60 (1910), 206–10.
101. This tradition that may ultimately root in speculations about the Pleiades and the astronomical causes for the Flood, on which see, e.g., *b. Rosh Hashanah* 11b–12a.
102. On the "gnostic" Norea, in relation to Jewish and Islamic traditions, see references and discussion in Stroumsa, *Another Seed*, 53–61.
103. It is important to recall, of course, also her initial caution that "[t]o claim that gender is constructed is *not* to assert its illusoriness or artificiality, where those terms are understood to reside within a binary that counterposes the 'real' and the 'authentic' as oppositional . . . [but rather] to understand the discursive production of the plausibility of that binary relation and to suggest that certain cultural configurations of gender take the place of 'the real' and consolidate and augment their hegemony through that felicitous self-naturalization" (Butler, *Gender Trouble*, 43).
104. For Butler, it is drag and trans-sexuality that exposes "gender reality" as lacking "reality," in the gap between seen and known: "even 'seeing' the body may not answer the question: *for what are the categories through which one sees*?" ("Preface 1999," *Gender Trouble*, xxi). Grappling with the history of optics may challenge us in other ways by pushing us to historicize even what now seems most natural to us about *seeing*.
105. The article typically cited as seminal in this regard is L. Mulvey, "Visual Pleasure and Narrative Cinema," *Screen* 16.3 (1975), 6–18. For a recent example of its application, particularly relevant for our purposes, see H. Morales, *Vision and Narrative*

in Achilles Tatius' Leucippe and Clitophon (Cambridge: Cambridge University Press, 2004), esp. 152–226.

106. R. Swenson, "Optics, Gender, and the Eighteenth-Century Gaze: Looking at Eliza Haywood's Anti-Pamela," *The Eighteenth-Century: Theory and Interpretation* 51.1–2 (2010), 27–43 at 29. Swenson continues by noting that "[r]ecent work has complicated how we think about gender, seeing, and agency, but the original and circular construct of gazer-as-agent needs another look. To date, critics have tended to invariably privilege the role of the spectator, reconstructing female spectators within or against the terms of Walter Benjamin's observant flâneur, Michel Foucault's Panoptic surveyor, or Jacques Lacan's (or Jean-Paul Sartre's) spectacle-turned-spectator. In short, recent work, while important, has not quite confronted the circular logic that must be unpacked if we are to reconstruct the historicized position of the (female) spectacle as either symbol or reality" (p. 29). Here too, my concern is less to question the power of the gaze as a technology of gender and more to question its uncritical application homogenously to all time and places, in circular readings and already-gendered modes of scholarly interpretation that interpret seeing as necessarily signaling (male) agency and (female) passivity.
107. Swenson, "Optics, Gender," 28.
108. Swenson, "Optics, Gender," 29.
109. For some examples, see A. Y. Reed, "Reading Augustine and/as Midrash: Genesis 6 in *Genesis Rabbah* and the *City of God*," in *Midrash and Context*, ed. L. Teugels and R. Ulmer (Piscataway, NJ: Gorgias, 2007), 74–90.
110. Rosen-Zvi, "Bilhah the Temptress," 75–76.
111. Rosen-Zvi, "Bilhah the Temptress," 67.
112. Contrast, e.g., Rosen-Zvi's reading of the *Testament of Reuben* in terms of a notion that "[g]aze, sight, and even intercourse only serve as mediators for the *real* struggle taking place *inside* the soul" (p. 84; italics mine). What I am here suggesting—following Shadi Bartsch—is that we may need to take seriously how ancient understandings of desire differ from modern ones, by virtue of optical theories often predicated on the permeability of the eye as a pathway into the body and soul alike; *Mirror of the Self: Sexuality, Self-knowledge, and the Gaze in the Early Roman Empire* (Chicago: University of Chicago Press, 2006).
113. See further A. M. Smith, *Ptolemy and the Foundations of Ancient Mathematical Optics* (Philadelphia: APS, 1999), 23–47. Explorations of the cultural consequences of such theories include D. E. Stewart, *The Arrow of Love: Optics, Gender, and Subjectivity in Medieval Love Poetry* (Lewisburg, PA: Bucknell University Press, 2003), 14–19.; S. C. Akbari, *Seeing through the Veil: Optical Theory and Medieval Allegory* (Toronto: University of Toronto Press, 2004), 23–36; S. Bartsch, *Mirror of the Self: Sexuality, Self-Knowledge, and the Gaze in the Early Roman Empire* (Chicago: University of Chicago Press, 2006), 55–67.
114. Smith, *Ptolemy and the Foundations of Ancient Mathematical Optics,* 23; italics mine. See also Bartsch, *Mirror of the Self,* 62–63, 67; she similarly stresses that

"almost all ancient schools of thought about optics, from the atomists to Plato, Euclid, and Ptolemy, put an emphasis on the tactile nature of sight, and several of them talk specifically in terms of penetration and touching in language that is literal, not metaphorical" (p. 59). On some of the social ramifications see, e.g., C. Barton, "Being in the Eyes: Shame and Sight in Ancient Rome," in *The Roman Gaze: Vision, Power, and the Body* (Baltimore: John Hopkins University Press, 2002), 216–35.

115. Bartsch, *Mirror of the Self*, 58.
116. I here focus on the latter in interaction with Bartsch, *Mirror of the Self*, etc., but one might pursue other lines of interpretation by reading the visuality of this work in terms of identity and empire, e.g., with S. Goldhill, "The Erotic Eye: Visual Stimulation and Cultural Conflict," in *Being Greek under Rome: Cultural Identity, the Second Sophistic, and the Development of Empire*, ed. Goldhill (Cambridge: Cambridge University Press, 2001), 154–94.
117. Trans. P. A. Clement, cited after Bartsch, *Mirror of the Self*, 70
118. Morales, *Vision and Narrative*, 130–35.
119. That is, in this case not generatively, with seed or semen, but rather destructively, with poison—as described, moreover, like the venom of a serpent, thereby evoking Genesis 2–3 as well as Lucretius's likening of the effluences emitted by seen objects to the slipperiness of a serpent's molted skin; 4.54–61.
120. One is reminded of Butler's famous assertion that "[g]ender is the repeated stylization of the body, a set of repeated acts within a highly rigid regulatory framework that congeal over time to produce the appearance of substance, of a natural sort of being" (*Gender Trouble*, 43–44)—in this case, bodies are posited to become substance as a result of seeing. Here, moreover, we may glimpse some hint that the fluidity so problematic in late modern contexts might be taken for granted in certain ancient ones; compare also pre-modern traditions about the fluidity of gender.
121. Bartsch, *Mirror of the Self*, 58. For some late antique examples of visuality and the soul in relation to pilgrimage, see Georgia Frank, *The Memory of the Eyes: Pilgrims to Living Saints in Christian Late Antiquity*. The Transformation of the Classical Heritage 30 (Berkeley: University of California Press, 2000), 102–33.

5

Magic, Abjection, and Gender in Roman Literature

Kimberly B. Stratton

LUCAN'S CIVIL WAR epic, *Pharsalia*, graphically describes the wretched depravity of the Roman civil war and the ensuing disintegration of civilized order and human dignity.[1] His depiction of the sepulchral witch, Erictho, is particularly arresting; she dwells in battlegrounds and cemeteries where she has continual access to the tools of her trade—decaying flesh, the cinders of cremated corpses, and the implements of death itself: nooses, crosses, and crucifixion nails (6.538–46). She also resides on the fringes of what it means to be human; she is emaciated and filthy, "oppressed by a Stygian pallor and weighed down with matted hair" (6.516–18). Erictho rejects human society not only spatially, by inhabiting tombs and going out only under darkened skies (6.518–20), but also ethically, by violating human corpses; she transgresses a primary tenet of civilized society—respect for the dead. She furthermore verges on the monstrous by cutting an unborn infant from the womb to make an infernal sacrifice and by slicing off the faces of men still caught in the throes of death, who hover at the boundary between this world and the next (6.554–59).

In Book Six of the *Pharsalia*, Erictho challenges both human and divine order through a necromantic rite in which she revives the corpse of a fallen soldier so he can report the outcome of the war, which is known only to the shades below. Erictho also sends a message back down to the infernal regions through a ritual that mingles the abhorrent with the erotic; she kisses the open mouth of a corpse, bites the tip of his motionless tongue, and whispers secret sacrileges into his icy cold lips (*gelidis infundit murmura labris arcanumque nefas*, 565–69). This image of a filthy hag tonguing a mutilated corpse sends chills up the spine and triggers an immediate and visceral pang of revulsion.

Lucan's portrait of Erictho epitomizes the characteristics of magic that have disturbed the western imagination for millennia. It is the stuff of which nightmares and witch-hunts are made. In this chapter I will also argue that Lucan's depiction of Erictho is quintessentially abject and that Julia Kristeva's theory of abjection can illuminate this and other literary representations of magic in Roman antiquity.

Portraits of filthy sorceresses, mutilating corpses and violating the dead, I propose, emerged out of, and reflected, a powerful corporal ideology that supported social hierarchy. In ancient Rome elite male bodies were regarded as naturally endowed with superior characteristics that justified their social privilege. Yet, even elite male bodies required cultivation, regulation, and manipulation to ensure that they conformed to these idealized standards, indicating awareness, on some level, of the fragility and artificiality of this corporal-based social hierarchy. The penal code served to enforce these artificial distinctions through a class-based punishment scheme that protected the ideal inviolability of elite bodies while publicly degrading the bodies of slaves, foreigners, and *humiliores* (the underclass), rendering their imagined difference a legal fact.[2]

In this chapter I will read ancient stories of witches, who transgress the boundaries of bodies, social mores, and even the threshold between life and death, against the corporal ideology that sought to protect the fragility and vulnerability of individual bodies, especially those of elite men like the authors of our texts. Their socially constructed identities and position in the hierarchy depended on demonstrating inviolability and self-control. The fear, therefore, of losing control, of being subjected to corporal violation and social inversion, I suggest, motivates many aspects of depictions of magic in Roman texts. It also resonates with the psychoanalytic category of abjection, which is why I have brought these two ideas together to illuminate a problematic feature of ancient magic.

Abjection—the revulsion experienced at confronting the wretchedness and fragility of human embodiment—is an idea developed from psychoanalysis by the French theorist Julia Kristeva. The use of psychoanalytic theory to illuminate ancient texts and societies has had a mixed reception.[3] Nonetheless, this chapter will engage the notion of abjection to nuance our analysis of women and magic against the backdrop of ancient corporal ideology. As my readings of various texts indicate, Kristeva's theory of abjection enables us to perceive a common thread working through diverse portraits of women's magic and links them not only to each other, but to larger psycho-social dynamics at play in ancient Rome. Furthermore, Kristeva's notion of the primal abject, which I discuss near the chapter's end, offers an explanation for one of the significant social questions prompted by studying ancient magic, namely, given that the material evidence reveals men were as likely to be practitioners of magic as women were, why does the literature associate women and magic so strongly? The concept of abjection has the potential to illuminate this anomaly.

Julia Kristeva and the Concept of Abjection

In *Powers of Horror: an Essay on Abjection*, Julia Kristeva formulates the notion of the abject as anything that "disturbs identity, system, order";[4] abjection forces us to confront our creatureliness. Kristeva develops this concept from psychoanalytic theory and extends it to an interpretation of religion, literature, and law. For Kristeva, society and individual psychology are interconnected: the individual emerges as a subject through internalizing the social-symbolic order, which is based in language. The same forces that work on society, therefore, can be seen to operate on the individual, and vice versa. As she formulates it, the concept of abjection explains individual psychological development as well as it illuminates the structures and dispositions in a diverse array of social products (legal, literary, and religious, among others). Because abjection can be used to illuminate not only aspects of individual psychology, but social products as well, I propose that it can help us understand why ancient magic generated strong feelings of fear and revulsion,[5] and why it was often associated with women.

Starting from the psychoanalytic work of Jacques Lacan and Melanie Klein, Kristeva describes the infant's earliest experiences as plenitude and continuity with the body of the mother; this connection with the mother begins prior to birth, but continues into the early prelinguistic stage, which Kristeva labels the "semiotic *chora*."[6] In this stage the infant is not yet aware of her own physical or psychic boundaries; everything is perceived as an extension of herself. Gradually, through the process of abjection—jettisoning whatever is unwanted, whether feces or unwanted food—a child develops an awareness of its own body and boundaries.[7] Through the basic actions of spitting out and excreting, the child discovers the boundaries of its body and begins to develop an awareness of herself as a distinct individual.[8]

For Kristeva, individuals emerge as subjects, first, through pushing away from continuity with the mother, and then by embracing language and the symbolic order, which structures the social world. The symbolic order—the arbitrary collective set of symbols that a society agrees to use—for Kristeva is associated with the father, patriarchy, and law; by embracing this the child is able to emerge as a self-aware and conscious subject (ego).[9] Subjectivity is thus quintessentially an entrance into language, which occurs part and parcel of rejecting the primal abject—the maternal *chora*.[10] While Kristeva uses the term "maternal" to refer to this relationship, the notion applies equally to any caretaker who nurtures the infant. In ancient Rome, elite children would have experienced this relationship primarily with a wet nurse (*nutrix*) and household slaves rather than with their own mothers.[11] Abjection operates not only on an individual psychoanalytic level, but also on a social level, where threats to boundaries, borders, and collective identities are hedged by laws, taboos, grammar rules, and rituals, all working to preserve social coherence through containment of the abject. This is where abjection theory can help illuminate ancient attitudes toward magic, at least on the part of elite men, who authored most of our ancient texts.

Experiences of abjection continue throughout one's life in response to objects and actions that threaten boundaries of the self or society. Kristeva writes, "It is thus not lack of cleanliness or health that causes abjection but what disturbs identity, system, order. What does not respect borders, positions, rules."[12] Anything abject reveals the fragility of our well-bounded selves and rationally controlled autonomy. In short, the abject is anything that reminds us of our origin and ultimate dissolution into death and disorder. Because Kristeva conceives the unconscious to be structured as a kind of language, abjection can also be found in the limits or breakdown of human communication, in the nonsense and chaos of foreign speech, expressed by the very word barbarian (*barbaros*).[13] Abjection operates on the societal level as well by demarcating social boundaries and projecting unwanted behaviors onto other people or groups, who then need to be repelled or eliminated as monstrous, bestial, and demonic.[14] In this way, abjection acts collectively to regulate socially approved behavior and to define a community's sense of identity.

Much of Kristeva's concept of abjection resonates with ancient corporal ideology, which both conceived elite bodies to be innately superior and inviolable and at the same time expressed concerns about protecting their integrity and cultivating the proper characteristics to reflect their presumed innate nobility.

Abjection and Greco-Roman Corporal Ideology

The social function of abjection, which defines communal boundaries by repelling unwanted behaviors and projecting them onto vilified others, illuminates what is at stake in many ancient depictions of magic, especially those that highlight socially transgressive behavior. Kristeva conceives the abject to function on three levels: anything that threatens the integrity of the physical body, individual identity, or society. Often, all three levels are manifest in depictions of magic; attacks on the integrity of individual bodies could threaten not only individual identity, but the stability and integrity of the social body.

This understanding of abjection can be helpful for analyzing Hellenistic and Roman societies in which social order was predicated on a clearly demarcated hierarchy. Nobility resided in the body; traits such as courage, grace, and self-mastery, which defined the noble classes, were regarded as inborn. Hellenistic novels, for example, demonstrate the notion that status is corporally located: despite being severed from their birth families and natal origins by misfortune, elite protagonists reveal their true identities by their beauty, noble carriage, and courage. Like a river to the sea, in these stories, inborn superiority leads children of nobility to their rightful place at the head of society.[15]

Despite the confident assertion of natural class-based characteristics and aptitudes that were displayed in a person's physiognomy, concern for ensuring that noble characteristics properly develop also occurs in ancient medical writings and philosophic literature, revealing a worry that "inborn" traits might not manifest without sufficient encouragement. For example, medical texts recommend that high-born infants receive special massages and swaddling techniques with the intention of directing their physical development in the proper manner; nurses were instructed to stretch and massage ligaments to impart correct posture and proportions for noble children in their care. Male and female infants, however, received different treatment, which was intended to inculcate the different types of behavior and physical characteristics considered most appropriate for their sex (Soranus *Gyn* 2.14–15).[16] Elite boys underwent education and rhetorical training to cultivate proper comportment, hand gestures, eye movements, and vocal modulation in order to display their masculinity, power, and persuasion. Not only did professional success in the legal or political realm depend on mastery of this corporal training (*askēsis*), but social standing and relationships among peers also relied upon these traits, which were subject to constant scrutiny and revaluation. One's social currency could precipitously fall with a misplaced facial expression, gesture of the hand, or crack in the voice, revealing an alarming fragility of status and social identity that undercut any conception of inborn character or nobility.[17]

A delicate hydraulic machine, controlled by humors and temperatures, the human body required vigilant care to maintain its proper operation and peak performance.[18] This mutability constituted the source of a body's vulnerability. Too much sex or not enough exercise could upset the fragile balance of humors, which determined a body's proper masculinity or femininity (Galen's *Hygiene* 5.2). Different regimes were prescribed for individuals based on sex and social status, in order to harmonize correctly the different humors in the body; improper observance of this protocol could deleteriously affect not only the proportion of masculine to feminine traits in the patient, but the sexual characteristics of their unborn children as well.[19]

This corporal ideology was graphically and vividly displayed in the realm of judicial punishment. Both Greece and Rome respected the integrity and inviolability of citizen bodies, which legally distinguished them from the bodies of slaves and foreigners.[20] The Roman arena in particular displayed this difference through gruesome and increasingly elaborate spectacles of capital punishment, visually reinforcing the hegemonic class system, which preserved certain classes of bodies from painful and humiliating degradation but subjected others to it as a form of edifying amusement.[21] Capital punishment was almost never inflicted upon a citizen of Rome in the Republic, especially one of high social rank. Rather, he would be banned from fire and water (*aquae et ignis interdictio*), which was tantamount to a social death, but did not violate the physical body of the citizen and allowed him to flee into exile.[22] During the Principate, two shifts gradually occurred: first, capital punishment for all orders became much more common as a result of newly enforced *maiestas* laws. Second, the distinction between slave/foreigner and citizen collapsed as Roman citizens of the lower orders were subjected to degrading and terrifying forms of punishment formerly reserved for conquered enemies and slaves.[23] These punishments, the *summa supplicia*, which included vivicombustion, crucifixion, and being thrown to beasts, were designed to inflict the greatest amount of suffering and degradation on victims. The contrast between noble and dignified deaths of the elite and the humiliating violation suffered by lower classes and slaves in the arena ideologically reaffirmed the division of rank between *honestiores* and *humiliores*. Social worth was demonstrated graphically by the sanctity and integrity of elite bodies versus the vulnerability and indignity of lower-class bodies.

This concern with the integrity and inviolability of elite bodies translated to sexuality as well. Because women's bodies were regarded as naturally designed to be penetrated and bear children, elite women posed a problem for the ideological identification of nobility with inviolability; as Jonathan Walters explains, elite women's high social status was in tension with "the 'naturally' demeaning nature of the act of being penetrated."[24] By opening their bodies for the gestation of another—distended, morphed into two at once—noble women also posed a potential danger to the honor of a family or to the certainty of paternity. As gateways to this world they could act as porous gaps in the security of a class-based social hierarchy; their bodies might nurture and permit entrance to an intruder from the wrong class. This unease with the openness of women's bodies was expressed medically and philosophically: women were conceived to be porous, mutable, and lacking self-control—women's bodies provided a foil for an elite masculine identity that was predicated on stability, certainty, guarded boundaries, and self-mastery.[25] In other words, as Kristeva argues, and I will discuss more fully below, women's bodies—especially mothers' bodies—provoked an experience of abjection and had to be hedged with restrictions, regulations, and taboos.

Literary Readings: Magic and Abjection in Roman Texts

Reading ancient representations of magic through the lens of ancient corporal ideology and the concept of abjection illuminates depictions of gruesome, threatening, and morbid rituals performed by female characters, and fosters an interpretation that goes beyond merely labeling them as misogynistic. Literary readings of magic and abjection can be divided into two main categories. First are stories in which magic triggers abjectionary revulsion by violating physical bodies, the sanctity of corpses, or the boundary between human and animal. These are cases in which the instability of personal identity is ultimately at stake. Second are stories in which magic violates the integrity of the social body by challenging gender roles and thereby destabilizing the hierarchy that rested on them.

Violating the Human Body

Corpses and Mutilated Bodies

I will begin with depictions of magical assault on individual bodies, which express anxiety over preserving a stable identity; depictions of witches, violating corpses, figure prime among these. The sanctity of the corpse is one of the most basic and universal dispositions of human society.[26] While practices vary widely, from burial to cremation to ritual consumption, all human societies ritualize their treatment of the dead; this ritual marks the corpse's transition from a living member of the community to becoming refuse that needs to be discarded. Outside this ritual safe-zone, encounters with corpses trigger a profound experience of abjection and remind one of the instability of life; the corpse is, after all, the ultimate waste product, whose castoff existence forces an awareness of our own certain dissolution.[27]

Ancient representations of magic cultivate this horror of the corpse with lurid depictions of necromantic rites that are conducted in cemeteries or with purloined body parts. Horace, for example, depicts two hags foraging for bones in a pauper's cemetery that had been converted into a park on the Esquiline (*Satire* 1.8). In this scene two hags harvest buried bodies for use in a magic spell. Their magic rite not only cultivates abjection by exposing corpses outside the hallowed rituals of burial and mourning, but also shows the limits of human subjectivity and the frailty of life: by using corpses for magic, human beings become mere objects. Garbage to be used and reused for ulterior purposes, they are dispossessed of agency. Kristeva writes, "The subject is unable to accept that its body is a material organism, one that feeds off other organisms and, in its turn, sustains them. The subject recoils from its materiality, being unable to accept its bodily origins, and hence also its imminent death."[28] Horace's satire ends when the old women flee; they have been frightened by a loud fart from the statue of Priapus, who is narrating the comic episode (1.8.46). The humor in *Satire* 1.8 results from the ironic tension created by juxtaposing an absurdly flatulent ithyphallic statue with the abjection of the women's corpse-magic. Because humor is an important strategy to circumscribe information that is unpalatable, it is no surprise to find humor and the abject combined here. Humor often attends abject topics such as excrement and body fluids.[29]

Apuleius's *Metamorphoses* also combines corpses and abjection with humor in its numerous depictions of magic. For example, the protagonist in the story, Lucius, witnesses the grotesque and horrifying ingredients used by Pamphile, the sorceress who is at the center of the novel's plot. Her magic apothecary includes: "body parts from corpses mourned and even buried; here some noses and fingers, there some flesh-covered nails of a crucified criminal, elsewhere the preserved gore of victims butchered, and a mutilated scalp wrenched from the teeth of wild animals" (3.17). She even employs pulsating entrails that were pulled from a living body (3.18). Like Erictho in Lucan's *Pharsalia*, Pamphile's magic relies substantially on the abject power of human corpses. It is as if the power of horror that these objects inspire by transgressing the boundaries between life and death—human subject and magical object—increases their potency to violate human autonomy and will. In fact, the entire novel revolves around the theme of abjection and human transformation: the opening lines of the novel invite the reader to enjoy a series of bawdy tales "so that you may be astounded at men's forms and fortunes, transformed into other shapes and in return restored, reciprocally bound" (1.1).[30] In other words, the novel focuses on the abject instability of identities; it is no wonder then that magic figures as a constant theme throughout.

In another episode of the *Metamorphoses*, two witches are stealing body parts from a corpse that has not yet been buried. In a comic yet unsettling incident they accidentally steal the facial organs of his sleeping guardian instead. Because the two men share the same name, the living Thelyphron, rather than the dead one, responds to the witches' magical summons (2.30). The mix-up is revealed when an Egyptian prophet (*Aegyptius propheta*) revives the corpse to reveal his murderers' identities (2.28). He also reveals that the nose and ears of the young man who watched his body the night before are wax replicas made by witches to conceal their theft. This story, while depicting an accidental episode of organ-harvesting from a still-living person (remember that Erictho and Pamphile are said to have done it deliberately), can be seen as triggering a strong sense of abjection; it reveals the fragile boundaries between life and death. A living person is harvested like a corpse, while sleeping, and a dead man is raised to expose the identity of his murderers. This story highlights the vulnerability and instability of the human body, whose anatomy and identity (little is more integral to a sense of identity than ones facial organs) are liable to theft. It also underscores the uneasy liminality of sleep, in which the living enter a state that resembles death and can, as in this episode, fall prey to terrifying circumstances when they are least aware and able to protect themselves. The dead, for their part, can be raised from eternal slumber with potent ritual actions.[31] In this story, magic functions as a narrative catalyst for revealing the inherent instability of the human form. As the title, *Metamorphoses*, would suggest, bodies and their social personae exist in fragile and uncertain conditions. Magic uncovers the inherent abjection of human existence in this book.

Another example where magic harnesses the abject power of death is Seneca's tragedy, *Medea.* The sorceress dresses in funerary attire, brandishes a torch snatched from a cremation pyre, and pours her own blood upon the altar (*Manet noster Sanguis ad aras*) as a libation to the goddess Hecate (797–810). This macabre ritual confounds the normal relationship between sacrificial victim and hierophant, as well as between sacred and defiling. Blood itself is abject and evokes revulsion: it signifies life when in the veins, but death when it escapes the body. Its flow signals vitality's ebb. In Medea's case, she mutilates her own body while confusing the boundary between life and death; her attire and ritual implements carry with them the contagion of the Underworld.

In all three portraits, abjection—marked by the presence of corpses, blood, and dismembered human bodies—signals the transgressive nature of magic rites and the female characters who perform them.

Confronting Bestiality

On the threshold between individual identity and social identity lie stories about magic effecting animal transformations. These stories reveal not only the insecurity of individual identity, they underscore the fragility of the category "human" upon which notions of society and civilization depend.[32]

In Apuleius's *Metamorphoses*, for example, Lucius is avidly curious about the workings of magic. He seduces a sorceress's apprentice to learn secrets of her mistress's magic art. After witnessing the sorceress Pamphile transform herself into a bird, Lucius demands the same, but he is accidentally turned into a braying ass. His lover grabbed the wrong vial and, voilà, Lucius is covered in hair and stands on four-hoofed feet. This episode signals the beginning of Lucius's quest to be restored to human form, a goal that is ultimately made possible by the goddess Isis after many entertaining and harrowing adventures. Animal transformation is a constant theme throughout the *Metamorphoses*. Not only does magic transform Pamphile into a bird and Lucius into a donkey, but one of the sorceresses (discussed previously, the one who stole the guardian's nose and ears), first appeared to him in the shape of a weasel (2.25). Add to this a tale Lucius hears about an innkeeper witch (*saga* 1.8) who turns her enemies into animals. She transforms an unfaithful lover into a beaver and turns a competing innkeeper into a frog (1.9). In these stories, satire joins hands with the abject. The novel is humorous and entertaining alongside its disconcerting and abject depictions of magic that serve to characterize the human condition.

In all these depictions—and one should not forget to include Circe's infamous spell in Homer's *Odyssey* (10.212), which converted Odysseus's sailors into swine—magical transformation reveals how artificial the distinction between humans and animals can be. By demonstrating the ease with which individuals slip from one category to the other, these stories highlight the arbitrary and easily transgressed nature of boundaries that human societies construct to separate themselves from beasts. Lucius's experiences as a donkey, in fact, reveal the cruel, barbaric, and inhumane behavior that human beings regularly exhibit toward animals. By violating the boundary presumed to separate humans from animals in these depictions, magic casts the reader face-to-face with the poverty of human pretenses to order and civilization, in other words, with the abject.

In addition to stories of magic that transform human victims into animals, other depictions use animal imagery to portray the sorceress herself as bestial. In Horace's *Epode* 5, Canidia's hair is entwined with vipers (15–16). Her friend Sagana has the streaming hair of a spiny sea urchin (28). In *Satire* 1.8 Canidia and Sagana claw in the dirt (*scalpere terram unguibus*) like wild animals looking for bones and buried body parts (26–27). Propertius similarly uses animal imagery in his *Elegies* to portray his lover's procuress/sorceress, whom he regards as greedy and an obstacle to his mistress. He accuses the procuress of digging out the eyes of a crow with her fingernail and of consulting screech owls and disguising herself in the skin of a wolf (4.5.14–18). These invective poems use animal imagery to vilify certain women and convey the transgressive character of magic. If, in these portraits, human bodies have no integrity or stability, what do depictions of magic reveal about threats to social boundaries? This is the question pursued in the following section.

Violating the Social Body

Kristeva describes acts against the integrity of the social body to be equally abject and revulsion-causing as acts that transgress the individual body. Just as confronting a disintegrated cadaver challenges our belief in the permanence of individual identity, confronting violent and evil acts challenges our trust in society's laws and religious prohibitions to shield us. Crime, especially violent crime, threatens security and stability on the social level, triggering a collective response to abjection. As Kristeva writes: "Any crime, because it draws attention to the fragility of the law, is abject, but premeditated crime, cunning murder, hypocritical revenge are even more so because they heighten the display of such fragility."[33] We encounter this type of collective abjection operating in many depictions of magic, where magic serves to violate social mores, gender roles, and basic human decency. Infanticide tops the list of all these categories.

Infanticide

Returning to Horace's *Epode* 5, Canidia's magic rite appears deadly serious and sinister, not ridiculous as it did in *Satire* 1.8, where flatulence disrupted the nefarious activities of two old women. In this text, a group of old crones starves a boy to death in order to distill yearning desire from his liver, which will become the main ingredient of a love potion. This act of infanticide horrifies us as readers. Dismembering rotting corpses on a battle field or mutilating the cadavers of crucified criminals triggers revulsion to decay and death. But murdering a boy to make an old hag's love potion (*amoris poculum*) evokes horror for its cruelty combined with trite venality.

In *Pharsalia*, Erictho commits the most heinous form of infanticide; she slices an unborn infant from its mother's womb to deliver the child to an early death on a smoldering altar as a sacrifice (6.558–59). Perverting the traditional roles of midwife and hierophant in the same act, her magic rite inverts proper Roman rituals in which a male priest sacrifices a domestic animal—not a child—to ensure divine protection, abundance, and fecundity.[34] This sacrifice appears especially horrendous given the vulnerability and liminality of pregnant women, who are in most societies granted special protection.

Erictho's obstetric intervention also provokes an experience of abjection by attacking the very source of life: the pregnant womb. The womb—and according to Kristeva, female genitalia more generally—arouses ambivalent emotions such as disgust, fear, and loathing.[35] Whereas Freud identifies fear of female genitals with the castration complex, Kristeva links it to abjection. The sight of a distended pregnant belly recalls with fascination and horror the fact that all human beings originate inside the body of another person. Life comes from life; human beings emerge embodied from another body to perpetuate the cycle of birth, death, and decay.[36]

Subverting Gender Roles

Lust constitutes a common element in Roman portrayals of women's magic. Canidia and her friend Sagana, for example, stop at nothing in their pursuit of ingredients for a love potion. In *Epode* 5 they are joined in their project—killing a young boy for his liver—by Folia of Ariminum, who is described as *masculae libidinis* (possessing a "masculine libido"). This designation could apply to virtually all the sorceresses of Latin literature, who almost unanimously use magic to pursue and subdue male objects of sexual desire or conceal acts of adultery, which I will discuss more fully below.[37] Horace presents these women as beyond their sexual prime and physically unappealing; they seek to dominate men whom they would have no hope of seducing without the coercive power of a love potion derived through murder.[38] This situation reverses ancient social custom, perceived to rest on natural order, according to which men seek sexual gratification with younger women, not the other way around.

In addition to inverting gender roles when women use magic to control men's libidos and gratify their own, the idea of a sexually voracious old crone evokes horror and revulsion. In *Epodes* 8 and 12 Horace describes with satiric delight the abhorrence of an old woman's body: her flabby chest and withered buttocks, which frame an anus like that of a flatulent cow, inspire nothing but vitriolic ridicule from the sexually flaccid poet. Here, again, humor is used to convey abjection, which eludes the bounds of normal language. Old women's bodies, in these satires, invoke the abjection associated with corpses. They remind us of death and our mortal origins. As Amy Richlin states about these depictions: "Old women themselves are repeatedly addressed as corpses; one woman is imagined as lusting in her grave.... In fact old women evoke the most intense expressions of fear and disgust, along with a sense that they constitute a sort of uncanny other."[39] In other words, sexually potent old women are quintessentially abject: they mingle the opposing poles of life and death, of fertility and decay; they transgress natural order in addition to social order.

An earlier Hellenistic portrait that anticipates this theme, Theocritus's *Idyll* 2 depicts a magic ritual that explicitly performs this gender role-reversal by melting and binding the male object while presenting the female subject as dominant and controlling.[40] In this poem, a love-struck maiden melts a wax figure of her lover (who has taken her virginity, but not made her a proper wife, 41) in order to make him melt with love for her. For the pain he has caused her she burns a bay leaf to make him burn; to force him to return to her she spins an *iunx* that will draw him back.[41] In each of these actions, she assumes a sexually active and controlling stance that inverts traditional sex roles and violates "natural" male mastery, challenging both masculine identity and one of the cardinal principles of social organization in ancient societies—patriarchy.[42] In virtually all Roman depictions of magic, women use sorcery to overturn traditional gender roles and usurp male sexual prerogative. From this social perspective, women's magic is highly abject; it undermines the fundamental basis of social order in antiquity—gender-based social hierarchy.

Adultery

The final abjectionary motif that recurs in Roman depictions of magic is adultery. In the majority of Roman depictions of magic, especially from the imperial period, women use spells to facilitate adultery or to pursue men for sexual relationships outside the confines of marriage.[43] In Apuleius's *Metamorphoses*, Pamphile transforms herself into a bird and manipulates pulsating intestines and other ghastly body parts to satisfy her insatiable lust. Although she is married, her magic compels handsome young men into her bed, where she violates their bodies as well as their masculine autonomy. The poet Tibullus similarly describes a magic rite that is replete with all the customary sepulchral elements, including "bones from a still-warm funeral pyre," that will enable his lover to deceive her husband and commit adultery with the poet (1.2.41–58). Another elegiac poet, Propertius, describes the magic powers of his lover's procuress, which she uses to deceive watchful husbands (4.5.5–18). In these literary portrayals, magic is associated not only with the pollution of corpses and bestiality of animals, but with the dangerous and abject quality of women's adultery.

While sex (*stuprum,* lit. defilement, dishonor) with unmarried freeborn women was a crime during the Republic,[44] it became much more serious after Augustus passed a series of moral reforms that made adultery and *stuprum* into public crimes to be tried by the State, rather than family crimes punished by the *paterfamilias*.[45] Catharine Edwards argues that concerns over adultery expressed at this time reflect less the actual moral decay of elite women in the late Republic, as some have argued, than the use of marital fidelity and women's chastity as potent symbols for Rome's social and political stability.[46] Women's simplicity and chastity were idealized as attributes of former times—before Rome's power and wealth corrupted the patrician class—and served a nostalgic and propagandistic purpose as part of Augustus's claim to restore the virtues and values of the Republic.[47]

Given the heavy symbolic load laid at the door of women's sexual comportment, depictions of women enlisting revolting forms of magic to gratify their lust in adulterous unions carried an especially potent ideological charge. As a crime, adultery threatens the very basis of patriarchy: women circumvent male control and surveillance to fulfill their own sexual agendas, generating significant and sometimes paralyzing doubts about paternity and, ultimately identity. Adultery thus challenges the entire hegemonic structure and corporal ideology of ancient society.

When viewed through the theoretical framework of abjection these depictions of women's craven magic and adulterous lust express deeper anxieties about preserving social order and safeguarding elite men's hierarchical privileges. This is clear in one final example for this section. In response to the announcement of his friend's engagement, Juvenal launches a vitriolic attack on women in an attempt to dissuade his friend from marriage. He reviles Roman women of his day for being unchaste, unfaithful, and sexually libidinous (esp. 329–34). They violate proper gender roles and break their most sacred vow of marriage by falsely presenting a foundling or illegitimate child to their husbands as an heir (558–605). Significantly, they also use magic to deceive and manipulate their husbands, driving the men literally insane with noxious potions (610–14). This passage, therefore, combines the abjectionary elements of magic that recur in ancient depictions and could be deemed a triumvirate of abjection: violating class boundaries through unregulated sexuality, overthrowing gender hierarchy, and violating men's corporal integrity.

Abjection of Magic in Practice

Manipulating men's libidos, either to guarantee their fidelity or seduce them, figures as a central goal of women's magic in Roman literary depictions. Significantly, erotic desire constitutes a primary motivating factor for a large proportion of actual spells performed in antiquity as well. According to John Gager, approximately one-fourth of extant curse tablets concern "matters of the heart."[48] The rest pertain to other areas of life in which competition and uncertainty led people to seek advantage through magical means.[49] Recently, Esther Eidinow has argued that "competition" is inadequate as an explanation for many of the curse texts.[50] Rather, she proposes that writing curses (along with oracle consultation) "were both strategies by which ordinary ancient Greek men and women, individually and collectively, expressed and managed aspects of the uncertainty and risk of everyday life."[51]

Whether we understand the motivation for ancient magic to be competition or risk management, it is important to point out that ancient magic primarily took the form of curses and binding spells (*defixiones, katadesmoi*).[52] That is to say, people framed their needs and desires in terms of harming or controlling other people. Even "love" spells sought to attract a particular person by causing him, or more often her, physical suffering as in the following example:

> Nab Euphēmia and lead her to me, Theōn, loving me passionately like a mad woman, and bind her fast (*katadēsate*) with unbreakable chains, super strong, hard as adamantine, for love of me, Theōn, and do not let her eat, nor drink, nor fall asleep, nor joke, nor laugh, but make her leap forth from every place and every house, and abandon father, mother, brothers, sisters, until she comes to me, Theōn, loving me, desiring me, right away, with an unceasing desire and manic love.[53]

To the extent that this type of magic violates the corporal integrity, autonomy, and social identity ("abandon father, mother, brothers, sisters") of its victim, it is abject. As Gager summarizes, ". . . all *defixiones* express a formalized wish to bring other persons or animals under the client's power, against their will and customarily without their knowledge. In some cases, the wish is expressed as an intention to inflict personal harm or death."[54] Scholars have debated the degree to which these violent intentions should be understood literally or figuratively. Gager argues that cursing uses hyperbolic metaphor, the primary purpose of which is expressive, such as shouting "kill the bum!" during a sports competition.[55] Faraone similarly argues that curses communicate through analogy: the intention is to render the victim useless *like* a corpse, not actually dead.[56] John Winkler proposes that the burning and suffering invoked in ancient attraction spells (*agōgai*) project the burning and suffering of unrequited love onto the desired object.[57] By ritually acting out and projecting the petitioner's feelings of frustration, *agōgē* spells allow for a resolution of the petitioner's psychic turmoil.[58] While these explanations make sense to a modern observer, who is familiar with the ideas of "splitting" and "projection" developed by psychoanalysis over the past century, most ancient observers regarded spells as dangerous and frightening because they were believed to work, and that is the starting point for understanding ancient magic's ability to elicit abjection.

Although this type of magic was not illegal everywhere in antiquity, it was often banned and generally regarded as a threat to society by operating surreptitiously against the bodies and minds of citizens.[59] It has been suggested, however, that someone laying a curse on their opponent may not have kept it a secret, intending that fear and hypochondria would harm the target of the spell as much or more than the spell itself.[60] In any case, magic threatened the social body through attacks on the bodies of individual persons, causing a gifted orator to become mute,[61] or a fast horse to break his leg,[62] or an enticing wife or courtesan to lose her charm.[63] Faraone has argued that in the agonistic context of ancient cities, curses and binding spells were frequently enlisted to promote or protect the interests of individuals and their families.[64] Moreover, he suggests, curses may have been the last recourse for "underdogs," who lacked the authority or power to protect themselves.[65]

While the leveling effect of *defixiones* that Faraone proposes may appear to legitimize the practice, two ancient accounts describe the fear, helplessness, and horror of those who found themselves victimized by magical attack. Tacitus reports the terrifying discovery of a curse enlisted against the heir to the imperial throne, Germanicus, and suspected of causing his untimely and painful death.

> It is a fact that explorations in the floor and walls brought to light the remains of human bodies, spells, curses, leaden tablets engraved with the name "Germanicus," charred and blood-smeared ashes, and other implements of witchcraft *(malefica)* by which it is believed the living soul can be devoted to the powers of the grave. (*Ann.* 2.69)

Three centuries later, the orator, Libanius, experienced a sacrilegious nightmare that he understood to portend "spells, incantations, and an attack by sorcerers." Following this dream he experienced a crisis in his career; by his own account "[his] oratory was undone" (1.246). He also suffered from an extended bout of gout, which he attributed to the same cause. One day, a desiccated chameleon was discovered in his classroom; "its head was tucked between its hind legs, one front leg was missing, and the other [leg] closed its mouth in silence" (1.249). After finding this mutilated creature, Libanius's situation began to ameliorate; the magic's power was apparently undone or weakened by its discovery.

While both stories of magical attack can be explained by other means—stress and hypochondria on the part of Libanius, poisoning on the part of Germanicus,[66]—it is clear from these accounts that harmful magic was readily suspected when people experienced a sudden and deleterious change of luck.[67]

Both these accounts also reveal the extreme horror of discovering evidence of magical attack and point to the abject nature of binding or nailing a figurine with the intention of causing surreptitious harm or, possibly, death. The magical violation of someone else's autonomy and physical well-being breaches not only the boundaries of her or his body, but interferes with her or his will and subjectivity. In this way magic threatens dissolution of the self, provoking an abject response of horror, revulsion, and fear.

Ancient literary depictions emphasize the subversive power of women's "love" magic. The material record suggests that erotic magic indeed constituted a significant percentage of extant spells, but surprisingly, given the literary stereotype, men comprise the overwhelming majority (86 percent) of petitioners in extant Greek erotic spells.[68] The primary danger of erotic magic, therefore, was not, as literature would suggest, women using it to subvert male authority and commit adultery, but rather men using it to manipulate women into sexual transgression; these erotic spells often explicitly seek to lead a dutiful wife or concubine from the bed of her husband to that of another man, violating the sanctity of the household and the patriarchal authority of men over their wives and mistresses (*PGM* IV.2755–61, LXI.29–30, IV.2756–58).[69] The material record, thus, presents an impression of ancient women as far more chaste and faithful than they are portrayed in literature;[70] it seems that women were more likely to be victims of men's predatory magic than mistresses of erotic magic themselves.[71]

Erotic magic, even when (or perhaps especially when) performed by men, causes abjection by undermining a central pillar of ancient society. The patriarchal system highly restricted sexual access to freeborn women in order to guarantee paternity and, consequently, social status through the orderly transmission of property between generations of men. By seeking to compel women into illicit sexual unions, men's erotic magic circumvented this system and undermined an important foundation of ancient Mediterranean culture. Fritz Graf has proposed that men of lower social classes may have used erotic magic to seduce women of higher classes, gaining a foothold through marriage into a higher social station.[72] Love magic also may have afforded families an acceptable explanation for the shameful misbehavior of their daughters, who dallied with men below their social station.[73] In either case, performing an attraction (*agōgē*) spell on a freeborn woman challenged the very foundation of hereditary social status, which is why the good reputations of respectable girls and women were so closely guarded; even a rumor of infidelity could raise questions about children's legitimacy and haunt a family.[74] In this way, men's erotic magic was as subversive and threatening as the adulterous magic of women stereotyped in literature.

The use of magic by subordinates to win favor from, or control the decisions of, a social superior constitute another aspect of magic that subverted corporal ideology and consequently resonates with abjection. The *Greek Magical Papyri*

(*PGM*) contain numerous spells that promise to curb someone's anger, or make the petitioner popular and persuasive. One such spell "to restrain anger" (*thumokatoxon*) and "to subordinate" (*hupotaktikon*) states: "Come to me, O God, who is not to be despised, O Daimon, and muzzle, subject, enslave (*katadoulōson*) so-and-so to so-and-so, and make him come under my feet" (VII.966–67). This spell challenges the very core of social identity based in corporal ideology; by giving someone the power to subordinate a social superior—even asking to enslave and humiliate him—this type of magic subverts the hierarchical principles on which ancient society depended. This ability to destabilize social order helps explain the depiction of magic as abject in so much of ancient literature, which reflects the perspective and values of the elite who produced it.

In addition to the subversive social effects of magic, many ritual practices performed as part of ancient spells could also be considered in terms of abjection. Like the magic of literary imagination, spells that were actually performed or found in recipe books of professional magicians often enlist ingredients and ritual actions associated with the abject. *Defixiones*, for example, were frequently left in cemeteries and request that the targets of the spells become cold and lifeless like corpses in the graves. While these requests were most likely meant metaphorically—cold and lifeless with respect to some person or skill rather than literally dead[75]—the site at which the curse tablets were deposited (graves) and the invocation of corpses both invite an encounter with mortality and corporal disintegration that are primary and primal components of abjection. Other spells include macabre ingredients such as parts of mutilated animals, blood, or body parts from someone who died violently (*biaiothanatos*),[76] and instruments of death such as gallows-wood (*PGM* V.74), or parts of a shipwrecked vessel (*PGM* V.65, VII.466). David Frankfurter describes the gruesome use of a fetus (*brephos*) in Roman Egypt to bind someone with malice.[77] These spells resemble in many ways the lurid depictions of magic from Roman literature of the first and second centuries CE, which, as we have already discussed, trigger abjection on many levels.[78] *PGM* IV.2145–2240, for example, closely approximates the necromantic rite performed by Erictho in Lucan's *Pharsalia*. It directs one to inscribe three Homeric verses on an iron lamella and attach it to a person on the point of death, who will then be able to answer any question (2155–57). It instructs: "Attach it to someone condemned and executed, tell him the verses in his ear, and he will tell you everything you wish" (2164–65). Further permutations of this spell involve writing with the blood of someone who died violently (*haimatos biaiou*, 2209), or burying it in the grave/tomb of someone who died untimely or by violence (*aōrou thēkēn/mnēma* 2216, 2222). A "Prayer to Selene" (*PGM* IV.2785–2890) capitalizes on abject imagery in its invocation of the moon goddess: her womb is said to be covered over with the scales of reptiles (2804–5); like Erictho, she dwells amid tombs and devours cadavers (2868–69). Significantly, she is also described as the source of life and death—"For all things are from you, and in you / eternal one (*aiōniē*), all things reach fulfillment (*teleuta*)" (2839–40). This links the goddess with the womb/tomb described by Kristeva as the primal abject.[79]

The use of nonsense language (*voces mysticae*) in many *defixiones*, especially from the later Roman Empire, constitutes another aspect of magic that can be understood in terms of abjection. Like "abracadabra," these magical words were charged with power and activated the spell when uttered. While these incomprehensible words and phrases have been explained as the appropriate language to communicate with numinous powers and their intermediaries, angels and demons,[80] they also suggest a breakdown of civilized human communication. They could even be considered a reversion to the pre-linguistic phase of infancy—when one experienced continuity with the source of life—or of neurosis, where rational discourse breaks down in the face of the unconscious and its phobias.[81] According to Kristeva, it is the ability to use language and symbols to communicate that initiates the infant's first steps into individuation from the maternal *chora*. The use of language enables the child to recognize the distinction between self and other; it provides the initial ordering of experience. Entrance into language and the symbolic realm more generally marks the beginning of subjectivity, the maintenance of which is secured throughout our lives by symbol systems, which mediate our experiences. As Noëlle McAfee explains, regarding Kristeva's theory of subjectivity, "The subject is an effect of linguistic processes. In other words, we become who we are as a result of taking part in signifying practices. There is no self-aware self prior to our use of language."[82] Nonsense, chaos, in short any breakdown of the symbolic order, thus, threaten our sense of meaning and threaten our very self.

In summary, the evidence for the actual practice of ancient magic, while only a pale reflection of the terrifying rituals portrayed in literature, nonetheless reveals many aspects that could trigger abjection. It enabled people to violate social hierarchy and usurp the benefits and privileges destined by Fortuna for those with higher birth, nobler ancestors, or greater talent. It interfered with female chastity and the patriarchal control over wives and daughters, which may also have contributed to transgressing social hierarchy and putting paternal identity in doubt. Most importantly, the ritual binding, burning, stabbing, and consigning to Hades that appear so often in extant spells violate the integrity of individual bodies and wills and provoke a strong revulsion that may explain the highly developed abjection of magic in literary depictions.

What has not been explained is why magic, which was performed by men in equal or greater numbers than women according to the material record, should be associated so strongly with women in the literary imagination. The answer, I propose, may lie in the connection Kristeva draws between primal abjection and women.

The Primal Abject, Women, and Magic

Kristeva identifies the root of all abjection to be the maternal body, which is both the source of our existence and the object from which we must separate to become distinct and autonomous beings. The term Kristeva uses, *chora* (womb or vessel), first appears in Plato's *Timeaus*, where it designates the original vessel of creation: "a receptacle (*hupodoxēn*), a sort of nurse (*tithēnēn*) of all generation" (49a). For Kristeva, *chora* is not so much the mother's womb as it is the sheltered, dependent relationship of the child to her caretaker. It is the space in which identity begins to emerge, "an articulation, a rhythm, but one that precedes language."[83] During this earliest stage of life, according to Kristeva, the infant's identity is contiguous with its mother's or caretaker's; the infant does not yet perceive her as a separate person, does not consider her to be an object to the infant's subject. Gradually the child emerges from this state of "plenitude without differentiation"[84] to become a thinking, speaking, and acting subject. This process, according to Kristeva, is accomplished through the act of abjecting. "The first 'thing' to be abjected is the mother's body, the child's own origin."[85] Kristeva argues,

> The abject confronts us, on the other hand, and this time within our personal archaeology with our earliest attempts to release the hold of *maternal* entity even before existing outside of her, thanks to the autonomy of language. It is a violent, clumsy breaking away, with the constant risk of falling back under the sway of a power as securing as it is stifling.[86]

For Kristeva, becoming an autonomous self occurs precisely through the act of abjection—first of the mother's body, which reminds us of our birth—and eventually, through the abjection of anything that threatens the body's boundaries, whether physically or symbolically. This separation is never complete. As the quotation above suggests, there always remains a fear of falling back into that comfortable abyss of primal unity and undifferentiated experience.[87] Abjection "preserves what existed in the archaism of pre-objectal relationship, in the immemorial violence with which a body becomes separated from another body in order to be."[88]

The maternal body thus presents an ever-present psychological danger for the child and for society, which must patrol it through taboos and prohibitions.[89] In fact, Kristeva identifies this fear of and desire for the mother as the origin of incest taboos. The mother's body "becomes a phobic 'object,'"[90] which must be abjected so that order, identity, and boundaries can be created. Roman depictions of lustful hags, performing seduction spells on young men, echo this revulsion toward the maternal body and a desire to proscribe the phobic place of origin. Satiric portraits that sexualize the aging female body transgress, and therefore reinforce, this primal taboo whose aim is to segregate sex and death. With their images of wilted flesh, these depictions force the reader to confront mortality, but more significantly, they invite the reader to consider that forbidden "place"—the uncanny womb/tomb, as seen in *PGM* IV.2785–2890, which according to Kristeva is the place of origin that lurks in our unconscious as the primal fear of our possible loss of self and dissolution back into the maternal body.[91] Depictions of women's magic invite the reader to contemplate that threat and to explore abjection as a violation of the social prohibitions that symbolically proscribe the mother's body and threaten to annihilate self and society.

Kristeva argues that not only is the mother abject, but all women become abject through an association with her: "Without a way of conceiving the mother that allows us to abject her and come to terms with that abjection, we abject all women."[92] Thus, fear that the maternal body poses a threat to individual autonomy and social order is projected onto all women, who categorically become the threatening Other. [93]According to Kristeva, it is through the ritualization of defilement—in an effort to contain and control primal abjection—that men have managed to relegate the female sex to the position of Other, identifying women with irrational and dangerous powers: "That other sex, the feminine, becomes synonymous with a radical evil that is to be suppressed."[94]

Kristeva thus draws a direct link between the mother's body, which the ego has to reject as abject in order for it to develop and for individual identity to emerge, and the position of women as Other. Through this association, the female sex as a whole comes to be identified with abjection, and regarded as a chaotic and dangerous power that needs to be brought under control by the patriarchal powers of law and social order. We see in her logic an explanation for the connection between women, abjection, and magic that pervades ancient representations of magic.

Conclusion

We have seen how depictions of magic in Roman literature express anxiety over controlling the stability and boundaries of the body, thus linking magic with abjection in the context of Roman corporal ideology, which sought to control rigid hierarchical boundaries through patrolling the comportment and integrity of individual bodies. Magic in these portraits engages abject materials such as corpses and defiling funerary implements; it dissolves human bodies, boundaries, and identities as well as it confounds the distinction between human and animal. Magic is imagined to violate social order by inverting gender roles and conferring on women prerogatives like sexual assertion that are traditionally reserved for men. These depictions suggest that the producers of these literary texts perceived magic as a disturbing and degrading threat to individual integrity and social order: in other words, as abject. The material evidence for ancient magic also indicates that much about ancient magic resonates with Kristeva's conception of abjection: it threatened individual autonomy, corporal sanctity, and patriarchal control over women; it employed macabre ingredients, contact with corpses, and nonsense language (*voces mysticae*) that were saturated with abjection. Thus, it would appear that, while literary depictions are highly exaggerated and stereotyped, the abjection they portray reflects the perception, among at least some people, that magic was transgressive and disturbing, violating boundaries of the body, identity, and social stability.

Furthermore, Kristeva's theory of the primal abject suggests that women are often associated with abjection through the mother's body. This may help clarify the frequent depiction of women's deleterious magic in ancient literature. While men were frequent users of magic in the ancient world, the identification of magic as abject appears to have contributed to the association of magic with women in the literary imagination. In fact, exaggerated and hyperbolic depictions of *women* practicing magic suggest that these gendered portraits helped to communicate the abject quality of magic. Women's Otherness concretized the Otherness of magic, and vice versa. Magic thus comes to be associated primarily with women in the ancient imagination, creating enduring stereotypes of sexually overwrought and infanticidal hags, whose sexuality violates the primal prohibition of the mother's body and its identification with chaos, disorder, and death.

Notes

1. I would like to thank Dayna Kalleres for encouraging me to develop a speculative idea I proposed in an earlier version of "Interrogating the Magic and Gender Connection" into a separate article to fill out the section on literary fantasy and stereotype. Expanding that initial paragraph into a full-blown chapter proved to be much more challenging than anticipated. I would like to extend my heartfelt appreciation to readers who contributed suggestions and insights along the way: Dayna Kalleres, David Frankfurter, Annette Reed, Nicola Denzey Lewis, Stephanie Cobb, Phil Webster, Connor Steele, and Miriam Peskowitz, who provided editing consultation. Dayna, in particular, has repeatedly offered helpful guidance and encouragement at moments when the project seemed stalled. All translations are my own as are any remaining mistakes.
2. See discussion and citations below.
3. Matthew Dickie, *Magic and Magicians in the Greco-Roman World* (New York: Routledge, 2001), 10–11, emphatically rejects psychoanalytic explanations of

ancient magic. See also criticisms in Marilyn B. Skinner, "*Ego mulier*: The Construction of Male Sexuality in Catullus," in *Roman Sexualities*, ed. Judith P. Hallett and Marilyn B. Skinner (Princeton, NJ: Princeton University Press, 1997), 132, of Freudian interpretations of Catullus's fraught relationship with his literary mistress.

4. Julia Kristeva, *Powers of Horror: An Essay on Abjection,* trans. Leon S. Roudiez (New York: Columbia University Press, 1982), 4.
5. This contrasts with the current trend in ancient magic studies to regard magic as merely another ritual technology among many available to promote/protect ones interests in competitive ancient Mediterranean societies, without pejorative connotations.
6. Kristeva, *Powers of Horror*, 14. This phase is pre-linguistic but not pre-symbolic. Kelly Oliver, *Reading Kristeva: Unraveling the Double-Bind* (Bloomington: Indiana University Press, 1993), 34, 43.
7. Kristeva, *Powers of Horror*, 13.
8. Ibid., 3.
9. Ibid., 13.
10. Elizabeth Grosz, *Sexual Subversions: Three French Feminists* (Sydney: Allen & Unwin; Boston: Unwin Hyman, 1989), 49.
11. Skinner, "*Ego mulier*," 132–33.
12. Kristeva, *Powers of Horror*, 4.
13. McAfee, *Julia Kristeva*, 29.
14. Ibid., 12–13.
15. Longus, *Daphnis and Chloe* 4.20–21, 30, 32; Chariton *Charea and Callirhoe* 5.9; Xenophon of Ephesus *An Ephesian Tale* 1.1, 1.2; Heliodorus *An Ethiopian Story* 1.20.
16. Soranos D'Éphèse, *Maladies des Femmes livre II*, ed. and trans. by Paul Burguière, Danielle Gourevitch, and Yves Malinas (Paris: Les Belles Lettres, 1990), 21–24. While Soranus never states that these techniques are explicitly intended for well-born children, his audience is clearly elite. See the discussion in Dale B. Martin *The Corinthian Body* (New Haven, CT: Yale University Press, 1995), 25–27.
17. Maud W. Gleason, *Making Men: Sophists and Self-Presentations in Ancient Rome* (Princeton, NJ: Princeton University Press, 1995), 63, 72 and *passim*, documents this very well.
18. Oribasius 3.31–34; and Galen *De alimentorum facultatibus* 474, 501–2, 528, 560 on the drying or cooling effects of certain foods; Galen *Hygiene* 6.2–5 on specific regimes to manage warm or cold dispositions and to treat pathological conditions. Elizabeth C. Evans, "Galen the Physician as Physiognomist," *Transactions and Proceedings of the American Philological Association*, vol. 76 (1945), 292–93.
19. Galen *Hygiene* 6.5 and Soranus *Gyn* 1.31 on the dangers of too much sex; Soranus *Gyn* 1.39 on deleterious effects on unborn children of female behavior during sex; Hippocrates *Regimen* 1.27 on following a particular dietary protocol to determine

the sex of a gestating fetus. Martin, *Corinthian Body*, 32–33; he reminds the reader on p. 37 that this conception of disease belongs primarily to the educated classes.

20. In Athens, for example, judicial torture (*basanos*) could be performed on slaves and foreigners but not citizens. Page du Bois, *Torture and Truth* (New York: Routledge 1991) 37. The refusal to allow one's slaves to be tortured was widely regarded as tantamount to confession since the testimony of slaves produced under duress was highly valued for its reliability (e.g., Demosthenes 30.37; Antiphon 1.6–12). In fact, some orators argued that slaves would only tell the truth *if* tortured, and unlike freemen, slaves revealed *only* truth when tortured (e.g., Lycurgus, against Leocrates, 29–31). Because philosophers, such as Aristotle, argued that slaves lacked independent reason (*logos*) and constituted extensions of their owners' bodies (*Pol.* 1255b), slaves were believed to respond more readily to physical suffering than free men did, who could, through exercise of reason, give false testimony and withstand intense pain (*Antiphon* 5.42, 49–50; *Isaios* 8.12). In fact, the ability to maintain silence despite extraordinary anguish was coded as an aristocratic virtue that marked a "natural" (*kata physin*) boundary between slave and free. See also Richard Bauman, *Crime and Punishment in Ancient Rome* (London: Routledge, 1996); and Peter Garnsey, *Social Status and Legal Privilege in the Roman Empire* (Oxford: Clarendon Press, 1970).

21. Cicero praised *munera* for this edifying capacity (*Tusc.* 2.41). See also Erik Gunderson, "The Ideology of the Arena," *Classical Antiquity* 15 (1996), 117; and Alison Futrell, *Blood in the Arena: The Spectacle of Roman Power* (Austin: University of Texas Press, 1997), 28–29.

22. The aversion to execution for citizens, especially nobles, was so ingrained that during the Catiline conspiracy, Pompey first had to declare that the conspirators renounced their citizenship before he could seek the death penalty for them as foreigners (Sall. *Cat.* 51.18). It is important to note that while capital punishment for Roman citizens (even members of the nobility) became more common during the Principate, nobles were not subjected to the degradation of the arena. Instead they were given the opportunity to commit suicide in the privacy of their homes. Bauman, *Crime and Punishment*, 12. Thus, even while the boundaries of their bodies were violated by the power of the emperor, demonstrating his ultimate and unchallengeable authority, their dignity remained intact. Courageous suicide was regarded as a noble form of death, which increased honor rather than detracted from it.

23. Garnsey, *Social Status and Legal Privilege*, 127; Bauman, *Crime and Punishment*, 133.

24. Jonathan Walters, "Invading the Roman Body: Manliness and Impenetrability in Roman Thought," in *Roman Sexualities*, ed. Judith P. Hallett and Marilyn B. Skinner (Princeton, NJ: Princeton University Press: 1997), 34, suggests that this ambiguity is responsible for Roman reticence to refer publicly to the sexual act within marriage.

25. Anne Carson, "Putting Her in Her Place: Woman, Dirt, and Desire" in *Before Sexuality: The Construction of Erotic Experience in the Ancient Greek World*, ed. David M. Halperin, John J. Winkler, and Froma I. Zeitlin (Princeton, NJ: Princeton University Press, 1990) 135–70, is the classic statement on this for Ancient Greece.

26. Bruce Lincoln, *Discourse and the Construction of Society: Comparative Studies of Myth, Ritual, and Classification* (New York/Oxford: Oxford University Press, 1989), 114.
27. Kristeva, *Powers of Horror*, 4.
28. Grosz, *Sexual Subversions*, 75.
29. I wish to thank Connor Steele for drawing my attention to the relationship between humor and abjection in so many of these texts.
30. Humor and abjection operate in tandem again in this text.
31. The ritual specialist who resuscitates the dead man is described as a prophet and is presented in respectful language. Nonetheless, temporary revivification of a corpse to reveal hidden knowledge, as in *Pharsalia*, appears uncanny, and conforms to the abject theme of the entire novel.
32. Kristeva, *Powers of Horror*, 12–13, original emphasis.
33. Ibid., 4.
34. Mary Beard, John North, and Simon Price, *Religions of Rome: Volume 1, A History* (Cambridge: Cambridge University Press, 1998), 297.
35. Kristeva, *Powers of Horror*, 33–35.
36. Ibid., 101.
37. See discussion in Stratton, *Naming the Witch*, 79–96.
38. Drawing on depictions such as this one, Matthew W. Dickie, "Who Practised Love-Magic in Classical Antiquity and in the Late Roman World?" *The Classical Quarterly* (New Series), 50, no. 2 (2000): 581–82 argues that, in fact, lust and the desire to attract men sexually motivate most women's magic in ancient Rome. See also Dickie, *Magic and Magicians*, 89–90, 178–81.
39. Amy Richlin, "Invective against Women in Roman Satire," *Arethusa* 17 (1984): 71.
40. See, for example, Christopher Faraone, "Sex and Power: Male-Targeting Aphrodisiacs in the Greek Magical Tradition," *Helios* 19 (1992): 92–103; Christopher Faraone, "Clay Hardens and Wax Melts: Magical Role-Reversal in Vergil's Eighth Eclogue," *CP* 84 (1989): 294–300; Faraone, *Ancient Greek Love Magic* (Cambridge: Harvard University Press, 1999), 153.
41. There are competing theories about how the *iunx* worked. See A.S.F. Gow, "ΙΥΓΞ, ΡΟΜΒΟΣ, Rhombus Turbo," *Journal of Hellenic Studies* 54 (1934): 1–13; Sarah Iles Johnston, "The Song of the *Iynx*: Magic and Rhetoric in *Pythian* 4," *Transactions of the American Philological Association* 125 (1995): 177–206; and Christopher Faraone, "The Wheel, the Whip and Other Implements of Torture: Erotic Magic in Pindar Pythian 4.213–19," *The Classical Journal* 88 (1993): 1–19.
42. Scholars have debated whether or not she represents a new liberated woman and changing social mores in Hellenistic Alexandria or behavior more representative of a courtesan. See Frederick T. Griffiths, "Home Before Lunch: The Emancipated Woman in Theocritus," in *Reflections of Women in Antiquity*, ed. Helene P. Foley (New York, London, Paris: Gordon and Breach Science Publishers, 1981), 247–74; and Faraone, *Ancient Greek Love Magic*, 154, who includes earlier bibliography for his position.

43. Interestingly, adultery does not figure as a theme in Greek representations of magic.
44. Susan Treggiari, *Roman Marriage:* Iusti Coniuges *from the Time of Cicero to the Time of Ulpian* (Oxford: Clarendon Press, 1991), 275–76.
45. Amy Richlin, "Approaches to the Sources on Adultery", *Reflections of Women in Antiquity,* ed. Helene P. Foley (New York: Gordon and Breach Science Publishers, 1981), 379–80, 382. Under the *lex Julia de adulteriis coercendis,* sexual liaisons between an unmarried freeborn woman and a man were treated the same as adultery, incurring the heavy penalty of exile, loss of half the woman's dowry and a third of her property. The man involved was also penalized, losing half his property and going into exile. See also Judith Evans Grubbs, *Women and the Law in the Roman Empire: A Sourcebook on Marriage, Divorce and Widowhood* (London and New York: Routledge, 2002), 83–84.
46. Catharine Edwards, *The Politics of Immorality in Ancient Rome* (Cambridge: Cambridge University Press, 1993), 34.
47. Edwards, *The Politics of Immorality,* 34. See also Kristina Milnor, *Gender, Domesticity, and the Age of Augustus* (Oxford and New York: Oxford University Press, 2005).
48. John G. Gager, *Curse Tablets and Binding Spells from the Ancient World* (Oxford: Oxford University Press, 1992), 78.
49. Gager, for example, organizes *Curse Tablets* around five main areas of human interaction characterized by competition; Christopher Faraone, "The Agonistic Context of Early Greek Binding Spells," in *Magika Hiera,* ed. Christopher Faraone and Dirk Obbink (New York, Oxford: Oxford University Press, 1991), 11, identifies competition between "rival tradesmen, lovers, litigants, or athletes concerned with the outcome of some future event" to be the primary social factor generating the production and consumption of ancient magic (*defixiones*).
50. Esther Eidinow, *Oracles, Curses, and Risk Among the Ancient Greeks* (Oxford; New York: Oxford University Press, 2007), 4.
51. Eidinow, *Oracles,* 4.
52. I am not including amulets that were apotropaic or medicinal in this discussion, but rather rituals that were recognized and labeled with one of the various terms for "magic." See Stratton, *Naming the Witch,* 12–15, 156.
53. Dierk Wortmann, "Neue magische Texte," *Bonner Jahrbücher* 168 (1968): 88–90; see also Gager, *Curse Tablets,* 105.
54. Gager, *Curse Tablets,* 21.
55. Ibid, 22.
56. Faraone, "The Agonistic Context", 8.
57. John Winkler, *The Constraints of Desire: The Anthropology of Sex and Gender in Ancient Greece* (New York: Routledge, 1990), 87–88.
58. Winkler, *The Constraints of Desire,* 89.
59. See Ramsay MacMullen, *Enemies of the Roman Order: Treason, Unrest, and Alienation in the Empire* (London: Routledge, 1966), chs. 3 and 4; Hans G. Kippenberg,

"Magic in Roman Civil Discourse: Why Rituals Could Be Illegal," in *Envisioning Magic: A Princeton Seminar and Symposium*, ed. Peter Schäfer and Hans G. Kippenberg (Leiden: Brill, 1997), 137–63; Robert K. Ritner, "The Religious, Social, and Legal Parameters of Traditional Egyptian Magic," in *Ancient Magic and Ritual Power*, ed. Marvin Meyer and Paul Mirecki (Leiden: E.J. Brill, 1995), 43–60; C. R. Phillips III, "*Nullum Crimen Sine Lege*: Socioreligious Sanctions on Magic," in *Magika Hiera*, ed. Christopher Faraone and Dirk Obbink (New York, Oxford: Oxford University Press, 1991), 260–76; James B. Rives, "Magic in the XII Tables Revisited," *Classical Quarterly* 52, no. 1 (2002): 270–90; James B. Rives, "Magic in Roman Law: The Reconstruction of a Crime," *Classical Antiquity* 22, no. 2 (2003): 313–39; Giuseppe Veltri, "Defining Forbidden Foreign Customs: Some Remarks on the Rabbinic Halakhah of Magic," in *Proceedings of the Eleventh World Congress of Jewish Studies, Div. C, Thought and Literature.*, vol. 1 (Jerusalem: World Union of Jewish Studies, 1994), 25–32; Collins, "Theoris of Lemnos and the Criminalization of Magic in Fourth-Century Athens," *Classical Quarterly* 51, no. 2 (2001): 477–93.

60. Gager, *Curse Tablets*, 21.
61. Cicero, *Brut.* 217 and *Orat.* 128–29; Libanius, 1.245–49. See Campbell Bonner, "Witchcraft in the Lecture Room of Libanius," *Transactions of the American Philological Association* 63 (1932): 34–44; and Christopher Faraone, "An Accusation of Magic in Classical Athens (AR. *Wasps* 946–48)," *Transactions of the American Philological Association* (1974): 119 (1989): 149–60.
62. SGD 167, DT 237. Cited in Gager, *Curse Tablets*, 55–56, 61.
63. DT 86, Dt 68. Cited in Gager, *Curse Tablets*, 85–86, 90.
64. Faraone, "The Agonistic Context", 10–11.
65. Faraone, "The Agonistic Context", 20. See also Frankfurter's and Ripat's contributions to this volume for thoughtful considerations of the petitioner's point of view. This study seeks to understand why magic generated such strongly abject depictions and was associated frequently with women's subversive activities; it is not intended to condemn or derogate the practice of magic in the ancient world.
66. L. Cilliers and F. P. Retief, "Poisons, Poisoning and the Drug Trade in Ancient Rome," *Akroterion* 45 (2000): 90.
67. The anthropologist E. E. Evans-Pritchard offers a seminal account of this phenomenon. E. E. Evans-Pritchard, *Witchcraft, Oracles, and Magic Among the Azande*, abridged with an introduction by Eva Gillies (Oxford: Clarendon Press, 1976), 18–32. See also Peter Brown, "Sorcery, Demons and the Rise of Christianity: From Late Antiquity Into the Middle Ages," in *Witchcraft Confessions and Accusations*, ed. Mary Douglas (New York: Harper & Row, 1972), 24–25, who notes specifically the case of Libanius.
68. Percentage derived from Faraone, *Ancient Greek Love Magic*, 43 n. 9. Jason of the Argonauts is a rare exception in Pindar's *Pythian Ode* 4:217. On the preponderance of male attraction spells, see also Gager, *Curse Tablets*, 244–45; Winkler,

Constraints, 72; and Fritz Graf, *Magic in the Ancient World*, trans. Franklin Philip (Cambridge: Harvard University Press, 1997), 185.

69. Matthew Dickie, "Who Practices Love-Magic," 567, argues that the female targets of erotic magic were largely prostitutes or lower-class women of ill-repute, who were sexually experienced and available or could be easily made available with magical assistance. Even in this case, however, magic would interfere with and subvert other men's rights to these women, including owners of prostitute-slaves and men in relationships with concubines. Dickie often cites evidence from early Christian writers, but in this case he does not. According to the stereotype in early Christian writings (first to third century), men used magic to target chaste virgins of the church. See note 71.
70. Faraone, *Ancient Greek Love Magic*, 166.
71. Only early Christian writings represent the situation more accurately, although there as well the portrayals of women's responses to men's magic conform to ideological and theological scripts and cannot be read as merely descriptive and unbiased. See Stratton, *Naming the Witch*, 138–39. Gager, *Curse Tablets*, 80–81, argues that even the relatively small number of erotic spells commissioned by women demonstrate female agency and sexual subjectivity. Of course, there is always the likelihood that women's magic tended to use more perishable household items that do not survive in the archaeological record, in which case the material record is skewed toward representing men's magic. See Richard Gordon, "Aelian's Peony: The Location of Magic in Graeco-Roman Tradition," *Comparative Criticism* 9 (1987): 64–65; and Richard Gordon, "Lucan's Erictho," in *Homo Viator: Classical Essays for John Bramble*, ed. Michael Whitby, et al. (Bristol: Bristol Classical, 1987), 231–41. See also Dickie, "Who Practices Love-Magic," 567, 573–76, for examples of erotic magic on behalf of women.
72. Fritz Graf, *Magic in the Ancient World*, 186.
73. Winkler, *Constraints*, 97.
74. Richlin, "Approaches to the Sources on Adultery at Rome," 391–93; Kate Cooper, *The Virgin and the Bride*, 13. While Edwards, *The Politics of Immorality*, 51–52, notes that there does not appear to have been much concern about confirming children's paternity in ancient Rome (despite the claim that aristocratic women were rampantly committing adultery), she does suggest that accusations and fears of poisoning symbolically reflect "concern with women's capacity to 'pollute' their husbands' lines by conceiving children in adulterous relationships."

    On the similar problem of establishing paternity in classical Athens, see Adele C. Scafuro, "Witnessing and False Witnessing: Proving Citizenship and Kin Identity in Fourth-Century Athens," in *Athenian Identity and Civic Ideology*, ed. Alan Boegehold and Adele Scafuro (Baltimore and London: Johns Hopkins University Press, 1994), 156–98; David Konstan, "Premarital Sex, Illegitimacy, and Male Anxiety in Menander and Athens," in *Athenian Identity and Civic Ideology*, ed. Alan Boegehold and Adele Scafuro (Baltimore and London: Johns Hopkins University

Press, 1994), 217–35; Cynthia Patterson, "The Case Against Neaira and the Public Ideology of the Athenian Family," in *Athenian Identity and Civic Ideology*, ed. Alan Boegehold and Adele Scafuro (Baltimore and London: Johns Hopkins University Press, 1994), 199–216; and Alan Boegehold, "Perikles' Citizenship Law of 451/0 B.C.," in *Athenian Identity and Civic Ideology*, ed. Alan Boegehold and Adele Scafuro (Baltimore and London: Johns Hopkins University Press, 1994), 57–66.

75. Gager, *Curse Tablets*, 22; Faraone, "The Agonistic Context", 8.
76. *PGM* I.248–49, eye of an ape or someone who died violently (*nekuos biothanatou*); *PGM* IV.2886, blood of someone who suffered violence (*Biaiou haima*); *PGM* VII.186–90 foot of a blood-eating gecko; *PGM* 11.45–49, brain and right hoof of black ram, brain of ibis, as well as clothing of someone who died violently. This spell also requires petitioner to walk backward, suggesting abjectionary inversion. *PGM* III.1–10 requires petitioner to drown a cat and blame violence on an enemy as a curse; *PGM* I.285, wolf's eye is an ingredient, but may be code for an innocuous plant substance. See Lynn R. LiDonnici, "Beans, Fleawort, and the Blood of a Hamadryas Baboon: Recipe Ingredients in Greco-Roman Magical Materials," in *Magic and Ritual in the Ancient World*, ed. Paul Mirecki and Marvin Meyer (Leiden: Brill, 2002) 359–77.
77. David Frankfurter, "Fetus Magic and Sorcery Fears in Roman Egypt," *Greek, Roman, and Byzantine Studies* 46 (2006): 37–62.
78. It is possible that literary depictions influenced the practice of actual magic. See Kimberly Stratton, "Magic in the Greco-Roman World up to and Including the Republic," in *Cambridge History of Magic and Witchcraft in the West*, ed. David J. Collins (New York: Cambridge University Press, forthcoming).
79. See the discussion of the Primal Abject, below.
80. Gager, *Curse Tablets*, 9–10; S. J. Tambiah, "The Magical Power of Words," *Man* 3 (1986): 171–208; Patricia Cox Miller, "In Praise of Nonsense," in *Classical Mediterranean Spirituality*, ed. A. H. Armstrong (New York: Crossroad, 1986), 481–505.
81. Kristeva, *Powers of Horror*, 6–7.
82. Noëlle McAfee, *Julia Kristeva* (New York: Routledge, 2004), 29.
83. McAfee, *Julia Kristeva*, 18.
84. Ibid, 35.
85. Ibid, 48.
86. Kristeva, *Powers of Horror*, 13, italics original.
87. Kelly Oliver, *Reading Kristeva: Unraveling the Double-Bind (Bloomington: Indiana University Press, 1993)*, 55.
88. Kristeva, *Powers of Horror*, 10.
89. Oliver, *Reading Kristeva*, 56.
90. Ibid, 58.
91. McAfee, *Julia Kristeva*, 48–49. This can be confirmed, perhaps, by Amy Richlin's findings that "female genitalia are compared in Latin with foul, wet, enclosed spaces and with the enclosure of the tomb." See Richlin, "Invective," 74.

92. Oliver, *Reading Kristeva*, 160.
93. "Nevertheless, no matter what differences there may be among societies where religious prohibitions, which are above all behavior prohibitions, are supposed to afford protection from defilement, one sees everywhere the importance, both social and symbolic, of women and particularly the mother." Kristeva, *Powers of Horror*, 70.
94. Kristeva, *Powers of Horror*, 70.

PART II

Gender and Magic Discourse in Practice

6

Magic Accusations against Women in Tacitus's Annals

Elizabeth Ann Pollard

IN HIS SYSTEMATIC study of "Women on Trial before the Roman Senate," Anthony Marshall counted in Tacitus a total of thirty-nine trials[1] that were prosecuted against women in the first century CE.[2] Nine of these thirty-nine trials, fully one-quarter, include what might be understood as accusations of the use of *artes magicae* in some form or another. Charges related to the *artes magicae* rank second in number only after *maiestas*, or treason, for which there were seventeen trials, and followed by a close third of adultery, of which there are eight trials. Several of these treason and adultery trials overlap with the cases concerned with *artes magicae*.[3]

What constitutes an accusation of *artes magicae* for the purposes of this counting? Some scholars have suggested that magic accusations were merely a convenient way to attack one's enemy.[4] In some of the later cases during the reign of the Julio-Claudians, especially the accusations by Agrippina Minor and her son Nero, convenient attack does seem to be *part* of what is happening. When desirous of removing a political opponent, a suggestion of *malum venenum* or of *divinatio* certainly seems to have been effective for this last Julio-Claudian. Throughout the first century CE, women could face accusations under a number of different guises, all of which are often translated into English as magic or sorcery: *maleficium*, *veneficium*, *venena*, *artes*, *carmina*, *devotiones*, and asking questions of *Chaldei* and *Magi*.

Before going any further with the legal definition of *artes magicae*, though, it is important to recognize the sociological aspects of magic accusations. Despite the potential pitfalls of such interdisciplinary enterprises, anthropological models can help us to get beyond what may have been transpiring legally; they can also help us to make sense of the social tensions at the heart of accusations of magic against women at imperial Rome. Groundbreaking work by Keith Thomas and Alan Macfarlane on the dynamics of witchcraft accusations in early modern

English villages has certainly demonstrated the value of such an approach and many scholars of witchcraft studies have since followed their example.[5] One heuristic that could help to explain the climate of witchcraft accusation at Rome in the first century CE is the model offered by Mary Douglas in her introduction to a collection of essays written to honor the retirement of Sir Edward Evans-Pritchard, whose *Witchcraft, Oracles, and Magic among the Azande* has been so influential on witchcraft studies since its publication in 1937. Douglas writes about how "ambiguous," "competitive," and "unregulated" relationships can lead to accusations of the use of magic. The relationships amongst the women in the Tacitean accounts certainly fit that description. Another of Douglas's categories for the accused, a person who "comes into an altogether anomalous position of advantage or disadvantage," is also a factor in understanding the accusations laid against certain women in Tacitus's *Annals*.[6] Douglas notes that when an accusation of the use of magic is laid against someone within a given community, in our cases women of the imperial ruling elite of Rome, the accused is either the member of a rival faction, a dangerous deviant, or an internal enemy with outside liaisons.[7] When the accused is a member of a rival faction, the accusation "redefine[s] faction boundaries or realign[s] faction hierarchy."[8] Douglas's model for witchcraft accusation sheds light not only on why certain women are accused of using *artes magicae* by their contemporaries, but also on the ways in which Tacitus crafts his accounts in order to magnify the accusations.

This chapter addresses the accusations of the use of *artes magicae* against women in Tacitus's *Annals* in three distinct sections. The first section briefly reviews some of the problems in defining *artes magicae*, focusing on the legal definitions in order to set the context for these accusations as they are reported by Tacitus. Section two examines closely the ways in which Tacitus shapes his accounts of the accusations against two women in particular: Munatia Plancina and Aemilia Lepida, prosecuted in the same year. Section two also reviews Tacitus's presentation of the accusations of *artes magicae* against other women. The third section extrapolates from these nine instances of magic accusations against women in Tacitus's *Annals* in order to draw some conclusions about how these accusations fit within Tacitus's history telling and how his depictions also reflected genuine sociological developments in first-century CE imperial Rome. Tacitus achieves more than merely the completion of his overall negative portrait of women in positions of power. An application of Douglas's theory shows how Tacitus's accounts demonstrate that accusations of *artes magicae* against women served three purposes: to help negotiate competitive and unregulated relationships between women of power, for example, the antagonistic relationship between Agrippina Maior and Munatia Plancina; to allow contemporary observers to deal with a group of people who are suddenly in an unexpected position of social power, such as the wives of governors and senators; and to allow for the realignment of factional hierarchy amongst noble families in the early Empire, especially the Aemilii Lepidi.

Legal Definitions of Artes Magicae

The debate concerning how to define "magic" in general, and in the Roman world in particular, has burned hotly in the last century. Much of this debate centers on how to differentiate magic from religion. Modern attempts simply to distinguish between what might be called magic and religion have focused on: the possible malignant goals of magic versus the beneficent intentions of religion,[9] the individual as opposed to the corporate aspect,[10] ritualism versus piety/belief,[11] the primitive as opposed to the evolved,[12] the peripheral as opposed to the central,[13] and similarly the foreign and hostile as opposed to the indigenous,[14] activity by women and low-class men as opposed to social superiors,[15] furtive/clandestine versus public,[16] coercive as opposed to supplicative,[17] accessing supernatural powers (right or wrong) for right or wrong ends[18] and the related illegal as opposed to legal.[19] Some attempts have been made to describe magic as a component of religion, similar to other rituals such as sacrifice or prayer.[20] Many attempts at defining magic categorize it as either "bad religion" as these previous dichotomies suggest, or when it comes to comparison to "medicine," magic is "bad science."[21] Ancient writers certainly expressed some of these distinctions, but there was by no means any consensus in antiquity on what set the *artes magicae* apart.

Recognizing the protean nature of magic in antiquity is certainly vital to any discussion of magic accusation. S. I. Johnston, examining contributions to the scholarship on the topic, urged the creation of provisional and flexible categories for the purpose of making progress in the study of magic.[22] P. Green, also reviewing books on magic, seems to favor getting away from the knots into which theoreticians on Greco-Roman magic have tied themselves and instead supports a more empirical approach.[23] Both Johnston and Green, from their unique perspectives, have advocated—I think rightly—pulling ourselves out of this definitional quagmire and moving forward with research on various topics broadly understood as magic in a Greco-Roman context. Attempting to grab onto any one or a few of these distinctions would invariably result in our missing intriguing pieces of evidence for this analysis of Tacitean accounts and would no doubt give a false sense of simplicity concerning these activities. By focusing on the distinctions the *Romans* made and the legal charges that Tacitus himself records, we can provide limits for the study without limiting ourselves by this modern terminological debate.

Roman legal sources refer to, and group together, the range of phenomena as *magicae artes*, *crimen magicae*, *maleficium*, *scelus maleficiorum*, *mathematica*, and *veneficium*.[24] Other contemporary terms for these phenomena that we see in the sources include *magia*, and the Greek terms *mageia*, *mageias* and *goeteia*.[25] The various spoken practices that are associated with these phenomena in the fictional representations, laws, and historical narratives include the Latin *nefarias preces*, *devotionibus ac maleficiis*, *carmina*, *devotiones*, *nenia*, *incantamenta* and, in Greek, *odas* and *epodai*.[26] These might be translated as spells or incantations.[27] The terms used in the fictional representations, laws, and historical narratives for ingredients that might be used in these practices include *venena*, *poculum amoris*, *amatoria*, *Medeides herbae*, *philtra*, in the Latin and, in the Greek, *philtra*, *kaka pharmaka*, *pharmaka lugra*, *pharmakon oulomenon*.[28] Each of these terms might be translated with the sense of potion. The names that the laws and the historical authors attach to the people who do these things include *magus*, *Chaldeus*, *maleficus*, *veneficus*, and *mathematicus*.[29] When the reference is to a woman who does these things in the fictional imaginings, the terms used are, in Latin, *saga* and *maga*, and in Greek, *mageousas*, *polypharmakos*, and *pharmakis*.[30] The problem with translating any of these terms into English is that the translation often involves forms of the words magic or witchcraft, both of which are replete with modern overtones. Clearly the Romans had a number of interrelated legal and literary terms for what is translated into English as magic, sorcery, poisoning, and astrology.

Unfortunately, Roman laws do not tell us who was punished or how often the laws were enforced. For that we must rely on historical accounts of trials that seem to be prosecuted on the legal and imaginative bases outlined here. Previous scholarly treatments of these trials have not focused on the relationship of gender to the accusations of the use of the *artes magicae*. R. S. Rogers, Ronald Syme, A. J. Marshall, and Richard Talbert generally focus more on the procedures rather than the crafted representations of the trials.[31] Marshall takes the procedural considerations one step further to explore how women's cases before the Senate suggest that women were more active political players than was generally thought to be the case. Still, none of these scholars considers how the recounting of the trials might reflect genuine sociological developments in the relationships among women at Rome. With this review of the classification of *artes magicae* in the laws complete, we can now turn to how Tacitus may indeed have shaped his accounts in such ways that make sense not only in literary, legal, and historical terms, but also in terms of modern sociological and anthropological theories of witchcraft accusation.

Tacitus's Crafting of the Cases against Munatia Plancina and Aemilia Lepida

The intricacies of accusation and its social function are particularly intriguing in Tacitus's juxtapositioning of two cases that occurred in the same year, 20 CE: the cases against Munatia Plancina and Aemilia Lepida. Family, class, and social connections play a prime role in how Tacitus shapes his depiction of these two cases. In Plancina's case, popular opinion was hotly against the woman who was acquitted; in Aemilia Lepida's case, popular opinion was very much in her favor, and yet she was convicted.

Before analyzing these cases, it is important to note that while Tacitus, as a writer, crafts his accounts to achieve certain ends, he is recounting events from the relatively recent past and, as a historian, must maintain some semblance of historical accuracy. Any analysis of Tacitus must keep that in mind. Francesca Santoro L'Hoir has expertly explored how Tacitus utilizes the rhetorical "topos of the unchaste poisoner" drawing from a range of source material including Greek tragedy, Cicero, and Quintilian.[32] Focusing on topoi and describing women such as Plancina, Agrippina, Pulchra, et al. as "characters" and "personae," however, denies these real women the agency and actions that inspired the historical accusations in the first place. Tacitus's rhetorical fashioning certainly influences what he emphasizes and even why the topos was profoundly effective, but his rhetoric does not explain what these historical agents did (or were thought by their contemporaries to have done), nor does it explain the historical circumstances within which the accusations balanced the complex, competitive nexus of the Roman aristocracy.

The limits of crafting in mind, then, we see that Tacitus does not lay bare the legal case against Munatia Plancina as directly as he might have. If "magic" were such a convenient stock charge, as Phillips and Matthews have suggested, why does Tacitus hold back?[33] It is certainly not because he is disinterested in writing about women. Book Three of the *Annals* is replete with discussions concerning women: including several trials for various crimes, a debate on whether or not wives should accompany their husbands into the provinces, and instances of Livia's continued influence on her son, Tiberius.[34] Plancina just so happens to be at the center of each of these issues. She was a woman of the nobility, with a censor and a consul in her near family and a close personal friendship with the empress Livia.[35] Livia's son, the emperor Tiberius, and Plancina's husband, Gnaeus Piso, had been consuls together in 7 BCE.[36] When Gnaeus later became governor of Syria, Plancina went with him into that province.

Annals 2.69–83 offers the most extended recounting of the death of Germanicus, the heir of Tiberius and darling of the Empire, and the involvement of Piso and Plancina in that death.[37] *Annals* 3.10–18 and 6.26.4 record the legal proceedings against Plancina and Piso that follow Germanicus's death.[38] Tacitus focuses on the charges against Piso, with only asides concerning Plancina here and there.[39] The passage in Tacitus which recounts the implements with which Piso allegedly facilitated Germanicus's death highlights many of the same activities classified as magic in both the fictional accounts and the law: the remains of human bodies, spells, curses, leaden tablets inscribed with Germanicus's name, charred and blood-smeared ashes, and other magical instruments that were thought to devote the soul to the powers of the grave.[40]

In Tacitus's account, the only link explaining Piso's knowledge of how to use these magical materials was Plancina's friendship with a certain Martina. Tacitus describes Martina as a woman who was infamous in Syria for poisonings (*infamis veneficiis*) and a dear friend of Plancina (*Plancinae percara*).[41] Vitellius and the other prosecutors of the case against Piso and Plancina summoned Martina to Rome to act as a witness.[42] But Martina never made it to court. She died under mysterious circumstances at Brundisium. Poison (*venenum*) was found knotted in her hair. Even though she had the means to kill herself with this hidden *venenum*, observers considered that suicide was unlikely.[43]

In Plancina's case, it is often what Tacitus does not explain that implicates Plancina all the more: this mysterious death of the one woman who might have been able to verify whence the poison was acquired and the secret talks that Livia seems to have had with Plancina.[44] When the verdict against Piso became clear, Plancina was even the last person to see her husband alive.[45] Tacitus suggests that foul play in Piso's death was likely. In one of Piso's final notes, which was read posthumously before the courtroom, Piso requested leniency for his children. With respect to Plancina, Piso said absolutely nothing, perhaps assuming that she had made her own arrangements.[46]

So, in Tacitus's account, why did Piso alone suffer for the crime if his wife was equally, if not more, guilty? Plancina clearly sided with her husband until the trial looked hopeless for him. Only at that point did she separate her own defense from his and call upon her ties with Livia in order to obtain her pardon.[47] Tacitus recounts that, even after Piso's death, a two-day trial took place to consider just the case against Plancina.[48] The *senatus consultum de Gnaeo Pisone Patre*[49] lists no specific charges against Plancina, noting only that there were numerous weighty charges lodged against her, *pluruma et gravissuma crimina*.[50] According to this senatorial decree, Plancina's relationship with Livia led to her acquittal. As mentioned earlier, these connections may have extended back at least twenty-seven years, to Tiberius's and Gnaeus's shared consulship. The *senatus consultum*'s praise of Julia Augusta, that is, of Livia, which is centered on her maternity of the princeps, his devotion to her, her kindness, her sparing use of her deserved great influence, attempts to justify Tiberius's intercession on Plancina's behalf at his mother's behest.[51] Plancina does not stand by her man as one might expect of the good Roman *matrona*; she flees to the protection of the most powerful woman in the Empire.[52]

The text of the senatorial decree dealing with Piso's case further records the senate's judgment as regards Piso and his children. The charges associated with the *artes magicae*, which receive so much attention in Tacitus, do not appear at all in this decree. How do we explain this silence? I would suggest that it is because

Plancina escapes punishment at the time of the trial that none of these charges actually appears in the *senatus consultum*, but instead, as regards Plancina, only a long, almost shame-faced, explanation of Tiberius's intercession at Livia's request remains. This lacuna in the *senatus consultum*, joined with Martina's crucial and unfulfilled role in the prosecution, suggests that Plancina, not Piso, was the one who would have been charged with these magical attacks. This is not merely an argument from silence. When Plancina receives her pardon, Tacitus reports that the gossip among the elite was that Plancina was a murderess (*interfectrix*) who had been rescued from the Senate, that Tiberius and his mother had defended Plancina (Piso is not mentioned), and that "consequently [Plancina] might now turn those drugs and arts (*venena et artes*), so favorably tested, against Agrippina [and] against her children."[53]

Tacitus makes it clear that Plancina, not Piso, was believed to be the mastermind of the *venena et artes*, which had led to Germanicus's death and Piso's downfall.[54] As Germanicus had lain dying, he claimed that he had been cut off by the wickedness of *both* Piso and Plancina.[55] Perhaps more telling was his deathbed assertion that he had fallen by the treachery of a woman (*muliebri fraude cecidisse*).[56] The final stamp of Plancina's guilt, Tacitus tells us, is that thirteen years later, only four years after Livia died, Plancina was "arraigned on charges well-known to the world."[57] She was found guilty and committed suicide. Once her highly placed ally Livia was gone, Plancina joined her husband in death.

Christopher Pelling discusses the narrative techniques by which Tacitus mirrors his characterizations of Piso and Germanicus; Piso's last letter as compared to Germanicus's closing speech, their response to threats, their republican ancestry, and their openness. Pelling notes that "Piso . . . finds his leading traits reinforced by the character of his wife. Violence, pride and truculence are hardly Germanicus's characteristics, though (interestingly) they are Agrippina's."[58] Perhaps Tacitus is working out the mirrored tellings of Piso and Germanicus even further through the depictions of their wives. While Plancina was the craftily presented user of *artes magicae* who ultimately gets her due, Agrippina Maior is the perpetual victim of *artes magicae*, either in the death or accusations of those close to her.

To sum up the magic accusations against Plancina, then, there is a senatorial decree that mentions very little about Plancina and nothing about magical charges and a heavily crafted historical account that lays on the charges thickly against the husband and includes enough detail and innuendo to implicate the woman who was initially pardoned but later found guilty. The *venena*, the *artes*, the blood-smeared ashes, and the leaden tablets all drew on the legal and literary imaginings of how *artes magicae* worked. There are hints of women's secretly shared knowledge, between Plancina and Martina and between Plancina and Livia, as well as suggestions of the mysterious "other" in the barbarous description of Martina and her poison-knotted hair that begins to call to mind such fictional characters as Canidia and Folia in Horace, with their remarkably unbound, and hence unmatronly, hair.[59] Plancina is a woman who does not know her proper place. Not keeping herself in the proper manner for ladies (*nec Plancina se intra decora feminis tenebat*), Plancina attended military exercises and involved herself in politics.[60] Finally, Tacitus also does not miss the opportunity to connect women's lust with the probable use of magical attacks. Tacitus's treatment of Germanicus's death closes with a recounting of a law passed to limit the lust (*libido*) of women by restricting the classes of women who could be prostitutes and another law that aimed to banish the rites of the Egyptians and Jews.[61] Although not explicitly linked by Tacitus, it seems that the historian might have assumed that his reader would easily have made the logical transition between discussions of legal prosecutions of *artes magicae* against Piso and Plancina and women's unbounded lust as epitomized by high-class prostitutes.[62] Again, with the reference to Egyptians and Jews, the Eastern and the lustful connections of *artes magicae*, so crucial to the case concerning Germanicus's death, are brought to the reader's mind.

In terms of the social implications, à la Mary Douglas, of these accusations, we have two women, Plancina and Agrippina Maior, with little direct access to power and few other means of social negotiation, battling it out through accusations of the use of *artes magicae*.[63] Women who were described as *atrox*, like Agrippina Maior and later her daughter, not only strived against other women but they also "aspire[d] toward a masculine role" in ways that genuinely seemed to threaten writers like Tacitus.[64] This is not just an empty literary threat, however; Agrippina Maior and Plancina are both characterized by Tacitus as *duces feminae*, women who place themselves at the heads of military forces.[65] These two women held unregulated positions of social power, and after the death of Germanicus, Agrippina found herself in an "anomalous position of social disadvantage," to use Mary Douglas's terminology. Agrippina, who went from the position of next-in-line to be empress of Rome to being merely the widow of Germanicus with no political future, was a woman who nevertheless held some claim to the vast client base of her dead husband. Her social connections are a central element of Tacitus's narrative: for example, Germanicus is said to have urged those who would prosecute Piso and Plancina for his impending death to consider Agrippina's role as granddaughter of Augustus, wife of Germanicus, and mother of six children (i.e., potential imperial heirs).[66] Agrippina exercised so much power and influence that even Tiberius seems to have been troubled by it: years later, in the context of magic accusations against her friend Claudia Pulchra, he refuses Agrippina's requests to remarry and tells her that she is not "a woman injured, if she lacked a throne."[67] When Agrippina's husband was killed, her basis for power through her marriage to the man designated to be the next emperor was cut out from under her. This unaccustomed position of social disadvantage would understandably have spurred her to lash out in some way against the powerful woman she saw as being to blame, Munatia Plancina. Germanicus seems to have seen this coming when on his deathbed he urged Agrippina to "strip herself of pride" and never to "irritate those stronger than herself by a competition for power (*aemulatione potentiae*)."[68] Accusations of using *artes magicae* would have been one way for Agrippina Maior to ignore Germanicus's pleas and to achieve retribution against her enemy Plancina.

The power and influence Plancina derived as the wife of a governor in such an important province as Syria, with its significant legionary strength and border with ever-threatening Parthia, would have put her in an "anomalous position of social advantage" that would have been uncomfortable for her contemporaries. Plancina presumably built up her own client base while accompanying her husband, Piso, when he served as governor in the province of Syria.[69] For example, her receipt of gifts from Vonones, the briefly reigning, Augustus-backed, Parthian ruler, certainly placed her at the heart of a very touchy foreign relations issue. The senator who comes to Piso's and presumably Plancina's legal defense (before she separated hers from his) demonstrates even further the nexus of social relations playing out in this magic accusation. This lawyer for Piso's, and likely Plancina's, defense is a Lepidus—either Manius or Marcus (the textual tradition is unclear).[70] This could be the Lepidus who was listed by Augustus as *capax imperii*, (i.e., capable of being his successor in lieu of Tiberius), or it could be his cousin.[71] Whichever Lepidus it is, coming to the defense of Piso and Plancina is a man from a powerful Republican family, members of which were a triumvir with Augustus and Antony and were even handpicked as Augustus's potential successors. This defense suggests that Plancina and her husband were aligned with a family that could challenge Tiberius's right to rule, and by Douglas's model, would be appropriate and expected targets of magic accusation.

The genuine social tension between Plancina, Agrippina, and their families continues in Tacitus's recounting of the case against Aemilia Lepida, who was also tried in 20 CE. Tacitus offers the case against Aemilia Lepida, former wife of Quirinius, yet another governor of Syria, as a clear foil to Plancina's role in Germanicus's death.[72] Whereas in the former case Tiberius interceded for Plancina's acquittal, in the latter case, Tiberius's position is more difficult to determine.[73] He does, however, ultimately deliver the final damning evidence that Lepida's slaves had revealed under torture, namely that she had made an attempt on her husband's life by *venena*. The charges brought against Aemilia Lepida, as Tacitus recounts them, demonstrate a certain unity. Her "rich and childless" ex-husband Publius Quirinius accused her of feigning to be a mother (*defertur simulavisse partum*). Adulteries (*adulteria*), poisoning (*venenum*), and inquiries made through the Chaldeans (*quaesitum per Chaldaeos*) with reference to the Caesarian house were added to the indictment (*adiciebantur*).[74] Tacitus's grouping of Aemilia Lepida's consultations of astrologers (*Chaldaei*), her alleged use of *venenum*, and her involvement in adultery should not be surprising given the later Roman law codes, which considered these crimes together as unpardonable offenses.[75]

But is there any closer relationship between the charges of poisoning, adultery, and illicit divination (all well within the range of expected legal magical charges) and those that Aemilia Lepida feigned birthing a child to Quirinius?[76] Breaking marital bonds is certainly typical of the lustful erotic *artes magicae* depicted in the contemporaneous novels. One need only call to mind the plots of the *magae* and *sagae* of Apuleius's *Metamorphoses* for this stereotype.[77] But what of the charges *de falsum*, of being a *suppostrix*? Such claims of illegitimate children may draw on the literary imagination of magic as well.[78] This linked charge is similar to one launched by the late first-century BCE poet Horace against Canidia, that famed literary practitioner of *artes magicae*. In the same rhetorical jab, Horace sneers with sarcastic irony that she is "no old woman practiced in scattering ashes among the graves of the poor" (in other words, the sepulchral wanderings old female magic-practitioners were known to do) and, two lines later, that "the midwife washed rags red with your blood, however robustly you, a woman in labor, leaped up" (in other words, insinuating that it was not her blood on the birthing rags, given her post-parturient spryness).[79] In the same breath, Horace links Canidia's magic use and faked childbirthing. It is not surprising that Aemilia Lepida would be prosecuted for *venena* and astrology, along with *falsum*, if the trope from Horace holds.

Family connections and potential client bases play a role here as well. As the wife of Quirinius, governor of Syria around the time of the birth of Jesus, Aemilia Lepida may have had close eastern associates much like Plancina's Syrian friend Martina.[80] In addition, at one point, Aemilia Lepida makes appeals to her ancestry in her own defense. Tacitus reports how when games interrupted her trial, Lepida showed up at the theater of Pompey with a number of distinguished women. With a weeping lamentation and invocation by name of her ancestors, including Pompey himself, Lepida stirred up so great a sympathy that the crowd, shedding tears, cried out against Quirinius that he was betraying a woman who had been the destined wife of Lucius Caesar (and, although Tacitus does not say it, hence a woman who might have been empress if her betrothed had not died an early death, making room for Tiberius's own designation as Augustus's heir-apparent).[81] Lepida's ancestry included not only Pompeius Magnus but also L. Cornelius Sulla. Aemilia Lepida appeals to the memory of that same Sulla whose *lex Cornelia de sicariis et veneficiis* in 81 BCE enabled prosecutions against those who used *malum venenum*.[82] Given her appeal to innocence through invoking the anti-*venena* name of Sulla and given her childless union with Quirinius, one wonders whether the *venena* that Lepida was accused of using were love-philters to attempt to have a child by Quirinius. Such love potions were included under the legislation that discussed *veneficium*.[83] Even more interesting is who comes to her legal defense, namely her brother Manius Lepidus. Once again the lack of clarity in the Tacitean manuscript tradition foils our ability to be certain that the Manius Lepidus who here defends his sister on magic charges is the one who was *capax imperii* (1.13) or the same one who defends Piso and Plancina (3.11). But this is a tantalizing detail, that Piso and Plancina as well as Aemilia Lepida are defended by members of the Lepidus family, cousins if not the same man, in a family that would no doubt have been even more powerful were it not for the Julio-Claudian hold on the principate. Given Aemilia Lepida's family, any child she might have borne (or alleged to have borne) would have posed a legitimate threat to the Julio-Claudian claim to absolute rule. The initial charge that Lepida made "Chaldaean inquiries into the Caesarian house" takes on a much more ominous and specific meaning.

Hence, in his reporting of the case against Aemilia Lepida, Tacitus freely draws on the literary and legal depictions of *artes magicae*. The trope of Canidia's questionable motherhood and the legal grouping of *venenum*, divination, and adultery demonstrate that borrowing. But this accusation is a historical event demanding explanation, not just a rhetorical or literary topos. As with Plancina, once again we see accusations as a tool against powerful women. In this case, Aemilia Lepida, a woman with powerful family connections, finds herself to be the object of accusation. One can see perhaps the third element of Douglas's model for accusation working itself out: that of the realignment of factional hierarchy. In this case, Aemilia Lepida's near relatives were *capax imperii*, and she herself might have been empress had her betrothed not met an untimely end. Her ancestry goes back not only to Pompey, the rival of Caesar, the founder of the now ruling line, but in addition, her family, the Aemilii Lepidi, is a powerful faction from the Republic that has very little power in the early Empire.[84] The accusations against her both draw on that family's traditional Eastern connections and serve to undermine her entire lineage. Thus, the manner in which her contemporaries accuse her and the way that Tacitus depicts the accusations, re-inscribing fictional stereotypes, reveal the multiple layers, both historical and stylized, of accusation and how they work to negotiate social relationships—not just between women but also among the powerful families from which these women come.

Other Accusations against Women Related to Artes Magicae *in Tacitus'* Annals

A brief recounting of each of the remaining trials of women for various *artes magicae* considers the exact charges lodged against these women, how Tacitus crafts these accounts, and how new light is shed on them by applying Douglas's theories of magic accusation. In 24 CE, Fabia Numantina was brought up on charges of *carmina* and *veneficium* after her ex-husband, Plautius Silvanus, was under suspicion for flinging his current wife out a window.[85] The thinking behind the charge was probably that Numantina's use of aphrodisiacs, or even the equivalent of what Faraone would call *philia* magic (to lure back her former husband), could have driven him insane to the point of killing his new wife. The ex-husband in question was the grandson of Urgulania, a close friend of Livia.[86] When Urgulania sent a dagger to her grandson, he took it as a hint to commit suicide. R. Develin argues that Tacitus uses the verb *credere* in this passage to distance himself from a conclusion he clearly wishes his readers to draw, namely that in this case when Urgulania sends the dagger it is a message from Tiberius (through Livia) to commit suicide.[87] The effect, if not intent, of Urgulania's intervention, was to shield Numantina from prosecution due to a lack of evidence as a result of her ex-husband's death. Thanks to her former grandmother-in-law's intercession, Numantina was subsequently acquitted of driving Plautius Silvanus insane with *carmina* and *veneficium*. Urgulania's involvement is particularly notable given that Plautius's and Numantina's trials come just after Calpurnius Piso's death prior to his trial on charges of keeping *venenum*.[88] This is the same Piso, brother and co-defender of Gnaeus, who had tried to bring Urgulania to court because of his anger about influence exerted on the state by Livia and Urgulania.[89] The same women's network of power (Livia-Urgulania) that had bothered Calpurnius Piso enough to bring a charge against Urgulania that resulted in his own death may have been at play in the vindication of Numantina. That a grandmother, at the behest of her friend Livia, would convince her own grandson to commit suicide amidst this climate of magic accusation demonstrates just how complex were the power struggles taking place among the nobility at this time and how accusations against women were one of the ways these struggles were negotiated.

Friends in high places, however, do not always aid one's case, but could prompt accusations, as we might expect from Douglas's sociology of witchcraft accusations. In 26 CE, Claudia Pulchra, second cousin of Agrippina Maior and widow of the Varus who famously lost three Augustan legions in the Teutoberg forest in 9 CE, was prosecuted by Domitius Afer and found guilty on charges of unchastity.[90] Other charges included having a certain Furnius as her lover, attempted poisonings and casting spells against the emperor (*veneficia in principem et devotiones obiectabat*).[91] Agrippina claims this prosecution has been undertaken solely to trouble her.[92] Pulchra's case firmly demonstrates how charges of sexual misconduct and treasonous plots could be linked with *artes magicae*, in particular *veneficia* and *devotiones*. For Tacitus, what Pulchra may or may not have done seems less important in this particular account than his desire to trace the character development of the grieving widow of Germanicus, Agrippina Maior, who resented being deprived of power as a result of the death of her husband, the former heir, and who was attacked through the targeting of her friends.

In the next generation of Germanicus's family, his daughter Agrippina Minor takes her mother's place as the thorn in the imperial side. Whereas Agrippina Maior and her friends had been the victims of magic use (Germanicus) and magic accusation (Claudia Pulchra), Agrippina Minor uses magic and magic accusation to her advantage.[93] More than twenty years after the trial of Claudia Pulchra, Agrippina Minor, allegedly out of jealousy, targets Lollia Paulina with charges of magic.[94] In 49 CE, Lollia is charged with consorting with Chaldeans (*obiceret Chaldeos*) and questioning *magi* (*magos interrogatum*), as well as seeking information from the image of Clarian Apollo about Claudius's marriage to Agrippina.[95] This wealthy former wife of Caligula had been a rival to the younger Agrippina when Claudius was choosing his next wife after the debacle of his marriage to the meretricious Messalina.[96] Claudius himself speaks against Lollia and she is exiled but soon afterward forced to commit suicide. Anthony Barrett suggests that these accusations against Lollia are consistent with "behavior considered typical of would-be traitors."[97]

What is really happening here may well be answered by Douglas's model for witchcraft accusations. These accusations are working out competitive and unregulated relationships among powerful women and their families, including especially the would-be wives of emperors. In this case, an imperial woman (Agrippina Minor) and wife of the emperor targets for accusation a former imperial wife with less social power and privilege in much the same way that less well-connected people are often targeted for accusations of witchcraft due to the perceived potential harm their envy could bring. There is more going on here, however, than jealous rivalry and deflecting envy. Lollia Paulina's wealth was extreme.[98] In other words, she had the money to make real trouble for the Julio-Claudian dynasty. Claudius says as much when he says that her resources for wickedness must be removed. To use Douglas's phrases, Lollia Paulina was clearly in a competitive relationship with Agrippina Minor (as a former imperial wife and a rival for Claudius), and her vast wealth afforded her an "anomalous position of advantage" that needed diffusing.[99]

Another case against a woman for consulting astrologers occurred later in the reign of Claudius. In 52 CE, Vibia and her son, L. Furius Arruntius Scribonianus, were indicted for their alleged attempts to inquire through Chaldeans into Claudius's death (*finem principis per Chaldeos scrutaretur*).[100] Her husband had been the L. Arruntius Camillus Scribonianus who had instigated an aborted revolt of Dalmatian legions under his command ten years prior. Tacitus makes explicit reference back to this revolt and Vibia's relegation by the Senate on account of it.[101] Tacitus raises suspicion that Camillus might have died by poison (*venenum*) while in exile for this revolt. It is quite possible that Tacitus is attempting to cast suspicion on Vibia for this poisoning along with her astrological consultations. Vibia is portrayed almost like a Plancina character: a fomenter of her husband's rebellious activities in the provinces, avoiding punishment for a decade and possibly capable of poisoning, as well.[102] She is a woman who, as a widow, is acting outside the expected role of a proper *matrona*. Along the lines of the sociological implications of witchcraft accusations, she could be seen as a member of a rival faction who must be brought down. In terms of the way that Tacitus stylizes his presentation, it is interesting to note that Tacitus presents this case just prior to the mention of the expulsion of astrologers from Italy and the reward voted to Pallas for his part in developing a law that penalized women who married slaves. The proposer of this reward is none other than the consul-designate Barea Soranus, whose daughter's astrological consultations contribute to his demise, as we shall see in the case of Marcia Servilia.[103] For Tacitus, his discussion of Vibia is consistent with treasonous concerns relating to *mathematici* and women who confound their social station with inappropriate marriages.

Agrippina Minor's interests take center stage again in the charges against Domitia Lepida in 54 CE.[104] Domitia Lepida was the mother of Messalina (the late wife of Claudius) and sister-in-law of Agrippina by the latter's earlier marriage to Cn. Domitius Ahenobarbus (cos. 32 CE) and sister-in-law of Claudia Pulchra (sister of her husband M. Valerius Messala Barbatus). Tacitus represents Domitia and Agrippina as rivals, especially for influence over young Nero. Suetonius suggests another cause for their animosity: the charges of adultery and incest between Agrippina's husband and his sister, this very same Lepida. According to Suetonius, these charges were only dropped due to the *mutatione temporum*.[105] The exact charges against Lepida were that she used *devotiones* against Agrippina and failed to keep her slaves in Calabria in check. Lepida was sentenced to death. In the case of Lepida, suggestions of undue political influence, both in her influence over Nero and her control over her slaves, and her aberrant sexuality with her brother combine with accusations of magical activity in the form of *devotiones*. Here we have a woman with access to power in ways that her contemporaries find problematic. In terms of Mary Douglas's model, the accusations against her serve not only to undercut a woman in an anomalous position of power, they also serve to realign factional hierarchy in the otherwise unregulated and competitive relationship that Domitia Lepida and Agrippina have for control over Nero. The charges also fall in line with the expectations of accusations being leveled by one in a position of social advantage against an envying social inferior.

Twice, then, in the cases of Lollia Paulina and Domitia Lepida, Tacitus depicts Agrippina's jealousy as leading to charges of *artes magicae* against her rivals. As already mentioned, Douglas's description of the sociological implications of witchcraft accusations helps to explain this. Yet, according to Tacitus, Agrippina herself was not above employing her own expert in the *artes magicae*. Just as Munatia

Plancina apparently made use of the services of her friend Martina, possibly even to poison Agrippina's father Germanicus, Agrippina Minor herself employed the services of a certain Locusta.[106] Mentioned by Tacitus as having been lately condemned on a poisoning charge (*nuper veneficii damnata*), Locusta is employed by Agrippina to do away with Germanicus's brother, her husband/uncle Claudius. Locusta seems to be in the long-term service of Nero and his mother, as the poisoner of Claudius, his son Britannicus by Messalina, and supplier of the poison Nero intended to take while fleeing Rome in 68 CE.[107] Locusta was ultimately put to death by Galba, the briefly ruling successor to Nero.[108] Agrippina's employment of Locusta's services suggests that even women who cast accusations were not above employing others for the exact same activity themselves.

Once Agrippina succeeded in attaining the rule for her son, two other trials of women on related charges are presented by Tacitus. The accusations against Junia Lepida in 65 CE are presented as part of Nero's plot to deal with his rival Silanus.[109] In fact, Junia Lepida, daughter of M. Junius Silanus (cos. 19 CE) and Aemilia Lepida (step-niece of Claudia Pulchra by her grandfather's second marriage), was a member of the family that was vehemently and litigiously pursued by Caligula, Claudius, and Nero. Barry Baldwin notes that "[t]o a degree, it may be necessary to condemn the regime for persecuting the name [Silanus]."[110] Here we see again Douglas's point about the way in which witchcraft accusations realign factional hierarchies. As they did with the Aemilii Lepidi, the Julio-Claudian emperors seem to have made good use of such accusations in order to subdue the Junii Silani. In the case at hand, Tacitus suggests that the charges against Junia are fabricated. The exact charges were incest with her brother's son and horrible rites of unholy matters (*diros sacrorum ritus*). In the case of this apparently trumped-up charge to pursue further the enmity of the imperial line against the Junii Silani, Nero resorted to accusations entirely consistent with the contemporary literary imagination; the combination of imprecise charges related to *artes magicae* and improper sexual conduct. The *diros ritus* recall the legal definitions of proper, as opposed to subversive, *religio*.

The final case of an accusation of a woman's use of *artes magicae* in Tacitus is presented as a tragic melodrama. In 66 CE, Marcia Servilia was accused of consulting astrologers on her father's behalf.[111] More specifically, Servilia was charged with paying magicians (*pecuniam magis dilargita esset*) to conduct magical rites (*magicos sacros*) in order to determine the safety of her family and the possibility that her father's trial would end well. The scene of her aged father, who was accused of *maiestas*, and Servilia in tears, having already become a widow at the age of twenty, seems to have been constructed by Tacitus to elicit pathos in his readers. After the daughter and father make pleas before the Senate on each other's behalf, they attempt to rush to embrace one another and are prevented by lictors who come between them. The filial piety and drama is heightened in that this case is described just before the death scene of her father's co-defendant, Thrasea and his wife Arria. Although Thrasea discourages her suicide, this Arria was sure to call to the audience's mind the story of her mother, the Arria who stabbed herself to show her husband that it did not hurt to commit noble suicide.[112] Recalling such *pietas* after Servilia's death for attempting to help her father, albeit through magical means, only highlights Tacitus's aims in relating Servilia's *magica sacra.* The illegality of her actions is minimized in the light of Tacitus's sympathetic treatment of this tearful, obedient, desperate daughter and her death at the hands of the despotic Nero.

The Social Function of Magic Accusations against Women in Tacitus's Annals

Following this review of the evidence for the accusations and trials for activities related to the *artes magicae* in Tacitus's accounts, a few summary conclusions are possible. First, the accusations are often reported in conjunction with some suggestion of sexual misconduct on the part of the accused, whether adultery, incest, or even claiming to have borne a child who does not exist. This grouping is consistent with many of the literary depictions. The linking of *adulterium* with *artes magicae* is likewise to be found in the laws. Although Plancina does not appear to have broken any sexual mores, she did commit other sacrilege, such as her ill-timed festive celebrations after Germanicus's death. Her inappropriate celebrations placed her outside the role of a proper Roman matron in much the same way that the licentiousness of the other accused women depicts them as transgressing the proper role of a wife and mother. Frequently, but not always, the accused is implicated in a treasonous plot (*maiestas*) against the emperor, or in some other uprising such as that of Vibia, who in 52 CE is implicated in her husband's earlier rabble-rousing in Dalmatia, or Domitia Lepida, whose slaves in 54 CE are apparently making trouble in Calabria. Such women were seen as grasping at political connections and power, which would be inappropriate for a woman to exercise. Accusing these women of magical activities was a sure way to undermine their authority.

In terms of these social connections, quite often the woman who is the object of these accusations either gets help from, or suffers as a result of, a woman connected with the imperial household. We see this in the aid that Plancina received from Livia and arguably that which Numantina received from Urgulania, a close friend of Livia. Alternatively, the woman could be attacked due to her friendly associations with an imperial woman as happens with Claudia Pulchra, whom Tacitus says is only charged due to her relationship with Agrippina, widow of Germanicus. In addition, making a powerful enemy in a woman of the imperial family could result in accusations of magic, which constitute one of the few ways that imperial women could attack others, as we see with Agrippina Minor against both Lollia Paulina and Domitia Lepida. Competitive relationships amongst women of the upper classes, which have few other ways of being resolved, could lead to accusations of the use of the *artes magicae,* as well as assistance to those who have been accused.

Similarly, competitive relationships amongst ruling families led to accusations of women's use of *artes magicae*. Plotting these nine women accused of *artes magicae* onto a family tree demonstrates that five of them are related to one another by ties of blood and/or marriage (Figure 1). Aemilia Lepida, Fabia Numantina, Claudia Pulchra, Domitia Lepida, and Junia Lepida can all be charted on the same stemma, the central relative being Paullus Aemilius Lepidus the consul of 34 BCE.[113] Perhaps the traditional Eastern affiliation of the Aemilii Paulli clan gave this family and its women an air of mystery and intrigue, as well as the eastern and African client base, which might have been thought to know something of the magical arts.[114] More recent history—namely the Aemilius Lepidus who was a triumvir, the one who was *capax imperii*, and the one potentially designated by Caligula as a successor—showed this family to be a legitimate rival for Julio-Claudian dominance. Attacking these women was a way of attacking this family. Regardless, with each accusation, the women of this family became more and more susceptible to such charges. When considering the case of Domitia Lepida, she might have been all the more vulnerable to the accusation given that her sister-in-law, niece, and great aunt had all been more or less successfully prosecuted on charges of *artes magicae.*

For Tacitus, individuals could be on all sides of the power dynamic implicit in accusations of the use of *artes magicae*. For example, Agrippina Minor is the *victim* of *maleficium, veneficium,* and *venena,* through her father Germanicus's death. She is a *user* in her employment of the skilled poisoner Locusta against her enemies. Finally she is an *accuser* in the cases against her rivals Lollia Paulina and Domitia Lepida. Accusations of the use of *artes magicae* in the *Annals* could be legitimate grounds for legal action, tools for women's bickering, and the stuff of farcical melodrama. Going beyond Tacitus, another important issue that should be mentioned is the way in which magic accusations hurled against women by other women (and the class distinctions between upper-class women like Agrippina Minor, who *employ* magic users, and the lower-class women such as Martina and Locusta, who are *experts* in magic use) re-inscribed the patriarchal structures that bound all these women. Amy Richlin, in a study of Roman women's religion, has rightly pointed out how women's "rituals may have been used by one class of women to express their power over another class of women."[115] This same co-optation may well be playing out in magic use and accusation. The phenomenon of women accusing women has long been of interest to scholars of witchcraft accusation in all historical periods, wishing to dig deeper than the assumption

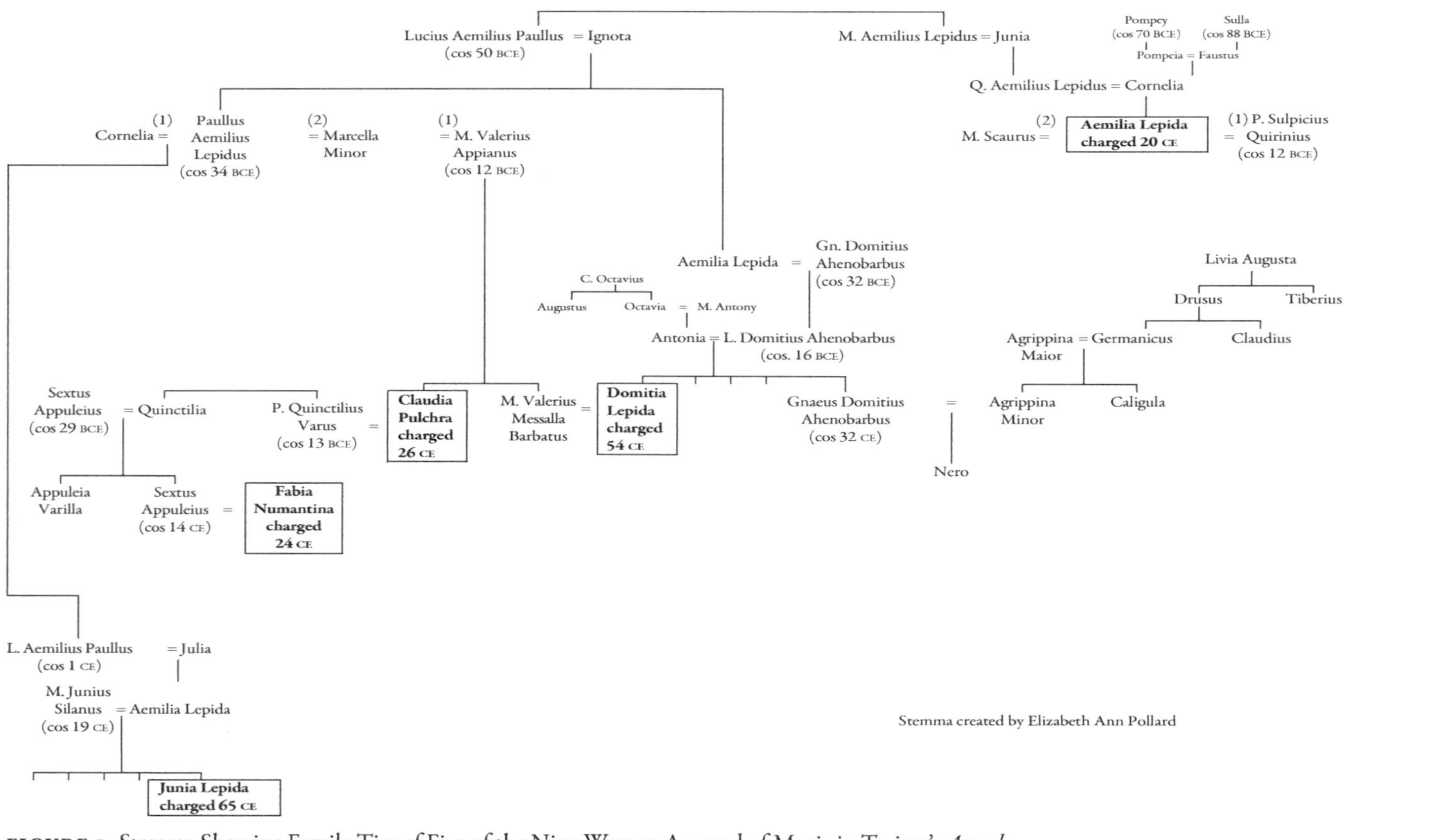

FIGURE 1 Stemma Showing Family Ties of Five of the Nine Women Accused of Magic in Tacitus's *Annals*.

that such accusations are blindly driven by misogyny, in order to determine women's complicity in those very accusations.[116] Application of Douglas's models for witchcraft accusation to this first-century context has revealed the strategic application of accusation by women against other women in order to work out their otherwise unmediated power struggles, with dramatic repercussions in the world of male politics.

In Tacitus's accounts of women's *artes magicae*, he moves from the serious charges against Plancina to the almost trivialized dramatic account of Servilia's astrological consultation, where this pious daughter, while being held apart from her father by lictors, begs in tears to be cleared of these exaggerated and trumped up charges. The prosecutable charges in Tacitus range from the use of *venena, carmina,* and *devotiones* and the hiring of professionals to accomplish these, to the consultation of astrologers, both *Chaldei* and *magi*. All the women accused in the courts are of the aristocracy. Of Martina and Locusta, the two experts, the former never has her day in court and the latter does not meet her end in the text of Tacitus. Six of our nine women are found guilty, and a seventh, Plancina, is initially acquitted through her friendship with Livia but convicted a decade later. An eighth, Vibia, is not mentioned as convicted or acquitted, only as spared by the emperor. In fact, only Fabia Numantina is acquitted of the charges against her. In Tacitus's accounts, these women are accused of having used *artes magicae* to gain the upper hand—either a better position for her husband, a better position for herself, or attempting to divine the future for the benefit of the men in her life. These charges are combined with women's sexual impropriety and their illegitimate attempts at social power in ways that are altogether consistent with the imaginings from the literary representations and the legal ideals.

Tacitus drew on the literary stereotypes of women who overstep sexual and social boundaries to transgress their appropriate roles as good wives and mothers. Perhaps to be expected, social connections among these noble, and often related, families determine the outcome of the trials. Friends in the highest of places, in our cases Livia Augusta and her close associate Urgulania, are the only possible deflectors of the charges of *artes magicae*. Enemies in the highest of places, whether the emperor or a powerful woman behind an emperor, such as Agrippina Minor with her influence over both Claudius and Nero, seem to guarantee a conviction. No consistent picture of the typical user, accuser, or victim of the *artes magicae* emerges. These charges are flung at women, by women and by men, in order to gain leverage within the ranks of the aristocracy. Lower-class magical experts, such as Martina and Locusta, are means to an end and are not prosecuted. Tacitus takes full advantage of this potential fluidity in who might accuse whom of using *artes magicae*. By making use of the trope of magical accusations, Tacitus casts these women in whatever light he desires: as unjustly acquitted, unjustly convicted by imperial rapacity, or convicted merely through the jealousy of another woman. It is worth noting, however, that quite often it is women who are accusing women of magic use. Given the female accusers, one would be hard-pressed to attribute these accounts merely to Tacitean, or even more broadly Roman, misogyny.

This discussion has drawn frequently from Mary Douglas's treatment of how accusations help to negotiate competitive and unregulated relationships. In our cases, these relationships are between women with power. Women such as Agrippina Maior and Munatia Plancina had few fora in which to play out their animosity and power struggles. Women's relationships of power with respect to one another had little formal outlet in Roman society. A woman in Agrippina Maior's situation, who was once next-in-line to be empress (as the wife of Germanicus the presumed heir), became much less powerful at his death. Against whom else might she lash out, but Plancina, the woman she felt had deprived her of her station? The second situation, which might precipitate an accusation of *artes magicae,* is a woman in an unexpected position of social power. Wives of governors in the provinces (such as Plancina and Aemilia Lepida in Syria), wealthy women such as Lollia Paulina, and female imperial advisors such as Domitia Lepida, certainly fall within that category. Finally, we turn to the possibility that these accusations could realign factional hierarchy or address an equilibrium that has been upset. Given the family stemma of several of the women prosecuted and its extension back to the Scipiones, a family conspicuously absent on the political scene since the demise of the Roman Republic, it is easy to see how the Lepidae might have presented a rival threat to the Julio-Claudian ruling elite. The accusations show a possible resolution of social tensions along the lines of what we might expect from sociological theory: the regulation of competitive relationships among women that otherwise had no formal rules, a diffusion of contemporary reaction against women in "anomalous positions of advantage," and, finally, the maintenance, worked out with the bodies and fates of women, of a balance of power amongst the ruling families of Rome.

Notes

1. This number includes the ten trials against women, which he catalogs as "dubious" senatorial trials.
2. Earlier versions of this material appear in my dissertation, *Magic Accusations Against Women in the Greco-Roman World from the First through the Fifth Centuries* CE (University of Pennsylvania, 2001), and were presented to the Social History of Formative Christianity Section at the annual meeting of the Society of Biblical Literature (2000) and to the Friends of Ancient History in Southern California (2003). I would like to thank those who have offered feedback to these

materials, most especially my doctoral thesis advisors, Ross S. Kraemer, Robert A. Kraft, and Brent D. Shaw, and the respondent to the paper at the Friends of Ancient History, Amy Richlin.

3. Anthony J. Marshall, "Women on Trial Before the Roman Senate," *EMC*, n.s., 34 (1990): 362–65, appendices A and B. During this same span of time, the first century CE, Marshall counts 122 trials against men.
4. Charles R. Phillips, "The Sociology of Religious Knowledge in the Roman Empire to AD 284," *ANRW* 16.3:2677–773 and Charles R. Phillips, "Nullum Crimen Sine Lege: Socioreligious Sanctions on Magic," in *Magika Hiera: Ancient Greek Magic and Religion*, ed. Christopher A. Faraone and Dirk Obbink (New York: Oxford University Press, 1991), 260–76; John Matthews, "Valentinian and Valens: Sex, Magic and Treason," Chapter in *The Roman Empire of Ammianus* (Baltimore: Johns Hopkins University Press, 1989), 204–31.
5. Keith Thomas, *Religion and the Decline of Magic* (New York: Oxford University Press, 1971) and Alan Macfarlane, *Witchcraft in Tudor and Stuart England* (New York: Harper & Row, 1970). For the potential pitfalls of historians' use of anthropological theories of magic, see Hildred Geertz, "An Anthropology of Religion and Magic, I," JIH 6 (1975): 71–89, a critique of Thomas, *Religion and the Decline of Magic* and Keith Thomas, "An Anthropology of Religion and Magic, I," *JIH* 6 (1975): 91–109, Thomas's defense of his use of anthropology.
6. Mary Douglas, "Thirty Years after Witchcraft, Oracles and Magic," in *Witchcraft Confessions & Accusations*, ed. Mary Douglas (New York: Tavistock, 1970), xxv.
7. Douglas, "Thirty Years," xxvii.
8. Douglas, "Thirty Years," xxvii.
9. Frazer and Leach compartmentalized magic, with religion, as a subset of *superstitio*, which was itself set in contrast to science (cited in Charles R. Phillips, "Seek and Go Hide: Literary Source Problems and Graeco-Roman Magic," *Helios* 21, no. 2 (1994): 107–14, 107 and n. 3). Marcel Mauss, *A General Theory of Magic*, trans. Robert Brain (London: Routledge & Kegan Paul, 1972), 22 notes: "... association with evil as an aspect of magical rites always provides humanity with a rough general notion of magic."
10. Émile Durkheim, *The Elementary Forms of the Religious Life*, trans. J.W. Swain (New York: Free Press, 1965), 60 makes the statement "There is no Church of magic . . . [t]he magician has a clientele and not a Church." Hendrik Versnel, "Some Reflections on the Relationship Magic–Religion," *Numen* 38, no. 2 (1991): 177–97, 179, describes magic as anti- or at least a-social, as well as exceptions to that rule. Similarly, Mauss, *General*, 24 declares that "[a] magical rite is any rite which does not play a part in organized cults."
11. Durkheim, *Elementary*, 57; William J. Goode, "Magic and Religion: A Continuum," *Ethnos* 14 (1949): 172–82; and Versnel, "Some Reflections", 179, who writes in particular about the technical action of a professional. This notion of ritualism

is closely related to the goal-oriented aspect often association with magic, as opposed to more "intangible long-term goals" often associated with religion; see Versnel, "Some Reflections," 178.

12. Frazer (1936), vol. 1, 423ff. sets forth his evolutionary model for the development of human thought from magic to religion to science (cited by I. C. Jarvie and J. Agassi, "The Problem of the Rationality of Magic," in *Rationality*, ed. Bryan Wilson [New York: Harper & Row, 1970], 175); Martin P. Nilsson, *Geschichte der griechischen Religion* (2 vols.; 3d ed.; Munich: Beck, 1967), 1:110–32 and Phillips, "Nullum Crimen," 266 and n. 46 for references. Mauss develops a similar model by which magic was the practice-ground for techniques which later shed their mystical component and become "automatic action." He notes at Mauss, *General*, 142: "We feel that techniques are like seeds which bore fruit in the soil of magic." Alan Segal, "Hellenistic Magic: Some Questions of Definition," in M. J. Vermaseren, ed., *Studies in Gnosticism and Hellenistic Religions presented to Gilles Quispel on the Occasion of his Sixty-Fifth Birthday* (Leiden: Brill, 1981), 359 adds an interesting twist to this dichotomy when he states "it is not necessarily true that the accuser would say that the 'magic' practiced is not religion... only that the practice was aggressive or primitive" with the intent "to harm society." See Stanley Jeyaraja Tambiah, *Magic, Science, and the Scope of Rationality* (Cambridge: Cambridge University Press, 1990), 47–50 for a discussion of Edward Tylor's late nineteenth-century discussion of the relationship between magic and primitive society.

13. I. M. Lewis, *Ecstatic Religion: An Anthropological Study of Spirit Possession and Shamanism* (Middlesex, England: Penguin Books, 1971).

14. Fritz Graf, "Excluding the Charming: The Development of the Greek Concept of Magic," in *Ancient Magic and Ritual Power*, ed. Marvin Meyer and Paul Mirecki (Leiden: Brill, 1995), 35–36, discusses the existence of this distinction even in the terminology *magos*, which "originated not so much from real observation of Persian religion or from the presence of Persian priests in Greek soil, but from a desire to designate certain ritual and ideological attachments as foreign, unwanted, and dangerous." Contrast this with Douglas's discussion in "Thirty Years," xxvi–xxx, of the witch accusation as leveled equally against both insiders and outsiders. As Segal, "Hellenistic Magic," 364, points out, Apuleius makes an interesting example with respect to his Isis initiation: "while the insider [Apuleius] distinguishes between magic and religion, his description of true religion matches some aspects of magical practice elsewhere."

15. Lewis, *Ecstatic*, 298–302. Although he is not arguing for any sort of distinction between "magic" and "religion," Lewis is useful for his distinction that, while women and low-caste men seek social redress through claiming to suffer amoral-spirit possession, social equals and superiors dealing with social inferiors are likely to make accusations of witchcraft against their opponents. Contrast with Phillips, "Seek," 109: "If I and other members of my elite group, guardians not only of literacy and religion but also of the whole societal *nomos* 'do it,' then it constitutes religion by

definition; the same activity in another group, especially one which for various sacred and secular reasons I dislike, becomes 'magic.'"

16. Hans Kippenberg, "Magic in Roman Civil Discourse: Why Rituals Could Be Illegal," in *Envisioning Magic: A Princeton Seminar and Symposium*, ed. Peter Shafer and Hans Kippenberg, SHR 75 (Leiden: Brill, 1997), 137–63, *passim*. Mauss, *General*, 23, differentiates between the religious acts that a "religious" professional might perform openly and in public and the magical rites which are done secretly in some obscure place.
17. Frazer (noted by Hendrik Versnel, "Beyond Cursing: The Appeal to Justice in Judicial Prayers," in Faraone and Obbink, eds., *Magika Hiera*, 177, and Graf, "Excluding," 35 and n. 21). Related to this is Bronisław Malinowski's idea that magic attempts to manipulate nature in order to achieve immediate goals, whereas religion is concerned with more transcendent issues (Bronisław Malinowski, *A Scientific Theory of Culture and Other Essays*, 200, as cited by Segal, "Hellenistic Magic," 350); Alan Segal, "On the Nature of Magic: Report on a Dialogue between a Historian and a Sociologist," in *The Social World of the First Christians: Essays in Honor of Wayne A. Meeks*, ed. L. Michael White and Larry Yarbrough (Minneapolis: Augsburg Fortress, 1995), 270–80, for the problematic relativism of "transcendental"; Goode, "Magic and Religion"; Leach (1964) for the "effort at control" which distinguishes magic from religion; and Versnel, "Some Reflections," 178.
18. Peter Brown, *Making of Late Antiquity* (Cambridge, MA: Harvard University Press, 1978), 1–26. Debates in Gospel accounts over the source of Jesus's power tap into this same issue; for this, see Segal, "Hellenistic Magic," 367–68.
19. Ritner cites Durkheim, Mauss, J. Z. Smith, P. Brown, and M. Smith for this distinction. See Robert Ritner, "The Religious, Social, and Legal Parameters of Traditional Egyptian Magic," in *Ancient Magic*, ed. Meyer and Mirecki 47, and notes 13 and 14 for full references. See also James Rives, "Magic in Roman Law: the Reconstruction of a Crime," *CAn* 22 (2003): 313–39.
20. Versnel, "Some Reflections," 181 and 194 n. 11. See also Graf (1991), 188–97, for a nuanced discussion of the structural similarities between prayer and spell (invocation, argument, wish/prayer), but ritual differences (namely how sacrifice in prayer creates community while a spell's sacrifice isolates the performer of the ritual from community).
21. Phillips, "Nullum Crimen," 266, for the connection of irrationality to magic; similarly, Phillips, "Seek," 108. Jarvie and Agassi, "Problem," 173–76 discuss the competition of magic and science for the same pragmatic goals.
22. Sarah Iles Johnston, "Describing the Undefinable: New Books on Magic and Old Problems of Definition," *HR* 43, no. 1 (2003): 50–54.
23. Peter Greene, "The Methods of Ancient Magic," *Times Literary Supplement* 5168 (2002): 5–6.
24. Terms for magic in the *Theodosian Code* are as follows: *magicae artes, Cod. Theod.* 9.16.3 and *Cod. Theod.* 9.16; *crimen magicae Cod. Theod.* 9.42.2; *maleficium, Cod.*

Theod. 9.16 *passim, Cod. Theod.* 9.38.7; *scelus maleficiorum, Cod. Theod.* 9.38.4; *mathematica, Cod. Theod.* 9.16.8; and *veneficium, Cod. Theod.* 9.38.3, 7 and 8. Eli Edward Burriss, "The Terminology of Witchcraft," *CP* 31 (1936): 137–45, offers an early, and quite thorough, discussion of terms for magic in Greco-Roman antiquity. More recently, Rives's ("Magic in Roman Law," 313) study of magic in Roman law argues for a shift "from a focus on harmful and uncanny actions to a concern with religious deviance" tracing the change through three "key moments": Sulla's 81 BCE law against poisoning, Apuleius's mid-second-century CE defense, and Paulus's *Opinions* of the third century CE.

25. *Magia* appears in the title of the twelfth- to thirteenth-century copy (f) of the eleventh-century (F) manuscript of Apuleius' *Apologia*, and both manuscripts apparently descend from a late fourth-century CE manuscript edition at Rome. For the Apuleian manuscript tradition, see Reynolds (1983), 15–18. Μαγεία appears in the context of the narrative on Simon Magus in the canonical Christian *Acts of the Apostles* 8.11, written in the late first or early second century CE. For the Greek term, μαγγείας, Heliod., *Aeth.* 6.15.1. For γοητεία, LSJ includes citations from Lucian's second century CE *Nigr.* 15, and Plotinus's third-century CE *Enn.* 4.4.44, among many others.

26. *Nefarias preces* (evil prayers), *magicos apparatos* (magical preparations), or *sacrificia funesta* (funereal sacrifices), *Cod. Theod.* 9.16.7; *devotionibus ac maleficiis*, Apul., *Met.* 9.29-31; *carmina et devotiones*, Tac., *Ann.* 2.69 on the implements used in the death of Germanicus; carmina used by Fabia Numantina in Tac., *Ann.* 4.22; *carmina et nenia* (and *libri carminum*) in Hor., *Epod.* 17.1–30; *carmina*, Juv., *Satires* 6.133; *incantamenta*, Amm. Marc. 16.8.2, 29.2.3; *devotiones* by Domitia Lepida in Tac., *Ann.* 12.64–65 and by Claudia Pulchra in Tac., *Ann.* 4.52; τινας ᾠδάς, Lucian, *Dial. meret.* 1.281, ἐπῳδαί, Lucian, *Dial. meret.* 4.1 and 4.4–5, Achilles Tatius, *Leucippe and Cleitophon* 2.7 and in Heliod., *Aeth.* 6.14.

27. When I use the term spell, it is to indicate a combination of words and accompanying ritualized actions that were thought by the user to achieve some desired end by marshaling supernatural powers. Attempts to draw sharp lines between magical spell and religious prayer, such as Versnel's (Hendrik Versnel, "Religious Mentality in Ancient Prayer," in *Faith, Hope and Worship: Aspects of Religious Mentality in the Ancient World* [Leiden: Brill, 1981], 1–64 and Versnel, "Beyond Cursing"), run the risk of perpetuating the unhelpful stereotypical distinction between "magic" and "religion." Graf's (1991) distinction (discussed in n. 20) is more useful.

28. *Venena*, Luc., *Civil War*, 6.430–506, Juv., 6.133; *venena et artes* of Plancina in Tac., *Ann.*, 3.17; *venena* by Aemilia Lepida in Tac., *Ann.* 3.22; *poculum amoris* in Prop. 2.1.51–54; *amatoria* in Amm. Marc. 29.2.3; *Medeides herbae, philtra* in Ov., *Ars Am.* 2.99–107; φίλτρα for describing Medea's potions in Plut., *Mor.* 139a; for the various descriptions of the drugs used by Circe, κακὰ φάρμακα, Hom., *Od.* 10.213, φάρμακα λύγρα *ibid.*, 10.236, φάρμακον οὐλόμενον *ibid.*, 10.394; Simaetha's φάρμακα in Theoc., *Id.* 2.15–16.

29. *Magus Cod. Theod.* 9.16.4 and *passim*, Tac., *Ann.* 12.22; *Chaldei, Cod. Theod.* 9.16.4 and Tac., *Ann.* 3.22, 12.22, 12.52; *maleficus, Cod. Theod.* 9.16 *passim; veneficus, Cod. Theod.* 9.16, *passim*, 9.38.3 and 8, Amm. Marc. 19.12.14-15; *mathematicus, Cod. Theod.* 9.16, *passim.*
30. *Saga*, Tib. 1.2.41–64 and Apul., *Met.* 2.8, 2.21; *maga*, Apul., *Met.* 2.5; *μαγεύουσας*, Achilles Tatius, *Leucippe and Cleitophon* 5.22; *πολυφάρμακος*, Medea in Hom., *Od.* 10.276; *φαρμακίς*, Lucian, *Dial. meret.* 1.281.
31. Robert S. Rogers, *Criminal Trials and Criminal Legislation under Tiberius* (Middletown, CT: American Philological Association, 1935) and Robert S. Rogers, "A Tacitean Pattern in Narrating Treason-Trials," *TAPA* 83 (1952): 279–311; Ronald Syme, *Tacitus* (Oxford: Clarendon, 1958) and Ronald Syme, *Augustan Aristocracy* (New York: Oxford University Press, 1986); Marshall, "Women on Trial," 333–66; and Richard J. A. Talbert, *The Senate of Imperial Rome* (Princeton, NJ: Princeton University Press, 1984); although Rogers, "Tacitean," 311, *does* note how Tacitus manipulates evidence "substituting the refutable for the undeniable, asserting the real to be only ostensible, and putting forward as actual and real the result of his own prejudiced thinking."
32. Francesca Santoro L'Hoir, *Tragedy, Rhetoric, and the Historiography of Tacitus' Annales* (Ann Arbor: University of Michigan Press, 2006), 158–95.
33. Here I take to heart K. Gilmartin Wallace's warning not to attempt "one more supposed demonstration of our superiority to Tacitus." There is truth to her admonition that "[i]f Tacitus does not know more about Roman history than we do . . . then there is no point in reading that preposterously difficult Latin" ("Women in Tacitus 1903–86," *ANRW* 33.5:3556–74, 3574).
34. Anthony J. Woodman and Ronald H. Martin, *The Annals of Tacitus: Book 3, Edited with a Commentary* (Cambridge: Cambridge University Press, 1996), 11–2, remark that "no other book of the extant *Annals* is framed by women, yet the frame is an apt reflection of the female presence which pervades Book 3." On the trial against Piso and Plancina in particular, see Woodman and Martin, *Annals*, 110–93.
35. To fix Plancina in the complicated nexus of Roman nobility at the beginning of the principate, Munatia Plancina was the granddaughter of L. Munatius Plancus, the censor of 22 BCE, the sister of the 13 CE consul of the same name, and the wife of Gnaeus Calpurnius Piso. See *PIR*^{2} (1970) no. 737, Werner Eck, Antonio Caballos, and Fernando Fernández, *Das Senatus Consultum de Cn. Pisone Patre* (Vestigia 48; Munich: Beck, 1996), 87–88, and Marshall, "Women on Trial," 342 and n. 23 for Munatia's family relations. Syme, *Augustan*, 374 and 429 only briefly discusses Plancina's trial and acquittal in two short paragraphs.
36. At the beginning of this consular year, Tiberius's mother Livia threw a party, inviting all the women of Rome (Dio Cass. 55.8.1). Perhaps it was at this party that a friendship was formed between Plancina and Livia, a friendship that led to Livia's intervention on Plancina's behalf when she was on trial for charges of murder almost three decades later. Syme, *Augustan*, 369, argues for Plancina as

Piso's second wife due to their age difference and the date of their eldest son's consulship. Possibly following Syme, Eck reasons that her oldest son having held the consulship in 27 CE suggests that he would have been born by 7 BCE. This would mean that Plancina was married to Piso when Livia threw her party to celebrate Tiberius's consulship. Syme, *Augustan*, 58, by different reasoning, suggests that Piso might have taken Plancina as his wife even earlier.

37. Dio Cass. 57.18.9–10, attributes the murder plot to both Piso and Plancina, writing that bones of men (*ὀστᾶ ἀνθρώπων*), lead curse tablets (*ἐλασμοὶ μολίβδινοι ἀρας τίνας μετὰ τοῦ ὀνόματος αὐτοῦ*) and poison (*φαρμάκῳ*) were used to kill Germanicus.
38. Suetonius's accounts of Germanicus's death do not mention Plancina at all, but instead describe Piso as an instrument of Tiberius's plan to do away with Germanicus; Suet. *Tib.* 52 and *Calig.* 2–3, where he mentions the *veneficia* and *devotiones* employed by Piso at the behest of Tiberius. Tac., *Ann.* 3.15–16, alludes to such involvement by Tiberius when he discusses the mysterious papers that Piso seemed to clutch throughout the trial but Piso killed himself (or was assassinated) before he could reveal their contents (presumably Tiberius's orders to kill Germanicus). Tacitus is very careful not to subscribe to either opinion, concerning whether Piso killed himself or was assassinated. Tacitus does remark that Plancina was the last person to see Piso alive.
39. According to the narrative analysis of Cynthia Damon, "The Trial of Cn. Piso in Tacitus' Annals and the Senatus Consultum de Cn. Pisone Patre: New Light on Narrative Technique," *AJP* 120, no. 1 (1999): 143–62. Tacitus uses a mirrored telling of the events in Books 2 and 3 to show that although Piso was able to diffuse the charge of *venenum*, he did not adequately address that of *devotiones* (Tac. 3.13.2, for the prosecution's accusations of both *venenum* and *devotiones*). Damon remarks that "Tacitus' defense (in Book 3), which was so well prepared to face the charge of poison, has nothing to say about the magical attacks . . . by putting the devotiones in the narrative and not discrediting them at the trial Tacitus recreates for the reader the suspicions that survived for generations after the fact" (Damon, "Trial," 157).
40. Tac., *Ann.* 2.69: et reperiebantur solo ac parietibus erutae *humanorum corporum reliquae, carmina* et *devotiones* et *nomen Germanici plumbeis tabulis insculptum, semusti cineres* ac tabo obliti aliaque *malefica* quis creditur animas numinibus infernis sacrari. The stock of Pamphile's workshop in Apuleius (*Met.* 3.17) included metal tablets and human body parts.
41. Gunhild Viden, *Women in Roman Literature: Attitudes of Authors under the Early Empire* (SGLG 57; Goteborg, Sweden: Acta Universitatis Gothobugensis, 1993), 45, argues that the Latin text uses chiasmus to implicate Plancina in the poisoning; *infamem veneficiis . . . Plancinae percaram* (2.74.2). *Ann.* 2.74: Isque (Marsus) *infamem veneficiis* ea in provincia et *Plancinae percaram* nomine Martinam in urbem misit . . . Marsus sent into the city a certain woman by the name Martina, *infamous in that province for poisonings* and a *dear friend to Plancina. In The Magician,*

the Witch, and the Law, Edward Peters's arguments concerning courtly witchcraft accusations in the medieval period suggest that magic accusations might be leveled by upper-class people against lower-class dependants of their rivals as a way to attack those rivals. Applying this model to the Roman period, we might expect that Martina would have been accused, not merely brought in as a witness. Perhaps the private prosecutorial nature of the Roman legal system explains why Martina would not herself be accused.

42. Tac., *Ann.* 2.74, for Vitellius's summons to Rome of Martina. Suet., *Vit.* 2 and Plin., *HN* 11.187 for Vitellius as the prosecutor of the case against Piso and Plancina. Surprisingly, Marshall, "Women on Trial," 356–57 does not include Martina on his list of women called as witnesses before the Senate. Granted she did not make it to trial, due to her mysterious death at Brundisium, but her involvement definitely deserves note in that context. This is all the more true if she gave relevant evidentiary testimony before her death, comparable to Urgulania's home interrogation by a praetor in 16 CE (Tac., *Ann.* 2.34.8), mentioned by Marshall, "Women on Trial," 356.
43. Tac., *Ann.* 3.7. Eck, Caballos and Fernández, *Senatus*, 153, mentions Martina as one who might have been called as a *testis*, had she not died at Brundisium. Such *testes cuiusque ordinis*, witnesses of every rank, are mentioned in the *SCP*, 1.25. Woodman and Martin, *Annals*, 121–22 discuss the difficulties of this passage, concerning how she died. They do note though, that although Germanicus's body has no marks of poison on it according to Tacitus, Suetonius (*Calig.* 1.2) and Dio Cass. (57.18.9) do comment on the traces of poison left on his body. They do not close the loop to suggest that Martina and Germanicus might have died by the same non-traceable poison. But they do suggest "that there seems no reason why Martina, an experienced and notorious poisoner should have committed suicide or be thought to have done so." All of this suggests that Plancina might have had a role in killing both Martina and Germanicus by the same means. Or else, it suggests that Tacitus is interested in making it seem that way.
44. Tac., *Ann.* 2.82; "*hoc egisse secretos Augustae cum Plancina sermones*" when describing the crowd's interpretation of the situation when hearing of Germanicus's failing health. Tacitus implicates Tiberius and Livia further, especially after Plancina's acquittal (3.17). Livia's intervention on Plancina's behalf, recorded in the *SCP* to be discussed shortly, certainly provides support for Tacitus's suggestion that these two women were in close contact.
45. Piso is last seen in the evening in his bedroom writing notes in his defense (Tac., *Ann.* 3.15–16).
46. Tac., *Ann.* 3.16: *de Plancina nihil addidit.*
47. Tac., *Ann.* 3.15.
48. Tac., *Ann.* 3.17.
49. The *SCP* makes reference to Plancina in lines 10 and 109–20. For texts of this decree, see Eck, Caballos and Fernández, *Senatus*, and David S. Potter, ed., "The Senatus Consultum de Gn. Pisone Patre" (trans. Cynthia Damon), *AJP* 120,

no. 1 (1999): 13–42. The entirety of vol. 120, no. 1 (1999) of *AJP* comprised articles devoted to this decree, following a joint session of the APA/AIA in Chicago, 1997. Other articles of interest include John P. Bodel, "Punishing Piso," *AJP* 120, no. 1 (1999): 43–63; Edward Champlin, "The First (1996) Edition of the Senatus Consultum de Cn. Pisone Patre: A Review," *AJP* 120, no. 1 (1999): 117–22; Damon, "Trial," 143–62; David S. Potter, "Political Theory in the Senatus Consultum de Cn. Pisone Patre," *AJP* 120, no. 1 (1999): 65–88; Richard J. A Talbert, "Tacitus and the Senatus Consultum de Cn. Pisone Patre," *AJP* 120, no. 1 (1999): 89–97; T. D. Barnes, "Tacitus and the Senatus Consultum de Cn. Pisone Patre (review article)," *Phoenix* 52, nos. 1–2 (1998): 125–48; David S. Potter, "Senatus Consultum de Cn. Pisone," *JRA* 11 (1998): 437–57; Alexander Yakobson, "The Princess of Inscriptions: Senatus Consultum de Cn. Pisone Patre and the Early Years of Tiberius' Reign," *SCI* 17 (1998): 206–24; Miriam Griffin, "The Senate's Story," *JRS* 87 (1997): 249–63; J. S. Richardson, "The Senate, the Courts, and the Senatus Consultum de Cn. Pisone Patre," *CQ* 47 (1997): 510–18.

50. *SCP* 1.109, translation and text in Potter, ed., "Senatus Consultum." Eck, Caballos, and Fernández, *Senatus*, 222–28, offer commentary on the acquittal of Plancina in the *SCP. Senatus Consultum de Cn. Pisone Patre* (lines 109–20); December 10, 20 CE. [Text and translation from Potter, ed., "Senatus Consultum," 13–41.]

> Concerning these matters the Senate decreed as follows: . . .
> THAT as far as the case of Plancina was concerned, against whom
> numerous weighty charges (*pluruma et gravissuma crimina*) had
> been lodged, since she admitted that she placed all hope in the
> compassion of our princeps and of the Senate, and since our princeps . . .
> interceded for Plancina at his mother's request, and received very just reasons
> made to him by her, as to why his mother wanted to obtain these concessions,
> the Senate deemed
>> THAT both Julia Augusta, who was most well deserving
>> of the republic not only because she gave birth to our princeps
>> but also because of her many great kindnesses to men of
>> every order—although she rightly and deservedly should havew
>> the greatest influence in what she requested from the Senate,
>> she used it most sparingly— and the very great devotion of our
>> princeps to his mother should be supported and indulged and
>
> THAT it was the Senate's pleasure
>> THAT the punishment of Plancina be remitted.

51. *SCP* 11. 115–19. Champlin, "First," 121 remarks that Livia's role in Plancina's acquittal "confirms the truly astonishing power of Julia Augusta (which has often been doubted)." Mireille Corbier, "Male Power and Legitimacy through Women: The Domus Augusta under the Julio-Claudians," in *Women in Antiquity: New Assessments*, ed. R. Hawley and B. Levick (New York: Routledge, 1995), 178–93, outlines the Augusta's powers.

52. The woman who stands by her man is a recurring positive exemplum for Tacitus. In *Hist.* 1.3 the good matrona is she who stands by her man (husband or son) for good or ill, exile or suicide. Anthony J. Marshall, "Ladies in Waiting: The Role of Women in Tacitus' Histories," *ASoc* 15–17 (1984–86): 167–84, 171–75, discusses Tacitus's emphasis on this model of the good woman/wife.
53. Tac., *Ann.* 3.17. Woodman and Martin, *Annals*, 181 argue that the coordination of *venena* and *artes* here should be equated to magical arts, hence depicting Plancina as a "witch" [*sic*]. For this terminology, they cite *TLL* 2.665.34ff, Butler-Owen on Apuleius' *Apol.* 25, and Burriss, "Terminology," 137.
54. See R. Develin, "Tacitus and Techniques of Insidious Suggestion," *Antichthon* 17 (1983): 64–95; Israel Shatzman, "Tacitean Rumors," *Latomus* 33, no. 3 (1974): 549–78, 564–67; and Inez Scott Ryberg, "Tacitus' Art of Innuendo," *TAPA* 73 (1942): 383–404, for discussions of Tacitus's proclivity to use such rumor and strong innuendo as I am suggesting here in the case of Plancina. Develin reviews various Tacitean suggestive techniques and the words Tacitus uses to signal uncertainty and alternatives, including *incertum, tradere*, and *credere*, as well as reporting variations of rumor. Although he does not examine Plancina in detail on her own, Develin, "Tacitus," 92, concludes similarly that "the real climax of suggestion [in Tacitus] involves Tiberius, Livia, Germanicus, and Piso, with incidentals." Shatzman, "Tacitean," 564–67, considers the use of rumor in Tacitus's account of Germanicus's death, but focuses much more on Piso than on Plancina. Ryberg, "Tacitus' Art," considers the death of Germanicus in detail, noting in particular the suspicion cast on Tiberius (and Livia) by Tacitus's telling. But, suspicion of Tiberius does not rule out that of Plancina as well. The devices Ryberg mentions as building up this innuendo include avoidance of direct accusations of crime, accusations reported as hearsay, accusations vocalized by another individual, and later referring to charges initially presented as rumors as fact, and finally "the innuendo which depends . . . on clever juxtaposition of ideas" ("Tacitus' Art," *passim* and 390). Although Ryberg does not mention it, some of Tacitus's word choice in this passage carries innuendo and insinuation of magic. Tacitus uses words that hint at magic, but actually mean something else. For instance, the phrase that precedes Germanicus's comment that he has died by female treachery is *tot bellorum superstitem* (the witness of so many wars, *Ann.* 2.71). The word for witness, *superstes*, calls to mind *superstitio*, a word often used in the context of discussing magic. In describing Plancina's inappropriate religious activities, Tacitus's audience hangs on his words when he says *magis insolenscente Plancina, (Ann.* 2.75) where *magis* functions adverbially and not as the ablative plural of *magus*, which could have implied the means by which Plancina pursued her *venena et artes*.
55. Tac., *Ann.* 2.71, *scelere Pisonis et Plancinae*.
56. Tac., *Ann.* 2.71; 2.69, for Germanicus's belief that he was poisoned by Piso.
57. Tac., *Ann.* 6.26.3, *petitaque criminibus haud ignotis*; also Dio Cass. 58.22.5 for Plancina's fate. Marshall, "Women on Trial," 353–54 and n. 55 include Plancina's

ultimate trial as one of those he classifies as dubious Senatorial trials. Where this conviction occurred is less important to my argument than the fact that these charges surfaced a second time, after the protection of Livia was removed.

58. Christopher Pelling, "Tacitus and Germanicus," in *Tacitus and the Tacitean Tradition*, ed. T. J. Luce and A. J. Woodman (Princeton, NJ: Princeton University Press, 1993), 84. Viden, *Women*, 38–47 also notices Tacitus's contrasting of Plancina and Agrippina but does not work it out with respect to *artes magicae*.
59. For worrisome knowledge transmission by female magic users, see, e.g., the pairing of Simaetha and Thestylis (Theoc., *Id.* 2), Canidia and her friends (Hor., *Epod.* 5), Meroe and Panthia as well as Pamphile and Photis (Apul., *Met.* 1.11–13 and 3.15–25), and the discussion in Elizabeth Pollard, "Magic Accusations against Women in the Greco-Roman World from the First through the Fifth Centuries CE" (PhD diss., University of Pennsylvania, 2001), 66–70 and 83. For the wild hair of witches, see, e.g., Hor., *Sat.* 1.8.24–26 (Canidia) and 5.16 and 5.27 (Folia).
60. Tac., *Ann.* 2.55.6 (Plancina with the military) and 2.58 (Plancina received gifts from Vonones) for Plancina's manly roles. Viden, *Women*, 44–45, provides more discussion of Plancina's unwomanly ways.
61. Tac., *Ann.* 2.85.
62. Christopher A. Faraone, *Ancient Greek Love Magic* (Cambridge, MA: Harvard University Press, 1999), 146–60 for prostitutes' use of aggressive/masculinized love magic. See also love elegists Ovid, Propertius, and Tibullus for the relationship between magic and the lena/procuress (K. Sara Myers, "The Poet and the Procuress: The Lena in Latin Love Elegy," *JRS* 86 (1996): 1–21).
63. In her discussion of Messalina, Sandra R. Joshel, "Female Desire and the Discourse of Empire: Tacitus's Messalina," *Signs* 21, no. 1 (1995): 50–82, 58, usefully reminds us "that Roman women in the upper classes had wealth and influence but, at the same time, no political roles and limited legal rights." This is not to say that women did not compete in realms of unofficial competition. Childbearing and marriage ties were certainly an unofficial locus of competition; certainly one ripe for magic use and magic accusation, as well. One need only think of the various love spells (e.g., DT 270.5–13, PGM 16.1–75, and PGM 15.1–21) and womb spells (e.g., *PGM* 7.260–71 and *PGM* 62.76–106) for evidence of that. For further discussion of this female competition, see Pollard, "Magic," 161–279, and Pauline Ripat, chapter 12 of this volume.
64. Michael Kaplan, "*Agrippina semper atrox*: A Study in Tacitus' Characterization of Women," in *Studies in Latin Literature and Roman History*, vol. 1, CL 164, ed. C. Deroux (Brussels: Collection Latomus, 1978), 411.
65. *Ann.* 1.69.1–4 for Agrippina and 2.55.6 for Plancina as *duces feminae*. For discussion, see Francesca Santoro L'Hoir, "Tacitus and Women's Usurpation of Power," *CW* 88, no. 1 (1994): 5–25, 12–13, and Kaplan, "*Agrippina*," 412.
66. Tac., *Ann.* 2.71. Her lineage and children are also a part of Tacitus's depiction of the melodrama as Agrippina returns to Rome with Germanicus's ashes (*Ann.* 2.75).

67. Tac., *Ann.* 4.52. In *Ann.* 4.53, Agrippina then tearfully pleads with Tiberius to allow her to remarry, but Tiberius refuses the request, wisely wary of the political power the widow of Germanicus could wield.
68. Tac., *Ann.* 2.72.
69. To contextualize Plancina's presence in Syria with her husband (and Aemilia Lepida's possible accompaniment of her husband to Syria twenty years earlier), note that it was only after Plancina's trial that Aulus Caecina suggested a law in the Senate prohibiting wives accompanying their husbands into the provinces. Richard A. Bauman, *Women and Politics in Ancient Rome* (New York: Routledge, 1992), 142–43 and 252, n. 32, discusses Tacitus's report (*Ann.* 3.33–34) of Caecina's proposal and his motivation for it (being bested by Agrippina in Germany). Raepsaet-Charlier, M-Th, "Epouses et familles de magistrats dans les provinces romaines aux deux premiers siècles de l'Empire," *Historia* 31 (1982): 56–69, 64–69, offers a catalog of evidence for eighty-nine women accompanying their governor-husbands into the provinces in the first two centuries CE. She also discusses the exact dating of the decree following Tacitus' chronology rather than that of Justinian's *Digest* (1.16.4). Anthony J. Marshall, "Roman Women and the Provinces," *ASoc* 6 (1975): 109–27 offers a general discussion of the role played by wives of provincial governors. Santoro L'Hoir ("Tacitus," 12–17 and *Tragedy*) has emphasized the echoes of Livy's account of the second-century BCE *lex Oppia* debate in Tacitus's account of the debate over governors' wives in the provinces. More recently, Santoro L'Hoir, *Tragedy*, 168–69 discusses the rhetorical relationship between female mobility, unchastity, and charges of adulteress/poisoner, but does not link this relationship to the debate about the presence of governors' wives in the provinces.
70. Tac., *Ann.* 3.11.
71. Tac., *Ann.* 1.13 for an M. or M'. Lepidus described by Augustus as *capax imperii*. Ronald Syme, "Marcus Lepidus, *Capax Imperii*," *JRS* 45 (1955): 22–33; repr., pages 30–49 in Ronald Syme, *Ten Studies in Tacitus* (Oxford: Clarendon, 1970) discusses this conundrum in detail. In this same passage, Tacitus notes that some traditions also put Gnaeus Piso on the list of Augustus's handpicked successors. That would make the rivalry between Agrippina and Plancina even more acute.
72. Tac., *Ann.* 3.22–23; Suetonius *Tiberius* 49. Tacitus himself juxtaposes these two cases at *Ann.* 3.24.1. See also Woodman and Martin, *Annals*, 209–23, for the trial of Aemilia Lepida. They note the juxtapositioning of it to Plancina's trial, but do not posit the effect this has on implicating Plancina further, as I argue here. Syme mentions her trial, but does not link it to Plancina (Syme, *Augustan*), 115. Frederick H. Cramer, *Astrology in Roman Law and Politics: Astrology in Rome until the End of the Principate* (MAPS 37; Philadelphia, PA: American Philosophical Society, 1954), 103–4, discusses her trial as typical of *maiestas* trials conducted by Tiberius to rid himself of troublemakers. Her trial is Cramer's case no. 2 of violations of the Augustan edict of 11 CE against astrology. This edict is recorded at Dio Cass. 56.25.5, and states that diviners (μαντεῖς) are forbidden to prophesy to

any person alone or ever to prophesy concerning death. The chronology in Suetonius's account makes it difficult to determine when the alleged crimes might have occurred. Suetonius suggests that a period of twenty years elapsed between their divorce and Quirinius's trial against her. Woodman and Martin, *Annals*, 212–13 discuss the difficulties in chronology. The date of their divorce is not crucial for my discussions, although if the instances of *venena*-use did occur twenty years earlier, they might have taken place while the couple was in Syria. Syme, *Augustan*, Table IV, shows this Aemilia Lepida (who later married Mam. Aemilius Scaurus). She is one generation before (and a distant cousin of) the Aemilia Lepida who married M. Junius Silanus (cos. 19) and was the mother of the Junia Lepida who was brought up on charges of incest and *diros sacrorum ritos* in 65 CE (*Ann.* 16.7–8).

73. D. C. A. Shotter, "Tiberius' Part in the Trial of Aemilia Lepida," *Historia* 15 (1966): 312–17 and G. B. Townend, "The Trial of Aemilia Lepida in AD 20," *Latomus* 21 (1962): 484–93.
74. Tac., *Ann.* 3.22.
75. *Cod. Theod.* 9.38.7 in 384 CE groups together as savage crimes (*scelera saeviora*) the following: treason (*maiestas*), poisoning (*veneficium*), magic (*maleficium*), seduction (*stuprum*), adultery (*adulterium*), and sepulcher violation (*violatio sepulchorum*). Santoro L'Hoir, *Tragedy*, 159–73, shows how these crimes are grouped in Ciceronian rhetoric.
76. Woodman and Martin, *Annals*, 212, note the frequent association of adultery and poisoning charges, although they do not posit the possible reasoning between this linking, i.e., the use of love potions.
77. One example from among many is, of course, Apuleius's richly drawn Meroe (*Met.* 1.7–13).
78. See Woodman and Martin, *Annals*, 210–11, for the themes of suppositious children in Greek and Roman comedy and the *lex Cornelia de falsis* as the possible grounds for this charge.
79. Hor., *Epod.* 17.47–52. Anne-Marie Tupet, *La magie dans la poésie latine I: Des origines à la fin du règne d'Auguste* (Paris: Société d'édition "Les Belles Lettres," 1976), 295, referencing Juv. 6.602–9, thinks this passage refers to the substitution of infants in wealthy upper-class houses. I would suggest rather that Horace's passage links magic-use and faked-childbirthing as the type of thing a "witch" might do.
80. Tacitus, *Ann.* 3.48 records a eulogy of Quirinius, for whom Tiberius proposed a public funeral. Following a 12 BCE consulship, Quirinius was governor of Syria and is mentioned in Luke 2.2. The possibility that the *venena*-use might have occurred while Lepida and Quirinius were in Syria is interesting: Lepida would have been charged with using *venena* in Syria while her husband was governor in the same way that Plancina, through Martina, had access to *venena* while her husband was governor of Syria.
81. Tac., *Ann.* 3.23.

82. *Digest* 48.8.3. *Cod. Theod.* 9.16.3 explored the issue of the intent of the user of *venenum*. Richard Gordon, "Imagining Greek and Roman Magic," in *Witchcraft and Magic in Europe: Ancient Greece and Rome*, ed. Bengt Ankarloo and Stuart Clark (Philadelphia: University of Pennsylvania Press, 1999), 255–56, provides further discussion of *malum venenum*. It should also be noted that other possible laws under which Aemilia Lepida might have been prosecuted include the *lex Cornelia de falsum* or the *lex Julia de adulteria*.
83. *Cod. Theod.* 9.16.3 for the use of *artes magicae* to turn virtuous minds to lust. Gordon, "Imagining," 256–57, for love potion use as *veneficium*.
84. Ronald Syme, *The Roman Revolution* (London: Oxford University Press, 1939), 494, well sums up the ill fate of the Aemilii Lepidi under the Julio-Claudian principate: "The last of them . . . succumbed to the evil destiny of his family—conspiracy and a violent death."
85. Syme, *Augustan*, Table XXVII shows Numantina's lineage in the Fabii line. Numantina is the daughter of Marcia (and Paullus Fabius Maximus cos. 11 BCE), and through her the granddaughter of L. Marcius Philipus (son of the second husband of Augustus's mother, Atia) (Tac., *Ann.* 4.22). Marshall, "Women on Trial," 353 and n. 52, case no. 32, lists this as a dubious trial before the senate.
86. Urgulania's *amicitia* with Livia is attested in Tac., *Ann.* 2.34.
87. Develin, "Tacitus," 75.
88. Tac., *Ann.* 4.21.
89. Tac., *Ann.* 2.34.
90. Syme, *Augustan*, 327 is careful to distinguish that the proper charge would have been *impudicitia*, not *adulterium*, since Pulchra was at this time a widow. See Ronald H. Martin and Anthony J. Woodman, *Tacitus Annals Book IV* (New York: Cambridge University Press, 1989), 216, for her family connections and Syme, *Augustan*, Table III and IV, for her family tree.
91. Tac., *Ann.* 4.52 and Dio Cass. 59.19.1. For Claudia Pulchra, Marshall, "Women on Trial," 344–45, case no. 9. Martin and Woodman, *Tacitus*, 215–18 discuss Pulchra's trial but do not discuss the charges and their implications in any detail. Cramer, *Astrology*, 256–57 discusses Pulchra as his case no. 3 of a violation of the 11 CE edict because Tiberius was the object of her spells.
92. Anthony A. Barrett, *Agrippina: Sex, Power and Politics in the Early Empire* (New Haven, CT: Yale University Press, 1996), 34–35 offers a discussion of the full import of Agrippina's comments to Tiberius. According to Barrett, Agrippina's claim that such a prosecution attacked a true descendant of Augustus (his granddaughter through Julia from his first marriage to Scribonia), as opposed to Tiberius (the adopted son, natural stepson of Augustus by his second wife Livia), would have played on Tiberius's anger at having been chosen successor to Augustus after so many other possible heirs had died.
93. Tac., *Ann.* 4.53 mentions Agrippina Minor's memoirs as a source for the ups and downs of her mother's life. One can almost imagine the daughter taking notes on

her mother's ill fortune when it comes to magic and magic accusation and then learning from that in order to turn magic and accusation to her own benefit.

94. Barrett, *Agrippina* provides a detailed biography of Agrippina Minor, discussion of the trials involving Agrippina, and an exhaustive bibliography. Barrett does not include any discussion concerning the nature of the magic-charges other than to mention in passing that they were typical in cases of treason. He does not treat these cases systematically and mostly recounts Tacitus's record of events. Judith Ginsburg, *Representing Agrippina: Constructions of Female Power in the Early Roman Empire* (New York: Oxford University Press, 2006) emphasizes the female rivalry.
95. Tac., *Ann.* 12.22 and Dio Cass. 61.32.4; Marshall, "Women on Trial," 349, case no. 22. Syme, *Augustan*, Table XI, for her ancestry. For Cramer, *Astrology*, 259–61 this case (his no. 5 for violations of the 11 CE Augustan edict) marks a turning point of when inquiries about the emperor become *maiestas*.
96. Tac., *Ann.* 12.1 for the marriage rivalry; Barrett, *Agrippina*, 57–58, 95–96 and 275–76, n. 6 discusses this rivalry and the wealth. Aemilian connections come up again in the context of Lollia Paulina's earlier marriage to Caligula. Caligula's sister Drusilla had married a member of this family and according to Dio was intended as a successor to Caligula (Barrett, *Agrippina*, 58).
97. Barrett, *Agrippina*, 107–8.
98. For Lollia Paulina's wealth, Plin., *HN* 9.117, Suet., *Calig.* 25.2, and Dio Cass. 59.12.1. She reportedly possessed emeralds and pearls to the amount of forty million sesterces.
99. Given Carol F. Karlsen's (*Devil in the Shape of a Woman: Witchcraft in Colonial New England* [New York: Norton, 1987]) arguments that women were targeted in late seventeenth-century New England for magic accusation because of inheritance issues, one wonders if that model may well have applied to Lollia Paulina as well, i.e., she was accused of magic as a convenient way to confiscate her money. Tacitus records that in her prosecution Claudius advocated stripping her of her property. That magic accusation and inheritance issues go hand in hand in the Greco-Roman context is certainly supported by Apuleius's *Apologia*, in which he spends almost as much time defending himself against charges that he was after Pudentilla's wealth as he does deflecting charges that he used magic to lure her into relationship.
100. Tac., *Ann.* 12.52 and *Hist.* 2.75; Dio Cass. 60.16.1–3; also Marshall, "Women on Trial," 351, his case no. 28. Syme, *Augustan*, 278, n. 62 and (1970), 99, n. 1, discusses the possibility that Vibia's actual name was Vinicia. Syme, *Augustan*, Table XV, shows her marriage into the family of M. Livius Drusus Libo. This is case no. 6 for Cramer, *Astrology*, 261–62, his case no. 6 of trials prosecuted under 11 CE Augustan edict.
101. Syme, *Augustan*, 278–79 for Camillus's revolt.

102. Although it does not fall into Douglas's categories for why magic accusation happens, it is worth noting here that many of the cases of magic accusations against women happen in conjunction with fears of external military threat. Plancina's accusation falls in the context of a threat of revolt in Germany; updates on the revolt of Tacfarinus in N. Africa are reported in conjunction with the trials of Aemilia Lepida and Numantina; a war in Thrace precedes Pulchra's accusation; fears about Mithridates precede Lollia's case. Mary Beth Norton's study of accusation at Salem (*In the Devil's Snare: The Salem Witchcraft Crisis of 1692* [New York: Knopf, 2002]) offers intriguing parallels. In this study she argues that the accusations of witchcraft in late seventeenth-century New England are best explained by the struggles the settlers were having with Native Americans. She argues that witchcraft accusations constructed by the afflicted girls had a great deal in common with fears of Indians and that those accused could be connected with mismanagement of the war front.
103. Tac., *Ann.* 12.53.
104. Tac., *Ann.* 12.64–65; Suet., *Ner.* 7.1 and 34.5; *PIR*^{3} D 180 (1933). Marshall, "Women on Trial," 354 and 365, and n. 57 lists this as a doubtful senatorial trial, instead suggesting that it was a trial that took place *intra cubiculum*. The case of Domitia Lepida is Cramer's case no. 8 in *Astrology*, 263–64 of the prosecution of the 11 CE edict.
105. Suet., *Ner.* 5.2.
106. *PIR*^{2} L 414 for Locusta.
107. For her poisoning of Claudius, Tac., *Ann.* 12.66; of Britannicus, *Ann.* 13.15; and her supplying of Nero's poison, Suet. *Ner.* 47.
108. Dio Cass. 64.3.
109. Tac., *Ann.* 16.8–9; Marshall, "Women on Trial," 349, case no. 23; Syme, *Augustan*, Tables XII and XIII for Junia Lepida, daughter of Aemilia Lepida (distant cousin of the Aemilia Lepida, wife of Quirinius, discussed above) and M. Junius Silanus (cos. 19 CE).
110. Barry Baldwin, "Executions, Trials and Punishment in the Reign of Nero," PP 22 (1967): 425–39, 428. Baldwin does not, however, deal with this prosecution of Junia Lepida in any detail nor does he focus on charges related to *artes magicae*.
111. Tac., *Ann.* 16.30–3 and Dio Cass. 62.26.3. Marcia Servilia is Marshall's case no. 24 (Marshall, "Women on Trial"), 349–50. Baldwin dismisses the case against Servilia's father, Q. Marcius Barea Soranus, without any direct mention of Servilia. His basic conclusion on this was, following Syme, that "Soranus was not quite a paragon" ("Executions," 438–39). Cramer, *Astrology*, 264–65, case no. 9 includes a discussion of the exact edict Servilia must have violated, that of 11 CE.
112. Mart. 1.13 recounts the story of the elder Arria's suicide encouragement-by-example to her husband A. Caecina Paetus (actually a co-conspirator of the husband of Vibia).

113. This is the father of the M. Lepidus (cos. 6 CE) as discussed in Syme, "Marcus," 30–49. In this article, Syme provides an extended discussion of the men of this lineage and Tacitus's favorable depiction of this powerful family with the capacity for rule. Paullus Aemilius Lepidus's (cos. 34 BCE) cousin's daughter is the Aemilia Lepida charged in 20 CE. His sister's granddaughter is the Domitia Lepida charged in 54 CE. Domitia Lepida is the sister in law of Claudia Pulchra, charged in 26 CE. Claudia Pulchra is the step-daughter of Paullus Aemilius Lepidus in his second marriage to Marcella (minor). In addition, Claudia Pulchra's aunt Claudia (sister of her father M. Valerius Appianus, cos. 12 BCE) was the second wife of P. Sulpicius Quirinius, Appianus's 12 BCE consular colleague and former husband of Aemilia Lepida, charged in 20 CE. Fabia Numantina is related to Claudia Pulchra through marriage. She marries Sex. Appuleius (cos. 14 CE), son of Quinctilia, Claudia Pulchra's sister-in-law through her marriage to P. Quinctilius Varus (cos. 13 BCE, of Teutoberger Wald fame). Finally, Junia Lepida is the great-granddaughter of Paullus Aemilius Lepidus. Those four women charged with offenses related to the *artes magicae* who do not fit neatly into this stemma are nonetheless of noble aristocratic background. Munatia Plancina, who married into the Gnaei Pisones (Syme, *Augustan*, 369 does point out that Munatia Plancina's own *nobilitas* was recent, either her father or grandfather being the *novus homo* consul in 42 BCE); Lollia Paulina (descended from L. Volusius Saturninus, cos. 12 BCE, and M. Aurelius Cotta); Vibia (or Vinicia); and Marcia Servilia.
114. The eastern connections of this family extend back to Lucius Aemilius Paullus the victor in the Third Macedonian War in 168 BCE and his son Publius Scipio Aemilianus Africanus, the final conqueror of Carthage in 146 CE.
115. Richlin "Carrying Water in a Sieve: Class and the Body in Roman Women's Religion," in *Women and Goddess Traditions*, ed. Karen King (Minneapolis: Fortress, 1989), 331–32.
116. On the inherent misogyny of witch-hunting and the idea of witch-hunting as woman-hunting/hating, see most notably Andrea Dworkin, *Woman Hating* (New York: E. P. Dutton, 1974), 118–50, Anne L. Barstow, *Witchcraze: A New History of the European Witch Hunts* (San Francisco: Harper Collins, 1994), *passim*, and Christina Larner, *Enemies of God: The Witch-Hunt in Scotland* (Baltimore: Johns Hopkins University Press, 1981), 3, 92–93, 197. Larner is sometimes critiqued by feminists (see especially Barstow) for her characterization of witchcraft accusations as "sex-related" but not "sex-specific." Diane Purkiss, *The Witch in History: Early Modern and Twentieth-Century Representations* (New York: Routledge, 1996), 7–29, challenges the way in which witchcraft/magic accusations have become an unexamined battle cry of a radical feminism divorced from historical reality. On women accusing other women, see Clarke Garrett, "Women and Witches: Patterns of Analysis," *Signs* 3, no. 2 (1977): 461–70, 462–63, and Lyndal Roper, *Oedipus and the Devil: Witchcraft, Sexuality and Religion in Early Modern Europe* (New York: Routledge, 1994), 199–225. For women testifying as witnesses against other women in witchcraft cases, see Clive Holmes, "Women and Witnesses," *PaP* 140 (1993): 45–78.

7

Drunken Hags with Amulets and Prostitutes with Erotic Spells: The Re-*Feminization of Magic in Late Antique Christian Homilies*

Dayna S. Kalleres

Introduction

By the early imperial period, Greco-Roman literature had constructed a deeply chiseled portrait of the witch—a harrowing image of a powerful, sexually voracious, female magical practitioner. Countless portraits have surfaced of a similar stripe: Horace's Canidia, Ovid's and Seneca's Medea, Apuleius's Pamphile, to name but a few.[1] We also have Juvenal's power-hungry Roman matriarchs dispensing *pharmakeia* with haphazard abandon and frequently fatal consequence.[2] Equally pervasive, though more humorous than frightening, are the descriptions of female healers. Old, drunken women offering amulets, incantations, and other magical wares soak the pages of Roman satire as well as moral discourse.[3]

Despite the existence of figures ready for Christian literary adaptation, Christian authors in the early imperial period generally turned away from female magical agency. When delineating boundaries marking the several dimensions of "true" Christian identity, as Kimberly Stratton has shown, authors instead presented women as "the victims of male magical predation, inverting the common stereotype of sorceresses enlisting magic to manipulate affections of male targets."[4] Stratton attributes this inversion to "Christianity's marginal status in the pre-Constantinian Empire" and locates a shift back to accusatory rhetoric aimed at women's illicit ritual activities after the third century.[5] While this was indeed the case and appearances of female magic in the ensuing centuries were infrequent, the full expression of such frightening imagery would lie dormant for the most part until the anti-witchcraft writings of the late medieval period.

The purpose here is to consider the occasional resurfacing of female magic in late antique Christian texts. And as we shall discover, though the appearances of female magic were rare, the surprising consistency of those images suggests that they served a narrowly circumscribed purpose. Ecclesiastical leaders were dealing with fragile and shifting positions of power in the evolving world of the post-Constantinian era; more to the point, they were grappling with the formidable challenge of extending the church's paternal reach deep into the growing number of families now entering the church. When and where church leaders were able to gain view into the domestic life of their flock, congregants' ritual practices were troubling to say the least. Church authorities often discovered a domestic sphere engaging in ritual practices hardly up to the ethical standards of the Christian church. In the church's endeavors to reshape the Christian family, if not indeed redefine family-church relations, female magic made a dramatic re-entrance into Christian discourse as an ever-present threat to the Christian family as the church struggled to maintain its ecclesiastical integrity. Often these families were situated in cities deeply rooted to a polytheist past.[6]

In this chapter, I will consider how patristic authors adapted certain Greco-Roman literary types of female magical practitioners in an effort, in a sense, to frighten the Christian household and family into existence: 1) "old drunken hags" who introduced healing magic into the Christian home and 2) prostitutes whose erotic magic lured Christian husbands out of the home, thus disrupting or even destroying families. The meager evidentiary pool limits my analysis to a few authors: Athanasius, Augustine, Basil of Caesarea, and Caesarius of Arles, with John Chrysostom dominating. Finally, I adopt Stratton's working definition of magic: that is, magic as a discourse of alterity. As Stratton explains, magic appeared in moments demanding identitarian clarity; authors deployed culturally familiar stereotypes that they then molded to demark localized, situational boundaries. Descriptions of magical practice, rather than reflecting a historical fact, functioned as a discourse: "dynamic, twisting, and contorting to meet the ideological needs of various situations."[7] To that end, magic in post-Constantinian Christian discourse served many of the same functions as magic in Greco-Roman literature from the late Republic and early Imperial periods; magic marked and/or constructed ritual and social aberrance. Images of female magical practice were discursive objects marking an Other, which measured the inverse construction of proper Christian identity both ritually and socially in specific, local situations of the post-Constantinian period. Therefore, I wish to clarify at the outset that I am reading these images with a view to their boundary-marking function rather than in a historically positivist manner.

I do not deny the plausibility that these images reflected actual socio-historical and cultural types: undoubtedly elderly women knowledgeable in *remedia* helped Christian children recover from illness and prostitutes dabbled in magic in an effort to retain their clients, many of whom were Christian husbands. What is unlikely—and what is unverifiable in any event—is that the authors surveyed here were referring to specific historical women and situations; rather, I consider how the authors drew upon well-known literary tropes in constructing their rhetorical invective and also played upon shared cultural knowledge to heighten the emotional tenor of that invective. With that caveat in place, let us move back toward the fourth century.

After Constantine: A New Ecclesiastical Presence in the Public and Private Spaces of Empire

The Council of Nicea (325 CE) dictated an imperial orthodoxy anticipating the development of an orthopraxy on a widespread, *public* scale. Bearing an imperially backed directive, ecclesiastical authorities stood in public spheres throughout the empire shaped by ceremonials, religious rites, processions, and calendars that were Roman. While these rituals reflected the Greek, Egyptian, and Syrian elements in particular localities, they were decisively non-Christian. Church leaders lacked the ritual traditions enabling an easy transition from the marginal and hidden to the public and visible.[8] Complicating matters, as Ramsay MacMullen pointed out long ago, ecclesiastical leaders now faced congregations full of individuals who had only recently turned to Christianity, many for a less than pious interest in social mobility.[9] To ecclesiastical leaders' general dismay, many congregants as well as clergy remained comfortable in their notion of a Christian identity that blended almost seamlessly into many of the non-Christian social, cultural, and religious arenas of life that had changed very little in the several years following 325 CE.[10]

This predicament fueled church leaders' endeavors to delineate a ritual divide between Christian versus non-Christian identity as well as divine versus demonic cosmology. In this discourse, church leaders conflated a demonized magic with an equally demonized *idolatreia* and *paganos superstitio*.[11] All three—*magia*, *idolatreia*, and *superstitio*—met their demise and thus their eradication from the public as well as most private spheres in two historical events: Christ's arrival followed by Constantine's victory.[12] In his *Oration in Praise of Constantine*, for example, Eusebius of Caesarea contended that with the rise of Constantine "those apostate spirits . . . who fastened on the souls of men"[13] would no longer be able to lend unconstrained power for "charms of forbidden magic, and the compulsion of unhallowed songs and incantations;"[14] demons could also no longer "[lurk] within their statues, or lay concealed in secret and dark recesses, eager to drink their libations, and inhale the odor of their sacrifices."[15] Athanasius of Alexandria featured Antony interrogating Greek philosophers: "Where are your oracles now? Where are the incantations of the Egyptians? Where are magicians' phantasms?"[16] All had suffered a mysterious decline in efficacy since the historical event of Christ's crucifixion: "Where the sign of the cross occurs, magic is weakened and sorcery has no effect."[17] In his *de Doctrina Christiana*, Augustine separated Christian ritual engagement with divine beings from pagan *superstitio*. The latter encompassed rituals devised "to consult and make agreements with demons on the basis of conventional and established signs"—such as "the many magical arts."[18] The catalog of forbidden practice consisted of the following: books of *augures* and *haruspices*, markings or characters, *praecantationes* (incantations), *ligaturae* (amulets), astrology, daily acts of superstition, interpretations of bodily twitches, to name a few.[19] Here Augustine conjoined *mageia*, idolatry, cult, and any manner of divination *technē*. In *de Civitate Dei*, Augustine again critiqued humanity's sinful inquisitiveness, leading to demonic communications "which they call magic (*magia*), or the more despicable term sorcery (*goēteia*) or more honorific (*theurgy*)."[20]

Descriptions of *female* magic, however, narrow the focus of ritual censure in a specific manner to speak to the issues of domestic orthopraxy and Christian family. Silly, old, drunken hags from the underbelly of urban life offered healing incantations for sick babies who were tended by nurses within the home who frantically affixed protective amulets to the infants' arms;[21] prostitutes used erotic magic to bind once obedient husbands in passionate infidelities that destroyed Christian families.[22] In parading such women before their congregations, church leaders intended a general warning regarding the dangers facing a Christian household in a still largely non-Christian world. Authors inserted more discriminating, subtle messages in the specific literary "type" of female magical practitioner as well as the individualized threat that each posed to the Christian family. In so doing, bishops and priests attempted to persuade their congregants to rely on the church's ecclesiastical and sacramental ritual protection over and above their own deeply embedded traditional ritual instincts. The church leaders surveyed here recognized that their task amounted to nothing less than a ritual conversion of the Late Roman household—in fact, a ritual conversion of the domestic sphere long overdue; likewise these leaders understood that such a conversion, if accomplished, would reconfigure or readjust social relations and power hierarchies in the family. Consequently, long before this could happen in reality, it must first take place much more dramatically and persuasively in sermonic description. To that end clerical leaders appear here and there in sermons performing the role of ecclesiastical *Pater familias*, ritually empowered as a caretaker for all members of a Christian family. And, indeed, eventually through prayer, blessings, and evolved usages of the sacraments, clergy would come to penetrate hidden domestic spheres and colonize what was once far beyond their reach. Bishops and priests would stand in areas that were once the exclusive territory of the Devil and its rituals.

Old Women Healers and Drunken Old Witches in Greco-Roman Literature

In *Homilia in Colossenses. 8,* John Chrysostom warns mothers tending sick children against inviting a "drunk and silly old woman" who promises healing through incantations. In *Ad Illuminandos catechesis.* 2, he similarly admonishes the recently baptized not to tarnish their seal by inviting "half-witted, drunken hags" into their homes to perform, we may reasonably presume, healing incantations. Athanasius chastises his congregation for a similar transgression.

> For the old woman pours a flood of words over you for twenty obol or, for a quarter of wine, she offers the invocation of a snake. And you stand like an ass, gaping wide, carrying upon your neck the filth of a four-footed animal, while deceiving the seal of the saving cross.[23]

It is important to realize that in using phrases such as "half-witted, drunken hags" John Chrysostom and Athanasius were baiting their sermons with rhetoric that would have undoubtedly caught the ears of culturally well-versed congregations. In these brief admonishments, each church father spoke in a deliberately provocative mixture of stock literary types that stretched back to Ancient Greek comedy because their urban audiences were still rooted in Greco-Roman literary culture. While the church used imagery lifted from Greco-Roman texts to demarcate Christian ritual identity, they also changed the imagery in the process. To comprehend fully the transformation, we need to understand what literary types circulated. How would audiences have reacted to the description of "half-witted, drunken hags," entering their homes and performing incantations and other magical practices? More to the point, how would they have responded to the added threat that such a transgression would compromise the power of their own baptismal seal?

The old female healer (*graus*, *anus*) is found throughout Greco-Roman literature.[24] We find her performing purification fumigations, incantations, amulet manufacture, snake charming, chasing away fevers, warding off the evil eye, and providing a variety of other services for the ill and diseased, as well as those emotionally or mentally compromised. While the literature clearly presumed that old women healers were permanent fixtures in the religious worlds of the ancient Mediterranean from classical Greece to late antiquity and far beyond, they occupied a humble, lowly position in the hierarchy of magic workers in the ancient world. It was precisely their debased, humble reputation, it would seem, which shielded them from the relentless anti-magic and demonizing rhetorical invective that would come to envelop male practitioners of questionable rituals (*augures*, *haruspices*, and astrologers, for instance, but also *magoi* and *goētes*) and that fundamentally constructed the frightening images of female sorcery in the early imperial period (Horace's Canidia or Apuleius's Pamphile). Intriguingly, the appearance or even mention of the old woman healer could also serve as an indictment of those who sought her help. Men who turned to her were superstitious and foolish individuals who had begun to slide precipitously down the slippery gendered scale of the ancient world. By contrast, women who turned to old women healers demonstrated their inherent mental limitations; women's innate irrationality left them prey to unscrupulous ritual practitioners. Clearly, wives needed firm guidance; the husband should have control over the purse strings.

In what follows I offer a brief survey of old women healers in the literature to give a sense of the wide range of services they offered as well as the ideological undercurrent conveyed in their presentation. Then we can begin to understand which aspects of this discourse within Greco-Roman literature the church fathers adapted for the task of colonizing the domestic sphere and crafting the ecclesiastical family.

In performing her most basic and base ritual skill, an old female healer possessed tremendously powerful saliva. Theocritus (third century BCE) mentions the ability of the *graus* to spit on her clients to protect them from the evil eye (*baskania*), a skill she could teach to any pupil sufficiently hydrated and willing to learn. Female ritualists were also known for their skills in amulet manufacture. As Diodorus Siculus remarks, for example, women (*yunaika*) made amulets with the inscribed name of Heracles, who was a wizard (*goēs*) from the Idaean Dactyli of Crete and "practiced charms and initiatory rites and mysteries."[25] Diodorus adds that the women also incorporated Heracles's own incantations into their practice. While his account conveys the tone of ancient ethnographic account, other descriptions present female ritual healing in a manner that casts an unmistakable and unflattering shadow over her clients. In the opening of Menander's *Phasma,* we meet Pheidas, a wealthy young man who had just seen a disturbing apparition of a beautiful woman; he complains to his slave, Syros, that he feels "strange and out of sorts." Presuming his master's complaints are the typical fare of the idle rich, Syros responds dismissively, "Find an empty medicine (*kenon pharmakon*) for your empty illness (*kenon*) and believe it's helping." Syros then counsels his master, Pheidas, to seek the aid of certain women (*yunaikes*) who are well-rehearsed in the art of magic; they who would encircle him, massaging and fumigating him. He further advises Pheidas to follow their actions and spray his body with water from three springs, adding salt and lentils.[26] The poet Tibullus characterizes the practices of female healers even less favorably.[27] In an effort to regain the affections of his Delia, who was tortured by nightmares, he worked together with an old female healer (*anus*); as she chanted her magical incantation (*magico carmine*), Tibullus scattered cleansing sulfur all around Delia. Once the healer left, Tibullus labored on to banish the "cruel dreams that had to be thrice propitiated with the offering of holy meal." Tibullus went so far as to wear a woolen headdress and ungirdled tunic; he performed nine vows to Trivia/Hecate in the dead of night. Anything for his beloved, who in the end still gave her affections to another. In *de Superstitio*, Plutarch ridicules those men whose *deisidaimonia* conjures horrifying, nightmarish apparitions in their sleep: "When, later, such persons arise from their beds, they do not contemn nor ridicule these things, nor realize that not one of the things that agitated them was really true, but trying to escape the shadow of delusion that has nothing bad at the bottom."[28] Such men mistake nightmares for frightening apparitions (*phantasma*) and in their deluded (*apates*) state foolishly seek help from conjurers (*agyrtai*) and sorcerers (*goētes*), who easily persuade them to call "the old woman (*graus*) who performs magical purifications (*perimaktrian*)."[29] They follow this with other similarly superstitious activities: dipping in the ocean, sitting on the ground all day, smearing mud, wallowing in filth, and other immersions.[30]

Elderly female healers emerge relatively unscathed in these descriptions. Their male clients, by contrast, are clear targets of rhetorical opprobrium; men's dependence on an old hag's magic not only reveals their unhinged, irrational, superstitious personality but that some kind of effeminizing passion has unraveled their masculinity. The old female healer with her purifications, incantations, and fumigations appears fleetingly in these descriptions; she functions only to confirm the disintegration of her client's masculinity.[31]

Elite male authors were no less sparing when criticizing women who hired *praecantrices* (female singers of incantations) to visit their households. Authors in the late Hellenistic/early Imperial period had particular contempt for female gullibility, which pushed out all common sense from the domestic sphere, allowing *praecantrices* and other female magic workers into the home. In Plautus's *Miles Gloriosus*, Periplectomenus humorously complains of the costs a witless wife demands to run a household:

> Please dear husband, give me some money, Mother needs a little present. Give me some cash to buy some candy; Give me some money to give next Sunday to the *praecantrici, coniectrici, hariolae atque haruspicae*. If I don't have the cash I'll enrage the lady who tells the future from my eyebrows.[32]

Before moving forward let us make a few observations regarding our sources, more specifically, what they can and cannot tell us. This literature strongly suggests that the healing rituals existed as well as the healers; however, the passages do not provide reliable insight into much else. Nonetheless, such descriptions do offer an important window into a robust discussion among the male elite, the cultured literati, as to the slow and steady harm such healing rituals inflict in society along gender lines. I am far from the first to make this suggestion; still I would like to comment further regarding the interpretation of the late antique materials. Even as scholars note the shifting ethical, theological, and ethical aspects of the now-Christian context in which we find old female healers in the post-Constantinian material, they read the figures themselves in a positive manner. That is to say, for example, interpreters treat John Chrysostom's descriptions of half-witted, drunken hags as confirmation that certain socio-religious roles (i.e., old female healer/witch) continued relatively unchanged from the Hellenistic period into late antiquity.[33] The only difference is that a thin, Christianized layer coated the surface of her spells in this later period. To that end, what I would like to draw attention to is the ways church leaders clung tightly to the old female healer in her original literary form and in what ways they attempted to re-fashion her. In reconfiguring elements of gender, old age, and magic within this Greco-Roman literary type for a Christian context, Christian leaders produced new figures bearing very specific, condemnatory messages regarding religious alterity and aberration. John Chrysostom, Athanasius, and Caesarius of Arles needed to project images of demonically aligned, old hags threatening the very souls of feverish Christian children in order to compel mothers to surrender their control over the domestic sphere and grant that power to church leaders whose ritual expertise could keep Christian family safe physically and spiritually. Referencing the old female healers exactly as they appeared in the literary tradition would have hardly achieved this goal.

To that end, we must consider how Christian authors not only absorbed this Greco-Roman type into Christian discourse, but how they transformed it. Here the first issue to consider is what new elements John Chrysostom and Athanasius add in the indictment of these female healers: both refer to them as drunken; John adds half-witted or silly. By adding these small descriptives to the *graus* who heals, John Chrysostom and Athanasius tap into a character type among the old female magical practitioners in Greco-Roman literature—one whose moral character is a central point of interest and a target for derision. Thus she proves quite a departure from our old female healer. And as such she, rather than her client, draws attention as a target of rhetorical invective.

A specific type of female magical practitioner associated with alcohol comes into sharp view rather dramatically in Roman literature during the Augustan era: the older female procuress (*lena*) turned sorceress (*saga*). Matthew Dickie understands the drunken, magic wielding *lena* to reflect a chronologically wide-sweeping social reality and situates her into his view of a sordid underworld of consumerized sex and magic: "a Demi-monde made up of prostitutes (*meretrices*) and procuresses (*lenae*) and of well-to-do young men who have nothing better to do with themselves than to have affairs with prostitutes."[34] Dickie describes a logical progression in the life of a prostitute: she gains a necessary proficiency in erotic magic, especially the more aggressive *agōgē* spells that were tools of the trade in her line of work.[35] Finally, of course, she consumes wine in copious amounts to soften the harsh realities of aging in a friendless, possibly homeless, and impoverished condition.

Leaving aside the question of the merits of this sociological model, I direct attention to the literary construction of these women. These women appeared in fragments before they exploded onto the pages of Roman love-elegy: a drunk, but non-magic practicing procuress in Herodas's 1st *Mime*; fleeting mention of an old woman offering ineffectual erotic incantations in Theocritius 2nd *Idyll*; and, of course, the trials and tribulations of *lenae* fill several scenes in the plays of Plautus.[36] When elderly *lenae* stumble drunkenly onto the pages of Roman elegiac poetry, however, their character has decidedly changed. Ovid, Sextus Propertius, and Tibullus, for example, hasten the physical disintegration of decrepit, wine-soaked hags while managing to magnify the dangers they pose to others in their necromantic arts;[37] we see *lenae* bleary-eyed with drink and yet capable of effecting aggressive and disturbing forms of magic.

In *Amores*, Ovid presents the *lena* Dipsas, who tried to instruct her girlfriend in the more canny skills of prostitution: "Don't give a free night because he's handsome; tell him to raise the cash from one of his men friends first. Easy does it while setting the trap but once he's caught squeeze him hard as you like."[38] Ovid harshly describes Dispas's "wispy white hair", "baggy cheeks", and "alcoholic eyes." In Ovid's words: "Rosey Dawn has never seen her sober." In stark contrast to her feeble appearance, the old woman (*anus*) possessed surprisingly deadly potency as the local witch (*illa magas artes*)—who "can reverse the flow of water, whirl the magic wheel, cull herbs, brew aphrodisiacs, guarantee the weather, cloud or sunshine, blood red stars . . . or a bloody moon . . . She's a night-bird—probably flits about in owlish feathers . . . And her eyes are twine-pupilled, glinting double. She's necromantic too and chants earth-splitting spells." Throughout the poem, Ovid manages to hold in tight, disquieting juxtaposition the shape of a doddering, inebriated buffoon dishing out advice to a young prostitute with that of a much more horrifying demonic creature capable of performing vicious and powerful dark forms of *goēteia*. Inexplicably, these contrasting figures inhabit the same body, and people deceived by Dipsas's apparent frailty would likely regret their mistake.

Sextus Propertius offers an almost identical characterization of his girlfriend's procuress, Acanthis, who could "blind watchful husbands with her skill."[39] In order to do so "she plucked out the eyes of undeserving crows with her nail." Acanthis also transformed her back into that of a nocturnal wolf (*nocturne lupo*) by "daring to impose the laws of the enchanted moon." Much to Propertius's dread, she seemed to plot against him as well. She consulted screeching owls about his blood and "read hippomanes, growths on a new born foal." Like Dipsas, Acanthis's magical power was paradoxically harnessed to a withering form: "I saw the phlegm congeal on her wrinkled neck and the bloody saliva passing through gaps in her teeth and her rotten breath expire on her paternal mats. . . ." Repeatedly, Propertius hoped for her death as he cursed her shade to suffer an alcoholic's perpetual thirst.

Aberrations like Dipsas and Acanthis emerge in Roman love elegy out of a rhetorical mixture of satirical disdain and horror. Ovid and Propertius express unrelenting disgust for the decrepitude of aging female flesh; the *lena*'s decaying female body is an abomination to behold; moreover, she reeks of alcohol. We could almost dismiss her entirely, but her frailty is an illusion; in fact, it is dangerously deceptive. Hidden inside the seemingly vulnerable, even infirm body, is a diabolic kind of magic. These *lenae* do not perform run-of-the-mill incantations or erotic magic; Ovid and Propertius describe living carcasses that enchant the moon, transform into other animals, and rip apart the living bodies of humans and animals. An old, garrulous, drunken woman, these poems insist, is never what she appears to be.

In the *Dialogue of Courtesans*, Lucian holds the world of old women, wine, prostitution, and erotic magic at an emotional distance. In *Dialogue* 4, the courtesan Melitta is desperate to recover a former lover who has fallen in love with another. As she laments to her friend Bacchis, "if we could only find an old women (*graus*), as I said! Her presence could save me." Bacchis offers "a most useful witch (*pharmakis*) of Syrian birth who is still quite fresh and firm."[40] Moreover, she could attest personally that the woman's skills in erotic magic were exemplary. Bacchis describes an elaborate ritual that involved the witch fumigating a piece of Bacchis's lover's clothing with sulfur and then whirling a rhombos around while singing incantations of "horrible and outlandish names." Her fee was low, only a drachma; likewise the old woman (*graus*) demanded a bowl of mixed wine which she then drank all by herself.

These women—old, ugly and drunken—stand apart from the elderly female healers in many respects. But there is one difference in particular that I would point out: they are not healers. In fact, their magic could cause significant harm. Likewise, authors give them reprehensible personalities, often matched by a repulsive physical appearance. While these drunken *lenae* and old *sagae* grab and hold the audience's attention, the old female healer is barely noticed. As the drunken *lena*/old *saga* is engaged in incantations and fumigations, the audience takes note of the horrors of rituals as well as the horrifying ritualists. By contrast, the prototype of the female healer functions to draw disapproving focus to those around them: superstitious and/or love-obsessed men and irrational women of the household. In the post-Constantinian period, Christian authors, aware of the individuated depth of these two different literary types from the magic world, fused them together in complex ways. A close reading, especially of John Chrysostom's passages, reveals a deliberate intermingling of the two sets of characteristics. Many within the audience would have been familiar with the full literary background of both and aware of the constituent parts coming together in the creation of the "half-witted and drunken woman" who could heal a feverish child. In the generation of her composite nature, however, she had been loosened from the predictable pattern of action and conventional teleological message defined in Greco-Roman literature. Thus she now had the potential to project a much more dangerous presence. Along with healing spells and bottles of wine, she brought something quite deadly into the houses of the physically sick—she smuggled in the Devil himself for the specific purpose of destroying Christian souls. Viewed from this angle, newly hybridized figures, who originated from the older world of Greco-Roman magic, could be made to bear a darker meaning as well as an urgent message in their Christian, post-Constantinian context.

Women's Ritual Space and Domestic Invisibility

Matthew Dickie has cited Chrysostom's silly, drunken hag as testimony of the Christianization of the old female healer in late antiquity.[41] While this may indeed have been the case, I would suggest also considering the role this woman and all female ritual practitioners, including the pious Christian mother, served in this sermon. They marked an essential divide between correct Christian practice and dangerous *idolatreia* as it related to the private, Christian, domestic sphere. To that end, we must consider the powerful image Chrysostom chose to arrange opposed descriptions of female ritual: a sick child. He selected an emotionally palpable image to insist upon an important theological point. Congregants were overly attached to an embodied life. Concern for the health of loved ones had led many, most especially mothers, to turn to questionable ritual healing. Attending to physical health to this degree ultimately risked spiritual death.

In late antiquity, survival was not an easy task. Disease, poverty, famine, natural disasters, imperial rule, and war conspired against the health and longevity of everyone regardless of socio-economic status. Constantine passed a law that recognized these hardships in an interesting way. Marking a divide between illicit magic and healing *remedia*, *Cod. Theod.* 9.16.3 (319 CE) condemned "the science (*scientia*) of those men who are equipped with magical arts (*magicis accincti artibus*)."[42] Individuals discovered to have harmed anyone were punished severely. But then the law starkly deviated, authorizing *remedia* intended for the healing of human bodies. The law also sheltered ritual actions that protected against natural disasters.[43] In the beginning of the fourth century, then, imperial law essentially legalized ritual *remedia*.

As the fourth century progressed, however, Christian rituals steadily gained footing in public spaces. Ecclesiastical rituals spilled from the church to the street in stational liturgies; martyr cults moved from distant cemeteries to crowd the city center.[44] Consequently, pagan cults—and once ambiguously treated ritual practices such as cult divination (e.g., *haruspices* and *augures*)—increasingly became the target of Christian opprobrium and imperial regulation. In relation to this overarching trend, church authorities censured traditional *remedia* (e.g., amulets, incantations, and phylacteries), which attended to the healing of the body. Such condemnation helped to construct an emerging notion of "Christian" ritual *remedia*. Baptism, the Eucharist, and the Sign of the Cross were promoted as an "ecclesiastical form of therapy" which treated the body, but more importantly, the soul.[45] In this discourse, sacramental rituals, martyr cults, and holy men offered powerful healing, while traditional rituals and ritual objects—involving amulets, incantations, and incubatory practices of questionable spiritual content—were increasingly condemned as illicit, demonic, and magical.

David Frankfurter has argued that Christian leaders' insistent polemic against such rituals—labeling them magic, *superstitio*, or demonic—attests to the degree to which lay Christians viewed traditional healing practices as normal.[46] Augustine's own comments incisively illustrate the wider ecclesiastical effort to address the inveterate ritual habits of many Christians: "someone comes along as you are lying there in a fever and in danger of death, and assures you that he can rid you of certain spells and charms . . . such things are from the *magi*."[47] Church authorities were sharply aware that physical illness could override one's adherence to religious boundaries, leading a person to choose cures that moved into dangerous ritual territory. In a Christian's physical health, late antique Christian authors found a literary crucible. In detailed depictions of sickness and disease plaguing innocent Christians, traditional ritual *remedia*—such as amulets, incantations, other folk practices, and healing sites—transmuted into the Devil's deceits. Likewise authors appropriated the categories of traditional healing to describe Christian rituals/sacraments—such as the sign of the cross or baptism—as powerful "*remedia* of Christ." They built a concept of Christian *remedia* in juxtaposition against a deliberately exaggerated account of non-Christian healing practices. To that end the silly, drunken hag provided a striking contrast to Christian orthopraxy. We see this in Athanasius of Alexandria's attack against congregants, which I quoted partially above and which follows, in more complete form. Athanasius criticized specifically their failure to realize the healing power of the cross when they instead turned to popular practices.[48]

> For the old woman pours a flood of words over you for twenty obol or, for a quarter of wine, she offers the invocation of a snake. And you stand like an ass, gaping wide, carrying upon your neck the filth of a four-footed animal, while deceiving the seal of the saving cross. Not only are the illnesses afraid of that seal, but also the entire crowd of demons fears and are astounded by it. For this reason, every sorcerer (*goēs*) is unsealed."[49]

AnneMarie Luijendijk astutely observes in her own contribution to this volume that Athanasius drew upon the characterization of drunken old women who performed magic in Apuleius's *Metamorphosis*. For his poor choice in ritual practitioners, Lucan was turned into a donkey. Athanasius, by contrast, described the potential for a far more consequential transformation. Anyone who entrusted his health to an old woman offering "amulets and sorceries" would jeopardize his religious and mental state.

> But if someone consulted amulets (*periapta*) and sorceries (*goēteiai mataia boēthemata*), let him know this clearly, that he has made himself instead of a believer, an unbeliever; instead of a Christian, a pagan; instead of wise, an idiot; instead of reasonable, an irrational person.[50]

We should read John's sermon in light of the larger Christianizing shift in the post-Constantinian church. His narrative of a sick child indicated a painful, but necessary, divide between what was and what was not Christian *remedia*. To that end, let us notice the manner in which this section begins in *Hom. in Col.* 8: John's depiction of a proper Christian mother. This "daughter of Abraham" who despite the illness and even potential death of her child, engaged in only one action: thanking God. "She made no amulets (*periapta*)" despite the overwhelming temptation to do so:

> Even though those [amulets] are unavailing, a mere cheat and mockery, still there were nevertheless those who persuaded her that they do avail, and she chose rather to see her child dead, than to put up with idolatry.[51]

Christianized—but not *Christian*—ritual practices abound in John's narrative world, serving to represent the confusing situation a mother in his congregation faced in a time of crisis. Not only did John attempt to acknowledge the ambiguity facing Christians who must select from an array of ritual choices in Antioch, he also presented the ease with which a person's ritual misstep could lead to a serious theological transgression.

> For these amulets (*periapta*), though they who make money by them are forever rationalizing about them, and saying, "we call upon God and do nothing extraordinary," and the like, and the old woman (*graus*) is a Christian "and one of the faithful," the thing is idolatry.[52]

In this post-Constantinian era, Christianization problematized—but in no way resolved— the dilemma of correct ritual practice. The legitimacy of traditional *remedia* had become a pressing issue as Christian rituals moved to take the public stage and church leaders grew increasingly anxious about what remained lurking within the private sphere. While a *defixione* might invite rousing and even unified rejection from the devout, and at the very least recognition of its theologically problematic nature from the lukewarm congregant, what about a verbal or written formula that simply invoked Jesus? Peter? The Trinity? Regardless of the ambiguity among his congregants, or precisely because of that ambiguity, John was unequivocal. Only one Christian remedy existed: "Sign the cross (*sphragison*)."[53]

John attempted to capture the tension, confusion, and anxiety that his congregation faced when such a crisis arose to test their orthopraxy. In *Hom. in Col. 8.*, he introduced women who automatically turned to tying the names of rivers as a form of protection; women chose amulets, incantations, old wives' tales (*graudeis mythous*) and spells (*grammata*) before they considered the sign of the cross for healing. They engaged in enigmatic rituals involving "soot, ash and salt" which protected against the evil eye. Likewise they believed "Christian" incantations offered by old women could offer real help; even if such rituals failed to heal the sick, at least their actions offered no further harm. By contrast, John insisted that these rituals were deadly due to their demonic nature: "this is that willingness of the devil to cloak our deceit and to give a deleterious drug in honey."[54] The body may have even been healed by these means, but at what cost to the soul?

Our drunken hag appears again couched in almost identical language in John Chrysostom's *Ad Illum cat.* 2 and seems to echo Athanasius's own reference to this character-type.[55] In the final moments of a sermon to those "about to be illuminated" through baptism, John castigated those who not only accepted amulets (*periapta*) but incantations (*epōdai*) "leading drunken and half-witted old women into [their] house."[56] Their presumed defense of such actions reveals the problematic ambiguity involving the status of healing rituals at this time:

> For when we deliver these exhortations, and lead [Christians] away, thinking that they defend themselves, they say, that the woman is a Christian who makes these incantations, and utters nothing else than the name of God. On this account I especially hate and turn away from her, because she makes use of the name of God, with a view to ribaldry. For even the demons uttered the name of God, but still they were demons.[57]

The drunken, silly, old hags of *Hom. in Col. 8.* and *Ad Illum. cat. 2* are striking in their similarity and, therefore, worth considering more closely. In *Hom 8 on Col.*, John had been discussing the issue of *idolatreia* when he suddenly turned to describe a mother who would rather sacrifice her child to fever than make healing amulets.[58] She would also reject women offering amulets and incantations. She understood that a "simple incantation" was the first step on a steady slope to idolatries that would lead her from her home to a pagan temple. John did not use words such as *mageia* or *goēteia*. He instead selected terms and descriptions designating specific ritual actions to suggest incriminatory practice: amulets, incantations, sprinkling of soot and ash, spells and old wives tales. While eschewing direct accusation of *maleficia* or *ars magica*, Chrysostom characterized these traditional *remedia* as "device(s) of Satan." His condemnation reached its height with the introduction of an old woman, who entered freely into the intimate, vulnerable space of a Christian home. She performed incantations bearing a fusion of Christian and non-Christian elements and a disarming interweaving of Greco-Roman literary types from harmless female healer to harmful, drunken *lena*. In this abbreviated mixture of easily recognizable literary portraits, John's audience listened to how simply demonic deceit could gain power over the weak, desperate, unsuspecting members of a Christian household. This was a woman, decrepit and old, hardly a threat and yet by inviting this "drunken and half-witted old woman" into a *Christian* home, a wife or female servant also invited the reversal of the epochal event of Christ's arrival.[59] In this new, not so easily navigable ritual world of burgeoning ecclesiastical Christianity, a person needed a strong guide to point out the proper ritual sources for healing and blessing that lead to salvation. To step off the ritual path, even slightly, was tantamount to stepping directly into the pit of damnation.

In *Ad Illum. cat. 2* again a drunken old woman entered a house, bringing in an obfuscating blend of Christian and non-Christian adjurational content.[60] Like *Hom. in Col. 8,* a heavy issue weighed in the background of the description. John contended that the use of Christianized, though certainly not Christian, *remedia* bore a heavy consequence.

> Do you not know what great result the cross has achieved? It has abolished death, has extinguished sin, has made Hades useless, has undone the power of the devil, and is it not worth trusting for the health of the body? It has raised up the whole world, and do you not take courage in it?[61]

A Christian who turned to old, apparently Christian women who performed healing incantations was not committing a minor ritual infraction. The same held true for the use of amulets and charms. Such an action, no matter how apparently innocuous in its familiarity, worked to reverse the cross's victory over the Devil and his devices. The Devil, eager to regain purchase over humanity, would use any means at his disposal.

Concerns regarding the fallout in a Christian domestic sphere from female ignorance and irrationality endure at least until the sixth century. Caesarius of Arles presented a similar scenario: a crisis of familial health forcing a mother to choose between Christian orthopraxy and magical *remedia*. Before speaking of the similarities in Caesarius's and John's descriptions, let us present the differences in their ecclesiastical situations. Arles experienced an idiosyncratic Christianization process. Christianity came to this Western city much later than it did to the Greek East; it did not grow slowly and organically but through larger conversions in the later fourth century. Consequently, as Klingshirn notes, Christianity "evolved as a local community religion designed with the needs of the peasants in mind."[62] Therefore, non-Christian folk healers and diviners held an inveterate position as "alternative givers of authority in the community" to a greater degree than in Antioch, for example. Like all cities in the Roman Empire from the third century on, Arles experienced "de-Romanizing shifts" and by the sixth century much of the public secular sphere had converted into private living space hidden from the eyes of the church. Caesarius expresses concerns regarding the invisibility and inaccessibility of the Christian domestic sphere, which he felt was more welcoming to the folk healers' *remedia* than a priest's sacraments. In light of this, he constructed a rhetorical invective against private healing practices which in certain ways bears an uncanny resemblance to John Chrysostom's condemnations.

In *Sermon 52* Caesarius addressed mothers who were incapacitated by "grief and terror" when faced with a sick child. Rather than entreating priests to anoint the sick child in blessed oil, according to Caesarius's characterization, they pursued a path that lead to the death of the soul: "Let us consult that soothsayer, diviner, fortune teller or herbalist. Let us sacrifice a garment of the sick person, a girdle that can be seen and measured. Let us offer some magical letters (*caracteres*), let us hang some charms on his neck (*praecantationes adpendamus ad collum*)."[63] Caesarius also reprimanded mothers who were only "apparently wise Christians." While they properly refrained from actively mixing demonic and divine healing themselves, they sent nurses or "other women through whom the Devil suggests these practices" to find *remedia* for their children. Therefore, despite precautions to remain pure themselves, such mothers still invited demons into their homes to execute what Caesarius described as the charms' cruel healings. Caesarius worked within the framework of John Chrysostom's earlier warnings, or at least within the general frame of the Greco-Roman literary trope. Women, as the practitioners/overseers of domestic health, were the means through which the Devil all too easily entered a Christian home. The Devil entered through non-Christian healing practices (magical and *remedia*) and practitioners, thus gaining unlimited access to the intimate spaces of a sick Christian's home during precarious, stressful times. Noticeably absent in Caesarius's list of the Devil's modes of domestic entry is our female healer with (or even without) her bottle of wine.

More insistently than John Chrysostom, Caesarius's sermons promoted—in a deliberate and sustained manner—what Klingshirn has described as an "ecclesiastical form of therapy."[64] He promoted the healing properties of the Eucharist—a campaign suited to this later age when the majority had been baptized at birth. Caesarius urged the sick to run to the church, "receive the Body and Blood of Christ, be anointed by the presbyters with consecrated oil, and ask these presbyters and deacons to pray over [the sick person] in Christ's name. If he does this, he will receive not only bodily health but also the forgiveness of his sins."[65] Caesarius's texts express the church's ritual evolution (in both the East and West) from the possibility of physical healing in ecclesiastical ritual in the fourth century to a guarantee in sacramental rites by the sixth century. As the Eucharist assumes a role as *remedia* for both soul *and body*, the elderly female healer, drunk or otherwise—at least in her ideological guise—fades from the Christian texts.

The Frightening World of Prostitutes and Magic in Greco-Roman Literature

In *Homilia in Romanos 24*, John Chrysostom warned of prostitutes (*pornai*) who "use incantations, libations, philters, potions and innumerable other things [to retain lovers]"; they also invoke the Devil, and use incantations to the dead (*nekuomanteia*) against their clients' wives.[66] They employed magic to make themselves more beautiful and used potions for abortions.

C. Faraone and M. Dickie have both approached Greco-Roman literary accounts describing prostitutes who engage in aggressive love magic. Each has relied heavily upon these texts in formulating their understanding of a lived reality in the ancient world and the situation of certain types of prostitutes within that world. In Faraone's sociological reading, prostitutes, especially those of a higher status referred to as *hetaira*, were engaged in a business practice that was gendered male; that is, they were autonomous or semi-autonomous economic agents, and in the effort to find and secure their clientele, the aggressive form of the *agoge* spell was an important tool of their trade; it was an effective as well as pragmatic means of sustaining their livelihood.[67] Matthew Dickie, by contrast, reads the literature in a somewhat positivist manner, flattening the ideological, symbolic and intertextual aspects of the characters and narratives in individual texts.[68] Dickie looks to magic-working prostitutes of literature (e.g., Simaetha, Canidia, the *sagae* of the Roman elegists, Lucian's Melitta and Bacchis) as testimony of a widespread belief in antiquity that prostitutes did practice magic freely.[69] He has also presented an easily legible, diachronic history of the magic-wielding prostitute and socio-economically autonomous *hetaira* from classical Athens through to late antiquity.[70]

Despite the methodological and perspectival differences separating them, Faraone and Dickie come together to posit that John Chrysostom's multiple warnings against prostitutes' magic offer clear evidence that her socio-religious "type" continues into late antiquity relatively unchanged.[71] Dickie also at times seems to absorb, rather uncritically, the literature's moralizing tone and exaggerated depictions into his reconstruction of the bleak world these women actually inhabited. Hence, we have his "demi-monde" of prostitutes, *lenae*, and male clients lurking in shadows beyond the brightly light civilization that comprised the rest of his ancient world.

Their claims are problematic in that they rest almost entirely on the evidence of John Chrysostom. Second, neither, in any serious manner, considers the wider context of the priest's descriptions in his sermons. Third, they neglect to examine the language John favors in his depiction of magic-wielding prostitutes. If they had, they would have noted Chrysostom's exclusive preference for the word *pornē* and *porneia* in several passages and then addressed the ambiguous meaning of the word. They would have also observed John's deep attachment to Pauline language in 1 Corinthians 6–7. In short, Dickie, and Faraone, who follows his lead, fail to address the constructed nature of passages written not just by any ecclesiastical leader, but by one who did not bear the name "Golden-Mouthed" by chance.[72] Consequently, both reflexively presume *that* rather than critically consider *if* Chrysostom's urgent warnings provide a clear, unadulterated view of a specific type of female magical practitioner who inhabited, if not inundated, the late antique urban environment.[73] What scholars have neglected, therefore, is how Chrysostom used local, cultural fears of prostitutes to develop a new Christian ethical concept and familial construction. However, Chrysostom was not relaying an account of actual women. He projected images of prostitutes—as familiar with the bones of the recently dead in the cemetery as they were with bodies of the recently aroused beneath the sheets—to persuade Christian families (especially husbands) to cling to their ecclesiastical leaders and view their bishop as the ultimate *Pater familias*. Chrysostom emphasized the urgency in managing one's emotions through a steady *Christianized* practice of moderation (*sōphrosynē*) especially in what was still basically a Greek city designed to incite desire (*epithymia*).

For John Chrysostom's strategy to be effective, the images would have to have a footing in reality. An element of socio-historical authenticity certainly informed his construction. And thus Dickie and Faraone are not entirely wrong in their readings. Christians associated with prostitutes, and prostitutes engaged in erotic magic in their business.[74] However, John's descriptions are not a useful piece in discovering how or how much this happened in Antioch. It was never John's intention to provide a verifiable history after all. He was determined to generate frightening projections of jealous, magic-wielding prostitutes and their ability to overturn Christian familial harmony in order to turn his congregation toward a particular mode of protective behavior: his idea of Christian *sōphrosynē*. In crafting prostitutes dabbling in erotic spells and other more harmful forms of magic, he drew upon a rich Greco-Roman literary archive of frightening courtesans. Several in John's urban, educated congregation would have had more than a passing familiarity with authors such as Lucian, Theocritus, Horace, and Ovid. More to the point, perhaps, this literature produced a deeply embedded, yet widespread, sense of unease at the prostitute's ability—both in her powers of sexual seduction and her magical potency—to dissolve a man's free will, thus ripping to shreds the delicate fabric of familial relations. Moreover, undoubtedly, Antioch's population circulated rumors of prostitutes seducing/enslaving clients through frightening magical practice. John's prostitutes, therefore, while not providing a transparent window into historical reality, do consciously reflect the literary and cultural specter of the vengeful, magic-practicing prostitute that still pervaded the late antique city. Now let us consider images of prostitutes and erotic magic in Greco-Roman literature. While the archive is quite rich, space permits only a few examples.

In his *Second Idyll*, Theocritus introduces the plight of Simaetha.[75] Simaetha frames the story of her torrid relationship with the younger Delphis by detailing the preparation and performance of the binding love spells (*katadesmoi philtroi*) that will bring him back. As she describes falling immediately and irreversibly in love with Delphis, she chants to the moon and to Hecate and aspires to make *pharmaka* as potent as Circe or Medea were able to concoct. As she portrays the first time she and Delphis had sex, she displays her skills with the rhombos and adds some of Delphis's possessions to a fire fumigating with bay leaves. Theocritus carefully constructs a portrait of a fearsome sorceress, driven single-mindedly by an erotic passion for a man who no longer wants her and has attached himself to another. But this seems only to enhance her resolve. She replays again and again in her mind the details of their short time together while strengthening her *katadesmoi* with fire spells and a "brayed lizard." Theocritus leaves the reader with the strong impression that erotic desperation and magical ability is dangerous, if not deadly, in an untethered, economically autonomous female. Indeed Delphis may be in danger of losing more than his free will if he does not immediately succumb, as Simaetha adds at the end: "Now with my love magic I will bind him, but if he vex me, so help me, Fates, he shall beat upon the gates of Hades, such evil drugs, I vow, I keep for him in my box, lore that I learned, Queen, from an Assyrian stranger." One cannot help but wonder if Simaetha has anyone else in mind who shall join Delphis on his journey to Hades should her binding spells fail. His new lover perhaps?

In Lucian's *Dialogue of Courtesans*, Bacchis, from our previous discussion, explains how easy it was for her to retrieve her lover, Phanias, who left her in anger and took up with another woman. For hardly any money at all, she was able to hire an old Syrian woman who could prepare binding spells to retrieve Phanias. In addition to fumigating his clothes with sulfur over a salted flame, the old woman also used the rhombos and sang incantations with "horrible and outlandish names." Seemingly helpless to resist the old woman's strong magic and unresponsive to the protests of both his new lover and his friends, Phanias immediately returned to Phoebis and he has never left her side again. The binding spell in effect ripped him immediately and irreversibly from his social embedment. The old woman also taught Bacchis a spell to turn Phanias against his new lover, Phoebis. Wherever Bacchis saw Phoebis's footprints, she should erase them and make her own in the opposite direction and say "I trample on you and am on top of you." Bacchis followed the old witch's instructions with the enthusiasm of a young apprentice. Lucian provides a fleeting, but provocative, glimpse of how an erotically infused love mixed with the fear of betrayal and abandonment might push a person to go beyond the erotic binding spell and seek extra magical insurance. As Lucian suggests, such a person could turn to even darker forms of magic that could reach deep into a lover's extended social and familial relationships, perhaps with fatal consequences.

Finally, other notorious literary figures warrant inclusion. Though these women are not clearly identified as prostitutes, they are characterized by their unbridled "masculine lust" for men.[76] Far from being a prostitute or a courtesan, the married Pamphile in Apulius's *Metamorphosis* has a notorious reputation for entrapping young men she lusted after and using especially frightening magic. Most infamously of all, perhaps, in *Epode* 5, Horace describes Canidia's desperation to win the love of Varus, who has forgotten her and sleeps around with every harlot.[77] She exclaims: "He walks free from my power by the charms of some more knowing witch . . . I'll prepare a stronger dose that will counter your disdain, and sooner shall the sky sink under the sea with all the earth spread over both than you not burn with passion for me." Horace describes in graphic detail Canidia's frightening appearance with her hair disheveled with vipers as she prepares a love potion capable of such potency. The main ingredients were liver and marrow harvested directly from a young boy who is held in captivity and starved to death over several days; he is buried to his neck, and meals were placed before him several times every day so that his eyes could easily see the food that would never again pass his lips.

The Sermonic Imagination of John Chrysostom: Horrifying Pornai *and Familial Sobriety*

After our brief tour of a few graphic, not to mention disturbing, images from the Greco-Roman archive, let us return to John Chrysostom's prostitutes. In *Hom. in Rom. 24,* Chrysostom warned of prostitutes (*pornai*) who "use incantations, libations, philters, potions and innumerable other things" to keep their married Christian clients as satisfied lovers.[78] Undoubtedly Antioch was a city that offered a home to prostitutes, *hetairai*, and as Dickie puts it "actresses-cum-prostitutes," especially given the importance of the theater. Here and in all of John's descriptions of female magic-wielding prostitutes, John preferred the word *pornē* and its cognates (*porneia, porneuomenai*) rather than other terms (*hetairai*). *Pornē* and *porneia* appear prominently in a set of texts important to Chrysostom's construction of Christian identity—the Pauline epistles. Indeed, 1 Corinthians 6–7 relies on the inherent ambiguity in *porneia* (prostitution, fornication, and general immorality) to emphasize the importance of maintaining strict boundaries of sexual and marital regulation over the human body and its desires until the Second Coming. This was not an easy task, given the body's carnal (*sarx*) nature. To step beyond these boundaries was to risk an inflammation of desire (*epithymia*) and fall into sexual depravity.

As Margaret Mitchell has explained, Chrysostom understood himself as a fourth-century Paul, and indeed we can sense the dualism of 1 Corinthians 6:15–19 standing behind many of the passages in which John projected images of prostitutes attacking families with magic.

> Do you not know that whoever is united to a prostitute (*pornē*) becomes one body with her? For it is said, "the two shall become one flesh (*sarx*)." But anyone united to the Lord becomes one spirit with him. Shun fornication (*porneia*)! . . . Or do you not know that your body is a temple of the Holy Spirit within which you can have from God, and that you are not your own. For you were bought with a price; therefore glorify God in your body (*sōma*).

A prostitute (*porne*) and prostitution (*porneia*) figuratively marked the nether-side of the border established upon one's entry into a Christian community. According to Paul in 1 Cor. 7, this Christian body is sustained at the individual, marital, and communal level by moderate living (*sōphrosynē*) until Christ's return. To abandon moderation, whether indulging in drunkenness (*methē*), luxuriousness (*aselgeia*), or extreme asceticism, was to risk rousing one's *epithumia*, thus relapsing into *porneia*.

Chrysostom wove Pauline *porneia* into his constructions of magic-working *pornai* and thus projected frightening images that would induce congregants to practice *sōphrosynē*. The Christian population was caught between two epochal events: Christ's incarnation and his eventual return. Consequently, Christians were still embodied and vulnerable to temptation and the rise of the passions. In *Hom. 24 on Rom.*, Chrysostom advised the extermination of the most deadly passions like "lust and anger." These emotions could erode one's self-control, and such a state would most certainly endanger one's chances at salvation. Instead congregants should "put on Christ" (*Rom.* 13.14)—a phrase Chrysostom interpreted in a Stoic manner—and manage their unwieldy flesh through behavioral moderation or *sōphrosynē*. They must carefully tend to the body's health without indulging its appetites to the point of excessive luxuriousness. In these sermons, Chrysostom did not forbid wine altogether but allowed a certain amount for the maintenance of one's health. He encouraged marriage as a means of avoiding sexual wantonness. Following the middle path between extreme asceticism and debauchery was the safest for embodied Christians until Christ's return.[79]

While Christ's own life offered an exemplar of embodied moderation, Chrysostom warned that Christians were not Christ. They should look to Christ's example, but strive within social structures provided to maintain healthy flesh in a carnal city. To that end, social and familial institutions were in place to support one's pursuit of *sōphrosynē*. Fornication was not forbidden; in fact, marital intercourse served as a safety valve for sexual desire.[80] Through such marital regulation, Christians could offer their own example of embodied propriety to non-Christians: "Let the Gentiles see that Christians know best how to indulge, and to indulge in an orderly way (*meta kosmou*)."[81]

While the institutional aids of marriage did exist, Antioch was a Greek city and thus the Devil's, with demonic advantage sewn into every aspect of embodied existence of the urban sphere. The Devil was everywhere "seeking to quench the light spirit."[82] Passions were easily stirred to licentiousness (*aselgeia*) and *porneia*. One must always be on guard and never sleep. To underline the dangers involved, Chrysostom offered an environment and activity familiar to a particular socioeconomic level that could easily tip one's behavioral balance: a banquet.

> For from banquets of that sort you have evil desires (*ai ponerai epithumiai*), and impurities and wives come to be scandalized, and prostitutes (*pornai*) in honor among you. Hence come the upsetting of families and evils unnumbered and all things are turned upside down, and you have left the pure fountain and run to the conduit of mire. For that prostitute's body (*to tēs pornes sōma*) body is mire (*borboros*), I do not ask any one else but you yourself who wallows in the mire, if you do not feel ashamed of yourself, if you do not think yourself unclean after the sin is over. Therefore I beg you flee from fornication (*porneia*).[83]

Here John warned against undermining the marital order that managed fleshly sobriety. When *pornai* or "*to tēs pornes soma*" took the place of wives in a husband's affections, a situation arose in which desire (*epithymia*) and licentiousness (*aselgeia*) increased. The wayward husband could anticipate the prostitute's inevitable pregnancy—a misfortune setting off a chain reaction of further malevolency. Pregnant and desperate, the prostitute would aggravate the situation by turning to magic to protect her interests. In so doing, she would advance her own damnation as well as destroy a Christian family. The precision of Chrysostom's description of magic's role in a Christian family's descent is worth considering. As he explained, the birth of an illegitimate child was abhorrent in and of itself.[84] But Chrysostom added that the prostitute, in a state of panic, would engage magic and potions to abort the fetus or commit infanticide. Moreover, at that point, her magic may reach beyond the child and the seduced husband to stretch deep into legitimate domestic terrain—John warned against "sorceries (*pharmaka*) applied not only to the womb but to the injured wife and there are plottings without number, and invocations of devils, and necromancies, and daily wars, and truceless fightings, and home-cherished jealousies."[85] While in the beginning the prostitute used comparatively innocuous magic—"incantations, and libations, and love-potions" to maintain her beauty and attract the husband—she would turn inevitably to darker magic as her dependency upon him deepened.[86]

John Chrysostom described a female ritual practitioner of harrowing potency. And yet, John carefully denied her agency in these crimes. Whatever the kind of magic the prostitute employed, Chrysostom placed the blame entirely upon the husband: "For even if the daring deed (*tolmema*) be hers, the cause (*aitia*) of it is yours." In other words, when a husband made the misstep of attending a banquet—where wine flowed and prostitutes enticed—he set off a chain reaction culminating in a desperate prostitute's necromantic schemes. The husband's decision to attend, and not the prostitute's magic, initiated the destruction of the marital institution protecting Christian *sōphrosynē*. "The upsetting of families, the wrongs due to children, the other ills unnumbered" could have all been avoided if husbands had only refrained from attending banquets where prostitutes and alcohol were in abundance.[87] In his inability to manage his desire for wine-soaked social and sexual intercourse—in short, to abstain from attending a Greek cultural practice—a Christian husband moved beyond, and indeed abandoned, Christianized domestic boundaries designed to produce legitimate children who would in turn reproduce Christian institutions that cultivated Christian *sōphrosynē*.

In this way, John departed from Greco-Roman literary tradition. The prostitute in this passage was not an active agent, if indeed she had any subjectivity. John situated her as *porneia* incarnate, describing her at one point as "*to tēs pornes soma*" —and, moreover, a body full of mire (*borboros*). Finally, rather than instruct the husband to flee the prostitute, he ambiguously begged him to flee *porneia*—a nameless, shapeless immorality that took the Christian husband to the *porne* or *to tēs pornes sōma*. This woman is a far cry from the strong figure of Simaetha or Canidia; she was only as powerful as the Christian husband allowed her to be. Her magic was only effective because he failed to regulate his desires and now that desire empowered her magical threat over his family.

John created an image of a prostitute who would not hesitate to employ erotic magic to tear a man's flesh from the communal body of Christ. Indeed if a Christian husband foolishly forgets *sōphrosynē* and succumbs to *porneia*, turning his limbs and joining them to a prostitute as described in 1Corinthians 2.15–16, the prostitute's magic is quite powerful and deadly. However, if a husband refrains from this initial surrender, she is impotent, her *agōgē* spells ineffectual.

> That we may then escape from all these, let us put on Christ and be with him continually. For this is what putting Him on is—never being

> without him, and having Him ever more visible in us, *through sanctification, through our moderation*.[88]

Similar themes surface in a well-known passage in *Hom. 37 on Matthew*. Once again John established in bold strokes the boundaries regulating proper embodied behavior. Marriage, family, house, and friends—all of these existed for the "health of the body and the benefit of the soul." And once again a barrage of *porneia* and necromantic magic conspired to tempt one into a wantonness subverting regulatory socio-familial order. Interestingly, however, while the message was the same, John positioned familiar elements of *porneia* and magic differently. Rather than a single event such as a Greek banquet, John offered an entire non-Christian environment, which held lapsarian inevitability for Christian men: the theater. The stage served as a literal and figurative setting for harlotry and magical temptation. *Porneia* was loosened from an individual female prostitute or body of the prostitute (*to tēs pornes soma*) and prismatically multiplied to intensify its malevolence. The passage is worth quoting in full.

> Why the tumult, and the satanical cries, and the devilish gestures? For first one, being a young man, wears his hair long behind, and changing his nature into that of a women, is striving both in aspect, and in gesture, and in garments, and generally in all ways, to pass into the likeness of a tender damsel. Then another who is grown old, in the opposite way to this, having his hair shaven, and his loins girt about, his shame cut off before his hair, stands ready to be smitten with the rod, prepared both to say and do anything. The women again, their heads uncovered, stand without a blush, discoursing with a whole people, so complete is their practice in shamelessness and thus pour forth all effrontery and licentiousness (*aselgeian*) into the souls of their hearers. And their one study is to pluck up all moderation (*sōphrosynē*) from the foundations, to disgrace our nature, to satiate the desire of the wicked *demon* (*emplesai tou ponerou daimonos tēn epithymian*). Yea, and there are both foul sayings and gestures yet fouler; and the dressing of the hair tends that way, and the gait and the apparel and voice and flexure of the limbs; and there are turnings of the eyes, and flutes, and pipes, and dramas, and plots; and all things, in short, full of the most extreme impurity (*aselgeia*). When then will you be sober again, I pray you, now that the devil is pouring out for you so much of the strong wine of fornication (*porneia*), mingling so many cups of unchastity (*akolasia*)? For indeed both adulteries and stolen marriages are there, and there are women playing the harlot (*porneuomenai*), men prostituting (*hetairokotes*), youths corrupting themselves (*malakizomenoi*): all there is iniquity to the full, all portends (*teratōdias*), all shame.[89]

As John would have it, this spectacle of gender subversion and moral perversion worked almost magically to transfix the Christian men within the audience.[90] The true intent of this entrancing display was a "plot against marriages."[91] And the result of gazing upon images was immediate: "Husbands [become] insupportable to their wives, wives contemptible to their husbands . . . how many husbands those *pornai* have severed from their wives, how many they have taken captive, drawing some even from the marriage bed itself, not suffering others so much as to live at all in marriage."[92] Drawing upon the rhetorical conventions regarding theatrical spectacle, John presented a mixture of sexual perversion and gender subversion splayed before an unprotected audience. As Blake Leyerle has so well explained, destruction of marital *sōphrosynē* was assured the moment a husband's eyes met these strange images. Hapless spectators (i.e., Christian husbands) were maliciously seduced and all too easily dragged from the safety of home, marriage, and family. However, this was not all: an entrancing *porneia* on stage gained added strength from the *goēs* standing behind the proverbial curtain. This strange spectacle of *porneia* comes complete with aggressive *agōgē* spell.

> The sorcerers (*goētes*) too. Whence are they? Is it not from [the theater] that in order to excite the people who are idoling without object and make the dancing men have the benefit of much and loud applause, and fortify *pornai* against those who live in moderation (*sōphronousais*), they proceed so far in sorcery (*magganeias*) as not even to shrink from disturbing the bones of the dead.[93]

John Chrysostom's rhetorical fugue forced the audience to a precipitous edge, persuading male listeners especially to despair of their ability to survive temptation if they stepped into this quintessentially Greek environment. And yet he retreated from the description of a Christian's complete destruction to speak of pleasures that could still maintain moderation: "You have a wife, you have children . . . you have a house."[94] These were the primary means, apotropaic in a sense, of warding off the perverse pleasures to be gained from a prostitute boy, harlot, and fortune-teller. Chastity of mind (*sōphrosynē*) could find fortification in other spectacles—rivers, grasshoppers, and attendance at the martyr shrines.

The underlying message here is clear. Yes, the world was treacherous. The Devil soaked through most of urban life with virulent temptations in a dizzying blend of male and female prostitutes, actresses, and gender subversion heightened by sorcery. But if one walked carefully—as one must until the end times—a person always bore the power to secure his/her own salvation. In one's behavior and daily interactions in the civic sphere, one "must rejoice in the Lord, not in the devil."

Conclusion

In the post-Constantinian era, old women undoubtedly manufactured healing amulets and performed incantations for the sick and diseased, and Christians purchased such *remedia* and indeed any kind of ritual objects they felt would bring healing to those suffering in their household. So too prostitutes practiced *agōgē* magic as did many in late antiquity, including married Christians; so too Christian husbands were hardly immune from indulging in licentious sexual activity outside of marriage, no matter how severe the divine punishments promised by their bishops. While patristic literature may provide a window into the social history of these practices, it is an intentionally contorted one and should not be trusted for a realistic account without corroborating archaeological and material evidence. A much more intriguing way of reading these texts involves how church fathers construct a frightening demonic threat in the deceptively harmless figure of a silly, drunken old woman with amulets and a desperate prostitute with erotic spells. In patching together elements of the Greco-Roman literary archive as well as drawing upon cultural ideas (and fears) of female magic, church fathers promoted the church's ritual power to heal and paternally protect the Christian family until Christ's return.

Notes

1. For example, Horace, *Satires* 1.8; *Epode* 5, 17; Seneca, *Medea*; Apuleius, *Metamorphosis* 1.8–13; 3.17–18. See the very helpful contribution of Barbette Spaeth's chapter 2 in this volume.
2. Juvenal, *Satire* 6.
3. Ovid, *Fast.* 2.571–83; Lucian, *Dialogues of Courtesans* 4; Ovid, *Philopseudeis* 9. Matthew Dickie, *Magic and Magicians in the Greco-Roman World* (London and New York: Routledge, 2001, 2003), 180–91, reads these and many other characters descriptively, assuming that they represent real people and professions; he thus uses this character type as evidence supporting his theory of the "prostitute-witch." By contrast, Kimberly Stratton, *Naming the Witch: Magic, Ideology, and Stereotype in the Ancient World* (New York: Columbia University Press, 2007), 83, questions Dickie's positivist reading by observing that old age and prostitution were part of "invective tropes in Roman discourse along with magic." See also the important comments in David Frankfurter's chapter 11 in this volume.
4. Stratton, *Naming the Witch*, 108. Cf. Stratton, "Male Magicians and Female Victims: Understanding a Pattern of Magic Representation in Early Christian Literature," *Lectio difficilior* 2/2004, http://www.lectio.unibe.ch.
5. Stratton, *Naming the Witch*, 108.
6. Two of the Christian authors (Athanasius, John Chrysostom) surveyed here are situated in cities well known for the Hellenistic roots: Alexandria and Antioch.

7. Stratton, *Naming the Witch*, 2, also 16–18.
8. Developed discussion of this point, Ramsay MacMullen, *Christianizing the Roman Empire* (AD 100–400) (New Haven, CT: Yale University Press, 1984), ch. 9.
9. Ibid.
10. Several church canons attest to the problem of congregants and clergy who engaged in magical and divinatory practices: Synod of Laodicea, Canon 36 [NPNF, second series, 14:123–24; PG. 137.1388]; Council of Ancyra, Canon 24[NPNF, second series, 14:74; PG 137.1190–1192]; Pseudo-Athanasian Canons 41, 71–72 [Wilhelm Riedel and W. E.Crum, ed. and trans., *The Canons of Athanasius of Alexandria* (London: Williams and Norgate, 1904; reprint, Amsterdam: Philo Press, 1973), Canon 41 (Coptic text, 88; English translation, 118), Canon 71 (Coptic text, 108; English translation, 135)]. For a discussion of the evidence suggesting the widespread problem of monastic or clerical "magic," David Frankfurter, *Religion in Roman Egypt: Assimilation and Resistance* (Princeton, NJ: Princeton University Press, 1998), 210–17; Frankfurter, "The Perils of Love: Magic and Countermagic in Coptic Egypt," *Journal of the History of Sexuality*, 10 3/4 (2001): 497–500.
11. "*Paganos superstitio*": *Cod. Theod.* 16.10.12.2 (392ce). See Michele Salzman, "*Superstitio* in the *Codex Theodosianus* and the Persecution of Pagans," *VC* 41 (1987): 172–88, 175, who notes the semantic continuity of *superstitio* from the early imperial to late Roman period by considering the legal context of *superstitio* denoted divination and magical practice.
12. For the demonization of magic in the late antique period, Valerie Flint, "The Demonisation of Magic and Sorcery in Late Antiquity: Christian Redefinitions of Pagan Religions" in *Witchcraft and Magic in Europe: Ancient Greece and Rome*, ed. Bengt Ankarloo and Stuart Clark (Philadelphia: University of Pennsylvania Press, 1999), 277–348; Flint, *The Rise of Magic in Early Medieval Europe* (Princeton, NJ: University of Princeton Press, 1991); Attilo Mastrocinque, *From Jewish Magic to Gnosticism* (Tübingen: Mohr Siebeck, 2005), 211–21. David Frankfurter, "Beyond Magic and Superstition" in *Late Ancient Christianity: A People's History of Christianity*, vol. 2, ed. Virginia Burrus (Minneapolis: Fortress Press, 2005), 255–312.
13. Eusebius of Caesarea, *de laudibus Constantini Oratio* 2.3 (PG 20.1325–27).
14. Eusebius of Caesarea, *de laudibus Constantini Oratio* 13.4 (PG 20.1397–99): *ἀλλὰ καὶ αὐτοὺς καταδέσμοις τισὶν ἀπειρημένης γοητείας, ἐκθέσμοις τε καὶ ἐπανάγκοις καὶ ἐπῳδαῖς, δυνάμεις ἀφανεῖς ἀμφὶ τὸν ἀέρα ποτωμένας, παρέδρους ἑατοῖς ἐφειλκύσαντο.*
15. Ibid.
16. Athanasius, *Vita Antonii.*78–79 (*SC* 400:124–376): *εἴπατε γοῦν, ποῦ νῦν ὑμῶν τὰ μαντεῖα; ποῦ αἱ τῶν Αἰγυπτίων ἐπαοιδαί; ποῦ τῶν μάγων αἱ φαντασίαι;*
17. Ibid.: *καὶ ἔνθα τὸ σημεῖον τοῦ σταυποῦ γίνεται, ἀσθενεῖ μὲν μαγεία, οὐκ ἐνεργεῖ φαρμακεία.*

18. Augustine, *De Doctrina Christiana* 2.20.30ff. (CCSL 32, 54): *vel ad consultationes et pacta quaedam significationum cum daemonibus placita atque foederata, qualia sunt molimina magicarum atrium*. Regarding Augustine's theory of demonic communication and ritual/religious identity, see R. A. Markus, "Augustine on Magic. A Neglected Semiotic Theory," *Revue des Études Augustiniennes* 40 (1994): 375–88; also Fritz Graf, "Augustine and Magic" in *The Metamorphosis of Magic from Late Antiquity to the Early Modern Period*, ed. Jan N. Bremmer and Jan R. Veenstra (Leuven; Paris; Dudley, MA: Peeters, 2002), 87–105.
19. Fritz Graf, "Augustine and Magic," 96.
20. Augustine, *De Civitate Dei* 10.9 (PL 41.13–804): *incantationibus et carminibus nefariae curiositatis arte compositis quam vel mageian vel detestabiliore nomine goetian vel honorabilore theurgian vocant*. As Graf illustrates, seeking a daemonic assistant (*parhedros*) for a binding spell, for instance, involves the same form of communication as the religious techniques involved in the pursuit of superior wisdom of the divine through an Apollo or a Sybil. Cf. J. B.Clerc, "Theurgica legibus prohibita. A propos de l'interdiction de la théurgie," *Revue des Études Augustiniennes* 42 (1996): 57–64.
21. John Chrysostom, *Homilia in Colossenses* (NPNF, first series, 13:298; PG 62.358). Cf. Basil of Caesarea, *Hom. in Ps.45.2* (PG 29.417) on the wearing of spells and characters around the necks of sick children.
22. John Chrysostom, *Homilia in Romanos 24*. (NPNF, first series, 11:518; PG 60.623); cf. John Chrysostom, *Homilia in Matthias 67*. (NPNF, first series 10:412; PG58.636–37).
23. Ibid.: *Καταντλεῖ γάρ σοι γραῦς διὰ κ́ ὀβολοὺς, ἢ τετάρτην οἴνου ἐπαοιδὴν τοῦ ὄφεως· καὶ σὺ ἕστηκας ὡς ὄνος χασμώμενος, φορῶν δὲ ἐπὶ τὸν αὐχένα τὴν ῥυπαρίαν τῶν τετραπόδων, παρακρου-σάμενος τὴν σφραγῖδα τοῦ σωτηρίου σταυροῦ. Ἣν σφραγῖδα οὐ μόνον νοσήματα δεδοίκασιν, ἀλλὰ καὶ πᾶν τὸ στῖφος τῶν δαιμόνων φοβεῖται καὶ τέθηπεν. Ὅθεν καὶ πᾶς γόης ἀσφράγιστος ὑπάρχει.*
24. Plutarch, *de Superstitio* 166a, 168a; Theophrastus, fr. 146 [F. Wimmer, Theophrasti Eresli opera quae superant Omnia vol. 3 (Leipzig 1862), 204–5]=Plutarch, *de Pericl.* 38.2; Dio. Laer., *On the Lives of the Philosophers* 4.54; Diod. Sic. 31.43.1; Theocritus, *2nd Idyll*; Lucian, *Dial. Meretr.*; Meander, *Phasma* 2–31. John Chrysostom, *Hom. 1 Cor.* (PG 61. 105–6).
25. Diodorus Siculus 31.43.1.
26. Menander, *Phasma* 2–31.
27. Tibullus 1.5.9–16.
28. Plutarch, 166a.
29. Ibid.
30. Ibid.
31. Plutarch, *de Superstitio* 166a–c, describes such men smeared with mud, wallowing in filth, casting themselves down face to the ground disgracefully—"his reasoning power is stuck in dreams, his fear is ever wakeful, and there is no way of escape or removal."

32. Plautus, *Miles Gloriosus* 690–95. For the term *praecantare* and its association with old female healers, see also Petronius, *Saturnalia* 131.5. In his monograph, *Magic and Magicians in the Greco-Roman World* (London, New York: Routledge, 2001), footnote 36, p. 340, Matthew W. Dickie very helpfully includes a fragment of Varro in which the Roman scholar criticizes women's tendency to consult *praecantrices* rather than doctors when it comes to their children's health: *ut faciunt pleraequae, ut adhibeant praecantrices nec medico ostendant.* Fr. 15, A Riese, *M. Terenti Varronis Saturarum Meippearum Reliquiae* (Leipzig, 1865).
33. Dickie, *Magic and Magicians*, 281ff.
34. Dickie, *Magic and Magicians*, 176.
35. Christopher A. Faraone, *Ancient Greek Love Magic* (Cambridge, MA: Harvard University Press, 1999), 146–56, has argued similarly, though from a more nuanced angle, seeing prostitutes' use of *agōgē* spells as another sign of their "aggressive masculinity," which he argues was perfectly natural given their status in public life: "once we realize that as a group they are in many ways quite similar to Greek men, especially in their economic autonomy and their education" 156.
36. The following plays of Plautus: *Curculio*, *Asinaria*, *Cistellaria*, *Mostellarria*, *Persa*, and *Truculentulus*.
37. Ovid, *Amores* 1.8; Tibullus, 1.5.49–56; Sextus Propertius, 4.5.
38. Ovid, *Amores* 1.8.
39. Sextus Propertius, 4.5.
40. Lucian, *Dial. Meretr.* 286.
41. Dickie, *Magic and Magicians*, 281–84.
42. Translation from Clyde Pharr, *The Theodosian Code and Novels, and the Sirmondian Constitution*, Corpus of Roman Law I (Princeton, NJ: Princeton University Press, 1952).
43. *Cod. Theod.* 9.16.3. The Latin reads: *scientia punienda et severissimis merito legibus vindicanda, qui magicis accincti artibus aut contra hominum moliti salutem aut pudicos ad libidinem deflexisse animos detegentur. nullis vero criminationibus implicanda sunt remedia humanis quaesita corporibus aut in agrestibus locis, ne maturis vindemiis metuerentur imbres aut ruentis grandinis lapidatione quaterentur, innocenter adhibita suffragia, quibus non cuiusque salus aut existimatio laederetur, sed quorum proficerent actus, ne divina munera et labores hominum sternerentur.*
44. For a meticulous guide to stational liturgies' development in late antique cities, John Baldovin, *The Urban Character of Christian Worship: The Origins, Development, and Meaning of Stational Liturgy* (Roma: Pont. Institutum Studiorum Orientalium, 1987); regarding the spread of martyr cult from cemeteries into the center of the late antique city, see Gillian Clark, *Christianity and Roman Society* (Cambridge: Cambridge University Press, 2004); also J. Leemans, W. Mayer, P. Allen, and B. Dehandschutter, eds., *"Let Us Die That We May Live": Greek Homilies on Christian Martyrs from Asia Minor, Palestine, and Syria (c. AD 350–AD 450)* (London and New York: Routledge, 2003), 3–22; Wendy Mayer with Bronwen

Neil, *St. John Chrysostom: The Cult of the Saints: Select Homilies and Letters* (Crestwood, NY: St. Vladimir's Seminary Press, 2006), 23. Liturgical practices and ecclesiastical regulations arising with martyr cult promoted a Christianization of the temporal and geographical dimensions of the late antique world; the classic studies of the transformation include R. A. Markus, *The End of Ancient Christianity* (Cambridge: Cambridge University Press, 1990) and E. D. Hunt, *Holy Land Pilgrimage in the Later Roman Empire AD 312–460* (Oxford: Clarendon Press, 1984). For a more recent as well as theoretically nuanced approach to this issue, David Frankfurter, ed., *Pilgrimage and Holy Space in Late Antique Egypt*, Religions in the Greco-Roman World 134 (Leiden: Brill, 1998).

45. For this phrase, William Klingshirn, *Caesarius of Arles: The Making of a Christian Community in Late Antique Gaul* (Cambridge: Cambridge University Press, 1994), 222.
46. David Frankfurter, "Beyond Magic and Superstition" in *Late Ancient Christianity*, ed. Virginia Burrus, *A People's History of Christianity*, vol. 2 (Minneapolis, MN: Ausburg Fortress Press, 2005), 255–260.
47. Augustine, *Serm.* 306e [Edmund Hill, trans., John E. Rotelle, ed., *Works of Saint Augustine* (Brooklyn: New City, 1990–99), 3:11, 277–78]. For a discussion of the Augustinian passage, David Frankfurter, "Beyond Magic and Superstition," 277–78.
48. Athanasius, *Fr. de Amul.* (PG 26.239–40). For a discussion of this passage, see Dickie, *Magic and Magicians*, 284.
49. Ibid.: Katantlei= *γάρ σοι γραῦς διὰ κ́ ὀβολοὺς, ἢ τετάρτην οἴνου ἐπαοιδὴν τοῦ ὄφεως· καὶ σὺ ἕστηκας ὡς ὄνος χασμώμενος, φορῶν δὲ ἐπὶ τὸν αὐχένα τὴν ῥυπαρίαν τῶν τετραπόδων, παρακρου–σάμενος τὴν σφραγῖδα τοῦ σωτηρίου σταυροῦ. Ἣν σφραγῖδα οὐ μόνον νοσήματα δεδοίκασιν, ἀλλὰ καὶ πᾶν τὸ στῖφος τῶν δαιμόνων φοβεῖται καὶ τέθηπεν. Ὅθεν καὶ πᾶς γόης ἀσφράγιστος ὑπάρχει.*
50. Athanasius, *De amuletis*, PG 26.1320.
51. Ibid.: [*Τὰ γὰρ περίαπτα καὶ αἱ γοητεῖαι μάταια βοηθήματα ὑπάρχουσιν.*] *Εἰ δέ τις αὐτοῖς κέχρηται, γινωσκέτω τοῦτο σαφῶς, ὅτι ἑαυτὸν ἐποίησεν ἀντὶ πιστοῦ ἄπιστον, ἀντὶ δὲ Χριστιανοῦ ἐθνικὸν, ἀντὶ δὲ συνετοῦ ἀσύνετον, ἀντὶ δὲ λογικοῦ ἀλόγιστον.*
52. John Chrysostom, *Hom. in Col. 8.* (NPNF, first series, 13:298; PG 62.358).
53. Ibid: "*Πιστὴ εἶ, σφράγισον.*" Several texts feature the sign of the cross as the ultimate weapon against magical and demonic rituals: for example, Cyril of Jerusalem, *Ad illum. cat.*, 13.36, describes the sign as a "powerful phylactery" (*μέγα τὸ φυλακτήριον*); see also Epiphanius, *Haer.* 1.2.30.7; 30.12.1–10. (PG 41.417, 426–27); Leonitus, *Symeon the Holy Fool*, 21–22; Martin of Braga, *Reforming the Rustics*, 16.
54. John Chrysostom, *Hom. in Col. 8.* (NPNF, first series, 13:298; PG 62.358).
55. John Chrysostom, *Ad illum. cat.* 2.5 (PG 49.240).
56. John Chrysostom, *Hom. in Col. 8.* (NPNF, first series, 13:298; PG 62.358): *μεθύουσα γραῦς καὶ ληροῦσα.*

57. John Chrysostom, *Ad Illum. cat.* 2.5 (PG 49.240).
58. John Chrysostom, *Hom. in Col. 8*. (NPNF, first series, 13:297–98; PG 62.357–59).
59. Ibid. Cf. Caesarius of Arles, *Serm.* 52.6. For other examples of women providing ritual ("magical") healing: John Chrysostom, *In epistulam ad Corinthos* [PG 61.106]; cf. Augustine, *Confessions* 1.7.11. By contrast, Ammianus Marcellinus, *Res Gestae* 29.2.26–28, describes a "simple-minded old woman" offering "harmless charms for fever" who was caught up in a vicious anti-pagan prosecution in Antioch.
60. Due to the fact that the language in *Hom. in Col. 8* and *Ad Illum. cat. 2* is so similar, the question lingers whether the old female healer has simply been accidentally duplicated in the process of manuscript transmission. I would argue against this in light of the fact that Chrysostom situates her quite specifically in each context to speak to a certain ritual dilemma. In the case of *Hom. in Col. 8.*, the problem is how one must adhere to orthopraxy in the domestic sphere; in the case of *Ad illum. cat. 2,* Chrysostom uses old female healers to delineate a boundary between the healing powers of the baptismal seal and non-Christian *remedia*, as well as gesture toward possible frailties of that seal, if one engages in heteropraxy.
61. John Chrysostom, *Ad Illum. cat.* 2.5 (PG 49.240).
62. William Klingshirn, *Caesarius of Arles: The Making of a Christian Community in Late Antique Gaul* (Cambridge: Cambridge University Press, 1994), 212.
63. Caesarius of Arles, *Sermons* 52.5. [*Saint Caesarius of Arles: Sermons*, FC 31 (Washington DC: The Catholic University of America Press, repr. 1971), 1: 262; CCSL103, 1: 232]. The Latin reads: *Illum ariolum vel divinum, illum sortilegum, illam erbariam consulamus; vestimentum infirmi sacrificemus, cingulum qui inspici vel mensurari debeat; offeramus aliquos caracteres, aliquas praecantationes adpendamus ad collum.*
64. Klingshirn, 222.
65. Caesarius of Arles, *Sermons* 19.5 [*Saint Caesarius of Arles,* 1:101].
66. John Chrysostom, *Homilia in Romanos 24*. (NPNF, first series, 11:520; PG 60.627): ἐπῳδὰς καὶ σπονδὰς καὶ φίλτρα καὶ μυρία ἕτερα μηχανῶνται . . . δαιμόνων κλήσεις, καὶ νεκυομαντεῖαι.
67. Faraone, *Ancient Greek Love Magic*, esp. 146–59. To this end, Faraone's study stands in line with the view of F. Graf, S. Iles Johnston, H. Versnel, and others who make a case for the practical, everyday use of magic in the ancient world. Furthermore, Faraone attends to the gender construction of the magical practitioner as well as the object of desire—while the aggressor in the *agoge* spell is coded masculine, the object of the binding spell, who loses all rational control once bound to the ritualist, is coded as feminine or effeminate.
68. In his article "Who Practices Love-Magic in Classical Antiquity and in the Late Roman World?", *The Classical Quarterly,* New Series, vol. 50, no. 2. (2000), 581, M. Dickie looks to magic-working prostitutes of literature (e.g., Simaetha, Canidia, the *sagae* of the Roman elegists, Melitta and Bacchis of Lucian's *Dial. Meretr.*) as

testimony of a widespread belief in the antiquity that prostitutes did practice magic freely. This belief was set against the contrary belief, also reflected in the literary account, that respectable wives did not practice magic.

69. Ibid.
70. In *Magic and the Magicians*, Dickie treats John Chrysostom's sermons as the primary evidence for prostitutes' magic in late antiquity. He compiles a list of magical practices from the following texts: *Virg. 52.* 52 [SC 125]; *fem. Reg.* 1 Dumortier; *Hom. 37 in Mt.* [PG 57. 257]; *Hom. In 1 Cor. 7.2* [PG 51.217] in addition to the texts we will treat below.
71. Basil of Caesarea, in *First Canonical Letter, 8* (Epistle 188.8 [PG 32.62ff.]), also classifies women who accidentally kill the men through erotic magic (magical love philters, incantations, magic knots) as intentional homicide. However, the status of the women is not clear: married, single, or prostitute? The text deals with a variety of ethical and legal issues Basil is subsuming into his episcopal purview.
72. Faraone, *Ancient Greek Love Magic*, 154–55: "The suspicion that prostitutes and mistresses used aggressive types of erōs magic is, moreover, widespread in later Mediterranean and European history. The church father John Chrysostom warns married men to stay away from such women because they use magic to alienate men from their wives, an accusation that recurs in Byzantine and medieval sources, in the especially detailed record of the Florentine and Venetian Inquisitors, in the trials and tribulations of the English royal house, and in sixteenth century Modena and modern Algeria." In his footnote for John Chrysostom he thanks M. Dickie for the reference to John Chrysostom In *Illud Propter Fornicationes Uxorem* (PG 51.216), a text we are not treating here.
73. This is especially clear in the list that Dickie provides, which is a lengthy list of magical practices John Chrysostom ascribes to prostitutes in several sermons.
74. Notice, for example, Dickie's reading of the *PGM* material in his article "Who Practices Love-Magic in Classical Antiquity."
75. Faraone, *Ancient Greek Love Magic,* 153–54, argues strongly and persuasively for Simaetha's identity as a courtesan, which includes a discussion of Simaetha's "appropriation of traditionally male forms of erotic magic."
76. Once again Simaetha is the center of much of Faraone's argument, 153ff.
77. Horace, *Epode 5*.
78. John Chrysostom, *Hom. in Rom. 24* (NPNF, first series, 11:520; PG 60.627): *ἐπῳδὰς καὶ σπονδὰς καὶ φίλτρα καὶ μυρία ἕτερα μηχανῶνται . . . δαιμόνων κλήσεις, καὶ νεκυομαντεῖαι.*
79. John Chrysostom, *Hom. in Rom. 24* (NPNF, first series, 11:518; PG 60.623).
80. For Chrysostom's indebtedness to Paul in his own preaching, see Margaret Mitchell, *The Heavenly Trumpet: John Chrysostom and the Art of Pauline Interpretation* (Louisville, KY: Westminster John Knox Press, 2002).
81. *Hom. in Rom. 24* (NPNF, first series, 11: 520; PG 60.626).
82. *Hom. in Rom. 24* (NPNF, first series, 11: 519; PG 60.625).

83. John Chrysostom, *Hom. in Rom.* 24 (NPNF, first series, 11: 520; PG 60.626).
84. Ibid.
85. John Chrysostom, *Hom. in Rom.* 24 (NPNF, first series, 11:520; PG 60.627): *φαρμακεῖαι λοιπὸν κινοῦνται, οὐκ ἐπὶ τὴν νηδὺν τὴν πορνευομένην, ἀλλ' ἐπὶ τὴν ἠδικημένην γυναῖκα, καὶ ἐπιβουλαὶ μυρίαι, και δαιμόνων κλήσεις, καί νεκυομαντεῖαι, καὶ πόλεμοι καθημερινοὶ, καὶ ἄσπονδοι μάχαι, καὶ σύντροφοι φιλονεικίαι.*
86. Ibid.: *Πολλαὶ γὰρ ὥστε ἐπιχαρεῖς γενέσθαι, καὶ ἐπῳδας καὶ σπονδὰς καὶ φίλτρα καὶ μυρία ἕτερα μηχανῶνται.*
87. Ibid.
88. John Chrysostom, *Hom. in Rom.* 24 (NPNF, first series, 11:520; PG 60.627)—emphasis mine: *διὰ τῆς ἁγιωσύνης ἡμῶν, διὰ τῆς ἐπιεικείας.*
89. John Chrysostom, *Hom. in Matt.* 37 (NPNF, first series, 10:249; PG 57.426–27).
90. Read the important treatment of this and similar passages in Blake Leyerle, "John Chrysostom and the Gaze," *Journal of Early Christian Studies* 1/2 (1993): 159–74; Leyerle, *Theatrical Shows and Ascetic Lives: John Chrysostom's Attack on Spiritual Marriage* (Berkeley: University of California Press, 2001), 42–74.
91. John Chrysostom, *Hom. in Matt.* 37 (NPNF, first series, 10:249; PG 57.427).
92. Ibid.
93. Ibid.
94. John Chrysostom, *Hom. in Matt.* 37 (NPNF, first series, 10:250; PG 57.428).

8

The Bishop, the Pope, and the Prophetess: Rival Ritual Experts in Third-Century Cappadocia

Ayşe Tuzlak

IN A LETTER to Cyprian of Carthage, dated 256 CE, a bishop by the name of Firmilian described some troubling events that had happened some twenty years earlier. A rash of earthquakes had wrecked buildings all over Cappadocia, Firmilian said. What is worse, the local Roman authorities blamed Christians for the damage,[1] bringing about a persecution that took the Christian community by surprise. Christians were forced to abandon their property and flee to areas that were not affected by either the natural or the political disaster.

In the midst of this upheaval, a strange figure entered the scene, and Firmilian thought that Cyprian ought to know something about her.

> Suddenly, a certain woman started up in our midst: she presented herself as a prophetess (*propheten se praeferret*), being in a state of ecstasy and acting as if she were filled with the Holy Spirit. But she was so deeply under the sway and control of the principal demons (*principalium daemoniorum impetu ferebatur*) that she managed to disturb and deceive the brethren for a long time by performing astonishing and preternatural feats (*admirabilia . . . et portentosa*).[2]

According to Firmilian, the evil spirits that resided in this woman gave her powers—strictly limited, but real nonetheless—that enabled her to mislead a number of well-meaning Christians. For example, the woman claimed that she could *cause* earthquakes. Firmilian insisted that this was not actually the case; her controlling demon, he said, had a "gift of foreknowledge" which allowed it to *predict* earthquakes that were going to happen by the will of God, creating the illusion of a power much greater than it actually possessed.[3]

Firmilian's letter, then, stands as an intriguing example of the work of those Christian authors who were attempting, as early as the late second century, to explain demonic epistemology and demonic agency in a world presumably controlled by an omnipotent and omniscient God. Christian understandings of demonic power—its limits, its relationship to God's sovereignty, and the role that human beings take in the manifestation of a demon's will on earth (whether it is through "magic" or "possession")—find expression in second- and third-century debates regarding sacramental theology.[4] Firmilian's possessed prophetess offers a very intriguing glimpse into this discourse, in particular the manner in which contemporary anxieties about possession, agency, gender, and sexuality could play into debates regarding ritual expertise and sacramental efficacy. Indeed, it is the ambiguous expression of this anxiety that I would like to take as the focus of this essay.

Firmilian never expresses an explicit opinion about whether the Cappadocian prophetess was consciously lying to her community, or whether, by contrast, she was as much of a dupe as her followers were. He does seem to imply that she was not in full control of her actions. He leaves the subjects of some of the verbs in this story ambiguous, leaving the reader unsure of which actions were performed by the demon and which were performed by the woman: *subegerat mentes singulorum ut sibi obedirent*;[5] *diceret etiam se in Judaeam et Hierosolymam festinare*;[6] *item et alium diaconum fefellit*.[7] G. W. Clarke supposes that the ambiguity is deliberate, though the limitations of English syntax force him to choose a subject when translating these passages (in all three cases, he chooses the masculine pronoun: "he so succeeded in subjecting the minds"; "he would say that he must be off to Judea and Jerusalem"; "he so managed to trick . . . a deacon").[8]

In any case, one thing on which Firmilian is very clear is that the demon could compel the woman to do unnatural things. It would "make her go in the very depths of winter through the bitter snow in bare feet."[9] Worse still, it managed to persuade a deacon and a presbyter ("a country fellow")[10] to sleep with the prophetess. Then, knowing through some sort of prognostication that its true nature was about to be discovered, the demon declared that the exorcist who was about to confront it was an unbeliever.

The demon's attempt to dismiss the exorcist's accusation was unsuccessful, but apparently so was the exorcism itself. Firmilian assures Cyprian that the exorcist "stoutly withstood" the demon and "succeeded in revealing that the spirit which had previously been thought holy was in fact thoroughly evil."[11] Yet he does not say that the exorcist managed to drive the demon out of the woman. Quite on the contrary, he continues to tell his story about their "illusions and trickeries" without any break in the narrative.[12]

What was worst of all about this episode, in Firmilian's view, was,

> that woman . . . employing a by no means despicable form of invocation (*inuocatione non contemptibili*), would pretend (*simularet*) to sanctify the bread and celebrate the Eucharist, and she would offer the sacrifice to the Lord not without the sacred recitation of the wonted ritual formula (*[non] sine sacramento solitae*).[13] And she would baptize many also, adopting the customary and legitimate wording of the baptismal interrogation (*baptizaret . . . multos usitata et legitima uerba interrogationis usurpans*). And all this she did in such a way that she appeared to deviate in no particular from ecclesiastical discipline (*ut nihil discrepare ab ecclesiastica regula uideretur*).[14]

With this paragraph, any lingering ambiguities about agency are sharply eliminated. "That woman" (*illa mulier*) performed invocations, and she dared (*ausa est*) to pretend (*simularet*) to sanctify the Eucharistic bread.

It seems ironic that Firmilian pins the responsibility for a sexual crime—the seduction of the rural clerics—on a demon rather than on the human woman that it had possessed. The word *spiritus* (which Firmilian prefers to *daemon*, at least in the singular) is grammatically masculine. To be fair, Firmilian does not use gendered language when talking about the spirit itself, and it seems that he chose the word *spiritus* only so that he could contrast the prophetess's "spirit" with the Holy Spirit that she mistakenly claimed to possess. Nevertheless, his story still creates an odd sexual tension between three masculine characters and the woman who is intimate with all of them.

But then Firmilian goes on to tell Cyprian that the false rituals were all performed by *that woman*: *she* baptizes, *she* celebrates the Eucharist, *she* recites the formulae. A few lines later, Firmilian backpedals and says that she was used *by* the demon to commit these ritual crimes (*nequissimus daemon per mulierem baptizavit*), just as she seems to have been used to commit sexual crimes.

Immediately apparent are the ambiguities in Firmilian's characterization of this prophetess and it is these anxieties about possession, agency, and ritual expertise that I would like to take as the focus of this essay. Firmilian's evident reluctance to ascribe any power to the woman—even while he must admit that her ritual and prophetic behavior had a dramatic impact on her community—illuminates the uncertainties that Christian authorities had about gender and power in this period. His frequent use of litotes ("by no means despicable . . . not without the sacred recitation . . . to deviate in no particular") can be seen as a literary attempt to grant the prophetess a kind of legitimacy and then withdraw it in the very same breath.

One thing that makes this exchange even more curious is its context. Though the story of the prophetess is most easily interpreted as a jab against a rival Christian sect, most likely the Montanists,[15] predicated in part upon a series of assumptions about what religious functions women could or could not serve, it is worth remembering that this narrative is only a brief digression in a long letter about the efficacy of the sacraments. The insults that Firmilian leveled against this unnamed woman are part of a much broader argument about who can access God's power and what can be done with it. This was a very contentious issue in the third century. Far from being an abstract theological debate, it was deeply entangled in the politics of the day,[16] with genuine repercussions for all the members of a young and unpopular religion.

Of course, Firmilian and Cyprian took the exclusion of women from ritual authority as axiomatic. They never seriously considered the possibility that a woman could legitimately baptize or celebrate the Eucharist. The prophetess's story provides not a point of debate but its opposite: namely, common ground for two powerful male interlocutors to take comfort in their shared outrage about their absent target.[17] For all that they disagreed on, Firmilian and Cyprian could take for granted that the prophetess's behavior was unnatural, outrageous, and offensive to God. This permits Firmilian to argue "backward" from the outlier case that he identifies, toward a more subtle and stable ritual theology that would stand *with* Cyprian's *against* that of the reigning pope.

And yet, to make this argument, Firmilian is forced to grant that a woman could persuade others to submit to her baptisms, which in turn implies that her authority is not necessarily rejected out of hand by everybody. This assumption brings narrative sense to Firmilian's story—the prophetess must have a clientele, after all—but it is in tension with his stated position that her lack of ritual power is self-evident and plainly dictated in scripture.

Firmilian tries to resolve this tension by making the demon into the true agent in the story. Since his primary concern is with ritual efficacy, replacing the Holy Spirit with a demon preserves the supernatural exchange of power that both he and Cyprian see as a crucial element of Christian sacraments. But though the presence of the demon may solve the *ritual* problem to Firmilian's satisfaction, it does not resolve the psychological or social issues raised by the prophetess and her authority within her community. This is an issue to which I will return later in the paper.

What, then, did Cyprian and Firmilian disagree about, if not the assumptions about this woman's gender and authority? This question calls for a brief digression about what would have been considered legitimate ritual authority in third-century North Africa.

Thaschus Cæcilius Cyprianus, better known as St. Cyprian, was the bishop of Carthage in the middle of the third century. His correspondence provides modern historians with interesting insights into pre-Nicene debates surrounding baptism, ordination, and martyrdom. Near the end of his life, Cyprian was engaged in an extended, and often very bitter, argument with the bishop of

Rome, known to history as Pope Stephen I, concerning the validity of baptism under certain circumstances.

Cyprian maintained that Christians who were baptized in a heretical church must be *re*baptized upon their return to the true church. Stephen disagreed, and his position is the one that eventually became dominant in many "mainline" denominations of Christianity, including Roman Catholicism. Today, if someone is baptized in a Protestant or Orthodox Church, and later converts to Roman Catholicism, she will not be expected to undergo a second baptism. Instead, it is assumed that the effects of the first baptism are actuated once the convert becomes a member of the Catholic Church, as the good intentions of the initiate at the time of her baptism achieve perfection at the time of her conversion.[18]

This was not a very common opinion in North Africa in Cyprian's time. At a council that convened at Carthage in the spring of 256 CE, seventy-one bishops who sought the right to rebaptize heretics signed a conciliar letter asking Stephen for permission to do so.[19] The heretics who were perceived as the greatest threat to Cyprian and his faction were the followers of a man named Novatian. It is important to understand that Novatian's error was not Christological, but ecclesiological. In other words, Cyprian had no quarrel with Novatian's views on salvation, the Trinity, the resurrection, the nature of God, the Biblical canon, and so on. All these elements of Novatian Christianity were perfectly orthodox, as Cyprian himself repeatedly admits.[20]

Rather, it was Novatian's perspective on the makeup of the church that caused offense to Cyprian. In Cyprian's opinion, Novatian was too much of a hardliner on the treatment of the "lapsed"—that is to say, Christians who avoided martyrdom by performing pagan sacrifices or bribing Roman officials. Novatian claimed that the church could not extend forgiveness to Christians who had weakened in the face of Roman persecution.

This was not a hypothetical issue in the third century. The Decian persecution was a constant threat for high-profile Christians. Cyprian himself was exiled to Kurubis (now Korba, Tunisia) in 257 CE. This forced him to address the conflict between ritual authority (such as that granted to bishops through ordination) and social status (popularly granted to martyrs, whose blessings were sometimes perceived to absolve sins) in a very direct way.[21] Even before his exile, Cyprian was engaged in a struggle to preserve episcopal authority against the claims of those who sought intercession from the recently martyred.[22]

So far as Cyprian was concerned, Novatian's ecclesiology—echoes of which can be seen in the confidence of "confessors" who survived the first round of persecutions and who earned significant social status as a result—demonstrated an alarming lack of faith in the power of the apostles and their successors.[23] Moreover, in setting himself up as a rival pope to Stephen, Novatian created division in the church—a particularly grievous sin in Cyprian's view. In his early letters,

Cyprian simply calls Novatian a schismatic, but by the time Firmilian's letter was written, he had been promoted to a full-blown heretic.

The broader point is that the authority that Cyprian and Firmilian seem to take for granted is significantly more unstable than they let on in their correspondence. In this light, it is possible to see Firmilian's story about the prophetess not as an attack on a heretical practice so much as a tactical retreat into the safe territory of gender roles. Cyprian could not always assert episcopal authority, even over his own presbyters,[24] and the reigning pope disagreed with him on critical issues in sacramental theology. It is therefore no wonder that Firmilian sought to reassure his fellow bishop with the story of a demon-possessed woman who caused some temporary social damage but whose trickeries were eventually and rightfully exposed. It is also no wonder that this attempt at reassurance is fraught with even more narrative and philosophical problems than it aimed to solve.

A first-time reader of Cyprian might be forgiven for missing the nuances of the discussion, since he spends most of his time arguing simply that Novatian is "fake and foreign";[25] that he is an arrogant traitor and flatterer, "frantic with greed";[26] that he left his father unburied and caused his wife to miscarry;[27] and that his sacraments are obviously total frauds, unsanctioned by God.[28] In a letter to Antonianus from 251 CE, Cyprian urges his fellow bishop to feel no curiosity about Novatian's teachings, since all that matters is that Novatian is *outside* the church.[29] In an argument that anticipates Firmilian's discussion of the prophetess and her careful baptismal wordings, Cyprian asserts that the ritual pronouncements of heretical clerics have no effect because they do not actually refer to anything:

> There is no one binding credal formula common to us and to schismatics, neither is there any common baptismal interrogation. For when *they* say "Do you believe in the forgiveness of sins and life everlasting through the holy Church?" they are being fraudulent . . . since they have no such church.[30]

To this day, historians argue about whether Cyprian had a consistent sacramental theology or whether his real gift was as a polemicist.[31] A decision need not be forced for the purposes of this chapter, since, as I will demonstrate below, both polemic and theology illuminate Cyprian's and Firmilian's assumptions about gender and authority.

In any event, the bishop of Rome denied the African bishops' request for permission to rebaptize heretics. Stephen argued that heretics should be received into the church with the ritual of laying on of hands, which he interpreted as a sign of penance. Cyprian asked sarcastically why the laying on of hands would do any good if rebaptism did not. His argument is worth quoting at length:

> If [the heretics] do possess the Holy Spirit, then we ask further: why do those who have been 'baptized' with them, when they come over to us, have hands laid on them for receiving the Spirit, whereas the Spirit would most assuredly have already been received at the time it could have been received had the Spirit been there? But if, on the other hand, no heretic or schismatic, being outside the Church, imparts the Holy Spirit, and if, for this reason, hands are laid on them in our Church so that with us they may receive what neither exists with them nor can be imparted by them, then, that being so, it is manifest that no forgiveness of sins either can be granted through those who beyond doubt do not possess the Holy Spirit themselves.[32]

The movement of the Holy Spirit is treated as if it were a physical exchange in this passage; as if grace itself were "contagious," so to speak.[33] Cyprian cannot see how the laying on of hands could reproduce the ritual efficacy of baptism, which he understands in a very specific, almost material way. Throughout his work, Cyprian speaks of the baptismal water as both *requiring* and *transmitting* purity. For instance, he cites Ezekiel 36.25 ("and I shall sprinkle over you clean water, and from all your uncleanness and all your idolatry you will be cleansed") to argue that the only water that can cleanse sins is water that has been sanctified by a bishop;[34] elsewhere he cites Exodus 14.27, where the Pharaoh is defeated once he reaches the water, to argue that the devil can only "persist in his malice" until he touches holy water, at which point he is stopped.[35]

Typically, Cyprian concludes his argument with an appeal, not to Christology, but to ecclesiology and to ritual practice:

> The conclusion must be, accordingly, that if they would wish to receive the forgiveness of sins . . . all without exception who come over from those adversaries and antichrists to the Church of Christ must be baptized with the baptism of the Church.[36]

The debate survives only in Cyprian's letters, and Stephen's responses have not been preserved in full.[37] However, Cyprian went on to create a voluminous correspondence on the matter, providing modern historians with a helpful, if slanted, view of the differing positions on the topic that circulated in the third century. It is as a part of this correspondence that Firmilian's letter survives.

What does any of this have to do with our Cappadocian prophetess? I think it is important to understand how Firmilian himself uses the story, what he believes it illustrates, and why he chose to put it into this particular place in his letter. We know much less about Firmilian than we do about Cyprian,[38] and his influence on the development of Christian doctrine has been slight. Cyprian's extant writings include dozens of letters and a handful of treatises and pamphlets, while all that survives of Firmilian's correspondence is the single letter that serves as the focus of this article. Therefore it is difficult, and perhaps even unfair, to speculate about Firmilian's opinion on baptism and prophecy.

Nevertheless, for all of its elusive brevity, the story about the prophetess raises interesting questions about gender, authority, agency, and ritual efficacy in third-century North Africa. A close but cautious reading of Firmilian can illuminate the way in which he uses this dramatically Other figure (a woman who baptizes, a demon who seduces ordinary men, a Jerusalemite in Cappadocia) to delve into issues of orthodoxy—and more importantly, orthopraxy.

Both Cyprian and Firmilian disagreed with Stephen on the topic of baptism, maintaining that anyone who was originally baptized outside the church must be rebaptized (or, as they would put it, baptized properly for the first time)[39] upon his or her conversion. At their most vitriolic, they could use shockingly abusive language when talking about the Bishop of Rome.[40]

Yet at the same time, both bishops acknowledge Stephen's authority, even to the point of defending that authority against the claims of Novatian, a man whose views of the sacraments were arguably more orthodox than Stephen's own, even by the bishops' own standards. Earlier in Stephen's career, before the relationship between the two men soured,[41] Cyprian admitted frankly to the importance of the episcopal seat at Rome:

> You, dearly beloved brother, far more than anyone else, are duty bound to bring honor upon [the martyrs' memory] by exerting the full weight of your personal authority (*gravitate et auctoritate tua*); after all, you are the one who has been appointed to replace and succeed them.[42]

Therefore, though it is somewhat anachronistic for the title of this chapter to refer to the bishop of Rome as the "Pope," it is fair to say that Cyprian maintains a grudging respect for the institutional hierarchy that gives Stephen his authority. Cyprian even admits that a heretic in Rome is somehow more damaging than a heretic in Carthage:

> They now have the audacity to sail off carrying letters from schismatics and outcasts from religion even to the chair of Peter, to the primordial church, the very source of episcopal unity; and they do not stop to consider that they are carrying them to those same Romans whose faith was so praised and proclaimed by the Apostle, into whose company men without faith can, therefore, find no entry.[43]

This is a letter to Stephen's predecessor, Cornelius—and a conciliatory one at that. Perhaps Cyprian developed a different opinion about the authority of the

Roman church when fierce disagreements with Stephen surfaced a few years later. Be that as it may, Cyprian clearly believed that there was Biblical backing for Rome's special position in Christendom.

How could Cyprian and Firmilian sustain the paradox between legitimate ecclesial authority and ritual correctness? Firmilian's enigmatic figure of the prophetess may supply a way to answer this question.

The scant scholarly literature on Firmilian's prophetess has tended to focus on the question of whether or not she was a Montanist. "Montanism" is a fourth-century name for a second- and third-century Christian sect[44] whose members believed, among other things, that when they entered ecstatic trances, the Holy Spirit would speak through them.[45] Many of the themes that pervade anti-Montanist literature appear in Firmilian's letter as well: women seizing authority that does not rightfully belong to them, demonic spirits persuading people that they are actually holy, bad baptisms and ordinations, false prophecy leading to heresy.[46]

Whether Firmilian's prophetess was "really" a Montanist is of limited relevance for my argument in this chapter, since the bishop's criticisms of her do not directly depend on her association with any particular sect. In fact, the opposite seems to be the case, since Firmilian does not seem to think that naming her heresy would give any extra traction to his narrative. Nevertheless, the problems that the proto-orthodox Christians had with the Montanists were haunted by some of the same uneasy ambiguities that are present in Firmilian's description of the prophetess (and he does mention his concern with the Montanists in the same letter that talks about the prophetess, suggesting that the two were connected, at least indirectly, in his mind).[47]

So how does Firmilian classify this prophetess? His own words are instructive. Primary, perhaps, is the fact that she is a woman (*mulier*). She is also "a false prophet and a heretic" (*pseudoprophetam et haereticum*),[48] "deeply under the sway and control of the principal demons" (*principalium daemoniorum impetu ferebatur*). Other nouns are harder to find; the rest of her description must be constructed with verbs. She is a person who "disturbs" (*sollicitaret*), "deceives" (*deciperet*), and "tricks" (*fefellit*) "many people" (*multos*)—both ritually and sexually. Most scandalously, she baptizes: *baptizaret, baptizavit*.

In Firmilian's perspective, this evidence is enough to condemn the prophetess utterly; it seems self-evident to him that nobody, not even the most stalwart members of the anti-rebaptism camp, could accept her initiations as legitimate. "Can it be that Stephen and his adherents extend their approval even to this baptism," he sneers, "especially as it came *complete with Trinitarian credal formula and the legitimate baptismal interrogation of the Church?*"[49] Firmilian cannot imagine the members of this woman's cult entering the catholic communion without being baptized all over again, and he uses her story as a way to prop up Cyprian's arguments to the same effect. (In fact, Cyprian said in a letter from the same year that what he endorsed was not *re*baptism at all, but simply baptism: what heretics do does not count.[50] Of course, if *heretics* rebaptize *their* converts, they are simply acting like "apes.")[51]

Christine Trevett argues that Cyprian would not have seen the Cataphrygian sect as particularly threatening, since he was sympathetic toward Christians who made ecstatic prophetic utterances and could, perhaps, have been one of them himself.[52] If this is true, Firmilian's account is propaganda designed to cast the worst possible light on the sect, and it was consciously crafted in a way that would have appealed to Cyprian's sensibilities.[53] Consider the fact that Firmilian categorizes the prophetess as an ecstatic, then goes on to assert that she performs all her rituals with careful attention to wording and gesture. Even within Firmilian's own narrative, then, multiple elements are suspended in tension.[54]

This raises the interesting possibility that the public alliance of Cyprian and Firmilian against Stephen might obscure a more complex relationship between them. If the two men disagreed about the role of prophecy or *extasis* in ritual, then Firmilian would have needed to get as much leverage as possible out of the characteristics of the prophetess that Cyprian would have found troubling as he did. The most obvious of these characteristics, of course, was her gender. The structure of his narrative, however, forces him simultaneously to affirm and deny the efficacy of the prophetess's rituals: Firmilian's theology cannot permit a woman to baptize effectively, but his story depends on the woman's social success for its horror and its subsequent call to action.

Cyprian was aware of this issue on some level, though he used a slightly different tactic in his approach to it. Instead of using demons to explain how a heretic could be both impotent and persuasive, he searched the Bible for illustrative examples. His favorite such example was the Biblical story of Kore, Dathan, and Abiram, three men who led a revolt against the Aaronite priesthood and who were punished by being swallowed by an earthquake. Cyprian frequently used this passage to demonstrate that a false priest angers God even if his theology and his ritual behavior are perfectly correct.[55]

Firmilian uses exactly the same example in this letter to Cyprian,[56] prompting G. W. Clarke, the editor of the letter collection, to accuse him of being "largely Cyprian *rechauffée*."[57] There is no doubt that Firmilian is sycophantically devoted to Cyprian. However, I believe that the unsolicited digression about the prophetess brings an interesting nuance into the discussion: Firmilian has his own vision of Christian ritual, and he is trying to persuade Cyprian to adopt it. Nevertheless, whatever incongruities may have existed between Cyprian and Firmilian, it is clear that in the view of both bishops, social and institutional boundaries are just as important as Christology and a female baptizer would threaten those boundaries. By juxtaposing the prophetess's inoffensive statements with her usurpation of a priestly role, Firmilian was able to spotlight exactly the sort of perversity that had upset Cyprian earlier. And by accusing her of being a sexual predator,[58]

Firmilian could develop the Biblical theme that orthodox theology could coexist with abhorrent behavior. His goal was to condemn Cyprian's *contemporary* enemies by describing an outrage from recent history.[59]

If Trevett is right about Firmilian's motives, then what we have here is an intriguing case of nested internecine disagreements about the efficacy of a sect's rituals. Though Firmilian is in almost slavish agreement with Cyprian on the topic of rebaptism generally, the story about the prophetess might be designed to win Cyprian over on the topic of spirit possession. In other words, if the two bishops disagree about anything, it is not whether the category of dangerous heretics, who need to be rebaptized *exists*; it is about whether ecstatic and spirit-possessed women fall into that category. The point is subtle enough that Firmilian is forced to make it dramatically, highlighting the elements of the prophetess's behavior that would anger Cyprian the most. But as a result, he puts more pressure on her gender than it can bear, and the story he tells is inconsistent as a result.

In any case, it seems clear that Firmilian's attack is not designed to bring anybody "back into the fold." The events surrounding the prophetess had already reached their conclusion at least two decades before this letter was written; according to Firmilian, an exorcist triumphantly exposed her lies despite the demon's noisy protests.[60] Even if the prophetess's personal followers still existed in 256 CE, they could not possibly have been the intended audience of a letter that was addressed to Cyprian, Firmilian's "most cherished brother."

This is a book about women, witchcraft, and magic in the world of antiquity, but I have mentioned neither witchcraft nor magic so far in this essay. Firmilian does not use any of the Latin words traditionally translated into English as "magician" or "sorcerer," and, so far as I have been able to discern, Cyprian does not address these topics in his extant corpus either.[61] Andrzej Wypustek makes the case that Montanism and other forms of ecstatic Christianity would have struck *pagan* authorities as sorcerous and illicit,[62] but the Christian authors under discussion in this chapter did not choose that vocabulary when crafting their accusations.

Unlike Wypustek, I do not believe that prophecy and possession—the phenomena that are ostensibly at issue in Firmilian's letter—are synonymous with magic or witchcraft, and all of these terms are considered profoundly problematic in our discipline anyway.[63] However, I think that what is at issue in Firmilian's story does address the broader question of *ritual expertise*, which is at the crux of any discussion about "magic." The narrative that one politically powerful man provides to another politically powerful man about the use and abuse of sacraments in the third century anticipates the arguments that Protestant and Roman Catholic Christians will have about the Eucharist a millennium later.[64] The models that these North African bishops use for their polemics differ from those that witch hunters will use in the Early Modern Period, but their concerns can be profitably compared.

Recent studies within the disciplines of religious studies and anthropology have tended to reject attempts to categorize actions as "magical" or "religious" based on their content. That approach was popular in the nineteenth century and much of the twentieth, but today, scholars usually prefer to categorize practices in terms of how they are *perceived*, both by the practitioners themselves and by their opponents. For the most part, the contemporary academic literature focuses on the rhetoric of accusation and self-identification, along with emic categories in the cultures that they study, rather than attempting to create checklists of "objectively" magical and religious acts.[65]

The case of Firmilian's prophetess illustrates a few of the reasons why this approach is useful. The "many" people she baptized obviously did not think she was evil or demon-possessed. Firmilian's implication that they were all duped by her demonic spirit does not bear scrutiny: the fact that they submitted to the baptism at all seems to suggest that they took for granted, at the very least, that a baptism by a woman could theoretically be valid. Therefore we cannot assume that everyone in Cappadocia was in agreement about what qualities might be possessed by legitimate spiritual authorities. Though patristic authors, including Firmilian and Cyprian, were quick to ascribe stubbornness and perversity to anyone who did not see things their way,[66] it seems likely that the people who disagreed with them often did so in good faith and for good reasons.

Thus it is neither accurate nor helpful to imagine the prophetess as misunderstanding or misrepresenting her own religion. There is, of course, the possibility that she was actually a charlatan who consciously misled people—nothing would have delighted Firmilian more. Late antique literature is filled with stories about people who used machinery or psychology to manipulate the public.[67] But even if this woman was a fraud, she was a fraud with significant authority within a community. We cannot escape the question of how, in a culture where it is supposedly self-evident that a woman does not have the authority to baptize, the prophetess managed to find baptizands. Given the existence of Montanism in that place and time, I think it is much more likely that she was a representative of a sect that constructed ritual authority differently than Cyprian and Firmilian did, particularly in terms of gender. *That* is what grated on the bishops.

The work of David Frankfurter helps a modern historian to situate Firmilian's narrative with more precision. In the past decade, Frankfurter has brought a precise, sophisticated vocabulary into the discussion of magic, priesthood, and prophecy by carefully outlining different categories of what he calls "ritual expertise." In his 2002 article "Dynamics of Ritual Expertise in Antiquity and Beyond: Toward a New Taxonomy of Magicians," Frankfurter demonstrates that it was common in various cultures in antiquity to demonize rival ritual experts as *magoi*, sorcerers, or witches.[68] In the case of Firmilian's letter, of course, the demonization is quite literal.

Rather than taking loaded terms like "magician," "priest," "wise woman," "miracle worker," and so on, as his starting points, Frankfurter identifies the common element that underlies all these classifications: namely, ritual expertise. He goes on to divide ritual experts into categories: their fit within the community (is their expertise recognized as inherited through a local family line, or do they wander from place to place, selling their services?); the source of their authority (books [or even just literacy], buildings, an existing hierarchy?); their physical proximity to the community (are they local, or must the client travel to see them?); the extent of their familiarity to that community (are they "ensconced in local tradition" or on the outskirts of it and alien to it?); their relationship with other local ritual experts (do they have powerful enemies who accuse them of performing black magic?). In light of these distinctions, the logic of the labels begins to present itself on its own terms.

Frankfurter draws upon a variety of examples from around the world and subtly traces distinctions between native and externally imposed categories. I will draw attention to only two elements of his argument here, namely those that pertain to the "witch" and the "prophet."

First, the witch: historians of religion have long recognized that accusations of witchcraft and sorcery are often exaggerated, or even fabricated outright, usually with the purpose of uniting the community against a perceived enemy.[69] To this Frankfurter adds the observation that the accusers frequently benefit materially from this process of invention. After all, *someone* needs to solve the problems that the "witch" creates with her curses, and who better than the trustworthy ritual expert? He writes:

> In every case one can see a relationship between the image of hostile magic (or sorcery or witchcraft) and the charisma of the one who identifies the problem, articulates its scope and nature, and provides effective remedies and *apotropaia* against it.[70]

Firmilian never explicitly refers to the Cappadocian woman as a magician or a witch, and he denies her claims to be a prophetess.[71] Within the context of his letter, then, she is nothing at all—it is telling that she is not even named. She is simply a cipher: a *mulier* who baptizes, but whose baptisms are so worthless that they must be redone, properly, by an expert whose authority and power are recognized by Firmilian's own religious institution. The characteristics of that institution are precisely the subject that Cyprian and Firmilian's correspondence is addressing: their concern is not about bad theology, but bad ecclesiology and bad ritual practice. At any rate, the prophetess poses no direct threat to any living Christian, proto-orthodox or otherwise; she is introduced by Firmilian as no more than an interesting historical curiosity. But she leaches authority from a church that demands unity and unanimity in the face of natural disasters (in her own time) and of political disasters (the context of Cyprian and Firmilian's correspondence). Thus Firmilian presents her story as a warning. His conclusion is consonant with Cyprian's perspective: "Our view," Cyprian writes around the year 254 CE, "is that without exception all heretics and schismatics are without any powers or rights whatsoever."[72]

J. Patout Burns argues that the ritual expertise of heretics created more of a crisis in North Africa, at the periphery of the Roman Empire, than it did for the bishops entrenched in the capital. For Burns, this explains why the bishop of Rome was so unresponsive to Cyprian's increasingly agitated letters.

> [Stephen] never perceived a threat to the purity or identity of his church; he never regarded schismatics at home or dissenters abroad as denizens of the demonic realm from which he must shield his church. Instead, he viewed them as rebels *within* the kingdom of Christ whom he must discipline and subject to his apostolic authority.[73]

Burns contrasts this with Cyprian's view, which required that his institution have complete control over the rituals "by which a candidate was separated from Satan and rejoined to Christ."[74] If modern scholarship is to talk about witchcraft accusations as a form of social and institutional boundary drawing, then the prophetess of epistle 75 is a perfect example.

Firmilian is eager to dismiss not only the validity of the baptisms that the woman administered to her followers, but also the woman's very agency. "What, then, are we to say about such a baptism, in which an evil demon baptized by means of a woman (*quo nequissimus daemon per mulierem baptizavit*)?"[75] According to both Firmilian and Cyprian, the power of remitting sins was granted by Jesus to the apostles, and, through the apostles, to bishops and to the churches they oversaw.[76] The seizure of this power by a woman was a disruption of the institutional and cosmic order. Trevett puts it well when she writes:

> The usurpation of priestly rights and rites underlies Firmilian's hostile presentation of the woman. Bishop Cyprian, he knew, was much concerned with catholicity, so in Epistle 75 Firmilian wrote of errorists who were "enemies of the one, catholic church in which we are", the adversaries "of us who have succeeded the apostles" and who asserted "unlawful priesthoods".[77]

Therefore, by Frankfurter's definition, the Cappadocian woman is a witch of the classic type. Her ritual power is socially compelling but ultimately hollow. She is said to be sexually rapacious, of easy but unnatural movements through the ice, and of demonically inspired predictions of earthquakes that are in themselves profoundly damaging to the church.

Frankfurter's observations about the *practical* value of this rhetoric are also apt. To put it crassly, the priests in Firmilian's camp are kept in business by re-baptizing the heretics that were misbaptized the first time. To put it perhaps a bit more charitably, the presence of a bad ritual expert permits Firmilian to elaborate on the qualities of a good one. The technical discussion on baptism and the argument with Stephen that make up the bulk of this very long letter are effectively illuminated by one very vivid example drawn from living memory.[78] (Clarke mentions in passing that he finds this story refreshing, if only because it is one of the few elements of Firmilian's letter that provides a glimpse of "the human context of the quarrel" about baptism.)[79]

Second, the prophet: Frankfurter's "prophet" is somewhat counterintuitively defined in terms of her marginality; though she is a product of her community, she is also, paradoxically, pitted against it. One of the things that characterizes a prophet, in Frankfurter's view, is her *newness*: she articulates "a new frame of reference: a new scheme of the cosmos and of social relations . . . new rituals, new protective amulets . . . and new healing rites."[80] Although Firmilian denies the woman's self-appellation, the mere presence of the word *propheten* in his narrative raises Biblical associations and the questions about legitimacy that accompany them; the *pseudo* that precedes the word does not fully efface the authoritative connotations that could easily have been canceled out had he chosen to call her a witch or a sorceress.

Within her own community, was this woman considered edgy and dangerous? Or was she part of a long-established tradition whose only enemies were outsiders like Firmilian? Was she a prophet in Frankfurter's sense, which is to say, someone who provided her followers with a new set of social relationships and initiation rites, and thus, by extension, a new vision of the cosmos? If Montanism had a foothold in the area, and if Cappadocian Montanist sects permitted women to baptize as well as to prophesy, then she may have been a charismatic but otherwise uncontroversial figure within her social circle. On the other hand, if local Montanists placed restrictions on gender roles and sexual behavior that excluded this woman's understanding of ritual authority, or if she was not a Montanist at all but some sort of renegade diviner and earth shaker who claimed that she truly belonged in distant Jerusalem,[81] then she really would have been a "prophet," but perhaps not in the sense that she imagined.

Unfortunately, we will not find our answers in Firmilian's letter. He treats the woman's followers, when he addresses them at all, with even less sensitivity and seriousness than he treats the woman herself; even one of her seductions is explained away by the fact that the man who was persuaded to share her bed was a "country bumpkin."[82] The male heretics in the Cyprianic correspondence, though perhaps more intensely reviled than our prophetess, are at least granted more agency; and yet, their stories do not include earthquakes or premonitions or walking barefoot in snow.

At any rate, the prophetess in Firmilian's letter is a rich source of Otherness over and against which the bishop could define good ritual: she is a woman, an ecstatic, a worker of *admirabilia*, and, oddly, a "heretic" (despite the fact that her orthodoxy and ritual propriety is beyond reproach even by Firmilian's own admission). All of these elements can bring into sharp relief the vision of ritual expertise that Cyprian and Firmilian were themselves developing. In addition, they provide a tantalizing glimpse of other, minority viewpoints. If they also cause us to reconsider scholarly distinctions between religion, heresy, and magic, then all the better.

Notes

1. Non-Christians frequently assumed that natural disasters were sent by the gods to punish towns with Christian populations, since Christians insulted those gods by denying their existence. Christians, for their part, argued that the natural disasters were sent by their God to punish the pagans who persecuted Christians. For numerous examples of this trope in patristic writings, see Graeme W. Clarke, ed. and trans., *The Letters of St. Cyprian*, 4 vols. (New York: Newman, 1984–1989), 4.264 n. 45.
2. This letter from Firmilian is preserved in Cyprian's correspondence (75.10.2). It is the only extant document by Firmilian, though we know of his activities through other authors (particularly Origen of Alexandria, who was his teacher [Euseb., *Hist. eccl.* 7.28.1]). Throughout this article, I use the translation and extended commentary by G. W. Clarke except when otherwise noted; all quotations of the letter are drawn from Clarke, *Letters*, vol. 4.
3. *Ep.* 75.10.2. This is an argument that Tertullian of Carthage had used a generation earlier. In his *Apologeticum* (22.8), Tertullian explains that "all spirits are winged" (*omnis spiritus ales est*), which allows them to know everything that is happening in the world the instant it happens, and to report it in the same instant. "Their swiftness of motion is taken for divinity," he explains. "Thus they would have themselves thought sometimes the authors of the things which they announce." He adds as a sly aside, "Sometimes, no doubt, the bad things are their doing, never the good."
4. In other words, Christians had already been asking the question of how their rituals might compel God to do things (is God "forced" to bestow grace upon a baptizand?); and this in turn raises the issue of how demons might act in the presence of perverse or mistaken ritual behavior, or in the absence of "good," protective Christian rituals.
5. *Ep.* 75.10.3.

6. *Ep.* 75.10.3.
7. *Ep.* 75.10.4.
8. Clarke, *Letters,* 4.85 and note at 4.266n50. In the last case, the demon does seem to be the subject of the verb, since he tricked the deacon *into sleeping with this woman* (*ut eidem mulieri commiscerentur*). In the other two cases, however, either subject fits the context.
9. 75.10.3.
10. Clarke, and most other commentators, take "*rusticum*" as an adjective. It could also mean the man's name was Rusticus. Even if this is true, however, the pun would not have been lost on Firmilian. Clarke, *Letters,* 4.266 n. 51.
11. *Ep.* 75.10.4.
12. According to Eusebius, the Montanist prophetesses Maximilla and Priscilla were also resistant to exorcism (*Hist. eccl.* 5.16.10, 5.16.16, 5.18.13). Eusebius blames the heretics' supporters for "preventing" the exorcism from working properly.
13. The Latin actually reads *sine sacramento,* but Clarke supplies a *non* in his translation since the sentence would be nonsense without it. For his justification see Clarke, *Letters* 4.267 n. 56.
14. *Ep.* 75.10.5.
15. It is likely that she belonged to the sect known as the Montanists. Christine Trevett provides a detailed justification for this identification in "Spiritual Authority and the 'Heretical' Woman: Firmilian's word to the church at Carthage," in *Portraits of Spiritual Authority: Religious Power in Early Christianity, Byzantium, and the Christian Orient*, ed. Jan Willem Drijvers and John W. Watt (Leiden: Brill, 1999), 48–50. I will discuss the significance of Montanism below.
16. The definitive work on Cyprian's tension with the Roman church, and his relationship with the Roman Empire as a whole, is J. Patout Burns, *Cyprian the Bishop* (London: Routledge, 2002).
17. Women frequently served this purpose for heresiologists in late antiquity. The case of Firmilian's prophetess is instructive since she is the primary character and yet is still anonymous; moreover, she is driven through her own narrative by a demon. Compare, for example, the story of Marcus, who (according to Irenaeus) flattered beautiful women by telling them they had prophetic gifts in order to seduce them (*Haer.* 13.3–5); or Simon Magus, who (according to Justin, Irenaeus, Hippolytus, and others) traveled from town to town in the company of his lover Helen, an ex-prostitute whom he introduced as his *ennoia* but who never gets a speaking part in his story (*Haer.* 23.2–3; *Ap.* 26; *Ref.* 6.14; a detailed study of the Simon legend can be found in Alberto Ferreiro, *Simon Magus in Patristic, Medieval, and Early Modern Traditions* [Leiden: Brill, 2005]). Firmilian's reluctance to grant the prophetess the status of a heresiarch, even as he uses her to make a point about heresy, suggests that her position in this story is suspended between the subject and the object of his debate with Cyprian.

18. This view was refined by another North African, Augustine of Hippo, in the fifth century. Discussion including extensive passages from relevant primary sources can be found in Pierre Pourrat, *Theology of the Sacraments* (St. Louis: B. Herder, 1910).
19. The minutes of the meeting are preserved in the *Sententiae episcoporum numero lxxxvii, de haeriticis baptizandis*, in *CSEL* 3:1 (435–61). A new critical edition has been published by Paolo Bernardini under the title *Le Sententiae episcoporum del concilio cartaginese del 256 e la loro versione greca* (Bologna: Edizioni Dehoniane, 2005) but I have not seen it.
20. See, for example, *Ep.* 69.7.1, where Cyprian argues that heretics affirm the same truths about their "church" as the orthodox do, but that the church itself doesn't exist for heretics. In *Ep.* 73.4.2, he says that heretics call on the name of God but it is the wrong God. To borrow the terminology of Gottlob Frege, Cyprian believes that heretical creeds have "sense" (*sinn*) but no "reference" (*bedeutung*).
21. Patout Burns provides insightful analysis of this phenomenon, and proposes a set of reasons for its development, in *Cyprian*, 82–84.
22. On the significance of the Decian persecution for the development of North African Christianity in general and Cyprian's theology in particular, see Patout Burns, *Cyprian*, 17–24 and *passim*.
23. *Epp.* 43.2.1–2, 52.2.5, 54.3.2–3. For the perspective of some clerics in Cyprian's camp, see *Ep.* 30.3, addressed to Cyprian by "the presbyters and deacons residing in Rome."
24. See Patout Burns, *Cyprian*, 80. Significantly, he entitles this chapter "The Revolt of the Presbyters."
25. *Ep.* 55.24.1.
26. *Ep.* 52.2.1.
27. *Ep.* 52.2.5.
28. *Ep.* 69.8.3.
29. *Ep.* 55.24.2, emphasis Clarke's. The Latin reads *scias nos primo in loco nec curiosos esse debere quid ille doceat, cum foris doceat.*
30. *Ep.* 69.7.1–2, emphasis Clarke's.
31. Patout Burns defends Cyprian's theology, calling his system "tightly argued" and "practical" (*Cyprian*, vii–viii). Maurice F. Wiles, by contrast, says that "the grounds and method of his theological reasoning are not of a kind to inspire confidence" ("The Theological Legacy of St. Cyprian," in *JEH* 14 [1963]: 139–49, 149).
32. *Manifestum est nec remissionem peccatorum dari per eos posse quos constet Spiritum sanctum non habere*, *Ep.* 69.11.3.
33. Of course, Cyprian would never use the language of contagion to talk about grace, though he frequently talks about heresy's power to contaminate innocent people; see, e.g., *Ep.* 67.3.1–2, where he cites Num 16.26 to make his point.
34. *Ep.* 70.1.3.
35. *Ep.* 69.15.1. Clarke calls this view "somewhat primitive," but I do not share his tendency to privilege the intellectual over the material (4.199 n. 6). For more on

Cyprian's view of the power of baptismal water to drive off demons, see Clarke, *Cyprian*, 4.175.

36. *Ep.* 69.11.3.
37. The relevant material is preserved in *Ep.* 74.1–3. Stephen's argument seems to have hinged on the ritual efficacy of Christ's name: see *Ep.* 75.9.1 and 75.18.1.
38. A handful of references to him survive in the work of Eusebius (*Hist. eccl.* 6.27, 6.46.3, 7.5.1–3 [citing Dionysius of Alexandria]), 7.7.5, 7.28.1, 7.30.3–5), Basil (*Epp.* 70, 188, *De Spiritu Sancto* 29.74), and Jerome (*Ep.* 33.4).
39. A common theme in Cyprian's work; see, e.g., *Ep.* 71.1.3.
40. In this letter alone, Firmilian calls Stephen arrogant, ignorant, crassly stupid, and a liar, and furthermore, he blithely compares him to both Judas and the Jews. For a catalog of these terms of abuse, see Clarke, 4.250. To be fair, Stephen seems to have engaged in some mudslinging of his own: according to Firmilian, he called Cyprian a "bogus Christ, a bogus apostle, and a crooked dealer" in a letter that has since been lost (*Epist.* 75.25.4).
41. So Clarke, *Cyprian*, 4.169n25, though arguably the argument for dating the letters in this way is circular.
42. *Ep.* 68.5.1.
43. *Ep.* 59.14.2.
44. Montanus's activity is fixed, following Eusebius, in the 170s. See Douglas Powell, "Tertullianists and Cataphrygians," *VC* 29, no. 1 (1975): 33–54, 41 for discussion of dating.
45. Their opponents also called them "Cataphrygians," since the sect had its start in Phrygia. The members of the sect seemed to prefer to refer to themselves by the name "the New Prophecy." For discussion, see Christine Trevett, *Montanism: Gender, Authority and the New Prophecy* (Cambridge: Cambridge University Press, 1996), 2.
46. I was particularly struck by the assertion that they would name local Phrygian cities Jerusalem (Eusebius, *Hist. eccl.* 5.18.3), an accusation that Firmilian also levels against his prophetess. For more on the conflict between proto-Catholic and Montanists regarding gender and authority, see Trevett, *Montanism*, especially chapters 3 and 4.
47. "Those called Cataphrygians, who try to claim they have new prophecies, can possess neither the Father nor the Son, because they do not possess the Holy Spirit," *Ep.* 75.7.3. Firmilian mentions Montanus by name in this passage, and dismisses the latter's visions as arising from the "spirit, not of truth, but of error" (*non veritatis Spiritum sed erroris*). The Montanists' theology was sound, like that of the prophetess, meaning that it was much harder to accuse them of heresy than it was to label Arians or Sabellians as heretics. Furthermore, the New Testament itself presents examples of what seem to be ecstatic utterances spoken during church gatherings (e.g., 1 Cor 12:1–12, 14:1–19; Acts 2:1–21), all of which take place long after the crucifixion. This makes it hard to condemn an ecstatic Christian for claiming to speak with the Holy Spirit's authority.

48. Firmilian uses this phrase in *Ep.* 75.9.1, immediately before introducing the story of the prophetess. It is arguable, but I think unlikely, that the phrase is not intended to apply to her.
49. *Ep.* 75.11.1, emphasis added.
50. *Ep.* 73.1.2.
51. *Ep.* 73.2.1.
52. For a persuasive argument in support of this view, see Cecil Robeck, *Prophecy in Carthage: Perpetua, Tertullian, and Cyprian* (Cleveland: Pilgrim, 1992).
53. Trevett, 57.
54. I am grateful to Ioana Georgescu for raising this issue with me at a recent conference.
55. The story appears in Num 16. Cyprian uses it frequently in discussions of legitimacy in the priesthood. For examples see *Ep.* 3.1.2, *Ep.* 67.3.2, *De Unitate* 18, etc.
56. *Ep.* 75.16.2.
57. "[Firmilian's letter] adds remarkably little to our understanding of the grounds of the controversy" (Clarke, *Cyprian*, 4.249).
58. If she was, in fact, a Montanist this would have been a highly ironic accusation since Montanists were frequently portrayed, even by their enemies, as being ascetics.
59. Trevett argues that Firmilian's verb *commiscerentur* permits the same ambiguity as the English phrase "slept with." If the prophetess was a celibate Montanist who engaged in the practice of *virgines subintroductae*—chaste bed-sharing—then she may well have been literally sleeping with men without committing any sexual misdemeanors ("Spiritual Authority," 58 and notes). Note, however, that Cyprian disapproved of *any* physical contact between men and dedicated virgins, as he explains at length in a letter about a different case (*Ep.* 4). There is no reason to believe that Firmilian disagreed with him on this. On the use of sexual slander among early Christians as a way to create and denounce "heretics" see Jennifer Wright Knust, *Abandoned to Lust: Sexual Slander and Early Christianity* (New York: Columbia University Press, 2006).
60. *Ep.* 75.10.4.
61. The word *veneficia* does appear in stock lists of sins of the flesh; see, for example, *On the Lord's Prayer*, ch. 16. But as far as I am aware, Cyprian spends less time discussing witchcraft and sorcery than he spends discussing the proper treatment of a man's beard.
62. Andrzej Wypustek, "Magic, Montanism, Perpetua, and the Severan Persecution," in *VC* 51, no. 3 (1997), 276–97.
63. In his careful analysis of the words *semeion* and *teras* in late antique literature, Harold Remus considers the oft-repeated claim that Christians and pagans differently valorize the language of "miracle" ("wonder," "monstrosity," "marvel," "horror"): "Does Terminology Distinguish Early Christian from Pagan Miracles?" *JBL* 101, no. 4 (1982), 531–51. To the question he puts in his title he answers "no." By contrast, Hendrik Versnel argues that modern distinctions between magic and

religion *can* be maintained in some ancient sources: "Some Reflections on the Relationship Magic–Religion," *Numen* 38, no. 2 (1991), 177–97. An excellent, up-to-date review of the literature is Michael Bailey, "The Meanings of Magic," *JMRW* 1 (2006): 1–23.

64. Though I disagree with his conclusions, Keith Thomas, *Religion and the Decline of Magic* (New York: Oxford University Press, 1971) provides numerous examples of popular Catholic attitudes toward the sacraments that Protestants would later classify as magical. See also Kevin C. Robbins, "Magical Emasculation, Popular Anticlericalism, and the Limits of the Reformation in Western France circa 1590," *JSH* 31, no. 1 (1997): 61–83, which argues that not only Catholic clergy, but Calvinist clergy too, were popularly believed to be magicians. For discussion of the impact of this Early Modern debate on later scholarship, see Jonathan Z. Smith, *Drudgery Divine: On the Comparison of Early Christianities and the Religions of Late Antiquity* (Chicago: University of Chicago Press, 1990). Smith famously argues that Protestant suspicion of ritual continues to influence theories of religion today.
65. The literature on this topic is immense, and the existence of this volume proves that questions about the definition of magic have not been settled. A number of excellent synopses and methodological studies exist. See, for example, Sarah Iles Johnston et al., "Panel Discussion: 'Magic in the Ancient World' by Fritz Graf," *Numen* 46, no. 3 (1999): 291–325, along with Graf's book itself (Cambridge, MA: Harvard University Press, 1999); see also Paul Mirecki and Marvin Meyer, eds., *Magic and Ritual in the Ancient World*, vol. 141 of *Religions in the Greco-Roman World* (Leiden: Brill, 2002) and Paul Mirecki and Marven Meyer, eds., *Ancient Magic and Ritual Power* (Leiden: Brill, 2001).
66. Cyprian in particular was incapable of understanding or having any sympathy for the motivations of those who left his church. He could not even imagine them as being honestly mistaken. For him, they were all "headstrong and stiff-necked" (*Ep.* 59.7.1).
67. The most famous example is probably the charlatan Alexander in Lucian's *The Lover of Lies*, a connection that Klawiter and Trevett both explore in the broader context of Montanism. For discussion, see Trevett, *Montanism*, 78, and Robert C. Klawiter, "The Role of Martyrdom and Persecution in Developing the Priestly Authority of Women in Early Christianity: A Case Study of Montanism," *CH* 49 (1980): 251–61.
68. In Mirecki and Meyer, eds., *Magic and Ritual*, 159–78.
69. This is particularly the case with studies of mediaeval European witch trials. The classic study is Peter Brown, "Sorcery, Demons, and the Rise of Christianity from Late Antiquity into the Middle Ages," in *Witchcraft Confessions and Accusations*, ed. Mary Douglas (London: Faber and Faber, 1977), 119–46. The argument that witch-hunts served to scapegoat unpopular groups was made forcefully by authors like Hugh Trevor-Roper, Joseph Klaits, and Anne Llewellyn Barstow. For bibliography see James A. Sharpe, "Witches and Persecuting Societies," *JHSoc* 3 (1990): 75–86.

70. David Frankfurter, "Dynamics of Ritual Expertise in Antiquity and Beyond: Towards a New Taxonomy of 'Magicians,'" in *Ancient Magic and Ritual Power*, ed. Paul Mirecki and Marvin Meyer (Leiden: Brill, 2001), 174.
71. *Propheten se praeferret et quasi sancto Spiritu plena sic ageret*, 75.10.2.
72. *Omnes omnino haereticos et schismaticos nihil habere potestatis ac iuris*, *Ep*. 69.1.1.
73. J. Patout Burns, "On Rebaptism: Social Organization in the Third Century Church," *JECS* 1 (1993): 367–403, 401; emphasis added.
74. Ibid., 402.
75. 75.11.1. This translation is my own. Clarke's rendering ("through the agency of a woman") is misleading, since agency is precisely what Firmilian is denying. The woman is the demon's instrument, by which (*per*) it does its work.
76. Firmilian addresses this in *Ep*. 75.16; Cyprian discusses apostolic succession in numerous places, but most clearly in *Ep*. 70.3.1.
77. Trevett, "Spiritual Authority," 56.
78. Though perhaps it is an imagined history, which would provide even more support for Frankfurter's point, Trevett raises the possibility that the character of the prophetess might be "a composite of various stereotypes and projected fears with regard to the kinds of teachers and teachings she was used to represent." Trevett, "Spiritual Authority," 44.
79. In his introduction to *Ep*. 75, *Cyprian*, 250.
80. Frankfurter, "Dynamics," 171.
81. See the intriguing reference to "Judaea an Jerusalem" in 75.10.3.
82. On which see n. 9.

9

Living Images of the Divine: Female Theurgists in Late Antiquity

Nicola Denzey Lewis

IN A PRIVATE estate near the city of Pergamum during the closing years of the fourth century, a teacher of philosophy named Sosipatra is surrounded by her husband and a gaggle of adoring students. They have gathered eagerly at her feet to hear their teacher expound on Platonist metaphysics. Midway through her lecture on the descent of the soul, Sosipatra falls into an oracular, corybantic (*korubantiasmos*) frenzy.[1] Her body, flailing then quiet, her eyes open wide in alarm and fixed at a distant point, she begins to speak after a brief silence:

> What is this? Look! My kinsman Philometor is riding in a carriage... but the carriage has been overturned in a rough spot in the road and both his legs are in danger! But wait: his servants have dragged him out unharmed, except that he has received wounds on his elbows and hands, though even these are not dangerous. He is being carried home on a stretcher, moaning loudly.[2]

A chill fills the air as Sosipatra's body slumps, passive. It is difficult to imagine the scene that follows next. When Philometor's servants arrive bearing their injured master, confirmation also arrives that Sosipatra's oracular utterance was completely accurate. Few around her express surprise. Still, from the event, Sosipatra's listeners conclude that their teacher is omnipresent (*pantaxou*) and omniscient, that "nothing happens without her being able to see."[3]

Sosipatra, who forms the focal point of this essay, is one of our most famous examples of a late ancient Platonist sage, many of whom were intimately—though complicatedly—involved in various types of ritual activities that could be called (both then and now) "magic." We know of her only from a sole extant source: Eunapius of Sardis's remarkable compendium of philosophers' biographies, his *Vitae philosophorum* or *Lives of the Philosophers and Sophists* (ca. 405

CE). Eunapius, born around 347 CE, had been trained by some of the finest teachers of the Eastern Mediterranean, including the sophist Chrysantius and the orator Prohaeresius. Intent to keep pagan spiritual traditions alive, he had been initiated into the Eleusinian Mysteries and had joined the college of the Eumolpidae. His markedly anti-Christian *Lives of the Philosophers and Sophists* contains the biographies of twenty-three Platonist teachers, of which Sosipatra's life is actually an extension or excursus on the life of her first husband, the philosopher Eustathius.

A thoughtful study of Sosipatra and her significance poses immediate and vexing challenges, which I will address in this chapter; I also hope to present a way to navigate through these challenges profitably. The first is an immediate, though general, question of what late ancient Platonists were up to—that is to say, it is a question of classification. Do we classify the hieratic or ritual activities that distinguished late Platonism from the merely "academic" pursuit of philosophy as "magic," or "religion"? By raising the question with such blunt, clumsy terms of classification, I am well aware of the history of debate on the usefulness of either term, as well as the complex relationship between the two.[4] Secondly, modern scholars have proceeded on the assumption that we can extract and reconstruct social history from our few late ancient sources. Yet the nature of the texts themselves—particularly as seen *within* their social context rather than as uncritical reflections of that context—invite caution. To put it more precisely, rather than to accept Sosipatra as a powerful and spiritually gifted woman who once lived and taught in late fourth-century Pergamum, can we instead be mindful as to how Eunapius constructed her as a character within the specific genre of late antique philosophical *bioi*? This is not to say that Sosipatra never existed beyond Eunapius's fictive construction of her. Rather, a more helpful question might be "what ideological work do these narratives do?" A sense of the narratological function of the magical in Eunapius will help us to further understand what sort of social functions Sosipatra might have served. Here, the recent work of Kimberly Stratton on "magic" as a discourse of alterity is instrumental for allowing us to see that narrative reflects and refracts the manner(s) in which people of the fourth century employed the discourse of "magic."[5] Finally, there is the issue of gender and magic—the topic of the present volume. In the case of Sosipatra, how did her gender affect the way in which she was perceived within late ancient pagan circles? What her supporters called her—and for that matter, what her opponents called her—had marked significance in the ideologically charged world of a nascent Christian empire. She is never called a magician (or a sorceress) by either group—at least, to the best of our knowledge. Eunapius assiduously avoids labeling, in any case. I believe this was deliberate, yet such bracketing of troubling words and concepts is no proof that Eunapius was unaware of the "problem" of Sosipatra. In fact, I argue here that Eunapius's entire narrative was crafted to defend her from charges of magic. How precisely he does this I will illuminate in the body of this chapter.

The Curious Life of Sosipatra

Eunapius's account of Sosipatra's life is fairly well articulated, full of curious tales and fine details. She was born near Ephesus into a wealthy family. From the outset, she was clearly a blessed child—any contact with her "seemed to bring a blessing on everything."[6] The first formal indication that Sosipatra was no ordinary child occurred when she was only five years old. One day, two old men "dressed in garments of skin" appear at her parents' country estate. First the old men persuade the steward to let them tend the estate's vineyards. The next season's harvest proves to be so prodigious that everyone in the estate wonders if the gods themselves had intervened to produce such bounty. This boon wins the old men the right to sit at the master's table where they express amazement at Sosipatra's beauty and charm. To her father, they note that the abundant vintage pales in comparison with the great feats of which they are capable. They implore the girl's father to turn Sosipatra over to their care, "to us who are more truly her parents and guardians."[7] The benefit to Sosipatra's family is clear: for five years they need not fear that she will ail or die, and her parents will receive a financial boon. But the real clincher is the cultivation of Sosipatra's spiritual potential: "Moreover, your daughter shall have a mind not like a woman's or a mere human being's."[8] With that, Sosipatra's father duly hands over his child to the mysterious visitors. Eunapius wonders if the men were indeed human at all, or if perhaps they were "heroes or demons or of some race still more divine." He hedges, at this point, on their hieratic pedigree: "into what mysteries they initiated her no one knew, and with what religious rite they consecrated the girl was not revealed even to those who were most eager to learn."[9]

When, years, later, the father reunites with the now-grown Sosipatra and her tutors, his daughter astonishes him with her knowledge of the precise details of his journey to her, "as if she had been driving with him."[10] At this point in the narrative, the secret is finally disclosed: the old men reveal that they are initiates into Chaldean lore, "but even this they told enigmatically and with bent heads."[11] The entire incident appears to have been an initiation or test of Sosipatra's readiness for further instruction, for while her father dozes at table after a meal, the old men "very tenderly and scrupulously handed over to her the whole array of garments in which she had been initiated, and added certain mystic symbols thereto; and they also put some books into Sosipatra's chest, and gave orders that she should have it sealed."[12] And then, as swiftly as they appeared, the old men are gone, returning to their sacred abode in the Western Ocean.

First and foremost, the old men had made a scholar out of their young charge. Like other great Platonist sages, Sosipatra could easily and publicly expound on poetry, philosophy, and rhetoric. At her base in Pergamum, the most famous teacher of philosophy in the city, Aedesius, proves no match for Sosipatra, whom Eunapius admiringly notes attracted throngs of adoring students who came to hear her teach philosophy in her home.[13] Yet Sosipatra's learnedness pales in comparison with her other skills. We have already witnessed two episodes of her "remote viewing" abilities. She also appears to have waking, prophetic dreams. In one story, Sosipatra decides to marry (clearly her own decision), choosing a fellow philosopher, Eustathius. On the eve of their marriage, she delivers a prophecy: she will bear him three children, "but all of them will fail to win what is considered to be human happiness. Yet as to the happiness that the gods grant, not one of them will fall short."[14] She also reports that Eustathius will die before her and earn a fitting place in the afterlife, but that she herself will receive a more distinguished favor from the gods; she will attain to an even higher celestial abode. In a prophetic dream-state, she informs her husband, "your station will be in the orbit of the moon, and you shall traverse the region below the moon with a blessed and easily guided motion." After a brief pause, she adds: "And I can tell you my own fate also." But then, Eunapius records, she again falls silent, troubled, before bursting out, "No, my god prevents me!"[15] Her prophecy concerning the lives of her children comes true, since, as Eunapius reports, Sosipatra's prophecies "had the same force as an immutable oracle, so absolutely did it come to pass and transpire as had been foretold by her."[16]

Sosipatra's remarkable talents do not end there. The "remote viewing" skills she exhibits when she recalls the details of her father's journey or sees Philometor's carriage overturn are also showcased in one final incident. After the death of her first husband, Eustathius, Sosipatra tells her favored student Maximus—whom she has asked to investigate an erotic spell for which she was the target—all the things he had done in a private ritual to level a counter-spell: she "described to Maximus his own prayer and the whole ceremony; she also told him the hour at which it took place, as though she had been present, and revealed to him the omens that had appeared."[17] The entire incident of Sosipatra's love spell is indeed an interesting one, to which I shall return presently; for our present purposes, however, I wish only to note that Eunapius's point to this story is, once again, to showcase Sosipatra's remarkable remote-viewing abilities.

Eunapius says little about Sosipatra's declining years. Widowed as she herself had predicted, Sosipatra returned with her three children to her own estate in Pergamum, where she forged a close romantic relationship with Philometor and where she was cared for by the great Platonist teacher Aedesius. Again, as she predicted, two of her children failed to win any acclaim. Only one, Antoninus, lives up to the example of his mother, traveling to Alexandria and immersing himself in the proper worship of the gods and their ancient rites. Like his mother, Antoninus has the gift of prophecy and prescience, predicting the destruction of the Alexandrian Serapeum in the spasm of violence that followed the Theodosian Decree of 391 CE.[18]

The "Holy Man," "Pagan Holy Men," and "Persons of Power"

The Gendered Holy Man

What do we make of Sosipatra's life? First, we must place her in the broader context of spiritual savants in late antiquity. In a now famous article published in 1971, historian Peter Brown introduced a series of essential characteristics of the late antique holy man: in a culture in transition, he was the new rural patron par excellence, a locus of divine power, an arbitrator in early disputes, a mediator between heaven and earth, and a thaumaturge.[19] But to bring the obvious to bear, in Brown's study two essential features were accepted without question: that the holy man was Christian, and that he was male.

Scholars in the past twenty years have redrawn the boundaries of Brown's field of inquiry. In two landmark articles published in 1977 and 1982, Brown's student Garth Fowden broadened his teacher's definition of "holy" to include pagan holy men, whom Fowden located in the Platonist circles of Rome, Alexandria, Athens, and Apamea from the third to the fifth centuries.[20] These circles became *loci* for a particular sort of divine power in late antiquity, providing a "widening frontier zone of philosophical mysticism."[21] Fowden's studies of the pagan "virtuosi of the spiritual life" introduced new paradigms for holiness within the context of Greco-Roman traditions and values.[22] In contrast to Brown's, Fowden's holy man was essentially urban and privileged, misanthropic and deeply private, a living *algama* or cultic image in a world where the public manifestations of pagan sacrality were becoming harder and harder to detect. Yet these pagan holy men shared with their Christian counterparts the power to manipulate their physical environment; they could summon up minor deities, bring rainstorms, foretell the future, and engage (like Sosipatra) in remote viewing and other acts of extrasensory perception. A few remarkable stories of their power remain: in 375 CE, for instance, the pagan philosophical hierophant Nestorius preserved Athens and Attica from destruction by earthquake, having been forewarned in a dream that Achilles had to be honored with public rites.[23] Later, the Athenian philosopher Proclus saved the same city from a disabling drought by summoning rain.[24] Even the emperor Julian—skilled in the hieratic arts he had learned from his Platonist spiritual masters—knew how to avert earthquakes and storms.[25] Thus pagan holy men exercised potent civic duties to protect citizens by controlling the forces of nature.

Although he is fully aware of the existence of Sosipatra and the famed late fourth-century Platonist philosopher, Hypatia of Alexandria—the two most famous Platonist female "holy men"—Fowden fails to raise the issue of gender in his studies of Platonist sages. This is not entirely surprising. The preferred ancient Greek term for "holy man," the *theios aner*, is resolutely gendered, raising at least the question of whether it would have been licit in antiquity to include a woman under such a clearly masculine designation. Presumably, Fowden merely included women under the category of *theios aner*, without intending to imply that a holy person (despite the gender-specific *aner*) had to be male. But others have chafed at the term. Rather than *theioi andres*, Anitra Bingham Kolenkow, for instance, prefers the term "persons of power."[26]

Women Philosophers

Ancient women were certainly drawn to philosophy. It was on the urging of Julia Domna that Philostratus wrote his biography of Apollonius of Tyana. Decades later, Alexander Severus's mother, Julia Mamaea, provided a military escort for the Christian philosopher Origen so that he might come to visit her.[27] Platonist circles included a large number of women devoted to philosophy. Galen writes of the elite woman Arria, wife of N. Nonius Macrinus, who sought to educate herself in Platonic philosophy.[28] We find included within Plotinus's study group in third-century Rome at least five women: Chione; Gemina and her daughter, Amphiclea; and Marcella.[29] Two of these women seem primarily to have been associated with the group through ties of matrimony, having married students of Plotinus; Marcella marries Plotinus's chief disciple, Porphyry of Tyre; Amphiclea marries Iamblichus of Chalcis.[30] Another woman, Arete, joined Iamblichus's philosophical circle in Syria. It is not clear whether women's participation in these circles extended beyond the roles of "hearers" or junior students. We do, however, have evidence that a century later, women contributed more actively to the intellectual life of these groups, even instructing men. In the fifth century, the great philosopher Proclus studied under Asclepigeneia, daughter of Plutarch, another renowned philosopher.[31] Inducted into Chaldean arts and theurgy by her father, Asclepigeneia passes along her knowledge to Proclus and, some say, to Hypatia of Alexandria herself.

Despite some achieved status as philosophical teachers, fifth-century women Neoplatonists are mentioned in our ancient sources primarily for the active role they play in supporting and raising scions for the great philosophical *diadoche* rather than as esteemed philosophers or holy women in their own right; they are primarily cultural continuators. The fifth-century philosopher Aedesia married the philosopher Hermeias and raised two more sons destined for philosophical fame, Ammonius and Heliodorus.[32] Although she was almost certainly skilled in hieratic arts, we know nothing of Aedesia beyond her status as a wife and mother to philosophers. Indeed, none of the women mentioned in our brief historical references is anywhere said to have divine talents or skills. Here, as a woman, Sosipatra stands alone—but she *is* aligned through her abilities with other male Platonist luminaries, including Plotinus and her own son, Antoninus.

"Magic" and "Religion" in Late Ancient Platonism

Theurgy

As we have seen, there were different ways in which the Platonist sage might exercise divine powers: through prescience and visions, oracular utterances, or control of the weather and earthquakes. But while modern scholars have noted these activities, they have failed to comment at length on their social significance. Instead, the preoccupation in contemporary scholarship on late ancient Platonism has been to ferret out details of its practice of theurgy (*theourgia*), a system of rituals designed to invoke divine powers and to connect human individuals with higher cosmic forces and processes. As an esoteric system developed in a largely hostile environment, the details of theurgy are difficult to discern from our extant sources. There is some indication that practitioners achieved a *unio mystica* with the Divine through ascent techniques, initially through mystical contemplation, but (some argue) then through more mechanical techniques, including the practitioner employing specific words, animating statues (*telestikê*), conjuring spirits, making hissing or popping noises, or employing stones, symbols, and a mystical spinning top, the *iynx* wheel.[33]

The theoretical underpinnings of theurgy were apparently outlined in the Chaldean Oracles, a collection of written sources attributed to a pagan thaumaturge named Julian who served in the Roman army under Marcus Aurelius and who, it was said, saved the army from a severe drought by calling down a rainstorm.[34] Garth Fowden has emphasized that Platonist theurgists considered their art to be not merely "Chaldean," but also Greek and Egyptian. Indeed, many of our later accounts of theurgic activities take place in or around Egypt. The early fourth-century Platonist Iamblichus associated the Chaldean Oracles with the Egyptian Hermetica; even more telling is the career of Sosipatra's son Antoninus, who sets himself up as a master theurgist in Canopus.[35]

In his study of fourth-century Platonist philosophy, Robert Penella takes for granted that Sosipatra must have been an adept in theurgy.[36] Eunapius certainly makes it clear that Sosipatra had been "fully initiated" into Chaldean mysteries. She appears to have passed on her knowledge—as well as her skills in oracular utterance and "omniscience"—to her son Antoninus. Antoninus, in turn, may have initiated the famous mathematician-philosopher Hypatia of Alexandria into theurgy, although this connection seems strained. The pattern of familial transmission of hieratic arts, however, holds true for what we know of Platonist religion in late antiquity. Sosipatra initiates her son; in Athens, Plutarch initiates his daughter Asclepigeneia who in turn passes on her knowledge to Proclus. Indeed, such familial transmission of theurgic arts was necessary in the charged social atmosphere of the late Roman Empire, and here, women played an active and necessary role as learned practitioners safely "behind the veil" of the public gaze.

But let us return to the term "theurgy," which proves to be problematic. Already in antiquity, some Christian critics of pagan philosophy saw "theurgy" as merely a fancy term for magic; Augustine dismisses "that which they call by the more despicable name of 'goetic magic' or by the more honorable one of 'theurgy.'"[37] Augustine's scorn is reflected in the opinions of even the most enlightened modern classicists, who saw Platonism as a late and degenerate form of Greek thought and theurgy as evidence for Platonism's pathetic descent into charlatan sorcery. In 1947, E. R. Dodds penned a seminal article that mischaracterized theurgy as, among other things, a form of automatic writing and a lowbrow "technique" of "vulgar magic."[38] Dodds saw theurgy as born of the desperation of the fading pagan elite class: "As vulgar magic is commonly the last resort of the personally desperate, of those whom man and God have alike failed," he wrote, "so theurgy became the refuge of a despairing intelligentsia which already felt *la fascination de l'abîme*."[39]

Subsequent generations of scholars since Dodds have attempted more nuanced analyses of theurgy.[40] One tactic has been to allow that theurgy was, in fact, a form of magic, but that magic itself should be revaluated as just one more value-neutral system of religious behavior. Thus Garth Fowden claimed that there was little practical difference between theurgy and magic: "after all, theurgy and magic depended for their success on the manipulation of the same network of universal sympathy; and many theurgical techniques are closely paralleled in the magical papyri."[41] Another tactic has been to see theurgy as "religion" rather than "magic." Jay Bregman, in his study of the philosopher-bishop Synesius of Cyrene, contends: "Theurgy implied a real religious commitment, which included a mystical notion that Greco-Roman civilization would collapse if the old gods, cults, and mysteries were abandoned."[42] Similarly, Kenneth Harl attests, "theurgic prayer, because it was activated by sacrifice, is best seen as a variant of traditional sacrifice supplicating divine power rather than as a magical spell summoning and bringing a supernatural power into servitude to human will."[43] Both Bregman and Harl see theurgy as a necessary adaptation of forms of pagan religiosity—notably sacrifice—that were no longer licit in a Christian empire. It was, therefore, a sociological response to the banning of sacrifices—first, public and nocturnal sacrifices by order of Constans and Constantius, then later, more comprehensively, by Theodosius I's edicts of 391–92 CE. There is, however, still within this view the conviction that theurgy must be rescued from the charge of being "magic" in the word's more reductive and negative sense: a byproduct of degenerate, extravagant Platonism, the mumbled incantations and crazy practices of the last generation of desperate pagans. Here, we are not so far from Dodds's world, even if in reaction to it.

One profitable direction is to look back to the sources themselves. What did the Platonist practitioners of theurgy think they were doing? They do not tell us, exactly, but they do make it clear that as far as they were concerned, it was certainly not magic, goetic or otherwise. Our first (and best) Platonist treatise on the subject, Iamblichus's *De Mysteriis Aegyptiorum*, distinguishes theurgy (there, a mystical ascent technique) from other forms of ritual act that depend (unlike theurgy) on the manipulation of physical objects according to systems of divine sympathies and antipathies.[44] Based on this, Polymnia Athanassiadi declares, "of course theurgy is not just a technique (though by a tenuous definition it can be this as well) but rather *a dynamic state of mind* [italics mine] varying from individual to individual."[45] Indeed, the Platonists themselves spent considerable effort distinguishing what they were doing from what they themselves considered magic. It is noteworthy then, that Eunapius emphasizes that Sosipatra produces her visions of the future *spontaneously* as a gifted seer, rather than as a practitioner of magic who needs a combination of preparatory techniques and material objects to conjure up a vision.

It soon becomes clear, however, that even among Platonists, "theurgy" did not mean simply one thing.[46] For Iamblichus in the early fourth century—and I suspect for Sosipatra in the late fourth century—theurgy was akin to a state of grace, in which the divine *dynamis* of a god came down to reside within the philosopher properly prepared to receive that power.[47] Whether or not we choose to call this "magic" is entirely subjective and ultimately unhelpful. Eunapius emphasizes that Sosipatra received her power not through any dangerous techniques by which a morally incontinent individual (from his perspective) might compel a god to do her will. Within most Platonist circles, therefore, theurgy was consistently positively assessed; not only did they not call it *mageia*, they took pains to distinguish one from the other. The sage Porphyry even railed against magic, claiming, for instance, that the gods had better things to do than be called down and manipulated to serve "the vilest of magicians"; it was the responsibility of the theurgist to instead go to the gods.[48] Iamblichus, meanwhile, categorically condemned divination using *charaktēres*:

> This bad and superficial type of divination, which is accessible to the great majority of people, uses falsehood and intolerable fraud; far from causing the presence of any god, it produces a movement of the soul that attracts

but a dim and ghostly reflection of the gods, which, because of its very debility, is sometimes disturbed by wicked demonic spirits.[49]

As for most Christians, they clearly saw theurgy as sorcery.[50] Here, "magic" and "sorcery" are merely the blunt tools of ugly rhetoric, not useful or accurate descriptors. The Platonist Isidore sought out oracular knowledge and worshiped the gods until Christians in Alexandria charged him with magic.[51] Later Byzantine Christian writers such as John Philoponnus certainly regarded Iamblichus as an arch-magician, since he claimed to obtain oracles by animating statues.[52] And although theurgy enjoyed prominence during the reign of Julian the Apostate—Julian studied with Maximus and appointed another theurgist, Chrysantius, to be the high priest (*archhiereus*) of Lydia—following Julian's death these same philosophers were tried and, in the case of Maximus, tortured and executed in 371 CE for crimes against the Empire. Interestingly, there were also other pagans who considered theurgy to be magic; the Platonist philosopher Eusebius of Myndus, for instance, railed against the theurgist Maximus and his use of magic that was merely the business of "crazy people who make a perverse study of certain powers derived from matter."[53]

Erotic Magic in Platonist Circles

There is one final incident in Sosipatra's narrative—strictly non-theurgical—that I feel compelled to include here, in part for what Eunapius does not say about either magic or theurgy, at least directly. After Eustathius's death, Sosipatra moves to Pergamum. There, a distant relative of hers, Philometor, falls passionately in love with her.[54] The entire incident is curiously told, and we sense Eunapius's hedging; Sosipatra feels the force of Philometor's love and shares it, but she is puzzled by its compulsive quality. She confesses to her student Maximus, "When Philometor is with me he is simply Philometor, and in no way distinguished from the crowd. But when I see that he is going away, my heart is wounded and tortured until it tries to escape from my breast."[55] She dispatches Maximus to display his piety (*theophiles epideixe ti*) to find out what ails her. Through a sacrificial rite, Maximus discovers that Philometor has placed an erotic spell on Sosipatra; to retaliate, he places a stronger counter-spell on Philometor. Maximus then returns to Sosipatra to find out whether his spell has worked. Not only does Sosipatra report no sensation of attraction to Philometor, she also recounts to him exactly what he had done to overcome the spell, what omens had appeared at the rite, and so on.[56]

The story is an interesting one, because Sosipatra is not the magician here but instead the helpless victim of an erotic spell. Furthermore, she herself does not work the counter-spell; instead, she enlists a student to do the deed. She subcontracts Maximus, in a sense, to provide an appropriate solution. It is also interesting—almost by way of an aside—what happens next. First comes the remote viewing incident I have already recorded above, in which Sosipatra explains to Maximus precisely what he did to cast the counter-spell, as if she herself had been in the room. At this, Maximus falls to his knees, convinced that Sosipatra possesses a divine nature. Considerably emboldened by the entire incident, Maximus confronts Philometor with his friends, adjuring him elliptically to cease "burning wood"—ostensibly (so Eunapius tells us) a reference to the sacrifice accompanying the erotic spell. Philometor is amazed at Maximus's (borrowed) knowledge; he immediately stops his forays into love spells, considers Maximus a powerful sage, and even ridicules his own foolish attempts to manipulate Sosipatra into loving him back. As for Sosipatra, she looks at him from this point with a "knowing and changed" (*gnosios kai diapherontos*) gaze, although it must be said that she still appears to be considerably smitten with him: the next story is that with which I began this essay, when Sosipatra interrupts her lecture to wring her hands at Philometor's mishap on the road to Pergamum.

What to make of this story? Eunapius clearly absolves Sosipatra of any direct involvement in the practice of magic, though his narrative evokes a world in which erotic magic is simply taken for granted as remarkably powerful, available to whomever might be motivated to use it, and which can be countered not by a more "academic" form of worship but only by the same system of spell casting; Sosipatra may be spiritually superior to mere mortals, yet she is unable to break the spell merely by virtue of being spiritually superior. In an environment where Sosipatra is vulnerable to the charges of practicing magic—not just by Christians but by rival philosophers—Eunapius employs a variety of moves: he insists a) that she was born different, thus her power was not "stolen" or coerced; b) that she was initiated into further arcane arts from childhood legitimately and appropriately; c) that her hieratic presence was a sign of the gods' favor to a persecuted community; and d) that (against her critics) her hieratic skills were exercises of "proper" divine gifts rather than illegitimate magic. Eunapius insures, ultimately, that Sosipatra comes across as being above reproach. Her theurgical skills run on an entirely different "track" from magic—at least, from love magic. Both are real, but one is manipulative, requiring a practitioner and a ritual system, while the other is spontaneous, passive, and requires no equipment.[57]

The Literary Factor

So far, following current scholarship, I have endeavored to consider the late antique pagan holy woman as a historical phenomenon. Nevertheless, we might be better off to consider the late antique thaumaturge as predominantly a construct within pagan hagiography, carefully crafted following specific sets or types of behavior governed by time-honored notions of divine power and blessedness. One recalls Roland Barthes's assertion: myth and ideology are "synonymous" and that there exists "an intimate relationship between realist representation and the imposition of ideological values."[58] The late antique hagiography is an ideologized *bios* constructed at a crucial moment in a community's collective identity construction. By nature, it is a constrained and conservative genre.

Platonists responded both directly and indirectly to the gradual demise of traditional forms of religiosity from the fourth to the sixth centuries. Eunapius's construction of Sosipatra, therefore, cannot be fully evaluated without an appreciation of the considerable task he had before him: to create an apologetic hagiography that presented Sosipatra as custodian to a set of esoteric traditions without divulging too much or making her a target of Christian (including imperial Christian) suspicions. Read in light of Ammianus Marcellinus's accounts of the witchcraft "trials" of fourth-century elite women—from which Sosipatra was mercifully spared—the biography of Sosipatra stands as a particularly remarkable example of the discourse of "magic" within one specific late pagan community.[59]

It is instructive to compare Sosipatra's *bios* in Eunapius with a similar account of a male Platonist sage: Porphyry of Tyre's biography of his teacher Plotinus (205–70 CE).[60] It should be said that Porphyry writes over a century before Eunapius, and if Eunapius knows of Porphyry's encomiastic biography, he certainly does not agree with Porphyry's adulation of Plotinus. It quickly becomes clear to a reader that Porphyry presents Plotinus as no mere professor of philosophy, but a *theios aner* set apart from mere mortals; he is a veritable spiritual savant. He never, however, describes Plotinus as a magician or a practitioner of theurgy.[61]

Let me rehearse a few scenes from Plotinus's biography to illumine the nature of Plotinus's supranormal skills in Porphyry's telling. In one, Plotinus appears to read Porphyry's thoughts, in what we might be tempted to call extrasensory perception.[62] In another, Porphyry alludes to having been present on more than one occasion when his teacher united, through mystic contemplation, with the One.[63] Plotinus's other skills include his special insight into people's character and foretelling the futures of the children in his care.[64] These are not incidents of magic as it tends to be classically defined—either now, or in late antiquity—but nevertheless, they show Plotinus to be no ordinary human.[65] Notably, he also displays skills very similar to those that Eunapius showcases of Sosipatra.

There is one particular incident in Plotinus's biography that bears recounting first. A rival philosopher, Olympius of Alexandria, tries to bring a "star-stroke" (*astrobolesai*) upon Plotinus by calling down malign astral influences. Plotinus feels these attacks viscerally, claiming that his limbs "were squeezed together and his intestines contracted 'like a money-bag pulled tight.'"[66] This particular Olympius is no career magician; he is a renowned philosopher, a fellow student of Ammonius Saccas—the man who taught philosophy to Plotinus and a host of other luminaries, including (possibly) the Christian Origen. Credentials notwithstanding, Porphyry dismisses Olympius as a pseudo-philosopher, presumably on the grounds that a true philosopher would not stoop to something as "vulgar" as magic. At any rate, Plotinus's power is sufficient enough that Olympius's attacks rebound. Plotinus turns the power back toward Olympius: "when he found his attempt recoiling upon himself, he told his intimates that the soul of Plotinus had such great power as to be able to throw back attacks on him on to those who were seeking to do him harm."[67]

To a generation of modern scholars, Plotinus typifies the hyper-rational scholar's scholar who would never deign to be involved in magic. Wilhelm Kroll described him as one who "raised himself by a strong intellectual and moral effort above the fog-ridden atmosphere which surrounded him."[68] After Plotinus's death, "the fog began to close in again," writes Dodds, "and later Neoplatonism is in many respects a retrogression to the spineless syncretism from which he had tried to escape."[69] Plotinus's involvement in rather sketchy activities—including the famous "séance" scene at the Iseum in Rome that E. R. Dodds wrote up as an appendix to his landmark study *The Greeks and the Irrational*—has therefore been excused as something to which he was merely dragged along by a more superstitious friend.[70]

But what interests me here are the points of coincidence between Porphyry's account of a magical "star-strike" on Plotinus against which he is able to use his personal power, and Eunapius's account of Philometor's erotic spell that Sosipatra's student annuls through a counter-spell. The pattern is certainly the same: an aggressor uses a spell to gain power over the victim of his obsessions, upon which the victim returns or rebounds the spell to the aggressor, thwarting him. Love, envy, and/or covetousness provoke the spell-caster; the victim of the spell clearly feels the effect of that spell—and in similar ways—until the spell is ultimately rendered powerless through a sort of counterstrike. In neither case, though, is this counterstrike construed as an act of counter-magic by the biographer recounting the narrative. Plotinus's own spiritual force is enough to have the spell against him rebound; he does not have to perform any kind of ritual redirection. Sosipatra, meanwhile, enlists a trusted ally to perform the necessary sacrifices and invocations; she herself does not deign to be directly involved, although she uses her powers of omniscience to dazzle Maximus by recounting the details of the acts that he performed alone. This remote-viewing sleight of hand allows the reader to marvel at Sosipatra's supramundane powers while simultaneously exonerating her, like Plotinus, from the charge of magic.

Given the thematic points of connection between Plotinus's and Sosipatra's involvement in magic, it is difficult to ascertain to what degree we should trust Eunapius's narrative. In our extant literature, the trope of the Platonist sage follows conventional lines. It is perfectly plausible to imagine—with Fowden and others—that Neoplatonists actively participated in "magic" and considered such events and actions commonplace, in which case Plotinus's and Sosipatra's victimization are related only circumstantially. On the other hand, it is possible that Eunapius included this particular narrative the way he did to make a broader point about what constituted divine power and what did not; thus Sosipatra's powers are brought into line with those of other *theioi andres* in late pagan *bioi* while being simultaneously demarcated from the powers of the magicians and ritual specialists of late antiquity.[71]

There is also the issue of Sosipatra's education. According to Roger Pack, Eunapius's account of the mysterious strangers who come to initiate Sosipatra follows an ancient trope, the *theoxenia*: that of the gods in disguise, who come to give those who welcome them a boon.[72] We find the best-known Classical variant in Ovid's *Metamorphoses* (8.620–724), where the elderly Philemon and Baucis offer hospitality to the disguised Jupiter and Mercury in their home; the couple begin to suspect something is not quite as it seems when their wine *krater* is miraculously replenished. Pack notes that the *theoxenia* trope follows three steps: 1) the first intimation of superhuman powers; 2) the host's reward; and 3) his departure at the bidding of the guests.[73] Although Pack is quick to point out that there are minor departures to the motif in Eunapius's account of Sosipatra's education, he rightly notes that our face-value reading of this narrative should be destabilized by its resonances with ancient folkloric themes. As he also points out, the thrust of Eunapius's account is not to emphasize Sosipatra's family's boon for welcoming the strangers to their house, but to consolidate Sosipatra's pedigree within mystical Platonism; Pack calls it "professionally valuable."[74] We find other parallel stories in similar literature that serve the same end: Pythagoras is taken by his father from Samos to Tyre to learn from the Chaldeans;[75] Democritus receives mystical instruction from the Chaldeans and Magi in Xerxes's retinue, when his father entertained the Persian king at Abdera.[76] What is remarkable and new, however—a point that Pack does not make—is that Eunapius employs these ancient motifs for the first time in describing the pedigree and skills of a woman.

The Problem of Gender

The historian of late antiquity Susan Ashbrook Harvey notes that late ancient Christian hagiographies were "almost exclusively the product of male writers."[77] These hagiographies were designed to reinforce specific ideas of gender, often through mimesis. Their authors deliberately molded a particular (and peculiar) literary form to conform to certain social expectations and, in turn, to shape them.[78] Thus Gregory of Nyssa's *Life of Saint Macrina* represents, in Susanna Elm's words, "our first image of the perfect Christian woman."[79] These texts provided important exempla for subsequent generations of Christian women.

Harvey cites the example of Melania the Elder, who diligently studied such hagiographies to draw examples for her own life. Christian hagiography, therefore, became a powerful medium for instruction and edification—even for social control.

The case is perhaps different for pagan *bioi* of late antiquity. Resolutely male-dominated, they represent forms of idealized behavior out of reach for the ordinary man. As for their usefulness as exempla for women, of the thirty-three sophists of Philostratus's *Lives of the Sophists*—which Eunapius used as his model for his *Lives*—not a single one is female. The only indication we have from the text that Philostratus knew of female philosophers is a brief and not particularly flattering account of a certain Philostratus the Egyptian, whom Philostratus reports was said to have studied philosophy with Cleopatra.[80] Although fully trained as a philosopher, Philostratus's peers considered him a mere sophist because of his association with "a woman who considered even the love of letters as a sensuous pleasure."[81] Sosipatra is the only woman mentioned among Eunapius's *Lives of the Philosophers and Sophists*; Eunapius goes so far as to apologize to the reader for including a woman in his compendium of men—as if it were well known that she had no right to be there. It is not clear whether Eunapius's notice was intended to be mimetic, or to be merely a sort of anecdotal history—the curiosity of a woman spiritual prodigy—although I suspect the latter is more likely. Sosipatra is never explicitly drawn as a moral exemplar, but as a remarkable divine child and divine woman, a bearer of ancient tradition and meaning. The few other female Platonists of which we know a small amount—notably Porphyry of Tyre's wife Marcella and Hypatia of Alexandria—never had biographies penned about them, although in the case of Hypatia we certainly encounter a significant overromanticization of her life story by those male authors, Christian and pagan, who wrote of her in passing.[82] Christian and pagan *bioi* and their divergent aims are reflected in a brief article by Arnaldo Momigliano, in which the historian contrasted Sosipatra with Macrina.[83] The comparison yields some interesting observations concerning the way in which the constraints of gender (and the dynamics of power) could be differently parsed out in the late fourth century. Macrina, engaged to be married in childhood, declares herself a "widow" at the death of her fiancé and remains a virgin throughout her life, isolated from men; Sosipatra, by contrast, marries twice and bears three sons, all of whom she trains in the hieratic arts. We find here two competing notions of *paideia*, but also radically different senses of what constitutes appropriate behavior for women.

Let us start with the competing notions of *paideia*. In 324 CE, the Emperor Licinius passed a law forbidding women from attending the "sacred schools of virtue"—that is, the philosophical schools of the Empire. He intended, most likely, to combat Christian philosophers, particularly female *didaskaloi*, but as a law it must have affected women's participation in pagan study groups as well.

Thus it is hardly surprising that two of our pagan holy women received their higher education from male family members. Porphyry explicitly states that he marries the pagan Marcella, who already had seven children, not so that he could have more children (presumably she was past the age of childbearing) but so that he could educate her.[84] Hypatia was educated in Platonism by her father, who had reached some degree of prominence as a philosopher and a mathematician. Sosipatra's education is somewhat more exotic. Despite its unconventional source, however, Sosipatra's knowledge is resolutely bookish. "Ever on her lips," reports Eunapius, "were the works of the poets, philosophers and orators"; even those books which others labored over to understand only incompletely, she could expound "with careless ease, serenely and painlessly."[85]

The cases of Sosipatra in Pergamum and Hypatia in Alexandria make evident that women teachers were valued in pagan philosophical schools, even into the fifth century. Still, they were uncommon. John Rist calls them "a comparative rarity in antiquity" and (from the ancient perspective) "a marvelous phenomenon."[86] Susanna Elm overstates her case when she claims "that pagan women achieved fame as eminent teachers of philosophy, especially in Alexandria, is well known."[87] In fact, Hypatia appears to be the only female teacher of philosophy in fifth-century Alexandria. Indeed, her fame likely stemmed from the fact that she was somewhat of a curiosity. For all her fame, her written philosophical works have not survived.

Theurgy had both male and female adherents, and although we know relatively little about theurgists of either gender, it is clear from the case of Sosipatra that women theurgists were highly valued.[88] Many of the gendered tropes invoked so often in the association of women and magic are entirely absent in the case of the pagan theurgical women of late antiquity, which is precisely why they are worthy of some consideration. It is significant, I think, that as theurgy went underground, women theurgists grew in prominence as private teachers of arcane wisdom who kept alive the ancient traditions of their families. For instance, the fifth-century Athenian Platonist Proclus—a fine rainmaker and thaumaturge—learned his theurgy from the pagan holy woman Asclepigeneia, who had learned these arts privately from her father, Plutarch.[89] As for Hypatia, there is no textual evidence that she practiced theurgy.[90] Her "holiness," therefore, was not explicitly hieratic, but rather a sort of numinous quality which she shared with all esteemed teachers of philosophy.[91] It is this quality that provoked Hypatia's students to address her with epithets such as "sacred," "divine," and "blessed"; Hypatia's students also all acknowledge her "divine spirit."[92]

But what do these texts indicate about the idealized behavior of women? Part of being a heroine in *bioi*—particularly, but not exclusively, in Christian *bioi*—was resisting the carnal advances of men. In their biographies, both Sosipatra and Hypatia spurn the advances of young male students who fall victim to their charms; their behavior provides the male hagiographer with the opportunity to deliver appropriately sage denouncements of the material world from the mouths of their heroines. When Maximus falls before her and proclaims her a goddess, Sosipatra delivers a pithy admonition: "Rise, my son. The gods love you if you raise your eyes to them and do not lean towards early and perishable riches."[93] Hypatia makes her point even more graphically; when her appeal to culture and the philosophical life fails to dissuade a young suitor, she contemptuously tosses a soiled sanitary napkin, "the symbol of unclean birth" at him, with the statement, "it is this, young man, that you love, and nothing of the Good."[94] The youth was so astonished by the display, the *Suda* reports, that his soul was turned to righteousness and he lived chastely ever after. We find here a good example of hagiography being used more for the purpose of directing and channeling male behavior—but we are conceptually now rather far from Sosipatra and Eunapius's overall handling of her story. We find there an apology for Sosipatra's femaleness without an attempt to fully subvert it to masculinity; compare, for instance, Eunapius's portrait of her with Xenophon's dialogue *Oeconomicus*, where when a man, Ischomachus, praises his wife's virtues, Socrates responds "Upon my word, Ischomachus, your wife has a truly masculine mind by your showing."[95] A woman who fulfills her duties capably becomes gendered male; in Xenophon's world, perfection is an exclusively male domain. Eunapius's view, by contrast, is that the perfect sage transcends human categories of gender: as Sosipatra's Chaldean teachers promise her father, "your daughter shall have a mind not like a woman's nor a mere human being's." Sosipatra is in no way inhibited by being a woman because she shares the divine Nous. Here, the contrast with late ancient Christian conceptions of women's spiritual power and authority—where women must first be "made male" before they can be made "holy"—is quite remarkable.[96]

Women, Magic, Sacrifice, and the Obsolescence of Oracles

Well before the closing of the last public school of philosophy by order of Justinian in 529 CE, the rise of Christianity had driven the traditional rites of Platonism underground. As early as the third century, Platonism was no longer necessarily a public enterprise. Fowden notes that there is no positive evidence that Plotinus ever gave formal lectures, nor had a large public following. We can ponder seriously, then, how many truly "public" male teachers of Platonism one would be likely to find in the fourth and fifth centuries. Most likely, Platonism flourished in a type of salon culture, accessed by the pagan elite, and under an increasing sense of the need for discretion and secrecy. Looking for a secure power base, Neoplatonism shifted back to the *domus*. One might imagine that women would have been ideally suited to teach within such a "salon culture." In the case of Sosipatra, Eunapius reports that she held a "chair of philosophy," which sounds very exalted until he clarifies that this chair was actually within her house.[97] After lectures with the renowned philosopher Aedesius, students flocked to Sosipatra's estate to study with the master herself. "Although there was none that did not greatly appreciate and admire Aedesius's erudition, Eunapius notes, "they positively adored and revered the woman's inspired teaching."[98] Hypatia, too, conducted a study circle in her house. According to the ecclesiastical historian Socrates, Hypatia made such attainments in literature and science, "as to far surpass all the philosophers of her own time . . . she explained the principles of philosophy to her auditors, many of whom came from a distance to receive her instructions."[99] This is not to say simply that late antique pagan holy women became more powerful as a consequence of their social location within the *domus*, but something rather more complex: traditional female virtues such as silence and obedience made them, in a sense, appropriate vectors for Platonist teachings that had necessarily to continue in an attitude of secrecy and utmost discretion.

The newly esteemed position of Platonist women teaching from the confines of their own homes correlates with another notable phenomenon: the increasing obsolescence of oracles. Women, needless to say, had traditionally held positions of power because of their oracular voices. The oracular woman was divested with foreknowledge, a power few mortals held. But by the fourth century, the great oracles of Delphi and Didyma (and their priestesses) had fallen silent.[100] At the same time, Polymnia Athanassiadi argues persuasively that late antique Christians fulminated—and legislated—not against the official, ancient sites of oracles, but against freelance divination and oneiromancy, of the sort that Sosipatra and her contemporaries practiced.[101] Thus oracles continued on in private oracle-seeking and oracle-delivering, and we see such evidence for women's roles in late antique oracles within Eunapius's account of Sosipatra; note the narrative with which I begin this essay, as Sosipatra falls into a "corybantic frenzy" while at home, surrounded by only a few dedicated (and duly awed) students. Her predictions, Eunapius notes, "had the same force as an immutable oracle."[102] Hypatia's student Synesius of Cyrene, too, refers to his teacher's words as "oracular utterances."[103] As in the case of passing along highly secretive theurgical teachings, pagan women's location within the domestic sphere worked to their advantage in the charged atmosphere of late antique religion and identity politics.

Conclusions

In her recent dissertation on theurgy, Carine van Liefferinge seeks to reexamine the difference between theurgy and magic, presenting theurgy as "the instrument for reviving pagan philosophy and politics."[104] She emphasizes the political dimension to theurgy, discussing who practiced it, what power it involved, whether or not it was practiced or promoted openly, what it augured for the Empire, and so on. In some way, it is fair to measure the health of the Empire (or, arguably, any political structure) by the degree of outcries of sorcery against its own members. In the fractious atmosphere of late antiquity, Christianity did not kill theurgy—it virtually created it. Theurgy drew upon forms of behaviors and ideologies designed to flourish underground.

The hieratic function of women—hardly unusual in traditional Greco-Roman religions—was, by the late fourth century, enhanced as women physically and functionally replaced functioning public oracular sites. The benchmark of the holy person was his or her power of prescience and the ability to utter oracular statements. In this atmosphere of persecution and necessary secrecy, women were ideally positioned to act as embodiments of tradition. From them, the last vestiges of ancient rites were delicately suspended. Sosipatra's power lay in her symbolic value to a community not as a sorceress, but as a powerful continuator of a wide range of pagan values: the miraculous qualities of foreknowledge and internal power, as well as the deeply domestic qualities of *pietas* and *paideia*. As an underground movement designed, on one level, to maintain traditionalism, Platonists could not afford to exclude women such as Sosipatra from their ranks; they were necessary to its survival—and perhaps even more vital because of their ability to teach privately, far from the bands of roving monks that despoiled the temples of the southern and eastern Mediterranean basin in the wake of the Theodosian Decrees.

Notes

1. Eunapius, *Lives of the Sophists* (trans. Wilmer C. Wright; LCL; Cambridge, MA: Harvard University Press, 1921). All excerpts of Eunapius in this chapter have been taken from this edition, although I have modified some translations where I have seen fit.
2. Eunap., *Lives* (Wright, 415).
3. Eunap., *Lives* (Wright, 416).
4. Upon examination, both terms seem to lose any objective meaning; they remain wholly unhelpful when applied to ancient materials. See Hendrik S. Versnel, "Some Reflections on the Relationship Magic–Religion," *Numen* 38, no. 2 (1991): 177–97; Alan Segal, "Hellenistic Magic: Some Questions of Definition" in M. J. Vermaseren, ed., *Studies in Gnosticism and Hellenistic Religion presented to Gilles Quispel on the Occasion of his Sixty-Fifth Birthday* (Leiden: Brill, 1981), 349–75. On "religion," see Talal Asad, *Genealogies of Religion: Discipline and Reasons of Power in Christianity and Islam* (Baltimore: Johns Hopkins University Press, 1993).
5. Kimberly B. Stratton, *Naming the Witch: Magic, Ideology, and Stereotype in the Ancient World* (New York: Columbia University Press, 2007).

6. Eunap., *Lives* (Wright, 401).
7. Eunap., *Lives* (Wright, 403).
8. Eunapius, *Lives* (Wright, 403).
9. Eunap., *Lives* (Wright, 405).
10. Eunap., *Lives* (Wright, 405). Sosipatra shows the same sort of "remote viewing" skills with her student Maximus (p. 413), on which, see below.
11. Eunap., *Lives* (Wright, 405).
12. Eunap., *Lives* (Wright, 407).
13. Eunap., *Lives* (Wright, 409).
14. Eunap., *Lives* (Wright, 411).
15. Eunap., *Lives* (Wright, 411).
16. Eunap., *Lives* (Wright, 411).
17. Eunap., *Lives* (Wright, 413).
18. Eunap., Lives (Wright, 417).
19. Peter Brown, "The Rise and Function of the Holy Man in Late Antiquity," *JRS* 61(1971): 80–101.
20. Garth Fowden, "The Platonist Philosopher and his Circle in Late Antiquity," *Philosophia* 7 (1977): 359–82 and Garth Fowden, "The Pagan Holy Man in Late Antique Society," *JHS* 102 (1982): 33–59.
21. Fowden, "Platonist Philosopher," 380.
22. Fowden, "Platonist philosopher," 381. See also Robert Lamberton, "Secrecy in the History of Platonism," in *Secrecy and Concealment*, ed. Hans G. Kippenberg and Guy G. Stroumsa (Leiden: Brill, 1995), 140–48; John M. Dillon, "An Ethic for the Late Antique Sage," in *A Cambridge Companion to Plotinus*, ed. Lloyd P. Gerson (Cambridge: Cambridge University Press, 1993), 331–32; H.-D. Saffrey, "Neoplatonist Spirituality: II. Iamblichus to Proclus and Damascius," in *Classical Mediterranean Spirituality*, ed. A. H. Armstrong (New York: Crossroad, 1989), 250–65, and Robert Kirshner, "The Vocation of Holiness in Late Antiquity," *VC* 38 (1984): 105–24.
23. Zos., *Historia Nova* 4.18.
24. Marinus, *Life of Proclus*, in *Neoplatonic Saints: The Lives of Plotinus and Proclus by Their Students*, trans. Mark Edwards (Liverpool: Liverpool University Press, 2000), 28–31.
25. Lib., *Orations* 15.71 and 18.177. On Julian's theurgical prowess, see P. Athanassiadi-Fowden, *Julian and Hellenism: An Intellectual Biography* (Oxford: Clarendon, 1981), esp. 161–91.
26. Anitra Bingham Kolenkow, "Persons of Power and Their Communities," in *Magic and Divination in the Ancient World*, ed. Leda Ciraolo and Jonathan Seidel (Leiden: Brill, 2002), 133–44.
27. Euseb., *Hist. eccl.* 6.21.
28. Gal., *De Theriaca,* 14.
29. Porph., *Plot.* 9.1–5; *PLRE* 1.202 (Chione) and *PLRE* 1.338 (Gemina I and Gemina II). See Robert J. Penella, *Greek Philosophers and Sophists of the Fourth Century: A Study in Eunapius of Sardis* (Leeds: F. Cairns, 1990), 61.

30. Porph., *Plot.* 9.4; *PLRE* 1.57.
31. *PLRE* 2.159; Marinus, *Life of Proclus*, 9.
32. Maria Dzielska, *Hypatia of Alexandria* (Cambridge, MA: Harvard University Press, 1995), 118.
33. See *Orac. chald.*, fr 110, fr 219 on the use of words. On the theurgical animation of statues, see Proclus, *Commentary on Plato's Parmenides*, ed. and trans. Glen Morrow and John M. Dillon (Princeton, NJ: Princeton University Press, 1997) 4.847; E. R. Dodds, "Theurgy and Its relation to Neoplatonism," *JRS* 37 (1947): 62–65.
34. John M. Dillon, *The Middle Platonists* (Ithaca, NY: Cornell University Press 1977), 393; R. T. Wallis, *Neoplatonism* (New York: Scribner, 1972); for editions of the Chaldean Oracles, see Hans Lewy, *Chaldaean Oracles and Theurgy* (Cairo: Institut Français d'Archéologie Orientale, 1956), most usefully the revised edition by Michel Tardieu, *REAug* 58 (1978); Édouard des Places, *Oracles chaldaïques*, 3rd ed., revised and corrected by A. Segonds (Paris: Société d'édition "Les Belles Lettres," 1996); Ruth Majercik, *The Chaldaean Oracles* SGRR 5 (Leiden: Brill, 1989). E. R. Dodds, "New Light on the Chaldaean Oracles," *HTR* 54 (1961): 263–73 is antiquated but still a landmark article.
35. Eunap., *Lives* (Wright, 416–17).
36. Penella, *Greek Philosophers*, 58–62.
37. August., *De civ. D.* 10.9.
38. Dodds, "Theurgy," 56, 64; see also A. A. Barb, "The Survival of the Magical Arts," in *The Conflict between Paganism and Christianity in the Fourth Century*, ed. A. Momigliano (Oxford: Clarendon, 1963), 100–123.
39. Dodds, "Theurgy," 59. Dodds's tendency to equate magic and theurgy had already been anticipated by the views of his friend Solomon Eitrem, whose unpublished work Dodds credits in his article (n. 4).
40. On theurgy as distinct from magic, see C. Zintzen, "Die Wertung von Mystik und Magie in der neuplatonischen Philosophie," *RM* 108 (1965), 71–100.
41. Garth Fowden, *The Egyptian Hermes* (Cambridge: Cambridge University Press, 1986), 133.
42. J. Bregman, *Synesius of Cyrene: Philosopher-Bishop* (Berkeley: University of California Press, 1982), 47. See also Anne Sheppard, "Proclus' attitude to Theurgy," *CQ*, n. s. 31 (1982): 212–24; Fowden, *Egyptian Hermes*, 126–50.
43. K. W. Harl, "Sacrifice and Pagan Belief in Fifth- and Sixth-Century Byzantium," *PaP* 128 (1990): 7–27, 13.
44. Iambl., *Myst.* See the recent critical edition by Emma C. Clarke, John M. Dillon, and Jackson P. Hershbell, *Iamblichus: On the Mysteries* (Atlanta: Society of Biblical Literature, 2003). Polymnia Athanassiadi, "Dreams, Theurgy and Freelance Divination: The Testimony of Iamblichus," *JRS* 83 (1993): 115–30.
45. Athanassiadi, "Dreams, Theurgy," 116. Another definition, farther down: "I would describe theurgy as the often involuntary manifestation of an inner state of sanctity deriving from a combination of goodness and knowledge in which the former

element prevails" (116). If this is the case, then Sosipatra indeed emerges as a master theurgist, since Eunapius is at pains not to portray her as a magician.

46. Recent scholarship has attempted, with varying degrees of success and no consensus, to typologize theurgy into, for instance, "high" and "low" forms—"low" representing, of course, something like what many people mean by "magic," from "high" or spiritual, mystical union with the One. See, for instance, Sheppard, "Proclus' attitude"; Dodds, "Theurgy," 62; Gregory Shaw, "Theurgy: Rituals of Unification in the Neoplatonism of Iamblichus," *Traditio* 41 (1985): 1–28, 6, 8–9.
47. For theurgy as akin to grace, see Athanassiadi, "Dreams, Theurgy," 120.
48. Porph., *Letter to Anebo*, 2.3a.
49. Iambl. *Myst.* 3.13.
50. See F. Martroye, "La repression de la magie et le culte des gentiles au IVe siècle," *RHDFE*, 4th ser. 9 (1930) 669–701, and Amm. Marc., *History* 19.19.12 on the witch trials of 359 CE.
51. Zach. Schol., *Life of Severus*, 16–17.
52. Phot., *Bibl. Cod.* 215, 173 B., cited in Athanassiadi, "Dreams, Theurgy," 129.
53. Eunap., *Lives* (Wright, 432–33).
54. The incident is included in Matthew W. Dickie, "Who Practised Love-Magic in Classical Antiquity and the Late Roman World?" *CQ*, n. s. 50, no. 2 (2000): 563–83, 580.
55. Eunap., *Lives* (Wright, 413).
56. Eunap., *Lives* (Wright, 413).
57. It is important to emphasize that the Frazerian division that emerges here between "religion" and "magic" stems not from my own interpretation, but from the sources themselves. The problem here is not one of modern definition, but how one ancient community articulated what it was that it was doing to outsiders. See, on this, Anitra Bingham Kolenkow, "A Problem of Power: How Miracle Doers Counter Charges of Magic in the Hellenistic World," in *Society of Biblical Literature: 1976 Seminar Papers*, ed. George MacRae (Missoula, MT: Scholar's Press, 1976), 105–10.
58. Roland Barthes, *Mythologies* (Paris: Editions du Seuil, 1957). The English translation is by Richard Howard, *The Eiffel Tower and other Mythologies* (New York: Hill & Wang, 1979); see also Roland Barthes, "L'effet du réel" in *Communication* 11 (1968): 84–89.
59. On the trials, see in particular Peter Brown, "Sorcery, Demons and the Rise of Christianity: from Late Antiquity into the Middle Ages," in Peter Brown, *Religion and Society in the Age of Saint Augustine* (London: Faber & Faber, 1971), 119–46. See also Ramsay MacMullen, *Enemies of the Roman Order* (Cambridge, MA: Harvard University Press, 1966), 95–127.
60. Porphyry, "On the Life of Plotinus and the Order of his Books," in *Porphyry on Plotinus. Ennead 1* (vol. 1 of *Plotinus*; ed. A. H. Armstrong; LCL; Cambridge, MA: Harvard University Press, 1966), 1.2–85.

61. Here, there is much debate in the scholarship as to what degree Plotinus actually practiced magic. See T. Hopfner, "*Mageia*," *RE* I 14, no. 1 (1928): 301–93; Lynn Thorndike, *A History of Magic and Experimental Science*, 2nd ed., vol. 1 (New York: Macmillan, 1929); Philip Merlan, "Plotinus and Magic," *Isis* 44 (1953): 341–48, 341; Arthur H. Armstrong, "Was Plotinus a Magician?" *Phronesis* 1 (1955–56): 73–79.
62. Porph., *Plot.* 11.
63. Porph., *Plot.* 23.
64. Porph., *Plot.* 11.
65. Merlan, "Plotinus and Magic," 341–48.
66. Porph., *Plot.* 10.10.
67. Porph, *Plot.* 10.5–9.
68. Kroll, quoted in Dodds, "Theurgy," 58.
69. Dodds, "Theurgy," 58.
70. E. R. Dodds, "A Séance at the Iseum," pt. 3 of appendix 2 in *The Greeks and the Irrational* (Berkeley: University of California Press, 1951); see also Armstrong, "Was Plotinus?" 73–79. See, though, Merlan's comments in "Plotinus and Magic": "we are in the thick of black magic at its blackest, and in the midst of the grossest magical practices" (344).
71. There may be a connection between the nature of these narratives and similar accounts of magic, ritual, and gendered power in Christian *bioi*—as in, for instance, Jerome's *Vit. Hil.* 21 and the *Historia Monachorum* 21; Palladius, *Lausiac History* 17. Many thanks to Dayna Kalleres for the reference.
72. Roger Pack, "A Romantic Narrative in Eunapius," *TPAPA* 83 (1952): 198–204.
73. Pack, "Romantic," 201.
74. Pack, "Romantic," 203.
75. Porph., *Life of Pythagoras* 1.
76. Diog. Laert., 9.34.
77. Susan Ashbrook Harvey, "Women in Early Byzantine Hagiography," in *That Gentle Strength: Historical Perspectives on Women in* Christianity, ed. L. L. Coon, K. J. Haldane, and E. W. Sommer (Charlottesville: University Press of Virginia, 1990), 36.
78. Harvey, "Women," 36.
79. Susanna Elm, *Virgins of God*: *The Making of Asceticism in Late Antiquity* (New York: Clarendon, 1996), 39.
80. Philostr., *VS* I. 5.
81. Philostr., *VS* I. 5.
82. On Marcella, see Porphryry, *Letter to Marcella*, trans. Kathleen Wicker O'Brian (Chicago: Scholar's Press, 1987); on Hypatia, see John Rist, "Hypatia," *Phoenix* 19(1965): 214–25. The best account of Hypatia's rather astonishing *Nachleben* is Emilien Lamirande, "Hypatie, Synésios et la fin des dieux: L'histoire et la fiction," *SR* 18, no. 4 (1989): 467–89 and, to a lesser extent, M. Alic, *Hypatia's Heritage:*

A History of Women in Science from Antiquity to the Late Nineteenth Century (Boston: Beacon, 1986).

83. Arnaldo Momigliano, "The Life of St. Macrina by Gregory of Nyssa," in *The Craft of the Ancient Historian: Essays in Honor of Chester G. Starr*, ed. J. W. Edie (Lanham, MD: University Press of America, 1985), 443–58.
84. Porph., *Letter to Marcella* 1 (O'Brian, 45).
85. Eunap., *Lives* (Wright, 409).
86. Rist, "Hypatia," 220.
87. Elm, *Virgins of God*, 249.
88. Silvia Lanzi, "Sosipatra, la teurga: una 'holy woman' iniziata ai misteri caldaici," *SMSR* 70, no. 2 (2004): 275–94.
89. Marinus, *Life of Proclus*, 28.
90. Dzielska, *Hypatia of Alexandria*, 62.
91. See Fowden, "Pagan Holy Man," 34: "Both Hierokles and Proklos assert that the Platonist succession was regarded by its representatives as 'holy.'"
92. Dzielska, *Hypatia of Alexandria*, 47.
93. Eunap., *Lives* (Wright, 413).
94. *Suda* 4.644.
95. Xen., *Oec.* X.1 (E. C. Marchant, LCL).
96. Much has been written on the theme of Christian women being "made male." See, for instance, E. Castelli, "Virginity and its Meanings for Early Christian Women," *JFSR* 2, no. 1 (1986): 61–88; Gillian Cloke, *This Female Man of God: Women and Spiritual Power in the Patristic Age, AD 350–450* (New York: Routledge, 1995); V. Burrus, "Is Macrina a Woman? Gregory of Nyssa's Dialogue on the Soul and the Resurrection," in *The Companion to Postmodern Theology*, ed. Graham Ward (Oxford: Blackwell, 2001), 249–64; V. Burrus, "Word and Flesh: The Bodies and Sexuality of Ascetic Women in Christian Antiquity," *JFSR* 10 (1994): 27–51.
97. Fowden, "The Platonist Philosopher," 337, citing Alan Cameron's work on the end of the ancient universities, notes that we have little information on public chairs of philosophy in the fourth century. It is unlikely that any city smaller than Rome, Constantinople, Athens, and Alexandria would have had public funds to support professors of philosophy.
98. Eunap., *Lives* (Wright, 469).
99. Socrates, *Hist. Eccl.* 8.9 (GCS 21, p. 111 Bidez).
100. Athanassiadi, "Dreams, Theurgy," 115.
101. Athanassiadi, "Dreams, Theurgy," 115.
102. Eunap., *Lives* (Wright, 411).
103. Synesius of Cyrene, *Letters* 10, 15, 16, 33, 81, 124, and 154 to Hypatia; she's referred to in 133, 136, 137, 159.
104. C. van Liefferinge, *La théurgie des Oracles chaldaïques à Proclus* (Liège: Centre international d'étude de la religion grecque antique, 1999).

10

Sorceresses and Sorcerers in Early Christian Tours of Hell

Kirsti Barrett Copeland

See the wretched women who left their needles, their spindles, and their distaffs, and became soothsayers; they cast spells (malie) *with herbs and images.*

DANTE ALIGHIERI, *Inferno*, Canto 20, ll.121-23[1]

In these cauldrons, a large number of sinners, murderers, greedy thieves, female sorcerers, and nobles who violently oppressed their fellow human beings with excessive taxes were boiling incessantly.

"The Fourth Court," *Visio Thurkhilli*[2]

TORMENTED IN THE fourth bulge of Dante's eighth circle of hell, soothsayers experience a horrific punishment. Condemned for fraud, these purveyors of the magical arts must spend eternity with their heads turned around one hundred and eighty degrees, walking backward in order to see where they are going. They weep as they circumambulate in this absurd procession of naked remolded human form. One by one, the pilgrim in Dante's *Inferno* meets the more notable individuals of Western history found in this bulge. Five are classical figures: Amphiaraus, known for deducing the outcome of the war against Thebes through augury;[3] Tiresias, the famous androgynous seer;[4] Arruns, a soothsayer who reads in the entrails of an ox the outcome of the war between Caesar and Pompey;[5] Manto, Tiresias's daughter and assistant;[6] and Eurypylus, who reputedly went to the Delphic oracle in the *Aeneid* (2.114). Three others are soothsayers of the thirteenth century, two of whom were in the employ of Frederick II: Michael Scot, Guido Bonatti, and Asdente.[7] All of those named, with the exception of Tiresias's daughter, and to some extent Tiresias himself, are male. Yet when Dante writes of the unnamed masses in the fourth bulge of the eighth circle, he turns to the stereotypical association of women and magic.

Another medieval vision, the *Vision of Thurkill* (early thirteenth century CE), underscores the perceived connection between women and magic by specifically listing "sorceresses" and not "sorcerers" in its description of souls boiling in cauldrons. In this vision, these "sorceresses," or literally "female sorcerers" (*veneficarum mulierum*), are the only ones in this list of five condemned categories to be marked as female.[8] Although the *Vision of Thurkill* expressly states that the theater of hell is populated with "people of different status and sex" (*homines diverse conditionis et utriusque sexus*),[9] patently female figures are far fewer than male ones. Thus the connection between women and magic operates in both directions in this vision; not only is magic associated with women through the labeling of the "sorcerers" as "female," but women are associated with magic since they are specifically condemned only for a few particular sins and magic is one of them.

As for Dante's female magicians, the pilgrim is instructed to look at these women who did not practice the appropriate feminine arts of sewing, weaving, and spinning yarn, but instead turned to aberrant crafts involving herbs and spells; thus, in the *Inferno*, spell casting is rendered a perversion of normal women's work. Moreover, although these women are referred to as "soothsayers" or fortunetellers (*'ndivine*) like those legendary seers mentioned by name in this canto, their methods are not augury and entrails reading, but rather spells, augmented with herbs and drawings, similar to the magical papyri of late antiquity. These women represent the rank and file magicians whose clients are not royalty, but normal, everyday men and women, seeking help in the fulfillment of certain desires, which are probably not limited to knowledge of the future, but include love spells and spells to cure their own illnesses as well as to inflict illnesses on others.

These commonplace magicians who provide magical spells and potions to men and women are the sort who populate the earliest Christian tours of hell, namely the *Apocalypse of Peter* (early mid-second century CE), its poetic reworking in *Sibylline Oracle* 2.195–338 (second to third century CE) and the *Apocalypse of Paul* (aka *Visio Pauli*, late fourth century CE). While the details about the types of magic condemned by these texts are slim, intriguingly, these early Christian tours of hell unequivocally portray *both* men and women practicing magic professionally, both men and women patronizing magicians as clients, and both men and women suffering as victims of magical attack. Thus, contrary to the medieval visions of hell discussed above, late antique visions of hell show no signs of an underlying assumption of an association between women and magic.

Tours of Hell

Although there are numerous visions of hell, magicians play a role in a surprisingly small number of them. For example, Jewish tours of hell from late antiquity concern themselves primarily with adultery, fornication, and slander, showing no interest in sorcerers or sorceresses. For this reason, they do not figure in this discussion.[10] Moreover, a number of the early and medieval Christian tours and visions of hell also contain no reference to magicians.[11] To my knowledge, practitioners of the magical arts primarily appear in the limited and related group of late antique tours of hell mentioned above, namely *Apoc. Pet.*, *Sib. Or.* 2.195–338, and *Apoc. Paul*. Additionally, magicians figure in some of the later descendants of *Apoc. Paul*, such as the *Greek Apocalypse of Mary* (aka the *Apocalypse of the Holy Mother of God Concerning the Chastisements* or the *Apocalypse of the Virgin*, ninth century CE?), the *Ethiopic Apocalypse of Mary* (seventh century CE or later), the *Ethiopic Apocalypse of Baruch* (seventh century CE or later), and the *Ethiopic Apocalypse of Gorgorios* (fourteenth century CE?).[12]

Apoc. Pet. is preserved in its entirety, and notably in the section where it mentions sorcerers and sorceresses, only in a late Ethiopic manuscript.[13] However, the revelation can be securely dated to the early second century thanks to its quotation as scripture by Clement of Alexandria.[14] This early date makes *Apoc. Pet.* not only the earliest Christian tour of hell to condemn magicians to an eternity of fire, but the earliest of all of the extant tours of hell, whether Jewish or Christian. We do not have to rely entirely on the Ethiopic manuscript for the contents of this early Greek apocalypse; two partial Greek manuscripts survive.[15] Unfortunately, neither Greek manuscript is extant at the chapter containing the sorcerers and sorceresses. However, *Apoc. Pet.* was recast into Greek poetry in *Sib. Or.* 2.195–338, and the sins listed in *Sib. Or.* 2 closely parallel those found in *Apoc. Pet.*, including the reference to sorcerers and sorceresses.[16]

Related to *Apoc. Pet.*, although probably not a direct literary descendant, is *Apoc. Paul*.[17] Likely a product of the end of the fourth century, *Apoc. Paul* begins with a preface dated to the year 388 CE and is first referred to in 416 CE by Augustine.[18] Unlike *Apoc. Pet.*, there is a wealth of manuscripts of *Apoc. Paul* in Latin, Coptic, Greek, and Syriac, as well as later versions in both Arabic and European languages. The best witnesses to the shape of the early Greek text are the long Latin version and the Coptic version; the extant Greek manuscripts are late abbreviations.[19] However, the late Greek recensions often provide a window into the vocabulary of the original *Apoc. Paul*. Hence, the Greek, Latin, and Coptic are all necessary in order to understand how this text in its earliest forms portrayed sorcerers and sorceresses. In contrast with witnesses to the earliest form of *Apoc. Paul*, which clearly depict male and female practitioners of magic, the later Latin recensions of *Apoc. Paul* as well as *Gk. Apoc. Mary* and *Eth. Apoc. Mary* and its descendants, *Eth. Apoc. Bar.* and *Apoc. Gorg.,* all reduce the unambiguous naming of both genders to inclusive masculine plurals.[20]

Whether the relationship between *Apoc. Pet.* and *Apoc. Paul* is direct or involves a common source, one thing is certain: they share not only the remarkably rare depiction of sorcerers and sorceresses, but also the explicitly inclusive formula "men and women" found throughout both of these tours of hell. The formulaic "men and women" used for crimes applicable to both genders is lacking in all of those early Christian tours of hell that do not include sorcerers and sorceresses, as well as in all of the Jewish tours of hell, which notably do not mention magicians. Thus, the earliest source for magical practitioners in hell—whether *Apoc. Pet.* or some original, no longer extant, tour of hell that influenced both *Apoc. Pet.* and *Apoc. Paul*—must have contained the formula "men and women" and also have treated sorcery as the shared provenance of both genders.

What Sort of Sorcery? Who Are the Sorcerers and Sorceresses?

Since all of the texts referred to in this article treat magic and magicians pejoratively, the definition of what is meant by magic will necessarily be the negative one espoused by Christianity. Collectively, these texts understand magic to be evil and a cause of harm, either physical or spiritual, to other individuals. They also imply that a magician performs magic at the behest of others. Beyond that, the words used and the few clues given vary between versions of individual texts and throughout the tradition. Within the many iterations of our few texts, we find many of the Greek and Latin terms for magicians: *pharmakos*, *goēs*, *magos*, *maleficus,* and *veneficus.* Since these terms are used broadly and imprecisely to label a variety of practices deemed inappropriate by the early church, the texts do not need to distinguish conclusively between different practices or to translate them accurately. But the vocabulary and setting of each text is suggestive of the crime of the magician, as it was understood by these early apocalypses.

Apoc. Pet. 12 and *Sib. Or.* 2.283 both refer to "sorcerers and sorceresses." The Greek terms used in *Sib. Or.* 2.283 are *pharmakoi* and *pharmakides* and presumably these are the Greek words underlying the Ethiopic version of *Apoc. Pet.* 12.[21] As with its cognate "pharmacist" in English, a *pharmakos* was known for dispensing drugs. In the ancient world, it was understood that of these drugs, some had healing powers and some could poison. The dual meaning of *pharmakon* as medicine or poison is already present in the archaic Greek of the *Odyssey* and the *Iliad.*[22] Likewise, Empedocles of Acragas in Sicily (492–432 BCE) was known both for being a sorcerer and for promising a student: "You shall learn all the *pharmaka* there are for ills and defence against old age."[23] Theophrastus's (370–285 BCE) *Historia Plantarum*, Bk. 9 also testifies to drugs that are deadly as well as to those that are beneficial.[24]

Of course, even from its first recorded usage in Homer, *pharmaka* could refer to goals that were less medical and more mystical. For example, in Book 10 of the *Odyssey*, Circe transforms Odysseus's men into animals using a *pharmakon* and likewise Odysseus transforms them back with another *pharmakon*.[25] Moreover, in Theocritus's (ca. 310–250 BCE) *Pharmakeutriai*, Simaetha, one of the "sorceresses" after whom the poem is named is not a professional practitioner and is only interested in creating an efficacious love spell.[26] Hence, *pharmakos* lacks the specificity in itself to reveal exactly what *Apoc. Pet.* 12 and *Sib. Or.* 2.283 condemn. It could be either the use and sale of poisons or the dispensing of love spells.

Apoc. Pet. 12 does not specify the sins of the sorcerers and sorceresses in its hell. The only clue it gives to the exact nature of their transgression may lie in the type of punishment to which they are subjected: these sinners spend eternity spinning on a "wheel of fire,"[27] calling to mind the punishment of Ixion in classical mythology.[28] *Apoc. Pet.* 11 contains two other indisputable references to punishments from classical mythology. In the first, men and women must repeatedly climb a hill and roll back down, recalling the infamous Sisyphean punishment of repeatedly pushing a rock up a hill only to have it roll back down.[29] In the second, birds eat away the flesh of sinners, just as an eagle consumed Prometheus's regenerating liver every day.[30] These two punishments are found consecutively in *Apoc. Pet.* and both answer for sins relating to the improper treatment of parents. The author chose the classical examples of humans who tricked and disobeyed the gods in order to illustrate the folly of not respecting and obeying one's parents. Thus, in these two cases, the deliberate parallels to classical punishments have some bearing on the punishment itself, raising the question, can Ixion's story, ending as it does on an eternal wheel of fire, shed any light on how *Apoc. Pet.* understands its sorcerers and sorceresses?

Ixion was not a sorcerer, so we are denied an easy connection between Ixion's story and the choice of punishment in *Apoc. Pet.* Ixion was placed on the wheel of fire for having tried to rape Hera, Zeus's wife, hardly a particular connection to sorcery.[31] However, Ixion was a Thessalonian king, a land associated in Greek and Roman imagination with magic and witchcraft.[32] Erictho, the super-witch of Lucan's (39–65 CE) *Pharsalia*, is from Thessaly, a place Lucan describes as home to witches so powerful that they can force the gods themselves to obey them (6, 435–40). Medea, the famous witch of the Argonaut cycles, collected powerful plants in Thessaly.[33] In a work roughly contemporaneous with *Apoc. Pet.*, Apuleius's (b. ca. 120 CE) *Metamorphoses*, the protagonist describes Thessaly as "universally acclaimed as the aboriginal crucible of the Art of Magic."[34] In *Metamorphoses*, there are three more Thessalonian witches: Meroe, Panthia, and Pamphile. If Ixion's punishment were, in fact, chosen for the sorcerers and sorceresses in *Apoc. Pet.*'s hell because of this Thessalonian connection with magic, it is all the more surprising that the text refers to both male and female sorcerers in hell, since Thessaly's literary reputation for magic points toward the stereotypical association of magic with female practitioners.

A simple element of Ixion's story that may illuminate the reason for the magical practitioner's punishment is that Ixion famously committed murder. He killed his father-in-law and became the first hero "to stain mortal men with kindred blood."[35] Even though Ixion killed his father-in-law by pushing him on top of burning coals, the association of his punishment with the sorcerers and sorceresses in hell may indicate that their crime is murder, even if they commit it through poison.

Sib. Or. 2.281–83 places special emphasis on the crime of killing one's kin in relation to sorcerers and sorceresses. As with *Apoc. Pet.*, sorcerers and sorceresses are listed as the final group punished in the litany of those tormented in hell. However, women who procure abortions occupy the penultimate place in *Sib. Or.* 2.281–82, whereas in *Apoc. Pet.*, women who procure abortions are fourth from the beginning out of seventeen separate punishments.[36] While *Sib. Or.* 2 and *Apoc. Pet.* do not always agree on the order of the punishments, usually the shift in order is much less pronounced; for example, usury and harm to widows and orphans appear merely in reverse order between *Apoc. Pet.* and *Sib. Or.* 2.[37] The movement of women who abort their children to a position directly before sorcerers and sorceresses suggests a possible connection between the two crimes: the reader could understand that sorcerers and sorceresses in *Sib. Or.* 2 provided *pharmaka* as abortifacient. Given the poetic nature of the *Sib. Or.* 2, understanding the sorcerers and sorceresses as accomplices of the women who abort would also provide tidy parallel bookends to the laundry list of punishments that began with those who "committed murder and all their accomplices."[38] Although the details are murky, the sinister nature of the sorcery committed by both men and women in *Apoc. Pet.* and *Sib. Or.* 2 appears to have some connection with the use of poisons for murder or abortion. At the very least there are few clues that would lead us credibly in other directions.

Although *Sib. Or.* 2.283 and, presumably, the lost Greek of *Apoc. Pet.* use only *pharmakoi/pharmakides* to describe sorcerers in hell, the different versions of *Apoc. Paul* 38 employ a wide range of Greek and Latin terms for magicians, including *pharmakos*, *goēs*, *magos*, *maleficus,* and *veneficus*. *Pharmakoi* appear in the late Greek recension of the text, strengthening the testimony of *Sib. Or.* 2.283 that this was the Greek word used in the earlier *Apoc. Pet,*, but the late Greek recension also adds *goētes*.[39] Like *pharmakos*, *goēs* can be translated as "wizard" or "sorcerer" but this word has mostly negative connotations going back to the fifth century BCE. In the late Greek recension of *Apoc. Paul*, little helpful context is provided to further define the crimes of the sorcerers; *pharmakoi* and *goētes* join "the whoremongers, and the adulterers, and those that oppress widows and orphans" in a bloody pit.[40] Probably the most one can say about these crimes is that they cause harm to other people, suggesting again that the sorcerer is punished in hell because he or she has inflicted pain upon innocent victims.

The Coptic version of *Apoc. Paul* 38 is more specific regarding the existence of victims of magical crimes. In this version, magicians (Coptic uses the Greek loan word *magos*) "bewitch men and women and they leave them suffering until they die."[41] The victims of the magicians may have been slowly poisoned, contributing to the emphasis on their long-lasting suffering. They may also be the victims of love spells, bewitched into desiring someone and suffering the accompanying torment described so well in both Greek and Coptic magical papyri.[42] Or the spell cast upon them may be far less poetic, seeking their destruction for such prosaic reasons as business competition, winning a court battle, or removing a political opponent.[43] The text is inconclusive, aside from suggesting that both "men and women" are among the victims who fall prey to the magicians' sinister art.

Finally, the long Latin version of *Apoc. Paul*, which is likely our best witness to the earliest Greek version of the apocalypse, provides one final clue to the nature of magical transgression—not only do the sorcerers (*malefici*) have victims, they also have clients. Their "evil magic arts" (*maleficia magica*) are "prepared for men and women."[44] Notably, the charge of *magica maleficia* was brought against Apuleius, according to his *Apology*.[45] In that context, the evil magic art in question was erotic magic: Apuleius was accused of inducing a wealthy woman to marry him through casting a love spell.[46] Thus, once again, both the Coptic and the long Latin suggest that the crime in question might be the provision of love spells to clients.

On another note, the meaning of *maleficium* extends not only to sorcery and enchantment, but also to fraud and deception. The latter point is significant since Dante's soothsayers are in the eighth circle of hell, the circle for those who committed fraud. Dante likely knew the long Latin version of *Apoc. Paul*, as Theodore Silverstein has shown based on several parallels between the texts.[47] Thus, even Dante, whose female soothsayers began this essay, knew a model of an early Christian tour of hell in which women were not particularly associated with magic.

The later Latin recension of *Apoc. Paul* 38 replaces *maleficia* with *veneficii*, using the legal designation for harmful magic of any kind.[48] Fritz Graf defines *veneficium* as follows: "The word refers first, it seems, to an action that brings on sudden death, either by the effective administration of a poison or by some other clandestine means."[49] Thus, although the long Latin and the Coptic of *Apoc. Paul* hint that the magicians in hell may be there for providing destructive love spells to clients, the later Latin recension returns the magician's crime to that implied in *Apoc. Pet.*, namely murder of another individual through magical means, perhaps through the administration of poison. Likewise, the *Gk. Apoc. Mary* refers to *pharmakoi*. It lists the *pharmakoi* along with "those who slay with the sword, and the women who strangle their offspring."[50] The commonly available English translation in the *Ante-Nicene Fathers* renders these *pharmakoi* not as "sorcerers," but simply as "poisoners."[51]

It is fair to say that our earliest tours of hell that refer to magic, *Apoc. Pet.*, *Sib. Or.* 2, and *Apoc. Paul*, never explicitly or implicitly include protective amulets or magic intended for the protection of crops in their definitions of sorcery. On these forms of magic, our texts are silent. The reason magic lands the sorcerer or sorceress in hell is the understanding that it inflicts suffering, usually deadly suffering, upon an innocent victim.[52]

"Men and Women," Women, and Men in Hell

As I mentioned in the preceding section, the long Latin and Coptic versions of *Apoc. Paul* state that the clients and victims of magicians include both "men and women" ("*uiris ac mulieribus*"; "*nrōme mn nehiome*").[53] They also refer to the magicians suffering in the bloody pit as "men and women," despite using only inclusive masculine plurals when referring to the magicians by their professional titles (*malefici*; *mmagos*).[54] The formula "men and women" also appears in *Apoc. Pet.* in reference to magicians in addition to the use of both a masculine plural and a feminine plural of sorcerer. The unambiguous gender-inclusive formula is found throughout hell in *Apoc. Pet.* and *Apoc. Paul*; however, it is usually avoided when a sin is perceived as being the exclusive provenance of one gender.

The formula "men and women" (*andres kai gunaikes*) appears in eight of the thirteen punishments found in the extant Greek of *Apoc. Pet.* and in fourteen out of the twenty punishments detailed in the Ethiopic text.[55] Insofar as the Greek is extant, the Greek and Ethiopic are remarkably parallel in the recipients of punishments that are marked by the formula. Together they include those who persecuted the righteous, those who blasphemed against the righteous, those who bore false witness, those who trusted in their riches, those who lent money at interest, men who lay with men as women and women who lay with women as men, idol makers, and those who abandoned God. Additionally, the Ethiopic includes those who did not honor their father and mother, slaves who did not obey their masters, those who did a charitable deed and saw themselves as righteous, and most importantly for this chapter, the sorcerers and sorceresses. All of these sins are seen as belonging equally to both genders and, with the exception of homosexuality, are not sexual sins. In *Apoc. Pet.*, sexual offenders either belong only to one gender or they are first described in terms of one gender and subsequently in terms of the other. The former is true of women who have abortions as well as the girls who lose their virginity.[56] The latter is true of adulterers; the visionary first notices women hanging by their hair and neck, which they used "to capture the soul [*sic*] of men for destruction." Only subsequently does he see "the men who lay with them in adultery . . . hang[ing] by their thighs in that place which burns."[57] Thus, *Apoc. Pet.* is not reluctant to lay the blame for a particular crime solely or primarily at a woman's feet. The choice not to do so with sorcery suggests that the text resists the common bias that women are more likely to dabble in the magical arts.

As in *Apoc. Pet.*, the vast majority of those suffering punishments in *Apoc. Paul* are introduced by the phrase "men and women."[58] For *Apoc. Paul*, this includes both sexual sins, such as adultery and same-sex acts, as well as non-sexual sins like usury and slander. However, the text still refers to "girls in black raiment" who lose their virginity "unknown to their parents."[59] Additionally, there are punishments expressly for priests, bishops, deacons, and lectors, which Paul only sees men suffering, no doubt because women did not hold these offices.[60] Thus *Apoc. Paul* also knows of sins belonging only to one gender and does not believe that sorcery falls in this category.

The majority of the later texts influenced by *Apoc. Pet.* and *Apoc. Paul* do not retain the equalitarian formula of "men and women." As I have shown, Dante and the *Vision of Thurkhill* emphasize the presence of large numbers of *female* sorcerers tormented in hell while the direct descendants of *Apoc. Paul* favor a more common and undefined masculine plural.[61] The only notable exception is *Gk. Apoc. Mary*, which does use the phrase "men and women" seven times.[62] It even utilizes the formula "men and women" in the same general passage in which it condemns the *pharmakoi*. However, roughly a page of text in the Greek edition intervenes between the two.[63] Thus, this late descendant of *Apoc. Pet.* and *Apoc. Paul* does not insist in the same way as the earlier texts that the reader understand the sorcerers as gender inclusive.

Other members of the complicated family tree of Jewish and Christian tours of hell, none of which mention sorcerers or sorceresses, also lack the formula "men and women." Most of the texts preserved in Latin, Coptic, or Greek refer primarily to "souls" (*animae*, *psychai*) or various non-gender-specific plurals.[64] Some of them do mention sins specified by gender. The *Epistle of Titus* describes women who "are sentenced to be punished by tortures in their breasts, these are women who lasciviously have yielded their bodies to men."[65] The *Acts of Thomas* 56 mentions "the souls of women who left their husbands and committed adultery" and the *Apocalypse of Ezra* speaks of a woman who "grudged to give her milk, but even threw her infants into the rivers."[66] As with the punishments directed specifically at women in *Apoc. Pet.* and *Apoc. Paul*, these punishments are for sexual sins or sins related to disposing of unwanted children, a byproduct of sexual sin. The Jewish texts preserved in Hebrew refer to "men" or "human beings" (*bene adam*) and sometimes they explicitly refer to "women" (*nashim, banot*) in the punishments, but again they lack both the formula and the reference to magic.[67] Given that the formula "men and women" existed for a short period of time in a limited number of texts, the question should be asked whether or not the inclusion of both male and female sorcerers and sorceresses can legitimately reveal anything about the attitudes of early Christians toward magicians and gender.

Social History, Magicians, and Hell

Unlike the magical papyri, the Christian tours of hell cannot provide hard evidence about the practice of magic. More akin to the classical and medieval literary depictions of magic, they can provide the modern reader with a window onto the prevalent stereotypes among certain Christians of the early centuries about magic and the role gender may or may not have played in its practice. In *Tours of Hell*, Martha Himmelfarb cautions against using the tours of hell, many of which are unmoored in time, to write any history, even social history.[68] She advocates treating the tours of hell primarily through their literary connections. By showing that many of the punishments are repeated from earlier texts, she illustrates her point that the presence of a particular punishment may merely be the remnant of an earlier time. However, she also concludes that, "One result of the study of a long-lived tradition like that of tours of hell is that it allows us to see how interests change."[69] These changes, these subtle variations in what can be a repetitive and sometimes surprisingly unimaginative genre, may indicate intentional choices made by the authors of the texts and shed light on shifting values or social conceptions.

In the preceding section, I demonstrate that neither the use of the phrase "men and women" nor the presence of magicians in hell is widely attested in the tradition of the tours of hell. Presumably, both *Apoc. Pet.* and *Apoc. Paul* were aware of multiple other tours that, unlike their common ancestor, contained neither the condemnation of magicians nor the formula "men and women." Himmelfarb argues that many of the punishments found in *Apoc. Pet.* come from sources, likely Jewish, which were shared with the later extant Jewish tours.[70] Given that both the explicitly equalitarian language and the sorcerers and sorceresses are absent from all of our extant Jewish tours, I presume that these features were also absent from any of their ancestors to which *Apoc. Pet.* might have had access. Thus, the author of *Apoc. Pet.*, having different possibilities from which to choose, decided to include the sorcerers and sorceresses and to use the deliberately inclusive language. Notably, the presence of both male and female sorcerers was so emphasized in *Apoc. Pet.* that when *Sib. Or.* 2 recast the vision of hell into a poetic form, it dropped the formula "men and women" used for most of the punishments, but it still kept "sorcerers and sorceresses."

For *Apoc. Paul*, one does not need to engage in speculation to the same degree as that required by *Apoc. Pet.* Arriving as it did two centuries later in the tradition, *Apoc. Paul* had numerous different visions of hell from which to draw. It certainly knew one of the sources of *Apoc. Pet.*, or possibly *Apoc. Pet.* itself, and it was aware of the *Apocalypse of Zephaniah* (or one of its sources), which lacks any reference to magic, in its fragmentary state, and does not use the formula "men and women."[71] Thus, the text in some sense chose to retain both the magicians and the equalitarian formula.

It may be, of course, that once the very early common source of *Apoc. Pet.* and *Apoc. Paul* contained both the magicians and the formula "men and women" that they became linked enough in the tradition that any early text which included magicians would be swayed to do so in an unambiguously inclusive way. But that in itself is significant. It means that the authors of *Apoc. Pet.* and *Apoc. Paul* did not experience sufficient cultural pressure to change the association; there was no reason in their eyes to render magic as the sole, or primary, propriety of women. Contrast this with our medieval examples, Dante's *Inferno* and the *Vision of Thurkill*, at least the former of which was likely to have been influenced by the widely disseminated Latin versions of *Apoc. Paul.* Both of these texts bear witness to an association between women and magic strong enough to induce them to underscore the connection at the expense of inclusive language. Thus, *Apoc. Pet.* and *Apoc. Paul* do attest to one early Christian view in which there is no particular association between women and magic.

It is also worth noting that an exclusive connection between women and magic is lacking despite the fact that in laying claim to the traditions of the Hebrew Bible, Christians were aware of a biblical model in which a female was particularly associated with both magic and the underworld, namely the Witch of Endor. In 1 Samuel 28:7, when Saul wishes to speak with Samuel his deceased father, he asks his servants to find him an "*'ishat ba'alat 'ov*," specifically, a woman who is a medium or necromancer. In this text, there is an assumption that the best person for the job Saul has in mind is a woman. In the earliest Christian exegesis, however, the fact that the witch of Endor is a woman is hardly even remarked upon.[72] Regardless of her gender, Origen makes her a type of Christ.[73] For other early Christians, the questions that surround her story have more to do with whether Samuel actually arose or whether it was an apparition of Samuel or a demon.[74]

Of the many other condemnations of sorcery in the Hebrew Bible, only one asserts a particular association between women and magic, namely Exodus 22:18, "You shall not permit a female sorcerer (*mekhashefah*) to live" (NRSV). However, elsewhere, masculine plurals are used or only male sorcerers are mentioned.[75] One passage in particular may be echoed in the early Christian tours of hell. Leviticus 20:27 reads, "A man or a woman (*'ish 'o 'ishah*) who is a medium or a wizard shall be put to death." Appearing only three times in all of the laws of Leviticus, this unambiguous naming of both genders is relatively rare. The other two occurrences of "a man or a woman" (Lev 13:29, 13:38) are in the context of whether or not particular diseases of the skin render an individual unclean. Thus, the gender-blind condemnation of magic found in the early Christian tours of hell may have its roots in Leviticus. However, the contrary examples of the Witch of Endor and Exodus 22:18 suggest that the tours of hell could have chosen between two different models of gender in relationship to magic. Presumably, the different authors chose to include both genders because that was the best reflection of the assumptions of their society.

However, some other early Christian literature does point to a connection between women and magic in that women are stereotypically weak victims seduced by male sorcerers. Irenaeus, the second-century bishop of Lyon and archheresiologist, wrote about a man named Marcus, whom he described as a "magician" (*magos*) who would create "love-potions" (*philtra kai agōgima*). Marcus, according to Irenaeus, used the potions and other magical means to seduce large numbers of women to his brand of Christianity.[76] Jerome, who cites Irenaeus roughly two centuries later, describes these women specifically as "weak."[77] Many of the Apocryphal Acts of the Apostles also attest to a widespread stereotype of weak women following after a male sorcerer. For example, in the *Acts of Paul and Thecla*, the charge of sorcery is directed against Paul, the hero of the text. The non-Christian men in the village whose wives have left them to follow the ascetic ways of the apostle shout, "Away with the sorcerer for he has misled all our wives."[78] Of course, the Apocryphal Acts do not believe their heroes to actually be sorcerers, but they do depict a society in which everyone understood that women were particularly susceptible to the ways of the magician.[79] As Todd Breyfolge writes about the fourth-century Priscillianists who were accused of heresy, "the presence of women evoked both heretical and magical connotations . . . Women were often associated with pernicious doctrines in Christian antiquity, at least in part because of their presumed weakness of mind and character."[80]

Despite the prevalence of this stereotype of weak women following male sorcerers in early Christian texts, this article has shown that for the early Christian tours of hell, there was no specific understanding that women either were or were not the primary practitioners of magic. We see neither an emphasis on women as sorceresses, like the biblical Witch of Endor or the classical Erictho, nor do we see a denial of them. *Apoc. Pet.* and *Apoc. Paul*, in sharp contrast to the medieval *Vision of Thurkhill*, underscore that for many early Christians, magic is understood to be the provenance of both genders, in its practitioners, in its clients and in its victims. Ultimately for these early tours of hell, the condemnation of magic is unconcerned with gender because the only pertinent question is salvation and damnation. As long as magic was practiced by both men and women, these texts needed to keep their threat of eternal punishment alive for both genders. Thus, the desire to affect the behavior of individuals obviously overwhelmed any interest in stressing the alterity of magic by associating it only with women.

Notes

1. Robert M. Durling, trans. with Ronald L. Martinez, *Inferno*, vol. 1 of *The Divine Comedy of Dante Alighieri* (New York: Oxford University Press, 1996), 311.
2. Paul Gerhard Schmidt, ed., *Visio Thurkilli: Relatore, ut Videtur, Radulpho de Coggeshall* (Leipzig: Teubner, 1978), 28; trans. mine. See also Eileen Gardiner, ed., "Thurkill's Vision," in *Visions of Heaven and Hell before Dante,* ed. Eileen Gardiner (New York: Italica, 1989), 232.
3. Stat., *Theb.*; Durling, *Inferno*, 313, note to ll. 31–36.
4. Ov., *Met.* 3.324–31, *Od.* 10. 490–95, 11.90–96, etc.
5. Luc., *Pharsalia* 1.585–638.
6. Stat., *Theb.*; Durling, *Inferno*, 314, note to ll. 52–56.
7. Durling, *Inferno*, 317, note to ll. 115–20.
8. Schmidt, ed., *Visio Thurkilli*, 28.
9. Gardiner, ed., "Thurkill's Vision," 226; Schmidt, ed., *Visio Thurkilli*, 19.
10. The absence of sorcerers and sorceresses is true for all of the Jewish tours of hell examined in Martha Himmelfarb, *Tours of Hell: An Apocalyptic Form in Jewish and Christian Literature* (Philadelphia: Fortress, 1983); Saul Lieberman, "On Sins and Their Punishments," in *Texts and Studies* (New York: Ktav, 1974), 29–56; Moses Gaster, "Hebrew Visions of Hell and Paradise," *JRAS* 23 (1893): 572–610; repr. in Moses Gaster, *Studies and Texts in Folklore, Magic, Medieval Romance, Hebrew Apocrypha and Samaritan Archaeology*, 3 vols. (London: Maggs Bros, 1925–28), 1:124–64; Michael E. Stone and John Strugnell, eds., "On the Torments of the Damned" in *The Books of Elijah Parts 1–2* (TTS 18, PsS 8; Missoula, MT: Scholars Press, 1979), 13–26.
11. For example, *Acts Thom.* 55–7, *Apocalypse of Zephaniah*, *Apoc. Ezra*, *Testament of Isaac*, *Vit. Pach.* SBo 88., Gregory the Great, *Dial.*, IV.37, *Furseus' Vision*, *Drythelm's Vision*, *Wetti's Vision*, *Charles the Fat's Vision*, *St. Patrick's Purgatory*, *Tundale's Vision*, *Monk of Evesham's Vision.*
12. The dates on these later texts are little more than guesses. For the dating of *Gk. Apoc. Mary*, see Montague Rhodes James, ed., *Apocrypha Anecdota: A Collection of Thirteen Apocryphal Books and Fragments*, vol. 2, no. 3 of *Texts and Studies*, ed. J. Armitage Robinson (Cambridge: Cambridge University Press, 1893; repr., Nendeln: Kraus Reprint Limited, 1967), 113: "if we place it in or about the ninth century we shall probably not be far wrong." *Eth. Apoc. Mary* mentions "Mohammadans," and hence must be after the seventh century; see M. Chaîne, trans., "Apocalypsis seu Visio Mariae Virginis," in *Apocrypha de B. Mariae Virginis*, CSCO, ScA 1/7 (1909), 43, 66. Wolf Leslau, *Falasha Anthology* (New Haven: Yale University Press, 1951), 64, dates *Eth. Apoc. Bar.* to the seventh century, but surely it must be later since it is dependent on *Eth. Apoc. Mary*. Leslau, *Falasha,* 80, calls his fourteenth-century date for the *Eth. Apoc. Gorg.* "reasonable enough."
13. Dennis D. Buchholz, *Your Eyes Will Be Opened: A Study of the Greek (Ethiopic) Apocalypse of Peter*, SBLDS 97 (Atlanta: Scholars Press, 1988), 157–244.

14. *Ecl.* 41.1–2, 48.1.
15. Thomas Kraus and Tobias Nicklas, *Das Petrusevangelium und die Petrusapokalypse: die griechischen Fragmente mit deutscher und englischer Übersetzung* (Berlin: de Gruyter, 2004), 101–30.
16. C. Alexandre, ed., *Oracula Sybillina* (Paris: Didot Fratres, 1869), 50–73.
17. For a detailed study of the indirect literary relationship between the two texts, see the arguments of Himmelfarb, *Tours*, esp. 140–47.
18. The preface of *Apoc. Paul* dates its own "discovery" to the co-consulship of Theodosius I and Cynegius in the year 388. See further Pierluigi Piovanelli, "Les origines de l'*Apocalypse de Paul* reconsidérées," *Apocrypha* 4 (1993): 25–64 and Kirsti Copeland, "Mapping the *Apocalypse of Paul*: Geography, Genre and History" (PhD diss., Princeton University, 2001), 21–35. For Augustine's witness to the *Apoc. Paul*, see 98 *Tract. Ev. Jo.*
19. For an edition of the long Latin manuscripts (Paris, Bibliothèque, Nouv. Acquis. lat. 1631; St. Gallen, Vadianus 317; Madrid, Escorial a. II. 30; and Codex 6, Stichtig Arnhemse Openbare en Gelders Wetenschappelijke Bibliotheek), see Theodore Silverstein and Anthony Hilhorst, eds., *Apocalypse of Paul: A New Critical Edition of Three Long Latin Versions* (Geneva: Patrick Cramer, 1997), 66–167; for an edition of the late Greek abbreviations (Monacensis Gr. 276 and Ambrosianus Gr. 895) see Constantinus Tischendorf, ed., *Apocalypsis Pauli*, in *Apocalypses Apocryphae* (Leipsig: Hermann Mendelssohn, 1866), 34–69; for translation and edition of the single extant Coptic manuscript (British Museum Oriental #7023), see Copeland, "Mapping the Apocalypse of Paul,"189–309.
20. For an edition of the later Latin manuscripts of the *Apoc. Paul* (Codex 362, Österreichische Nationalbibliothek, Vienna; Codex 856, Universitätsbibliothek, Graz; Codex C 101, Zentralbibliothek, Zürich), see Silverstein and Hilhorst, eds., *Apocalypse of Paul*, 170–207; for the edition of the *Gk. Apoc. Mary* (Cat. MSS Bodl. i. 659), see James, ed., *Apocrypha Anecdota*,114–26 (123); for the Latin translation of the *Eth. Apoc. Mary* see M. Chaîne, trans., "Apocalypsis seu Visio Mariae Virginis," 43–68 (66); for an English translation of the *Eth. Apoc. Bar.* and the *Eth. Apoc. Gorgorios*, see Leslau, *Falasha*, 57–91 (74, 87).
21. Alexandre, *Oracula Sybillina*, 68. For the *Ethiopic Apoc. Pet.*, I must rely on the literal translation of Buchholz, *Your Eyes Will Be Opened*, 225.
22. Fritz Graf, *Magic in the Ancient World* (Cambridge, MA: Harvard University Press, 1997), 28.
23. Empedocles, DK 31 F 111; G. S. Kirk, J. E. Raven, and M. Schofield, trans., *The Presocratic Philosophers*, 2nd ed. (Cambridge: Cambridge University Press, 1983), 285, cited after Graf, 33.
24. John Scarborough, "Pharmacology," *OCD*, 3rd ed., 1154–55; John Scarborough, "The Pharmacology of Sacred Plants, Herbs, and Roots" in *Magika Hiera*, ed. Christopher Faraone and Dirk Obbink (New York: Oxford University Press, 1991) 139–54 (esp. 146–52).

25. Graf, *Magic in the Ancient World*, 28.
26. Georg Luck, "Witches and Sorcerers in Classical Literature," in *Witchcraft and Magic in Europe*, ed. Bengt Ankarloo and Stuart Clark (Philadelphia: University of Pennsylvania Press, 1999), 93–158 (120).
27. *Eth. Apoc. Pet.* 12:5, trans., Buchholz, 224–25.
28. Ixion's wheel, see: Apollod., *Epit.* 1.20, Verg., *G.* 4.480, Pind., *Pyth.* 2.21ff., etc. For the wheel as fiery see Scholiast on Eur., *Phoen.* 1185. The fiery wheel is also known from vase paintings reproduced in Charles Mills Gayley, *The Classic Myths in English Literature and in Art.* (Boston: Ginn & Co., 1911), 358; cited after John E. Hankins, "The Pains of the Afterworld: Fire, Wind, and Ice in Milton and Shakespeare," *PMLA* 71, no. 3 (Jun., 1956): 482–95 (492).
29. Hom., *Od.* 11.593.
30. Hes., *Theog.* 507–616.
31. One could argue that Ixion's desire to possess someone is echoed in the love spells. However, Ixion did not use any sort of spell in attempting to achieve his goal.
32. David Walter Leinweber, "Witchcraft and Lamiae in the 'The Golden Ass,'" *Folklore* 105 (1994): 77–82 (78); Matthew W. Dickie, "Who Practised Love-Magic in Classical Antiquity and the Late Roman World?," *CQ*, n.s., 50, no. 2 (2000): 563–83 (582).
33. Ov., *Met.* 7.160ff.
34. 2.1; Jack Lindsay, trans., *Apuleius: The Golden Ass* (Bloomington: Indiana University Press, 1960), 50.
35. Pind., *Pyth.* 2.30ff, trans, Gregory R. Crane, ed., *Perseus Digital Library* (cited 24 January 2007; http://www.perseus.tufts.edu).
36. *Eth. Apoc. Pet.* 8, *Gk. Apoc. Pet.* 26.
37. *Eth. Apoc. Pet.* 9–10, *Gk. Apoc. Pet.* 31–2; *Sib. Or.* 2.268–71.
38. *Sib. Or.* 2.256; Ursula Treu, trans., "Christian Sibyllines," in *New Testament Apocrypha*, vol. 2, ed. Edgar Hennecke and Wilhelm Schneemelcher, trans. R. McL. Wilson (Louisville, KY: Westminster/John Knox Press), 658–63 (661).
39. Tischendorf, ed., *Apocalypses Apocryphae*, 60.
40. *Revelation of Paul* 38, *ANF* 8:579.
41. Copeland, "Mapping the Apocalypse of Paul," 216, 277.
42. Love spells tormenting the object of desire are countless. For example, the *Erotic Spell of Cyprian of Antioch* reads as follows: "She must not eat or drink, slumber or sleep, for her garments burn her body, the sky's lightening sets her afire, and the earth beneath her feet is ablaze. The father must have no mercy upon her; the son must show her no pity; the holy spirit must give no sleep to her eyes, for her remembrance of god and her fear of him flee away from her, and her thoughts, her intentions, and her mind turn to devilry, as she hangs upon desire, longing, and disturbance because of N. son of N." For this and other examples in the Coptic Christian tradition, see Marvin W. Meyer and Richard Smith, eds., *Ancient Christian Magic: Coptic Texts of Ritual Power* (Princeton, NJ: Princeton University Press,

1994), 153–64 (155). Or for another example, see Karl Preisendanz, ed., *Papyri Graecae Magicae* (Stuttgart: Teubner, 1973–74), IV.1496–1595 (Betz, 67): "Inflame her and turn her guts inside out, suck out her blood drop by drop, until she comes to me." Betz contains numerous other love spells as well.

43. See examples collected in Gager, *Curse Tablets and Binding Spells from the Ancient World* (Oxford: Oxford University Press, 1992).
44. *Apoc. Paul* 38, trans. J.K. Elliott, ed., *The Apocryphal New Testament* (Oxford: Clarendon,1993) 635; Silverstein and Hilhorst, eds., *Apocalypse of Paul*, 144–45.
45. Graf, *Magic in the Ancient World*, 66.
46. *Apol.*, 83, 1.
47. Silverstein and Hilhorst, *Apocalypse of Paul*, 17–18. Theodore Silverstein, "The Vision of St. Paul: New Links and Patterns in the Western Tradition," *AHDLMA* 34(1959): 199–248, esp. 199–201. See also Tamás Adamik, "The *Apocalypse of Paul* and Fantastic Literature," in *The Visio Pauli and the Gnostic Apocalypse of Paul*, ed. J. N. Bremmer and István Czachesz (Leuven: Peeters, 2007), 144–57, esp. 156–57.
48. Silverstein and Hilhorst, eds., *Apocalypse of Paul*, 194.
49. Graf, *Magic in the Ancient World*, 47.
50. *Gk. Apoc. Mary* 23, in *ANF* 9.172.
51. Ibid.
52. *Eth. Apoc. Mary* and its descendant *Eth. Apoc. Bar.* do not speak of poisoning but rather of writing magical texts (Chaîne, trans., *Apocrypha*, 66; Leslau, trans., *Falasha*, 74). *Eth. Apoc. Gorg* condemns "those who were soothsayers, used divination, led (men) astray through idols, birds, and charms, and abandoned His law" (Leslau, trans., *Falasha*, 87). These texts do appear to condemn magic for its own sake, not just because of its victims.
53. Silverstein and Hilhorst, eds., *Apocalypse of Paul*, 144; Copeland, ed., "Mapping the Apocalypse of Paul," 277. Some of my comments on the gender-inclusive formula derive from Kirsti Copeland, "Gender and the Afterlife in Roman Egypt," (paper presented at the annual meeting of the Society of Biblical Literature, San Antonio, Texas, November 21, 2004), 1–3, 10.
54. Ibid. The English translation of the Syriac version of the *Apoc. Paul* found below Tischendorf's edition of the Greek suggests that this version, like the *Apoc. Pet.*, contains both the formula "men and women" as well as the specific genders in the professional title, "witches and wizards." Tischendorf, ed., *Apocalypses Apocryphae*, 60.
55. *Gk. Apoc. Pet.* 27–34 (note the order is reversed to "*γυναῖκες καὶ ἄνδρες*" in 28, 30, 34); Kraus and Nicklas, *Das Petrusevangelium und die Petrusapokalypse*, 112–17, 119–20. *Eth. Apoc. Pet.* 7:1, 8:5, 9:1, 9:3–4, 9:6, 10:1–2, 10:6–7, 11:2, 11:8, 12:1, 12:5; Buchholz, *Your Eyes Will Be Opened*, 196–97, 204–5, 208–17, 220–25.
56. *Eth. Apoc. Pet.* 8, 11.
57. *Eth. Apoc. Pet.* 7; Buchholz, *Your Eyes Will Be Opened*, 199, 201.

58. The phrase is used fifteen times; see *Apoc. Paul* 31, 32, 37 (twice), 38 (twice), 39 (three times), 40 (four times), 42.
59. *Apoc. Paul* 39; Elliott, *Apocryphal New Testament*, 635.
60. *Apoc. Paul* 34–36.
61. Of all of the later texts mentioned in this paper, only the *Vision of Thurkill* appears to have escaped the wide-reaching influence of the *Apoc. Paul.*
62. *Gk. Apoc. Mary* 3–5, 12–14, 23 (*ANF* 9.169–72).
63. *Gk. Apoc. Mary* 23; James, *Apocrypha Anedocta*, 122 (ἀνδρῶν τε καὶ γυναικῶν), 123 (φάρμακοι).
64. E.g., *(Apocr.) Ep. Tit.*, l. 400–418 (Stone and Strugnell, *Books of Elijah*, 14, 15): *animae peccatorum, alii, hii. Acts Thom.* 55–57 (Elliott, trans., *Apocryphal New Testament*, 470–71; R. A. Lipsius and M. Bonnet, eds., *Acta Apostolorum Apocrypha*, vol. 2 [Leipzig: Hermann Mendelssohn, 1898], 171–74): ψυχαὶ. *Testament of Isaac* 9 (K. H. Kuhn, trans., "The Testament of Isaac," in *Apocryphal Old Testament* [ed. H. F. D. Sparks; Oxford: Clarendon, 1984], 423–39 [435]; K. H. Kuhn, "The Sahidic Version of the Testament of Isaac," *JTS*, n.s., 8, no. 2 [1957]: 225–39 [234]): ⲈⲨⲘⲎⲎϢⲈ ⲘⲮⲨⲬⲎ *(ψυχαί)*, ⲚⲢⲈϤⲈⲢⲚⲞⲂⲈ, ⲚⲢⲰⲘⲈ. *Vit. Pach.* SBo 88 (Armand Veilleux, trans., *The Life of Saint Pachomius and His Disciples*, vol. 1 of *Pachomian Koinonia*, CSS 45 [Kalamazoo, MI: Cistercian Publications, 1980], 114–16; L. Th. Lefort, ed., *Pachomii Vita bohairice scripta*, CSCO, SCo 3/7 [1925]): ⲚⲒⲮⲨⲬⲎ *(ψυχαί)*, ϨⲀⲚⲘⲞⲚⲀⲬⲞⲤ *(μονάχοι)*. *Apoc. Ezra* (*ANF* 8:571–74; Otto Wahl, ed., *Apocalypsis Esdrae* [Leiden: Brill, 1977], 25–34): τῶν ψυχῶν τῶν ἁμαρτωλῶν, τοὺς ἁμαρταλοὺς, τὸ γένος τῶν ἀνθρώπων.
65. Stone and Strugnell, *Books of Elijah*, 14.
66. *Acts Thom.* 56 (Elliott, trans., *Apocryphal New Testament*, 470); *Apoc. Ezra* (*ANF* 8:573).
67. Stone and Strugnell, *Books of Elijah*, 16–23, passim. Sometimes בני אדם does refer explicitly to men who sinned against or with women and hence is not always an inclusive masculine plural.
68. Himmelfarb, *Tours*, 5.
69. Himmelfarb, *Tours*, 5.
70. Himmelfarb, *Tours*, 131–34, 169, 171.
71. K. H. Kuhn, "The Apocalypse of Zephaniah," in *Apocryphal Old Testament*, 919–24.
72. See for example: Justin, *Dial.* 105, Tertullian, *An.* 57.8.
73. Patricia Cox, "Origen and the Witch of Endor: Toward an Iconoclastic Typology," *AThR* 66, no. 2 (1984): 137–47.
74. Klaas Smelik, "The Witch of Endor, I Samuel 28 in Rabbinic and Christian exegesis till 800 AD," *VC* 33, no. 2 (1979): 160–79.
75. E.g., Lev 19:26, 31, 20:6; Deut 18:10–11; 2 Kings 21:6, 23:24; Isa 8:19; 19:3; Mal 3:5.
76. Irenaeus, *Haer.* 1.13 (*ANF* 1:334–6; W. Wigan Harvey, ed., *Libros quinque adversus haereses* [Cambridge: Typis Academicis, 1857; repr., Ridgewood, NJ: Gregg, 1965], 114–27, esp. 120–22).

77. Jerome, *Ep.* 7.5 "To Theodora" (*NPNF*, Series 2, 6:156).
78. *Acts Paul* 15 (Elliott, trans., *Apocryphal New Testament*, 367). See also *Acts Phil.*, "Of the Journeyings of Philip the Apostle," (*ANF* 8:498–499).
79. I suspect that these charges lobbied at the apostles in the Apocryphal Acts of the Apostles reflect the accusations of sorcery primarily from "proto-orthodox" Christians, much like Irenaeus's accusations of Marcus, and not from the practitioners of traditional Greek or Roman religion.
80. Todd Breyfogle, "Magic, Women, and Heresy in the Late Empire: The Case of the Priscillianists," in *Ancient Magic and Ritual Power*, ed. Marvin Meyer and Paul Mirecki (Boston: Brill, 2001), 435–54 (445).

PART III

Gender, Magic, and the Material Record

11

The Social Context of Women's Erotic Magic in Antiquity

David Frankfurter

THIS CHAPTER WILL proceed in three parts.[1] First I consider problems in, and two recent models for, comprehending ancient women's recourse to erotic spells: what kinds of women engaged in such rites and with what goals in mind? Second, I examine the role of individual agency—self-determination and creativity—in women's magic as a way of addressing critical social situations. Finally, I argue that women's recourse to erotic spells points inevitably to situations of economic and social crisis, the solution to which would be a secure relationship with a particular man. This point, developed on comparative grounds, does not obviate women's real erotic passion but states merely that for many women this passion had a social context.

The Courtesan and the Goodwife

A number of recent publications on ancient magic have presented us with two quite different images of men's and women's motivations for erotic magic, a discrepancy that takes us to the very intersection of gender, sexuality, society, and ritual expression. In one, both women and men seek stable connubial relationships with occasional recourse to magical spells, although men express their desires in more coercive, violent terms. In the other, both men and women of a particular ilk, especially prostitutes, seek to exploit each other sexually through magic. These two images of erotic magic proceed from divergent interpretations of, first of all, a lively and evocative literature, from classical through late antique times, that describes in alternately sympathetic, horrifying, and ludicrous terms men's and women's recourse to magic spells to resolve their sexual desires. Secondly, balancing these *literary* vignettes is the great corpus of ritual manuals, binding tablets, and inscribed magical objects in which actual spells were designed and deployed for use throughout the Mediterranean world from the fifth century BCE on through late antiquity. Most of the erotic spells in this corpus are clearly for men seeking (at least) sex with women, and they are worded with a degree of aggression that has given many modern scholars pause:

> Let her not be able to sleep for the entire night, but lead her until she comes to his feet, loving him with a frenzied love, with affection and with sexual intercourse. For I have bound her brain and hands and viscera and genitals and heart for the love of me, Theōn.... Grab Euphēmia and lead her to me, Theōn, loving me with a frenzied love, and bind her with bonds that are unbreakable, strong and adamantine, so that she loves me, Theōn; and do not allow her to eat, drink, sleep, or joke or laugh but make (her) rush out of every place and dwelling, abandon father, mother, brothers, and sisters, until she comes to me, Theōn, loving me, wanting me (with a) divine, unceasing, and a wild love. And if she holds someone else to her bosom, let her put him out, forget him, and hate him, but love, desire, and want me; may she give herself to me freely and do nothing contrary to my will.[2]

Why the commanding, explicit, even sadistic tone? Does the language reflect the real desires of the male subject, and if so, should we infer an essential violence in ancient men's sexuality? Or does the language have some *latent* meaning or function in expressing or verbalizing desire—the projection of the subject's own state of anguish, or vengeance for the object's refusal?[3] And given that the preponderance of these sexual-compulsion spells—called *agōgai*—are the work or commission of men, what manner of erotic magical spells did women utilize in their lives, if literary sources have any validity in asserting they sometimes did? With what data and which social models *can* we discuss women's erotic magic? This is the topic of this chapter.

For Christopher Faraone most women in antiquity simply did not use or think in terms of *agōgai*, whose violent language—indeed, inheriting the language of the curse—reflected *men's* verbally declarative efforts to extract single women from the social confines of the patriarchal domus (father or occasionally husband). Their ultimate goal, in the words of one spell, would be "eternal"—presumably marital—love and sex with the chosen woman: " . . . so that Theodotis, daughter of Eus, . . . be subservient, obedient, eager, . . . in unending intercourse for all the time of her life."[4] Women's interests, Faraone argues, are reflected in the range of potions, ointments, and charms—*philia* ("affection magic")—that wives use in classical literature to *maintain* marital bonds and sexual devotion, a ritual effort related more to the protective spell than the curse. Ironically, men's own fears of such wifely powers fed into various caricatures of domestic sorcery.[5]

A few women's spells, however, do adhere to the more coercive *agōgē* formulation, such as this fifth-century CE lead tablet:

> From the hour that I write this let Sextilius, son of Dionysia, not sleep; let him burn in madness, let him neither sleep nor sit nor speak but hold me, Septimia, daughter of Amoena, in [his] mind. Let him burn with love and desire for me; let the spirit and heart of Sextilius, son of Dionysia, burn with love and desire for me, Septimia, daughter of Amoena . . . Let him not touch sleep but burn with love and desire for me, let his spirit and heart combust, all the parts of the whole body of Sextilius, son of Dionysia.[6]

Such aggressive expressions of desire, drawing their language and adamance from the masculine spells, Faraone tentatively attributes to the culture of courtesans.[7] Faraone's picture of women's own erotic magic, then, is part of a larger scenario whereby men and (usually married) women deploy separate types of magical spells to maintain (in the case of wives) or disrupt (in the case of single men) domestic bonds as part of the normal negotiation of Mediterranean social life, with sequestered girls and straying husbands.[8]

Matthew Dickie, on the other hand, sees no intrinsic masculinity in the *agōgai* spells, which he suggests were customarily adjusted for women's own quests for sexual hook-ups.[9] Loose women, girls, and courtesans were all apparently on the prowl for sexual adventure. Placing women's erotic magic in historical context involves for Dickie

> the very real possibility . . . that there were twelve-year-old girls who ran away from home to Alexandria for adventure and who slept freely with men, not always taking payment for their services. There were no doubt other types of sexually active women who were neither prostitutes nor wives. Women who were divorced or separated from their husbands will have been one; widows will have been another.[10]

At the same time, the men who deployed erotic *agōgai* "were not trying to secure the undivided attentions and affections of a maiden of good family, but were more concerned to bring to their beds for their own exclusive enjoyment women who had been known to gratify the sexual needs of other men"—to wit, prostitutes and courtesans.[11] For Dickie, indeed, the prostitute and the lascivious youth, each pursuing the other's exclusive sexual attentions with *agōgai*, constituted the dominant social context for erotic magic through late antiquity.[12] This *demi-monde* of competition, exploitation, and crass gratification, to be found (Dickie asserts) in virtually every ancient city and village, would match the pictures of magical activity drawn by Roman authors like Lucian, Petronius, Apuleius, and, especially, those of Christian persuasion like Clement of Alexandria and John Chrysostom of Antioch. Chrysostom, for example, asserts that:

> Many women, in order to come off as pleasing, devise incantations and libations and love-potions and countless other things. . . . For spells are prepared, one after another, not only on the prostituted womb [i.e., for abortion] but also against the victimized wife, with countless plottings, invocations of demons, and necromancies, (all resulting in) daily battles and irreconcilable conflicts, and domestic squabbles.[13]

For Chrysostom the city is a veritable jungle of predatory sorceresses and demons, against which the Christian should protect herself and her family in every way.[14] But if many scholars would regard such assessments as little more than the polarizing rhetoric of an anxious bishop, Dickie judges them historically reliable, revealing a real situation. Magic, the purview of predatory women, not only disrupted the home, he asserts; it also served as "an *integral part* of the *equipment* of a courtesan . . . [that] is needed to make sure that lovers are drawn to her and remain faithful to her."[15] Magic and its remains—spells, manuals, literary vignettes—signify depravity in both economy and sexuality—an underworld separate from and predatory on the family. The sequestered girl and chaste wife have no use for such spells.

Dickie's model certainly allows for a more dynamic women's eroticism, a broader sense of sexual desire, and a greater agency in women's magical expression than Faraone's world of *philia* spells. However, his relegation of this eroticism, and magic itself, to the *demi-monde* of courtesans and adulteresses—thus distancing magical practices from normative Mediterranean society—is both unnecessarily restrictive and (in Dickie's presentation) frankly moralistic. Indeed, in many ways Dickie simply replicates as history the caricatures and censure of Christian authors.[16]

What difference do these two models make to the understanding of women's use of erotic magic? At the level of historicity they contrast quite vividly. Were prostitutes in fact the predominant female users of erotic spells? What other women used erotic spells, and in what situations? For Faraone, many women used erotic spells, if mostly of the milder *philia* type. For Dickie, good women shunned magic, but bad women used every kind of spell. The models also differ in their very understanding of women's ritual acts as expressions of aggression and desire and in relationship to social systems like marriage and the family. For Dickie erotic magic was fundamentally anti-social and predatory, while for Faraone erotic magic included types that were expressly, even anxiously protective of marriage and the family.[17]

Contributing to the ambiguity of women's magic that both scholars try to resolve are the various caricatures of sorceresses that inform ancient literature and even some spell-manuals. The common picture in Greco-Roman literature of a lascivious older woman who uses barbaric utterances and nocturnal rites to bind some unwitting youth reflected, *pace* Dickie, not a real social type but rather the folklore of the night-witch—*strix*, *gello*, or *lilith*—who eats children and drains men's potency.[18] These literary sorceresses, like Lucian's Bacchis and Apuleius's Pamphilē, may also have reflected broader suspicions of women's real ritual efforts to protect home and marriage, turning demon-vigilant mothers into anti-domestic witches.[19] In the service of entertainment, literary sorceresses allowed both the objectification of suspicions and a controlled, even ludicrous representation of night-witch fears.[20] Thus their depiction, and even their allusion in Christian sermons, reflected ancient cultural thinking *about* women's magic, and their powers vis-à-vis sexuality in particular.

Such caricatures of the predatory sorceress do envision magic as a depraved, predatory activity that crystallizes women's lustful nature and shunts her into an underworld of obscene practices and desires. But they also occasionally suggest that women did engage in magical practices in such domains as sex and the family. Our task is then to assemble a more circumspect historical-social model for women's use of magic, especially erotic spells, that does not simply reify caricatures. We need to gain a broader sense of magic as a private pursuit embedded in social realities—to tease apart situation, formulation, actor, object, and audience. How, that is, can we understand real women's recourse to erotic magic as an understandable social strategy, one that is not selfish and coercive but rather self-assertive, even desperate? This question brings us to the element of *agency* in magic.

Magic and Ritual Agency

What is involved—emotionally, socially, economically—when a person engages in coercive ritual expressions, whether by a god's mediation or by the sheer force of the spell?[21] Does it imply a shift from the religious sphere to that of sorcery, from the public and positive to the nocturnal and aggressive? Or should we gather that magic, like religion, extended throughout public and private life with a range of applications and rites, each specific to the situation?

Research on magic in societies ancient, pre-modern, and modern has shown the extent to which this sphere of ritual we call magic (according to most second-order, "etic" definitions) is woven so thoroughly through life that people often are hard-pressed to distinguish it from religious or other ritual endeavors.[22] Indeed, it is often hard to define a category "magic" across protective, healing, divinatory, erotic, and cursing spheres of ritual expression. As Bronislaw Malinowski showed at the beginning of the twentieth century, magic clusters particularly around insecure and liminal situations in life and supplements rather than replaces instrumental action.[23] Thus we find spells, amulets, and magical gestures especially around the protection of travelers, pregnancy and children, health, home, animals, and the like.[24]

But the insecure and liminal experiences that tend cross-culturally to invite magic as a supplement to instrumental activity obviously extend also to social tensions: hostilities, rivalries, the control of obstinate family members, or the release of love-objects from family control. John Winkler classically introduced this context to frame men's erotic *agōgē* spells, arguing that men had but little else at their disposal to express their desire for women enmeshed in tightly controlled patriarchal households; and whether or not we accept this scenario for all *agōgai* it does alert us to the idea that some such broader social context would have governed the recourse to magic.[25] For example, in the case of two Coptic spells meant to strike particular men impotent we might hypothesize a crisis similar to Winkler's scenario but from the other side, as it were: to *guard* a particular woman's virginity. The clients, that is, were probably fathers or mothers concerned lest their daughters fall for the seductions of some inappropriate suitors.[26]

The social crises that motivate recourse to magic certainly go beyond sex, however, and extant spells display the innumerable tensions and anxieties of local culture. A woman doubtless besieged by malicious gossip implores the powers to "close, seal, stop up and dull their wits and close the mouths of all mankind, . . . so that they are not able to speak with her or converse with her, except for good things, from this day and forever."[27] For similar reasons a man asks angels to silence a woman, "that you give to her mouth and her nose a closing and a silence and a weariness and a bridle and a shackle and a dumbness to her mouth . . . and [do likewise to] everyone who thinks evil against him."[28] A woman calls down divine judgment on her son's girlfriend or fiancée, for she has "separated my son from me so that he scorns me. You must not listen to her, O [God . . .] if she calls up to you. You must strike her womb and make her barren. You must consume the fruit of her womb. You must make a demon descend upon her, [who will cast] her into troubles and illness and great affliction."[29] An assemblage of *tabellae defixiones* from a house in Roman Corinth invokes Hermes of the Underworld to bring just vengeance on a particular woman while asking at the same time to "make me fertile"—suggesting a woman contending with the public humiliation of barrenness.[30] And the following two spells seek to bind women through their body parts, quite likely in connection with their erotic allures. A fourth-century BCE lead tablet seeks to "record"—to inscribe coercively the name of—"Isias, the daughter of Autoclea, with Hermes the Restrainer. Restrain her near you. I bind Isias before Hermes the Restrainer—the hands, the feet of Isias, the whole body."[31] In contrast, the following Coptic formula was written and purveyed generically, to restrain the beauty and attention of *any* woman:

> with hatred and strife and loathing, in the face of N, daughter of N, so that at the moment that [I] write your names, along with your figures and your amulets, on a potsherd, and light a fire under it until it is charred, you must char the face of N, daughter of N, in the presence of the entire generation of Adam . . . that at the moment that they see the face of N, daughter of N, when they hate it and its speech, her face must receive no favor, and her work must not be established for all eternity.[32]

We cannot, of course, be certain of the gender of the clients of these last two spells nor of the precise nature of the rivalries in which they seek to intervene magically. However, their sexual implications, specifying body parts that would presumably pose erotic allure (body, face), suggest that the female objects of the spells are constructed as romantic rivals or interlopers. In all these spells, and the many others like them, magic follows social situations in which personal desire is opposed by others' wills, social constraints, or simply an inability to proceed: erotic desire for a domestically circumscribed girl or paternal protection of a girl from a suitor; a mother's resentment for her son's girlfriend and the latter's influence; a woman's sense of threat from other women, whether in sexual rivalry or marital devotion. In such cases, the deployment of the spell might augment public negotiations or might constitute the only allowable form of expression in otherwise foregone circumstances—offering a sense of power and control, of objectified sentiments, and the hope of real efficacy.[33]

But when we speak of magic as recourse or as displaced emotional expression we often forget the intricate procedures involved in launching the spells whose texts have come down to us. In the "hierarchy of means" by which ancient people chose to engage the practice of magic at home or in the wider world it could be a protracted process, from consultation with experts and collection of materials to "performing" the spell, depositing the materials, and perhaps letting it be known that a curse or *agōgē* was deployed against a particular person.[34] And it is the complexity of this process that highlights the effort and the *agency* of the individual herself. Magic, in many ways, is fundamentally about agency, and the artifacts of magic reflect the agency—the creativity and self-determination—of historical individuals in trying to secure their lives, protect their property, extricate themselves from danger, or, in the cases we have been examining, negotiate the frustrations of the close-knit society. By emphasizing agency we see the subject or initiator of the spell as one who takes expressive action on her own behalf and who negotiates creatively between immediate circumstances, authentic sentiments, and various modes of authority (gods, names, myths, phrases), usually with the help of a ritual expert.

Consider, for example, Esrmpe, a young Egyptian wife of the late first century CE, who deposited a plea to the local mortuary god Osiris at his shrine, as had long been a customary way of resolving domestic crises in Egypt.[35] In this case Esrmpe's plea had been transcribed in a hybrid alphabet of Greek and Egyptian letters ("Old Coptic") that she herself could read aloud before the shrine or that would be legible to others. After announcing herself, she proceeds:

> My lord Osiris, (Lord) of Hasro! I complain to you, do justice to me and Hor, the (son) of Tanesneou, concerning what I have done to him and what he has done to me. Namely, he does not make love with me, I having no power, I having no protector-son. I am unable to help (myself), I am childless (?). There is no one who could complain concerning me before you because of Hor. . . . I complain to [you . . .] . . . Osiris, listen to my calls![36]

The papyrus continues with a succession of invocations and names of Egyptian gods. We are thus confronted with a young woman handling that most fraught of experiences in traditional societies, infertility, with implications for her social status (as with the Corinthian tablets, above, p. 324) as much as for the marital relationship. Here, of course, the cause of infertility appears quite clearly in Esrmpe's speech. We should presume, then, that this appeal to Osiris followed and complemented a succession of efforts on Esrmpe's part to get Hor to make love to her. What is particularly noteworthy is Esrmpe's own agency in, first, learning the procedure for supernatural appeal, then dictating the letter to the scribe, then getting herself out to the shrine, and then reading the letter aloud and depositing it nearby.

Consider, secondly, Prosodion, a wife and mother in 2–1 BCE Knidos (Asia Minor), who leaves a lead tablet by a statue of Demeter in a local shrine that *dedicates*—probably *anieroi*—

> to Demeter and Kore and the gods with Demeter, whoever is taking away [my] husband . . . Nakōn, from his children. Do not let Demeter . . . be merciful to her—whoever receives [sex] from Nakōn—[thus] adding to the misery of Prosodion, but let Prosodion be blessed, her and her children in every way . . .[37]

Here again the social crisis—the implications of the anonymous "other woman" for Prosodion's status and her children's livelihood—quite clearly frames the ritual efforts. Prosodion's use of a lead tablet at the (notably public) Demeter shrine, worded as an appeal to the goddess to "dedicate," not kill or bind, her rival, reflect adherence to some established local practice, as some thirteen other tablets were found in the same place; and we should presume some aid and guidance in Prosodion's completion of the ritual process.

But if Esrmpe's and Prosodion's expressions of agency in seeking resolution were matched by traditional, publicly accepted sequences of acts that focused on recognized shrines, a fourth-century BCE woman apparently had to confront her problems in a more secretive manner, getting her appeal inscribed on a lead tablet and burying it with a corpse that could act as messenger:

> Of Thetima and Dionysophon the ritual wedding and the marriage I bind by a written spell, as well as (the marriage) of all other women (to him), both widows and maidens, but above all of Thetima; and I entrust (this spell) to Macron and to the *daimones*. And were I ever to unfold and read these words again after digging (the tablet) up, only then should Dionysophon marry, not before; may he indeed not take another woman than myself, but let me alone grow old by the side of Dionysophon and no one else. I implore you: have pity for [Phila?], dear *daimones*, [for I am indeed bereft?] of all my dear ones and abandoned. But please keep this (piece of writing) for my sake so that these events do not happen and wretched Thetima perishes miserably.[38]

It would be a mistake to draw too much of a contrast between this spell and Esrmpe's appeal simply on the basis of "public" versus "secretive" acts. Both cases involved individual ritual agency, mortuary locations as ritual sites, and probably a web of social consultations up to the point of the spells' depositing. For their respective cultures, neither was any more "religious" than "magical." For our reconstruction of the motivations and agency of women's magic, Phila's spell should strike us much like Esrmpe's plea for its "beseeching prayer to the *daimones* . . . through which Phila expresses her deeply felt despair in front of a formidable threat: the prospect of her consort, Dionysophon, marrying another woman." As the editor of this spell argues, "the simplest and most straightforward interpretation [would be] that Dionysophon had decided to repudiate his wife in order to conclude a new marriage. In case she had no close relatives who could support her, she would find herself in a situation not very different from that of a dismissed concubine."[39]

In such straits, Phila carries out a series of acts, from deciding to resort to magical means to consulting with others to figure out the procedure, then writing or commissioning the lead binding spell, linking it to and then burying it with the corpse ("Macron"), and then perhaps the tactical insinuation to the couple that their wedding has been "fixed." This series of acts reflects considerable agency in dealing with a critical situation. To understand magic in life we must accept agency and deliberate action themselves as factors in magical efficacy, regardless of their ultimate effects on a situation.[40]

While I will address the broader social implications of such incidents of women's magic in the next section, here I simply want to emphasize this feature of agency in negotiating social crises and apparently irresolvable situations through ritual efforts. Those efforts, from verbalizing the situation by means of the spell, to conducting the gestures and activities needed to launch the spell, and from consulting ritual experts in family or community to informing the victims, all give the performer a sense of efficacy, even power, in circumstances she could not otherwise influence or change, and they allow her to express in action sentiments she could not properly or publicly articulate. Agency, then, comprises the individual's efforts to articulate intolerable social situations through the stages of private ritual when public resolution is forestalled, impossible, or seems to require corollary efforts.

Women's Desires, Women's Straits

So often we imagine this agency in selfish terms, magic as the route for satisfying one's own desires rather than society's. The many ancient spells for gaining magical advantage in sports or business or law court seem certainly to endorse this assumption, as do curses. Employing magic in these cases seems tantamount to soliciting the professional "hit," cheating a system that depends on social contracts and rationality, and certainly exceeding such "religious" routes as the pious appeal for a god's intervention.

Men's *agōgai* spells, in all their aggressive sexual demands, have invariably been put in the same selfish context. Indeed, for Dickie the *demi-monde* of conniving prostitutes and dissolute youth reeks of selfish exploitation, in which magic serves only to capture moneyed johns or to monopolize courtesans' favors. Yet, as Winkler and others have argued, the Greek and Roman materials can be understood in another way: as expressions of chaotic emotional states in situations of tight social constraints. They do convey their clients' authentic states of desire, even for sex and monopolized favors, but the desire is imagined, constructed, and articulated according to cultural realities of power-relations and family constraints, such as who can marry whom, who controls a woman's sexuality, where women can go, how children will be supported, what sexual fulfillment might mean, and what languages for desire and fantasy are available. They reflect the psychology of crisis and liminality.

And so also for women's erotic spells, which, in the generally gender-dichotomous worlds of antiquity, ought to reflect quite different social contexts from men's. While the surviving spells certainly convey emotional or erotic desire, I want to argue that they also reflect the social or economic straits that could result if the arrangement sought were *not* secured through sexual or marital bonds.

That is, women's erotic spells—both *philia* and *agōgai*— should be read against the backdrop of the client-woman's social and economic precariousness, the resolution of which might come through securing sexual bonds with—and thus devotion from—a particular man. "Wives," says a character in Seneca, "pull their marriages together by magic arts and prayers."[41] However, the merit of this social/economic approach is that it covers *not only* married women maintaining their husbands' affections and young women's efforts to gain husbands, but also prostitutes, whose real livelihoods (in contrast to literary portrayals such as Lucian's) were actually quite precarious and temporary.[42]

Faraone's own characterization of women's *philia* (marital affection) spells alerts us already to social and economic implications, for in these cases, conducted usually with potions and gestures, women seek to *maintain* marital bonds against some threat to affection—a rival woman, for example. The "magic," as it were, is not selfish so much as bent on the wife's security in social status, economic stability, and of course marital harmony. As one Greek manual from Egypt prefaces a spell, "[This one attracts a woman] to a man. The same one [makes (men) steadfast] and faithful."[43] But the same efforts at securing social status and livelihood should motivate the women's *agōgai* that coercively draw men or even break apart or prevent rivals' relationships. Consider Phila's spell to prevent Dionysophon's wedding to Thetima rather than herself (above, p. 327), or another lead tablet binding one "Aristokudes and the women who will be seen with him. May he not marry any *other* woman or young maiden."[44] What the client imagines herself as gaining through these spells is certainly more than just sex and attention; it is marriage, with its concomitant social security. The same motivations seem likewise to lie behind those spells that curse other women's marriageability out of what we should probably presume to be rivalry for specific men: a papyrus from Byzantine Egypt by which the client seeks to afflict Martha with such illness that she "puts aside marriage . . . yea, Jesus Christ, you must dissipate her hope so that no one desires to assist her,"[45] or another fourth-century BCE lead tablet, restraining Theodora from advancing her relationship with one Charias:

> May she be unmarried [*atelēs*] and whenever she is about to chat with Kallias and with Charias—whenever she is about to discuss deeds and words and business . . . words, whatever he indeed says. I bind Theodora to remain unmarried to Charias and (I bind) Charias to forget Theodora and (I bind) Charias to forget . . . sex with Theodora.[46]

There is, to be sure, a cold insistence in declaring hopefully Theodora's abandonment, but such language is sensible both in the context of a social conflict not otherwise resolvable and as generic to the spell itself in its efforts at linguistic completeness.

As Faraone portrays, women resorted to sexual magic even after marriage had been secured, to maintain men's affection and devotion but also to curse the inevitable interlopers and mistresses, as in the following from Christian Egypt, meant to restrain a man's sexual drive with some woman who is evidently not the client:

> . . . His penis must not become hard, it must not have an erection, it must not ejaculate, he must not have intercourse with Touaien daughter of Kamar or any woman, whether wild or domesticated,[47] until I myself call out, but may it dry up, the male organ of Pharaouo son of Kiranpales. He must not have intercourse with Touaein daughter of Kamar, he being like a corpse lying in a tomb. . . [48]

We know from cross-cultural analogues that such impotency spells were typically meant to work *beyond* the marriage bed—with the Touaiens of the village—and, as here, reversible at home ("until I myself call out").[49]

So, across these various spells to bind, coerce, and curse lovers, rivals, and disruptors, we begin to get a sense of ancient women's broader magical efforts to secure domestic stability and negotiate rivalries—often, it seems, in situations in which they could wield few other forms of power, such as against other women. Indeed, to comprehend the kinds of women's straits that framed their aggressive spells it is again useful to recall Phila's *agōgē* (above, p. 327), a response to the desperate position of losing the very kind of rivalry for a potential husband that the last few spells sought to preempt. For many women, married or courtesans, a man's abandoning them for another woman would pose not just emotional heartbreak but also a loss of social status, economic support, and danger to children.[50] In this broad sense, a woman's erotic desire for a man and his companionship would often be enmeshed with her anxiety for the security and livelihood that the man and his economic attentions could provide, and so her strategy for gaining or maintaining that security might involve *both* cultivating her own erotic allure *and* deploying magical spells to bind the man or curse her rivals.[51]

This context would seem to frame one Domitiana's attempt to bind Urbanus for marital purposes, that he become "loving, tormented, and sleepless with desire and love for her, so that he may take her into his house as his wife [*symbios*]. Unite them in marriage [*gamō*] and as spouses [*symbiountas*] in love for all the time of their lives. Make him as her obedient slave, so that he will desire no other wife or maiden apart from Domitiana alone."[52] It should similarly frame one Capitolina's efforts to bind Nilos, that he should love her "with a divine passion, and in every way you will be for me an escort [*akolouthos*] as long as I want, that you might do for me what I wish and nothing for anyone else, and that you might obey no one save only me, Capitolina, and that you might forget your parents, children, and friends."[53] The adamant, coercive tone of these spells reflects the intensity of the women's desire, to be sure, but even more the security and stability that a *symbios* or an *akolouthos* might offer.

This interweaving of ancient women's erotic desire with their efforts to avoid economic and social insecurity is most clearly illustrated in historical and ethnographic materials from modern cultures. These materials provide not only similar (and similarly aggressive) erotic spells but also clear social contexts for their deployment. Indeed, in these modern materials erotic spells serve as a principal expression of agency for women in demonstrably insecure circumstances. Women in modern Honduras, for example, may enjoy the benefits of matrilinear property inheritance, but they need to conduct their lives within a male-dominated society in which men, who work away from the village, bring in the preponderance of income. Women's common use of sex spells on men, which draw on family-based traditions of spell-formulation, have as a self-declared goal financial rewards for themselves and their children. Sex spells provide the women with an arena for action and self-determination.[54] Even more starkly, women in 1970s Belize depended entirely on men as economic providers even while job instability and mobility contributed to unstable family structures. With little to keep men except their sexual allure, women resorted to a variety of erotic binding spells, using food and material assemblages. This erotic magic sought

> to control the sexual behavior of the male in two rather different ways: 1) the woman seeks to guarantee that the man returns to her even if there is sexual involvement with other women, and 2) she tries to limit the sexual potency of the male so that he can accomplish sexual intercourse with her alone.[55]

One is reminded of the Coptic impotency spells mentioned earlier. Of course, as this same ethnographer goes on to observe, Belizean men's suspicions of these very acts fed into common stereotypes of women's sorcery and thus contributed to a general tension between men's and women's subcultures. But the same methods and motivations for women's sexual binding spells (and the same defensive caricatures of women) have been preserved in inquisition records from early modern Brazil, Mexico, and Spain.[56] María Helena Sanchez Ortega has assembled extensive evidence for a women's magical subculture in early modern rural Spain that made extensive use of erotic magic. The following two spells exemplify the aggressive imagery involved in binding men sexually:

> *NN,/ Wherever you are,/I send you this nail;/I strike you with this passion./Soon you will come for my love—/For my love, captured and bound.*[57]

> *Bring me three willow rods;/Sharpen them on Barabbas's molars;/Carry them through hell./Drive one into his mind,/So that he won't forget me;/Another into the heart,/So he will come when I desire;/Another into his back,/So he will answer my call.*[58]

Such erotic spells, whether to secure absolute physical and psychic devotion or (as some hope) to cause impotence, must at one level reflect a genuine erotic longing on the part of the women. However, they do so—Sánchez Ortega argues—within a context of economic dependency. Much as in modern Belize, a husband's or lover's sexual interest meant financial support and status, while his abandonment for another woman's erotic allures meant financial and social insecurity. So "despite their assertions" of raw erotic desire, Sánchez Ortega concludes,

> these enamored women were not satisfied merely with having their love reciprocated. Their aspirations and amorous passion extended to the total control of the beloved's will, and the reasons for desiring such control had little to do with the admired mystical sighs of their religious sisters' passion. Our enamored women, practitioners of magic, were essentially pragmatic souls who realized that they must obtain masculine support at all costs, so as not to be socially devalued.[59]

Passion and economic needs, even status insecurity, *in combination* led women to deploy erotic magical spells to gain and hold men's sexual interest. At the same time magic itself—the sequence of ritual preparations and performances—expressed agency on the part of women: their creative, active intervention in the unpredictabilities of affection and love, in the daunting competition for devoted partners, and in the social vagaries and constraints of a traditional society.

Conclusion

By crediting the women clients behind erotic *agōgai* (and other aggressive spells related to sexuality) with this agency we achieve a subtler, more empathetic understanding of magic in everyday life. And by postulating broader socio-economic implications behind women's efforts to secure men or curse rivals for certain men we gain also a larger paradigm for understanding women's motivations for deploying erotic spells and aggressive spells against others. With this paradigm we do not need to rely on alleged social distinctions between women using *philia* and women using *agōgai*, for necessity and crisis (or simply the predilections of ritual experts) can impel a range of types of wording, whether the client is an anxious prostitute, an anxious maiden, or an anxious wife and mother. Nor do we need to entertain misogynist stereotypes of conniving prostitutes and virtuous goodwives and their respective proclivities to magic, for the model proposed here would cover both social worlds in regard to women's ritual strategies to gain and preserve status and livelihood in various social worlds.[60] Most importantly, the eroticism and sexual rivalry behind the spells we have seen emerge as fundamentally *social* phenomena, enmeshed in the realities of women's lives, not proclivities of the individual or mysteries of the heart.

In the end, however, the agency of these women in deploying these spells—out of emotional distress, in the face of looming misfortune, and often against institutional censure— simply verified for the larger culture the fearful stereotype of women as sorceresses—predators on male potency and on each others' social and romantic fortunes. Simply accusing another woman of erotic sorcery might go far in resolving a situation of sexual rivalry or marital threat. Yet ritual agency itself—the preparation of real sexual binding spells—perseveres despite, and often in response to, these cultural suspicions and mythic nightmares of magical power and its female wielders.[61]

Notes

1. Abbreviations: *ACM* = Marvin Meyer and Richard Smith, eds., *Ancient Christian Magic: Coptic Texts of Ritual Power* (San Francisco: HarperSanFrancisco, 1994); *CTBS* = John G. Gager, ed., *Curse Tablets and Binding Spells from the Ancient World* (New York: Oxford University Press, 1992); *DT* = *Defixionum Tabellae*, ed. A. Audollent (Paris: Fontemoing, 1904; repr. Frankfurt: Minerva, 1967); *DTA* = *Inscriptiones Graecae* 3.3 Appendix (Berlin: Reimer, 1897); *GMPT* = *The Greek Magical Papyri in Translation*, ed. H. D. Betz (Chicago 1986); Kropp 1–3 = Angelicus M. Kropp, *Ausegewählte koptische Zaubertexte* 1–3 (Brussels: Fondation égyptologique Reine Élisabeth, 1930–31); *PGM* = *Papyri Graecae Magicae*, ed. K. Preisendanz (Stuttgart 1973–74). I am indebted to the Casablanca Group and to Henk Versnel for invaluable criticisms of earlier drafts.
2. *Suppl. Mag.* 45, ll.6–9, 43–52 = *PGM* CI = *CTBS* 30 (tr.). This spell, from fifth-century CE Egypt, was written on papyrus and wrapped around two embracing wax figures, which were melted together, and then the assemblage sealed in a pot and presumably buried.
3. John J. Winkler, "The Constraints of Desire: Erotic Magical Spells," *The Constraints of Desire: The Anthropology of Sex and Gender in Ancient Greece* (New York: Routledge, 1990), 71–98. See also John Gager, *CTBS*, 78–85; Bernadette J. Brooten, *Love Between Women: Early Christian Responses to Homoeroticism* (Chicago: University of Chicago Press, 1996), 73–113; Lynn LiDonnici, "Burning for It: Erotic Spells for Fever and Compulsion in the Ancient Mediterranean World," *GRBS* 39 (1998): 63–98; and Hendrik S. Versnel, "An Essay on Anatomical Curses," in

Ansichten griechischer Rituale: Geburtstags-Symposium für Walter Burkert, ed. Fritz Graf (Stuttgart & Leipzig: Teubner, 1998), 217–67, esp. 247–64.

4. *Suppl. Mag.* 38 = *CTBS* 34. See Christopher A. Faraone, *Ancient Greek Love Magic* (Cambridge, MA: Harvard University Press, 1999), 41–95.
5. Faraone, *Ancient Greek Love Magic*, 120–21, 128–31. See also Richard Gordon, "Magic as a Topos in Augustan Poetry: Discourse, Reality and Distance," *Archiv für Religionsgeschichte* 11 (2009): 209–28, esp. 219–22 on the relationship of the lore of women's magic and the literary synthesis of the witch, antithesis of the home.
6. *DT* 270, tr. Author.
7. See Faraone, *Ancient Greek Love Magic*, 149–60.
8. See also Winkler, "Constraints of Desire," 97–98.
9. Matthew Dickie, "Who Practised Love-Magic in Classical Antiquity and in the Late Roman World," *CQ* 50, no. 2 (2000), 565–67.
10. Dickie, "Who Practised Love-Magic?," 572.
11. Dickie, "Who Practised Love-Magic?," 569.
12. Matthew Dickie, *Magic and Magicians in the Greco-Roman World* (London and New York: Routledge, 2001), 176.
13. John Chrysostom, *Hom. Rom.* 24 (= *PG* 60: 627), tr. author. On classical caricatures of sorceresses see also Ov., *Am.* 1.8; 3.7.27–38. On Christian representations, see, e.g., Jerome, *Vit. Hil.*; Theodoret, *Hist. Rel.* 8.13; *Hist. Mon. In Aeg.* 21.17; and in general, David Frankfurter, "The Perils of Love: Magic and Counter-Magic in Coptic Egypt," *JHSex* 10 (2001): 480–500, and Silke Trzcionka, *Magic and the Supernatural in Fourth-Century Syria* (London and New York: Routledge, 2007), 81–100.
14. See further Trzcionka, *Magic and the Supernatural*, 106–9, 122–25, on Chrysostom's views of magical dangers to the Christian. Dayna Kalleres offers an incisive picture of Chrysostom's demonological worldview in "City of Demons: Violence, Ritual, and Christian Power in Late Antiquity" (Berkeley: University of California Press, 2014).
15. Dickie, *Magic and Magicians*, 84 (emphasis mine); cf. 79–95, 188–89, 302–3.
16. See Dickie, *Magic and Magicians*, vii; See also David Frankfurter, review of *Magic and Magicians in the Greco-Roman World*, by Matthew Dickie, *BMCR* (2002.02.26; accessed 7 July 2014; http://bmcr.brynmawr.edu/2002/2002-02-26.html).
17. See Esther Eidinow's incisive discussion of the two models in *Oracles, Curses, and Risk Among the Ancient Greeks* (Oxford: Oxford University Press, 2007), 208–12.
18. On night-witches, see Richard Gordon, "Lucan's Erictho," *Homo Viator: Classical Essays for John Bramble*, ed. M. Whitby and P. Hardie (Bristol: Bristol Classical Press, 1987), 231–41, and "Imagining Greek and Roman Magic," in *Witchcraft and Magic in Europe: Ancient Greece and Rome*, ed. Bengt Ankarloo and Stuart Clark (Philadelphia: University of Pennsylvania Press, 1999), 159–275, esp. 204–10; and Sarah Iles Johnston, "Defining the Dreadful: Remarks on the Greek Child-Killing

Demon," in *Ancient Magic and Ritual Power*, ed. Marvin Meyer and Paul Mirecki (Leiden: Brill, 1995), 361–87; and more broadly on the use of the night-witch to inform the understanding of everyday magic: Norman Cohn, *Europe's Inner Demons* (Chicago: University of Chicago Press, 1993), 162–66, 211–33, and Richard Kieckhefer, "Avenging the Blood of Children: Anxiety over Child Victims and the Origins of the European Witch Trials," in *The Devil, Heresy and Witchcraft in the Middle Ages: Essays in Honor of Jeffrey B. Russell*, ed. Alberto Ferreiro (Leiden: Brill, 1998), 91–109. Both Lucian, *Dial. meret.* 1, and Ovid, *Amores* 1.8, combine the sorceress and the night-witch. More broadly on literary construction of the sorceress, see Kimberly B. Stratton, *Naming the Witch: Magic, Ideology, and Stereotype in the Ancient World* (New York: Columbia University Press, 2007), 71–105.

19. On the fears and caricatures of women's real ritual activities see Winkler, "The Constraints of Desire," 90–91; Faraone, *Ancient Greek Love Magic*, 110–21; and esp. Rebecca Lesses, "Exe(o)rcising Power: Women as Sorceresses, Exorcists, and Demonesses in Babylonian Jewish Society of Late Antiquity," *JAAR* 69, no. 2 (2001), 343–75.
20. Lucian, *Dial. meret.* 4; Apul., *Met.* 2.5. See also Dickie, "Who Practised Love-Magic?," 577–79.
21. For ancient materials Versnel distinguishes these two approaches to verbalizing efficacy: the "appeal or prayer for justice" and the magical spell proper. See his "Beyond Cursing: The Appeal to Justice in Judicial Prayers," *Magika Hiera: Ancient Greek Magic and Religion*, ed. Christopher A. Faraone and Dirk Obbink (New York: Oxford University Press, 1991), 60–106, and "Essay on Anatomical Curses," 233–35. While agreeing that the appeals for justice can often imply the client's submission to civic religion and judicial tradition rather than a more individualized sort of resolution, I do not view the distinction as sufficiently clear at the level of ritual consultation and performance to warrant an absolute division in mentality and religious/social world. Furthermore, the choice of a spell's wording, between "declarative" and "imploring," may often be regional or specific to the expert. For example, an expert with more formal affiliation with a temple might provide clients with spells of the "appeal" formulation, while one more marginal to religious institutions might deal in spells that depend merely on verbal efficacy.
22. See especially Andromache Karanika, "Folk Songs as Ritual Acts: The Case of Work-Songs," *Finding Persephone: Women's Rituals in the Ancient Mediterranean*, ed. Maryline Parca and Angeliki Tzanetou (Bloomington, IN: Indiana University Press, 2007), 137–53.
23. Bronislaw Malinowski, "Magic, Science and Religion" [1925], *Magic, Science and Religion and Other Essays* (New York: Beacon, 1948; repr. Prospect Heights, IL: Waveland, 1992), esp. 28–36, on which see Stanley Jeyaraja Tambiah, *Magic, Science, and the Scope of Rationality* (Cambridge: Cambridge University Press, 1990), 70–73.
24. In this sense Malinowski's model works also with Arnold van Gennep's observations of the clustering of rites around those in—or encountering those in—liminal

periods or life-stages. See his *Rites of Passage*, tr. Monika B. Vizedom and Gabrielle Caffee (Chicago: University of Chicago Press, 1960 [1908]).

25. Winkler, "The Constraints of Desire."
26. *ACM* 86 = Heidelberg kopt. 682; *ACM* 87 = Strasbourg copt. 135.
27. T-S NS 321.96, ll. 16–20, ed. and trans. M. J. Geller and Dan Levene, "Magical Texts from the Genizah (with a New Duplicate)," *JJS* 49, no. 2 (1998): 334–40.
28. *ACM* 102 = Würzburg 42.
29. *ACM* 93. Cf. SB 3.6264, a letter in which a woman complains about her daughter-in-law or son's fiancée: Roger S. Bagnall and Raffaella Cribiore, *Women's Letters from Ancient Egypt* (Ann Arbor: University of Michigan Press, 2006), 282.
30. I. Corinth 125–26, ed. R. S. Stroud, *Corinth XVIII.6: The Sanctuary of Demeter and Kore. The Inscriptions* (Princeton, NJ: Princeton University Press, 2013), 104–15.
31. *CTBS* 19 = Margherita Guarducci, *Epigrafi sacre pagane e cristiane*, vol. 4 of *Epigraphica Greca* (Rome: Instituo Poligrafico dello Stato, 1978), 248–49.
32. *ACM* 105 (Heidelberg kopt. 681).
33. Cf. Winkler, "Constraints of Desire," 87–89 on mastery and control through projection in the magical spell.
34. See especially Richard Gordon, "*Quaedam veritatis umbrae*: Hellenistic Magic and Astrology," *Conventional Values of the Hellenistic Greeks*, SHC 8, ed. P. Bilde and T. Engberg-Pedersen (Aarhus, Denmark: University Press, 1997), 146–49; and compare Gerda Senger's description of a woman's consultation with experts in modern Egypt to resolve her anger at her husband for seeing another woman: *Women and Demons: Cult Healing in Islamic Egypt* (Leiden: Brill, 2003), 47–48. On reconstructing magical procedures in antiquity see Emmanuel Voutiras, *Dionysophontos Gamoi: Marital Life and Magic in Fourth Century Pella* (Amsterdam: Gieben, 1998), 90–102.
35. In general on such letters to the dead or to mortuary gods, see Alan H. Gardiner and Kurt Sethe, *Egyptian Letters to the Dead* (London: Egypt Exploration Society, 1928), 1–12; George R. Hughes, "A Demotic Letter to Thoth," *JNES* 17 (1958): 1–12; and Edward Wente, *Letters from Ancient Egypt* (Atlanta: Scholars Press, 1990), 210–20.
36. Helmut Satzinger, ed. and trans., "The Old Coptic Schmidt Papyrus," *Journal of the American Research Center in Egypt* 12 (1975): 37–50 (translation emended). See Satzinger, "Die altkoptischen Texte als Zeugnisse der Beziehungen zwischen Ägyptern und Griechen," *Graeco-Coptica: Griechen und Kopten im byzantinischen Ägypten*, ed. Peter Nagel (Halle: Martin-Luther-Universität, 1984), 137–46, and brief discussion by David Frankfurter, "A Plea to a Local God for a Husband's Attentions," *Religions of Late Antiquity in Practice*, ed. Richard Valantasis (Princeton, NJ: Princeton University Press, 2000), 230–31 (cf. also *ACM* 1). I revisit the content and context of this plea in "'It is Esrmpe who appeals!' Place, Object, and Performance in the Quest for Pregnancy in Roman Egypt," to be published in the proceedings of the Princeton University conference "Placing Ancient Texts: The Rhetorical and Ritual Use of Space" (2014).

37. *DT* 5, ed./trans. (with adjustments) Eidinow, *Oracles, Curses, and Risk*, 389, with discussion at 215.
38. Voutiras, trans., *Dionysophontos Gamoi*, 15–16.
39. Voutiras, *Dionysophontos Gamoi*, 55, 82.
40. On the efficacy of magical spells and petitions, whether through the actor/client's own cathartic performance of ritual acts or through the tactical publicizing of the spell or petition, see Hendrik Versnel, "Writing Mortals and Reading Gods: Appeal to the Gods as a Dual Strategy in Social Control," *Demokratie, Recht und soziale Kontrolle im klassischen Athen*, Schriften des Historischen Kollegs 49, ed. David Cohen (Munich: Oldenbourg, 2002), 68–72.
41. Seneca, *Hercules Oetanus*, ll. 452–53, trans. Georg Luck, *Arcana Mundi, Magic and the Occult in the Greek and Roman Worlds* (2nd ed.; Baltimore: Johns Hopkins University Press, 2006), 121.
42. See, e.g., Lucian, *Dial. meret.* 1 and 4; cf. Theoc., *Id.* 2.23–32; Theodoret, *H.R.* 8.13. Arguments for the historical reliability of Lucian's courtesans include Dickie, *Magic and Magicians*, 9–11, 190; Faraone, *Ancient Greek Love Magic*, 149–51; and now Edward E. Cohen, "Free and Unfree Sexual Work: An Economic Analysis of Athenian Prostitution," in *Prostitutes and Courtesans in the Ancient World*, ed. Christopher A. Faraone and Laura K. McClure (Madison: University of Wisconsin Press, 2006), 95–124, esp. 108–12. But contrast Laura K. McClure, "Introduction," *Prostitutes and Courtesans in the Ancient World*, 3–18, and Kate Gilhuly, "Bronze for Gold: Subjectivity in Lucian's *Dialogues of the Courtesans*," *AJP* 128 (2007): 59–94, both on the dubiousness of using this work for the history of prostitution. For reconstructing the historical realia and social world of prostitution the indispensable study is Thomas A. J. McGinn, *The Economy of Prostitution in the Roman World: A Study of Social History and the Brothel* (Ann Arbor: University of Michigan Press, 2004), esp. 14–71. Lucian's courtesans themselves admit some economic precariousness: *Dial. meret.* 3, 6.
43. *M[onimous / autous poiei] kai pistikous*. *PGM* LXXVIII, ed. Priesendanz 2: 207, trans. (emended) O'Neil, *GMPT*, 299.
44. *CTBS* 23 = DTA 78. Compare Dickie's odd interpretation in "Who Practised Love-Magic?" 575–76.
45. *ACM* 100 = Aberdeen copt. Ms. The same scribe produced *ACM* 101.
46. *CTBS* 22, p. 90 (= *DT* 68). The last two spells invite other scenarios, of course, such as a man's vengeance against a woman who spurned him or a community's punishment of a deviant through her hopes for social status. But the resemblances across these last series of spells suggest a similar scenario: women using magical rites to "fix" rivals for the men they hoped to marry.
47. *Oute čoout oute tefnē* (from *tbnē* ?). The adjectives indeed pertain to animals, perhaps reflecting the tendency in spells to list and enumerate for completion's sake, or perhaps reflecting the client's wry assessment of the man's sexual preferences. On the use of zoological analogies see Frankfurter, "Perils of Love," and *Evil Incarnate:*

Rumors of Demonic Conspiracy and Satanic Abuse in History (Princeton, NJ: Princeton University Press, 2006), 15–26.

48. *ACM* 85 = Chicago Oriental Institute 13767, ed. Elizabeth Stefanski, "A Coptic Magical Text," *American Journal of Semitic Languages and Literatures* 56, no. 3 (1939): 305–7.
49. See, e.g., Laura Hobson Herlihy, "Sexual Magic and Money: Miskitu Women's Strategies in Northern Honduras," *Ethnology* 45, 2 (2006): 143–59, esp. 152. A Byzantine legend tells the story of a woman who consults a ritual specialist (*pneumatikos anthropos*) to deal with her unfaithful husband and his new mistress. The specialist offers such magical recourses as the husband's death, demonic possession, or—notably—impotency (*maranō . . . autou epithumian*); but, the woman says, "I want nothing else . . . but that he loves and cherishes me" (ed. Lennart Rydén, *The Life of St. Andrew the Fool* [Uppsala, Sweden: Almqvist & Wiksell, 1995], 2: 170–72).
50. See, e.g., Ilias Arnaoutoglou, "Marital Disputes in Greco-Roman Egypt," *Journal of Juristic Papyrology* 25 (1995): 11–28, esp. 22–24.
51. Such socio-economic scenarios are perhaps less applicable to the few female homoerotic *agōgai* like *PGM* XXXII.1–19 and *Suppl. Mag.* 42. As Brooten, *Love Between Women*, makes clear, the possible scenarios for such couples' relationships are extensive (105–9).
52. *CTBS* 36 = *DT* 271, ll. 30–32, 43–45, ed. G. Adolf Deissmann, "An Epigraphical Memorial of the Septuagint," *Bible Studies*, trans. Alexander Grieve (2nd ed. Edinburgh: T. & T. Clark, 1909), 271–300, with translation from Gager, *CTBS*. On this woman's *agōgē* see Faraone, *Ancient Greek Love Magic*, 29 n.124, 62–63, 149–50.
53. P. Alex. Inv. 491 = *PGM* XV.1–5 (ed. Preisendanz 2: 133), trans. Hock, *GMPT* 251.
54. Herlihy, "Sexual Magic and Money."
55. M. Kenyon Bullard, "Hide and Secrete: Women's Sexual Magic in Belize," *Journal of Sex Research* 10, no. 4 (1974): 259–65 (quotation p. 261).
56. E.g., Ruth Behar, "Sexual Witchcraft, Colonialism, and Women's Powers: Views from the Mexican Inquisition," *Sexuality and Marriage in Colonial Latin America*, ed. Asunción Lavrin (Lincoln: University of Nebraska Press, 1989), 178–206; María Helena Sánchez Ortega, "Sorcery and Eroticism in Love Magic," *Cultural Encounters: The Impact of the Inquisition in Spain and the New World*, ed. Mary Elizabeth Perry and Anne J. Cruz (Berkeley: University of California Press, 1991), 58–92; Carole A. Myscofski, "The Magic of Brazil: Practice and Prohibition in the Early Colonial Period, 1590–1620," *History of Religions* 40, 2 (2000): 153–76; Laura de Mello e Souza, *The Devil and the Land of the Holy Cross: Witchcraft, Slavery, and Popular Religion in Colonial Brazil*, trans. Diane Grosklaus Whitty (Austin: University of Texas Press, 2003 [1986]), 142–52; Ramón A. Gutiérez, "Women on Top: The Love Magic of the Indian Witches of New Mexico," *JHSex* 16, 3 (2007): 373–90.

57. Recited 1655 by Laura Garrigues at Valencia, from Sánchez Ortega, "Sorcery and Eroticism in Love Magic," 64.
58. Recited by Isabel Bautista at Castile, from Sánchez Ortega, "Sorcery and Eroticism in Love Magic," 75.
59. Sánchez Ortega, "Sorcery and Eroticism in Love Magic," 62; see also further conclusions on p. 84.
60. See Mary O'Neil, "Magical Healing, Love Magic and the Inquisition in Late Sixteenth-Century Modena," *Inquisition and Society in Early Modern Europe*, ed. Stephen Haliczer (Totowa, NJ: Barnes & Noble, 1987), 88–114, esp. 98–105, in which priests and prostitutes figure prominently as ritual experts for erotic spells.
61. See especially Lesses, "Exe(o)rcising Power"; Cohn, *Europe's Inner Demons*, 162–66, 211–33; Robin Briggs, *Witches and Neighbors: The Social and Cultural Context of European Witchcraft* (New York: Viking, 1996), 163–68, 259–86; and Gutiérez, "Women on Top."

12

Cheating Women: Curse Tablets and Roman Wives

Pauline Ripat

IN BOOK FOUR of Virgil's *Aeneid*, Queen Dido of Carthage is faced suddenly with the realization that Aeneas, her lover, is leaving her. Without him, she is ruined; she has sacrificed all for him—her reputation, her honor, the safety of her people. She begs him to stay, for without him, she will quite literally die. Aeneas, *pius* Aeneas, the model of behavior for Roman men, tells her to stop scorching him with her complaints (*desine meque tuis incendere teque querelis*).[1] She turns to the practice of love magic, and by the end of the book, to curses. Though the scene is fictional, Aeneas's refusal to recognize Dido's difficulties, and Dido's resort to magic and curses, probably resonated with many members of Virgil's ancient audience. Aeneas's apathy, at the very least, is reflected in our literary sources' lack of interest in women's problems, and as a consequence we hear very little about the real problems that real women might have experienced. At the same time, curse tablets found in the archaeological record[2] indicate that cursing often afforded an anxious or troubled person a perceived remedy. The evidence of curse tablets is therefore doubly important: first, it can provide indirect information about the type of problems or anxieties commonly experienced by ancients, including women; second, as secretive attempts to unleash unearthly and destructive powers upon another, curse tablets may be considered as evidence for women's actual, rather than imagined, "magical" activity. Roman women's use of curse tablets has not received much attention, however.[3] This chapter seeks to demonstrate the potential benefits of such an inquiry by gathering and contextualizing Greek and Latin curse tablets from Italy and the western provinces that name as their victims slave women or freedwomen. I shall argue that these are best considered the work of female practitioners, wives seeking to protect their relationships from the victims, whom they perceive as interlopers. The context, which did not allow for "real" action, but rather demanded "magical" action on the part of wives, will then be knit together from a consideration of Roman ideals of behavior and scattered details of actual experience, sifted from necessarily eclectic sources. The position of wives could be extremely precarious should their husbands philander within the household, and cursing was one possible mode of self-preservation for wives caught in the eddies of a domestic hierarchy unmoored. This observation allows for further consideration of the discrepancy between the stereotype of women's magical activity and women's plausibly "real" magical activity.

The Evidence: Cursing Women

Curse tablets (*defixiones, katadesmoi*), in David Jordan's oft-quoted description, "are inscribed pieces of lead, usually in the form of small, thin sheets, intended to influence, by supernatural means, the actions or welfare of persons or animals against their will."[4] Curse formulas on these lead sheets generally aimed at restricting the victim's abilities. This was done by magically "binding" the victim's physical characteristics or personal attractions outright with a direct formula, or by magically encouraging the victim through "persuasive analogy" to become as dull as the lead upon which the curse was inscribed, as backward as the letters in which the formula was written, or as lifeless, boring, or silent as the corpses into whose graves curse tablets were often dropped for the perusal of the infernal deities or dead. Sometimes a lead or clay "voodoo doll" was included for good measure (often ritually twisted or entombed in its own tiny coffin).[5] Christopher Faraone argues that in Greek society wielders of curse tablets did not intend to end their victims' lives, but only to inhibit their abilities. Some Roman practitioners were evidently unaware of, or unconcerned for, Greek etiquette of curse tablet use, however, and instead occasionally demanded their victims' annihilation in no uncertain terms.[6] A cluster of first-century BCE curse tablets from Rome, for example, exhort death, destruction, and ruin upon their targets.[7] The antipathy of practitioners for their victims, and thus the practitioners' reason for inscribing curse tablets, was rooted in competitive contexts: the curses aim to improve the practitioners' chances for success by reducing the competition's chances—or at times by removing the competition entirely. The ever-increasing corpus of curse tablets, drawn from all corners of the Greek and Roman worlds, and spanning a millennium, testifies to the enduring popularity of the strategy in the courts, the circus, the theater, the world of business, and in affective relationships.[8]

The last category is of interest here. "Separation curses" (*Trennungszauber*), as they are generally called, aim to divide two people who are, or who are suspected to be, in an intimate relationship. One member of the couple is the practitioner's rival for the attentions of the third person. Some curse tablets clearly fall into this category. Consider, for instance, the demand "may Quintula never again be with Fortunalis!" found on a tablet from first-century CE Spain.[9] The identification of other tablets as separation curses might be less sure; for example, a variety of scenarios could be suggested for a third-century tablet from Noricum. The formula bids "infernal Jove and infernal Juno . . . to hand over to the shades below Aurelius Sinnianus Caeserianus," whose name has been inscribed upside down; it then adds "thus, Silvia do you perceive your husband turned upside down, in the same way as his name has been written."[10] The placement of both the victim and the practitioner in these (for lack of a better term) "love-triangles" is also not a foregone conclusion. Is the practitioner a would-be home-wrecker, or a partner seeking to remove an interloper? It need not be the same situation for every curse. However, I argue for the probability of two statements: first, the tablets that target slave women, and perhaps also those that target freedwomen, are best understood as "separation curses" that have arisen from "love-triangle" situations; second, the practitioner behind this kind of tablet is the wife of the victim's master or patron. Before engaging in these discussions, it is worth first describing the evidence in question.

A handful of curse tablets targeting slave women exist. The earliest found thus far is an extremely corrupt tablet from second-century BCE Pompeii, found in a tomb, cursing Philematium, the slave of Hostilius.[11] A series of first-century BCE tablets from Morgantina target one "Venusta, slave of Rufus."[12] A tablet from Augustan Rome, discovered among some graves, aims to render a slave woman's attractions no better than a corpse ("Just as the corpse who is buried here is unable to speak or make conversation, thus may Rhodine be corpse-like and be neither able to speak nor able to make conversation with M. Licinius Faustus.")[13] Another contemporary lead tablet from Rome, folded up and wrapped with an iron wire, appears to offer a slave woman as a sacrifice to the infernal gods ("Danae, the new slave of Capito. May you have this woman as a welcome victim, and may you devour Danae").[14] Another Augustan tablet, this time from Spain, grimly points out "Dionysia, slave of Denatia" to the gods below.[15] From a grave in Minturnae in Latium comes a second-century CE tablet that was folded and pierced by a nail; its formula seeks to ensure that a slave woman will be utterly unsuccessful ("Infernal gods, I hand over to you . . . Tyche, the slave of Carisus, that everything she does should turn out against her. Gods below, I commit to you her limbs, complexion, figure, head, hair, shadow, brain, forehead, eyebrows.")[16] Intriguing too is a fourth or fifth-century terracotta tablet from Pannonia, which wishes that Zimia be pursued by "gorgon-killing Athena" for her sexual debauchery.[17] Not to go unmentioned are a few tablets identifying victims whose names or descriptions indicate that they were freedwomen. One from Cumae curses "Naevia Secunda, the freedwoman of Lucius,"[18] while a tablet from Campania contains only the name Claudia Helena;[19] a second-century CE curse from Messina identifies the victim, Valeria Arsinoe, as a bitch in heat.[20]

The number of these tablets is admittedly small in comparison to the corpus of curse tablets as a whole. This observation should not undercut their significance, however. Numbers do not matter much; remains of curse tablets of any sort can never give statistical information about the percentage of the population that used them in particular situations. The evidence of curse tablets gives instead indication of what was *possible*; here, we see that slave women in parts of Italy and other parts of the western empire might be targeted as victims of curses from the late republican period onward. Furthermore, curse tablets in the archaeological record are merely the most physically enduring examples of a variety of "magical" means thought to accomplish similar purposes. Indeed, the end, not the means, was the critical factor in formulating charges of "magical" activity. The notorious confusion between poison and curses by the late republic, at least, is the result of the similarity of imagined outcome—the weakening or death of the purported victim.[21] And cursing did not require a lead tablet. On the contrary, evidence suggests that a spoken formula, perhaps accompanied by ritual actions, might be deemed as effective.[22] Furthermore, Pliny the Elder describes stones that were believed to have the power to punish private enemies and engender discord.[23] In short, the curse tablets in question here represent the absolute minimum of attempts to curse slave women; the unrecoverable real number of attempts might have exceeded this handful in exponential figures.

Some of the curses described above are clearly separation curses, others less so at first blush. But the identity of all of these as the work of wives seeking to curse their husbands' slaves is the most probable scenario. A variety of necessary conditions for the use of curse tablets create a process by which other possible scenarios and practitioners are eliminated. Wielders of curse tablets in general are thought to have shared certain common concerns. As curse tablets grow out of the soil of competition, practitioners perceived the victim as a rival, that is, someone in whose place they could imagine themselves, or alternatively, whom they imagined intended to take their own place. The removal of a rival was critical for success in a particular situation that is often hinted at on the tablet; but this short-term success was an important step toward the achievement of a broader goal.[24] As one person's success was equally understood as another's failure, and one's reputation, and perhaps even self-perception, depended on the opinion of others, the ultimate goal of the practitioner was assurance of honor and avoidance of public humiliation.[25] The neutralization of the rival and thus success was not assured to the practitioner by other, more legitimate means, such as the invocation of law, or the application of social pressure—other powers had to be prevailed upon. Though it has been suggested that in Greek society, cursing one's rivals to ensure the honor of one's family might have been deemed acceptable, the same cannot be said for Roman society.[26] Certainly a general's curse of Rome's enemies was honorable, and provisional self-curses were requisite for sealing treaties, but real or suspected curses by private individuals were at once socially despicable actions and legal crimes.[27] It must then be concluded that cursing was not undertaken lightly and therefore that it was a Roman practitioner's last, and possibly only, recourse when faced with a personal crisis.

Thus, when it comes to curses that target women of lowly, indeed, the lowest status, that is, the people in Roman society who were least protected by law and social custom, we must identify a situation in which a slave woman could be imagined as a rival for a male's attention and the practitioner could be perceived as vulnerable, in the sense of being unable to control the outcome of the conflict by invoking law or social norms. The curse tablets themselves offer no reason to suspect them as the products of competition between prostitutes, the scenario posited for some Greek curse tablets against women.[28] The arena of personal relationships then seems a better choice. Spurned lovers seeking revenge can be crossed off the list of possibilities straight away. Curses deriving from just that situation survive in the archaeological record, but differ from the examples cited above in that they include a fair amount of detail about the situation that has necessitated the vengeance curse, and often name the practitioner.[29] It must also be doubted that the practitioners are would-be interlopers, perhaps other slaves, seeking to dissolve a slave woman's pre-existing relationship and so to win the man for herself. Removal of the current favorite could not mean that favor would automatically fall upon the practitioner, rendering the use of a curse tablet somewhat pointless as a way to achieve such a goal.[30] Furthermore, understanding these tablets as attempted "crimes of passion" on the part of jealous women bent on destroying the happiness of others is to embrace the stereotype of women's magical behavior,[31] and to do precisely what the stereotype encourages its audience to do, that is, to look no further.

Look further we must. The most obvious scenario is a situation in which a woman's husband is engaging in a relationship with a slave, the victim. Unlike sex with a woman who was another's wife, or with a woman who had the legal capacity to marry, a man's sexual relations with a slave was not considered adultery by law or social custom.[32] These relations might be regarded as shameful because they suggested a lack of self-control, but it is nevertheless clear that sexual use, indeed, abuse, of slaves by masters was endemic.[33] As the next section will demonstrate, such situations had the potential to create serious, even potentially tragic, circumstances for a wife, yet a wife suffering the ill effects of her husband's relationship with a slave enjoyed no legal avenues of redress, nor social validation of her problems.[34] Secretive strategies, practices both illegal and illaudable, might be the only alternative. This, then, is the context for curses.

Ideals of Behavior and Collapsed Household Hierarchies

Much attention has been devoted to the legal position of wives within the Roman family, less attention has been paid to their treatment.[35] In Roman social hierarchies, a person's status was supposed to dictate treatment, meaning that one's own status was manifested in the attitudes and behavior of others. The insufficiently respectful attitudes of others were keenly felt insults, and excessive respect shown to one of undeserving status was felt to cheapen social distinctions.[36] In theory, social expectations of behavior and symbolic markers of status ensured that a Roman *matrona* ought never to have perceived herself as sufficiently similar to a slave or freedwoman for a situation of rivalry to develop. The reality, however, could be quite different. The household hierarchy, envisioned through ideal lenses as solid, in reality rested delicately upon the fulcrum of a husband's behavior toward his wife in conjunction and comparison with his behavior toward other members of the household.[37] It cannot be doubted that the position of *matrona* deserved respect. But respect for a position does not necessarily translate into respect for the person occupying it, and the real treatment a wife experienced within the household might not be commensurate with her social deserts should the guarantor of her privilege, her husband, undermine her by showing excessive favor to another.[38] The overlap between ideals of uxorial and servile behavior and the rewards for each presented by one and the same man, husband and master, introduced a potentially equalizing force amongst the women in the household. The following discussion describes the ideals that were expected to confirm a wife's position, but which in reality might open the door to a wife's destabilization, and the concomitant possibility of rivalry with a household inferior for influence with her husband. The consequences for a wife should such transpire could be ruinously dire—and the appeal of curses as a means by which to re-establish a collapsed hierarchy all the greater.

A stable household hierarchy, and a wife's elevated position within it, was supposed to be secured by the presence of marital *concordia*, or harmony between husband and wife. Scholars disagree over the degree of intimacy and warmth this ideal was meant to betoken between conjugal partners, but it is certainly suggestive of marital fondness and mutual goodwill that was manifested negatively in the absence of quarrels.[39] Achievement was wrought by actions from each partner.[40] A wife ought to exhibit proper wifely behavior,[41] including sexual fidelity, proficient household management, and *obsequium* to her husband. This last term translates flatly as "obedience," but the meaning takes its hue from the relationship it serves. Susan Treggiari notes *obsequium* in a marital relationship means more "compliance" than "obedience," while the same word in the context of a freedman-patron relationship means more "obedience" than "compliance."[42] However, the chameleon-like quality of the word ensures that expectations of marital *obsequium* could be pulled between opposite poles of agreeability and submissiveness depending upon the individuals and the relationship. For example, the ideal that a wife should shape her own interests to those of her husband has as its corollary pressure on a wife to subordinate all of her own desires to his; the sunny stipulation that a wife ought to be generally agreeable and pleasant shadows the darker expectation that a wife ought to endure her husband's habits without argument, and adopt a conciliatory attitude in the face of his anger.[43] Manifestations of wifely *obsequium* might thus converge upon those of servile *obsequium*. The line between servile and wifely *obsequium* is further obscured if the concept is considered from the point of view of the recipient, that is, as the general demeanor owed to a man by all his inferiors—wives, slaves, and children.[44] But a husband's acknowledgement of a wife's *obsequium* ought to differ from a master's acknowledgment of a slave's, or a patron's of a freedman's, and so distinguish a wife from the others. Here we come to the husband's contribution to marital *concordia*: a husband ought to reward his wife for her good behavior by treating her with due respect and honor, thereby elevating her position above his other inferiors within the larger household. A wife's position was, in short, supposed to be one of unique regard, as we can also see in Sallust's scorn of the polygamous Numidians, whose habits render no wife special and all equally cheap.[45] Marital *concordia* might then be imagined as a constant, cyclical exchange of attitude and acknowledgment on the part of each spouse, a presence that manifested itself as a stable household hierarchy, unthreatened by quarrels and divergent goals.[46] It is a bond that both parallels, and dovetails with, other relationships between disparate members of the familial hierarchy, investing those relationships too with meaning.

The echo of conjugal *concordia* in the other asymmetrical relationships within the household, however, in addition to the overlap of ideals of wifely and servile behavior, risked a confusion between wives and slaves. Indeed, wives and slaves were often collapsed in literature and rhetoric. Patricia Clark observes that the language of slavery was often used to describe a wife's duties and expected behavior toward her husband, with the point that the vocabulary was meant to be *metaphorical* and that the metaphorical nature of this language might be conveyed through elusive devices such as tone of voice.[47] William Fitzgerald outlines the fantasy of the slave as a "second self," one who anticipates a master's wishes before they have even been voiced;[48] in this sense, a good slave is the most perfect of wives. In Plautus's *Menaechmi*, a husband, angry with his wife for her inability to keep out of his affairs and to stop nagging, literally dresses his prostitute mistress up as his wife by giving her his wife's cloak, with the words "since you alone live compliant to my ways (*meis morigera moribus*)."[49] But in reality, wives were not slaves, and Richard Saller describes the symbolic markers of a wife's privileged status within the household. These included forms of address—the expectation that a wife be addressed as *domina*, for example—and also unique responsibilities, such as the *matrona*'s central role in the performance of household cult. Public festivals such as the *Matralia* and *Ancillarum Feriae* underlined the expected difference between matronly and servile sexual mores. In short, marital *concordia* and these kinds of indicators at once suppressed identification between the two categories of women, and distinguished a wife's privileged position within the household.[50]

Or at least they were supposed to. On the one hand, ideals are ideals because they are difficult to achieve; on the other it might also be suspected that these markers bolstered a necessary distinction that was not otherwise very clear, and that lack of clarity sometimes prevailed. We might note the ubiquity of the "jealous wife" in the literary sources, and observe that there are very few people of whom wives are not potentially jealous—dead wives, daughters, stepdaughters, in addition, of course, to concubines and household slaves.[51] We do not have to accept as cause the pettiness often implied by the sources to think that perhaps wives often felt insecure despite their position and the symbolic markers of its status. Pomponia's crossness at her husband's preference for his slave Statius's meal-planning skills over her own alerts us that "privileges" characteristic of status were not necessarily glamorous, and that a wife's pride in domestic proficiency was easily trespassed upon in a household with trusted slaves.[52] Tacitus's statement that Agrippina could not accept her son Nero's freedwoman lover as a rival (*aemula*) hints that status alone might not be the issue, but rather the degree of influence over, or favor with, the person through whom a woman's authority was derived.[53] Collapse of the household hierarchy therefore threatened, a wife's command of respect flagged, and rivalry between a wife and a household slave loomed, when the positive acknowledgment expected of a husband was manifested instead by the same man, this time as master, toward a slave. Such a situation menaced particularly when the "good slave" was also, like the wife, a lover. Though sexual jealousy might be aroused, we must doubt it as a wife's sole motivation for considering a slave a foe, despite the insinuations of the sources.[54] To do so would require that we posit a different set of social values for Roman men and for Roman women regarding the use of slaves. However, if a husband's relationship with a slave progressed beyond the merely sexual into one of affective reciprocity, it risked mimicking the exchanges between husband and wife and confusing which was the woman to whom wifely privilege, favor, and credibility ought to adhere.

Sexual relations were an expectation of marital *concordia*. Their lack was a harbinger of discord, and a situation likely to become a topic of conversation among the household, or even possibly further afield. For example, Suetonius states knowingly that the end of Tiberius and Julia's marital *concordia* was first signaled by his absence from her bed.[55] Sexual intimacy promoted emotional intimacy too, which ideally extended to the sharing of secrets and counsel. Good wives were to keep no secrets from their husbands, and good husbands found value in a wife's advice.[56] We see both the expectation of sharing thoughts and sexual relations as the avenue in the excuse offered for Augustus's habit of sleeping with married women: he was merely learning what his adversaries, their husbands, were up to.[57] A husband's sexual relationship with a slave was therefore most likely the beginning, not the end point, of a situation of wife-slave rivalry within the household. Challenges existed within the behaviors that sexual relations could foster between the couple—intimacy, trust, sharing of secrets and advice, themselves the markers of a wife's privileged position. It is evident that an attitude of increased confidence adopted by a slave in response to a master's favor could be seen as offensive even to other members of the family—Plutarch, for instance, reports Cato's son's distaste for the way the widower Cato's servile concubine made her way "rather too boldly (*thrasyteron*)" to Cato's bedchamber. The confidence of a slave favored by a husband might easily be interpreted as disrespect by a wife, and this attitude on the part of one whose identity demanded the opposite was a deliberate humiliation. Furthermore, the unchecked self-assurance of one slave, if noticed by the rest of the household, could signal to them a chink in the hierarchy and so risked diminishing the wife's authority over them too. This is no doubt what Salvian, a Christian source, means when he observes that a husband, who has taken up with the slave girls, has undermined his wife's authority in the household.[58] But these behaviors were pregnant with yet further threats.

If it can be accepted that a wife might perceive a slave, and particularly a favored slave woman, as a rival, we must also address the possibility that a slave woman might actively participate in this rivalry too. It must be said that slaves had no choice in the participation in sexual relations with a master. But a master's favor was a critical factor in the quality of a slave's life, in a slave's chances for manumission, and even in life as a freed person.[59] Slaves might court it. Shows of affection, respect, and loyalty might gain it. The laments of masters, disabused of their previous belief that the regard of their slaves was genuine, pepper our sources. A telling example is the curse laid upon a certain Acte on a Roman tombstone:

> Here are inscribed the eternal marks of shame of Acte, a freedwoman, a treacherous, tricky, hard-hearted poisoner . . . Manumitted for free, she went off with an adulterer, cheated her patron and took away his slaves, a girl and a boy, as he lay in bed, leaving him an old, lonely, despoiled man, broken-hearted. And the same curse (is laid upon) Hymnus and those who went away with Zosimus.[60]

Acte, it seems, had once been thought a trusted, loyal, and loving slave—and evidently also one who had the makings of a good wife. There is no suggestion that Acte unseated a wife in this inscription, and it is possible that Acte had never expressed the fondness that the disappointed husband-patron now thought she had pretended. But this example shows that intimate relations with a master could translate into real benefits for a slave—and we must suspect that some slaves, even slaves of married husbands, capitalized on this possibility.[61]

Competition is an inherent characteristic of hierarchies in which advancement is possible. As we have seen in the discussion of the competitive contexts that produced curse tablets, a competitor might identify the reduction of a rival as an avenue to success. Thus, a slave woman fostering relations with her master, even if she did not initiate them, might well perceive the value in increasing her own worth at the expense of the wife's. Intimacy and attendant favor might be promoted through the sharing of secrets; these secretive confidences might consist of reports on the wife's activities, otherwise unknown to her husband.[62] This strategy had the two-fold advantage of demonstrating the questionable loyalty of the wife and her unworthiness as the keeper of secrets, while presenting the contrasting loyalty and worthiness of the slave as their revealer. This very situation was in fact enshrined in a public matron's festival, the Matralia, celebrated annually on June 11 in honor of Mater Matuta. "Why is it that it is forbidden to slave women to set foot in the shrine of Matuta, and why do the women bring in one slave woman only and slap her on the head and beat her?" Plutarch asks.[63] Ovid provides the response. Ino, whose myth formed the basis of the ritual for Matuta queried by Plutarch, was in the habit of secretly supplying farmers with seed; this was revealed to Ino's husband by her slave girl, his lover. Ovid addresses Ino, "you yourself indeed denied it, but rumour affirmed it."[64] The commemoration of this mythological tale by matrons collectively suggests a sense of empathetic affinity was thought to exist between Ino and matrons in general from common experience.[65] Artemidorus provides non-mythological evidence of the possibility of such a chain of events in his book on dream interpretation. In his collection of significant dreams for the prognostication of dreams for future clients, culled from all over the Mediterranean, including Rome and Italy, he includes the following:

> A woman dreamt that a handmaid in her service borrowed her portrait, which had been drawn on a tablet, and also her clothes, since she intended to participate in a procession. Soon afterwards, the handmaid destroyed the woman's marriage by her slander and caused her injuries and abuse.[66]

Particularly noteworthy is the implication in the details of the dream that the slave girl not only removed the wife, but even appropriated her position in terms of privilege, if not in name.

Also important is the role widespread gossip played in the myth of Ino, and is implied to have played in the unseating of Artemidorus's unhappy dreamer. A wife whose credibility with her husband was waning in inverse proportion to the waxing of a slave's was in a very precarious position. Clark identifies the vulnerability of a wife who did not enjoy the alliance or protection of a household superior to household slaves' gossip;[67] worse, gossip need not stop at the garden gate—a wife might discover her purportedly dirty laundry hung out for the general viewing of the neighborhood. Slaves, as the constant observers of the lives of the free members of the household, were potential repositories of scandalous information, pipelines through which a household's secrets and troubles might be betrayed.[68] Another passage in Artemidorus's book reveals a chilling prospect, one he implies was commonly realized: dreams of a swollen tongue signify "often [that] the dreamer's wife has been slanderously accused of being an adulteress."[69] Gossip of this sort was expected to cause antipathy between husband and wife—note, for example, that dreams of beating one's wife point her out as a bona fide adulteress[70]—and reduced a woman's reputation to that of a common whore with its suggestion that she embraced not the virtue of matronly chastity, but the unbridled and indiscriminant lustful vices ascribed to slaves. Indeed, this dichotomy was celebrated in its own religious festival, the *Ancillarum Feriae*, on July 7, mentioned above, in commemoration of a time in early Roman history when the willing promiscuity of female slaves saved the chastity of Roman women from assault.[71] But a wife who was willing to entertain other men was a traitor.[72] If reports were believed, her divorce would inevitably follow, sealing her disgrace, and any prospects for another marriage were ruined. In the unlikely event that bad reputation was not enough to keep suitors at bay, law would crush her prospects; according to the jurist Modestinus, "women accused of adultery cannot marry during the lifetime of their husbands, even before conviction."[73]

In sum, then, wives might well find themselves bereft of the markers of their identity, cheated of the respect and protection their position was supposed to afford. To make things more difficult, the real identity problems a wife might be experiencing were obscured by the fact that she retained her social position—she *was* still the wife—and that her position retained all the social symbols of her status identified by Saller. She might therefore have had difficulty in explaining precisely *how* or *why* she felt that she was not receiving proper respect, or why another was receiving too much—a problem presented by the murky overlap of ideals of wifely and servile behavior, and also by the fact that insult can conceal itself in solicitous clothing, allowing it to lurk below the radar of proof.[74] Open avenues of redress were lacking. Non-adulterous relationships in and of themselves were not considered cause for grievance in either law or social opinion. Indeed, ideals of wifely behavior encouraged supreme *obsequium* in situations of a husband's infidelity.

Augustine's mother Monica never started a jealous quarrel with philandering Patricius. So far from being jealous of Scipio Africanus's slave lover was Tertia Aemilia that she willingly freed the woman after her husband's death. Livia, an exemplar's exemplar, was reputed to have taken no notice of Augustus's peccadilloes, and even to have procured lovers for him.[75] The wife who valued *concordia* above her own concerns earned praise, and those who voiced concerns were interpreted as selfish grousers, threatened *concordia*, and earned opprobrium.

Yet to do nothing risked much; a wife might find herself open to the insubordination or gossip of the household, and possibly even to the slander of the neighborhood. But complaints to a husband about his or others' behavior might earn censure for bringing discord to the marriage, and possibly even bring about divorce; the philandering emperor Augustus, for example, claimed that he set Scribonia aside because he could no longer endure her waspish ways.[76] Sympathetic support from family and friends might be hard to find; Plutarch advises brides to consider their husbands' taking of servile lovers as a sign of respect for themselves (as their husbands will not trouble them with unseemly behavior), while Augustine, in response to a plea for advice from a woman whose husband has taken a lover, chastises her for driving him to the arms of another woman by being insufficiently compliant to his wishes.[77] Even if a wife could convince her family of misuse by her husband, her family might encourage her to soldier on.[78] Leaving the marriage, a legal possibility, exposed a woman to gossipy suspicions that she had been adulterous, and was leaving her husband in favor of a lover;[79] it furthermore meant leaving any children behind with their father, and abandoning them to the specter of a chilly stepmother.[80]

It is important to recognize that even the empathetic support of other women might be similarly lacking to individual troubled wives, despite the communal celebrations of the Matralia. Plutarch gives indirect evidence that support *might* be offered in his specific instructions to wives to deem meddlers and troublemakers those who point out a husband's abuses. But not all women disagreed with Plutarch's advice. Augustine, for example, reports his virtuous mother offering similar instruction to women, though perhaps for slightly different reasons.[81] Leaving aside questions of justice, the ideal of wifely uncomplaining compliance was an avenue by which conflict might be minimized or avoided, and was thus a tactic for women to gain some measure of control in their relationships. Augustine comments that those who did not follow his mother's strategy (*institutum suum*) to avoid making demands on their husbands were "kept under and abused" (*subiectae vexabantur*). Indeed, Livia's affability is said to have made her "master over Augustus" (*tou Augustou katekratēsen*). In this light, to its adherents the wifely ideal offered not subjection, but freedom from quarrel and abuse; complaints against a husband were counterproductive, and their makers might therefore be viewed as self-destructive lost cases.[82]

In short, a wife whose status was being undermined might well find herself in a state of both personal crisis and social isolation. Self-preservation might call for extreme measures—to be visited upon the rival. Artemidorus, for example, mentions a slave girl who had "provoked the jealous wrath of her mistress and suffered countless evils."[83] Her tragic dreams included visions of Andromache, only one of the many slave women abused by their mistresses in the literary sources. At this point it is useful to address the charge often laid against wives, to the effect that they punished the household slaves too harshly. Clark has suggested that this might be understood as the result of misplaced anger over tensions arising from the strained relations between husband and wife.[84] It might equally have been the case that wives sought to conceal the vulnerability of their position and establish their superiority within the household by exercising the usual markers of social difference: physical violence, abusive language, ridicule.[85] As discussed above, abuse of a slave girl by matrons figured as a central act of the Matralia, a festival meant to distinguish between them.[86] On an individual level, however, similar behavior within a household brought discord, and with it censure. A wife in an intractable and desperate situation might therefore choose a different avenue to security within the household. Curses to hinder or do away with a household rival, such as those described above, offered the advantage of being undertaken in secret. The impression of ideal behavior was thus maintained, and accusations of disrupting the household's harmony were deflected, while the promise of achievement of a very necessary goal was offered: the re-establishment of position by removing the perceived problem-maker(s)—rivals for privilege, spreaders of undermining gossip. In this sense, we must understand the separation curses less as attempts to protect relationships than as attempts to protect the practitioners within relationships. It is a fine distinction, but one that places our focus where it ought to be: on the practitioner's real vulnerability, and on her dependence upon a man as the mediator of her position, not on the man himself as the desired goal.

It cannot be said how often a woman would have found herself in a situation of rivalry with a slave woman. It cannot even be said how many married couples had slaves or freedmen attached to their households in the first place. We also cannot know how often curse tablets, or their vocalized counterparts, or their relatives—amulets and potions—were sought out by the wives who did find themselves in the dire straits of an identity crisis due to circumstances beyond their control. The literary sources certainly dwell upon women's physical violence against slaves, but are mostly silent about women's magical aggression against these same people. This lack of comment, however, is probably more a function of the relative secrecy in which curses were undertaken in comparison with the obviousness of physical abuse, in addition to the fact that women's cursing and poisoning really only drew men's attention when they imagined themselves to be the target.[87] We should furthermore not expect mainstream sources that are uninterested in detailing women's real problems to be interested in providing much information about genuine attempts to remedy them. But hints do survive, not only in off-hand references in literature to curses that aimed to silence hostile tongues and gossip,[88] but also in the more prosaic sources of information about the lives of ordinary people. There is, for example, the suggestively terse horoscope recorded in Vettius Valens's second century collection:

> In the same year he freed (his) concubines because Jupiter in the (6th) locus of slaves took over from Venus. In the 46th year he had troubles and reverses in affairs of property and because of female persons, quarrels, and the death of two concubines; for the transfer (of power) was from Venus to Saturn in the (7th) locus of marriage and from sun to Mars and Jupiter.[89]

It of course cannot be said for certain that an anxious wife was at the bottom of the quarrels or deaths mentioned here. But when the evidence of curse tablets is set within a web of different considerations—ideals of wifely behavior, social consequences of failing to exhibit them, and their location in the territory of household hierarchy, itself largely unregulated by law—we must conclude three things: first, women might experience some very real and intractable difficulties in marriage; second, the need to dig deeply into our sources to find information about wives' real problems and their remedies does not point to the nonexistence of the difficulties, but rather to the lack of recognition they earned; and finally, and as a consequence, that curses may well have offered a final and necessary resort to self-help for some, perhaps many, women.

Women and Magic

In conclusion, then, it is worth addressing the stereotype that associated women with magical activity in a mutually denigrating relationship in Greek and Roman antiquity. Modern scholars have tended to adopt one of three approaches to the literary stereotype of "women's magic," usually presented as the malevolent actions of a jealous, lust-crazed, or power-hungry female. At the risk of oversimplification, the first (and most traditional) approach has been to accept descriptions of motives and practices as accurate; the second has been to treat such descriptions as groundless male fantasy, aimed at the denigration of women as irrational, selfish, and wanton; the third has been to identify magic as a subjective label that tended to alight on women's challenges, or perceived challenges, to established hierarchies.[90] But if "magic" were to be defined as secretive attempts to direct destructive unearthly powers against another, attempts that were recognized as illegal acts even by the practitioners themselves, we must conclude that the kinds of curses considered here qualify as "real" magical activity by women. Furthermore, as they are directed at social and legal inferiors—slave women, not elite men—the motivations and contexts of these curse tablets do not jibe well with either the stereotype or its various interpretations. Instead, women's "real magic" is best understood as the product of real, but unrecognized, problems women might face—and so also, and more importantly, as indication of the same.

Thus, if "women's magic" is to be located anywhere, the curse tablets discussed here and their context suggest it ought to be placed at the intersection of two dynamics. The first is the general denial of "real" problems to anyone but wealthy, free Roman men. If authority was the reward of the ability to shoulder responsibility and the problems that came with it, then the inverse of this relationship is that those with little authority have fewer problems, and none of consequence.[91] Thus the poor have fewer problems than the rich,[92] slaves have fewer problems than the free,[93] women have fewer problems than men,[94] even female slaves have fewer problems than male slaves.[95] Furthermore, any problems that might be suspected as legitimately women's tended to be reinterpreted in antiquity as men's. For example, a wife's barrenness was a husband's concern, as it thrust upon him the difficult choice of divorce or no progeny, while a woman's (purported) adultery caused a husband untold grief and embarrassment.[96] Even a wife's bruised face might be recast as a husband's woe—her behavior forced him to expose his own foible, lack of self-control.[97] It is a truism that a problem must be recognized before it can be dealt with. The evidence of the curse tablets gives indication of just one of possibly many problems experienced by women that went unrecognized because they developed in hierarchies that were negatively unstable for women alone.

The stereotypes that facilitated the denigration of women's attempts to deal with unrecognized problems as selfish and petty form the second dynamic. Distress over a situation that was denied the status of a real problem rendered a woman a tiresome complainer; attempts to deal with an unrecognized problem were the excessive acts of a selfish glutton for undeserved power. Distortion in the popular imagination of the contexts and motives of women's use of magical forms ensured that the real contexts of their use would never be explored.[98] Misrepresentation of women's magic took the form not only of hags performing erotic magic by moonlight to win young lovers, but also of styling the selfish magical actions of men as "womanly." The best example occurs in a well-known passage by Tacitus, in which Germanicus, the nephew and heir of the emperor Tiberius, bemoans his own murder by the "womanly treachery" (*muliebris fraus*) of Piso, his political nemesis. At first glance, *muliebris* strikes as a specific reference to the hand Plancina was suspected to have lent, while *fraus*, the specific agent of death, is of course the confused array of poisons and curse tablets that Piso had supposedly procured to usher Germanicus out of life.[99] But the meaning of "womanly treachery" is greater than the sum of its parts. It is surely to be understood as a package that comprises both means and context, and so highlights the perversity of the circumstances of Germanicus's death. A great leader, defender, and future hope of the Roman community has been sacrificed to the petty jealousies of an inferior being through a sideways attack: this, then, is *muliebris fraus*, and cursing, poisoning, "magic," is to be understood as merely an exponent of a broader negative concept of "womanish" behavior as selfish, destructive, and unsporting.[100]

In short, the collision of these two dynamics—failure to recognize women's difficulties and the stereotype that ultimately served to portray as individual failings the real problems that some, and perhaps many, women might experience as inevitable outcomes of systemic structures—precipitated women's use of magic. Abusive behavior, real or magical, need not be admired to encourage sensitivity to the desperate situations that may have given rise to it. Indeed, refusal to recognize women's less laudable behavior or failure to investigate its contexts lands us in precisely the same place as does embracing unquestioningly negative stereotypes of women's "natural" proclivity to irrationality, jealousy, excessive violence, pettiness, and selfishness—without avenues of inquiry by which to try to understand the real experiences of real women.

Notes

1. Verg., *Aen* 4.360.
2. In the following *DT* = Auguste Audollent, *Defixionum Tabellae* (1904. Reprint, Frankfurt: Minerva, 1967); tablet numbers rather than page numbers are provided.
3. Curse tablets have generally been approached through the lens of language rather than society. See David R. Jordan, "A Survey of Greek *Defixiones* Not Included in the Special Corpora," *GRBS* 26 (1985): 152, for rationale; cf. Hendrik S. Versnel, "Beyond Cursing: The Appeal to Justice in Judicial Prayers," in *Magika Hiera: Ancient Greek Magic and Religion*, ed. Christopher A. Faraone and Dirk Obbink (New York: Oxford University Press, 1991), 90, where the consideration of Greek and Latin tablets is encouraged. Christopher A. Faraone, *Ancient Greek Love Magic* (Cambridge, MA: Harvard University Press, 1999), 146–60, discusses women's use of "male" erotic magic, including a form of curse tablet. Emmanuel Voutiras, *Dionysophontos Gamoi* (Amsterdam: J.C. Gieben, 1998) publishes and contextualizes a Greek curse tablet by a woman seeking to ensure her marriage to a particular man. Elizabeth Pollard, "Magic Accusations against Women in the Greco-Roman World from the First through the Fifth Centuries CE," (PhD diss., University of Pennsylvania, 2001) discusses women's use of curse tablets against thieves.
4. Jordan, "Survey," 152; see David R. Jordan, "New Greek Curse Tablets (1985–2000)," *GRBS* 41 (2000): 5–6 for a more precise definition of *defixio*. I shall use the looser term "curse tablet" to refer to curse formulas inscribed on tablets. John

Gager, *Curse Tablets and Binding Spells from the Ancient World* (New York: Oxford University Press, 1992), 3–41, offers an excellent introductory discussion of curse tablets in general. William Brashear, "The Greek Magical Papyri: An Introduction and Survey; Annotated Bibliography (1928–1994)," *ANRW* II 18.5: 3380–684, at (1995): 3443–44 n. 340, provides references to the major collections of curse tablets and seminal discussions; to his list Jordan, "New Greek Curse Tablets," should be added.

5. Christopher A. Faraone, "The Agonistic Context of Early Greek Binding Spells," in Faraone and Obbink, *Magika Hiera*, 5–11, describes the usual formulas on Greek tablets. See also Daniel Ogden, "Binding Spells: Curse Tablets and Voodoo Dolls in the Greek and Roman Worlds," in *Witchcraft and Magic in Europe: Ancient Greece and Rome*, ed. Bengt Ankarloo and Stuart Clark (Philadelphia: University of Pennsylvania Press, 1999), 1–90. Note that Latin tablets often adhere less precisely to prescribed formulas.
6. Faraone, "Context," 4–10; the opinion that this holds true also for Roman tablets is found in Fritz Graf, *Magic in the Ancient World* (Cambridge, MA: Harvard University Press, 1999), 145–46.
7. William Sherwood Fox, *The Johns Hopkins* Tabellae Defixionum (Baltimore: Johns Hopkins University Press, 1912): *male perdat, male exseat, male disperdat.* Note also as examples the tablets discussed by Heikki Solin, "Analecta Epigraphica LXVII–LXXVIII," *Arctos* 15 (1981): 121 and *"Eine Fluchtafel aus Cremon," Arctos* 21 (1987): 130–31, and Maurice Besnier, "Récents travaux sur les defixionum tabellae latines, 1904–1914," *RevPhil* 44 (1920): 6 no. 3.
8. Gager, *Curse Tablets*, 42–174, provides examples and discussion of curse tablets from the major competitive categories. Not all curse tablets fall neatly under these headings; see, e.g., Versnel, "Beyond Cursing," esp. 68 on "prayers for justice"; John Winkler, "The Constraints of Eros," in Faraone and Obbink, *Magika Hiera*, 214–43, and Faraone, *Ancient Greek Love Magic*, 41–95 on spells of erotic attraction.
9. Josep Corell, "Drei *Defixionum Tabellae* aus Sagunt (Valencia)," *ZPE* 101 (1994): 280–6. Cf. Gabriella Bevilacqua, "Un incantesimo per odio in una defixio di Roma," *ZPE* 117 (1997): 291–93, and *DT* no. 139 for other clear separation curses from the Roman west. *DT* no. 135, a tablet that curses a woman on one side and a man on the other, is less certain, as is *DT* no. 138, *DT* no. 191, and *AE* (1907) 30, no. 99, and the tablet published by Josep Corell, "*Defixionis Tabella* aus Carmona (Sevilla)," *ZPE* 95 (1993): 261–68. Faraone, "Context," 13 n. 59, gives reference to separation curses from the Greek east; Gager, *Curse Tablets*, 85–92, provides translations of some of these.
10. *AE* (1950) 41, no. 112; Rudolf Egger, "Liebeszauber." *JÖAI* (1948): 112–20; Emilio Garcia-Ruiz, "Estudio linguistico de las *defixiones* Latinas no incluidas en el corpus de Audollent," *Emeritas* 35 (1967): 56 no. 2. Cf. *DT* no. 100, for another tablet from first century CE Germany that seems to emerge from a similar situation.

11. There have been various editions; see *CIL* 4.925, Attilio Degrassi, *Inscriptiones Latinae Liberae Rei Publicae* (Florence: La Nuova Italia, 1963), 322–23, and Garcia-Ruiz, "Estudio linguistico," 56 no. 14.
12. Ned Nabers, "Lead Tabellae from Morgantina," *AJA* 70 (1966): 67–68, and "Ten Lead Tabellae from Morgantina," *AJA* 83 (1979): 463–64; Margherita Guarducci, *Epigrafica Greca IV: epigrafi sacre pagane e cristiane* (Rome: Instituo Poligrafico dello Stato, 1978), 250–51; Faraone, "Context," 18–19; Jaime Curbera, "Venusta and Her Owner in Four Curse Tablets from Morgantina," *ZPE* 110 (1996): 295–97.
13. For this tablet, see *DT* no. 139, *CIL* 1.818 and 6.140.
14. *DT* no. 138; *CIL* 1.819 and 6.141.
15. Heikki Solin, *Eine neue Fluchtafel aus Ostia* (Commentationes Humanarum Literarum Societas Scientiarum Fennica 42.3; Helsinki: Helsingfors, 1968), 27 no. 22.
16. *DT* no. 190; *CIL* 10.8249.
17. Franjo Barišić, "Une *defixionis tabella* grecque de Progar en Srem," *Archaeologia Iugoslavica* 11 (1970): 23–28.
18. *DT* no. 196.
19. *CIL* 4.9252; Solin, *Eine neue Fluchtafel*, 30 no. 40; Jordan, "Survey," 181.
20. Jordan, "Survey," 178 no. 114; Gager, *Curse Tablets*, 214–15 no. 116; Versnel, "Beyond Cursing," 64–65 suggests that this is perhaps best understood as a revenge curse rather than a pre-emptive strike. It is possible that the curse against Zimia ought to be understood in the same way.
21. On the confusion between curses, curse tablets, and poisons, see, e.g., Cic., *Brut.* 217, *Or. Brut.* 129; Tac., *Ann.* 2.69–73; Gager, *Curse Tablets*, 258 no. 156; Ramsay MacMullen, *Enemies of the Roman Order* (Cambridge, MA: Harvard University Press, 1966), 124–25; Hendrik S. Versnel, "*Kolasai tous hēmas toioutous hēdeōs blepontes* 'Punish Those Who Rejoice in Our Misery': On Curse Texts and *Schadenfreude*," in *The World of Ancient Magic: Papers from the First International Samson Eitrem Seminar at the Norwegian Institute at Athens, 4–8 May 1997* (Papers from the Norwegian Institute at Athens 4), ed. David. R. Jordan, Hugo Montgomery, and Einar Thomassen (Bergen: Paul Åströms Förlag, 1999), 133; Naomi Janowitz, *Magic in the Roman World* (London: Routledge, 2001), 12; James Rives, "Magic in Roman Law: the Reconstruction of a Crime," *CA* 22 (2003): 313–39 discusses definitions and Roman law, while classic and recent bibliography is given in "Magic in the XII Tables Revisited." *CQ* 52 (2002): 270 nn. 3 and 4. Laws against cursing/poisoning are recounted by Paulus, *Sent.* 5.23.15–18, and Modestinus, at *Dig.* 48.8.11.13. Marcianus at *Dig.* 48.8.20.3, differentiates between potions for good and potions for harm.
22. E.g., *CIL*, 8.2756; Catull., 7.9–12; Ov., *Am.* 3.7.27–30, and *Met.*, 7.161; Plin., *HN* 28.19.
23. Plin., *HN* 37.164 and 182.
24. Cf. Faraone, *Ancient Greek Love Magic*, 41–95, on the use of "transitory violence" in magic to achieve a stable relationship.

25. Faraone, "Context," is the locus classicus for this discussion; see also Versnel, "*Kolasai*," for the attainment of honor and avoidance of shame as driving forces.
26. E.g., Faraone, "Context," 17–20; cf. Versnel, "Beyond Cursing," 62–63.
27. This is particularly true for women's use of poisons/curses. Note, e.g., Tacitus' identification of the poisoning/cursing of Germanicus at *Ann.* 2.71 as "womanly deceit" (*muliebris fraus*), discussed below; Prop., *Elegies* 2.31/32.27, praises a woman for not having sullied her reputation by poisoning (*non tua deprenso damnast fama veneno*). See Versnel, "Beyond Cursing," 76, for discussion of women laboring under slanderous suspicions of misdeed in this regard; cf. also Gager, *Curse Tablets*, 246–48, and Faraone, *Ancient Greek Love Magic*, 114. Matthew Dickie, *Magic and Magicians in the Greco-Roman World* (New York: Routledge, 2001), 133–34 discusses *venefica* as a term of abuse. Ulp., *On the Edict* 33, (*Dig.* 48.20.3) notes that a woman's dowry would be confiscated if she were convicted of poisoning. For legitimate (i.e., political) uses of curses, see, e.g., Herman Dessau, ed., *Inscriptiones Latinae Selectae*, vol. 1 (Chicago: Ares, 1979), no. 190; René Cagat, ed., *Inscriptiones Graecae ad Res Romanas Pertinentes*, vol. 3 (Chicago: Ares, 1975), no. 137; Diod. Sic., *Library of History*, 37.11; Livy, *History of Rome*, 5.41.3, 8.9.4–8.10.14, 9.10.3, 10.28.14–18; and Macrob., *Sat.*, 3.9.
28. E.g., Dickie, *Magic and Magicians*, 85–87, 104–6; Faraone, *Ancient Greek Love Magic*, 150–60 discusses courtesans' use of other kinds of magic, i.e., *agōgē* spells to attract lovers or *philia* magic if in a monogamous relationship.
29. Versnel, "Beyond Cursing," 68, and see *DT* no. 198 for an example; cf. the fullness of the explanation for the curse which curse laid upon the freedwoman Acte in a tombstone inscription (Franz Buecheler, *Carmina Latina Epigraphica* [Leipzig: Teubner, 1895], 95), discussed below.
30. Cf. Faraone, *Ancient Greek Love Magic*, 96–131, for discussion of devices (amulets, lotions, potions) used for engendering fond feelings for a practitioner in a victim.
31. E.g., Dickie, *Magic and Magicians*, 175–92.
32. Susan Treggiari, *Roman Marriage* (Oxford: Clarendon Press, 1991), 262–319, discusses laws and perceptions surrounding Roman adultery. It is possible that not all women with adulterous husbands wished to dissolve their marriages by availing themselves of the laws at their disposal; perhaps we should understand some curse tablets against free women as the attempts of those wives who wished to preserve them. Note, e.g., a tablet from Britain: "Tacita, hereby accursed, is labelled old like putrid gore" (trans. R.P. Wright); see Robin G. Collingwood and M. V. Taylor, "Roman Britain in 1930," *JRS* 21 (1931): 248, and R. P. Wright, "Roman Britain in 1951," *JRS* 42 (1952): 103. Consider also a tablet from North Africa that curses a certain Saturnina and her reproductive abilities, published by Paul Roesch, "Une tablette de malédiction de Tébessa," *Bulletin d'archéologie algérienne* 2 (1966–1967): 231–37.
33. See Patricia Clark, "Women, Slaves, and the Hierarchies of Domestic Violence: The Family of St. Augustine," in *Women and Slaves in Greco-Roman Culture:*

Differential Equations, ed. Sheila Murnaghan and Sandra R. Joshel (London: Routledge, 1998), 120–21, for the ideal of the self-controlled *paterfamilias*. For the suggestion of shame, see, e.g., Val. Max., *Memorable Doings and Sayings*, 6.7.1, and Quint., *Inst.* 5.11.34–35. This last is quoted and discussed by Keith Bradley, *Slavery and Society at Rome* (Cambridge: Cambridge University Press, 1994), 28, who also notes (49) that "the owner's sexual access to slaves was regarded as conventional." Artem., *Oneirocritica*, 3.30, recounts dreams that indicate the dreamer will fall in love with a slave girl; cf. also Sen., *Ben.*1.9.4.

34. Contrast the recognition that adultery as defined by law was an injury to a wife in Sen., *Ep.* 94.26. Cf. Treggiari, *Roman Marriage*, 313 and n. 287, however, for ancient advice to wives to pretend not to notice.
35. See, e.g., Judith Evans Grubbs, *Women and the Law in the Roman Empire* (London: Routledge, 2002) with bibliography.
36. Tac., *Ann.* 13.26, describes complaints that lack of respect (*inreverentia*) for patrons was running roughshod among freedmen, and recounts the argument that ungrateful freedmen ought to be re-enslaved; at *Ann.* 14.39, Tacitus bemoans the obedience shown by a Roman general and army to a freedman of Nero.
37. This description assumes the household was not multi-generational, and that the husband was thus the *paterfamilias*. On the probability of this scenario, see Richard Saller, *Patriarchy, Property and Death in the Roman Family* (Cambridge: Cambridge University Press, 1994). A husband's mother might still be a presence; in this situation, her approval of a wife was also necessary for a wife's authority within the household to stand firm. See Clark, "Women," 115–16.
38. E.g., Dio Cass., *Roman History*, 59.26.9.
39. Contrast, e.g., Keith Bradley, *Discovering the Roman Family* (Oxford: Oxford University Press, 1991), 6–8, 128, Suzanne Dixon, *The Roman Family* (Baltimore: Johns Hopkins University Press, 1991), 83–90, and Treggiari, *Roman Marriage*, 245–51.
40. Treggiari, *Roman Marriage*, 245–51; Clark, "Women," esp. 116–17.
41. Emily Hemelrijk, "Women's Demonstrations in Republican Rome," in *Sexual Asymmetry: Studies in Ancient Society*, ed. Josine Blok and Peter Mason (Amsterdam: J. C. Gleben, 1987), 217; Susan Fischler, "Social Stereotypes and Historical Analysis: The Case of the Imperial Women at Rome," in *Women in Ancient Societies*, ed. Léonie J. Archer, Susan Fischler, Maria Wyke (London: Routledge, 1994), 117; and Moses Finley, "The Silent Women of Rome," in *Sexuality and Gender in the Classical World: Readings and Sources*, ed. L. McClure (Oxford: Blackwell, 2002), 148, note that the ideals of women's behavior did not change over the course of Roman history.
42. Treggiari, *Roman Marriage*, 238–41.
43. On optimistic readings of wifely *obsequium*, see Treggiari, *Roman Marriage*, 229–30, 238–40, 255–57; for the more pessimistic realizations of the same, see Clark, "Women," passim. Cf. Artem., *Oneirocritica*, 2.32, who praises the wife who "gives ground" in conflict. Note also Plut., *Mor.*, 139 F, 140 C, 141 A and F; the Sabine

women set the standard at Livy, *History*, 1.13, and Anna has the proper wifely attitude at Verg., *Aen.*, 4.423. Note that the otherwise virtuous Aemilia (Val. Max., *Memorable*, 6.7.1) is allowed to be peevish at Livy, *History*, 38.57.7. Contrast Sen., *Ben.* 4.27.5 for a rare remark about men who are difficult to live with.

44. E.g., Artem., *Oneirocritica*, 1.24.
45. Sall., *Iug.* 80.6–7. See Treggiari, *Roman Marriage*, 250, who also cites Tac., *Germ.*, 18.1.
46. Clark, "Women," 109, describes this ideal configuration as one at whose center are the husband and wife, "bound by mutual ties of marital affection . . . [with] children, dependents, freedmen and freedwomen, and assorted household slaves . . . envisaged as ranging outward from this centre in concentric spheres."
47. Clark, "Women,"115–16, 118–19. Note that the parallels might manifest themselves in other ways too: unfaithful concubines might be charged with adultery by their married lovers according to Roman law, e.g., *Digest of Justinian*, 48.5.14; see Treggiari, *Roman Marriage*, 280. Faraone, *Ancient Greek Love Magic*, 157, remarks upon the use of wifely *philia*-producing magic by mistresses and prostitutes in stable relationships.
48. William Fitzgerald, *Slavery and the Roman Literary Imagination* (Cambridge: Cambridge University Press, 2000), 13–31.
49. Plaut., *Men.*, 102; 114–18, describes the wife's habits. Note that the wife's father blames her for the whole state of affairs at lines 787: "how many times have I told you to be compliant?" *quotiens monstravi tibi vero ut morem geras?* See Treggiari, *Roman Marriage*, 229–230 for *morigera* in comedy as the forerunner of *obsequium* as an ideal of wifely behavior.
50. Richard Saller, "Symbols of Gender and Status Hierarchies in the Roman Household," in Murnaghan and Joshel, *Women and Slaves in Greco-Roman Culture: Differential Equations*, ed. S.R. Joshel and S. Murnaghan (London and New York: Routledge, 1998), 85–91; Hemelrijk, "Women's Demonstrations," esp. 222–24, also remarks upon the lack of "sisterhood" among women of different statuses.
51. E.g., Prop., *Elegies*, 4.11.89–90 (dead wife); Philostr., *VA*, 1.10.2 (daughter); Plut., *Cic.*, 41.7 (stepdaughter); Tac., *Ann.* 13.12–13 (daughter-in-law); Plut., *Mor.*, 144 C (cf. 140 B, 144 A), Artem., *Oneirocritica*, 4.59, Juv., *Sat.*, 6.475 (slave girls); Petron., *Sat.*, 69 (slave boy); see Apul., *Met.*, 5.30 for mistresses as "torture" (*angor*) for wives.
52. Cic., *Att.*, 5.1.3–4. Treggiari, *Roman Marriage*, 243–4, cites epitaphs bearing witness to the ideal of wifely domesticity. Cf. J. E. Hulett Jr., "Social Role and Personal Security in Mormon Polygamy," *American Journal of Sociology* 45 (1940): 547, reporting upon the dynamics within polygamous Mormon households: children report mothers in tears when their fathers assigned menial domestic chores to a different wife, because "in polygamy these duties were regarded as prerogatives of symbolic status about as often as they were regarded as onerous and thankless tasks, and often were cherished as such." Cf. also Jessie Embry, "The Effects of Polygamy on

Mormon Wives," *Frontiers: A Journal of Women's Studies* 7 (1984): 59, for competitiveness between wives in polygamous unions over status markers.

53. Tac., *Ann.*, 13.12–13; cf. also Plut., *Mor.*, 143 A–B, and *SB* 3.6264, a second-century CE letter from a mother to a son, blaming her daughter-in-law for turning him against her. Translated with commentary in Roger Bagnall and Raffaelle Cribiore, *Women's Letters from Ancient Egypt* (Ann Arbor: University of Michigan Press, 2006), 282.
54. Cf. Graf, *Magic in the Ancient World*, 159, who only rarely allows jealousy as the motivation for a curse tablet; separation spells are not among the few. For sexual jealousy being the main motivation, see, e.g., Petron., *Sat.*, 69, Artem., *Oneirocritica*, 4.59, Juv., *Sat.*, 6.475–76.
55. Suet., *Tib.*, 7.3
56. See Treggiari, *Roman Marriage*, 238, 243–45, 253–56, for discussion, and for tombstone avowals of the value of a wife as good counselor; cf. also Artem., *Oneirocritica*, 3.37, for dreams of whetstones signifying wives, as sharpening aids for tasks at hand. Augustus is said to have cooled toward Maecenas after the latter told his wife about Murena's conspiracy (Suet., *Aug.*, 66). The sharing of secrets is a sign of amicable and affectionate intimacy at Artem., *Oneirocritica*, 1.78 and 2.80, and Sen., *Ep.*, 3.2.
57. Suet., *Aug.*, 69.
58. Plut., *Cat. Mai.*, 24.2; Salvian, *De Gubernatione Dei*, 7.4.17; note Apul., *Met.*, 5.30 for Venus's humiliation at household insubordination.
59. We might note a curse tablet whose curse is entirely contained within the wish that its servile and freedman victims will be removed from the favor of their master/patron, published by Heikki Solin, "Analecta Epigraphica," *Arctos* 22 (1988): 141–46.
60. See Buecheler, *Carmina*, 95; text and translation given by Richmond Lattimore, *Themes in Greek and Latin Epitaphs* (Urbana: University of Illinois Press, 1962), 124.
61. Not every slave or freedman was necessarily cynical in the expression of respect and love for a master/patron; see, e.g., *CIL* 11.1273: *hic aliis obiit, vivit liberate suavis patronus*. Cited and discussed by Treggiari, *Roman Marriage*, 246.
62. E.g., Tac., *Ann.*, 14.60 (in a perversion of the expected, Octavia's slaves are tortured in an attempt to make them falsely implicate their mistress in an adulterous affair), and Prop., *Elegies*, 3.6 (Cynthia's slave is to report to Propertius her doings and thoughts). Cf. also Suet., *Aug.*, 65.2, Val. Max., *Memorable*, 2.5.3.
63. Plut., *Quaest. Rom.*, 16 (*Mor.*, 267D); see also Ov., *Fast.*, 6.481–82.
64. Ov., *Fast.*, 6.551–57.
65. Saller, "Symbols," 89; Celia Schultz, *Women's Religious Activity in the Roman Republic* (Chapel Hill: University of North Carolina Press, 2006), 54–55, cites a group dedication to Matuta by matrons; she also notes (69) that Matuta had some male worshippers as well.

66. Artem., *Oneirocritica*, 5.53, in R. J. White, trans., *The Interpretation of Dreams:* Oneirocritica *by Artemidorus* (Torrance, CA: Original Books, 1990), 242. See Artemidorus's prologue to his first book for his account of the geographical breadth of his research (provided in White, *Interpretation*, 21–22).
67. Clark, "Women," 116, 125; cf. Virginia Hunter, *Policing Athens* (Princeton: Princeton University Press, 1994), 89, 96–118, discusses the detrimental effect of gossip in the Athenian household and the role of slaves in spreading it. Note that *DT* no. 139, mentioned above, curses primarily the slave Rhodine, and in some detail, so that she will be separated from M. Licinius Faustus; but at the end four other people are mentioned. A scenario of spreading gossip seems possible.
68. Victoria Pagán, *Conspiracy Narratives in Roman History* (Austin: University of Texas Press, 2004), 17–18; e.g., Cicero, *Comment. pet.*, 17, alerts a candidate to the impact of gossip emanating from one's own household on one's public image. Household gossip is probably at the root of Artemidorus's (*Oneirocritica*, 4.59) revelations about the sexual habits of a particular client and the consequent lack of significance of his dreams. Plutarch warns wives not to listen to the gossip of those who would try to rile her with tales of her husband's infidelities at *Mor*. 143 F.
69. Artem., *Oneirocritica*, 1.32, trans. White, *Interpretation*, 47; see also 2.27 for dreams signifying false accusations.
70. Artem., *Oneirocritica*, 2.48; see also 2.13.
71. Treggiari, *Roman Marriage*, 311, 314; Saller, "Symbols," 88; Suet., *Tib*., 35.2 remarks upon the perversity of matrons behaving like prostitutes.
72. See most recently Holt Parker, "Why Were The Vestals Virgins?" *AJPh* 125 (2004): 563–601.
73. *Digest of Justinian*, 23.2.26 in Theodore Mommsen and Paul Krueger, eds., *The Digest of Justinian* (trans. Alan Watson; Philadelphia: University of Pennsylvania Press, 1985).
74. Cf. Plaut., *Men*., 787–805 for a wife who can only convince her father of her misuse by providing concrete evidence.
75. August., *Conf*., 9.9; Val. Max., *Memorable*, 6.7.1; Suet., *Aug*., 71, cf. Dio Cass., *Roman*, 58.2.5.
76. Suet., *Aug*. 62. Finley, "Silent Women," 151 suggests her complaints centered on his extra-marital affairs; cf. Suet., *Aug*., 71 and Dio Cass., *Roman*, 58.2.5. Plut., *Mor*., 141 A records Aemilius Paulus's witticism about his pinching shoe of an ex-wife.
77. Plut., *Mor*., 140 B; August., *Ep*., 262.
78. See Quint., *Inst*., 7.8.2 with Clark, "Women," 121; cf. also one of the possible readings of P. Würzb. 21 given in Bagnall and Cribiore, *Women's Letters*, 279–80. Contrast, however, Sen., *Ben*., 4.27.5.
79. Jane Gardner, *Women in Roman Law and Society* (Bloomington: Indiana University Press, 1986), 260–61; Treggiari, *Roman Marriage*, 294. Remarriage also cast doubt on her character; see Publius Syrus, *Maxims*, 381: "A woman who marries many times displeases many husbands," in Jane Gardner and Thomas Wiedemann,

trans., *The Roman Household: A Sourcebook* (London: Routledge, 1991), 46. Apul., *Met.*, 5.30 alludes to the abuse a woman without a man's protection might suffer.

80. For concerns over stepmothers, see, e.g., Artem., *Oneirocritica*, 3.29; Prop., *Elegies*, 4.11.86; Life *of Aesop* 37; Scriptores Historiae Augustae *Marcus*, 29.10; Sen., *Helv.*, 2.4. Note also Parker, "Vestals," 591.
81. Plut., *Mor.*, 143 F-144 A; August., *Conf.*, 9.9.
82. Dio Cass., *Roman*, 58.2.5; cf. also Clark, "Women," 110–13. Margaret Madden and Ronnie Janoff-Bulman, "Blame, Control, and Marital Satisfaction: Wives' Attributions for Conflict in Marriage," *Journal of Marriage and the Family* 43 (1981): 663–74, present more recent findings that (in the late seventies, at least) wives who were willing to accept blame for arguments that developed out of their husbands' actions (e.g., buying power tools for a private hobby with money specifically set aside for household items, flirting with other women) were generally much more satisfied in their marriages than those who did not accept responsibility, because they felt that they exercised control over conflict.
83. Artem., *Oneirocritica*, 4.59, trans. White, *Interpretation*, 219.
84. See Clark, "Women," 123–25 for examples and discussion of violent wives.
85. Dio Chrys., *3 Fort.*, 6–7 describes the methods of humiliation used to demonstrate social superiority over another.
86. Schultz, *Women's Religious*, 147; Saller, "Symbols," 89.
87. On poisoning in particular, see Parker, "Vestals," esp. 589–90.
88. Ov., *Fast.*, 2.571–582, for a woman binding hostile tongues; cf. Arn., *Adv. nat.*, 1.43.5. See Prop., *Elegies*, 4.7.35–46, for courtesans poisoning rivals.
89. Provided and translated by Otto Neugebauer and Henry B. Van Hoesen, *Greek Horoscopes* (Philadelphia: The American Philosophical Society, 1959), 107.
90. E.g., Dickie, *Magic and Magicians*, reads literary descriptions uncritically; contrast the interpretations of, e.g., Graf, *Magic in the Ancient World*, 64, 185–90; Mary Beard, John North, and Simon Price, eds., *Volume 1: A History*, vol. 1 of *Religions of Rome* (Cambridge: Cambridge University Press, 1998), 215–27; Faraone, *Ancient Greek Love Magic*, 170–71; Janowitz, *Magic*, 86–96; and Parker, "Vestals," passim.
91. See, e.g., Cic., *Har. resp.*, 1.1, and *Rep.*, 2.39–40, for unequal distribution of responsibility and authority.
92. E.g., Hor., *Sat.*, 1.1.76–79; Tac., *Ann.*, 14.60.3; Artem., *Oneirocritica*, 4.17.
93. E.g., Mart., *Epigrams*, 9.92; Epictetus, *Diatr.* 4.1.33.
94. E.g., Val. Max., *Memorable*, 9.1.3.
95. Artem., *Oneirocritica*, 1.50.
96. Treggiari, *Roman Marriage*, 284–85, 462.
97. Clark, "Women," 119. Note Val. Max., *Memorable*, 6.7.1, where Tertia Aemilia, wife of Scipio Africanus, is praised for pretending not to notice his affair with a slave girl, and thus not exposing his lack of self-control.
98. Sandra Joshel, *Work, Identity and Legal Status at Rome* (Norman, OK: University of Oklahoma Press, 1992), 6–7, observes the effect of a stereotype is the

maintenance of the status quo of inequitable divisions of power by suppressing inquiry into the reality of situations.

99. Tac., *Ann.*, 2.69–71.

100. Note also Val. Max., *Memorable*, 2.5.3, Ptol., *Tetr.*, 4.9.200, Artem. *Oneirocritica*, 2.32; Prop., *Elegies*, 4.4.51, presents Tarpeia as longing to have some magic with which to betray the Romans more quickly; Livy, *History*, 6.5.1d, recounts how the Romans chose *not* to resort to the underhanded method of removing Pyrrhus by poison.

13

Saffron, Spices, and Sorceresses: Magic Bowls and the Bavli

Yaakov Elman

THREE IMPORTANT COLLECTIONS of Babylonian magic bowls have been published in the last few years, thus adding to our collection of published texts, and it seems an appropriate time to revisit the question of the relationship of the Sasanian rabbinic elite to the use of amulets and (perhaps) magic bowls, and to investigate yet another issue which has not yet been settled in any definitive way: the question of whether women were involved in the production of these bowls.

The overwhelming majority of these bowls are composed in some dialect of Babylonian Aramaic, and many of them include themes or characters already familiar to us from the Babylonian Talmud—rabbinic figures such as R. Joshua b. Perahiah or R. Hanina b. Dosa; angelic names; biblical verses; the theme of divorce as a means of ridding one's house of demons; and, in one case, as we shall see, an incantation that appears in part in the Talmud (hereafter: the Bavli). Indeed, the Bavli itself is filled with demons and demonology, and so it would seem probable that the culture of Sasanian Jewish Babylonia provided fertile ground for the later development of magic bowl praxis.

The Bavli expresses concern regarding women as sorceresses (bSanh 67a, ySanh 7:13 [25d]), which combined with the ubiquity of women as clients of the bowls, would suggest the role of women as producers of bowls as well as consumers. Indeed, this was the basic argument of Rebecca Lesses's recent study of the question of women as exorcists.[1] It seems to me that the arguments she raised may be strengthened and broadened, and the second section of this chapter is devoted to considering the role of women not only as consumers, victims, and perpetrators of incantatory attacks, but also as producers of their prophylactic, the magic bowls. In so doing, I will attempt to unravel part of the riddle posed by an incantation quoted in the Bavli. In the following, I hope to examine both questions; the combination will shed light on the role of women in the production of magic bowls.

The Bowls in the Bavli

First I will begin with a discussion of the bowls themselves—what we know of their provenance and possible evidence for their use by Jews of the Talmudic period—before addressing the question of women's role in their production. James Montgomery, in his collection, dates the bowls as follows, based on the Nippur archaeological evidence: "The lowest dating then is the seventh century, on the basis of the Cufic coins, and this dating is to be pushed back, if it be modified at all, because of the ease with which small coins slip down through the soil. The archaeological evidence then for the terminus ad quem is the seventh century (probably its beginning), with a fair leeway back into the preceding century."[2] However, as he himself notes, "magical literary forms are peculiarly persistent . . . And so our texts, copied and recopied as precious magical prescriptions, repeated possibly by laymen long after the school of sorcery had ceased to exist, may have extended over a series of centuries."[3] While it may be that it occurred to a sixth-century exorcist to employ a common household item—an earthenware bowl, as material for an amulet, we may safely assume that something in the practice of producing amulets impelled him to do this. Since some of these incantations have a long history, going back to ancient Babylonian times, we may well expect to find traces of this development in earlier documents. I suggest that one link in this chain may be found in the Babylonian Talmud.

An overlap between the texts of these bowls and the Babylonian Talmud has been identified. First, the name of Amemar, a fifth- to sixth-generation Babylonian sage, who lived in the second half of the fourth century—250 years before the Nippur bowls were created, appears in a recently published British Museum magic bowl. Second, another published bowl has recently been identified by Christa Müller-Kessler and Theodore Kwasman as having been written in Talmudic Aramaic.[4] Moreover, despite the consensus view that the Bavli does not contain any reference to these bowls, a new look at the terminology of the bowls themselves indicates that the use of magic bowls is likely attested in the Bavli itself. This is as it should be, since, by its nature such a practice did not spring up overnight and spread to all the various Babylonian religious and ethnic communities—Persian, Christian Syriac speakers, Jewish Aramaic, Manichaean, and Mandean.

Primary is the question of whether magic bowls are mentioned in the Bavli. The usual Hebrew/Aramaic term for an amulet is *qemeᶜa*, a word that appears some thirty-four times in the Bavli, almost always in contexts in which it is clear that the amulet was made of leather or "roots," that is, medicinal herbs. It is also clear from the discussions in which these references occur that they had a medical purpose, but also that demons were conceived to be the cause of disease. In the bowls themselves, the word *qemeᶜa* is used to describe a bowl.[5]

The reason the Bavli employs the term *qemeᶜa* mostly for herbs used for medicinal purposes is that these passages relate to the prohibition of carrying an amulet on the Sabbath unless its medical efficacy has been established (mShab 7:2). If it is proven to heal, one may carry it despite prohibitions against carrying objects on the Sabbath. In subsequent discussions the term appears in conjunction with (leather) phylacteries or medicinal herbs (bShab 61a)—all items that could be worn or carried. Thus, the Bavli's redactors simply had no occasion to refer to these bowls in legal discussions since they were usually buried or left hidden somewhere. The other reason seems to be that they were not considered forbidden "Amorite practices" (*darkei ha-Emori*) because they were considered both medicinal and effective (Shab 67a). Since demons were believed to cause disease, the connection is clear. (See discussion below.)

The essential parameters of the permitted use of amulets are set forth in bShab 61a–b. The factors to be considered are proven effectiveness when produced by one who has established himself or herself an expert by having succeeded in manufacturing effective amulets three times, or that the amulet itself has proved effective three times. Legally speaking, the sex of the manufacturer is irrelevant. And indeed, since women were suspected of engaging in magical practices (see bSanh 67a and ySanh 7:13 [25d]) where it states, "most witches are female"), it is likely that they would be called upon to foil the magical practices of others.[6] Unfortunately, this is not made explicit in bShab 61a–b where "expert" producers of amulets are discussed:

> [On the Sabbath he may not go out . . .] nor with an amulet, whether it be from an expert.
>
> R. Papa said: Do not think that both the man [producing the amulet] and the amulet must be approved, but as long as the man is approved, even if the amulet is not approved [it may be worn on the Sabbath]. This may be proved as well [from the text of the mishnah], for it is stated: Nor with an amulet, whether it is not from an expert—but it is not stated: if it is not approved. This proves it.
>
> Our Rabbis taught: What is an approved amulet? One that has healed [once], a second time and a third time; whether it is an amulet in writing or an amulet of roots, whether it is for an invalid whose life is in danger or for an invalid whose life is not in danger. [It is approved] not [only] for a person who has [already] had an epileptic fit, but even [merely] to ward it off. And one may tie and untie it even in the street, provided that he does not secure it [61b] with a ring or a bracelet and go out therewith into the

street, for appearances' sake (*mar'it ayin*) [that the people who see him not think that it is worn for ornamentation].

But was it not taught: What is an approved amulet? One that has healed three men simultaneously?

There is no difficulty: one is to approve the man [who produced it], and one is to approve the amulet.

R. Papa said: It is obvious to me that if three amulets [are successful for] three people, each [being efficacious] three times [even for the same person], both the producer and the amulets are [henceforth] approved, but not the producer. [But] R. Papa asked: What if three amulets [are efficacious] for one person? The amulets are certainly not rendered approved; but does not the producer become approved or not? Do we say: Surely, he has healed him. Or perhaps, it is this man's fate to be susceptible to writing [that is, to amulets, but the producer is not approved]?

[The question] stands over.[7]

We see here that amulets are approved for use and can even be worn on the Sabbath if they have proved themselves effective three times or have been made by someone who has produced an amulet that healed three times. The language used for the producer is masculine, leaving open the question regarding women's potential involvement in their manufacture. Could this test have been used for magic bowls? On first consideration, since the bowls were supposed to protect the house against demons, or to expel them, how could the client (or a rabbi?) know that the bowl had been successful? However, since bowls were often written for specific maladies, a successful cure could be registered. R. Papa's test could be applied to the bowls. Furthermore, it is clear from the following discussion that amulets could be written on more substantial materials, such as on the handles of vessels. Generally speaking, the most common vessels in use were made of clay, a matter confirmed both by literary references in classic rabbinic literature and by archaeological finds. This passage in bShab 61b attests to the writing of amulets on handles of utensils—presumably made of clay, making at least a partial analogy with our magic bowls:

It was asked: Do amulets have sanctity or perhaps they do not have sanctity?

In regard to what law [was this asked]? Shall we say: In regard to saving them from a fire? Then come and hear: Benedictions [of prayer in writing]

> and amulets, though they contain the [divine] letters and many passages from the Torah, may not be saved from a fire [on the Sabbath], but are burnt where they are. Again, if in regard to storing them away [when worn out], come and hear: If it [the Divine Name] was written on the handles of utensils or on the legs of a bed [for magical purposes], it must be cut out and stored away. Rather, [the question is] what about entering a privy with them? Have they sanctity, and it is forbidden, or perhaps they have no sanctity, and it is permitted?
>
> Come and hear: Nor with an amulet, if it is not from an expert. This [implies that] if it is from an expert, one may go out [with it]; now if you say that amulets possess sanctity, it may happen that one needs a privy, and so come to carry it four cubits in the street [so as to store it outside the privy].
>
> The reference here is to an amulet of roots [which certainly does not possess sanctity].
>
> But was it not taught: Both a written amulet and an amulet of roots?
>
> The reference here is to an invalid whose life is in danger [and so he may take it with him into the privy].
>
> But was it not taught: Both an invalid whose life is in danger and one whose life is not in danger [thus including both categories]?
>
> Rather, [this is the reply:] since it heals even when he holds it in his hand, it is well.[8]

Here the amuletic text is written on less fragile materials—the handles of utensils or even on the legs of a bed, which are quite a departure from other uses of the word *qemeᶜa*, but these are still portable, not buried in the ground as magic bowls were. However, although these amulets seem not to have been used against demons, but rather disease, it is clear, as noted above, that demons could be the cause of disease, and a "cure" for one could be considered as a remedy for the other. For example, another text (bPes 111b) details the use of two amulets against demons that inhabited a certain tree:

> [The demons] of sorb-bushes are [called] *shidei* [demons]. A sorb–bush which is near a town has not less than sixty *shidei* [haunting it]. What is the difference? In regard to writing an amulet [against them].

> A certain town-official went and stood by a sorb-bush near a town, at which he was set upon by sixty demons and his life was in danger. He then went to a scholar who did not know that it was a sorb-bush haunted by sixty demons, and so he wrote a one-demon amulet for it. Then he heard how they suspended a *hinga* [a musical instrument] on it [=the tree, perhaps to dance around it], and sing thus: "The man's turban is like a scholar's, [but] we have examined the man and he does not know 'Blessed art Thou' [the opening formula of a blessing]." Then a certain scholar came who knew that it was a sorb-bush of sixty demons and wrote a sixty-demon amulet for it. Then he heard them saying: "Clear away your vessels from here."[9]

This amulet was apparently written not only for that occasion or person, but was of a more permanent nature, a sort of "real estate" amulet that was left on a tree, not too dissimilar from a magic bowl left in a house. Note that when the demons discover the amulet, they leave the tree entirely—"Clear your vessels from here!" It was thus designed to expel the demons from the tree, just as bowls were designed to expel demons from the house. The amulet effectively rid the tree of demons, just as a bowl was intended to do for a person's property. It seems unlikely that we are dealing with an amulet written with ink on parchment. There is also no indication that this amulet was specifically written for the person affected; moreover, it was not buried beside or under the tree, but rather hung on it, and therefore exposed to the weather. Thus it has no direct analogy with either bowls or amulets that were worn by private individuals.

Why was a tree in the public domain treated in this fashion? The story tells us. It was located near a town, and was a constant source of danger to passersby. And now we proceed to an exceedingly interesting incantation preserved in both the Bavli (Pes 110a-b) *and* in a recently published bowl from the British Museum collection.

> Amemar said: The chief of the sorceresses told me: He who meets sorceresses should say thus: "Hot dung in perforated (or: divided—YE)[10] baskets for your mouths, O ye witches! May your heads become bald, the wind carry off your crumbs, your spices be scattered, the wind carry off the new saffron which ye are holding, ye sorceresses: as long as He showed grace to me and to you, I had not come among (you); now that I have come among you, your grace and my grace have cooled."[11]

Before discussing this incantation's wider implications, we should say a few words about the text. The translation of the term "scatter your crumbs" (*prhykhy*) (פרחייכי) is conjectural. In light of the mention of saffron, I would suggest that it should be rendered as "caper," a well-attested meaning of *parha'*. The play on *perah*, "flower," is evident; the phrase could then mean "may your capers fly away," which fits the mention of saffron in the continuation. Continuing along this line, let us examine the phrase "may you become bald" (*qrh qrhykhy*) (קרח קרחייכי). Michael Sokoloff in his *Dictionary of Babylonian Jewish Aramaic*, suggests a reading of *qrh qrdyky*, but notes that this is also unclear. I suggest that we understand *qrdykh* as referring to castor oil or, perhaps, the bean.[12] The word *qrh* is attested in Montgomery 18, where *perah* is a metathesized variant of *ᶜaraq*, "to flee" (see Montgomery's glossary). The meaning of *qrh qrhykhy* in that case would be "may your castor oil (plants?) flee," which better conforms to the parallel stichs that follow.

While saffron is known as an expensive herb used both for medical and magical purposes, the question is whether capers and castor oil or plants have magical use. Caper plants do have medicinal uses, among others as a diuretic. This would conform to the well-known laxative effect of castor oil, which may perhaps, with all due hesitation, point to a meaning of "to cause diarrhea" for *ᶜaraq*. It would also fit the curse of "hot dung." Could this be a specific incantation against these ailments?

At any rate, this use of common medicinal herbs for magical purposes conforms to the extensive use of such herbs in the Greek magical papyri. As John Scarborough puts it:

> The Greek, Coptic, and demotic texts known as Papyri Graecae Magicae mention over 450 plants, minerals, animal products, herbs, and other substances as presumably "pharmaceutically active" in the recorded spells, incantations, formulas and imprecations. The texts in the collection are dated generally to Roman and Byzantine Egypt (c. 30 B.C.–c. 600 A.D.), but several instances of drug lore (e.g., the multi-ingredient incense called *κῦφι*) indicate a heritage going back many centuries, probably to dynastic Egypt . . . The *Papyri Graecae Magicae* have yielded a trove of insights on how Jew, Christian, and pagan perceived their world; and an important facet of our fresh understanding of these precious documents that emerge from beliefs of "common people" is the pharmacology of magical and sacred plants and drugs.[13] Thessalus's *Powers of Herbs* specifically mentions "saffron crocus."[14]

Now, Amemar is not referring to an amulet, but to an incantation to be recited for protection against witches that one encounters. Significantly, this incantation also appears almost verbatim on a magic bowl, thus indicating that these incantations could be employed in various magical contexts. However, this alone does not mean that the bowl was manufactured for Jews, since Jewish themes appear on bowls that were clearly made for and by non-Jews. These include not only divine and angelic names, but also the name of an early Palestinian sage, R. Joshua b. Perahiah.

The relevant part of the magic bowl—035A of J. B. Segal's collection (BM 91735; 1886-1-9, 3)—is as follows:

> Qr qrryky pr prryky. Your spices are scattered, your gates fly away, and I have loosened (their) hinges. The blast demon (carries off) the new saffron which you grasp. Show me favor and he will show you favor. Now we scattered upon you—from now qr qrryk the witch.[15]

Moreover, as Segal points out, parts of this extract appear on another magic bowl.

Segal suggests that the presence of "Heb. verses from the Bible and a garbled version of a passage from BT Pesahim indicates the Jewish authorship of this text." The biblical verses (Num 10:35 and Is 44:25) may do so, but the presence of an incantation with no particular religious affinities can hardly be considered proof of Jewish origin in a highly syncretistic cross-cultural context. It is highly unlikely that a later bowl manufacturer simply copied a passage from the Talmud. For one thing, it is virtually certain that the Bavli was not available in written form before the middle of the eighth century, as David Rosenthal has shown,[16] and anyone with enough erudition to extract this incantation from the huge mass of the Bavli would himself have been a rabbinic scholar of note.

The corruptions in the text indicate that in all likelihood the manufacturer copied this part of the incantation from another bowl in which the lower register of the four words was effaced. She/he thus reconstructed them as best he/she could, and only missed two letters, twice converting two *het*s into *resh*es, and missing two *hets*.

However, the consistency of the misreading almost suggests that they were intentional, though the intention is unclear. Could the scatological nature of the curse formula have motivated such a change? As it happens, none of the Bavli's scatological terms has survived in the bowl unscathed, nor do we have "hot dung in perforated baskets!"

The inter-confessional nature of these incantations argues for the role of women in their manufacture. Clearly, the essential marketing requirement for them was that they proved themselves effective, no matter who produced them. If this commerce crossed religious lines, why would it not cross gender ones as well, especially when women had the reputation of being proficient in sorcery? The question is whether Jewish women at this time were literate. However, studies of literacy over the last generation have demonstrated that the ability to write encompasses a continuum, and, as I have shown elsewhere, by some standards even a successful rabbi need not have been all that literate—a powerful memory was far more important.[17] Moreover, the type of literacy needed to produce a magic bowl is fairly minimal, as demonstrated by a number of fairly corrupt—or even unreadable—magic bowls. In our case, the bowl contains six unreadable words that apparently did not impair the effectiveness of the bowl, at least in the view of the manufacturer.

The question is why he/she did not emend the text or substitute another one? One possibility is that this text had proved effective, or that this was the only text the manufacturer knew. Possibly the text was highly regarded, either because of its Talmudic connections—an unlikely possibility at this date, or that it was an incantation believed to have been supplied by witches themselves. If the latter were the case, what would have been more effective than to have "set a witch to foil a witch"? Of course, the number of corrupt texts and indecipherable or only partly decipherable bowls indicates that the clients seldom took the trouble to read them, or that they were incapable of doing so. Presumably they relied on the reputation of the manufacturer.

It is clear that some bowl makers worked with a standard text, since we find duplicate or even triplicate bowls, with only the names of the clients changed; see Montgomery 10, 11, and 18, for example, and he himself quotes two others in this series. Thus, the amount of literacy required was merely sufficient for the maker to write the names of the clients. Another possibility is that the manufacturer did not have another text at her/his disposal, and could not "wing it."

The *materia magica* are also "low tech." The Talmud itself generally requires quite involved substances for its spells, as do the Greek magical papyri; this spell was devised against witches who employed expensive, but common, household items: capers, castor oil, saffron, and "spices." The bowl mentions only saffron and spices. However, the bowls usually rely on spells, divorce formulae and the like, and seldom if ever mention the *materia magica* employed by the witches against whose pernicious influence they have been written.

To conclude the first part of this inquiry, the possibility that the word *qemeᶜa* can include, or rather, did include magic bowls within its range of meaning does not constitute evidence of the bowls' existence in Talmudic times. However, it should be noted that our dating of the bowls rests on the excavations at Nippur, and the bowls found there were published by Montgomery and, much more recently, by Müller-Kessler,[18] number a bit over a hundred, but the bowls in Segal's collection of British Museum bowls, of which 120 can be deciphered,[19] and that of Levene of the Mussaieff bowls (around twenty, plus another published later),[20] and those published by Gordon (twenty-three) and Shaked and Naveh (twenty-two)[21] were not found *in situ*, and their provenance is unknown. Can some of these 186 or more bowls have been of Talmudic provenance? The possibility is worth considering, if only because of the ambiguity of *qemeᶜa*, and the consideration that such "technologies" do not arise and flourish suddenly.

Women in the Bowls

Above, we raised the possibility that women also produced magic bowls. Generally speaking, we have a lot less information about the manufacturers of these bowls than we do about the clients, who are mentioned by name in these custom-made bowls. In short, the clients are male and/or female, as are their enemies and the spirits and demons that afflict them. However, the divine protective powers, or the wielders of such powers, are all male—from God or gods in all the variety of their names or persons, and the angels, all the way to such figures as R. Joshua b. Perahiah. Judged by these, we are not far from the situation in which the gynecological profession practiced, a bit more than a generation ago: though all its clients were female, all its practitioners were male, though of course bowls were written for both men and women. Nor is any help to be gained from the apotropaic figures named in cures for female ailments, for the argument can always be made that the exorcist was not a woman any more than he was R. Joshua b. Perahia, the Second Temple rabbinic figure that appears so often in these incantations, or occasionally R. Hanina b. Dosa, an early Palestinian rabbi (in Levene's *Corpus* M156).[22]

I would add another consideration. Women sometimes commissioned these bowls, and in some cases for gynecological problems. Moreover, the demoness Lilith is frequently invoked as the source of the danger or problem, as are human women—daughters-in-law and mothers-in-law, especially, are frequently invoked as the one casting the spell requiring exorcism; why not "set a thief to catch a thief"? Finally, as Rebecca Lesses has pointed out, since women are stigmatized as sorceresses, why not assume that they were exorcists as well?[23] However, she leaves the question open, and it is within that context that the following comments are offered.

How can such a model be disproved for the magic bowls? The easiest proof would be a bowl whose manufacturer/exorcist identified herself as someone's daughter. Unfortunately, however, whether male or female, the bowls' fashioners generally remain steadfastly anonymous. Luckily, as we shall soon see, this is not always the case.

If these were only hypothetical considerations, we might well hesitate. Thus, in two of the bowls published by Cyrus Gordon and in one of the bowls published by Montgomery, women exorcists seem to be named, though they cannot be definitely connected with the writing of the bowls. In the former, "the women named on the bowls utter a formula that refers to going up on the roof and speaking with the demons," and in one of the latter, "a man and a woman utter the incantation in turn."[24]

J. B. Segal's recent edition of the British Museum bowls further pierces the veil of anonymity, as does one published by Levene in his *Corpus*. There are at least three bowls in which the name(s) of the exorcist(s) are mentioned, and in two of them, the exorcists are women. Text 049A (BM 135563; 1971-2-29, 1) was apparently inscribed by (or by direction of?) one Gušnazdukt daughter of Ahat, who speaks in the first person in the opening of the incantation,[25] and in 036A (BM 91776; 1980-4-15, 16), we have Kwaršid Gušnas son of Dustay and a woman, whom Segal assumes is his wife, Zebinta daughter of Zaywi.[26] While only two bowls are thus described, we must remember that Segal notes only one other exorcist, Maifarhad of text 041A.[27] We may add to this small group one Pabak son of Kufitai of Montgomery no. 2 (CBS 2945), which may be the second Montgomery bowl referred to by Lesses.[28] And Mihlad and Baran sons of Mirdukh in a bowl published by Levene (M163), if they were exorcists. The "press and binding" was manufactured against Isha son of Ifra Hurmiz "under the feet and command and authority of this Mihlad and (this) Baran sons of Mirdukh. Šamiš king of the gods!"[29] Thus, surprisingly, a third of the admittedly small corpus of named exorcists are female! And, it is interesting to note that Gušnazdukt's bowl is written in Talmudic Aramaic, as demonstrated by Müller-Kessler.[30] Thus, a total of six women are mentioned in connection with these incantations. And although we cannot be certain that they were the producers of these bowls, their ubiquity within the small corpus of bowls that does contain the names of sorcerers makes that probability more likely.

With this indication, we may reexamine these texts for indications of female authorship or involvement with a bit more confidence, especially those bowls commissioned by women or for women. Text 25 in Isbell's collection (Montgomery 13 [CBS 8694]) was written for one Bahmandukt, daughter of Sama,[31] who apparently suffered from some malady or syndrome that prevented her marriage from being consummated (vaginitis?). Montgomery, with perhaps a Victorian sensibility, assumed that this was "a charm for a certain woman against the reproach of barrenness, that her husband may love her and she may have children by him," and points to this text and his no. 28 "as love charms, bear[ing] the closest relation to the Greek erotic incantations."[32]

In a recent article, Michael Morony notes that this couple commissioned two bowls, one by the husband and one by the wife:

> The bowl commissioned by 'Epra [=the husband] for himself and Bahmandūk is against the Lilith in their house, while that commissioned by Bahmandūk is to get 'Epra to come to Bahmandūk, his wife, inside his house so that she will give birth.[33]

It is difficult to understand why 'Epra's presence in the house was necessary for Bahmanduch to give birth rather than to conceive! Nevertheless, whatever the exact nature of Bahmanduch's problem(s), they are undoubtedly "female," and the bowl would seem to have been commissioned by the wife.

And yet only male powers are invoked. Nevertheless, this bowl may contain a hint that will enable us to discern a way of unraveling this paradox. Here is the relevant text, as translated by Montgomery first, followed by Isbell, the latter with several important changes. Here is Montgomery's text: 13:

> (1) Closed are the mouths of all races, legions (2) and tongues from Bahmanduch bath Samai. (3) And the angel Rahmiel and the angel Habbiel and the angel Hanniniel, (4) these angels, pity and love and compassionate and embrace Bahmanduch (5) daughter of Sama. Before all the sons of Adam whom he begat by Eve, we will enter in before them; from their clothing they will clothe her and from their garments they will garb her, the garment of the grace of God. (7) With her they will sit, on this side and on that, driving away (demons?), as is right. In the name of YHWH-in-Yah, El-El the great, (8) the awful, whose word is panacea, this mystery is confirmed, made fast and sure forever and ever.
>
> (9) Hark a voice in the mysteries! Hark the voice of....., the voice of a woman, a virgin travailing and not bearing. Quickly be enamored, (10) be enamored and come Ephra bar Saborduch to the marrow of his house and to the marrow of Bahmanduch daughter of Sama. (11) his wife.

Who are the "we" who will enter before them in l. 5? Is there then a team of exorcists? Moreover, what is the nature of Bahmanduch's ailment? Montgomery, followed by Isbell and Morony (see below), takes *hvl* (חבל) to mean "travail," but in all other occurrences takes it to mean "injure, destroy." Neither Segal nor Levene register "travail" as a possibility in their collections; unfortunately, the root does not appear in Müller-Kessler's *Zaubershalentexte*.[34] In any case, the problem is not that Bahmanduch's labor is not proceeding. I would take *hvl* (חבל) to refer, as it usually does in these texts, to demonic injury, and, as noted above, the malady is not barrenness, but inability on Bahmanduch's part to allow consummation of the marriage. Note that the incantation is meant to allow the husband to enter both the house and to "come . . . to the marrow of . . . his wife," as Montgomery renders it.

Thus, Montgomery's "come . . . to the marrow of his house" is an attempt to render *lgvf bytyh vlgv gvfh dbhmndvkh* (לגוף ביתיה ולגו גופה דבהמנדוך), where *lgvf* (לגוף) should clearly be read without the *peh*, and thus rendered as "into his house"—*lgv bytyh*—לגו ביתיה, and, it should be noted, a wife in Talmudic literature is often called 'of the house.' This may thus be a reference to the wife herself.

Isbell, in his Text 25, provides this translation:

> (1) Closed are the mouths of all of them—nations, legions, and (2) languages from Bahmanduk the daughter of Sama. (3) And may these angels—the angel Rahmiel, the a[ngel] Habbiel, and the angel [Ha]nniniel—(4) love, honor, be gracious (to) and embrace Bahmanduk (5) daughter of Sama in the presence of all the sons of Adam [whom he f]athered by Eve. Let us enter before them. (6) They will clothe her with their clothing, [they will c]over her with their garments, the cloak of the kindness of God. (7) With her they are sitting all around (giving) grace as it is appropriate in the name of YHWH who is Yah, El-El, the Great, (8) the fearful, whose Word is full salvation. This mystery is certified, established and confirmed forever and ever . . . .[35]
>
> (9) . . . the sound of the woman, the young woman who travails but does not give birth. . . . (10) . . . let Epra son of Shabroduk enter his house and the body of Bahmanduk daughter of Sama. (11) (She is like) a young woman who travails but does not give birth. (She will become) like fresh myrtle (used) for crowns. Amen and amen. (12) Confirmed and established is salvation from the heavens for Bahmanduk daughter of Sama. (13) . . . Amen. Amen. Selah. Salvation and peac[e from] the heavens forever and [ever] and ever.

First, two linguistic notes. Whatever the religion of the writer of the bowl, the divine names are definitely Jewish, even though his/her client bore a Persian name; as so often is the case, names are no indication of religious or ethnic origin. Both Jews and Christians bore Persian names. Again, we should note that the word *betulta*, whatever its meaning in ancient Semitic languages,[36] clearly *does* mean "virgin" here, as Montgomery translated, though with a question mark. In l. 10 *ni'vl* (ניעול) clearly refers to Epra and should not be translated a "let us enter" but "let him enter," as Isbell has it. Montgomery renders it as "come Epra . . . ," but does not explain the grammatical form. While the bowl is not composed in Talmudic Aramaic—note the *yrhmn yhbbvn* (יחבבון ירחמן) of l. 4, we do find bowls with a mixture of forms. This variety of the imperfect third masculine prefixes within one text was recently noted by Levene in his notes to M102: "eleven with ני, ten with לי, and two with י"![37] Indeed, this mixture of forms may well indicate that while the incantation might have required an archaic form, the writer's native Babylonian Aramaic broke through in places. I would suggest that the ניעול in our bowl is a similar case.

I would then translate ll. 9–10 as follows:

> The voice of the virgin wife, who is injured but does not give birth . . . and let ʿEpra son of Saborduch enter his house and into the body of Bahmanduch daughter of Sama his wife.

There is no need to deny *betulta* its natural meaning because of Isbell's mentor's opinion of the cognate in Ugaritic texts. And again, if the woman cannot engage in marital relations, conception, and thus, birth, is impossible.

All in all, then, it would seem that Bahmanduch remained a virgin even after her marriage, since the marriage could not be consummated. We are then to take "enter the body of his . . . wife" literally.

At first glance we have only male powers invoked: three angels, all with names denoting comfort or love, and, of course, the God invoked is presumably male. But "the sons of Adam" are clearly not sons, for Bahmanduk is to be clothed and covered with their clothing. Since the problem is one that involves her assuming the feminine role in sexual intercourse, it is difficult to imagine that she should be dressed as a male, and so "sons of Adam" would seem to refer to women, who thus are taking part in the ceremony described in this *historiola*, or perhaps the ceremony accompanying the burial of this bowl. It would thus seem likely, in light of the evidence presented above, that at least one woman exorcist participated in this ceremony, and that women's clothes were used in it.

Here then we have a bowl that seems to allow for the participation of women in the exorcism. However, it seems to me that we can go a bit further. The scholarly consensus on this matter seems to be that unless we have proof positive that women could act as exorcists, we must assume that this role was limited to males, despite the fact that it is clear that in many cultures extending over thousands of years, witchcraft was considered a female role. When we consider the names of women mentioned in connection with exorcism, as noted above, it becomes more and more probable that women did function as exorcists in the ritual associated with this bowl.

A few years ago, Dan Levene published a magic bowl from the Moussaieff collection (164).[38] The bowl is replete with Jewish texts and themes, including biblical verses and a quotation from a mishnah, and does not have any non-Jewish elements. Indeed, Levene notes that this "use of the Mishna in this bowl is equivalent to the established manner and tradition in which we are used to seeing biblical verses used in Jewish incantation texts, attesting to the holy status that the text of the Mishna (the Oral Torah) had acquired in late antiquity."[39]

The bowl contains a series of exorcisms of apparently escalating effectiveness, introduced by the formula "And if you do not depart and go out of the house of PN, etc." (E1), followed by three iterations of "if not" (E2–E5), and concluding with another "And if you do not flee and go out from the house of PN" (E6). E2–E4 read as follows, in Levene's translation:

E2 I shall bring against you the shard of a fortunate man and I shall defile you.
E3 And if not
I shall bring against you the staff (11) of a leprous man and I shall strike you.
E4 And if not
I shall bring against you a rod of seven pieces that seven sorcerous women are riding and their eight ghosts.
E5 And if not
I shall bring against you water from the mouths of seven people with gonorrhea/discharge and I shall pour [it] on you and I shall remove you.

And finally, E6 culminates with the threat of being "under the ban of Rabbi Joshua bar Perahia, amen amen selah."

Here too while the seven sorcerous women are definitely female—*shb nshy hrsht'*(שב נשי חרשתא), the verb "riding" is masculine *rkhbyn* (ר(כ)בין), and their ghosts seem to relate to women—*shvlnythvn* (שולניתהון). One wonders whether the "seven people with gonorrhea/discharge"—*shb' zbyn* (שבע זבין)—do not include women, *zbvt* (זבות)?

Thus, in Segal's British Museum catalog, the following text opening 005A (BM 91745; 1980-4-15, 8):

> (1) Overturned, overturned. Overturned be the heavens, overturned the earth, overturned the stars, overturned the planet, overturned the curse, overturned the hour, overturned a curse of the mother, overturned a curse of the daughter (2) and of the mother-in-law, far and near, standing afar and standing near. Upon his knees kneeling and upon his face falling, with his mouth cursing.[40]

The last sentence reads in Aramaic *lyṭ 'l byrkhh rkvh v'l 'nfyh nfl bpvmyh:* ליט על בירכה רכבה ועל אנפיה נפל בפומיה, with cavalier disregard for endings. Since mothers, daughters, and mothers-in-law are mentioned, why not translate the last sentence as feminine?

In 066A (BM 108819; 1914-2-14, 45), we have the following:

> (1) This amulet sorcery and curses and curses and shall not approach Overturning, overturning, overturned be the earth, overturned the heavens [overturned the heavens], overturned all (2) overturned be the streets, overturned of the daughter-in-law who stands in the fields and in the town, the temple, the synagogue, and the cemetery, that (3) kneeling, upon his face striking.

While the Aramaic reads *rkbh ʿl ʾfh shqfh*: רכבה על אפה שקפה.

Once again, given the ambiguity of the orthography, and the presence of women—mothers, daughters, and daughters-in-law, why not translate these sentences in the feminine?

Montgomery 13 raises another issue that is pertinent to the question of whether women produced some of these bowls: their purpose. Thus, Lesses noted that:

> Because some of the bowls were made for women, and some were probably produced by women, we can know in a more direct manner what those women's concerns and needs were in particular areas of their lives—health and disease, pregnancy, childbirth, children's health, sexual anxieties, and fears of malevolent human (male and female) and demonic attack (which is not to say that men did not share these concerns).[41]

In another useful study, Michael G. Morony has investigated the sociological data that can be garnered from the corpus of published bowls; indeed, he has produced a database of names of clients, relationships, etc. In a pioneering attempt, he employs his database to investigate the structure of the households of the clients who commissioned these bowls, and attempts to relate that to matters such as language. He found 119 households, mostly in Aramaic (73 percent), the rest in Mandaic (21 percent), and Syriac (5 percent). Again, of these 119 households, 66 percent were monogamous couples, with or without children. In a further breakdown, Morony notes that:

> Of the 79 monogamous households 61 percent (48) had male heads (in which everything belonged to the man). However, 30 percent (24) of the monogamous households were what might be called joint families, in which the house, possessions, and children belonged to the man and woman equally . . . About 9 percent (7) of monogamous household had female heads; everything belonged to the woman even though a man was present . . . There appears to have been substantial diversity in the nature of households.
>
> Was such diversity threatening? Could it have contributed to insecurity? It is easy to understand insecurity in a single-parent household or among individuals living alone (about one-quarter of the total sample). But nuclear family households (two-thirds of the total sample) may also have had difficulty supporting themselves without extended family networks (for which there is little evidence in the texts). They were on their own. This explains the importance of children and of conflicts over property among

> heirs as former households/families split up to form new ones from one generation to the next.[42]

Morony goes on to suggest that, while "these circumstances were not necessarily new or unique in sixth century Iraq, but may have been aggravated by contemporary changes."

> One working hypothesis would relate the proliferation of incantation bowls in certain places to increased social tensions resulting from agricultural development during the sixth century, to its effect on the native rural population, and to the insecurity of forcibly imported labor. Social tensions and insecurity may also have been increased by socioreligious changes among these populations, including the effect of religious change on the position of women, and the mortality caused by the great plague pandemic of the sixth century and recurring outbreaks of plague that lasted until the mid-eighth century.[43]

There is no question that the great outbreaks of Black Plague from 542 CE on had a great effect on the population of Mesopotamia; elsewhere I have traced its effect on the position of women in Sasanian law,[44] and Morony himself traced its economic consequences as reported in the Syriac chronicles.[45] I have even suggested that the absence of a particular concern for plague—as opposed to drought and war—in the Babylonian Talmud suggests that it was closed before 542 CE. But by the same token we do not find this as a particular concern within the corpus of magic bowls.[46]

To return to our major concern, however, the prominent position of women as clients, and their concerns in these bowls—and here I refer to matters of social relations and not only gynecological problems, increases the possibility that women served as exorcists as well. Certainly, the mention of Gušnazkukt daughter of Ahat and Zebinta daughter of Zaywi as involved in the exorcism supports Lesses's surmise. And if my surmise that bowls are potentially included in the Babylonian Talmud's use of the word *qemeᶜa* is borne out, the rabbis' assumption that women were involved in sorcery, and thus exorcism, will be as well.

There is another aspect to this question that should be considered. Who else but women sorceresses would be more likely to draft an ordinary household item into the technology of expelling a household nuisance? Does the opaque language of R. Papa's *qemeᶜa* include magic bowls produced by women? Taking all the facts into consideration—that women did produce bowls in the post-Talmudic era, that women sorceresses provide Amemar with an incantation that also appears in part in a magic bowl, and that the same term is used both for amulets and bowls, the likelihood is great. Would

Amemar, or one of his contemporaries, have sought out the services of this "head of the sorceresses" as an exorcist? If Amemar transmitted her spell, we must presume that he considered it efficacious. If he would not have employed her to write a bowl for him, I suspect that it would have been more for reasons of rabbinical honor than any lack of respect for their powers. At worst, this head of the sorceresses' guild, shall we say, was at worst a respected colleague. At what point she or one of her guild members would have invented the new and improved technology of demon removal must for the moment remain moot.

Notes

1. Rebecca Lesses, "Exe(or)cising Power: Women as Sorceresses, Exorcists, and Demonesses in Babylonian Society of Late Antiquity," *JAAR* 69 (2001): 343–75; in particular, see her discussion of the assumptions shared by the rabbis and the bowls on p. 366.
2. *Aramaic Incantation Texts from Nippur*, ed. James A. Montgomery (Philadelphia: The University Museum, 1913), 103–4.
3. Montgomery, *Aramaic*, 102.
4. Christa Müller-Kessler, "A Unique Talmudic Aramaic Incantation Bowl," *JAOS* 120 (2000): 159–65.
5. See Montgomery, *Aramaic*, 2:1, 10:17, 29:5; Dan Levene, *A Corpus of Magic Bowls: Incantation Texts in Jewish Aramaic from Late Antiquity* (London: Routledge, 2003), M108:2, M155:9, M123:1, M138:1, M155:9; and some nine times in Müller-Kessler's collection (q.v.). The alternate designation, *kasa'*, appears twice in Montgomery (7:13 and 31:1), once in Levene (M107:1), and not at all in Segal or Müller-Kessler.
6. See *b. Sanh.* 67a and *y. Sanh.* 7:13 [25d] and the chapter by Rebecca Lesses in this volume.
7.

[לא יצא איש...] ולא בקמיע בזמן שאינו מן המומחה.
אמר רב פפא: לא תימא עד דמומחה גברא ומומחה קמיע, אלא: כיון דמומחה גברא, אף על גב דלא מומחה קמיע. דיקא נמי, דקתני ולא בקמיע בזמן שאינו מן המומחה ולא קתני בזמן שאינו מומחה - שמע מינה.
תנו רבנן: איזהו קמיע מומחה? כל שריפא, ושנה, ושלש. אחד קמיע של כתב, ואחד קמיע של עיקרין. אחד חולה שיש בו סכנה ואחד חולה שאין בו סכנה, לא שנכפה - אלא שלא יכפה. וקושר ומתיר אפילו ברשות הרבים, ובלבד שלא יקשרנו [סא עמוד ב] בשיר ובטבעת ויצא בו ברשות הרבים - משום מראית העין.
והתניא: איזהו קמיע מומחה - כל שריפא שלושה בני אדם כאחד! –
לא קשיא, הא - למחויי גברא, הא - למחויי קמיעא.
אמר רב פפא, פשיטא לי: תלתא קמיעי לתלתא גברי, תלתא תלתא זימני - איתמחי גברא ואתמחי קמיעא. תלתא קמיעי לתלתא גברי, חד חד זימנא - גברא איתמחי, קמיעא לא איתמחי. חד קמיע לתלתא גברי - קמיעא איתמחי, גברא לא איתמחי.

בעי רב פפא: תלתא קמיע לחד גברא מאי? קמיעא – ודאי לא איתמחי: גברא איתמחי או לא איתמחי? מי אמרינן: הא אסי ליה, או דילמא: מזלא דהאי גברא הוא דקא מקבל כתבא? – תיקו.

8.

איבעיא להו: קמיעין יש בהן משום קדושה או דילמא: אין בהן משום קדושה?
למאי הילכתא! אילימא לאצולינהו מפני הדליקה - תא שמע: הברכות והקמיעין, אף על פי שיש בהן אותיות ומענינות הרבה שבתורה - אין מצילין אותן מפני הדליקה, ונשרפים במקומן. אלא לענין גניזה. - תא שמע: היה כתוב על ידות הכלים ועל כרעי המטה - יגוד ויגנזנו. - אלא ליכנס בהן בבית הכסא, מאי? יש בהן קדושה - ואסיר, או דילמא: אין בהן קדושה ושרי? – תא שמע: ולא בקמיע בזמן שאינו מן המומחה. הא מן המומחה - נפיק. ואי - אמרת קמיעין יש בהן משום קדושה - זמנין דמיצטריך לבית הכסא, ואתי לאיתויינהו ארבע אמות ברשות הרבים! - הכא במאי עסקינן - בקמיע של עיקרין.
והתניא: אחד קמיע של כתב ואחד קמיע של עיקרין! –
אלא, הכא במאי עסקינן - בחולה שיש בו סכנה. –
והתניא: אחד חולה שיש בו סכנה ואחד חולה שאין בו סכנה! –
אלא, כיון דמסי, אף על גב דנקיט ליה בידיה - נמי שפיר דמי.

9.

פרחא דבי זרדתא - שידי. הא זרדתא דסמיכה למתא - לא פחתא משיתין שידי. למאי נפקא מינה - למיכתב לה קמיעא.
ההוא בר קשא דמתא דאזיל וקאי גבי זרדתא דהוה סמיך למתא, עלו ביה שיתין שידי ואיסתכן. אתא לההוא מרבנן דלא ידע דזרדתא דשיתין שידי היא, כתב לה קמיע לחדא שידא. שמע דתלו חינגא בגויה, וקא משרו הכי: סודריה דמר כי צורבא מרבנן, בדיקנא ביה במר דלא ידע ברוך. אתא ההוא מרבנן דידע דזרדתא שיתין שידי הוה, כתב לה קמיעא
דשיתין שידי. שמע דקא אמרו: פנו מנייכו מהכא.

10. The manuscripts contain many variants of this form—בזי, בוען, בזיע, בזוי, בזין, בזיא, טיעי, but none but the last affects the meaning.

11.

אמר אמימר, אמרה לי רישתינהי דנשים כשפניות: האי מאן דפגע בהו בנשים כשפניות - נימא הכי: חרי חמימי בדיקולא בזייא לפומייכו נשי דחרשייא, קרח קרחייכי, פרח פרחייכיעמוד ב] [איבדור תבלונייכי, פרחא זיקא למוריקא חדתא דנקטיתו נשים כשפניות . אדחנני וחננכי לא אתיתי לגו. השתא דאתיתי לגו - קרחנני וחננכי.

12. For the oil, see Sokoloff, 1038b s.v. *qidra'*, and Immanuel *Löw*, *Flora der Juden,* vol. 1 (Hildesheim: Olms, 1967), 608.

13. John Scarborough, "The Pharmacology of Sacred Plants, Herbs, and Roots," in *Magika Hiera: Ancient Greek Magic & Religion*, ed. Christopher A. Faraone and Dirk Obbink (New York: Oxford University Press, 1991), 156–57.

14. Ibid., 155–56.

15.

קר קרריכי פר פרריכי איתבדר תבלוניכי פרחו ת(רעי)ך ופרקית ניסביך (זיקא) למוריקא חדתא (בדרנא בך) דנקיטתו אחנני חנא וחניך השתא (בדרנא בך) למן השתא .... קר קרריך חרשותא

16. See David Rosenthal, *Mishnah Avodah Zarah: Mahadurah Biqortit u-Mavo*, vol. 1 (Jerusalem: Hebrew University, 1980), 96–106.
17. Yaakov Elman, "Orality and the Redaction of the Babylonian Talmud," *Oral Tradition* 14, no. 1 (1999): 52–99.
18. Christa Müller-Kessler, *Die Zauberschalentexte in der Hilprecht-Sammlung, Jena, und weitere Nipur-Texte anderer Sammlungen* (Wiesbaden: Harrassowitz Verlag, 2005).
19. J. B. Segal, *Catalogue of the Aramaic and Mandaic Incantation Bowls in the British Museum*, with a contribution by E. C. D. Hunter (London: British Museum Press, 2000).
20. Levene, *Corpus*, 124, ll. 3–4.; for the new bowl, see n. 25.
21. See Levene, *Corpus*, 1, where a few other bowls' publications are mentioned.
22. See n. 15 for the reference.
23. Lesses, "Exe(or)cising" 361–62.
24. Ibid., p. 362.
25. Segal, *Catalogue*, 92–93.
26. Segal, *Catalogue*, 75–77; the identification is on p. 25.
27. Segal, *Catalogue*, 83–85.
28. Montgomery, *Aramaic*, 121–26.
29. Levene, *Corpus*, 122, ll. 3–4 (see n. 9).
30. Montgomery, *Aramaic*, 102.
31. Montgomery reads: "Samai," which Isbell emends to "Sama" without comment. The reason seems to be that the name appears in that form in l. 13, and also in Montgomery 1 (CBS 8693), but why emend in favor of the shorter form? The frequent variation of Aha and Ahai indicates that either is possible. See Montgomery's note on this name ad l. 4 of Text 1 (pp. 118–19).
32. Montgomery, *Aramaic*, 179.
33. Michael G. Morony, "Magic and Society in Late Sasanian Iraq," in *Prayer, Magic, and the Stars in the Ancient and Late Antique World*, ed. Scott Noegel, Joel Thomas Walker, and Brannon M. Wheeler (University Park, PA: Pennsylvania State University Press, 2003) 81–107; the quote is from p. 105.
34. Müller-Kessler, *Die Zauberschalentext* (see above, n. 8).
35. Isbell, 75–76.
36. Isbell states, on the authority of *Ugaritic Textbook*, 377–8, that "there is no word in the Near Eastern languages that by itself means a virgo intacta."
37. Levene, *Corpus*, 44.
38. Dan Levene, "'If You Appear as a Pig': Another Incantation Bowl (Mousaieff 164)," *JSS* 52 (2007): 59–70.
39. Ibid., 67.
40. Segal, *Catalogue*, 46.
41. Lesses, "Exe(or)cising," 367.
42. Morony, "Magic," 105–6.

43. Ibid., 106–7.
44. See Yaakov Elman, "Marriage and Marital Property in Rabbinic and Sasanian Law," in *Rabbinic Law in Its Roman and Near Eastern Context*, ed. C. Hezser (Tübingen: Mohr-Siebeck, 2003), 227–76.
45. Michael G. Morony, "Michael the Syrian as a source for Economic History," *Hugoye: Journal of Syriac Studies* 3 (2000; cited August 8, 2010; http://syrcom.cua.edu/Hugoye/Vol3No2/HV3N2Morony.html.
46. Note that the listing of the root נגע in Montgomery's glossary (p. 294) merely relates to the word יגע "touch" in Montgomery, *Aramaic*, 16:4, and is in company with "Leprosy" and "Stroke." See also M117 in Levene, *Corpus*. However, these all relate to some skin disease, similar to those in Leviticus.

14

Victimology or: How to Deal with Untimely Death

Fritz Graf

PAST RESEARCH ON magic in the Greco-Roman world has almost exclusively focused on some standard sources, on literary texts of all epochs that talk about magic, and on the lead curse tablets and Greco-Egyptian magical papyri that attest to its practice. In this contribution, I will look at a different group of texts, the stone inscriptions that were set up at graves: in the past, they have been somewhat neglected in research on magic and sorcery in the ancient world. They were not the work of ritual specialists as were the papyri and the lead curse tablets, nor do they reflect the fictionalization of magic that is dominant in the literary texts. The texts I discuss here deal all with the problem of a sudden and unexpected death (and, by extension, with a few other instances of a sudden and unexpected crisis) and with the way some people in the Greek and Roman world reacted to it: they blamed malevolent human beings for using sorcery to destroy a beloved family member. This mechanism is far from being confined to the ancient world, but it has, as we will see, its own specific physiognomy in the societies of the Roman Empire.[1] Thus, analyzing these texts, I will not only present rich material that hitherto has been rarely studied; I will also embed it in a more general theory of witchcraft and try to understand the gender structure that is visible behind these texts.

An Alexandrian Epigram

The collection of antiquities in the French *Bibliothèque Nationale* in Paris contains, as part of its Froehner Collection, a dark stone with a long grave epigram; it comes from late Ptolemaic Alexandria and was written around the year 100 BCE. The text is composed in iambics, and it has been inscribed by a somewhat unprofessional hand.[2] Here is the text in my translation:[3]

"Thermis, worthy one, greetings."

"Lords of the *daimones* down there and you, noble Persephassa, Demeter's Daughter: Admit this unfortunate and shipwrecked guest, me Thermis, born to her father Lysanias, the noble wife and companion of Simalos. If someone has directed the terrible Erinyes of poison/spells[4] against my entrails and my life, do not, immortal gods, send him any other fate than one that is similar to what I have been suffering—I who now dwell down here, having left behind, in three months[5] of a wasting illness, the fruits of life, bereft of what Earth, Giver-of-All, gives to humans, of my children, Lords, and of my husband,[6] whose soul existed for me only, and sweet was my life with my spouse. I have already forgotten all this, wretched me, and in my grief I pronounce a curse: 'Make them go to the big deep Vault of Hades and the Gates of Darkness, utterly deprived of their children and their city. But may all my children enjoy an unharmed and blessed life, as may my husband, arriving at old age's time.' And if there is even small respect for prayers in Hades, may this curse reach those to whom I address it."

"While I sing the Muses' song of my life with you, a song sweet and mournful at the same time, Thermis my spouse, I promise you this: the children I have from you, I will raise them in a way that is worth my love to you, my wife, and I will keep Lysas as an equal to my children. I will do this out of recognition, for blameless were the ways of your life."

We hear two voices in this epitaph, the voice of the deceased, Thermis, a young wife and mother, and the voice of the surviving husband, Simalos (I have distinguished them in my translation by inverted double commas). Simalos opens with the customary formulaic address to a deceased person, basically a greeting. Then Thermis begins to speak. She starts with a short prayer to the Underworld gods, asking them to admit her to their realm; such a prayer is rare in these texts. At the same time, her introduction gives the necessary information about her name, family, and personal situation. Then she laments her fate, the terrible way of her death that she ascribes to *pharmaka*, poison, or spells (more on this below); she curses the person or persons responsible for her death and prays for blessings for her young children and her husband. His voice closes the inscription: he promises to care for all her children, those from their common marriage as well as the boy Lysas about whom we know nothing; maybe she has born him from another man, either in a very short former marriage or even out of wedlock.

Both voices, the one of the deceased person and the one of the survivor, are conventional in Greek grave epigrams; but it is rare that they are combined into a complex dialog beyond the grave, as they are here. It shows the intensity of the feelings of the mourning husband, who must have written this text himself rather than have it commissioned to a professional poet or scribe: given the disjunction between the poetic style and the mediocre lettering, the husband who set it up for his wife invested more care in formulating the text than in having it written on stone. He is very conscious of its poetic form, to the extent that he invokes the Muses in a way only a poet would. At the same time he uses not the high style and widely used elegiac couplets or hexameters, but the simpler iambics that are relatively rare in grave epigrams. Among other uses, iambics are the meter of curse poetry and thus might be thought as apt for this text with its elaborate curse, but they are also somewhat easier to handle; even so, the writer allows himself some syntactic awkwardness when he copes with the requirements of the meter.[7] The intense emotions that made Simalos write these verses must have been caused by the fact that Thermis died relatively young, with her children still well under age; but, more importantly, these emotions resulted also from the remarkable and cruel way she died, killed by a wasting illness that lasted for three long and terrible months.[8]

Thermis, however, does not simply talk about her death that has cut short a happy marriage: she retaliates by cursing whoever did this to her. The unknown perpetrators shall suffer the same terrible death, and their children shall die as well: the entire family shall be made to disappear from the face of the earth "with all their roots" (v. 17). The divinities of her present realm, Persephone and her *daimones*, shall help this curse to become true—as, somewhat unexpectedly, these same divinities are also asked to help to fulfill the prayer for long life and happiness of Thermis's husband and children.

Although they were Greek speakers, neither Simalos nor Thermis will presumably have belonged to the city's affluent upper class.[9] But they could afford a somewhat ambitious monument, so they certainly were well off. The literary form of the text and the fact that Simalos wrote it himself makes me think that he must have been a minor intellectual, a mid-level official or a scribe perhaps.

The epigram combines two topics that by themselves are seldom attested in antiquity, and more rarely combined, although they belong intimately together. One topic is the explanation of an unexpected death by an evil spell; the other is the curse that the victim puts on the (mostly unknown and even unknowable) person who sent such a spell, in order to take her revenge.

Sorcery and Sudden Death

Many pre-modern societies coped with the extraordinary disruption of life caused by an unexpected and early death of a person by accusing someone of having caused it through sorcery; the same mechanism was available for other instances of a sudden crisis. E. E. Evans-Pritchard has given an anthropological description and explanation of this mechanism among the Azande of Sudan that is still a classic; Jeanne Favret-Saada did the same for the Bocage, a rural region of contemporary France. In a much wider perspective that aimed at a historical phenomenology of human reactions to death, the Swiss folklorist and classicist Karl Meuli collected a wealth of evidence from European folklore on death customs and beliefs that contain many cases of the same mechanism.[10]

Two Literary Cases

Among our literary sources, the death of the young prince Germanicus in the fall of 18 CE is perhaps the most prominent case where an unexpected death led to the suspicion of poisoning and to rumors and private accusations of sorcery; it must have been a *cause célèbre* in its time. According to Tacitus, who left us a detailed account of the affair, the emperor Tiberius had sent Germanicus as a special envoy to the province of Syria, to sort out administrative problems.[11] The many colorful and otherwise unattested details of Tacitus's account might go back to the memoirs of Germanicus's daughter, Agrippina the Younger; Tacitus used these "memoirs of an outspoken woman" for other details of his historical narrative.[12] The young prince was immediately confronted with obstruction by the regular provincial governor, Cn. Calpurnius Piso, who was backed by his ambitious wife, a personal friend of Augustus's widow Livia; when Germanicus was absent in Egypt, Piso undid most of his measures. When Germanicus returned to an atmosphere of heavy tension, he fell suddenly ill and died very quickly. Friends and family suspected poison and magic; and although the naked corpse was publicly exhibited to demonstrate that it showed no trace of poison, a search of Germanicus's personal quarters led to incriminating material hidden in his rooms that pointed to foul play ("human body parts, spells and consecrations with Germanicus's name inscribed in lead tablets"). Tacitus even has a name for the female specialist Piso had employed, a certain Martina, "famous for her potions;" she conveniently died shortly afterward on her way to Italy. The emperor initiated a trial against Piso and his wife; she was acquitted (by personal intercession of Livia, as the rumor went), and her husband committed suicide before the final verdict.[13] Three decades ago, archaeologists found a version of the senatorial minutes of this trial on a bronze tablet in Spain; it is a version that had been edited for wider publication and sent to the provinces. This text shows that the senate focused its accusation on the political aspect of the affair and refrained from any allusion to the more grisly, and more scandalous, side of the story: the accusation of sorcery remained rumor and family lore.[14]

Less well known is that in another trial an early and sudden death was used as part of the accusation—and rejected almost as quickly as in the case of Germanicus. When, in about 158 CE, the young philosopher Apuleius was tried for magic in the law court of the governor of the province Africa Proconsularis, the accuser made him responsible not only for the love magic with which he attracted a wealthy and much older widow, thus snubbing and angering the family of her former husband who had hoped to keep the money in the family, but also accused Apuleius of having caused the death of his friend Pontianus, the son of his wealthy wife and thus his stepson. Pontianus died of a (presumably somewhat prolonged) illness when he was away from his hometown in Carthage.[15] The accuser quickly dropped the latter charge, however, before the trial began. Again, the unexpected death of an otherwise healthy young man triggered the suspicion of sorcery that, again, remained family lore and was not tried in court.[16]

Inscriptions (Mainly) from the Greek East: Pharmakeia *and Cunning Stealth*

Grave inscriptions from both the Greek East and the Latin West preserve more cases, albeit with less telling details than the two literary accounts. Some are as straightforward as the epigram from Alexandria, others are more allusive, and some cases are disputed and need more thought.[17]

Some inscriptions from the Greek world formulate the accusations in a way similar to the Alexandria epigram that accuses someone of having "directed the terrible Erinys of *pharmaka* against my entrails and my life" (line 6). An inscription from Side in Cilicia, for a girl or a young unmarried woman, "Hermione, daughter of Hermogenes, from Aigeai," is as direct as it is short: Hermione is described as *pepharmakeumenē*, "the victim of *pharmaka*," that is, as we shall see, "poisoned" or "bewitched."[18] We lack a context, but the wording points to a routine suspicion of sorcery rather than to accidental or intentional poisoning. A grave inscription for a young doctor on the island of Thasos, states that although buried in his home city, he had died abroad from the effects of *pharmaka*.[19] Somewhat more cautiously, another inscription from Alexandria formulates the accusation as a suspicion only: "in case someone gave her *pharmaka*."[20]

Two almost identical Greek inscriptions from late Hellenistic Rheneia, the small island off Delos, are not grave inscriptions but curses.[21] But since they explain the untimely death of a girl through *pharmakeía*, and Rheneia served as the cemetery of the island of Delos on which it was forbidden to bury someone,[22] the two inscriptions must come from two graves, the curse replacing the usual epitaph. Both texts date to the late second or early first century BCE and were written by Hellenized Jews, presumably Palestinian traders who settled in the international trade center that the island of Delos had become in this period. The wording of both texts is identical, with the sole exception of the name of the victim (Marthina in one case, Heraklea in the other one), and they were inscribed at about the same time, to judge from the letterforms. They invoke Iahwe (in a formula known from the Septuagint) to take revenge "on those who have cunningly murdered or poisoned poor Marthina/Heraklea who died before her time (*ahōrous*), unjustly shedding her innocent blood";[23] a relief of two raised hands depicts the gesture of invocation that accompanied the curse prayer. The circumstances under which these young girls died are unclear, to us as well as to their families. They died in a way that triggered the suspicion of foul play to which someone—the parents? the community?—reacted with the invocation of an all-powerful god to punish the unknown culprits; to inscribe it on stone guaranteed the permanence of the speech act involved, as in the case of the leaden curse tablets. Since we possess only these two monuments, we cannot know whether something unusual caused this suspicion or whether this was a standard way of dealing with the sudden death of young people in this specific community. We can only state that the way the texts describe the accusation insists on the stealthy character of the killing: the formula "those who have cunningly (*dolōi*, by secret action) murdered or poisoned," describes any secret way of killing, in an almost overly precise way.

All these inscriptions ascribe an untimely death to the use of *pharmaka*. The term *pharmakon* is notoriously ambiguous, and not only in the well-known sense that its core meaning, "powerful substance," denotes both poison and healing drug. More importantly in our context, the Greek term does not distinguish between what we would call natural and what we would call supernatural actions of these substances; such a distinction is far from self-evident outside modern Western thinking.[24] This explains (and makes otiose) several scholarly discussions, such as the debate of how to understand the "destructive (*dēlētēria*) *pharmaka*" against whose purveyors the magistrates of fifth-century BCE Teos uttered a public curse—did they think of poison or of sorcery? The correct answer is: both at once.[25] For a similar reason, the Roman *lex Cornelia* of 78 BCE was directed against *sicarii et venefici*: people who killed visibly with a weapon in their hand (the *sicarii*) and thus left a clear trace of their action by openly penetrating the body, and those who killed secretly, by poison and/or sorcery, without leaving a clear trace on the body.[26] Or, to put it in the language of ritual performance: the *pharmakon* Socrates used against a headache, a certain leaf and a spell, would work only when the two, substance and speech act, were combined; otherwise the herb leaf would remain simply a herb leaf and the spell a string of harmless or strange words that have no consequence.[27] In the same way that spell and herb must be combined in order to heal, a poisonous plant kills only when combined with a spell.

Pharmakeia retained this double meaning ("double" according to our cosmology) throughout antiquity. In his *Laws*, Plato tried to differentiate between *pharmakeia* "that damaged bodies with substances, according to natural laws" and a second type that "does harm . . . with sorcery, spells, and so-called *defixiones*;" the specialist for the first type was the doctor, for the second type the seer and interpreter of miracles.[28] In Plato, this differentiation went together with the overall constitution of a field of magic that was separated from and opposed to religion or medicine; this happened in the fifth and fourth centuries BCE, among philosophers and scientific doctors.[29] In the case of *pharmakeia*, however, Plato's differentiation had not much impact; it remained unheeded for the rest of antiquity', and beyond, as medieval lexicography shows.

In the tenth-century Byzantine Lexicon *Suda*, *pharmakeia* is treated as almost synonymous with *mageia* and *goēteia* being as one of three Greek terms for magic among which it has to be differentiated and more closely defined:

> *Goēteia* (wizardry), *mageia* (magic) and *pharmakeia* (sorcery/poisoning) are different from each other; they all were invented by the Medes and Persians. "Magic" is the invocation of beneficent demons with a good intent, as are for example the oracles of Apollonius of Tyana. "Wizardry" is used for the calling up of a corpse through invocations; therefore it takes its names from the laments and dirges that happen at the grave. *pharmakeia* is when through some lethal concoction something is given to somebody through the mouth as a magic potion.[30]

This group of definitions is well established among learned Byzantines; it might go back, through several removes, to the introduction of a late antique book of spells where the use of these books was justified in a Christian environment in which magic usually had a very bad image and magical books were proscribed.[31] In the last reckoning, however, the distinctions could well go back to a non-Christian source; part of it seems to be known to Augustine in his polemics against Porphyry.[32] The use of a substance and its preparation by a human are the central elements in this definition of *pharmakeia*.

This explains why the two curse inscriptions from Rheneia describe the death also as "murder by cunning stealth" (*dolōi phoneusantas*). A similar description appears in other texts. An inscription from Pisidia, set up by a husband on the grave of his wife and his son, invokes Helios, the Sun god who sees everything, as a possible avenger: "If she died of her own fate, then let it be; but if by stealthy hands, Helios, look after it!"[33] An epitaph from Amisos (Pontos) for a twenty-year-old woman calls upon "the divine light" (that is the Sun god) to revenge her death "if cunning stealth (*dolos*) killed me."[34] And the grave inscription from Salamis on Cyprus for "Kalliope who died age 28" invokes Helios to send "the laments of those who died young" after the unknown stealthy plotter (*epiboulos*): his children shall die an early death as well.[35] A large pair of raised arms with open hands accompanies this text, as it accompanies the two texts from Rheneia.[36]

These texts invoke a powerful and all-knowing divinity to revenge the death, sometimes in a conditional phrase ("if cunning stealth killed me"). Humans cannot know for certain whether there was foul play, and even if they know, they rarely know who did it; the gods—mostly Helios who sees everything—know and will take revenge. Helios is invoked in many cases in which it is impossible to find human justice, especially when a person has committed perjury: in another curse text from Delos, someone complained that a woman did not give back a deposit, against the oath she took. The text again combines the invocation of Helios with a description of the typical gesture: "Theogenes . . . raises his hands to Helios and the Pure Goddess."[37]

This Delian text, although describing the gesture, does not depict it, unlike the Rheneia texts or other epitaphs that implore Helios. An epitaph from Pessinus for a young man, Menodoros, invokes Helios to revenge "whoever laid hands on him, unless it was the violence of a god."[38] The short epitaph with the accompanying image of a pair of raised arms are an addition to a grave monument built by his mother during her lifetime for herself and another son of hers, the young Gallus Asclepius who seems to have died of natural causes. His brother Menodoros was still alive at the time of this inscription, and the mother expected him to outlive her for many years; hence, the text does not mention him. But he unexpectedly died when the monument was still very recent; his grief-stricken mother suspected witchcraft as a reason and added not only the name of her second son, but also a curse against the unknown perpetrators.

The verb that describes Menodoros's death, "to lay hands on" (*enkheireō*), appears in a Latin guise in an epitaph from the Via Appia for the slave girl Timothea, and it again goes together with the invocation to the Sun god and a pair of hands: after a standard grave text, the writer added the invocation: "Sol, I hand over to you who raised his hand against her."[39] A second Latin inscription from the same grave complex on the Via Appia is inscribed on the back of a stele with a standard grave inscription by a couple for their son Callistus; it is an invocation that again is accompanied by two raised hands.[40] This added text uses the grave of an untimely dead, an *ahōros* in the Greek terminology, to address a curse against the unknown murderers of one Severa. This recalls the role that *ahoroi* and *biaiothanatoi*, "those who died early and those who died through violence," play in binding spells that are routinely deposited in their graves: they are often treated as one single category of deceased who willingly help to harm the living, out of frustration about their own short life.[41]

More ambiguity surrounds a group of texts where injustice done and justice sought is central. A closed formulaic group seeks revenge "if someone (in one case "man or woman") has wronged the deceased" (or very similar formulas). Three or perhaps four of the texts come from the Southern shore of the Black Sea, one from Sicily; none concerns a young person (the Sicilian epitaph has been dedicated to a sixty-two-year-old mother).[42] But they all refuse to accept a specific death as natural and suspect foul play; this brings them close to all the other texts collected here. Even if the writers of the epitaphs hesitate to spell out clearly what they mean, it is murder that cannot be traced—that is: *pharmakeia*; open violence would have left a trace and made the conditional phrase unnecessary.

In some cases, such as the one of Menodoros, open violence cannot be fully excluded. This has good reasons: the relatives who were devastated by an untimely death regarded an act of harmful magic as not very different from open murder with a weapon, except that in the latter case they could invoke the law, at least if they knew the culprit. But since the majority of these cases unquestioningly lead one to the assumption of sorcery, this is the more likely explanation here as well.

Things get even murkier when there are invocations to Helios that accompany a standard grave inscription that informs the reader only about the deceased and perhaps the persons who took care of the monument, but is silent about the cause of death. A few inscriptions, all but one from around the Southern shore of the Black Sea, preface an otherwise standard grave text with a short invocation of the god as avenger, such as a stele from Pleuramis in the borderland between Northern Galatia and Pontus that was dedicated by a couple for their two children, Maxima and Maximos; its upper margin carries the invocation "Helios, do justice!"[43] A text from Sestos has a longer invocation to Helios, placed between the picture of two raised arms with open palms: "Lord Helios, look upon us: they shall not escape you!"; a husband dedicated it for his wife.[44] As such, none of these texts gives an unambiguous reason for the invocation of Helios, beyond the suspicion of foul play. But an unambiguous text from Amisos helps to clarify the situation.[45] Amisos is on the western part of the South coast of the Black Sea; it thus is part of the same region. The text ascribed the death of a young man to *dolos*: this refers to the suspicion of *pharmakeia* and most likely explains the other four texts.[46]

Texts from the Roman West: The Evil Hands of a Sorceress

Latin texts appear to be somewhat more outspoken than those of the Greek East.[47] One text, a grave inscription for a four-year-old child, outrightly accuses a *saga*, a witch, for the death, and warns the parents:[48]

> The most cruel hand of a witch has killed me, while she remains on earth and causes damage through her craft. Parents, guard your children, lest grief will attach itself to your heart.

Another text, from Roman Africa, is the grave inscription of a twenty–eight-year-old woman who, like Thermis, died from a slowly killing disease: "Bewitched by spells, she was lying ill for a long time, as life was forced out from her."[49] The grave inscription of a young freewoman in Salona (Dalmatia) who died when twenty-three years old—"at a flourishing age" (*florente aetate*)—after an illness of a year and five months, ascribes this painful death to sorceresses, *veneficae*, whoever they were.[50] The inscription from Rome that curses Acte, a former slave who married her master, for having caused the death of this elderly gentleman, calls her *venenaria* and *dolosa*.[51] According to a late and presumably Christian text from Bulgaria, a young wife "died through sorcery," (*per maleficia de secolo obit*).[52] A final text from Rome for a young girl contains the reference to stealthy action (*dolus*) known from the Greek texts, but names the culprit, the freedman Atimetus; the deceased prays to the gods that he may hang himself, with a formula that is also known from the curse against Acte.[53]

There is no instance among these Latin texts where we would doubt that we deal with what in our thinking too would be sorcery. The victim is "bound down by spells," (*carminibus defixa*) (in a rather technical way of speaking); the accusation is *maleficium*, "sorcery," again in a rather technical sense; the texts talk of *veneficae*, "sorceresses," and they even have a name for one culprit, Atimetus the freedman; no Greek text mentioned an agent. Thus, on the Latin side the categorical systems seems neater, and it might appear that magic has crystallized itself out from the sorcery/poisoning complex as its own category. But this is only partially true, if at all: the two literary texts, Tacitus's account of Germanicus's death and Apuleius's self-defense, show that here too poison and what we would call magic are inseparable. Apuleius had to prove that he was neither an expert in exotic poisons nor in strange rites that made him worship terrible demons, and he countered with the claims that he was a scientist and a pious man. Germanicus's naked body was publicly exposed on the marketplace of Antiochia, and "it showed no sign of poison": the suspicion then was there. At the same time, there is the report on the typical instruments of *defixio* found in his room: the two things supplement each other, or even the same thing.

Accordingly, in the few epigraphical texts that directly refer to *venenum*, "poison," we can assume that the authors really imagined that the death had been administered by harmful potent substances. But as in the case of Germanicus, the deceased were young—a three-year-old boy in one case,[54] a young man of twenty-five who "defended himself against injustice" in another one.[55] We do not know in either case whether the relatives also prosecuted the suspected poisoner or whether they were content with publicizing their anonymous suspicion on a tombstone; but as explanation of an untimely death through stealthy means, the texts are not alien to the overall group.

First Results

Overall, I counted thirty-five grave inscriptions from the Greek and Roman world that suspect foul play as the reason for death; the vast majority belongs to the second and third centuries CE. The number could double if one adds those epitaphs from the Greek East that exhibit a pair of raised hands, but without an invocation to a divinity to avenge an untimely death. Franz Cumont and Louis Robert had explained this symbol in this way (adding only the possibility that the hand might also refer to a manifest murder committed by someone either unknown or unassailable); more recently, scholars felt more inclined to explain the raised hands as a reference to the divine protection of a grave.[56] A close analysis of some clusters, however, has shown that there is no unambiguous evidence for a tomb curse whereas a vast majority of the cases concerns epitaphs for children and adolescents, the rest for people whose death could be felt to be premature by those left behind. There is no need to assume that any of the tombstones with raised hands referred to divine protection of the grave.

The age of the deceased, however, needs some clarification. Following the lead of Cumont, some scholars called them young. But this needs qualifications: although there are children and adolescents among them, some are married and have children (as has the woman in the Alexandria epigram from which I started, or as Germanicus); the victim of Acte was an elderly gentleman of sixty-two years. What counts, then, is not the numerical age, but the unexpectedness of the death that caused unusual grief to those left behind and made them suspect foul play. Louis Robert called them "les morts prématurés": this is correct, if understood not as an objective fact but as a subjective interpretation.

A final point concerns the distinction between death through witchcraft and through murder that I mentioned earlier. There are good reasons to regard all the cases I have reviewed as closely related. For one, among the thirty-five cases I collected there are very few cases that are ambiguous as to violent murder; the vast majority of the cases either talks unambiguously about sorcery or clearly points to it. Secondly, although the age spectrum is wide, there is a surprisingly large number of children and young women among the victims, much more than one would expect if we dealt with violent murder. Furthermore, epitaphs for the victims of murder *manu armata* are usually quite outspoken, in the Greek as in the Roman world, and they do not fit into the group discussed here.[57] And finally, the inscriptions fit into a rather closed chronological frame: very few precursors are late Hellenistic, the main group belongs to the second and third century CE. This again makes them a surprisingly homologous group. In doubtful cases, then, sorcery is a much more likely cause of death than a violent killing.

Alternative Explanations of Sudden Death

Thirty-five texts (or, with the stones that show the raised hands without an explanation, more than seventy) is a relatively small number of cases among the thousands of ancient grave inscriptions that suggest sorcery as cause of death; I have added the two most prominent cases from the literary record. The number is otherwise very small given that such a reaction to premature death was and is widespread in many societies, albeit to a varying degree; few societies go as far as Evans-Pritchard's Azande and ascribe every death to sorcery.[58] But Greeks and Romans of the Imperial epoch certainly believed in the damaging power of sorcery and binding spells. In the age of Nero, the Elder Pliny generalized this belief into a widely held fear: "Nobody is not afraid to fall victim to an evil spell."[59] Three centuries later, the famous case of the orator Libanius again shows the power of such beliefs: the orator and his friends ascribed a series of psychosomatic problems that he suffered to the spells of nasty rivals; we would rather call it Libanius's mid-life crisis.[60] Accordingly, at least in late antiquity some amulets both in Greek and in Latin protected from this danger, although again there are fewer than one would expect.[61] Furthermore, only one of the epigraphical texts aims its accusation at a concrete person, the freedman Atimetus; in all the others, the suspected perpetrator remains anonymous, and there are no trials connected with these cases. In his famous trial, Apuleius was accused of being a sorcerer, but the accusation of having killed Pontianus was dropped immediately; and the trial of Cn. Calpurnius Piso dealt exclusively with high treason and dereliction of a governor's duty, not with sorcery. Why are there so few cases, then, that offer sorcery as an explanation?

One obvious answer would simply be that, ordinarily, such accusations were not recorded on a gravestone. By its very nature, this assertion is not easily proved or disproved. But the fact that longer inscriptions both in Greek and in Latin are usually rather detailed as to the circumstances of death, especially when they deal with an unexpected death, seems to militate against such a simple explanation, as does the possibility of adding the symbol of the raised hands.

Another answer could be that the same society had other mechanisms of dealing with the problem caused by an early death, and these mechanisms were at least as widespread. Many grieving parents or recently married spouses accused not a human "witch" but an envious and malevolent divinity or demon of having caused death; even when these epitaphs give envy, *phthonos* as the single cause for death, it is a demonic power, not the envy of human neighbors that is accused.[62] In a somewhat cruel twist, the parents could be made to feel guilty themselves: many grave inscriptions from Phrygia prohibit violation and unauthorized use of a grave by someone from outside the family and add the threat that those who would not obey "would fall victim to untimely fate": either he or his children would die young.[63]

Another alternative explanation was that the grieving relatives could comfort themselves by believing that the dead had been introduced into Elysium, or turned into a hero, a divinity, or even a star.[64] This saved the beloved dead from the horrors of the Underworld, as did, in other contexts, the initiation into a mystery cult, attested for some young deceased and perhaps implied in all inscriptions that promised a special place in the Underworld.[65] The resulting cult with its regular sacrifices, or simply the gaze to the nightly sky to spot the one star, preserved the memory of the deceased daughter, son, or spouse in a much more constructive way than any accusation of sorcery would have done. The same is true for the few parents who preferred to use the arguments offered by philosophy; although these arguments could be much less conclusive, they still carried weight, as is shown by Plutarch's *Consolation to my Wife*, written after the death of their young daughter Timoxena.[66]

In theory, these ways of reacting to an unexpected death are not mutually exclusive. In practice, they never occur together and thus must be regarded as different methods to cope with such a loss: this helps explain the paucity of cases in which people suspected sorcery. But it leads to another question. Why did people choose the solution they chose, then? Or, to put it differently: what were the reasons some people suspected foul play, *pharmakeia*/sorcery, and others did not? Can we distinguish specific circumstances?

The Circumstances of Witchcraft Accusations

Some inscriptions that contain accusations of sorcery will help us to broaden our approach and find yet another answer to the question why people were choosing the explanation they chose. Almost all of these inscriptions again deal with unexpected death, a few with other matters.

Cursing the Perpetrators

The Alexandrian inscription from which we started contains not only an accusation of *pharmakeia*, but also a curse against the anonymous perpetrator and his or her entire family. It is not the only inscription in our group to do this: all the invocations to Helios are curses, technically spoken; and the texts from Rheneia (nos. 5 and 6) are explicit curses that invoke Iahwe as a revenger. There are other curses in the grave inscriptions, and they may be relevant for our topic as well.

In pre-modern societies, a curse is a judicial instrument that is used when other legal steps to punish a culprit are impossible, for whatever reason. In such a situation, humans called upon their gods for just retribution, and they could make this curse public to make it more effective.[67] At the end of an ascending chain of political responsibility, we find the gods; they take over as the enforcers of retribution when humans are unable to do so, and they are called into action by a curse. In public contexts, a curse is used to punish offenders because there was no human authority left to enforce a punishment. In private contexts, curses are more often used because one did or could not invoke the public authorities for help, either because there was no law available, because the accuser could not make a case that would stand in court, or because they were not wealthy enough for litigation. In both spheres then, the public and the private, a curse was a powerful instrument to enforce justice.

Many among the grave inscriptions that contain curses fit into this same pattern.[68] A complex case that leads back to magic comes from Imperial Rome; it can be pieced together from the two inscriptions on an impressive funerary altar for one Iunia Procula who died at the age of eight years (note 51). The main inscription on the front side of the altar gives the name of the deceased girl, after the indication of her age (*vixit annos VIII menses XI dies V*) and the information that she left father and mother in grief. The name of the person who had the monument made not only for his daughter, but also for himself and another person, the freedman M. Iunius Euphrosynus, occupies the bottom line of this side; the name of the second person, presumably his wife, has been intentionally erased.

A second, lengthy inscription on the back of the same monument explains the erasure and reveals the social drama that led to it. It is written in (rather shaky) iambics. Fittingly enough for this meter, it is a curse, as is the Alexandrian grave epigram: although at this time iambics could be used for all sorts of purposes, their function as medium of public blame and curse in earlier poetry could still be accessible:

> Here is written the eternal disgrace of the freedwoman Acte, sorceress, faithless, treacherous, with a hard heart: a nail and a hemp rope to hang her neck, and boiling pitch to burn her evil breast! Freed for nothing, she followed an adulterer, cheated on her master and abducted the servants, a maid and a boy, while her master was lying in bed, so that the old man, left alone, pined away. (And for Hymnus and Zosimus who followed the same disgrace).[69]

The curse was pronounced against the freedwoman Acte, a "sorceress": she cheated on the man who freed her without charge (presumably to live with her), and when he fell sick, she robbed him of everything, including some of his servants; Hymnus and Zosimus, who are cursed as an afterthought and whose Greek names indicate that they must be slaves, might well be the adulterer and the eloping slave boy. Thus, it is her name that has to be reconstituted in the erasure on the front side.[70] Thus, we can guess the drama in the house of M. Iunius

Euphrosynus.[71] A Greek freedman himself, as his Greek *cognomen* shows, he fell in love with the Greek slave girl Acte and freed her, trading freedom for sex; his claim that he freed her without asking to be paid is true only in a financial sense. But she cheated on him; and when he fell ill after the death of his small daughter Iunia Procula, presumably their common child, she left him and took his two slaves with her; Iunius did not survive the shock. His heirs suspected magic (love magic as the root of his infatuation, binding spells as the reason for his illness, or both), banned her from the family tomb, cursed her and, as an afterthought, added the slaves that followed her to the curse.[72] The curse was inscribed on the tomb of Iunia Procula because she was dead "before her time," an *ahōros* in Greek terminology, and thus was thought to be an ideal messenger and helper with the Underworld gods to whom a curse was implicitly addressed.[73] In theory, Euphrosynus's heirs could have brought Acte to court, as did the relatives of the widow Apuleius married in African Oea. But presumably Acte had moved out and disappeared from Rome; and at any rate, litigation was costly and more of an upper-class matter.

Another grave curse deserves mention more because of its unusual nature than because it deepens our theoretical understanding. It is the gravestone of a sacred cobra and comes from Ptolemaic Memphis in Egypt:[74]

> Stop in front of the impressive stone on the crossroads, stranger, and you will find something frozen in writing; and pouring forth your voice, lament me who went early to the Underworld, me the long-lived aspis, killed through evil hands. What do you gain, most terrible man, that you robbed me of this life? My children will always be with you and your off-spring! I was not alone on earth when you killed me, but there are as many animals on earth as there are grains of sand on the beach of the sea. They will send you to Hades not as the first, but as the last, having witnessed with your eyes the death of your off-spring.

The snake, by nature long-lived, has suffered an early death through a murderous hand; someone else mummified and buried it and added a rather grandiloquent poem that justifies why humans are bitten and killed by snakes in a curse that has almost cosmological dimensions.[75]

These curses are not substantially different from other curses we can read on gravestones; since ancient tombstones were not hidden away in cemeteries but lined the major roads outside a town, for every passerby to read, this was tantamount to the publication of a private curse. In one text, a husband curses those to whom his deceased wife had made a down payment, in case that these persons would refuse to pay him back and thus exacerbate his heavy loss.[76] There were laws against such an embezzlement, but they need incontrovertible ancient proof, and that might have been difficult to obtain in a situation where one party to the payment was dead; furthermore, the grave inscription acted preemptively and must have intended to shame the debtors into compliance. From another text, it becomes clear that an old man cursed his brother on the deathbed for having cheated him his entire life; he then had this curse inscribed on the tombstone as a public revenge.[77]

Rumor and Witchcraft Accusations

Several Hellenistic inscriptions on lead, dedicated in the sanctuary of Demeter in Cnidos, invoke Demeter, Persephone, and the underworld divinities around them as avengers in a situation where no other help was available—the theft of a cloak by an unknown party or the loss of a bracelet that could not be pegged on a thief caught in the act, or the refusal to give back a sum of money for which, foolishly, the lender never had asked for a receipt. Three texts concern *pharmakeia*. In a very fragmentary inscription, a woman calls upon Demeter as an avenger against whoever "has made a *pharmakon*, a potion, an ointment or a spell against me or someone of us."[78] This then remained a suspicion, for whatever reason, against which the presumed victim wanted to protect herself. Similar suspicions become visible in rare oracular answers from the sanctuaries of Dodona and Claros; the client of the oracle asked the god for more information before taking counter-measures or for ideas about these measures.[79] In Cnidos, two other women defended themselves against such accusations. One invoked the goddess against "whoever says that I make a *pharmakon* against my husband"[80]: this, then, is a rumor that the petitioner wanted to stop—if we can take the present tense literally, she was accused of still being at it, and her husband might have been ill, but he was still alive.[81] The second text is more serious, and more circumstantial: the writer called the wrath of the goddess upon herself, "if ever I have given Asklepiadas a *pharmakon* or intended something evil in my heart against him, or called a woman to the temple so that she, for three half-drachmas, would remove him from among the living."[82] The seriousness of the self-curse must mean that Asklepiadas had died, and that his death was ascribed, directly or indirectly, to the sorcery/poisoning of the speaker, with several rumored stories of how she went about her crime, either doing it herself or engaging someone else, a local sorceress. Slander and rumor again, then, but of a more insidious kind, destined to ruin the reputation and the social standing of a widow.

A very different text comes from further east and is dated a few centuries later. In one of the so-called "confession inscriptions" from Eastern Lydia, a woman named Tatias is accused of having used a *pharmakon* against her son-in-law who suddenly had become insane. She defended herself with a public confession of her innocence, invoking the local god, Men, in a self-curse. She promptly died:

this proved both her guilt and the god's power. Shortly afterward her son had a fatal accident: this made the god's point even more clear.[83] The mechanism, then, is very similar to what we perceive in Cnidos. Misfortune strikes a family; a suspicion of foul play arises and is directed against a woman (the wife of a deceased or ill husband, the mother-in-law of a mentally ill man). The rumor spreads, and the woman has to defend herself publicly by having recourse to the gods.

Thus, many or perhaps all of these accusations of sorcery were accompanied by and based on rumor. Rumor must also have played a vital role in Apuleius's case: Apuleius himself provoked the sorcery trial in a desperate attempt to stop the local gossip.[84] And in his account of Germanicus's death, Tacitus relied heavily on the rumors that were running in the family: to use rumors as comments on the actors of his *History* was a firm part of his historiographical method.[85]

Sorcery and Social Stress

These few cases, more eloquent on the internal dynamics that surrounded accusations of *pharmakeia* than the more reticent grave epigrams, help to understand what has been going on, and they tie in with sociological and anthropological theory. Social anthropologists have long agreed that ideas of witchcraft and sorcery are indicators of underlying social or cultural stress and provide "channels for the expression of hostility" present in social relations; in this reading, witchcraft beliefs in a very general sense are present in most societies.[86] In the course of the debate, however, simplistic models have been rightly challenged, and it has become clear that a witchcraft accusation is always "a complex therapeutic-narrative-mythological construct."[87] In a chapter of her *Natural Symbols*, Mary Douglas proposed a theoretical model to understand what sort of societies develop what sort of witchcraft beliefs.[88] "By and large witchcraft beliefs are likely to flourish in small enclosed groups, where movement in and out is restricted, when interaction is unavoidably close, and where roles are undefined or so defined that they are impossible to perform" (108); in such groups, "the body politic tends to have a clear external boundary, and a confused internal state in which envy and favoritism flourish." This model certainly works for the cases of Germanicus and of Apuleius. In Germanicus's case, we can define the groups as the courtly élite or, more narrowly, the group of Roman aristocrats and administrators in Syria who had Tiberius's ear but functioned outside any institutional control; for Apuleius, the group is the extended family of Apuleius's wife Pudentilla that comprised her sons, her two brother-in-laws, and Apuleius himself. In the case of Germanicus, Tiberius had (either by design or by administrative bungling) never defined the respective competences of Cn. Calpurnius Piso, the governor of Syria, and Germanicus, the emperor's special envoy to this same province. This resulted in conflicts, both between the two men and between their wives, Agrippina and Plancina, revealing how closely knit this group was, similar to British administrators in India or Kenya. And when Germanicus died unexpectedly after a prolonged illness, Piso and his wife were accused of *veneficium*, especially, we can assume, by Germanicus's widow Agrippina, who had a knack for publicity. In Apuleius's case, roles were hopelessly embroiled once the itinerant young philosopher married the mother of his best friend; the brothers of her deceased husband used the accusation of magic as a weapon in the competition with Apuleius for her considerable estate. Apuleius's role was much more problematical than that of Cn. Piso, since he was an outsider, being a philosopher and a foreigner; in his *Apology*, he was at pains to prove that in truth he fitted well into provincial upper-class society.[89] In both cases, these groups existed in an environment that functioned differently from their own internal workings. The Roman state retained most of its role definitions for public office and the traditional rules for competition even under the changed conditions of the Imperial system; there was no room for witchcraft accusations in the senatorial trial of Piso and his wife. The same must have been true, albeit perhaps to a lesser degree, for the way the political and social life of the province Africa was functioning in Apuleius's time; Apuleius could provoke a trial of sorcery in order to clear himself of all suspicions.

The inscriptions studied above that give details of *pharmakeia/veneficium* (Cnidos, Phrygia, the case of Acte) confirm the sociological analysis, although we have much less data than in the two literary cases. Some inscriptions deal with the narrow world of the ancient Mediterranean household, and they point to the loosely defined roles that were characteristic for it. The Greek *oikos* is patrilinear and patriarchal, with roles that were always open to definition, depending on how well one got along with the patriarch. Wives and their mothers were the dangerous intruders in such a male-defined *oikos*: this explains why the wife of a deceased or ill husband or the mother-in-law of a mentally ill man was easily targeted; they were the least well-defined members of the household. In Roman society, with its clear-cut dichotomy between free masters and unfree slaves, *libertae* and *liberti* are persons who are in an ambivalent social position, no more slaves and not yet full citizens. Suspicions of sorcery could target them from early on, as a story shows that is preserved by Pliny the Elder but goes back to the early second century BCE. According to Pliny, C. Furius Cresimus, a freedman who had become a very successful landowner and farmer, was accused of magically moving his neighbors' crops onto his own fields; he could convince his townsmen that this was gossip that resulted from envy.[90] If the household itself is one of a freedman and the mistress is a former slave girl elevated to freedom and the conjugal bed of the master, a girl who perhaps is also much younger than the master, the problems of role definition and the tensions that result from them are even greater.

Other inscriptions, as well as the case of Cresimus, show social dynamics outside the family at work, in the face-to-face situations that characterized the life in an ancient village and in the village-like neighborhoods of ancient cities; the inscription from Alexandria that formed the starting point of this investigation must belong to such a background. Here, social stress is inevitable, and it is in rumor and gossip that such stress found focus and relief.[91] Against a reading that stresses the normativity of rumor, I would underline its cognitive function that has been described as "collective process of reducing uncertainty." In the dialogic process that creates rumor, sudden and vague fears that result from unexpected events are focused on specific actions that then could be ascribed to specific individuals who would serve as scapegoats.[92] In most of our cases, we see or we can at least assume that gossip and rumor surrounded these untimely deaths: to look for the action of an evil human perpetrator and her supernatural ritual power was an accepted way of dealing with the high emotional stress generated by the loss of a young family member, a child, or a wife. Rumors must have been especially rampant when a young man suddenly died while he was embroiled in legal or other fights to defend himself, as in the singular text from Heba in Tuscany (see note 55). But whereas such rumors would often lead to the witchcraft trials in early modern Europe or to the formal ritual procedures among Evans-Pritchard's Azandes, such trials were rare in the ancient world, as we saw, and curses were much more often used to take revenge on the sorcerer.[93] This has to do with the fact that sorcery sits somewhat uneasily in the Greek and Roman judicial system. Although not all Greek cities had laws against sorcery or *pharmakeia*, some are attested, from Plato's imaginary laws to the real Imperial edicts in the Theodosian code, and we know about a few trials that were based on these laws.[94] But even where there were laws, there existed major obstacles to such trials. In a pragmatic view, murder through *pharmakeia* was difficult to prove, for good reason. Before the rise of modern forensic techniques, most poisonous substances could not be traced; thus, the accusation of *pharmakeia* often enough could be nothing more than a slander without much evidence; neither the facts nor the perpetrator were easily determined. As importantly, the crimes that the curse was to punish were mostly a domestic affair, and the house stayed as much as possible outside the legal system of Greek and Roman society. Accusations of magic entered the public space especially when the political structures themselves began to show signs of stress, as they did in the third century CE, or in the fragile political world of fourth-century BCE Athens.

The key role of rumor helps to understand the sometimes tantalizingly vague language of many of the epitaphs we have been dealing with: as we have seen, their writers often do not use an unambiguous and "technical" term, such as *pharmakon* or *venenum*, but prefer to allude to what has happened in ambiguous language, or they embed it in a conditional clause. It is not something about which people talked freely and openly. To suspect someone in one's community of having had a hand in the death of a child or a young wife was bad enough, to point fingers openly and make clear accusations is a risk to social peace that one wanted to avoid. And who would know whether one invited death and destruction upon oneself by being too outspoken?

Social stress, then, and the rumors that go with it are a convenient overall explanation. We are mostly concerned with the closed world of the Mediterranean house or with the face-to-face world of the ancient village or city. If we discern social status, we see the ambivalent persons of freed slaves as the prime targets and marked social disequilibrium as the dominant circumstance. In the two cases from Delos, we might deal with immigrants in a multicultural environment, another instance of social tensions and unresolved social positioning. About a century earlier another immigrant or rather grandson of an immigrant, the Egyptian priest Apollonios, had overcome a similar social conflict with the local Greek merchants by what they undoubtedly regarded as magic, although Apollonios himself preferred to ascribe it to the power of his god. When his enemies tried to prevent the planned construction of a new temple to Apollonios's god Sarapis by bringing him to court, they suddenly were unable to speak, and Apollonios won. To tie the tongue of one's courtroom adversaries was an established practice of ancient magic.[95]

At the same time, the model has its limitations. According to Mary Douglas "envy and favoritism" are characteristics of the internal dynamics of the small groups we deal with; envy leads to binding spells and other magical attacks, as André Bernard tried to generalize for the ancient world.[96] In our material, however, envy plays a different role: it is rarely articulated as a trigger for magical attacks, more often it is a demonic force that can provide an alternative explanation for an early death. Again, we detect a strong hesitation against witchcraft accusations all over the ancient world, a hesitation that might well have to do with the fundamental cohesion of the small groups we deal with: over the vindictive disruption of the group that would have been the result of a witchcraft accusation, individual group members preferred the accusation of an envious superhuman force.[97] Only outsiders such as (former) slaves or unnamed and thus undefined humans were acceptable targets of such accusations.

We can also discern regional variations that must feed on specific local traditions, most clearly along the Northern coast of Asia Minor: such variations resist the uniform sociological model by bringing in a moment of choice based on tradition. This emphasizes the insight that very often we are unable to understand the choices made by the individual local actors in each instance. "The crucial point to note here (to cite again a social anthropologist) is that such explanations are not applied indiscriminately, still less 'irrationally.' They belong to local logic of explanation, and they are applied in cases that within such local logic call for special focus and attention."[98] Not all comparable situations led to an accusation of witchcraft: the model is not predictive, it is only descriptive. Not even during the European witch craze, all domestic or public social and cultural tensions lead to witchcraft accusations.[99] In order to understand the single instance, we need much more information than we can even hope to obtain. This means that, in all epigraphical cases, these specific reasons are unrecoverable, since they are rooted in details of individual lives and local traditions to which we do not have access any more, unlike the modern social anthropologists who deal with living societies. Inscriptions preserve only what the indigenous writer chose to tell us, and that in most cases excludes the trivial details of life that are so valuable to the social anthropologist.

Results

Two positive results of this inquiry have to be highlighted, beyond the agnosticism that results from our fragmentary record. One is the insight into the relatively small number of sorcery accusations that are attested in this record, given the large number of grave inscriptions for young people, and given that this explanatory mechanism was so well established in many other cultures. Ancient societies, both in Greece and in Rome, did not easily yield to such accusations, and even if they did, the accusations remained mostly on the level of suspicion, rumor, and gossip, and did not make it into the courtrooms. "Real" witches, that is, were very rare in the world of Imperial Greece and Rome, unlike what ancient and modern fiction would make us believe.

The other insight that deserves to be stressed is that there is no clear genderization of the persons accused of having caused an early death through *pharmakeia*. Often, the person remains undefined, both as to gender and to identity. In a few cases, a woman is accused, such as the courtesan Theoris of Lemnos in a notorious case of love magic in fourth-century Athens; the otherwise unknown Martina in connection with Germanicus's death; the "evil" *liberta* Acte or an anonymous *saga* in Imperial Rome, or unspecified *veneficae* in another Roman epigram.[100] More rarely, the accused is a man—the philosopher Apuleius, an unknown *magus* in a Clarian oracle from Western Asia Minor, the freeman Atimetus in Imperial Rome.[101] Compared to the stereotype of the female witch that we find in Greek and Roman literature, the reality "on the ground" is much more complex.[102]

Abbreviations

BE	*Bulletin Épigraphique*
CIL	*Corpus Inscriptionum Latinarum*
CLE	Franz Bücheler, Alexander Riese, Ernst Lommatzsch, eds., *Carmina Latina Epigraphica*. 3 vols. (Leipzig: Teubner, 1895. 1897. 1926)

IG	*Inscriptiones Graecae*
I.Délos	*Inscriptions de Délos*
PGM	Karl Preisendanz, ed., *Papyri Graecae Magicae*, 2 vols. (Leipzig and Berlin: Teubner, 1928–1931, revised ed. by Albert Henrichs 1973–1974)
SGOst	Reinhold Merkelbach and Josef Stauber, eds., *Steinepigramme aus dem griechischen Osten*, 5 vols. (Stuttgart and Leipzig: Teubner and München: Saur 1998–2004)
SEG	*Supplementum Epigraphicum Graecum*
ThesCRA	*Thesaurus Cultus Rituumque Antiquorum* (Los Angeles: Getty, 2004–2006)

Notes

1. In what follows I do not make terminological differentiations between sorcery and witchcraft. None of the definitions tried in scholarship are convincing, and scholars have underlined "the complex and shifting boundaries of indigenous conceptualizations," (Pamela J. Stewart and Andrew Strathern, eds., *Witchcraft, Sorcery, Rumors and Gossip* [Cambridge: Cambridge University Press, 2003], 2), with reference to Lucy Mair's warning of "overdefinition," in Lucy Mair, *Witchcraft* (London: World University Library, 1969), 21. An earlier and much shorter version of my thoughts on this text has been published in Sabrina Buzzi et al., eds., *Zona Archaeologica. Festschrift für Hans Peter Isler zum 60. Geburtstag* (Bonn: Habelt, 2001), 183–91. I thank Sarah Iles Johnston for manifold help and input.
2. Louis Robert, *Inscriptions grecques* (vol. 1 of *Collection Froehner*; Paris: Éditions des Bibliothèques nationales, 1936), 122 no. 77; see also Louis Robert, *Hellenica* (vol. 2; Limoges: Bontemps, 1942), 122f.; Werner Peek, *Grab-Epigramme* (vol. 1 of *Griechische Vers-Inschriften*; Berlin: Akademie-Verlag, 1955), 1875; Étienne Bernand, *Inscriptions métriques de l'Égypte gréco-romaine* (Paris: Belles Lettres, 1969), 209 no. 46. Robert added two more cases in Louis Robert, *Opera Minora Selecta* (vol. 7 of *Épigraphie et antiquités grecques*; Amsterdam: Hakkert, 1990), 235 n. 40 (orig. *Journal des Savants* 1973, 172 n. 40).
3. The Greek I follow is the one of Bernand, *Inscriptions métriques*, except for some details of interpunction.
4. *φάρμακα* in Greek. The *φάρμακα* are an Erinys, a destructive underworldly demon: compare Aesch. *Septem* 70 where Eteokles calls the curse of his father an "overpowering Erinys," Ἐρινὺς μεγασθενής.
5. Robert, *Hellenica*, 123, understands "three months" as the time passed after her death and puts a comma after *μῆνας*. This, however, interrupts the fiction of a timeless voice of the deceased.
6. Peek, *Grab-Epigramme* puts a stop after *κἀνδρός* and reads *οὐ*. This turns the following into a rhetorical question, which simplifies the syntax but adds an unconvincing flourish; Bernard does not follow, and rightly so.

7. The vocabulary often aspires to be poetical, and combinations such as οἰκτρὰς Ἐρινῦς φαρμάκων (7) are quite ambitious (but well done), as is the entire verse 17. The syntax in v. 13f. is rather convoluted, and my translation is approximate only.
8. The illness, φθίσις in l. 10, is far from specific: it can have been almost any long, drawn-out disease.
9. The names, however, would not forbid such an assumption. Whereas the name Thermis appears only here, Simalos is rather common; one Simalos, son of Timarchos, from Salamis on Cyprus, is a friend of a courtier, admiral and secretary of Ptolemy II, *I.Délos* 1533 and 1534.
10. Edward E. Evans-Pritchard, *Witchcraft, Oracles and Magic Among the Azande* (Oxford: Clarendon, 1937); Jeanne Favret-Saada, *Les mots, la mort, les sorts: La sorcellerie dans le Bocage* (Paris: Gallimard, 1977). Karl Meuli's ambitious project was never finished, for an overview see his paper "Lateinisch 'morior'—deutsch 'morden'" in Karl Meuli, *Gesammelte Schriften*. ed. Thomas Gelzer (Basel: Schwabe, 1975), 439–44. See also Richard Kieckhefer, *Magic in the Middle Ages* (Cambridge: Cambridge University Press, 1989), 180f. on the European Middle Ages. Combining social anthropology with the psychoanalytic theory of Melanie Klein, Michele Stephen, "Witchcraft, Grief, and the Ambivalences of Emotion," *AEth* 27 (1999): 711–37 proposed a psychoanalytical reading in order to explain the crosscultural presence of the connection.
11. Tac., *Ann.* 2.53–61, 69–74; 3.12–19. See Anne-Marie Tupet, "Les pratiques magiques à la mort de Germanicus," *Mélanges Pierre Wuillemier* (Paris: Gallimard, 1980), 345–52; see also Elizabeth Ann Pollard in this volume.
12. On the Younger Agrippina's memoirs as a rare source about her mother, Germanicus's wife, see Tac., *Ann.* 4.53; my citation is from Ronald Syme, *Tacitus* (Oxford: Clarendon, 1958), 277.
13. For details on the magical rites in Tac., *Ann.* 2.69, see also Suet., *Calig.* 3 (*veneficiis et devotionibus*). On the sorceress Martina, Tac., *Ann.* 3.7.
14. Werner Eck, Antonio Caballos, and Fernando Fernández, *Das Senatus Consultum de Cn. Pisone Patre* (Vestigia 48; Munich: Beck, 1996).
15. This becomes clear from *Apol.* 96.5f.: Apuleius refers to letters Pontianus sent him from his travel to and his stay in Carthage, "some when he still was healthy, some when he already was ill" (*litteras... praemisit ... quas adhuc validus, quas iam aeger*).
16. Apul., *Apol.* 2: "He [*Aemilianus, the main accuser*] clamored that I killed Pontianus, the son of his brother. But when he should have signed to the official accusation, he immediately forgot about him." *Pontianum fratris sui filium, quam paulo prius occisum a me clamitaret, postquam ad subscribendum compellitur, ilico oblitus est.*
17. For a full and detailed catalog with extensive justifications for my choices, see my paper in *Zeitschrift für Papyrologie und Epigraphik* 162(2008), 139–150; see also the catalogs of Franz Cumont, "Il sole vindice dei delitti ed il simbolo delle mani alzate," *MPARA*, n.s., 1 (1923): 65–80, Franz Cumont, "Deux monuments du culte solaire," *Syria* 14

(1933): 385–95, and Gudmund Björck, *Der Fluch des Christen Sabinus*, (PU 8; Uppsala: Almqvist & Wiksell, 1938).

18. Side (Pamphylia), short epitaph in prose, second/third century CE: George E. Bean, *The Inscriptions of Side* (Ankara: Türk Tarih Kurumu Basimevi, 1965), no. 152; Johannes Nollé, *Side im Altertum* (IGSK 44; Bonn: Habelt, 2001): 528 no. 206.
19. *IG* 12:8 no. 540. In an only marginally less open way, an epigram from the island of Andros ascribed the death of a young athlete from a noble family who was buried together with his son to the action of "unholy plants," *IG* 12:5 no. 764, an easy circumlocution for poison.
20. For Arsinoe *áōros* ("who died untimely"); late second/early third century CE: *Sammelbuch* 1323; Cumont, "Il sole vindice", 76 no. 22; Björck, *Der Fluch*, 29 no. 11.
21. One is today in Bukarest, the other in Athens; late second/early first century BCE—*SIG*[3] 1181; *Corpus Inscriptionum Iudaicarum* 1 no. 725; Björck, *Der Fluch*, 29 no. 11; *I.Délos* 2532; for two other curses from Delos, see *I.Délos* 2531 (from the sanctuary of the Foreign Gods), and *IG* XI 1296 (*ThesCRA* 3, 251 no. 15).
22. Hdt. 1.64; Thuc. 3.104.1.
23. ἐπὶ τοὺς δόλωι φονεύσαντας ἢ φαρμακεύσαντας τὴν ταλαίπωρον ἄωρον Μαρθίνη/Ηρακλέαν ἐκχέαντας τὸ ἀναίτιον αἷμα ἀδίκως. "They shed innocent blood, the blood of their sons and daughters" is *Psalm* 105.38 (LXX: ἐξέχεαν αἷμα ἀθῷον, αἷμα υἱῶν αὐτῶν καὶ θυγατέρων); the juncture is also used in the opening letter of 2 *Maccabees* 1.8, written less than a century earlier than the two inscriptions.
24. As we are reminded by Philippe Descola, *Par-delà nature et culture* (Paris: Gallimard, 2005).
25. The so-called *Dirae Teorum*, published with a short commentary in Russell Meiggs and David Lewis, *A Selection of Greek Historical Inscriptions to the End of the Fifth Century* B.C. (Oxford: Clarendon, 1989 [1969]): no. 30.
26. For the ancient sources of the lex Cornelia see Crawford 1996: 749–53; on its use in cases of magic James Rives, "Magic in Roman Law: the Reconstruction of a Crime," *CAn* 22 (2003): 312–39.
27. Plato, *Chrm.* 155e.
28. Plato, *Leg.* 11.932e–933b: σώμασι σώματα κακουργοῦσα κατὰ φύσιν against μαγγανείαις τέ τισιν καὶ ἐπωιδαῖς καὶ καταδέσεσι λεγομέναις [...] βλάπτειν.
29. See Marcello Carastro *La cité des mages. Penser la magie en Grèce ancienne* (Grenoble: Millon, 2006).
30. *Suda*, s.v. γ 365: γοητεία καὶ μαγεία καὶ φαρμακεία διαφέρουσιν· ἅπερ ἐφεῦρον Μῆδοι καὶ Πέρσαι. μαγεία μὲν οὖν ἐστιν ἐπίκλησις δαιμόνων ἀγαθοποιῶν δῆθεν πρὸς ἀγαθοῦ τινος σύστασιν, ὥσπερ τὰ τοῦ Ἀπολλωνίου Τυανέως θεσπίσματα. γοητεία δὲ ἐπὶ τῶι ἀνάγειν νεκρὸν δι' ἐπικλήσεως, ὅθεν εἴρηται

ἀπὸ τῶν γόων καὶ τῶν θρήνων τῶν περὶ τοὺς τάφους γινομένων. φαρμακεία δὲ ὅταν διά τινος σκευασίας θαναταφόρου πρὸς φίλτρον δοθῆι τινι διὰ στόματος.

31. According to Ada Adler in her notes on the *Suda* gloss, the immediate source is the ninth-century Chronicle of George the Monk, C. de Boor, ed. (*Georgii Monachi Chronicon* [vol. 1; Leipzig: Teubner, 1904], 74). But a very similar differentiation is found a century before that in Pseudo-Nonnus, *Commentarii ad carmina S. Gregorii* 64 (PG 38,491 attributed to Cosmas of Jerusalem); on the collection of spells see Gustave Przychozki, "De commentarii cuiusdam magici vestigia," *ByzZ* 22(1913): 65–71. I thank Anthony Kaldellis for his help with these intricacies of Byzantine scholarship. For magical books: Zachariah, *Vita Severi* 60–68; Callinicus, *Vita Hypatii* 43; vgl. *Codex Theodosianus* 9.16.12 (astrology).
32. August., *De civ. D.* 10.9.
33. Ramsay 1888: 265 no. 6; William R. Ramsay, *The Cities and Bishoprics of Phrygia* (Oxford: Clarendon, 1895), 339 no. 187; Cumont, "Il sole vindice", 75 no. 12; Björck, *Der Fluch*,, 26 no. 3; Bean 1959: 109 no. 78; see also *BÉ* 1961, 739.
34. Ca. 200 CE; J. G. C. Anderson, Franz Cumont, and Henri Grégoire, *Recueil des inscriptions grecques et latines du Pont et l'Arménie* (SPo 3; Brussels: Lamertin, 1910), 75 no. 15; Björck, *Der Fluch*, 25 no. 2.
35. Second century CE; Franz Cumont, "Nuovi epitaffi col simbolo della preghiera al dio vindice," *APARA*, 3rd ser., Rendiconti 5 (1926–1927); Björck, *Der Fluch*, 27 no. 5; Jean Pouilloux, Paul Roesch, and Jean Marcillet-Jaubert, *Corpus épigraphique* (SaCh 13; Paris: Boccard, 1987), no. 198.
36. The original editors mistakenly called the Salamis text a *defixio*; Cumont, "Deux monuments" corrected them.
37. Delos, *I.Délos* 2531, invocation to Helios and Ἁγνὴ Θεά, i.e. the Greek goddess Atargatis (I translate the introduction: *Θεογένης [— —] | κατ' ἀναγίου(?) αἴρει τὰς χεῖρας | τῷ Ἡλίῳ, καὶ τῇ ἁγνῇ θεᾷ*), and one from Stephen Mitchell, *The Ankara District: The Inscriptions of North Galatia* (vol. 2 of *Regional Epigraphic Catalogues of Asia Minor*; Oxford: B.A.R., 1982), no. 242, a regular epitaph with an added curse for the possibility that a deposit which the deceased woman had made before her death would not be restituted to the widower.
38. 175–200 CE: Pierre Lambrechts and R. Bogaert, "Asclépios, archigalle pessinontien de Cybèle," in *Hommages à Marcel Renard*, ed. Jacqueline Bibauw, vol. 2, CL102 (Brussels: Collection Latomus, 1969), 404–14, esp. 412–14; see also Marc Waelkens, *Die kleinasiatischen Türsteine. Typologische und epigraphische Untersuchungen der kleinasiatischen Grabreliefs mit Scheintür* (Mainz: Von Zabern, 1986), 291 no. 753; Johan Strubbe, *The Inscriptions of Pessinous* (IGSK 66; Bonn: Habelt, 2005), 84 no. 53).
39. *CIL* VI 3, 14099; Dessau, *ILS* 8497[a]; Cumont, "Il sole vindice", 65: *Sol, tibi commendo qui manus intulit ei.*
40. *CIL* VI 3, 14098; Dessau, *ILS* 8497; Cumont "Il sole vindice", 65.

41. On these two groups, see Sarah Iles Johnston, *Restless Dead. Encounters between the Living and the Dead in Ancient Greece* (Berkeley: University of California Press, 1999), 127–99. The same can be seen in the curse against the "witch" Acte, below n. 51.
42. Amisos (Pontus), today in the Musée du Louvre in Paris, prose epitaph; imperial epoch: Alphonse Dain, *Inscriptions grecques du Musée du Louvre. Les textes inédits* (Paris: Les Belles Lettres, 1933), 41 no. 34. A freedman.—Saatli (Northern Galatia), prose epitaph; imperial epoch: *MAMA* 7.402; Mitchell, *Ankara District*, no. 362; *SEG* 40,1219. Husband and son, dedicated by wife and two brothers.—Sogluca (Northern Galatia), prose epitaph; third century CE: Mitchell, *Ankara District*, no. 246. Wife, no age given.—Yalta museum, prose epitaph; imperial epoch: *Vestnik Drevnei Istorii* 51 (1955), 174–76 (perhaps imported from the same region).—Licodia Eubea (Sicily), prose epitaph, third/fourth century CE: *IG* XIV 254; Maria Teresa Manni Piraino, *Iscrizioni Greche Lapidare del Museo di Palermo* (Palermo: Flaccovio, 1973), no. 18. Widow, sixty-two years old; dedicated by her daughter.
43. Anderson, Cumont and Grégoire, *Recueil des inscriptions*, no. 258; Cumont, "Il sole vindice," 75 no. 16. Other texts from the same region: (a) Dorylaion (North Eastern Phrygia), prose epitaph, third century CE: *Živa Antica* 44 (1994), 170 no. 26 (*SEG* 44, 1994, no. 1059).
44. *CIG* 2016d; Johannes Krauss, *Die Inschriften von Sestos und der thrakischen Chersones*. (IGSK 19; Bonn: Habelt, 1980), no. 66.
45. See n. 42.
46. In the Greek grave inscription of a young girl from Bostra in Northern Arabia (imperial epoch; Philippe Le Bas and William Henry Waddington, *Voyage archéologique en Grèce et en Asie Mineure* [vol. 3; Paris: Firmin-Didot et Cie, 1870], no. 1928; Björck, *Der Fluch*, 31 no. 17; Maurice Sartre, Les inscriptions grecques et latines de la Syrie [13:1; Paris, 1982], no. 9363), the deceased curses those who killed her by "using bad words," ***kakologoûntes***. This verb is rare and otherwise not used for spells but for slander (or, even more rarely, for bad style), but bad words that cause a death might well be spells that caused a girl's death.
47. See Iiro Kajanto, "On the 'freedom of speech' in Latin epitaphs," *Latomus* 27 (1968): 187–88; but there are many more examples than he gives, e.g., *CIL* II 2968 *a latronibus interfectus* (not the only case); III 2399 *interfecta annorum X causa ornamentorum* "killed at age 10 because of her jewelry"; or VIII 2268 *a tauro deceptus "tricked by a bull"*; *Année Épigraphique* 1997 no. 339 *ab inimico suasus, gladio interfectus* "lured by the enemy, killed by the sword," about a one-year-old boy and his father.
48. Rome, from the Esquilin, now in Verona; metrical epitaph, before 31 CE (?): *CIL* VI 3, 19747; *CLE* 987.
49. *CIL* VIII 2756; *CLE* 1604; Björck, *Der Fluch*, 31 no. 16.—The husband was an officer in the military unit that could have been involved with the arrest of Perpetua

and her fellow Christians, as Andrzej Wypustek, "Magic, Montanism, Perpetua, and the Severan Persecution," *VC* 51, no. 3 (1997): 276–97, esp. 283 has pointed out.

50. *CIL* III 2197 = *CLE* 1534B.
51. Late first/second century CE; *CIL* VI 3, 20905; *CLE* 95. The curse is inscribed on the back of the grave altar for their common daughter Procula who died as a child (which of course might have precipitated the marital crises of Acte and her master/husband); the spirit of this child is thus used as the carrier of the curse, see also above note 39.
52. Fourth or fifth century CE: Veselin Beševliev, *Spätgriechische und spätlateinische Inschriften aus Bulgarien* (Berlin: Akademie Verlag, 1964), 135 no. 2.
53. Second century CE: *CIL* VI 2, 12649; Björck, *Der Fluch*, 32 no. 20.
54. Teate (Chieti), prose epitaph; uncertain epoch: *CIL* IX 3030.
55. Heba (Tuscany), now in the museum of Grosseto; late Republic/early imperial epoch: Heikki Solin, "Analecta Epigraphica LXVII–LXXVIII," *Arctos* 15 (1981): 101–23, 105f.
56. Most prominently Marie-José Morant, "Mains levés, mains supines, à propos d'une base funéraire de Kadyanda (Lycie)," *Ktema* 24 (1999): 289–94.
57. For Latin inscriptions, see the indices of *CIL* under the entry *mortes singulares.*
58. See the remarks of Robin Briggs, *Witches and Neighbours. The Social and Cultural Context of European Witchcraft* (London: HarperCollins, 1996), 63 on the small number of such accusations even during the European witch-craze.—I thus disagree with Robert, *Inscriptions grecques*, 55, and Hendrik S. Versnel, "*Kolasai tous hēmas toioutous hēdeōs blepontes* 'Punish Those Who Rejoice in Our Misery': On Curse Texts and *Schadenfreude*," in *The World of Ancient Magic: Papers from the First International Samson Eitrem Seminar at the Norwegian Institute at Athens, 4–8 May 1997* (ed. David R. Jordan, Hugo Montgomery, and Einar Thomassen; PNIA 4; Bergen: Paul Åströms Förlag, 1999), 125–62. esp. 133, who assume a vaguely large number of cases.
59. *Defigi quidem diris precationibus nemo non metuit* Plin., *HN* 28, 19.
60. Still the most important interpretation: Campbell Bonner, "Witchcraft in the Lecture Room of Libanius," *Transactions of the American Philological Association* 63 (1932): 34–44; see also Fritz Graf, *Magic in the Ancient World* (Cambridge, MA: Harvard University Press, 1997) 164f.
61. See the remarks of Christoph Schäublin, in Thomas Gelzer, Michael Lurje, and Christoph Schäublin, *Lamella Bernensis. Ein spätantikes Goldamulett mit christlichem Exorzismus und verwandte Texte* (BzAl 124; Stuttgart: Teubner, 1999), 85f.
62. A good collection and discussion of the evidence is still lacking. But see Anne-Marie Vérilhac, *ΡΑΙΔΕΣ ΑΩΡΟΙ: Poésie funéraire* (Athens: Athens Academy Press, 1978), 2.199–201 and Johnston, *Restless Dead*, 193 for a selection of texts and a discussion; see also Renate Schlesier, "Zauber und Neid. Zum Problem des bösen Blicks in der antiken griechischen Tragödie," in *Tradition und Translation.*

Festschrift für Carsten Colpe (ed. Christoph Elsas and Hans G. Kippenberg; Berlin: de Gruyter, 1994), 96–112 and Thomas Rakoczy, *Böser Blick. Macht des Auges und Neid der Götter. Eine Untersuchung zur Kraft des bösen Blicks in der griechischen Literatur* (CM 13; Tübingen: Gunter Narr Verlag, 1996) for a literary perspective.

63. A list of instances for this hexametrical curse (*ὅς ἂν προσοίσει χεῖρα τὴν βαρύφθονον | οὕτως ἀώροις περιπέσοιτο συμφοραῖς*: "whoever will lay a hand full of envy on it, shall fall victim to an untimely fate") in Johan Strubbe, ARAI EPITUMBIOI. Imprecations against Desecrators of the Grave in Greek Epitaphs of Asia Minor. A catalog (IGSK 52; Bonn: Habelt, 1997), 123; a variation of the same curse dedicates the perpetrator to black Hekate's demons, *Ἑκάτης μελαίνης περιπέσοιτο δα[ί]μοσιν*, *MAMA* 10,189 (Appia in Phrygia; 212–220 CE). On the curse to lose one's children see below, note 75.

64. On heroization, see Fritz Graf, *Nordionische Kulte* (Rome: Institut Suisse, 1985), 131f.; catasterism: Franz Cumont, *Lux perpetua* (Paris: Geuthner, 1949), 290–305 and Vérilhac, *PAIΔEΣ AΩPOI,* 2, 325–30. Greek epigrams relating to young deceased in Vérilhac, *PAIΔEΣ AΩPOI,* vol. 1 nos. 197 (among "the children of the gods"), 198 (new Ganymedes), 199 (among the Olympians), 200–201 (star); a sarcophagus for a senator's young daughter, Robert Cohon, "A Muse Sarcophagus in Its Context," *AA* (1992): 109–19.

65. A collection of Greek epigrams in Vérilhac, *ΠAIΔEΣ AΩPOI,* vol. 1, nos. 192–94, 196–97; a Latin text *CLE 1233* (Thessaly, Bacchus); much vaguer, e.g., *IG* XII:7,115 (Arkesine, late Hellenistic), again in Peek, *Grab-Epigramme*, (above, n.1) no. 1155 and Vérilhac, *ΠAIΔEΣ AΩPOI*, vol. 1 no. 95 (a sixteen-year-old boy, victim of a shooting accident). None of the burials that contained the so-called Orphic Gold Tablets seems to have belonged to a young person, Fritz Graf and Sarah Iles Johnston, *Ritual Texts for the Afterlife. The Bacchic Gold Tablets* (London: Routledge, 2012).

66. *Mor.*, 608a–612a; see Rudolf Kassel, *Untersuchungen zur griechischen und römischen Konsolationsliteratur* (Zetemata 18; Munich: Beck, 1958).

67. See the list of texts in Fritz Graf, "Malediction," in *Thesaurus Cultus et Rituum Antiquorum*, vol. 3 (Los Angeles: The J. Paul Getty Museum, 2005), 247–70. Still important is Erich Ziebarth, "Der Fluch im griechischen Recht," *Hermes* 30 (1895): 57–70. An inscription from the island of Chios, written in the later sixth century BCE, illustrates this mechanism almost in a textbook way. The text, promulgated by the political authorities of the island state, orders the authorities to set up border markers, presumably to mark land confiscated during one of the political upheavals of the epoch. In such a partisan atmosphere, the temptations to remove the markers must have been great. Therefore, the law stipulates a heavy fine for any person who would remove a marker; and it defines the enforcing magistrate and the magistrate who supervises the enforcement. Each supervising magistrate in turn is threatened with a fine for neglecting his duty, all the way up the hierarchy; each time, the next level enforces the fine, the following level supervises

the enforcement. The highest magistrate, however, is treated differently, for good reasons: a fine cannot be enforced any more, since there is no higher political authority. Instead, he is cursed in case he would neglect to enforce a fine due to a removal of a border marker by an inferior magistrate. Lillian H. Jeffery, *The Local Scripts of Archaic Greece* (Oxford: Clarendon, 1990), 336f.

68. A typical case is a Roman grave inscription for a certain Grattius, a twenty-three-year-old man who was killed in an unspecified act of street violence. The very nature of the crime makes it almost impossible to determine a culprit, and the Roman legal system that left investigation and prosecution to private initiative made a trial under those circumstances impossible. We hear Grattius's voice that wishes that his attacker might die in the same way: "This I wish: may you die, yourself crucified in a bad way . . . and pay the fine that you deserve." A grave inscription from Imperial Egypt, set up for three sailors who were killed in a river port, invokes the god Sarapis as the avenger of this crime; the perpetrators remained unknown, and it is unclear whether anyone investigated the crime. In a rare instance from Syria, the murderer was unassailable because he was a senior administrator, and the family of the victim ("killed for nothing") understandably did not dare to bring him to court. In another isolated case, the relatives of the victim did not curse the actual killer but another person involved in the case who, however, could not be reached by the law: in the grave epigram of a young man killed by the lover of his wife, the deceased, one Aphrodisios, curses his wife ("may Zeus ruin her!"). The actual murderer might well have been brought to court for murder, but no ancient law would incriminate the wife as well (at least not without clear evidence of her help); but the relatives who had the stone put up obviously regarded her as guilty as her lover.

69. *Hic stigmata aeterna Acte libertae scripta sunt| venenariae et perfidae, dolosae, duri pectoris:| clavom et restem sparteam ut sibi sollum alliget | et picem candentem pectus malum commurat suum. | manumissa gratis secuta adulterum | patronum circumscripsit et ministros, ancillam et puerum,| lecto iacenti patrono abduxit | ut animo desponderet solus relictus spoliatus senex. | e[t] Hymno [et] eadem stigmata secutis Zosimum.*

70. *Act*]*e* is given in *CLE* 95; maybe [*Actae liberta*]*e* or, more officially, [*Iuniae M. l. Acta*]*e* (nine letters).

71. For a more detailed analysis of the social realities see Judith Evans Grubbs, *Women and the Law in the Roman Empire* (London: Routledge, 2002), 232–36.

72. Hymnus and Zosimus obviously are slave names again. This curse against two male slaves does not fit to the accusation that she took "a maid and a boy" with her: either the syntax has to be understood differently ("his slaves, his maid, and his house-boy" instead of "his slaves, namely a maid and a house-boy"), or one of the two males named in the final line is her lover.

73. They are the usual messengers in the binding spells of the Greek Magical Papyri, e.g., *PGM* IV 296ff.; Johnston, *Restless Dead*, 127–99. See also Grubbs, *Women*, 241f.

74. Peek, *Grab-Epigramme*, no. 1313; Bernand, *Inscriptions métriques*, no. 102: *στῆθι λάον κατενῶπα τελώριον ἐν τριόδοισι, | ξεῖνε, καὶ εὑρήσεις γράμματι ῥηγνύμενον·| ἠὺ δ' ὄπα προχέων στενάχιζέ με τήν προμολοῦσαν | εἰς ἐνέρους ὁσίην ἀσπίδα τηλέβιον | δυσμενέων ὑπὸ χερσί· τί σοι πλέον, αἰνότατ' ἀνδρῶν,| ἐστίν, ὅτι ζωῆς τῆσδέ με ἀπεστέρεσας; σοὶ γὰρ ὁμοῦ καὶ ἔρεσσι κέλωρ' ἐμὰ θεσπέσι' ἔσται· | οὐκ οἴημ ἐπὶ γῆς ἔκτανες οὖσαν ἐμέ,| ἀλλ' ὅσα περ ψάμαθος παρὰ θῖν' ἁλὸς ἔσχεν ἀριθμά,| τόσσον ἐπιχθόνιοι θῆρες ἔχουσι γένος· | ἦ σὲ μὲν οὐχ ὕπατον, πύματον δ' Ἀΐδην. πελάσουσι,| ὄμμασι δερκόμενον σῶν ἐρέων θάνατον.*

75. The curse that the culprit should see his children die appears also in Phrygian grave inscriptions; see Louis Robert, "Malédictions funéraires grecques," in *Compte-Rendus de l'Académie des Inscriptions et Belles-Lettres* (1978), 242–89; repr., in *Opera Minora Selecta* (Épigraphie et antiquités grecques 5; Amsterdam: Hakkert, 1989), 697–745, esp. 260–64; Strubbe, ARAI EPITUMBIOI, 287.

76. Josef Zingerle, "Heiliges Recht." *JÖAI* 32 (1926): 5–72: Beiblatt 50 (Björck, *Der Fluch*, 29f. no. 13) (Galatia).

77. Mopsuhestia, Cilicia; lost according to Le Bas and Waddington, *Voyage*, no. 1499; found and independently republished by V. W. Yorke, "Inscriptions from East Asia Minor," *Journal of Hellenic Studies* 18 (1898): 306–27, esp. 307 no. 3; new readings and an excellent discussion in Zingerle, "Heiliges Recht," 54–68 no. 2. The text *also SEG* 6, 786 and Björck, *Der Fluch*, 30 no. 15.

78. Wolfgang Blümel, *Die Inschriften von Knidos* (IGSK 41; Bonn: Habelt, 1992), no. 154. Demeter's name is lost, the goddess is simply called *δέσποινα*, "Lady", in l. 16.

79. Two inquiries in Dodona (Hellenistic; both suspect a woman): Anastasios-Ph. Christidis, Sotiris Dakaris and Ioulia Vokotopoulou, "Magic in the Oracular Tablets from Dodona," in *The World of Ancient Magic. Papers from the First International Samson Eitrem Seminar at the Norwegian Institute at Athens 4–8 May 1997*, ed. David R. Jordan, Hugo Montgomery, and Einar Thomassen, PNIA 4 (Bergen: The Norwegian Institute at Athens, 1999), 67–72, esp. 68 no. 1 (infertility, the suspect is a man) and 70 no. 4 (the suspect is a woman). Public inquiry in Claros: Reinhold Merkelbach and Johannes Stauber, "Die Orakel des Apollon von Klaros," *EpA* 27 (1996): 1–53; repr., in Reinhold Merkelbach, *Philologica. Ausgewählte Kleine Schriften* (Stuttgart: Teubner, 1997), 155–218, esp. 25 no. 11, and Reinhold Merkelbach and Johannes Stauber, eds., *Steinepigramme aus dem griechischen Osten* (5 vols.; Stuttgart: Teubner and München: Saur, 1998–2004), 1 no. 03/02/01; see Fritz Graf, "An Oracle against Pestilence from a Western Anatolian Town," *ZPE* 92 (1992): 267–78.

80. Graf, "An Oracle against Pestilence," 150.

81. This explanation fits the text better than an alternative that sees her using erotic magic in order to preserve an otherwise improbable marriage, as in the case of Apuleius.

82. Graf, "An Oracle against Pestilence," 147.

83. Georg Petzl, "Die Beichtinschriften Westkleinasiens." *EpA* 22 (1994), 88 no. 69, with earlier bibliography.
84. Apul., *Apol.* 1.5–6.
85. "Tacitus is a great reporter of rumors, unconfirmed stories that cast a bleak shadow over the emperors," Roland Mellor, *Tacitus* (London: Routledge, 1993), 42.
86. The citation from Clyde Kluckhohn, *Navaho Witchcraft* (Boston: Beacon, 1967), 88; another pioneering study is Max G. Marwick, *Sorcery in its Social Setting. A Study of Northern Rhodesian Cevia* (Manchester: Manchester University Press, 1965); he titled a paper "Witchcraft as a Social Stress-Gauge," *AJSc* 26 (1964): 263–68.
87. Gábor Klaniczay, *The Uses of Supernatural Power. The Transformation of Popular Religion in Medieval and Early-Modern Europe* (Princeton, NJ: Princeton University Press, 1990), 156 à propos Favret-Saada, *Les Mots.*
88. Mary Douglas, *Natural Symbols: Explorations in Cosmology* (London: Barrie & Rockliff, 1970), esp. ch. 7, "The Problem of Evil."
89. See Graf, *Magic in the Ancient World*, 65–88 and the essays in Hammerstaedt et al., *Apuleius. De magia* (Darmstadt: Wissenschaftliche Buchgesellschaft, 2002).
90. See the story told by Plin., *HN* 18.41–43, after Calpurnius Piso F 33.
91. Rumor is widely researched, especially in social psychology; for its connection with sorcery see Stewart and Strathern, *Witchcraft*, 29–58; for a history of rumor that starts with Hesiod, Hans-Joachim Neubauer, *The Rumour: A Cultural History* (trans. Christian Braun; New York: Free Association Press, 1999).
92. For a short introduction to the cognitive approach Prashant Bordia and Nicholas DiFonzo, "Problem Solving in Social Interactions on the Internet: Rumor as Social Cognition," *SPQ* 67 (2004): 33–34; the normativity was stressed by Max Gluckman, "What is Gossip About? An Alternative Hypothesis," *Man* 2 (1967): 278–85.
93. On the process that could transform gossip into judicial or ritual processes see Stewart and Strathern, *Witchcraft*, 17.
94. There is no comprehensive account for the Greek world. On Athens see Derek Collins, "Theoris of Lemnos and the Criminalization of Magic in Fourth-Century Athens," *CQ* 51 (2001): 477–93; on Ptolemaic Egypt, Jean L. Tondriau, "Notes ptolémaïques. I: Accusations de magie contre des souverains lagides," *Aegyptus* 28 (1948): 168–77. On the other hand, in about 450 BCE the magistrates of the Eastern Greek city of Teos publicly cursed whoever would use *pharmaka deleteria*, "destructive sorcery," against the city and its citizens; see the inscription in Meiggs and Lewis, *Selection*, no. 30. There is much more on Rome; see Carlo Castello, "Cenni sulla repressione del reato di magia dagli inizi del principato fino a Costanzo II," in *VIII° Convegno Internazionale dell'Accademia Romanistica Constantiniana*, ed. G. Crifò and S. Ciglio (Naples: Edizioni Scientifiche Internazionali, 1991), 665–92, Detlef Liebs, "Strafprozesse wegen Zauberei. Magie und politisches Kalkül in der römischen Geschichte," in *Grosse Prozesse*

der Römischen Antike (ed. Ulrich Manthe and Jürgen von Ungern-Sternberg; Munich: Beck, 1997), 146–58, and Nicole Zeddies, *Religio et sacrilegium. Studien zur Inkriminierung von Magie, Häresie und Heidentum (4.–7. Jh.)* (Frankfurt am Main: Peter Lang, 2003).

95. On this case, see Helmut Engelmann, *The Delian Aretalogy of Sarapis* (EPRO 44; Leiden: Brill, 1975); for another case, Cic., *Brut.* 217; for a selection of actual *defixiones* that attempt to damage legal adversaries see John G. Gager, *Curse Tablets and Binding Spells from the Ancient World* (New York: Oxford University Press, 1992), 116–50.
96. The citation is from Douglas, *Natural Symbols*, 113; André Bernand, *Sorciers grecs* (Paris: Fayard, 1991).
97. This confirms the interpretation of Greek explanations of reproductive failure that Johnston, *Restless Dead*, 184–99 proposed; I cite her conclusions, 199: "The continuing integrity of the *oikos* in its extended sense, of such groups as the phratry and of the polis as a whole would have been significantly threatened if the alternative explanation—surreptitious attacks by the living—had arisen between members of the smaller groups."
98. Stewart and Strathern, *Witchcraft*, 2003: 8.
99. See the remarks of Klaniczay, *Uses*, cited above note 78.
100. Theoris of Lemnos: [Demosth.] *C. Aristogeiton* 25. 77–79; more in Collins, *Theoris*, 477–93. Martina: Tac., *Ann.* 3.7.
101. Clarian oracle: above note 53 and 79.
102. On the literary stereotype, see Barbette Spaeth in this volume; for a possible explanation John J. Winkler, *The Constraints of Desire: The Anthropology of Sex and Gender in Ancient Greece* (New York: Routledge, 1990) and John J. Winkler, "The Constraints of Eros," in *Magika Hiera: Ancient Greek Magic and Religion*, ed. Christopher A. Faraone and Dirk Obbink (New York: Oxford University Press, 1991), 214–43; see also Graf, *Magic in the Ancient World*, 185–90.

15

A Gospel Amulet for Joannia (P.Oxy. VIII 1151)

AnneMarie Luijendijk

STROLLING THE STREETS and markets or visiting houses and churches in late antique Antioch, Syria, one would notice women and children wearing amulets around their necks.* At least, the practice caught the eye of the prominent preacher John Chrysostom, who voiced his disapproval of it in several of his sermons. From the ambo of the Antiochean church, Chrysostom asked his congregation: "Do you not see how women and little children suspend Gospels from their necks as powerful amulets, and carry them about in all places wherever they go?"[1] This practice of wearing gospel amulets among the female members of his congregation clearly concerned the golden-mouthed preacher, for he also mentioned it in another homily, exclaiming:

> And what are these amulets and borders? Since they were continually forgetting God's benefits, he commanded that his wonders be inscribed on little books and that these should be suspended from their hands . . . which they call phylacteries, as now many of our women have Gospels hanging from their necks.[2]

Given Chrysostom's condemnation of Jewish practice in other sermons, his equation of the women's gospel amulets to Jewish phylacteries is a strong criticism.[3] Instead of carrying around physical objects inscribed with gospel passages, he advised his audience to memorize them, to "write the commands of the Gospel and its laws" upon their minds.[4]

Around the same time that Chrysostom objected to women and children wearing gospel amulets, an otherwise unknown Christian woman called Joannia from Oxyrhynchus, Egypt, commissioned a similar amulet, tied it up in a small roll, and wore it around her neck to seek healing from severe bouts of fever. Several publications have reprinted the text of this charm, but apart from short comments it has not received a fuller scholarly discussion.[5] A careful analysis of this amulet in its late antique, local Egyptian context suggests not only the medical conditions that likely prompted Joannia to obtain it, but also significantly complicates the picture evoked by Chrysostom. It helps us to see the widespread use of amulets and the context that occasioned such interferences by church leaders. Additionally, I will demonstrate that Joannia's amulet, in its use of canonical scripture, liturgical allusions, Christian scribal practices, and in its invocation of local saints, gives us a different view of "orthodoxy" than a church authority like John Chrysostom promoted. This orthodoxy could include practices like wearing amulets. My study also finds that, despite the polemic of certain church leaders focusing on women and their particular affinity for amulets, men played central roles both in the production of such amulets and in their regular use. Thus I shall argue in this chapter that Joannia's amulet, rather than demonstrating a divide between religion and magic, exposes those categories as identity markers for creating a legitimate and socially acceptable Christian practice, identity markers that have little to do with daily needs and practices.

My approach in this chapter of studying the "social life" of a papyrus amulet is grounded in scholarship on material culture.[6] I emphasize that we cannot consider small papyrus documents as this as hermeneutically simple.[7] As we will see, these seemingly insignificant everyday objects participate in the larger discourse of healing, religion, and power with the writings of elite male ecclesiastical writers. Therefore, I pay attention to the rhetoric not only of elite church leaders, but also to the rhetoric of the amulet.

Joannia's Amulet

A long, narrow strip of papyrus of 4.4 x 23.4 cm preserves in fifty-six short lines a healing amulet for Joannia, the daughter of Anastasia, also known as Euphemia (P.Oxy. VIII 1151).[8] The oblong format facilitated the amulet's use, making it easy to roll up and wear on one's body, whether simply tied with string or put in a small container.[9] Indeed, this papyrus was found tied up into a tiny packet; therefore, we can assume that Joannia wore the document on her body, probably suspended from her neck.[10]

The amulet is written in a professional style of handwriting fashionable in the fifth century CE, thus roughly contemporary with Chrysostom's preaching.[11] Common Christian scribal contractions (so-called *nomina sacra*) and crosses feature in the text.[12] It also quotes or alludes to biblical passages (viz. Revelation, the gospels of John and Matthew, Joel, and Psalms) and invokes God, Jesus and his mother Mary, as well as a host of saints.

The amulet reads:[13]

> † Flee, hateful spirit, Christ drives you out. The son of God and the Holy Spirit have gained advantage over you.
>
> God of the sheep pool, rescue Joannia, to whom Anastasia alias Euphemia gave birth, from every evil.
>
> † In the beginning was the word and the word was with God and God was the word. All things came into being by him and without him not anything came into being that has come into being.
>
> Lord † Christ, son and word of the living God, the one who healed every disease and every sickness, heal and look upon your female slave Joannia also, to whom Anastasia alias Euphemia gave birth, and expel from her and put to flight every fever-heat and every kind of chill, quotidian, tertian and quartan and every evil, on account of the prayers and entreaties of our mistress, the God-bearer, and of the glorious archangels and of John, the holy and glorious apostle and evangelist and theologian, and of saint Serenus and of saint Philoxenus and of saint Victor and of saint Justus and of all the saints.
>
> Upon your name, Lord God, I have called, the wondrous and supremely glorious (name) and fearful for your enemies. Amen. †

The people mentioned by name in the amulet—Joannia, its wearer, and her mother, "Anastasia who is also called Euphemia"—are not otherwise known.[14] What we shall discover about Joannia—why she obtained her amulet and from whom—comes from a contextualization of this amulet. That contextualization begins at the site where the papyrus was found.

Bernard P. Grenfell and Arthur S. Hunt excavated this piece among thousands of other papyrus fragments at the site of the ancient Egyptian city of Oxyrhynchus.[15] As we will see, a close observation of the saints invoked in the amulet reveals that the amulet was also locally produced in that city. The final section of our amulet's text invokes Mary the mother of God, the evangelist John, saints Serenus, Philoxenus, Victor, Justus, and—to make sure that no saint was left out—"all the saints." We have evidence that the saints named in the amulet were closely identified with Oxyrhynchus: Mary, "the Mother of God," enjoyed great popularity in Egypt as a whole and also in Oxyrhynchus, where a church was dedicated to her.[16] Saint Victor, too, was worshiped widely in Egypt and he had a shrine in Oxyrhynchus as well.[17] The three other saints invoked by name in the papyrus, Philoxenus, Justus, and Serenus, each had a sanctuary in Oxyrhynchus, and documents from that city frequently mention them, but they hardly ever appear in documents from other localities.[18] Moreover, that same city also boasted a sanctuary for John the Evangelist. This in and of itself is a noteworthy fact, because, as Arietta Papaconstantinou remarks, Oxyrhynchus was the only Egyptian city at this time to have a church dedicated to him.[19] The allusion to the story of Jesus healing at the pool by the Sheep Gate (John 5:2)[20] and the quotation from the Johannine Prologue (John 1:1, 3) also suggest that the composer of our amulet had a special affinity with the fourth evangelist.[21] This brief tour of Oxyrhynchite shrines and their saints indicates that it is highly likely that Joannia had commissioned her amulet in Oxyrhynchus, invoking the locally worshiped saints to help her recover from illness.[22]

Exorcising Fevers

People in antiquity commissioned amulets for manifold purposes, ranging from a desire for sex to the protection of the home and restoring health.[23] The latter, iatromagical function of amulets was a common one, and one we see also in our piece.[24] Its opening lines contain an exorcism: it exhorts a "hateful spirit" to flee and uses a direct address to convince the spirit that "Christ drives you out."[25] Joannia wanted to be released from that spirit and all evil, reflecting the common ancient opinion that evil spirits cause illnesses.[26] The phrase "flee, evil so-and-so, divine power so-and-so drives you out" occurs as a standard formula in many amulets.[27] Such exorcistic exclamations for the hateful spirit to flee are "'performative' incantations in which the disease/daemon is directly addressed" and consist of the recitation of a formula while performing a ritual act.[28] I picture Joannia during the ritual session that may have taken place when she purchased her amulet: she said its text out loud in her own voice, probably in a "repeat after me" fashion with the writer of the amulet, for she, as most people in antiquity, may have been illiterate.[29] As an accompanying ritual gesture, she crossed herself at the places indicated in the document. Indeed, according to Joannia's compatriot Athanasius of Alexandria, making the sign of the cross causes demons to flee.[30]

While ancient authors depicted women as burning with a sexual desire that prompted them to fabricate predatory lust spells,[31] our papyrus amulet tells that Joannia suffered from the heat of fever. Commands in the text phrased in the imperative, such as "drive out," "rescue," "heal and look upon," and "expel and put to flight," suggest that Joannia was sick when she commissioned the amulet.[32] Unlike others, who wore phylacteries for protection against sickness and evil forces, Joannia obtained hers when she already experienced symptoms of fever and chills.[33]

In his article on "Incantations and Prayers on Inscribed Greek Amulets," Roy Kotansky observed that "during the Roman Empire the treatment of diseases with amulets seems to have required the proper diagnostic identification of the ailment, and we find that the texts found on amulets often indicate the specific diseases for which they are written."[34] This is indeed also the case in Joannia's amulet, as it describes her illness in detail. The mention of "every fever-heat and every kind of chill, quotidian, tertian and quartan" suggests that Joannia may have suffered a form of what now is diagnosed as malaria. Feeling alternately hot and cold and having recurring, intermittent fevers constitute the clinical symptoms of malaria, an infectious disease transmitted by mosquitoes.[35] Malaria has a devastating effect on the health of infected people, including anemia, splenomegaly, jaundice, and kidney failure, leading to weakness and often death. Even less aggressive forms of malaria "act as a contributing factor to morbidity and mortality."[36] Still a debilitating and deadly disease in the tropics and subtropics, daily killing as many as two thousand children in Africa alone, malaria in antiquity was a prevalent and equally deadly pestilence around the Mediterranean, as recent studies have shown.[37] In the inhabitable fertile strip of land along the Nile, with its marshes and canals, this "marsh fever" could thrive. Evidence of malaria has already been found in Egyptian mummies from ca. 3200 BCE.[38] The struggle against the illness in this region can be seen also in the substantial number of fever amulets from antiquity.[39] Irina Wandrey posits a connection between the large number of fever amulets from that period and the increase of malaria in Late Antiquity caused by neglect of irrigation canals.[40]

Malaria affects children and pregnant women more than men.[41] We do not know whether Joannia was an infant or an adult woman, for the amulet does not reveal her age. She may have been only a girl. Children in antiquity were vulnerable to illness and premature death; as Roger Bagnall states, "nearly one-third of all children died before their first birthday and more than two-fifths by the age of five."[42] No wonder that parents—mothers and grandmothers in particular—equipped their offspring with protective spells. A mother called Maria had purchased an expensive parchment amulet against "every cold and every fever" for her child, "Phoibammon, the son."[43] In the "discourse of ritual censure," such private practices for the guarding of children also surface in the writings of Christian authors.[44] In a sermon attributed to Athanasius of Alexandria and transmitted in Coptic, the preacher abhors this habit of attaching amulets to children that he locates in towns and villages.[45] John Chrysostom disapprovingly refers to "amulets and bells . . . hung from [a baby's] hand, and the scarlet woof, and the other things full of extreme folly" and the writer of a *scholium* on Gregory Nazianzus objects to "the bits of colored thread around wrists, arms, and necks; and the moon-shaped plates of gold, silver, or cheaper material, which foolish old women fasten upon infants."[46] In chapter 7 of this volume, Dayna Kalleres sharply dissects ecclesiastical rhetoric against women's domestic ritual practices.[47] If Joannia acquired her amulet as an adult woman, she could have contracted the disease when pregnant. While men are susceptible to this disease as well, the fact that women and children are particularly vulnerable to malaria and its effects puts the penchant to slander them over the use of magic and amulets (as we heard in Athanasius's and Chrysostom's sermons) in a different light.[48] It also raises the question as to whether amulets remained so widely used precisely because they were more useful than categories of official and popular religion.

Historiola *for Healing*

In a comment on this amulet, Gary Vikan drew attention to its magical and aretalogical aspects:

> On its most basic level this amulet draws its power from the invocation of the sacred name, and thereby from the primal, magical belief that such names share in the being and participate in the power of their bearers. But this papyrus is magical as well on a secondary, "aretalogical" level, since the power of the deity, as if this were Isis, is also being invoked through a recitation of His most glorious deeds.[49]

Indeed, amulets explicitly claim their purposes—in Joannia's case curing her from fever and chills and all evil—by appealing to "glorious deeds" as persuasive precedents.[50] In amulets and spells, "an abbreviated narrative that is incorporated into a magical spell," termed *historiola*, encapsulates the precedent and operates, as David Frankfurter states, "as the performative transmission of power from a mythic realm articulated in narrative to the human present."[51] Joannia's fever amulet refers to previous healing acts of Jesus recounted in the Gospel of John and the Gospel of Matthew, the two most popular gospels in the ancient church. First, by referring to the "sheep pool" it claims a precedent in the story of Jesus healing a man at the so-called Bethzatha pool by the Sheep Gate in Jerusalem, narrated in John 5:2-15.[52] As a second analogy, Joannia's amulet mentions Jesus's all-encompassing therapeutic powers: his ability to heal "every disease and every sickness," a stock phrase in the Gospel of Matthew (Matt 4:23, 9:35, 10:1) and quotation of the Greek text of Deuteronomy 7:15. Its appearance in other amulets makes clear that this was considered a particularly powerful—and indeed widely applicable—phrase.[53] Another healing amulet (P.Oxy. VIII 1077, Oxyrhynchus, sixth century CE) reads:

> Curative Gospel (*iamatikon euaggelion*) according to Matthew. And Jesus went about all of Galilee, teaching and preaching the gospel of the

> kingdom, and healing every disease and every disease and every infirmity among the people. And his fame spread into all of Syria, and they brought him those who were ill, and Jesus healed them.[54]

Yet another amulet against fever and illness, written for a woman in the fifth or sixth century (SB XIV 11495, provenance unknown), also incorporates a quotation from Matthew's Gospel as *historiola*. Following lines from the credo, it reads in translation:

> Because you then (*pote*) cured the people's every infirmity and disease . . . Jesus! . . . because when you went into the house of Peter's mother-in-law, who was sick with fever, the fever left her, also now (*kai nun*) we beseech you, Jesus, heal now your female slave, who wears your holy name, of every sickness and (every) fever and every ague and every headache (?) and every witchcraft and every evil spirit. In the name of the Father, the Son and the Holy Spirit.[55]

In addition to the biblical phrase of "every disease and every illness," this amulet also appeals to the story of Jesus curing Peter's mother-in-law from fever (paraphrasing Matt 8:14-15), which I find an especially well-chosen biblical precedent for the healing of women with febrile symptoms. The words "then you cured, . . . also now heal" make the precedent explicit. In the amulet's theology, Jesus is an ongoing actor.[56]

The final sentence in Joannia's amulet cleverly weaves together several biblical phrases. It invokes "the name of the Lord God," not the host of magical names we find in some other amulets. Although not a direct quotation, the three adjectives used to modify the Lord God's name—wondrous, supremely glorious, and fearful—are reminiscent especially of the Psalms and other liturgical language.[57] The words "I have called on your name, Lord God," hark back to Joel 3:5: "everyone who calls on the name of the Lord shall be saved," a sentence quoted also in Romans 10:14 and Acts 2:21. With its implied appeal to salvation this phrase makes for a fitting conclusion for a healing amulet.[58]

Many other Christian amulets use gospel quotations and several show a preference for the *incipit* of one of the canonical gospels, just as Joannia's amulet cited the three opening verses of the Gospel of John.[59] Some amulets record the opening sections of all four gospels.[60] I contend that John Chrysostom, in the sermons cited above, as well as contemporary writers, refer to such amulets with gospel quotations as "small gospels."[61] Instead of picturing women and children walking around with miniature codices of entire gospels tied around their necks, we should imagine these gospel amulets as the Jewish *tefillin* (φυλακτήρια), amulets with biblical excerpts.[62] I concur with Claudia Rapp's assessment that "we see the use of extracts from scripture, *pars pro toto*, to evoke the power of the *entire* Word of God."[63] Thus in these amulets the quotations from gospel *incipits* represent the whole message of the gospel, while also the historiola and references to specific healing episodes appeal to the mythical acts of Jesus, thereby creating a small but very powerful text.

Priestly Production

How did Joannia obtain this gospel amulet? Given the proficient handwriting and especially the standard phraseology in the document, she probably did not pen the charm herself but turned to a specialist.[64] Indeed, many spells and amulets display a trained style of handwriting, indicating that professional religious experts were involved in their production.[65] Such specialists show up frequently in literary sources and many aspects in amulets and magical handbooks make clear that putting together amulets was considered a business.[66] Joannia thus probably also paid for her amulet. The economic aspect of amulet production plays a part in the invectives against the makers of amulets, as we shall see.

Some texts associate amulets with old women, as the *scholium* to Gregory of Nazianzus's speech mentioned above. In a passage attributed to the fourth-century bishop Athanasius of Alexandria, the feisty church leader accuses his parishioners of using "amulets and sorceries" when sick and turning to old women. Staking out clear divisions between those who use amulets and those who do not, Athanasius ridicules people who turn to a female expert:

> And if someone consulted [amulets and sorceries], let him know this distinctly, that he has made himself instead of a believer, an unbeliever; instead of a Christian, a pagan; instead of an intelligent person, an unintelligent one; instead of an intellectual, an irrational person. For the old woman pours a flood of words over you for 20 obol, or, for a quarter of wine, a snake's invocation. And you stand as an ass, gaping wide, carrying upon your neck quadruped's dirt, while deceiving the seal of the cross's salvation. Not only are the illnesses afraid of that seal, but also the whole dense crowd of demons fears and wonders at it. Whence also every wizard is unsealed [i.e., unbaptized].[67]

In this passage that is rich in rhetoric and allusions, Athanasius sorts people that wear amulets into the undoubtedly unflattering category of unbelieving, unintelligent, and irrational pagans. By mentioning an ass, I suggest that he alludes to Apuleius's well-known book *Metamorphoses*, where an out-of-hand magical act turns the main character, Lucian, into a donkey.[68] In thus making fun of people who obtain healings from an old woman (*graus*), who, he asserts, received payment either in pocket change or wine, Athanasius plays on the stereotype of the old woman as the bibulous sorceress, a familiar face in ancient polemics against magic. From Athanasius's invective it is not clear, however, whether the old woman is a Christian or not.[69] Chrysostom's parishioners apparently obtained amulets from women who were Christians, even believers.[70] Second-century satirist Lucian of Samosata linked old women with exorcisms. For him, believing that an exorcism would cause fevers or inflammations to flee in fear—the very idea encapsulated also in our amulet—amounted to "old wives' fables" (*graōn muthoi*).[71] This episode caused Matthew Dickie to note that

> in the Hellenistic Greek world and in Rome certain areas of magic were the peculiar preserve of women, and old women especially. These are not the more spectacular forms of magic-working, but the run-of-the-mill cures and snake-charmings that the speaker in Lucian's *Philopseudeis* feels even old women can perform.[72]

Here and throughout his study on *Magic and Magicians in the Greco-Roman World*, Dickie situates women among magic's bottom rungs, stating: "women generally occupied a lowly position in the hierarchy of magicians in the Roman Empire."[73] Instead of accepting the rhetoric of these authors, we can also interpret such invectives as indications of the activities of female religious experts who practiced healings.[74] Someone like Joannia may have consulted a female expert for health care. Kalleres argues convincingly that the feminization of magic in the writings of church leaders serves to denote the divide between orthopraxy and idolatry.[75]

Instead of imagining the maker of our gospel amulet as a female healer, internal evidence from the amulet itself and external evidence from ancient Christian writings suggests that Joannia collaborated with a religious expert from among the clergy, which was presumably mostly male at this time. In Egypt, local priests associated with sanctuaries traditionally performed rites and ministered to ritual needs such as the preparation of amulets. In his article "Ritual Expertise in Roman Egypt and the Problem of the Category 'Magician,'" Frankfurter convincingly made the case for the "continuity of the role of the ritual specialist" from Egyptian priest to Christian holy man, priest, or monk.[76] We should situate these "ritual experts" not on the margins of society, Frankfurter argued, but as fulfilling a principal role in the social and religious life of their communities.[77]

The scribal execution of Joannia's amulet indeed points to such a clerical milieu: the experienced handwriting, the use of *nomina sacra* (Christian scribal features that abound also in literary manuscripts), and the crosses placed at crucial points in the text. Moreover, the content suits that group, notably the biblical quotations and allusions to Revelation, the Gospels of John and Matthew, Joel and Psalms and, as we will see next, the similarity with liturgical prayers. This signaled to the client the expertise of the manufacturer and thus the efficacy and legitimacy of this Christian amulet.

In an article on the reception of the biblical phrase "healing every illness and every disease," Theodore de Bruyn shows the resemblance in expression between amulets and Christian liturgical prayers. In a prayer for "oil of the sick," attributed to mid-fourth-century bishop Sarapion of Thmuis, the analogy in language and imagery is especially striking.[78] The prayer reads:

> We call upon you, the one having all authority and power, the savior of all people, Father of our Lord and Savior Jesus Christ, and we implore you that healing power of your only-begotten may be sent out from heaven upon this oil. May it become to those who are anointed . . . for a rejection of every disease and every sickness (*eis apobolēn pasēs vosou kai pasēs malakias*), for an amulet warding off every demon, for a departing of every unclean spirit, for a taking away of every evil spirit (*eis aphorismon pantos pneumatos ponērou*), for a driving away of all fever and chills and every weakness (*eis ekdiōgmon pantos puretou kai rhigous kai pasēs astheneias*), for good grace and forgiveness of sins, for a medicine of life and salvation, for health and wholeness of soul, body, spirit, for perfect strength. Master, let every satanic energy (*pasa energeia satanikē*), every demon, every plot of the opposing one, every blow, every lash, every pain, or every slap in the face, or shaking, or evil shadow (*skiasma ponēron*) be afraid of your holy name, which we have now called upon (*to onoma sou hagion, ho epekalesametha nun hēmeis*), and the name of the only-begotten; and let them depart from the inner and the outer parts of these your servants so that the name of Jesus Christ, the one who was crucified and risen for us, who took to himself our diseases and weaknesses and is coming to judge the living and the dead, may be glorified.[79]

While Joannia's amulet and Sarapion's prayer differ in many respects, the similarities are nevertheless significant: the driving out of evil spirits, the fevers and chills, the precedent of Jesus's healing, the calling upon God's name. As De Bruyn noted, "the preparation and use of amulets was similar to the preparation and use of oil," and both came from a clerical milieu.[80] In his book *Curse Tables and Binding Spells*, John Gager suggests that the use of magical letters in the composition of *defixiones* augmented the expert's status and credibility as magician.[81] Similarly, I propose that the specialized biblical and liturgical language with matching scribal practices and the selection of appropriate local saints signaled to the client the expertise of the manufacturer of this Christian amulet. Did Sarapion (or whoever composed the prayer) side with the positions

Athanasius and later Chrysostom advocated, writing the prayers as an alternative to amulets? Given the fifth- and sixth-century dates of these amulets, I consider it more likely that these clergy composed amulets that reflected liturgy as a way to legitimize them—thereby actively participating in the larger discourse about the permissibility of amulets.

Looking beyond Joannia's amulet we find evidence that further supports the assumption that a clergy member composed it.[82] Canons of church councils record accusations against priests manufacturing amulets and engaging in magic and divination. A canon from the late fourth-century church synod held in Laodicea, Phrygia Pacatiana (modern-day Turkey), repudiates clergy for composing amulets for their flock, and in addition excommunicates the wearers of such:

> They who are of the priesthood, or of the clergy, shall not be magicians, enchanters, mathematicians, or astrologers; nor shall they make what are called amulets, which are chains for their own souls. And those who wear such, we command to be cast out of the Church.[83]

The mere fact that the bishops at the council addressed the topic indicates that their clerical colleagues did in fact provide this service.[84]

An incident reported by Shenoute of Atripe, another fifth-century contemporary of Joannia, gives further evidence that these activities were highly contested:

> In the moments of suffering however, [there are some who] when they fall into poverty or become ill—or indeed other temptations—abandon God and have recourse to enchanters or oracles or . . . other deceptive things: just as I myself have seen—the snake's head bound to the hand of someone, and another with the crocodile tooth bound to an arm, another with fox claws bound to his legs: especially as there was a magistrate who told the latter that he was wise to do so. Indeed, when I reproachfully asked him whether it was the fox claws that would heal him, he said: "It was a great monk who gave me them saying, Bind them to you, and you will recover."[85]

In this case, a monk provided the iatromagical supplies for the healing of an unspecified illness, much to the dismay of the influential abbot.

The fourth-century Canons of Pseudo-Athanasius of Alexandria excommunicate priests' sons who read magical books: "If they shall find [one of the sons] of the clergy concerned with books of magic, he shall be estranged from the fellowship of Christ."[86] One wonders where these sons found those magical books. Did they take them perhaps from their priestly fathers' bookshelves? Indeed, studies of amulets and magical books preserved in the papyrological record have shown that most amulets were copied from a grimoire,[87] and a charm such as Joannia's would fit neatly into a Christian priest's library. In any case, we witness here again the close association of priests with magic causing the disapproval of the upper-level clergy.[88] In view of this internal and external evidence, Joannia most likely acquired her amulet from a local priest or monk.

The production of an amulet like Joannia's probably happened at a church or shrine. Indeed, as we have seen, all the saints mentioned in our piece had places of worship in Oxyrhynchus. At the site of another ancient Egyptian city, Antinoë, archaeologists found an archive of oracular texts at a shrine for Saint Collu-thus, which revealed that trained scribes on the shrine's staff practiced divination there.[89]

With regard to visiting shrines for what some would call magical practices, a Coptic sermon attributed to Athanasius of Alexandria merits a citation. Its author scolds parents that bring their children to enchanters, whom he equals with demons, and exhorts them instead to bring their sick offspring to a church or martyr shrine for healing.

> Every one who takes his children to enchanters is no different from him who brings them to demons. Instead of bringing your children to enchanters, bring him to the martyria of the martyrs and he will be healed.[90]

As Frankfurter has argued, statements like these relate to orthopraxy: "to edit out of proper religious conduct this range of gestures and materials by associating them with the realm of the demonic."[91] It also suggests that people visited shrines for healing. Joannia—or, if she was a girl, her parents—probably also went to a shrine and left with an amulet, one professionally produced by a monk or priest.[92]

The fact that our amulet was in all likelihood commissioned from a clergy member at a local church or shrine demonstrates the battle that preachers such as Chrysostom, Athanasius, and Shenoute faced. It also evokes the question whether Athanasius's and John Chrysostom's "old women" could be young male clergy, earning additional income while helping with healing? In other words: to what extent are these church leaders acting against colleagues in the clergy whose theology, economics, and practices they resisted?

Church leaders not only condemned those who made amulets, they disapproved of amulets completely, including the practice of wearing them. Chrysostom, in the passage quoted at the beginning of this chapter, exhorted his congregants not to wear amulets, like their Jewish fellow citizens, but rather to learn gospel passages by heart. In his preaching, the bishop clustered women wearing amulets together with Jews wearing phylacteries.[93] Both Jews and women function as the groups from which categories of magic and heresy are coined. In other words, they are the quintessential Other.

Like his colleague Chrysostom in the East, Augustine, bishop of Hippo in Northern Africa, frowned upon those who wore amulets, although without tying them to Jewish practices. In a tractate on the Gospel of John, Augustine considered sick people who relied on amulets deplorably weak. Instead, he suggested that people suffering from headache or fever place a gospel manuscript near their head:

> When you have a headache, we commend you if you put the gospel by your head and do not hurry to an amulet. For human frailty has come to this, and men who hurry to amulets must be so lamented that we rejoice when we see that a man, confined to his bed, is tossed by fever and pain and yet has placed no hope anywhere else except that he put the gospel by his head, not because the gospel was made for this but because it has been preferred to amulets.[94]

Thus these influential Christian leaders, Chrysostom and Augustine, favored the Gospel as the word of the Lord above any amulet's protective claims and analogies of healing. Yet in shrines and churches one could find a priest or monk who would work together with a local woman and her sufferings to manufacture an amulet with *nomina sacra*, crosses, gospel quotations, and liturgical formula. These clergy and the wearers of these amulets thus tie into exactly the same evangelical powers that ecclesiastical leaders also recognized, however, in a manner that the latter would deem heretical.

The real significance of studying texts such as Joannia's amulet is therefore that it allows us to witness the paradoxical reality of women visiting shrines for amulets, on the one hand, and preachers railing against women's magical piety, on the other. Thus in exposing the constructed nature of the rhetoric of the church leaders, we obtain a better, if more complex, understanding of practiced religion.

Appendix: Greek text of Joannia's amulet, P.Oxy. VIII 1151[95]

†φεῦγε π̣ν̣(εῦμ)α̣ | μεμισιμένον, | Χ(ριστό)ς σε διώκει· | προέλαβέν σε | ὁ υἱὸς τοῦ θ(εο)ῦ καὶ | τὸ πν(εῦμ)α τὸ ἅγιον.| ὁ θ(εὸ)ς τῆς προβατι|κῆς κολυμβή|θρας, ἐξελοῦ τὴν | δούλην σου | Ἰωαννίαν ἣν | ἔτεκεν Ἀναστασία | εἱ καὶ Εὐφημία | ἀπὸ παντὸς κακοῦ.| † ἐν ἀρχῇ ἦν | ὁ λόγος καὶ ὁ λόγος | ἦν πρὸς τὸν θ(εὸ)ν καὶ | θ(εὸ)ς ἦν ὁ λόγος.| πάντα δι' αὐτοῦ | ἐγένετο κ(αὶ) χωρεὶς | αὐτοῦ ἐγένετο | οὐδὲ ἓν ὃ γέγονεν.[96]*| κ(ύρι)ε †Χ̣(ριστ)έ, υἱὲ καὶ | λόγε τοῦ θ(εο)ῦ τοῦ | ζοντος, ὁ ἰασάμε|νος πᾶσαν νόσον | καὶ πᾶσαν μαλακίαν | ἴασαι καὶ ἐπίσκεψαι | καὶ τὴν δούλην σου | Ἰωαννίαν ἣν ἔτεκεν | Ἀναστασία ἡ καὶ | Εὐφημία, καὶ ἀπο|δίωξον*

καὶ φυγάδευ|σον ἀπ' αὐτῆς πάντα |πυρετὸν κ(αὶ) παντοῖον | ῥῆγος ἀμφημερινὸν | τριτεον τεταρτεον | καὶ πᾶν κακόν. εὐχε̂ς | κ̣α̣ὶ πρεσβίαις τῆς |δεσποίνης ἡμῶν τῆς | θεοτόκου καὶ τῶν | ἐνδόξων ἀρχαγγέ|λων κ(αὶ) τοῦ ἁγίου καὶ ἐν|δόξου ἀποστόλου κ(αὶ) | εὐαγγελιστοῦ κ(αὶ) θεο|λόγου Ἰωάννου κ(αὶ) τοῦ | ἁγίου Σερήνου κ(αὶ) τοῦ | ἁγίου Φιλοξένου κ(αὶ) τοῦ | ἁγίου Βήκτωρος κ(αὶ) τοῦ |ἁγίου Ἰούστου κ(αὶ) πάντων | [τῶ]ν ἁγίων. ὅτι τὸ ὄνομά | σου, κ(ύρι)ε ὁ θ(εό)ς, ἐπικαλεσά|[μ]ην τὸ θαυμαστὸν | καὶ ὑπερένδοξον καὶ | φοβερὸν τοῖς ὑπε|ναντ̣ί̣ο̣ι̣ς. ἀμήν †

Apparatus

2 l(ege) *μεμισημένον*; 5 *υϊος* pap.; 11, 30 *ϊωαννιαν* pap.; 13 l. *ἡ*; 23 *υϊε* pap.; 25 l. *ζῶντος*, *ϊασαμενος* pap.; 28 *ϊασαι* pap.; 36 l. *ῥῖγος*; 37 l. *τριταῖον τεταρταῖον*; 38-9 l. *εὐχαῖς κ̣α̣ὶ πρεσβείαις*; 42 *αρχαγγελων* with dot over second *gamma*, pap.; 46 *ϊωαννου* pap.; 49 l. *Βίκτορος*; 50 *ϊουστου* pap.; 54 *ϋπερενδοξον* pap.

Notes

*. In writing this article, I have benefitted much from the generous help and insightful comments of David Frankfurter, Melanie Johnson-DeBaufre, Sarit Kattan-Gribetz, and Laura Nasrallah. I presented this paper in the "Christianity in Egypt: Scripture, Tradition, and Reception" -consultation at the Society of Biblical Literature, New Orleans, November 2009, and thank the audience for their engaging questions.

1. John Chrysostom, *Stat.* 19.14 (NPNF^{1} 9:470) (trans. W. R. W. Stephens, slightly modified). Iconographically, Egyptian mummy portraits from the Fayum Oasis depict children and women with amulets, see Barbara Borg, "*Der zierlichste Anblick der Welt . . .*" *Ägyptische Porträtmumien* (Zaberns Bildbände zur Archäologie; Mainz: Philipp von Zabern, 1998), 52, and Roy Kotansky, "Incantations and Prayers for Salvation on Inscribed Greek Amulets," in *Magika Hiera: Ancient Greek Magic and Religion*. ed. Christopher A. Faraone and Dirk Obbink (New York: Oxford University Press, 1991), 107–37, at 114 and 130 note 47.

2. John Chrysostom, *Hom. Matt.* 72 (PG 58: 669). The Greek reads: *Καὶ τίνα ταῦτά ἐστι τὰ φυλακτήρια καὶ τὰ κράσπεδα; Ἐπειδὴ συνεχῶς ἐπελανθάνοντο τῶν εὐεργεσιῶν τοῦ Θεοῦ, ἐκέλευσεν ἐγγραφῆναι βιβλίοις μικροῖς τὰ θαύματα αὐτοῦ, καὶ ἐξηρτῆσθαι αὐτὰ τῶν χειρῶν αὐτῶν· (διὸ καὶ ἔλεγεν· Ἔσται ἀσάλευτα ἐν ὀφθαλμοῖς σου·) ἃ φυλακτήρια ἐκάλουν· ὡς πολλαὶ νῦν τῶν γυναικῶν Εὐαγγέλια τῶν τραχήλων ἐξαρτῶσαι ἔχουσι.*

3. See, for instance, Robert L. Wilken, *John Chrysostom and the Jews: Rhetoric and Reality in the Late 4th Century* (TCH 4; Berkeley: University of California Press, 1983) and Charlotte E. Fonrobert, "Jewish Christians, Judaizers, and Christian Anti-Judaism," in *Late Ancient Christianity: A People's History of Christianity*, vol. 2, ed. Virginia Burrus (Minneapolis: Fortress Press, 2005), 234–54,

306–9, esp. 236–43. On magical practices in Chrysostom's Antioch, see Silke Trzcionka, *Magic and the Supernatural in Fourth-Century Syria* (London: Routledge, 2007).

4. John Chrysostom, *Stat* 19.14 (NPNF[1] 9:470), trans. Stephens, slightly modified: "Here there is no need of gold or property, or of buying a book; but of the will only, and the affections of the soul awakened, and the Gospel will be your surer guardian, carrying it as you want then, not outside, but treasured up within; yea, in the soul's secret chambers." The preacher encouraged the members of his audience to repeat Matt 5:34 to themselves (ibid. 9:470–71).

5. For instance, Karl Preisendanz, ed., *Papyri graecae magicae. Die griechischen Zauberpapyri.* 2nd ed., ed. Albert Henrichs SWC (München: Saur, 2001), 2:212–3 (P 5b); C. Wessely, "Les plus anciens monuments du christianisme écrits sur papyrus (II)," PO 18 (1924), 417–20; John Garrett Winter, *Life and Letters in the Papyri* (The Jerome Lectures; Ann Arbor: University of Michigan Press, 1933) 188; Gary Vikan, "Early Byzantine Pilgrimage *Devotionalia* as Evidence of the Appearance of Pilgrimage Shrines," in *Akten des XII. Internationalen Kongresses für christliche Archäologie: Bonn, 22.–28. September, 1991*, ed. Ernst Dassmann, Josef Engemann (JAC 20, no. 1; Münster: Aschendorffsche Verlagsbuchhandlung, 1995) 377–88 at 387; Marvin W. Meyer and Richard Smith, eds., *Ancient Christian Magic: Coptic Texts of Ritual Power* (Princeton, NJ: Princeton University Press, 1994), 40–41 (no. 16); Jane Rowlandson et al., eds., *Women and Society in Greek and Roman Egypt* (Cambridge: Cambridge University Press, 1998), 82 (no. 66); David Frankfurter, "Amuletic Invocations of Christ for Health and Fortune," in *Religions of Late Antiquity in Practice,* ed. Richard Valantasis; Princeton Readings in Religions (Princeton: Princeton University Press, 2000) 340–43, at 342 (Text B); Arietta Papaconstantinou, *Le culte des saints en Égypte des Byzantins aux Abbassides. L'apport des inscriptions et des papyrus grecs et coptes* (Paris: CNRS 2001) 342–43; Paul Mirecki, "Evangelion-Incipits Amulets in Greek and Coptic: Towards a Typology," in *Proceedings of the Central States Regional Meeting of the Society of Biblical Literature and the American Schools of Oriental Research* 4 (2001), 143–53 at 146 (no. 3); Theodore de Bruyn mentions this amulet in his "Appeals to Jesus as the one 'who heals every illness and every infirmity' (Matt 4:23, 9:35) in Amulets in Late Antiquity," in *The Reception and Interpretation of the Bible in Late antiquity: Proceedings of the Montreal Colloquium in Honour of Charles Kannengiesser*, ed. Charles Kannengiesser, Lorenzo DiTommaso, and Lucian Turcescu (Leiden: Brill, 2008), 65–81, esp. at 67.

6. Arjun Appadurai, ed., *The Social Life of Things: Commodities in Cultural Perspective* (Cambridge: Cambridge University Press, 1986).

7. See also AnneMarie Luijendijk, "*Greetings in the Lord:*" *Early Christians and the Oxyrhynchus Papyri* (HTS 60; Cambridge, Mass.: Harvard University Press, 2008), esp. 233.

8. *Editio princeps* Arthur S. Hunt, P.Oxy. VIII 1151 (1911) 251–53. For the reading of lines 38–39, see Dieter Hagedorn "Bemerkungen zu Urkunden," *ZPE* 145 (2003): 224–27 at 226.
9. Other Christian amulets of this format are, for instance *PGM* P 15a (4–5 x 24 cm, provenance unknown, sixth century), PSI VI 719 (=P 19; 25 x 5.5. cm, Oxyrhynchus, fourth or fifth century), P. Cairo Cat. 10696 descr. (= *PGM* P 5c; provenance unknown; 6.4 x 26.4 cm, fifth or sixth century), P.Turner 49 (Suppl. Mag. 31; 40 x 3 cm, provenance unknown, fifth or sixth century). See also Daniel and Moltomini, Suppl. Mag. 1:86–87, who mention that "Egyptian parallels for the at times extremely oblong format are numerous."
10. On the condition of the papyrus when found, see Hunt, P.Oxy. VIII 1151, 251. For evidence that certain charms were worn from the neck, recall John Chrysostom and the mummy portraits mentioned in endnote 1. A fragment from a magical handbook provides instructions for making an amulet, specifying that it should be worn around the neck. It reads: "Protect him, NN, whom NN bore . . . attach (it) around the neck." [*φ*]*ύλαξον τὸν δ(εῖνα) ὃν ἔτ*[*εκεν ἡ δ(εῖνα)* | [*π*]*ερίαξον περὶ τὸν τρά*[*χηλον)*] (Suppl. Mag. 80 = P.Reinach II 89.1–2).
11. Hunt (P.Oxy. VIII 1151, 251) mentions that the handwriting resembles a book hand: "it is written in a clear upright hand, approximating to a literary type." He dated it to the fifth century CE with a question mark (ibid). The writer consistently wrote a dieresis over neighboring vowels and made some vowel exchanges (*omicron* for *omega*, *eta* for *iota*, *epsilon* for *alpha iota*); all common iotacisms in papyri and even in literary manuscripts.
12. The writer penned 12 *nomina sacra* for the words Spirit, Christ, God, Lord; all terms that are commonly contracted in Christian manuscripts. Therefore, the amulet is visually Christian. For the visual aspect of *nomina sacra*, see Larry W. Hurtado, "The Earliest Evidence of an Emerging Christian Material and Visual Culture: The Codex, the Nomina sacra and the Staurogram," in *Text and Artifact in the Religions of Mediterranean Antiquity: Essays in Honour of Peter Richardson*, ed. Stephen G. Wilson and Michel Desjardins (SCJ 9; Waterloo, ON: Canadian Corporation for Studies in Religion, 2000), 271–88 at 277. In magical documents *nomina sacra* also occur in less-than-orthodox contexts. An interesting use in this amulet occurs in its first line: the word for spirit (*πνεῦμα*) appears written as a *nomen sacrum*, $\overline{\underset{.}{\pi}\underset{.}{\nu}\underset{.}{\alpha}}$, although it here indicates not the Holy Spirit (as it does in line 6), but explicitly a "hateful spirit" (*π̣ν̣(εῦμ)α̣ μεμισιμένον*). Other examples of this use of the *nomen sacrum* for evil spirits are P.Coll.Youtie 91.5 and P.Turner 49.4.
13. For the Greek text, see the appendix.
14. The amulet mentions the name of its bearer twice: "Joannia, to whom Anastasia alias Euphemia gave birth" (lines 11-3, 30-2). The name Joannia occurs only infrequently in Greek papyrus documents and literary texts: Friedrich Preisigke, *Namenbuch, enthaltend alle griechischen, lateinischen, ägyptischen, hebräischen . . . Menschennamen* (Heidelberg: Selbstverlag des Herausgebers, 1922), 155; Daniele

Foraboschi, *Onomasticon alterum papyrologicum* (Milano: Varese Istituto Editoriale Cisalpino, 1971), 153; Dieter Hagedorn, ed., *WörterListen* (http://www.zaw.uni-heidelberg.de/hps/pap/WL/WL.pdf, accessed March 11, 2009), 59. No extant examples of this name form a match with the Joannia from this amulet since they date to different periods and thus must indicate different persons by the same name. Moreover, none of these texts come from Oxyrhynchus, the site where our amulet was found. The names Anastasia and Euphemia show up in the papyrological record, but the double name "Anastasia alias Euphemia" occurs only here and a match with Joannia's mother in other documents cannot be made. Indicating matrilineal instead of patrilinear descent is a common feature of Greek amulets from the first century CE on. According to Jaime Curbera "the magical use of maternal lineage was originally a distorted representation of the onomastic practices found in ancient Egyptian texts. Its wide diffusion was due to the congruence between this reversal of Graeco-Roman norms and a general representation of magical practice as the inversion of normal practice." See Jaime B. Curbera, "Maternal Lineage in Greek Magical Texts," in *The World of Ancient Magic. Papers from the First International Samson Eitrem Seminar at the Norwegian Institute at Athens, 4–8 May 1997*, ed. David R. Jordan, Hugo Montgomery, Einar Thomassen; Papers from the Norwegian Institute at Athens 4 (Bergen: Norwegian Institute at Athens, 1999), 195–204 at 201.

15. For excavation reports, see Bernard P. Grenfell and Arthur S. Hunt, "Excavations at Oxyrhynchus (1896–1907)," in *Oxyrhynchus: A City and Its Texts*, ed. A. K. Bowman, et al. (London: Egypt Exploration Society, 2007), 345–68 (reprinted from the *Egypt Exploration Fund: Archaeological Report*, Egypt Exploration Society, London).
16. P.Oxy. XI 1357, a liturgical calendar for the year 535-56, records a three-day celebration for the nativity of Christ in the church of "saint Mary." See Arietta Papaconstantinou, "La liturgie stationnale à Oxyrhynchos dans la première moitié du 6e siècle. Réédition et commentaire du POxy XI 1357," *REBy* 54 (1996): 135–59, at 140, line 30. Papaconstantinou comments: "Cette église est bien connue à Oxyrhynchos" (ibid., 146).
17. Saint Victor occurs frequently in papyri and inscriptions. See Arietta Papaconstantinou, *Le culte des saints en Égypte des Byzantins aux Abbassides. L'apport des inscriptions et des papyrus grecs et coptes* (MB: Paris: CNRS, 2001), 62–68 ("ΒΙΚΤΩΡ").
18. Based on this and other papyri, Papaconstantinou, *Culte des saints*, 204, concludes that "Philoxène est, avec Juste et Sérénos, le troisième grand saint local d' Oxyrhynchos. Dans cette ville, les attestations documentaires sont très nombreuses, alors qu'elles sont presque inexistantes ailleurs." For Philoxenus, see Papaconstantinou, *Culte des saints*, 203–4 ("*ΦΙΛΟΞΕΝΟΣ*"). There is a sanctuary for the saint at Oxyrhynchus, and even an oracle, as evidenced by three oracle tickets (P.Harr. I 54, P.Oxy. VIII 1150, and P.Oxy. XVI 1926). A saint Justus appears in papyri from Oxyrhynchus (GLP II 78, P.Laur. II 46; P.Oxy. VI 941, VIII 1151, X 1131, XI 1357,

XXVII 2480, PSI VII 791, and P.Stras. V 395 and also in inscriptions on three lamps, perhaps also found at Oxyrhynchus, see Papaconstantinou, *Culte des saints*, 108 ("ΙΟΥΣΤΟΣ"). A martyr shrine for Saint Justus appears in papyri from the fifth century and later (ibid., 108–9). For Serenus, see Papaconstantinou, *Culte des saints*, 187–88 ("ΣΕΡΗΝΟΣ"). The saint is mentioned in multiple papyri and in an inscription from Saqara (Saq. 219). Again, he has a sanctuary in Oxyrhynchus. A papyrus from Heracleopolis (sixth century) mentions the saint in an invocation for health (BGU III 954= PGM 9): *ἅγιε Σερῆνε πρόσπεσε ὑπὲρ ἐμοῦ ἵνα τελείως ὑγιάνω* (lines 29–30, quoted from Papaconstantinou). This amulet for a man called Silvanus, it was "found folded and tied up with red thread" and included the Lord's prayer (see for instance, E. A. Judge, "The Magical Use of Scripture in the Papyri," in *Perspectives on Language and Text: Essays and Poems in Honour of Frances I. Anderson*, ed. E. W. Conrad and E. G. Newing (Winona Lake, IN: Eisenbrauns, 1987), 339–49, at 340–41).

19. Papaconstantinou, *Culte des saints*, 115–16 ("ΙΩΑΝΝΗΣ ΕΥΑΓΓΕΛΙΣΤΗΣ"). The fourth evangelist appears in P.Oxy. VIII 1151, XI 1357, PSI VIII 953 and VBP IV 65. His name also appears on a set of three spoons (SB I 5977) and in an inscription from Wadi Sarga. As Papaconstantinou concludes, Oxyrhynchus is the only city in late antique Egypt with a sanctuary for John the Evangelist (ibid., 116).

20. This phrase may also have Mariological connotations, for tradition has it that the Virgin Mary was born near this pool by the Sheep Gate. See Mary Cunningham, *Wider than Heaven: Eighth-Century Homilies on the Mother of God* (Crestwood, NY: St. Vladimir's Seminary Press, 2008), 61n36: "The tradition that Mary was born near the "probatic" pool by the Sheep Gate in Jerusalem (John 5.2), where her parents had a house, appeared early although it is not attested in the New Testament or the *Protevangelion* of James. In the fifth century, a church was built at this site to commemorate the Virgin's nativity." Kosmas Vestitor (eighth to ninth century) narrates in a homily: "For [Mary's] ancestral home was situated near the pool by the Sheep Gate in Jerusalem, according to the text, where Christ [who was] also our God raised up and cured the man who had lain as a paralytic for thirty-eight years (cf. John 5.1–9), since he was about to go forth from that house symbolically as the Shepherd of rational sheep" (ibid., 141).

21. On the popularity of the Gospel of John at Oxyrhynchus, apparent from the many papyrus fragments with its text, see David C. Parker, *An Introduction to the New Testament Manuscripts and Their Texts* (Cambridge: Cambridge University Press, 2008), 323.

22. In his *Curse Tablets and Binding Spells from the Ancient World* (Oxford: Oxford University Press, 1992), 13, John G. Gager, writing on the choice of deities in curse tables and binding spells (*defixiones*), makes the following observation: "In general, two factors seem to have governed the selection of gods and spirits and their names: first, local customs and beliefs; and second, the recipes available through the formularies owned and used by local experts. In this sense," Gager continues,

"we may use what we read on *defixiones* as a reasonably accurate measure of prevailing beliefs at particular times and places."

23. Theodore de Bruyn and Jitse Dijkstra's definition of an amulet comprises these different applications: "all texts that were written to convey in and of themselves – as well as in association with incantation and other actions – supernatural power for protective, beneficial, or antagonistic effect . . ." ("Greek Amulets and Formularies from Egypt Containing Christian Elements: A Checklist of Papyri, Parchments, Ostraka, and Tablets," *BASP* 48 [2011]: 163-216 at 168).
24. See also Kotansky, "Inscribed Greek Amulets," 107. For an overview of different types of amulets, see William M. Brashear, "The Greek Magical Papyri: An Introduction and Survey; Annotated Bibliography (1928–1994)," in *ANRW* 18.5:3380–684, at 3494–3506.
25. Exorcisms are common Christian practices, see, for instance, Eric Sorensen, *Possession and Exorcism in the New Testament and Early Christianity* (WUNT157; Tübingen: Mohr Siebeck, 2002). The phraseology "flee hateful spirit" harkens back to Rev 18:2 "'Fallen, fallen is Babylon the great! It has become a dwelling-place of demons, a haunt of every foul spirit, a haunt of every foul bird, a haunt of every foul and hateful beast'" (NRSV) (*Ἔπεσεν, ἔπεσεν Βαβυλὼν ἡ μεγάλη, καὶ ἐγένετο κατοικητήριον δαιμονίων καὶ φυλακὴ παντὸς πνεύματος ἀκαθάρτου καὶ φυλακὴ παντὸς ὀρνέου ἀκαθάρτου καὶ μεμισημένου*).
26. Kotansky, "Inscribed Greek Amulets," 117.
27. According to Daniel, "the main outlines of a *φυλακτήριον*" are "a command to a god to protect a person from named or unnamed evils" (R. W. Daniel, "Some *φυλακτήρια*," *ZPE* 25 (1977), 145 (commenting on P.Yale II 130 = SB XIV 12113). Moltomini and Jordan noted: "*φεῦγε, ὁ δεῖνα* (the evil), *ὁ δεῖνά* (a divine power) *σε διώκει*. . . . In virtually all of these passages, *φεῦγε vel. sim.* occurs in the first position" (Suppl. Mag. 25, 1: 71). See also Kotansky, "Inscribed Greek Amulets," 117, 119.
28. The expression comes from Kotansky, "Inscribed Greek Amulets," 119 and is based on the work of anthropologist Stanley Jeyaraja Tambiah, "Form and Meaning of Magical Acts: A Point of View," in *Modes of Thought: Essays on Thinking in Western and Non-Western Societies*, ed. R. Horton and Ruth Finnegan (London: Faber, 1973), 199–229. Tambiah, in turn, was influenced by John Langshaw Austin's *How to Do Things With Words*, 2nd ed., ed. J. O. Urmson and Marina Sbisà (WJL, 1955; Cambridge, MA: Harvard University Press, 1975).
29. Rowlandson, *Women and Society*, 281: "For the spell to be effective, women must have intoned the magic words in their own voices, or risked attaching their beloved to whoever recited the charm." The legibility of the handwriting supports the claim that the spell was intended to be read out loud. See also Kotansky, "Inscribed Greek Amulets," 110, and David Frankfurter, "Narrating Power: The Theory and

Practice of the Magical *Historiola* in Ritual Spells," in *Ancient Magic and Ritual Power*, ed. Marvin Meyer and Paul Mirecki (Leiden: Brill, 1995), 457–76 at 463. On (il)literacy, see William V. Harris, *Ancient Literacy* (Cambridge, MA: Harvard University Press, 1989) and recently, William A. Johnson and Holt N. Parker, eds., *Ancient Literacies: The Culture of Reading in Greece and Rome* (Oxford: Oxford University Press, 2009).

30. *εἰ γὰρ τοῦ σταυροῦ γενομένου, πᾶσα μὲν εἰδωλολατρεία καθηρέθη, πᾶσα δὲ δαιμόνων φαντασία τῷ σημείῳ τούτῳ ἀπελαύνεται* (Athanasius, *C. gent.* 1:27–9; R. W. Thomson, ed., *Athanasius. Contra gentes and de incarnatione* [Oxford: Clarendon Press, 1971]).

31. Kimberly Stratton has skillfully exposed such labels in her *Naming the Witch: Magic, Ideology, and Stereotype in the Ancient World* (Gender, Theory, and Religion; New York: Columbia University Press, 2007), especially 79–96. It is worth noting in this context a group of erotic magical texts, in which, as Lynn LiDonnici has shown, elite men wish fevers on their female victims. Lynn R. LiDonnici, "Burning for It: Erotic Spells for Fever and Compulsion in the Ancient Mediterranean World," *GRBS* 39 (1998): 63–98.

32. Kotansky, "Inscribed Greek Amulet," 119–20, distinguishes two different uses of the imperative in amulets: "some contain 'performative' incantations in which the disease/daemon is directly addressed (e.g., the *φεῦγε* formula) and some are simple prayers that use and imperative to bid the deity to take action . . . the use of the imperative form of the verb *ἀπολαύνειν* ('to drive away, to expel') suggests the driving out of an already sedentary and chronic ailment."

33. An example of a phylactery that protected against fever is P.Oxy. VI 924, for a woman named Apia (fourth century, Oxyrhynchus). It reads: "Verily guard and protect Aria from ague by day and quotidian ague and ague by night and slight fever and . . . All this thou graciously do in accordance with thy will first and with her faith, since she is a slave of the living God, and in order that thy name may be glorified for ever" (trans. Grenfell and Hunt, P.Oxy. VI 924, 290, slightly adapted).

34. Kotansky, "Inscribed Greek Amulets," 116. This specificity extended into the Byzantine period, as we see in Joannia's and other later amulets.

35. For the description of the clinical symptoms of malaria, I depend on Walter Scheidel, *Death on the Nile: Disease and the Demography of Roman Egypt* (Leiden: Brill, 2001), 75–91, and François Retief and Louise Cilliers, "Malaria in Graeco-Roman Times," *AC* 47 (2004) 127–37, at 128–29. Not all scholars would agree with this diagnosis, Fischer-Elfert cautions: "Malaria mag sich hinter dem einen oder anderen Fieber-Rezept verbergen, nur stimmen die Symptome in den Texten nie zur Gänze mit der einen oder anderen Form dieser Krankheit überein" (Hans-W. Fischer-Elfert, "Heilkunde im Alten Ägypten," in *Zwischen Magie und Wissenschaft*, 43–54, at 51). This is, in my opinion, because the ancients had a different concept of sickness.

36. Scheidel, *Death on the Nile*, 75.
37. For studies on malaria in antiquity, see Cheston B. Cunha, "Prolonged and Perplexing Fevers in Antiquity: Malaria and Typhoid Fever," *IDCNA* 21 (2007): 857–66; Retief and Cilliers, "Malaria in Graeco-Roman Times," 127–37; Robert Sallares, *Malaria and Rome: A History of Malaria in Ancient Italy* (Oxford: Oxford University Press, 2002), and Paul F. Burke, Jr., "Malaria in the Greco-Roman World: A Historical and Epidemiological Survey," *ANRW* 37.3:2252–81. Thomas Fuller, "Spread of Malaria Feared as Drug Loses Potency," *The New York Times*, January 26, 2009, mentions the death of the African children in our time.
38. Sallares, *Malaria and Rome*, 31; Scheidel, *Death on the Nile*, 76.
39. In William Brashear's catalogue of Greek iatromagical amulets, fever forms by far the largest category ("The Greek Magical Papyri" [ANRW II 18.5], 3500). A search on the TM Magic website gives fifty results for "type = fever;" forty of these are Greek, the rest are Coptic (ten; one is bilingual Greek-Coptic) and Aramaic (one). See F. Naether and M. Depauw, *TM Magic* (cited March 11, 2009, http://www.trismegistos.org/magic/index.php). Fever amulets for women are, for instance, Greco-Egyptian: P.Tebt. II 275, for a woman named Tais (Tebtynis, third century); Suppl. Mag. 3, for a woman named Helene (= P. Haun. III 50; third century, provenance unknown); Suppl. Mag. 9, for a woman named Techosis (=P.Michael. 27; third to fourth century, provenance unknown); Christian: Suppl. Mag. 23, for a woman named Kale (=P.Haun. III 51; fifth century, provenance unknown); Suppl. Mag. 25, for a woman named Gennadia (fifth century, provenance unknown); Suppl. Mag. 31, for an unnamed woman (=P.Turner 49; fifth or sixth century, provenance unknown).
40. "The postulated virulence and geographical extent of the often fatally ending variants of malaria in the period of the downfall of the Roman Empire and in the early Byzantine years coincide with the heyday of Late Antique and Early Medieval magic, when healing magic 'against fever and shivering' was widespread. It seems quite probable that a close connection exists between the spread of malaria and the increase of folk medicinal and magical healing and protective practices . . .," Irina Wandrey, "Fever and Malaria 'For Real' or as a Magical-Literary Topos," in *Jewish Studies Between the Disciplines (Judaistik zwischen den Disziplinen): Papers in Honor of Peter Schäfer on the Occasion of His 60th Birthday*, ed. Klaus Herrmann, Margarete Schlüter, and Giuseppe Veltri (Leiden: Brill, 2003), 257–66 at 265.
41. Retief and Cilliers, "Malaria in Graeco-Roman Times," 129. For pregnant women, infection with malaria leads to a lower birth weight of infants, and a higher incident of stillbirths and death of newborns (see Scheidel, *Death on the Nile*, 75). On the current situation in Africa, see Fuller, "Spread of Malaria Feared."
42. Roger S. Bagnall, *Egypt in Late Antiquity* (Princeton, NJ: Princeton University Press, 1993), 182. See also Roger S. Bagnall and Bruce W. Frier, *The Demography of Roman Egypt* (CSPESPT 23; Cambridge: Cambridge University Press, 1994).

43. Edition: Pieter J. Sijpesteijn, "Amulet against Fever," *ChrEg* 57 (1982): 377–81. The text is written on fine parchment. See Meyer and Smith, eds., *Ancient Christian Magic*, 99–100 (no. 52), and David Frankfurter, "Beyond Magic and Superstition," in *Late Ancient Christianity: A People's History of Christianity*, ed. Virginia Burrus, vol. 2 (Minneapolis: Fortress Press, 2005), 255–84, 309–12, at 280. See also Dayna Kalleres's discussion in chapter 7 of this volume on Chrysostom's praise for a mother who did not acquire an amulet for her sick son (Chrysostom, *Hom. 8 on Col. 8*) and Dayna Kalleres, "Old Hags with Spells and Prostitutes with Potions: The Re-Feminization of Magic in Post-Constantinian Christianity," 4.
44. Expression from Frankfurter, "Beyond Magic and Superstition," 257.
45. ϩⲟïⲛⲉ ⲉⲩⲙⲟⲩⲣ ⲛ̄ϩⲉⲛⲫⲩⲗⲁⲕⲧⲏⲣⲓⲟⲛ ⲉⲛⲉⲩϣⲏⲣⲉ ⲉⲁⲩⲧⲁⲙⲓⲟⲟⲩ ϩⲓⲧⲛ̄ⲧⲧⲉⲭⲛⲏ ⲛ̄ⲛ̄ⲣⲱⲙⲉ, ⲛⲁï ⲉⲧⲟ̄ ⲙ̄ⲙⲁ ⲛ̄ⲟⲩⲱϩ ⲛ̄ⲛ̄ⲇⲁⲓⲙⲱⲛ. L. Th. Lefort, "L'homélie de S. Athanase des papyrus de Turin," *Muséon* LXXI (1958), 5–50, 209–39; at 36 (Coptic) and 226 (French translation).
46. Chrysostom, *In Epistulam I ad Corinthios hom* (PG 61.105–106) and *Basilii Aliorumque scholia in S. Gregorii Naz. Orationes* (PG 36.907), translation both Stander, "Amulets," 57.
47. Kalleres, "Re-Feminization of Magic," 4.
48. In a document from the year 316, two Oxyrhynchite public physicians report to the *logistes* Valerius Ammonianus on the condition of a man who suffered from fever (P.Oxy. VI 896.33).
49. Vikan, "Early Byzantine Pilgrimage Devotionalia," 387.
50. The expression is adapted from Gager ("persuasive analogies," *Curse Tablets*, 13), who based it on the work of Tambiah, "Form and Meaning of Magical Acts," 199–229. Tambiah, writing about magical practices of the Zande in Africa, notes: "in most Zande magical rites (especially those considered important by the people concerned), the analogical relation or comparison and the wished-for effect is stated *verbally* simultaneously with or before the carrying out of the so-called 'homoeopathic' act (of influencing certain objects by manipulating other objects which resemble them)." (ibid., 213). The situation is slightly different here: In the case of Gager's *defixiones* and Tambiah's Zande magic, in Joannia's and other amulets, the analogy is purely verbal, referring to an action in the past that functions as precedent. As far as I can ascertain, these amulets are not accompanied by ritual acts other than the reciting and making the cross sign, as noted above.
51. Frankfurter, "Narrating Power," respectively at 458 and 464. Frankfurter observes, "*historiolae* most often are employed in healing spells (as opposed to love or curse spells), perhaps because situations of illness, accident and childbirth were so dire in antiquity as to require more dramatic invocations of divine power than were possible with mere directives, prayers or commands" (ibid. 461).
52. Another amulet, written on an ostracon, also refers to the same passage in John 5 (PGM O 3; seventh or eighth century; provenance unknown; English translation Meyer, *Ancient Christian Magic*, 32–33, no. 6).

53. See also Theodore de Bruyn, "Appeals to Jesus as the one 'who heals every illness and every infirmity' (Matt 4:23, 9:35) in Amulets in Late Antiquity," in *The Reception and Interpretation of the Bible in Late Antiquity: Proceedings of the Montreal Colloquium in Honour of Charles Kannengiesser*, ed. Charles Kannengiesser, Lorenzo DiTommaso, and Lucian Turcescu (Leiden: Brill, 2008), 65–81. De Bruyn collected seven amulets that contain this Matthean expression.
54. Translation Meyer, *Ancient Christian Magic*, 33, no. 7.
55. Translation William Brashear, P.Turner 49, 193 (slightly modified).
56. See also Frankfurter: "the *historiola* . . . works . . . as a guarantee or rationale, an explicit precedent, for the directive utterance, the command, which is the central speech-act" ("Narrating Power," 469).
57. A TLG search for name (ὄνομα) near supremely glorious (ὑπερένδοξος) indicates interestingly that the adjective mostly applies to Mary, the god-bearer. In the Septuagint, the adjective occurs in Dan 3:53 and Odes 8:53, 56.
58. καὶ ἔσται πᾶς, ὃς ἂν ἐπικαλέσηται τὸ ὄνομα κυρίου, σωθήσεται, Joel 3:5 LXX.
59. Another gospel amulet, opening with John 1:1–11, is P.Köln VIII 340: "Amuleto con NT Ev. Jo. 1, 1–11" (fifth or sixth century, unknown provenance).
60. See for instance, P.Oxy. XVI 1928 verso (fifth or sixth century, Oxyrhynchus); PSI VI 719 (=P 19; Oxyrhynchus, fourth or fifth century), P. Cairo Cat. 10696 descr. (= *PGM* P 5c; provenance unknown; fifth or sixth century) and P. Vindob. G 348, a sixth- or seventh-century amulet (ed. R. W. Daniel, "A Christian Amulet on Papyrus," *VC* 37 [1983] 400–404).
61. See, for instance, Isidore of Pelusium (Egypt), Epistle II 150 "To Epimachus" (PG 78. 604C): ὥσπερ νῦν [αἱ γυναῖκες τὰ] Εὐαγγέλια [τὰ] μικρά, "just as now [women] (carry) small gospels." I should note that the words αἱ γυναῖκες, "the women," were apparently absent in Migne's manuscript of Isidore's text and supplied by him, probably based on John Chrysostom.
62. On *tefillin*, see Yehudah B. Cohn, *Tangled up in Text. Tefillin and the Ancient World* (BJS 351; Providence, RI: Program in Judaic Studies, 2008). Cohn argues that "the word *tefillin* originally described the function of the amulet that it signified as a prayer for long life (ibid., 2).
63. Claudia Rapp, "Holy Texts, Holy Men, and Holy Scribes. Aspects of Scriptural Holiness in Late Antiquity," in *The Early Christian Book*, ed. William E. Klingshirn and Linda Safran (CUA; Washington, DC: Catholic University of America Press, 2007), 194–222 at 202.
64. See also Papaconstantinou, *Culte des saints*, 343. Professional handwriting does not necessarily exclude a woman writer. Kim Haines-Eitzen has collected substantial evidence for female scribes and calligraphers from antiquity; see Kim Haines-Eitzen, *Guardians of Letters: Literacy, Power, and the Transmitters of Early Christian Literature* (Oxford: Oxford University Press, 2000), chapter 2: "'Girls Trained for Beautiful Writing': Female Scribes in Roman Antiquity and Early Christianity," 41–52.

65. See, for instance, David Frankfurter, *Religion in Roman Egypt: Assimilation and Resistance* (Princeton, NJ: Princeton University Press, 1998), 224–37; Gager, *Curse Tablets*, 4–12; Robert Ritner, "Egyptian Magical Practice under the Roman Empire: The Demotic Spells and their Religion," *ANRW* 18.5:3333–79 at 3357–58.
66. Chrysostom acknowledges the business aspect of amulets: "For the amulets, even though those who make money from them (*χρηματιζόμενοι*) philosophize endlessly, . . . the matter is idolatry" (*Ad Colossenses* VIII 5, PG 62:358). Frankfurter again draws a parallel between indigenous Egyptian priests (*hry-tp*) and Christian clergy: just as the former supplemented their income, "so also in Coptic Egypt monks and priests could apply their scribal learning, their training in efficacious words and chants, their memorized prayers to folk life" (Frankfurter, "Ritual Expertise," 129).
67. Τὰ *γὰρ περίαπτα καὶ αἱ γοητεῖαι μάταια βοηθήματα ὑπάρχουσιν. Εἰ δέ τις αὐτοῖς κέχρηται, γινωσκέτω τοῦτο σαφῶς, ὅτι ἑαυτὸν ἐποίησεν ἀντὶ πιστοῦ ἄπιστον, ἀντὶ δὲ* Χριστιανοῦ *ἐθνικὸν, ἀντὶ δὲ συνετοῦ ἀσύνετον, ἀντὶ δὲ λογικοῦ ἀλόγιστον. Καταντλεῖ γάρ σοι γραῦς διὰ κ΄ ὀβολοὺς, ἢ τετάρτην οἴνου ἐπαοιδὴν τοῦ ὄφεως· καὶ σὺ ἕστηκας ὡς ὄνος χασμώμενος, φορῶν δὲ ἐπὶ τὸν αὐχένα τὴν ῥυπαρίαν τῶν τετραπόδων, παρακρου—σάμενος τὴν σφραγῖδα τοῦ σωτηρίου σταυροῦ. Ἣν σφραγῖδα οὐ μόνον νοσήματα δεδοίκασιν, ἀλλὰ καὶ πᾶν τὸ στῖφος τῶν δαιμόνων φοβεῖται καὶ τέθηπεν. Ὅθεν καὶ πᾶς γόης ἀσφράγιστος ὑπάρχει.* (Athanasius, *De amuletis*, PG 26.1320).
68. Apul., *Met.* III 24.
69. Dickie, *Magic and Magicians*, 284: "Athanasius says nothing about the old woman's introducing Christian elements in her ritual and maintaining that she was one of the faithful. It may be that such women did not yet exist in Alexandria." I interpret this passage as directed polemically against Christian women who practice healing.
70. *καὶ Χριστιανή ἐστιν ἡ γραῦς καὶ πιστή*, Chrysostom, *Ad Colossenes* VIII 5 (PG 62.558).
71. The section reads in translation: "If, then, you do not first convince me by logical proof that it takes place in this way naturally, because the fever or the inflammation is afraid of a holy name or a foreign phase and so takes flight from the swelling, your stories still remain old wives' fables." (Lucian, *Lover of Lies* 9 [Harmon, LCL]). Lucian has a passage on a magical statue that can "send fevers upon whomsoever he will" (ibid., 349). People offered the statue money for a cure, for instance, from a fever: "votive offerings or payment for a cure from one or another of those who through him had ceased to be subject to fever" (ibid., 351).
72. Dickie, *Magic and Magicians*, 246.
73. Ibid., 245.
74. Dickie discusses a section of Philostratus, *Life of Apollonius of Tyana*, for what he terms a category of "mendicant holy women." He concludes that this "affords a glimpse of a world that is almost wholly lost to us in which humble people consult elderly mendicant holy women about their flocks, but it also inadvertently tells us

of a hierarchy amongst seers and magicians in which old women with some sort of pretension to holiness who go from community to community begging stand on the very bottom rung of the ladder" (ibid., 249). See, however, in a different context, Stratton's remark (*Naming the Witch*, 83) that old age is a component of the ancient diatribe against magic and more generally, David Frankfurter's review of Dickie's book (BMCR 2002.02.26 at http://bmcr.brynmawr.edu/2002/2002-02-26.html).

75. Kalleres, "Re-Feminization of Magic," 5.
76. David Frankfurter, "Ritual Expertise in Roman Egypt and the Problem of the Category 'Magician,'" in *Envisioning Magic: A Princeton Seminar and Symposium*, ed. Peter Schäfer and Hans G. Kippenberg (SHR 75; Leiden: Brill, 1997), 115–35, especially 127.
77. Ibid., 116.
78. De Bruyn, "Appeals to Jesus," 76.
79. Maxwell E. Johnson, *The Prayers of Sarapion of Thmuis: A Literary, Liturgical and Theological Analysis* (OrChrAn 249; Rome: Pontificio Istituto Orientale, 1995), 66 (Greek)—67 (English translation, adapted). Johnson dates these prayers to the mid-fourth century (ibid., 148).
80. De Bruyn, "Appeals to Jesus," 79.
81. On unintelligible magical signs and letters in spells, Gager (*Curse Tablets*, 10) remarked that "For the anxious client, what mattered was the belief that the *magos* possessed the special knowledge to get these names and titles right . . . We should also consider the likelihood that there was an element of status enhancement for professionals in maintaining a core of 'unintelligible' discourse, for this left the client with little choice but to assume that the specialist alone, through superior wisdom, understood the meaning and significance of this higher language."
82. In his writings, Frankfurter has illuminated different aspects of the involvement of clergy in practices traditionally labeled as "magic," see, for instance, his *Religion in Roman Egypt* and other works cited below.
83. Canon 36, translation Henry R. Percival, *The Seven Ecumenical Councils* (NPNF, Series 2) 14:151.
84. In the literature we find individual late-antique bishops and presbyters accused of engaging in magical practices. These charges, however, seem to belong to polemics grounded in doctrinal differences and aim at the deposing of these men. For several interesting cases, see Dickie, *Magic and Magicians*, 262–72.
85. Shenoute, Acephalous Work A14. Edition: Tito Orlandi, ed., *Shenute: Contra Origenistas* (CDMCL; Rome: C. I. M., 1985), 18; English translation: Tito Orlandi, "A Catechesis Against Apocryphal Texts by Shenoute and the Gnostic Texts of Nag Hammadi," *HTR* 75 (1982): 85–95 at 90. On this text see also Frankfurter, "Ritual Expertise," 127 and David Frankfurter, "Syncretism and the Holy Man in Late Antique Egypt," *JECS* 11(2003): 339–85 at 375.

86. Canon 71: ⲈⲨϢⲀⲚϬⲚ̄ⲞⲨ[Ⲁ Ϩ̄Ⲛ̄Ⲛ̄ϢⲎ]ⲢⲈ Ⲛ̄ⲚⲈⲔⲖⲎⲢⲒ[ⲔⲞⲤ Ⲉ]ϤⲔⲰ̣[ⲦⲈ] ϨⲒϨⲈⲚ Ϫ[ⲰⲰ]ⲘⲈ Ⲙ̄ⲘⲀⲄⲒⲀ, ⲈⲨⲈⲀⲀϤ Ⲛ̄ϢⲘⲘⲞ ⲈⲦⲔⲞⲒⲚⲰⲚⲒⲀ Ⲙ̄ⲠⲈⲬ̄Ⲥ̄, Walter Crum in W. Riedel and Walter E. Crum, *The Canons of Athanasius of Alexandria* (London: Williams and Norgate, 1904), 108 (Coptic), 135 (translation). The Arabic translation confirms the reading "sons" (ibid., 47).
87. P.Oxy. LVI 3834 (third century; Oxyrhynchus), for example, is such a handbook. It consists of six fragmentarily preserved spells; the sixth begins with "in case of fever" but then the text breaks off. On the topic of copying from handbooks in general, see D. R. Jordan, "New Reading," ZPE 74 (1988), 239. Jordan notes here: "the use of formularies by writers of love charms on papyrus was so common that it would be unusual if the writer of our charm had composed *ad hoc*. The text of this formulary would of course not have had the personal names as here but rather the abbreviation."
88. Frankfurter mentions another example of a "(Christian) village priest in sixth-century Upper Egypt 'who practiced astrology and magic. This occupation returned to him a great quantity of money. It was revealed to the bishop not to let him offer the holy sacrifice [Eucharist] anymore'" (Frankfurter, "Ritual Expertise," 128, quoting the Arabic Synaxarium Jacobite [128n33]).
89. See Frankfurter, *Religion in Roman Egypt*, 194–95.
90. ⲢⲰⲘⲈ ⲚⲒⲘ ⲈϤϤⲒ Ⲛ̄ⲚⲈϤϢⲎⲢⲈ ⲔⲞⲨⲒ̈ ⲈⲢⲀⲦⲞⲨ Ⲛ̄ⲚⲢⲈϤⲘⲞⲨⲦⲈ, ⲚϤ̄ϢⲞⲂⲈ ⲖⲀⲀⲨ ⲀⲚ ⲈⲠⲈⲦⲠⲢⲞⲤⲈⲚⲈⲄⲄⲈ Ⲙ̄ⲘⲞⲞⲨ Ⲛ̄Ⲛ̄ⲆⲀⲒⲘⲰⲚ. ⲈⲠⲘⲀ ⲆⲈ ⲈⲦⲢⲈⲔϪⲒ Ⲛ̄ⲚⲈⲔϢⲎⲢⲈ ⲈⲢⲀⲦⲞⲨ Ⲛ̄Ⲛ̄ⲢⲈϤⲘⲞⲨⲦⲈ, ϪⲒⲦϤ̄ ⲈⲘ̄ⲘⲀⲢⲦⲨⲢⲒⲞⲚ Ⲛ̄Ⲙ̄Ⲙ̄ⲀⲢⲦⲨⲢⲞⲤ ⲀⲨⲰ ϤⲚⲀⲖⲞ. Lefort, "L'homélie de S. Athanase," 39.
91. Frankfurter, "Beyond Magic and Superstition," 258, cf. 265–66.
92. See also Frankfurter, "Amuletic Invocations," 314: "the wording . . . suggests the work of ecclesiastical scribes rather than of freelance wizards."
93. In addition to the passages cited above, see also his polemics against the use of Jewish healing amulets in *Adv. Iud.* 8.5–7(PG 48.937ff) and *Adv. Iud.* 1.7.5–11 (PG 48.854–55).
94. August., *In Evang. Iohan.* 7.12.1, translation John W. Rettig, *St. Augustine: Tractates on the Gospel of John 1–10* (FC 78; Washington, DC: Catholic University of America Press, 1988), 165.
95. Edition from Hunt, P.Oxy. VIII 1151, 252; lines 38–39 adapted according to Dieter Hagedorn, "Bemerkungen zu Urkunden," *ZPE* 145 (2003) 224–27 at 226.
96. The amulet's text follows John 1: 1, 3, without the phrase *οὗτος ἦν ἐν ἀρχῇ πρὸς τὸν θεόν* (John 1:2). This omission does not represent a known textual variant. The amulet's author may have deemed it redundant. By writing *οὐδὲ ἓν ὃ γέγονεν*, the scribe followed a version of the text also known from, for instance, the corrector of P75 and the Sahidic translation; it is the reading that the editors of the NA27 preferred. Some early witnesses read *οὐδὲν ὃ γέγονεν* (P66).

Bibliography

Abusch, Ra'anan. "Rabbi Ishmael's Miraculous Conception: Jewish Redemption History in Anti-Christian Polemic." In *The Ways That Never Parted: Jews and Christians in Late Antiquity and the Early Middle Ages*, edited by Adam H. Becker and Annette Yoshiko Reed, 307–43. Tübingen: Mohr/Siebeck, 2003.

Abusch, Tzvi. "The Demonic Image of the Witch in Standard Babylonian Literature: The Reworking of Popular Conceptions by Learned Exorcists." In *Religion, Science, and Magic: In Concert and in Conflict*, edited by Jacob Neusner, Ernest S. Frerichs, and Paul V.M. Flesher, 27–60. New York: Oxford University Press, 1989.

Adamik, Tamás. "The Apocalypse of Paul and Fantastic Literature." In *The Visio Pauli and the Gnostic Apocalypse of Paul*, edited by J. N. Bremmer and István Czachesz, 144–57. Leuven: Peeters, 2007.

Adler, William. *Time Immemorial: Archaic History and its Sources in Christian Chronography from Julius Africanus to George Syncellus*. Washington, DC: Dumbarton Oaks, 1989.

Adler, William and Paul Tuffin. *The Chronography of George Synkellos*. Oxford: Oxford University Press, 2002.

Akbari, S. C. *Seeing through the Veil: Optical Theory and Medieval Allegory*. Toronto: University of Toronto Press, 2004.

Alexander, Philip, trans. "3 [Hebrew Apocalypse of] Enoch." In *The Old Testament Pseudepigrapha*, edited by James Charlesworth, 1:223–315. Garden City, NY: Doubleday, 1983–1985.

Alexandre, C., ed. *Oracula Sybillina*. Paris: Didot Fratres, 1869.

Alic, M. *Hypatia's Heritage: A History of Women in Science from Antiquity to the Late Nineteenth Century*. Boston: Beacon, 1986.

Alighieri, Dante. *Inferno*. Vol. 1 of *The Divine Comedy of Dante Alighieri*. Translated by Robert M. Durling. With Ronald L. Martinez. New York: Oxford University Press, 1996.

American Heritage Dictionary of the English Language, s.v. "witch." 4th ed. Boston: Houghton Mifflin, 2000.

Anderson, Alan, and Raymond Gordon. "Witchcraft and the Status of Women—the Case of England." In *Witchcraft, Women, and Society*. Vol. 10 of *Articles on Witchcraft, Magic, and Demonology*, edited by Brian Levack, 27–40. New York: Garland, 1992.

Anderson, J. G. C., Franz Cumont, and Henri Grégoire. *Recueil des inscriptions grecques et latines du Pont et l'Arménie*. Studia Pontica 3. Brussels: Lamertin, 1910.

Anderson, Janice Capel. "Reading Tabitha: A Feminist Reception History." In *A Feminist Companion to the Acts of the Apostles*, edited by Amy-Jill Levine, 22–48. London: T. & T. Clark, 2004.

Ankarloo, Bengt, and Stuart Clark, eds. *Witchcraft and Magic in Europe: Ancient Greece and Rome*. Philadelphia: University of Pennsylvania Press, 1999.

The Ante-Nicene Fathers. Edited by Alexander Roberts and James Donaldson. 10 vols. 1885–1887. Reprint, Peabody, MA: Hendrickson, 1994.

Appadurai, Arjun, ed. *The Social Life of Things: Commodities in Cultural Perspective*. Cambridge: Cambridge University Press, 1986.

Apollonius Rhodius. *Argonautica*. Translated by R.C. Seaton. Loeb Classical Library. Cambridge, MA: Harvard University Press, 1980.

Apps, Lara and Andrew Gow. *Male Witches in Early Modern Europe*. Manchester: Manchester University Press, 2003.

Apuleius. *Metamorphoses (The Golden Ass)*. Translated by J. Arthur Hanson. Vol. 1. Loeb Classical Library. Cambridge, MA: Harvard University Press, 1989.

Aramaic Incantation Texts from Nippur. Edited by James A. Montgomery. Philadelphia: The University Museum, 1913.

Armstrong, Arthur H. "Was Plotinus a Magician?" *Phronesis* 1 (1955–1956): 73–79.

Arnaoutoglou, Ilias. "Marital Disputes in Greco-Roman Egypt." *Journal of Juristic Papyrology* 25 (1995): 11–28.

Asad, Talal. *Genealogies of Religion: Discipline and Reasons of Power in Christianity and Islam*. Baltimore: Johns Hopkins University Press, 1993.

Athanassiadi, Polymnia. "Dreams, Theurgy and Freelance Divination: The Testimony of Iamblichus." *Journal of Roman Studies* 83 (1993): 115–30.

Athanassiadi-Fowden, P. *Julian and Hellenism: An Intellectual Biography*. Oxford: Clarendon, 1981.

Audollent, Auguste. *Defixionum Tabellae*. Paris: Fontemoing, 1904. Reprint, Frankfurt: Minerva, 1967.

Austin, John Langshaw. *How to Do Things with Words*. 2nd ed. Edited by J. O. Urmson and Marina Sbisà. William James Lectures, 1955. Cambridge, MA: Harvard University Press, 1975.

Bagnall, Roger S. *Egypt in Late Antiquity*. Princeton, NJ: Princeton University Press, 1993.

———. "Linguistic Change and Religious Change: Thinking about the Temples of the Fayoum in the Roman Period." In *Christianity and Monasticism in the Fayoum*

Oasis, edited by Gawdat Gabra, 11–19. Cairo: American University in Cairo Press, 2005.

Bagnall, Roger S., and Raffaelle Cribiore. *Women's Letters from Ancient Egypt*. Ann Arbor: University of Michigan Press, 2006.

Bagnall, Roger S. and Bruce W. Frier, *The Demography of Roman Egypt*. Cambridge Studies in Population, Economy, and Society in Past Time 23. Cambridge: Cambridge University Press, 1994.

Bailey, Michael. "The Meanings of Magic." *Journal of Magic, Ritual & Witchcraft* 1 (2006): 1–23.

Baldwin, Barry. "Executions, Trials and Punishment in the Reign of Nero." *La Parola del Passato* 22 (1967): 425–39.

———. "Women in Tacitus." *Prudentia* 4 (1972): 83–101.

Bamberger, B. J. *Fallen Angels*. Philadelphia: Jewish Publication Society of America, 1952.

Barb, A. A. "The Survival of the Magical Arts." In *The Conflict between Paganism and Christianity in the Fourth Century*, edited by A. Momigliano, 100–123. Oxford: Clarendon, 1963.

Bar-Ilan, Meir. "Witches in the Bible and in the Talmud." In *Approaches to Ancient Judaism*, edited by Herbert Basser and Simcha Fishbane, 5:7–32. Atlanta: Scholars Press, 1993.

Barišić, Franjo. "Une *defixionis tabella* grecque de Progar en Srem." *Archaeologia Iugoslavica* 11 (1970): 23–28.

Barnes, T. D. "Tacitus and the Senatus Consultum de Cn. Pisone Patre (review article)." *Phoenix* 52, nos. 1–2 (1998): 125–48.

Barrett, Anthony A. *Agrippina: Sex, Power and Politics in the Early Empire*. New Haven, CT: Yale University Press, 1996.

———. *Livia: First Lady of Imperial Rome*. New Haven, CT: Yale University Press, 2002.

Barstow, Anne L. *Witchcraze: A New History of the European Witch Hunts*. San Francisco: Harper Collins, 1994.

Barthes, Roland. "L'effet du réel." *Communication* 11 (1968): 84–89.

———. *Mythologies*. Paris: Editions du Seuil, 1957.

Bartman, Elizabeth. *Portraits of Livia: Imaging the Imperial Woman in Augustan Rome*. Cambridge: Cambridge University Press, 1998.

Barton, C. "Being in the Eyes: Shame and Sight in Ancient Rome." In *The Roman Gaze: Vision, Power, and the Body*, edited by David Fredrick, 216–35. Baltimore: John Hopkins University Press, 2002.

Bartsch, Shadi. *Ideology in Cold Blood: A Reading of Lucan's* Civil War. Cambridge, MA: Harvard University Press, 1998.

———. *Mirror of the Self: Sexuality, Self-knowledge, and the Gaze in the Early Roman Empire*. Chicago: University of Chicago Press, 2006.

Bauckham, Richard J. "The Fall of the Angels as the Source of Philosophy in Hermias and Clement of Alexandria." *Vigiliae Christianae* 39 (1985): 319–30.

Bauman, Richard. *Crime and Punishment in Ancient Rome*. London: Routledge, 1996.

Bauman, Richard. *Women and Politics in Ancient Rome*. New York: Routledge, 1992.

Bean, George E. *The Inscriptions of Side*. Ankara: Türk Tarih Kurumu Basimevi, 1965.

Beard, Mary, John North, and Simon Price, eds. *Volume 1: A History*. Vol. 1 of *Religions of Rome*. Cambridge: Cambridge University Press, 1998.

Behar, Ruth. "Sexual Witchcraft, Colonialism, and Women's Powers: Views from the Mexican Inquisition." In *Sexuality and Marriage in Colonial Latin America*, edited by Asunción Lavrin, 178–206. Lincoln: University of Nebraska Press, 1989.

Ben-Yehuda, Nachman. *Deviance and Moral Boundaries: Witchcraft, the Occult, Science, Fiction, Deviant Sciences and Scientists*. Chicago: University of Chicago Press, 1985.

———. "Witchcraft and the Occult as Boundary Maintenance Devices." In *Religion, Science, and Magic in Concert and in Conflict*, edited by Joseph Neusner, Ernest S. Frerichs, and Paul V. M. Flesher, 229–61. Oxford: Oxford University Press, 1989.

Bernand, André. *Sorciers grecs*. Paris: Fayard, 1991.

Bernand, Étienne. *Inscriptions métriques de l'Égypte gréco-romaine*. Paris: Société d'édition "Les Belles Lettres," 1969.

Bernardini, Paulo. *Le Sententiae episcoporum del concilio cartaginese del 256 e la loro versione greca*. Bologna: Edizioni Dehoniane, 2005.

Berthelot, M. and C. É. Ruelle. *Collection des anciens alchimistes grecs*. 2 vols. Paris: Steinheil, 1888.

Beševliev, Veselin. *Spätgriechische und spätlateinische Inschriften aus Bulgarien*. Berlin: Akademie Verlag, 1964.

Besnier, Maurice. "Récents travaux sur les 'Defixionum tabellae latines,' 1904–1914." *Revue de philologie, de littérature et d'histoire anciennes* 44 (1920): 5–30.

Betz, Hans Dieter, ed. *The Greek Magical Papyri in Translation, Including the Demotic Spells*. Chicago: University of Chicago Press, 1992.

Bevilacqua, Gabriella. "Un incantesimo per odio in una defixio di Roma." *Zeitschrift für Papyrologie und Epigraphik* 117 (1997): 291–93.

Bhabha, Homi K. *The Location of Culture*. London and New York: Routledge, 1994.

Bhayro, Siam. "The Use of *Jubilees* in Medieval Chronicles to Supplement Enoch: The Case for the 'Shorter' Reading." *Henoch* 31.1 (2009): 10–17.

Björck, Gudmund. *Der Fluch des Christen Sabinus*. Papyrus Upsaliensis 8. Uppsala, Sweden: Almqvist & Wiksell, 1938.

Black, Matthew. *Apocalypsis Henochi graece*, with Albert-Marie Denis, *Fragmenta pseudepigraphorum quae supersunt graeca una cum historicorum et auctorum Iudaeorum hellenistarum fragmentis*. Leiden: Brill, 1970.

———. *The Book of Enoch, or 1 Enoch*. Studia in Veteris Testamenti pseudepigraphica. Leiden: Brill, 1985.

———. "The Twenty Angel Dekadarchs at 1 Enoch 6:7 and 69:2." *Journal of Jewish Studies* 33 (1982): 227–35.

Blakely, S. *Myth, Ritual and Metallurgy in Ancient Greece and Recent Africa*. Cambridge: Cambridge University Press, 2006.

Bloch, R. H. *Medieval Misogyny and the Invention of Western Romantic Love*. Chicago: University of Chicago Press, 1991.

Blümel, Wolfgang. *Die Inschriften von Knidos*. Inschriften griechischer Städte aus Kleinasien 41. Bonn: Habelt, 1992.

Blundell, Sue. *Women in Ancient Greece*. Cambridge, MA: Harvard University Press, 1995.

Bodel, John P. "Punishing Piso." *American Journal of Philology* 120, no. 1 (1999): 43–63.

Boegold, Alan. "Perikles' Citizenship Law of 451/0 B.C." In *Athenian Identity and Civic Ideology*, edited by Alan Boegehold and Adele Scafuro, 57–66. Baltimore and London: John Hopkins University Press, 1994.

Bohak, Gideon. *Ancient Jewish Magic*. Cambridge: Cambridge University Press, 2008.

———. Review of *Naming the Witch: Magic, Ideology, and Stereotype in the Ancient World*, by Kimberly B. Stratton. *Journal for the Study of Judaism* 39 (2008) 445–46.

Bonner, Campbell. "Witchcraft in the Lecture Room of Libanius." *Transactions of the American Philological Association* 63 (1932): 34–44.

Boor, C. de. *Georgii Monachi Chronicon*. Vol. 1. Leipzig: Teubner, 1904.

Bordia, Prashant and Nicholas DiFonzo. "Problem Solving in Social Interactions on the Internet: Rumor as Social Cognition." *Social Psychology Quarterly* 67 (2004): 33–34.

Borg, Barbara. "*Der zierlichste Anblick der Welt* ...." *Ägyptische Porträtmumien*. Zaberns Bildbände zur Archäologie. Mainz: Philipp von Zabern, 1998.

Boyarin, Daniel. *Border Lines: The Partition of Judaeo-Christianity*. Philadelphia: University of Pennsylvania Press, 2004.

———. "Gender." In *Critical Terms for Religious Studies*, edited by M. C. Taylor, 117–35. Chicago: University of Chicago Press, 1998.

———. "On Stoves, Sex, and Slave-Girls: Rabbinic Orthodoxy and the Definition of Jewish Identity." *Hebrew Studies* 41 (2000): 169–88.

Boyer, Paul, and Stephen Nissenbaum. *Salem Possessed; the Social Origins of Witchcraft*. Cambridge, MA: Harvard University Press, 1974.

Bovenschen, Sylvia. "The Contemporary Witch, the Historical Witch, and the Witch Myth." *New German Critique* 15 (1978): 83–119.

Bowen, Nancy R. "The Daughters of Your People: Female Prophets in Ezekiel 13:17–23." *Journal of Biblical Literature* 118 (1999): 417–33.

Bradley, Keith. *Discovering the Roman Family*. Oxford: Oxford University Press, 1991.

———. *Slavery and Society at Rome*. Cambridge: Cambridge University Press, 1994.

Brakke, David. *Demons and the Making of the Monk: Spiritual Combat in Early Christianity*. Cambridge, MA: Harvard University Press, 2006.

Brashear, William. "The Greek Magical Papyri: An Introduction and Survey; Annotated Bibliography (1928–1994)." In *Aufstieg und Niedergang der römischen Welt: Geschichte und Kultur Roms im Spiegel der neueren Forschung* 18.5:3380–684.

Part 2, *Principat*, 18.5, edited by H. Temporini and W. Haase. Berlin: Walter de Gruyter, 1995.

Brauner, Sigrid. *Fearless Wives and Frightened Shrews: The Construction of the Witch in Early Modern Germany*. Edited by Robert H. Brown. Amherst: University of Massachusetts Press, 1995.

Bregman, J. *Synesius of Cyrene: Philosopher-Bishop*. Berkeley: University of California Press, 1982.

Bremmer, Jan N. "Why Did Medea Kill Her Brother Apsyrtus?" In *Medea: Essays on Medea in Myth, Literature, Philosophy, and Art*, edited by James J. Clauss and Sarah Iles Johnston, 83–100. Princeton, NJ: Princeton University Press, 1997.

Breyfogle, Todd. "Magic, Women, and Heresy in the Late Empire: The Case of the Priscillianists." In *Ancient Magic and Ritual Power*, edited by Marvin Meyer and Paul Mirecki, 435–54. Boston: Brill, 2001.

Briggs, Robin. *Witches and Neighbours. The Social and Cultural Context of European Witchcraft*. London: HarperCollins, 1996 [republished: Oxford: Blackwell, 2002].

Brooten, Bernadette J. *Love Between Women: Early Christian Responses to Homoeroticism*. Chicago: University of Chicago Press, 1996.

Brown, Peter. *Making of Late Antiquity*. Cambridge, MA: Harvard University Press, 1978.

———. "The Rise and Function of the Holy Man in Late Antiquity." *Journal of Roman Studies* 61 (1971): 80–101.

———. "Sorcery, Demons and the Rise of Christianity: from Late Antiquity into the Middle Ages." In *Religion and Society in the Age of Saint Augustine*, edited by Peter Brown, 119–46. London: Faber and Faber, 1971.

———. "Sorcery, Demons, and the Rise of Christianity from Late Antiquity into the Middle Ages." In *Witchcraft Confessions and Accusations*, edited by Mary Douglas, 119–46. London: Faber and Faber, 1977.

Buchholz, Dennis D. *Your Eyes Will Be Opened: A Study of the Greek (Ethiopic) Apocalypse of Peter*. Society of Biblical Literature Dissertation Series 97. Atlanta: Scholars Press, 1988.

Buecheler, Franz. *Carmina Latina Epigraphica*. Leipzig: Teubner, 1895.

Bullard, M. Kenyon. "Hide and Secrete: Women's Sexual Magic in Belize." *Journal of Sex Research* 10, no. 4 (1974): 259–65.

Burke, Paul F., Jr. "Malaria in the Greco-Roman World: A Historical and Epidemiological Survey." In *Aufstieg und Niedergang der römischen Welt: Geschichte und Kultur Roms im Spiegel der neueren Forschung* 37.3:2252–81. Part 2, *Principat*, 37.3. Edited by H. Temporini and W. Haase. Berlin: Walter de Gruyter, 1996.

Burghartz, Suzanna. "The Equation of Women and Witches: A Case Study of Witchcraft Trials in Lucerne and Lausanne in the Fifteenth and Sixteenth Centuries." In *Witchcraft, Women, and Society*, edited with introductions by Brian P. Levack. Volume 10 of *Articles on Witchcraft, Magic, and Demonology* (New York: Garland, 1992)

Burriss, Eli Edward. "The Terminology of Witchcraft." *Classical Philology* 31 (1936): 137–45.

Burrus, Virginia. "Is Macrina a Woman? Gregory of Nyssa's Dialogue on the Soul and the Resurrection." In *The Companion to Postmodern Theology*, edited by Graham Ward, 249–64. Oxford: Blackwell, 2001.

———. "Word and Flesh: The Bodies and Sexuality of Ascetic Women in Christian Antiquity." *Journal of Feminist Studies in Religion* 10 (1994): 27–51.

Butler, E. M. *The Myth of the Magus*. Cambridge: Cambridge University Press, 1948.

Butler, Judith. *Gender trouble: Feminism and the Subversion of Identity*. London: Routledge, 1990.

Buzzi, Sabrina, D. Käch, E. Kistler, E. Mango, M. Palaczyk, and O. Stefani, eds. *Zona Archaeologica. Festschrift für Hans Peter Isler zum 60. Geburtstag*. Bonn: Habelt, 2001.

Cagat, René, ed. *Inscriptiones Graecae ad Res Romanas Pertinentes*. Vol. 3. Chicago: Ares, 1975.

Cantarella, Eva. *Pandora's Daughters: The Role and Status of Women in Greek and Roman Antiquity*. Baltimore: The Johns Hopkins University Press, 1987.

Carastro, Marcello. *La cité des mages. Penser la magie en Grèce ancienne*. Grenoble: Millon, 2006.

Carson, Anne. "Putting Her in Her Place: Woman, Dirt, and Desire." In *Before Sexuality*, edited by David M. Halperin, John J. Winkler, and Froma I. Zeitlin, 135–69. Princeton, NJ: Princeton University Press, 1990.

Castelli, Elizabeth. "Virginity and Its Meanings for Early Christian Women." *Journal of Feminist Studies in Religion* 2, no. 1 (1986): 61–88.

Castello, Carlo. "Cenni sulla repressione del reato di magia dagli inizi del principato fino a Costanzo II." In *VIII° Convegno Internazionale dell'Accademia Romanistica Constantiniana*, edited by G. Crifò and S. Ciglio, 665–92. Naples: Edizioni Scientifiche Internazionali, 1991.

Chaîne, M., trans. "Apocalypsis seu Visio Mariae Virginis." In *Apocrypha de B. Mariae Virginis*, 43–68. Corpus Scriptorum Christianorum Orientalium. Scriptores Aethiopici 1/7, 1909.

Champlin, Edward. "The First (1996) Edition of the Senatus Consultum de Cn. Pisone Patre: A Review." *American Journal of Philology* 120, no. 1 (1999): 117–22.

Charles, R. H. *The Book of Enoch*. Oxford: Clarendon Press, 1912.

Charlesworth, James, ed. *The Old Testament Pseudepigrapha*. 2 vols. Garden City, NY: Doubleday, 1983–1985.

Christidis, Anastasios-Ph., Sotiris Dakaris, and Ioulia Vokotopoulou. "Magic in the Oracular Tablets from Dodona." In *The World of Ancient Magic. Papers from the First International Samson Eitrem Seminar at the Norwegian Institute at Athens 4–8 May 1997*, edited by David R. Jordan, Hugo Montgomery, and Einar Thomassen. Papers from the Norwegian Institute at Athens 4, 67–72. Bergen: The Norwegian Institute at Athens, 1999.

Chrysostom, John. *Ad populum Antiochenum de statuis*. Translated by W. R. W. Stephens. In vol. 9 of *The Nicene and Post-Nicene Fathers*, Series 1. Edited by Philip Schaff. 1886–1889. 14 vols. Reprint, Peabody, MA: Hendrickson, 1994.

Cilliers, L., and F. P. Retief. "Poisons, Poisoning and the Drug Trade in Ancient Rome." *Akroterion* 45 (2000): 88–100.

Clark, Patricia. "Women, Slaves, and the Hierarchies of Domestic Violence: The Family of St. Augustine." In *Women and Slaves in Greco-Roman Culture: Differential Equations*, edited by Sheila Murnaghan and Sandra R. Joshel, 109–29. London: Routledge, 1998.

Clark, Stuart. *Thinking with Demons: The Idea of Witchcraft in Early Modern Europe*. Oxford: Oxford University Press, 1997.

Clarke, Emma C., John M. Dillon, and Jackson P. Hershbell. *Iamblichus: On the Mysteries*. Atlanta: Society of Biblical Literature, 2003.

Clarke, Ernest G. *Targum Pseudo-Jonathan of the Pentateuch*. With collaboration by W. E. Aufrecht, J. C. Hurd, and F. Spitzer. Hoboken, NJ: Ktav, 1984.

Clarke, Graeme W., ed. and trans. *The Letters of St. Cyprian*. 4 vols. New York: Newman, 1984–1989.

Clauss, James J., and Sarah Iles Johnston, eds. *Medea: Essays on Medea in Myth, Literature, Philosophy, and Art*. Princeton, NJ: Princeton University Press, 1997.

Cloke, Gillian. *This Female Man of God: Women and Spiritual Power in the Patristic Age, AD 350–450*. New York: Routledge, 1995.

Coblentz Bautch, Kelley. "Amplified Roles, Idealized Depictions: Women in the Book of the Jubilees." In *Enoch and the Mosaic Torah: The Evidence of Jubilees*, edited by G. Boccaccini and G. Ibba, 338–52. Grand Rapids, MI: Eerdmans, 2009.

———. "Decoration, Destruction, and Debauchery: Reflections on 1 Enoch 8 in Light of 4QEn[b]." *Dead Sea Discoveries* 15 (2008): 79–95.

———. "What Becomes of the Angels' Wives? A Text-Critical Study of 1 Enoch 19:2." *Journal of Biblical Literature* 125.2 (2006): 766–80.

Cohen, Edward E. "Free and Unfree Sexual Work: An Economic Analysis of Athenian Prostitution." In *Prostitutes and Courtesans in the Ancient World*, edited by Christopher A. Faraone and Laura K. McClure, 95–124. Madison: University of Wisconsin Press, 2006.

Cohn, Norman. *Europe's Inner Demons*. New York: New American Library, 1975. [Republished: Chicago: University of Chicago Press, 1993]

Cohn, Yehudah B. *Tangled up in Text. Tefillin and the Ancient World*. Brown Judaic Studies 351. Providence, RI: Program in Judaic Studies, 2008.

Cohon, Robert. "A Muse Sarcophagus in Its Context." *Archäologischer Anzeiger* (1992): 109–19.

Collingwood, Robin G., and M. V. Taylor. "Roman Britain in 1930." *Journal of Roman Studies* 21 (1931): 215–50.

Collins, Derek. "Theoris of Lemnos and the Criminalization of Magic in Fourth-Century Athens." *Classical Quarterly* 51 (2001): 477–93.

Columella, Lucius Junius Moderatus. *On Agriculture (De Re Rustica)*. Translated by E. S. Forster and Edward H. Heffner. 3 vols. LCL. Cambridge, MA: Harvard University Press, 1941–1955.

Connelly, Joan Breton. *Portrait of a Priestess: Women and Ritual in Ancient Greece*. Princeton, NJ: Princeton University Press, 2007.

Cooper, Kate. *The Virgin and the Bride: Idealized Womanhood in Late Antiquity*. Cambridge, MA: Harvard University Press, 1996.

Copeland, Kirsti B. "Gender and the Afterlife in Roman Egypt." Paper presented at the annual meeting of the Society of Biblical Literature. San Antonio, Texas, November 21, 2004.

———. "Mapping the Apocalypse of Paul: Geography, Genre and History." PhD diss., Princeton University, 2001.

Corbeill, Anthony. *Controlling Laughter: Political Humor in the Late Roman Republic*. Princeton, NJ: Princeton University Press, 1996.

Corbier, Mireille. "Male Power and Legitimacy through Women: The Domus Augusta under the Julio-Claudians." In *Women in Antiquity: New Assessments*, edited by R. Hawley and B. Levick, 178–93. New York: Routledge, 1995.

Corell, Josep. "*Defixionis Tabella* aus Carmona (Sevilla)." *Zeitschrift für Papyrologie und Epigraphik* 95 (1993): 261–68.

———. "Drei *Defixionum Tabellae* aus Sagunt (Valencia)." *Zeitschrift für Papyrologie und Epigraphik* 101 (1994): 280–86.

Corpus inscriptionum iudaicarum. Edited by J. B. Frey. 2 vols. Rome, 1936–1952.

Corpus inscriptionum latinarum, consilio et auctoritate Academiae litterarum regiae Borussicae editum. 16 + vols. Berlin: Walter de Gruyter, 1863–.

Cox, Patricia. "Origen and the Witch of Endor: Toward an Iconoclastic Typology." *Anglican Theological Review* 66, no. 2 (1984): 137–47.

Cramer, Frederick H. *Astrology in Roman Law and Politics: Astrology in Rome until the End of the Principate*. Memoirs of the American Philosophical Society 37. Philadelphia, PA: American Philosophical Society, 1954.

Crane, Gregory R., ed. *Perseus Digital Library*. Cited January 24, 2007. http://www.perseus.tufts.edu/hopper/.

Cumont, Franz. "Deux monuments du culte solaire." *Syria* 14 (1933): 385–95.

———. "Il sole vindice dei delitti ed il simbolo delle mani alzate." *Memorie della Pontificia Accademia Romana di Archeologia*, n. s. 1 (1923): 65–80.

———. *Lux perpetua*. Paris: Geuthner, 1949.

———. "Nuovi epitaffi col simbolo della preghiera al dio vindice." *Atti della Pontificia Accademia Romana di Archeologia*, 3rd ser., Rendiconti 5 (1926–1927): 67–78.

Cunha, Cheston B. "Prolonged and Perplexing Fevers in Antiquity: Malaria and Typhoid Fever." *Infectious Disease Clinics of North America* 21 (2007): 857–66.

Curbera, Jaime. "Venusta and Her Owner in Four Curse Tablets from Morgantina." *Zeitschrift für Papyrologie und Epigraphik* 110 (1996): 295–97.

Cypriani, Thasci Caecili. "Epistula 75." In *Opera Omnia*, edited by Guilelmus Hartel. Corpus Scriptorum Ecclesiasticorum Latinorum. Volume 3, no. 2, 810–27. Vienna: Apvd C. Geroldi Filium Bibliopolam Academiae, 1871.

Dain, Alphonse. *Inscriptions grecques du Musée du Louvre. Les textes inédits*. Paris: Société d'édition "Les Belles Lettres," 1933.

Damon, Cynthia. "The Trial of Cn. Piso in Tacitus' Annals and the Senatus Consultum de Cn. Pisone Patre: New Light on Narrative Technique." *American Journal of Philology* 120, no. 1 (1999): 143–62.

Daniel, R. W. ed. "A Christian Amulet on Papyrus." *Vigiliae christianae* 37 (1983): 400–404.

Davila, James. *The Provenance of the Pseudepigrapha: Jewish, Christian, or Other?* Leiden: Brill, 2005.

Dean-Jones, Lesley. "The Politics of Pleasure: Female Sexual Appetite in the Hippocratic Corpus." *Helios* 19, nos. 1–2 (1992): 72–91.

De Beauvoir, Simone. *The Second Sex*. Translated and edited by H. M. Parshley. New York: Vintage Books, 1989.

De Bruyn, Theodore. "Appeals to Jesus as the one 'who heals every illness and every infirmity' (Matt 4:23, 9:35) in Amulets in Late Antiquity." In *The Reception and Interpretation of the Bible in Late antiquity: Proceedings of the Montreal Colloquium in Honour of Charles Kannengiesser*, edited by Charles Kannengiesser, Lorenzo DiTommaso, and Lucian Turcescu, 65–81. Leiden: Brill, 2008.

Degrassi, Attilio. *Inscriptiones Latinae Liberae Rei Publicae*. Florence: La Nuova Italia, 1963.

Deissmann, G. Adolf. "An Epigraphical Memorial of the Septuagint." In *Bible Studies*, 2d ed., translated by Alexander Grieve, 271–300. Edinburgh: T. & T. Clark, 1909.

De Jonge, M. *Pseudepigrapha of the Old Testament as Part of Christian Literature: The Case of the Testaments of the Twelve Patriarchs and the Greek Life of Adam and Eve*. Leiden: Brill, 2003.

———. *Studies on the Testaments of the Twelve Patriarchs: Text and Interpretation*. Leiden: Brill, 1975.

———. *Testamenta xii patriarcharum*. 2nd ed. Pseudepigrapha veteris testamenti Graece 1. Leiden: Brill, 1970.

Demos, John Putnam. *Entertaining Satan: Witchcraft and the Culture of Early New England*. New York: Oxford University Press, 1982.

———. "Underlying Themes in the Witchcraft of Seventeenth-Century New England," *The American Historical Review* 75, no. 5 (1970)

Descola, Philippe. *Par-delà nature et culture*. Paris: Gallimard, 2005.

Des Places, Édouard. *Oracles chaldaïques*. 3rd ed. Revised and corrected by A. Segonds. Paris: Société d'édition "Les Belles Lettres," 1996.

Dessau, Herman, ed. *Inscriptiones Latinae Selectae*. Vol. 1. Chicago: Ares, 1979.

Develin, R. "Tacitus and Techniques of Insidious Suggestion." *Antichthon* 17 (1983): 64–95.

Dickie, Matthew. *Magic and Magicians in the Greco-Roman World*. New York: Routledge, 2001.

———. "Who Practiced Love-Magic in Classical Antiquity and the Late Roman World?" *The Classical Quarterly*, n. s. 50, no. 2 (2000): 563–83.

Dillon, John M. "An Ethic for the Late Antique Sage." In *A Cambridge Companion to Plotinus*, edited by Lloyd P. Gerson, 331–32. Cambridge: Cambridge University Press, 1993.

———. *The Middle Platonists*. Ithaca, NY: Cornell University Press, 1977.

Dillon, Matthew. *Girls and Women in Classical Greek Religion*. London: Routledge, 2002.

Dimant, Devorah. "'The Fallen Angels' in the Dead Sea Scrolls and in the Apocryphal and Pseudepigraphic Books Related to them." PhD diss., Hebrew University of Jerusalem, 1974.

Dittenberger, W., ed. *Sylloge inscriptionum graecarum*. 4 vols. 3d ed. Leipzig, 1915–1924.

Dixon, Suzanne. *The Roman Family*. Baltimore: Johns Hopkins University Press, 1991.

Dodds, E. R. "New Light on the Chaldaean Oracles." *Harvard Theological Review* 54 (1961): 263–73.

———. "A Séance at the Iseum." Pt. 3 of appendix 2 in *The Greeks and the Irrational*. Berkeley: University of California Press, 1951.

———. "Theurgy and Its relation to Neoplatonism." *Journal of Roman Studies* 37 (1947): 62–65.

Doherty, L. E. "Sirens, Muses, and Female Narrators in the *Odyssey*." In *The Distaff Side: Representing the Female in Homer's Odyssey*, edited by B. Cohen, 81–92. Oxford: Oxford University Press, 1995.

Douglas, Mary. *Natural Symbols: Explorations in Cosmology*. London: Barrie & Rockliff, 1970.

———. *Purity and Danger: An Analysis of Concepts of Pollution and Taboo. 1969*. London: Routledge and Kegan Paul, 1978.

———. "Thirty Years after *Witchcraft, Oracles and Magic*." In *Witchcraft Confessions & Accusations*, edited by Mary Douglas, xiii–xxxviii. New York: Tavistock, 1970.

———, ed. *Witchcraft: Confessions and Accusations*. New York: Tavistock, 1970.

duBois, Page. *Torture and Truth*. New York: Routledge, 1991.

Durkheim, Émile. *The Elementary Forms of the Religious Life*. Translated by J. W. Swain. New York: Free Press, 1965.

Durrant, Jonathan B. *Witchcraft, Gender, and Society in Early Modern Germany*. Studies in Medieval and Reformation Traditions. Vol. 124. Leiden: Brill, 2007.

Dworkin, Andrea. *Woman Hating*. New York: E. P. Dutton, 1974.

Dzielska, Maria. *Hypatia of Alexandria*. Cambridge, MA: Harvard University Press, 1995.

Easterling, P. E. *Sophocles: Trachiniae*. Cambridge: Cambridge University Press, 1982.

Eck, Werner, Antonio Caballos, and Fernando Fernández. *Das Senatus Consultum de Cn. Pisone Patre*. Vestigia 48. Munich: Beck, 1996.

Edwards, Catharine. *The Politics of Immorality in Ancient Rome*. Cambridge: Cambridge University Press, 1993.

Efron, Joshua. "The Deed of Shimeon ben Shatah in Ascalon." Appendix to *Jewish and Hellenistic Cities in Eretz Israel*, by Aryeh Kasher. Tübingen: Mohr/Siebeck, 1990.

Egger, Rudolf. "Liebeszauber." *Jahreshefte des Österreichischen Archäologischen Institutes in Wien* 37 (1948): 112–20.

Eidinow, Esther. *Oracles, Curses, and Risk Among the Ancient Greeks*. Oxford: Oxford University Press, 2007.

Elgvin, Torleif. "Jewish Christian Editing of the Old Testament Pseudepigrapha." In *Jewish Believers in Jesus*, edited by Oskar Skarsaune and Reidar Hvalvik, 278–304. Peabody, MA: Hendrickson, 2007.

Elliott, J. K., ed. *The Apocryphal New Testament*. Oxford: Clarendon, 1993.

Elm, Susanna. *Virgins of God: The Making of Asceticism in Late Antiquity*. New York: Clarendon, 1996.

Elman, Yaakov. "Marriage and Marital Property in Rabbinic and Sasanian Law." In *Rabbinic Law in Its Roman and Near Eastern Context*, edited by C. Hezser, 227–76. Tübingen: Mohr/Siebeck, 2003.

———. "Orality and the Redaction of the Babylonian Talmud." *Oral Tradition* 14, no. 1 (1999): 52–99.

Embry, Jessie. "The Effects of Polygamy on Mormon Wives." *Frontiers: A Journal of Women's Studies* 7 (1984): 55–61.

Engelmann, Helmut. *The Delian Aretalogy of Sarapis*. Études préliminaires aux religions Orientales dans l'Empire Romain 44. Leiden: Brill, 1975.

Eshel, Esther and Hanan. "New Fragments from Qumran: 4QGen^{f}, 4QIsa^{b}, 4Q226, 8QGen, and XQpapEnoch." *Dead Sea Discoveries* 12 (2005): 134–57.

Eunapius. *Lives of the Sophists*. Translated by Wilmer C. Wright. Loeb Classical Library. Cambridge, MA: Harvard University Press, 1921.

Evans-Pritchard, Edward E. *Witchcraft, Oracles and Magic Among the Azande*. Oxford: Clarendon, 1937.

Fantham, Elaine, Helene Peet Foley, Natalie Boymel Kampen, Sarah B. Pomeroy, and H. A. Shapiro, eds. *Women in the Classical World: Image and Text*. New York: Oxford University Press, 1994.

Faraone, Christopher A. "An Accusation of Magic in Classical Athens (AR. *Wasps* 946–48)." *Transactions of the American Philological Association (1974–)* 119 (1989): 149–60.

———. "The Agonistic Context of Early Greek Binding Spells." In *Magika Hiera: Ancient Greek Magic and Religion*, edited by Christopher A. Faraone and Dirk Obbink, 3–32. New York: Oxford University Press, 1991.

———. *Ancient Greek Love Magic*. Cambridge, MA: Harvard University Press, 1999

———. "Clay Hardens and Wax Melts: Magical Role-Reversal in Vergil's Eighth Eclogue." CP 84 (1989): 294–300.

———. "Deianira's Mistake and the Demise of Heracles: Erotic Magic in Sophocles' *Trachiniae*." *Helios* 21 (1994): 115–36.

———. "Sex and Power: Male-Targeting Aphrodisiacs in the Greeks Magical Tradition." *Helios* 19 (1992): 92–103.

———. "The Wheel, the Whip and Other Implements of Torture: Erotic Magic in Pindar Pythian 4. 213–19." *The Classical Journal* 88 (1993): 1–19.

Favret-Saada, Jeanne. *Les mots, la mort, les sorts: La sorcellerie dans le Bocage*. Paris: Gallimard, 1977.

Ferrary, J. "Lex Cornelia de sicariis et veneficiis." *Athenaeum* 79 (1991): 417–34.

Ferreiro, Alberto. *Simon Magus in Patristic, Medieval, and Early Modern Traditions*. Leiden: Brill, 2005.

Festugière, A.-J. *La révélation d'Hermès Trismégiste*. Reprint, Paris: Les Belles Lettres, 2006.

Finley, Moses. "The Silent Women of Rome." In *Sexuality and Gender in the Classical World: Readings and Sources*, edited by Laura K. McClure, 147–56. Oxford: Blackwell, 2002.

Fischer-Elfert, Hans-W. "Heilkunde im Alten Ägypten." In *Zwischen Magie und Wissenschaft*, edited by Georg Scwedt, 43–54. Berlin: Akademie Verlag, 1991.

Fischler, Susan. "Social Stereotypes and Historical Analysis: The Case of the Imperial Women at Rome." In *Women in Ancient Societies*, edited by Léonie J. Archer, Susan Fischler and Maria Wyke, 115–33. London: Routledge, 1994.

Fishbane, Simcha. "'Most Women Engage in Sorcery': An Analysis of Sorceresses in the Babylonian Talmud." *Jewish History* 7 (1993): 27–42.

Fitzgerald, William. *Slavery and the Roman Literary Imagination*. Cambridge: Cambridge University Press, 2000.

Flint, Valerie. "The Demonisation of Magic and Sorcery in Late Antiquity: Christian Redefinitions of Pagan Religions." In *Witchcraft and Magic in Europe: Ancient Greece and Rome*, edited by B. Ankarloo and S. Clark, 277–348. Philadelphia: University of Pennsylvania Press, 1999.

Flower, Harriet I. *The Art of Forgetting: Disgrace and Oblivion in Roman Political Culture*. Chapel Hill: University of North Carolina Press, 2006.

Foley, Helene. *Female Acts in Greek Tragedy*. Princeton, NJ: Princeton University Press, 2001.

Fonrobert, Charlotte. "Jewish Christians, Judaizers, and Christian Anti-Judaism." In *Late Ancient Christianity: A People's History of Christianity*, edited by Virginia Burrus, 2:243–54. Minneapolis: Fortress, 2005.

———. *Menstrual Purity: Rabbinic and Christian Reconstructions of Biblical Gender*. Stanford, CA: Stanford University Press, 2000.

———. "Women's Bodies, Women's Blood: The Politics of Gender in Rabbinic Literature." PhD diss., Graduate Theological Union, 1995.

Foraboschi, Daniele. *Onomasticon alterum papyrologicum*. Milano: Varese Istituto Editoriale Cisalpino, 1971.

Fowden, Garth. *The Egyptian Hermes*. Cambridge: Cambridge University Press, 1986.

———. "The Pagan Holy Man in Late Antique Society." *Journal of Hellenic Studies* 102 (1982): 33–59.

———. "The Platonist Philosopher and his Circle in Late Antiquity." *Philosophia* 7 (1977): 359–82.

Fox, William Sherwood. *The Johns Hopkins* Tabellae Defixionum. Baltimore: Johns Hopkins University Press, 1912.

Frank, Georgia. *The Memory of the Eyes: Pilgrims to Living Saints in Christian Late Antiquity. The Transformation of the Classical Heritage 30*. Berkeley: University of California Press, 2000.

Frankfurter, David. "Beyond 'Jewish Christianity': Continuing Religious Subcultures of the Second and Third Centuries and Their Documents." In *The Ways that Never Parted: Jews and Christians in Late Antiquity and the Early Middle Ages*, edited by Adam H. Becker and Annette Yoshiko Reed, 131–43. Minneapolis: Fortress Press, 2007.

———. "Beyond Magic and Superstition." In *Late Ancient Christianity: A People's History of Christianity*, edited by Virginia Burrus, 2:255–312. Minneapolis: Fortress Press, 2005.

———. "Dynamics of Ritual Expertise in Antiquity and Beyond: Towards a New Taxonomy of 'Magicians.'" In *Ancient Magic and Ritual Power*, edited by Paul Mirecki and Marvin Meyer, 159–78. Leiden: Brill, 2001.

———. *Evil Incarnate: Rumors of Demonic Conspiracy and Satanic Abuse in History*. Princeton, NJ: Princeton University Press, 2006.

———. "Fetus Magic and Sorcery Fears in Roman Egypt." *Greek, Roman, and Byzantine Studies* 46 (2006): 37–62.

———. "The Legacy of Jewish Apocalypses in Early Christianity: Regional Trajectories." In *Jewish Apocalyptic Heritage*, edited by J.C. VanderKam and W. Adler, 129–200. Minneapolis: Fortress Press, 1996.

———. "Narrating Power: The Theory and Practice of the Magical *Historiola* in Ritual Spells." In *Ancient Magic and Ritual Power*, edited by Marvin Meyer and Paul Mirecki, 457–76. Leiden: Brill, 1995.

———. "The Perils of Love: Magic and Counter-Magic in Coptic Egypt." *Journal of the History of Sexuality* 10 (2001): 480–500.

———. "A Plea to a Local God for a Husband's Attentions." In *Religions of Late Antiquity in Practice*, edited by Richard Valantasis, 230–31. Princeton, NJ: Princeton University Press, 2000.

———. *Religion in Roman Egypt: Assimilation and Resistance*. Princeton, NJ: Princeton University Press, 1998.

———. Review of Matthew Dickie, *Magic and Magicians in the Greco-Roman World*. *Bryn Mawr Classical Review* 2002.02.26: http://bmcr.brynmawr.edu/2002/2002-02-26.html.

———. "Ritual Expertise in Roman Egypt and the Problem of the Category 'Magician.'" In *Envisioning Magic: A Princeton Seminar and Symposium*, edited by Peter Schäfer and Hans G. Kippenberg. Studies in the History of Religions 75, 115–35. Leiden: Brill, 1997.

———. "Syncretism and the Holy Man in Late Antique Egypt." *Journal of Early Christian Studies* 11 (2003): 339–85.

Fraser, K. A. "Zosimus of Panopolis and the Book of Enoch: Alchemy as Forbidden Knowledge." *Aries* 4.2 (2004): 125–47.

Freud, Sigmund. *Jokes and Their Relationship to the Unconscious*. New York: Moffat Ward, 1916.

Friedlander, Gerald, trans. *Pirke de-Rabbi Eliezer*. 4th ed. New York: Sepher-Hermon, 1981.

Fuller, Thomas. "Spread of Malaria Feared as Drug Loses Potency," *The New York Times*, January 26, 2009.

Futler, Alison. *Blood in the Arena: The Spectacle of Roman Power*. Austin: Texas University Press, 1997.

Gager, John G. *Curse Tablets and Binding Spells from the Ancient World*. New York: Oxford University Press, 1992.

Galen. *On the Properties of Foodstuffs (De alimentorum facultatibus)*. Translated by Owen Powell. Cambridge: Cambridge University Press, 2003.

Garcia-Ruiz, Emilio. "Estudio linguistico de las *defixiones* Latinas no incluidas en el corpus de Audollent." *Emérita* 35 (1967): 55–89.

Gardiner, Alan H., and Kurt Sethe. *Egyptian Letters to the Dead*. London: Egypt Exploration Society, 1928.

Gardiner, Eileen, ed. "Thurkill's Vision." In *Visions of Heaven and Hell Before Dante*, edited by Eileen Gardiner, 219–36. New York: Italica, 1989.

———, ed. *Visions of Heaven and Hell Before Dante*. New York: Italica, 1989.

Gardner, Jane F. *Women in Roman Law and Society*. Bloomington: Indiana University Press, 1986.

Gardner, Jane F., and Thomas Wiedemann. *The Roman Household: A Sourcebook*. London: Routledge, 1991.

Garnsey, Peter. *Social Status and Legal Privilege in the Roman Empire*. Oxford: Clarendon Press, 1970.

Garrett, Clarke. "Women and Witches: Patterns of Analysis." *Signs* 3, no. 2 (1977): 461–70.

Gaster, Moses. "Hebrew Visions of Hell and Paradise." *Journal of the Royal Asiatic Society* 23 (1893): 572–610. Reprinted in Moses Gaster. *Studies and Texts in Folklore, Magic, Medieval Romance, Hebrew Apocrypha and Samaritan Archaeology*, 1:124–64. London: Maggs Bros, 1925–1928.

Gayley, Charles Mills. *The Classic Myths in English Literature and in Art*. Boston: Ginn & Co., 1911.

Gedif, T., and H. Jürgen Hahn. "The Use of Medicinal Plants in Self-Care in Rural Central Ethiopia." *Journal of Ethnopharmacology* 87.2–3 (2003): 155–61.

Geertz, Hildred. "An Anthropology of Religion and Magic, I." *Journal of Interdisciplinary History* 6 (1975): 71–89.

Geller, M. J., and Dan Levene, eds. and trans. "Magical Texts from the Genizah (with a New Duplicate)." *Journal of Jewish Studies* 49, no. 2 (1998): 334–40.

Gelzer, Thomas, Michael Lurje, and Christoph Schäublin. *Lamella Bernensis. Ein spätantikes Goldamulett mit christlichem Exorzismus und verwandte Texte*. Beiträge zur Altertumskunde 124. Stuttgart: Teubner, 1999.

Gennep, Arnold van. *Rites of Passage*. Translated by Monika B. Vizedom and Gabrielle Caffee. Chicago: University of Chicago Press, 1960.

Gilhuly, Kate. "Bronze for Gold: Subjectivity in Lucian's *Dialogues of the Courtesans*." *American Journal of Philology* 128 (2007): 59–94.

Ginsburg, Judith. *Representing Agrippina: Constructions of Female Power in the Early Roman Empire*. New York: Oxford University Press, 2006.

Ginzberg, L. *The Legends of the Jews*, trans. H. Szold. 7 vols. Reprint, Baltimore: Jewish Publication Society, 1998.

Gleason, Maude W. *Making Men: Sophists and Self-Presentation in Ancient Rome*. Princeton, NJ: Princeton University Press, 1995.

Gluckman, Max. "What is Gossip about? An Alternative Hypothesis." *Man* 2 (1967): 278–85.

Goff, Barbara. *Citizen Bacchae: Women's Ritual Practice in Ancient Greece*. Berkeley: University of California Press, 2004.

Goldhill, Simon. "The Erotic Eye: Visual Stimulation and Cultural Conflict." In *Being Greek Under Rome: Cultural Identity, the Second Sophistic, and the Development of Empire*, edited by Simon Goldhill, 154–94. Cambridge: Cambridge University Press, 2001.

———. *Language, Sexuality, Narrative, the Oresteia*. Cambridge: Cambridge University Press, 1984.

———. *The Poet's Voice: Essays on Poetics and Greek Literature*. Cambridge: Cambridge University Press, 1991.

Goodare, Julian. "Women and the Witch-Hunt in Scotland." *Social History* 23 (1998): 288–308.

Goode, William J. "Magic and Religion: A Continuum." *Ethnos* 14 (1949): 172–82.

Goodnow, Katherine J. *Kristeva in Focus: From Theory to Film Analysis*. New York: Berghahn Books, 2010.

Goodyear, F. R. D. *The Annals of Tacitus, Vol II. Annals 1.55–81 and Annals 2*. New York: Cambridge University Press, 1981.

———. "Women and the Witch-Hunt in Scotland," *Social History* 23 (1998)

Gordon, Richard. "Aelian's Peony: The Location of Magic in Graeco-Roman Tradition." *Comparative Criticism* 9 (1987): 59–95.

———. "Imagining Greek and Roman Magic." In *Witchcraft and Magic in Europe: Ancient Greece and Rome*, edited by Bengt Ankarloo and Stuart Clark, 159–275. Philadelphia: University of Pennsylvania Press, 1999.

———. "Lucan's Erictho." In *Homo Viator: Classical Essays for John Bramble*, edited by M. Whitby and P. Hardie, 231–41. Bristol: Bristol Classical Press, 1987.

———. "*Quaedam veritatis umbrae*: Hellenistic Magic and Astrology." In *Conventional Values of the Hellenistic Greeks*, edited by P. Bilde and T. Engberg-Pedersen. Studies in Hellenistic Civilization 8, 146–49. Aarhus: University Press, 1997.

Gounaropoulou, Loukretia, and M. B. Hatzopoulos, *Ἐπιγραφὲς Κάτω Μακεδονίας. Τεῦχος Α΄ Ἐπιγραφὲς Βεροίας*. Athens, 1998.

Gow, A. S. F., ed. *Theocritus*. 2d ed. Vol. 1. Cambridge: Cambridge University Press, 1952.

———. "*ΙΥΓΞ, ΡΟΜΒΟΣ*, Rhombus Turbo." *Journal of Hellenic Studies* 54 (1934): 1–13.

Graf, Fritz. "Excluding the Charming: The Development of the Greek Concept of Magic." In *Ancient Magic and Ritual Power*, edited by Marvin Meyer and Paul Mirecki, 29–42. Leiden: Brill, 1995.

———. *Magic in the Ancient World*. Translated by Franklin Philip. Cambridge, MA: Harvard University Press, 1997.

———. "Malediction." In *Thesaurus Cultus et Rituum Antiquorum*, 3:247–70. Los Angeles: The J. Paul Getty Museum, 2005.

———. "Mythical Production: Aspects of Myth and Technology in Antiquity." In *From Myth to Reason? Studies in the Development of Greek Thought*, edited by R. Buxton. New York: Oxford University Press, 1999.

———. *Nordionische Kulte*. Rome: Institut Suisse, 1985.

———. "An oracle against Pestilence from a Western Anatolian Town." *Zeitschrift für Papyrologie und Epigraphik* 92(1992): 267–78.

Graf, Fritz, and Sarah Iles Johnston. *Ritual Texts for the Afterlife. The Bacchic Gold Tablets*. London: Routledge, 2007.

Greenberg, Moshe. *Ezekiel 1–20*. Anchor Bible 22. Garden City, NY: Doubleday, 1983.

Greene, Peter. "The Methods of Ancient Magic." *Times Literary Supplement* 5168 (2002): 5–6.

Grégoire, Henri. *Recueil des inscriptions grecques-chrétiennes d'Asie mineure*. Paris: Leroux, 1922.

Grenfell, Bernard P., and Arthur S. Hunt. "Excavations at Oxyrhynchus (1896–1907)." In *Oxyrhynchus: A City and Its Texts*, edited by A. K. Bowman, R. A. Coles, N. Gonis, D. Obbink, and P. J. Parsons, 345–68. London: Egypt Exploration Society, 2007.

Griffin, Miriam. "The Senate's Story." *Journal of Roman Studies* 87 (1997): 249–63.

Griffiths, Frederick T. "Home Before Lunch: The Emancipated Woman in Theocritus." In *Reflections of Women in Antiquity*, edited by Helene P. Foley, 247–74. New York, London, Paris: Gordon and Breach Science Publishers, 1981.

Grossfeld, Bernard. "Bible, Translations." In *Encyclopedia Judaica*, 4:841–51. Jerusalem: Keter, 1972.

Grosz, Elizabeth. *Sexual Subversions: Three French Feminists*. Sydney: Allen & Unwin; Boston: Unwin Hyman, 1989.

Grubbs, Judith Evans. *Women and the Law in the Roman Empire*. London: Routledge, 2002.

Guarducci, Margherita. *Epigrafi sacre pagane e cristiane*. Vol. 4 of *Epigrafica Greca*. Rome: Instituo Poligrafico dello Stato, 1978.

Gunderson, Erik. "The Ideology of the Arena." *Classical Antiquity* 15 (1996):113–151.

———. *Staging Masculinity: The Rhetoric of Performance in the Roman World*. Ann Arbor: University of Michigan Press, 2000.

Gutiérez, Ramón A. "Women on Top: The Love Magic of the Indian Witches of New Mexico." *Journal of the History of Sexuality* 16, no. 3 (2007): 373–90.

Hagedorn, Dieter. "Bemerkungen zu Urkunden." *Zeitschrift für Papyrologie und Epigraphik* 145 (2003): 224–47.

———, ed. *WörterListen*. Cited 11 March 2009. http://www.zaw.uni-heidelberg.de/hps/pap/WL/WL.pdf.

Haines-Eitzen, Kim. *Guardians of Letters: Literacy, Power, and the Transmitters of Early Christian Literature*. Oxford: Oxford University Press, 2000.

Hall, Edith. *Inventing the Barbarian: Greek Self-Definition through Tragedy*. Oxford: Clarendon, 1989.

Hallett, J. *Fathers and Daughters in Roman Society: Women and the Elite Family*. Princeton, NJ: Princeton University Press, 1984.

Halpern Amaru, Betsy. *The Empowerment of Women in the Book of Jubilees*. Leiden: Brill, 1999.

Hammer, Reuven, ed. and trans. Sifre: A Tannaitic Commentary on the Book of Deuteronomy. New Haven, CT: Yale University Press, 1986.

Hammerstaedt, Jürgen, P. Habermehl, Francesca Lamberti, A.M. Ritter, and P. Schenk, eds. *Apuleius. De magia*. Darmstadt, Germany: Wissenschaftliche Buchgesellschaft, 2002.

Hankins, John E. "The Pains of the Afterworld: Fire, Wind, and Ice in Milton and Shakespeare." *PMLA* 71, no. 3 (June 1956): 482–95.

Hansen, Chadwick. *Witchcraft at Salem*. New York: G. Braziller, 1969.

Hanson, Paul. "Rebellion in Heaven, Azazel, and Euhemeristic Heroes in 1 Enoch 6–11." *Journal of Biblical Literature* 96 (1977): 195–233.

Harl, K. W. "Sacrifice and Pagan Belief in Fifth- and Sixth-Century Byzantium." *Past and Present* 128 (1990): 7–27.

Harris, William V. *Ancient Literacy*. Cambridge, MA: Harvard University Press, 1989.

Harvey, Susan Ashbrook. "Women in Early Byzantine Hagiography." In *That Gentle Strength: Historical Perspectives on Women in Christianity*, edited by L. L. Coon, K. J. Haldane, and E. W. Sommer, 36–59. Charlottesville: University Press of Virginia, 1990.

Harvey, W. Wigan, ed. *Libros quinque adversus haereses*. Cambridge: Typis Academicis, 1857. Reprint, Ridgewood, NJ: Gregg, 1965.

Hastrup, Kirsten. "Iceland: Sorcerers and Paganism." *Early Modern European Witchcraft: Centres and Peripheries*, ed. Bengt Ankarloo and Gustav Henningsen. Oxford: Clarendon Press, 1990.

Heimann, Paula. "Certain Functions of Introjection and Projection in Early Infancy." In *Developments in Psycho-Analysis*, edited by Joan Riviere, 122–67. Psychoanalysis Examined and Re-Examined. London: Hogarth, 1952.

Heine, Ronald D., ed. *Montanist Oracles and Testimonia*. Macon, GA: Mercer University Press, 1989.

Heinemann, Evelyn. *Witches: A Psychoanalytic Exploration of the Killing of Women*. Translated by Donald Kiraly. London: Free Association Books, 2000.

Heller, B. "La chute des anges: Schemhazai, Ouza et Azaël." *REJ* 60 (1910): 206–10.

Hemelrijk, Emily. "Women's Demonstrations in Republican Rome." In *Sexual Asymmetry: Studies in Ancient Society*, edited by Josine Blok and Peter Mason, 217–40. Amsterdam: J. C. Gleben, 1987.

Hengel, Martin. *Rabbinische Legende und frühpharisäische Geschichte: Schimeon ben Shatach und die achtzig Hexen von Askalon*. Heidelberg: Winter, 1984.

Herlihy, Laura Hobson. "Sexual Magic and Money: Miskitu Women's Strategies in Northern Honduras." *Ethnology* 45, no. 2 (2006): 143–59.

Hester, Marianne. *Lewd Women and Wicked Witches: A Study of the Dynamics of Male Domination*. London; New York: Routledge, 1992.

Hesiod. *Theogony, Works and Days, Shield*. Translated by Apostolos N. Athanassakis. Baltimore: Johns Hopkins University Press, 1983.

Hijmans, B. L., Jr. "Significant Names and Their Functions in Apuleius' Metamorphoses". In *Aspects of Apuleius' Golden Ass*, edited by B. L. Hijmans Jr. and R. Th. Van Paardt, 116–17. Groningen: Bouma's Boekhuis, 1978.

Himmelfarb, Martha. *A Kingdom of Priests: Ancestry and Merit in Ancient Judaism*. Philadelphia: University of Pennsylvania Press, 2011.

———. *Tours of Hell: An Apocalyptic Form in Jewish and Christian Literature*. Philadelphia: Fortress, 1983.

Hollander H. W., and M. de Jonge, *The Testaments of the Twelve Patriarchs: A Commentary*. Leiden: Brill, 1985.

Holmes, Clive. "Women and Witnesses." *Past and Present* 140 (1993): 45–78.

Homer. *The Odyssey*. Translated by A.T. Murray. Vol. 1. Loeb Classical Library. Cambridge, MA: Harvard University Press, 1984.

Hopfner, T. "*Mageia*." *Realencyklopädie für protestantische Theologie und Kirche* I 14, no. 1 (1928): 301–93.

———. *Odes and Epodes*. Translated by C. E. Bennett. Cambridge, MA: Harvard University Press, 1988.

Horovitz, Chaim Saul, and Louis Finkelstein, eds. *Sifre Deuteronomy*. Berlin: Gesellschaft zur Forderung der Wissenschaft des Judentums, 1939. Reprint, New York: Jewish Theological Seminary of America, 1969.

Horovitz, H. S., and I. A. Rabin, eds. *Mekhilta de-Rabbi Ishmael*. 2d ed. Jerusalem: Bamberger and Wahrman, 1960.

Howard, Richard. *The Eiffel Tower and other Mythologies*. New York: Hill & Wang, 1979.

Hughes, George R. "A Demotic Letter to Thoth." *Journal of Near Eastern Studies* 17 (1958): 1–12.

Hulett, J. E., Jr. "Social Role and Personal Security in Mormon Polygamy." *American Journal of Sociology* 45 (1940): 542–53.

Hunter, Virginia. *Policing Athens*. Princeton, NJ: Princeton University Press, 1994.

Hurtado, Larry W. "The Earliest Evidence of an Emerging Christian Material and Visual Culture: The Codex, the Nomina Sacra and the Staurogram." In *Text and Artifact in the Religions of Mediterranean Antiquity: Essays in Honour of Peter Richardson*, edited by Stephen G. Wilson and Michel Desjardins. Studies in Christianity and Judaism 9, 271–88. Waterloo, ON: Canadian Corporation for Studies in Religion, 2000.

Husain, Shahrukh, ed. *Daughters of the Moon: Witch Tales from around the World*. Boston: Faber & Faber, 1994.

Hutton, Ronald. "The Global Context of the Scottish Witch-Hunt." In *The Scottish Witch-Hunt in Context*, edited by Julian Goodare, 16–32. Manchester: Manchester University Press, 2002.

Ilan, Tal. "Cooks/Poisoners; Healers/Killers; Religion/Witchcraft: Jewish Women's Religious Life at Home." *Haushalt, Hauskult, Hauskirche. Zur Arbeitsteilung der Geschlechter in Wirtschaft und Religion*, E. Klinger et al., 107–23. Würzburg Echter Verlag, 2004.

———. *Jewish Women in Greco-Roman Palestine*. Tübingen: Mohr/Siebeck, 1995.

———. *Silencing the Queen: The Literary Histories of Shelamzion and Other Jewish Women*. Tübingen: Mohr/Siebeck, 2006.

———. "Woman in the Apocrypha and the Pseudepigrapha." In *A Question of Sex? Gender and Difference in the Hebrew Bible and Beyond*, edited by D. W. Rooke, 126–44. Sheffield, UK: Sheffield Phoenix, 2007.

Institoris, Heinrich. *Mallevs Maleficarvm in Tres Divisvs Partes*. Frankfurt am Main: Apud Nicolaum Bassaeum, 1580.

Isaac, Ephraim. "1 (Ethiopic Apocalypse of) Enoch." In *The Old Testament Pseudepigrapha*, edited by James Charlesworth, 1:5–89. Garden City, NY: Doubleday, 1983–1985.

Jakov, Daniel, and Emmanuel Voutiras, art. "Prayer, Greek." In *Thesaurus Cultus et Rituum Antiquorum*, 3:120–23. Los Angeles: The J. Paul Getty Museum, 2005.

James, Montague Rhodes, ed. *Apocrypha Anecdota: A Collection of Thirteen Apocryphal Books and Fragments*. Vol. 2, no. 3 of *Texts and Studies*. Edited by J. Armitage Robinson. Cambridge: Cambridge University Press, 1893. Reprint, Nendeln: Kraus Reprint Limited, 1967.

Janowitz, Naomi. *Magic in the Roman World*. London: Routledge, 2001.

Jarvie, I. C.. and J. Agassi. "The Problem of the Rationality of Magic." In *Rationality*, edited by Bryan Wilson, 173–93. New York: Harper and Row, 1970.

Jastrow, Marcus. *A Dictionary of the Targumim, the Talmud Babli and Yerushalmi, and the Midrashic Literature*. New York: Pardes, 1950.

Jeffers, Ann. "Magic From Before the Dawn of Time: Understanding Magic in the Old Testament: A Shift in Paradigm (Deuteronomy 18:9–14 and beyond)." In *A Kind of Magic: Understanding Magic in the New Testament and Its Religious Environment*, edited by Michael LaBahn and Bert Jan Lietaert Peerbolte, 123–32. London: T&T Clark, 2007.

Jeffery, Lilian H. *The Local Scripts of Archaic Greece*. Oxford: Clarendon, 1990.

Jellinek, A. *Bet ha-midrash*. Jerusalem: Sifre Vahrmann, 1967.

Jensen, Anne. *Frauen im frühen Christentum*. Traditio Christiana. Bern: Peter Lang, 2002.

Johnson, Maxwell E. *The Prayers of Sarapion of Thmuis: A Literary, Liturgical and Theological Analysis*. Orientalia Christiana Analecta 249. Rome: Pontificio Istituto Orientale, 1995.

Johnson, William A., and Holt N. Parker, eds. *Ancient Literacies: The Culture of Reading in Greece and Rome*. Oxford: Oxford University Press, 2009.

Johnston, Sarah Iles. "Defining the Dreadful: Remarks on the Greek Child-Killing Demon." In *Ancient Magic and Ritual Power*, edited by Marvin Meyer and Paul Mirecki, 361–87. Leiden: Brill, 1995.

———. "Describing the Undefinable: New Books on Magic and Old Problems of Definition." *History of Religions* 43, no. 1 (2003): 50–54.

———. *Restless Dead. Encounters Between the Living and the Dead in Ancient Greece*. Berkeley: University of California Press, 1999.

———. "The Song of the *Iynx*: Magic and Rhetoric in *Pythian* 4." *Transactions of the American Philological Association* 125 (1995): 177–206.

Johnston, Sarah Iles, John G. Gager, Martha Himmelfarb, Marvin Meyer, Brian Schmidt, David Frankfurter, and Fritz Graf. "Panel Discussion: 'Magic in the Ancient World' by Fritz Graf." *Numen* 46, no. 3 (1999): 291–325.

Jordan, David R. "New Greek Curse Tablets (1985–2000)." *Greek, Roman and Byzantine Studies* 41 (2000): 5–46.

———. "A Survey of Greek Defixiones Not Included in the Special Corpora." *Greek, Roman and Byzantine Studies* 26 (1985): 151–97.

Joshel, Sandra R. "Female Desire and the Discourse of Empire: Tacitus's Messalina." *Signs* 21, no. 1 (1995): 50–82.

———. *Work, Identity and Legal Status at Rome*. Norman, OK: University of Oklahoma Press, 1992.

Judge, E. A. "The Magical Use of Scripture in the Papyri." In *Perspectives on Language and Text: Essays and Poems in Honour of Frances I. Anderson*, edited by E. W. Conrad and E. G. Newing, 339–49. Winona Lake, IN: Eisenbrauns, 1987.

Juvénal. *Satires*. Edited and translated by Pierre de Labriolle and François Villeneuve. Paris: Les Belles Lettres, 1964.

Kaibel, Georgius. *Epigrammata Graeca ex lapidibus conlecta*. Berlin: Reimer, 1878. Reprint, Hildesheim: Olms, 1965.

Kajanto, Iiro. "On the 'Freedom of Speech' in Latin Epitaphs." *Latomus* 27 (1968): 187–88.

Kalleres, Dayna. "Exorcising the Devil to Silence Christ's Enemies: Ritualized Speech Practices in Late Antique Christianity." PhD diss., Brown University, 2002.

Kamensky, Jane. "Female Speech and Other Demons: Witchcraft and Wordcraft in Early New England." *Spellbound: Women and Witchcraft in America*, ed. Elizabeth Reis, Worlds of Women. Wilmington, DE: Scholarly Resources, 1998.

Kaplan, Michael. "*Agrippina semper atrox:* A Study in Tacitus' Characterization of Women." In *Studies in Latin Literature and Roman History*, edited by C. Deroux. Vol. 1. Collection Latomus 164, 410–17. Brussels: Collection Latomus, 1978.

Karanika, Andromache. "Folk Songs as Ritual Acts: The Case of Work-Songs." In *Finding Persephone: Women's Rituals in the Ancient Mediterranean*, edited by Maryline Parca and Angeliki Tzanetou, 137–53. Bloomington, IN: Indiana University Press, 2007.

Karlsen, Carol F. *Devil in the Shape of a Woman: Witchcraft in Colonial New England.* New York: Norton, 1987.

Kassel, Rudolf. *Untersuchungen zur griechischen und römischen Konsolationsliteratur.* Zetemata 18. Munich: Beck, 1958.

Kee, Howard Clark, trans. "Testaments of the Twelve Patriarchs." In *The Old Testament Pseudepigrapha*, edited by James Charlesworth, 1:775–828. Garden City, NY: Doubleday, 1983–1985.

Kervinen, Timo, and Antero Heikkinen. "Finland: The Male Domination." *Early Modern European Witchcraft: Centres and Peripheries*, ed. Bengt Ankarloo and Gustav Henningsen. Oxford: Clarendon Press, 1990.

Kieckhefer, Richard. "Avenging the Blood of Children: Anxiety over Child Victims and the Origins of the European Witch Trials." In *The Devil, Heresy and Witchcraft in the Middle Ages: Essays in Honor of Jeffrey B. Russell*, edited by Alberto Ferreiro, 91–109. Leiden: Brill, 1998.

———. *Magic in the Middle Ages*. Cambridge: Cambridge University Press, 1989.

Kippenberg, Hans. "Magic in Roman Civil Discourse: Why Rituals Could be Illegal." In *Envisioning Magic: A Princeton Seminar and Symposium*, edited by Peter Shafer and Hans Kippenberg, 137–63. Studies in the History of Religions 75. Leiden: Brill, 1997.

Kirk, G. S., J. E. Raven, M. Schofield, trans. *The Presocratic Philosophers*. 2nd ed. Cambridge: Cambridge University Press, 1983.

Kirshner, Robert. "The Vocation of Holiness in Late Antiquity." *Vigiliae christianae* 38 (1984): 105–24.

Klaits, Joseph. *Servants of Satan: The Age of the Witch Hunts*. Bloomington: Indiana University Press, 1985.

Klaniczay, Gábor. *The Uses of Supernatural Power. The Transformation of Popular religion in Medieval and Early-Modern Europe*. Princeton, NJ: Princeton University Press, 1990.

Klawiter, Frederick C. "The Role of Martyrdom and Persection in Developing the Priestly Authority of Women in Early Christianity: A Case Study of Montanism." *Church History* 49 (1980): 251–61.

Klein, Melanie. "On Identification." In *New Directions in Psycho-Analysis: The Significance of Infant Conflict in the Pattern of Adult Behaviour*, edited by Melanie Klein, Paula Heimann, and R. E. Money-Kyrle, 309–45. New York: Basic Books, 1955.

———. "Some Theoretical Conclusions Regarding the Emotional Life of the Infant." In *Developments in Psycho-Analysis*, edited by Joan Riviere, 198–236. Psychoanalysis Examined and Re-Examined. London: Hogarth, 1952.

———. "On the Theory of Anxiety and Guilt." In *Developments in Psycho-Analysis*, edited by Joan Riviere, 271–91. Psychoanalysis Examined and Re-Examined. London: Hogarth, 1952.

Klijn, A. F. J. *Seth in Jewish, Christian and Gnostic literature*. Leiden: Brill, 1977.

Kluckhohn, Clyde. *Navaho Witchcraft*. Boston: Beacon, 1967.

Knibb, M. A. "The Book of Enoch or Books of Enoch? The Textual Evidence for 1 Enoch." In *The Early Enoch Literature*, edited by G. Boccaccini and J. J. Collins, 21–40. Leiden: Brill, 2007.

———. *The Ethiopic Book of Enoch: A New Edition in Light of Aramaic Dead Sea Fragments*. 2 vols. Oxford: Clarendon, 1978.

Knust, Jennifer Wright. *Abandoned to Lust: Sexual Slander and Early Christianity*. New York: Columbia University Press, 2006.

Kolenkow, Anitra Bingham. "Persons of Power and Their Communities." In *Magic and Divination in the Ancient World*, edited by Leda Ciraolo and Jonathan Seidel, 133–44. Leiden: Brill, 2002.

———. "A Problem of Power: How Miracle Doers Counter Charges of Magic in the Hellenistic World." In *Society of Biblical Literature: 1976 Seminar Papers*, edited by George MacRae, 105–10. Missoula, MT: Scholars Press, 1976.

Konstan, David. "Premarital Sex, Illegitimacy, and Male Anxiety in Menander and Athens." In *Athenian Identity and Civic Ideology*, edited by Alan Boegehold and Adele Scafuro, 217–35. Baltimore and London: Johns Hopkins University Press, 1994.

Kotansky, Roy. "Incantations and Prayers for Salvation on Inscribed Greek Amulets." In *Magika Hiera: Ancient Greek Magic and Religion*, edited by Christopher A. Faraone and Dirk Obbink, 107–37. New York: Oxford University Press, 1991.

Kraemer, David. *Jewish Eating and Identity Through the Ages*. New York: Routledge, 2007.

———. "Problematic Mixings: Foods and Other Prohibited Substances in Rabbinic Legislation." *Review of Rabbinic Judaism* 8, no. 1 (2005): 35–54.

Kraemer, Ross Shepard. *Her Share of the Blessings: Women's Religions among Pagans, Jews, and Christians in the Greco-Roman World*. New York: Oxford University Press, 1992.

Kraft, R. A. "The Pseudepigrapha in Christianity." In *Tracing the Threads: Studies in the Vitality of Jewish Pseudepigrapha*, edited by J. Reeves, 55–86. Atlanta: Scholars Press, 1994.

Kraus, Thomas, and Tobias Nicklas. *Das Petrusevangelium und die Petrusapokalypse: die griechischen Fragmente mit deutscher und englischer Übersetzung*. Berlin: Walter de Gruyter, 2004.

Krauss, Johannes. *Die Inschriften von Sestos und der thrakischen Chersones*. Inschriften griechischer Städte aus Kleinasien 19. Bonn: Habelt, 1980.

Kristeva, Julia. *Powers of Horror: An Essay on Abjection*. Translated by Leon S. Roudiez. New York: Columbia University Press, 1982.

Kropp, Angelicus M. *Ausegewählte koptische Zaubertexte*. 3 vols. Brussels: Fondation égyptologique Reine Élisabeth, 1930–1931.

Kuhn, K. H. "The Sahidic Version of the Testament of Isaac." *Journal of Theological Studies*, n. s. 8, no. 2 (1957): 225–39.

Kugel, James. *The Bible as It Was*. Cambridge, MA: Harvard University Press, 1999.

Lagogianni-Georgakarakos, Maria. *Die Grabdenkmäler mit Porträts aus Makedonien*. Corpus signorum imperii Romani. Griechenland 3:1. Athens: Academy, 1998.

Lamberton, Robert. "Secrecy in the History of Platonism." In *Secrecy and Concealment*, edited by Hans G. Kippenberg and Guy G. Stroumsa, 140–48. Leiden: Brill, 1995.

Lambrechts, Pierre and R. Bogaert. "Asclépios, archigalle pessinontien de Cybèle." Pages 404–14 in *Hommages à Marcel Renard*. Edited by Jacqueline Bibauw. Vol. 2. Collection Latomus 102. Brussels: Collection Latomus, 1969.

Lamirande, Emilien. "Hypatie, Synésios et la fin des dieux: L'histoire et la fiction." *Studies in Religion* 18, no. 4 (1989): 467–89.

Lanzi, Silvia. "Sosipatra, la teurga: una 'holy woman' iniziata ai misteri caldaici." *Studi e materiali di storia delle religioni* 70, no. 2 (2004): 275–94.

Larner, Christina. *Enemies of God: The Witch-Hunt in Scotland*. Baltimore: Johns Hopkins University Press, 1981. [Also published: London: Chattto and Windus, 1981.]

Larson, E. "The Relation between the Greek and Aramaic Texts of Enoch." In *The Dead Sea Scrolls: Fifty Years after Their Discovery*, edited by L. H. Schiffman, E. Tov, and J. C. VanderKam, 434–44. Jerusalem: Israel Exploration Society, 2000.

Lattimore, Richmond. *Themes in Greek and Latin Epitaphs*. Urbana: University of Illinois Press, 1962.

Lauterbach, Jacob Z., ed. *Mekilta de-Rabbi Ishmael*. 3 vols. Philadelphia: Jewish Publication Society of America, 1935.

Lawlor, H. L. "The Book of Enoch in the Egyptian Church." *Hermathena* 30 (1904): 178–83.

———. "Early Citations from the Book of Enoch." *Journal of Philology* 25 (1897): 164–225.

Le Bas, Philippe and William Henry Waddington. *Voyage archéologique en Grèce et en Asie Mineure*. Vol. 3. Paris: Firmin-Didot et Cie, 1870.

Lefkowitz, Mary R. "Influential Women." In *Images of Women in Antiquity*, edited by Averil Cameron and Amélie Kuhrt, 49–64. Detroit: Wayne State University Press, 1983.

Lefort, L. Th. "L'homélie de S. Athanase des papyrus de Turin." *Muséon* 71 (1958): 5–50, 209–39.

———, ed. *Pachomii Vita bohairice scripta*. Corpus Scriptorum Christianorum Orientalium. Scriptores Coptici 3/7, 1925.

Leinweber, David Walter. "Witchcraft and Lamiae in 'The Golden Ass.'" *Folklore* 105 (1994): 77–82.

Leslau, Wolf. *Falasha Anthology*. New Haven, CT: Yale University Press, 1951.

Lesses, Rebecca. "Exe(o)rcising Power: Women as Sorceresses, Exorcists, and Demonesses in Late Antique Judaism." *Journal of the American Academy of Religion* 69 (2001): 343–75.

———. "They Revealed Secrets to Their Wives: The Transmission of Magical Knowledge in 1 Enoch." In *With Letters of Light—Otiyot Shel Or: Studies in Early Jewish Apocalypticism and Mysticism in Honour of Rachel Elior*, edited by D. Arbel and A. Orlov, 196–222. Berlin: De Gruyter, 2010.

Levack, Brian P., ed. *Witchcraft, Women, and Society*. Vol. 10 of *Articles on Witchcraft, Magic, and Demonology*. New York: Garland, 1992.

Levene, Dan. *A Corpus of Magic Bowls: Incantation Texts in Jewish Aramaic from Late Antiquity*. London: Routledge, 2003.

———. "'If You Appear as a Pig': Another Incantation Bowl (Mousaieff 164)." *Journal of Semitic Studies* 52 (2007): 59–70.

Lewis, I. M. *Ecstatic Religion: An Anthropological Study of Spirit Possession and Shamanism*. Middlesex, UK: Penguin Books, 1971.

Lewy, Hans. *Chaldean Oracles & Theurgy*. Cairo: Institut Français d'Archéologie Orientale, 1956.

Libanius. *Libanii Opera, Vol. 1, Fasc. 1: Orationes I–V*. Edited by Richardus Foerster. Lipsiae: Teubner, 1963.

———. *Libanius' Autobiography (Oration I): Greek Text Edited with Introduction, Translation, and Notes*. Edited by A. F. Norman. London: University of Hull Publications, 1965.

LiDonnici, Lynn. "Beans, Fleawort, and the Blood of a Hamadryas Baboon: Recipe Ingredients in Greco-Roman Magical Materials." In *Magic and Ritual in the Ancient World*, edited by Paul Mirecki and Marvin Meyer, 359–77. Leiden: Brill, 2002.

———. "Burning for It: Erotic Spells for Fever and Compulsion in the Ancient Mediterranean World." *Greek, Roman and Byzantine Studies* 39 (1998): 63–98.

Lieberman, Saul. *Order Mo'ed*. Vol. 3 of *Tosefta Ki-Fshutah: A Comprehensive Commentary on the Tosefta*. New York: Jewish Theological Seminary of America, 1962.

———. "On Sins and Their Punishments." In *Texts and Studies*, 29–56. New York: Ktav, 1974.

———. ed. *The Tosefta: The Order of Mo'ed*. New York: Jewish Theological Seminary of America, 1962.

Liebs, Detlef. "Strafprozesse wegen Zauberei. Magie und politisches Kalkül in der römischen Geschichte." In *Grosse Prozesse der Römischen Antike*, edited by Ulrich Manthe and Jürgen von Ungern-Sternberg, 146–58. Munich: Beck, 1997.

Lincoln, Bruce. *Authority: Construction and Corrosion*. Chicago: University of Chicago Press, 1994.

———. *Discourse and the Construction of Society: Comparative Studies of Myth, Ritual, and Classification*. New York/Oxford: Oxford University Press, 1989.

Lindsay, Jack, trans. *Apuleius: The Golden Ass*. Bloomington, IN: Indiana University Press, 1960.

Lipsius, R. A., and M. Bonnet, eds. *Acta Apostolorum Apocrypha*. 2 vols. Leipzig: Hermann Mendelssohn, 1898.

Lloyd, G. E. R. *Magic, Reason, and Experience: Studies in the Origin and Development of Greek Science*. Cambridge: Cambridge University Press, 1979.

Loader, W. R. G. *Enoch, Levi and Jubilees on Sexuality*. Grand Rapids, MI: Eerdmans, 2007.

Loraux, Nicole. *Les enfants d'Athéna*. Paris: Éditions la Découverte, 1984.

———. *The Experiences of Tiresias: The Feminine and the Greek Man*. Translated by Paula Wissing. Princeton, NJ: Princeton University Press, 1995.

———. "Herakles: The Super-Male and the Feminine." In *Before Sexuality*, edited by David M. Halperin, John J. Winkler, and Froma I. Zeitlin, 21–52. Princeton, NJ: Princeton University Press, 1990.

———. *The Invention of Athens: The Funeral Oration in the Classical City*. Translated by Alan Sheridan. Cambridge, MA: Harvard University Press, 1986.

Lovén, Lena Larsson. "LANAM FECIT: Woolworking and Female Virtue." In *Aspects of Women in Antiquity*, edited by Lena Larsson Lovén and Agneta Strömberg, 85–95. Jonsered, Sweden: Paul Aströms Förlag, 1998.

Löw, Immanuel. *Flora der Juden*. Vol. 1. Hildesheim: Olms, 1967.

Lucan. *Civil War*. Translated by J.D. Duff. Loeb Classical Library. Cambridge, MA: Harvard University Press, 1977.

Lucian. *Lucian*. Translated by A. M. Harmon, K. Kilburn, and M. D. MacLeod. 8 vols. Loeb Classical Library. Cambridge, MA: Harvard University Press, 1959.

Luck, Georg. *Arcana Mundi: Magic and the Occult in the Greek and Roman Worlds. A Collection of Texts*. 2d ed. Baltimore: The Johns Hopkins University Press, 2006.

———. "Witches and Sorcerers in Classical Literature." In *Witchcraft and Magic in Europe: Ancient Greece and Rome*, edited by Bengt Ankarloo and Stuart Clark, 93–158. Philadelphia: University of Pennsylvania Press, 1999.

Luijendijk, AnneMarie. *"Greetings in the Lord:" Early Christians and the Oxyrhynchus Papyri*. Harvard Theological Studies 60. Cambridge, MA: Harvard University Press, 2008.

MacCormack, Carol, and Marilyn Strathern, eds. *Nature, Culture and Gender*. Cambridge: Cambridge University Press, 1980.

MacDonald, Dennis. "Virgins, Widows, and Paul in Second Century Asia Minor." *Society of Biblical Literature Seminar Papers* 16 (1979): 169–72.

MacFarlane, Alan. *Witchcraft in Tudor and Stuart England*. London: Routledge & Kegan Paul, 1970. [Republished: New York: Harper & Row, 1970.]

MacMullen, Ramsay. *Christianizing the Roman Empire* (AD 100–400). New Haven, CT: Yale University Press, 1984.

———. *Enemies of the Roman Order: Treason, Unrest, and Alienation in the Empire*. Cambridge, MA: Harvard University Press, 1966. [Also published: London: Routledge, 1966.]

McAfee, Noëlle. *Julia Kristeva*. Routledge Critical Thinkers. New York: Routledge, 2004.

McLachlan, Hugh, and J. K. Swales. "Witchcraft and the Status of Women: A Comment." In *Witchcraft, Women, and Society*, edited with introduction by Brian P. Levack. Vol. 10 of *Articles on Witchcraft, Magic, and Demonology*. New York: Garland, 1992.

Madden, Margaret E., and Ronnie Janoff-Bulman. "Blame, Control, and Marital Satisfaction: Wives' Attributions for Conflict in Marriage." *Journal of Marriage and the Family* 43 (1981): 663–74.

Maher, Michael, ed. and trans. *Targum Pseudo-Jonathan: Genesis*. Aramaic Bible 1B. Edinburgh: T. & T. Clark, 1992.

Mair, Lucy. *Witchcraft*. London: World University Library, 1969.

Majercik, Ruth. *The Chaldaean Oracles*. Studies in Greek and Roman Religion 5. Leiden: Brill, 1989.

Malinowski, Bronislaw. "Magic, Science and Religion." In *Magic, Science and Religion and Other Essays*, by Bronislaw Malinowski, 17–92. New York: Beacon, 1948. Reprint, Prospect Heights, IL: Waveland Press, 1992.

Manni Piraino, Maria Teresa. *Iscrizioni Greche Lapidare del Museo di Palermo*. Palermo: Flaccovio, 1973.

Manning, C. E. "Canidia in the Epodes of Horace." *Mnemosyne* 23 (1970): 393–401.

Marek, Christian. "Der höchste, beste, grösste, allmächtige Gott. Inschriften aus Nordkleinasien." *Epigraphica Anatolica* 32 (2000):129–46.

Marinus. *Life of Proclus*. In *Neoplatonic Saints: The Lives of Plotinus and Proclus by Their Students*, translated by Mark Edwards, 28–31. Liverpool: Liverpool University Press, 2000.

Marshall, Anthony J. "Ladies in Waiting: The Role of Women in Tacitus' Histories." *Ancient Society* 15–17 (1984–1986): 167–84.

———. "Roman Women and the Provinces." *Ancient Society* 6 (1975): 109–27.

———. "Women on Trial Before the Roman Senate." *Echos du Monde Classique*, n. s. 34 (1990): 333–66.

Martin, Lauren. "The Devil and the Domestic: Witchcraft, Quarrels and Women's Work in Scotland." *The Scottish Witch-Hunt in Context*, ed. Julian Goodare. Manchester and New York: Manchester University Press, 2002.

Martin, Ronald H., and Anthony J. Woodman. *Tacitus Annals Book IV*. New York: Cambridge University Press, 1989.

Martinez, Ronald L., and Robert M. Durling. Introduction and notes to *Inferno*, by Dante Alighieri. Vol. 1 of *The Divine Comedy of Dante Alighieri*. Translated by Robert M. Durling. New York: Oxford University Press, 1996.

Martroye, F. "La repression de la magie et le culte des gentiles au IVe siècle." *Revue historique de droit français et étranger*, 4th ser. 9 (1930): 669–701.

Marwick, Max G. *Sorcery in its Social Setting. A Study of Northern Rhodesian Cevia.* Manchester: Manchester University Press, 1965.

———. "Witchcraft as a Social Stress-Gauge." *Australian Journal of Science* 26 (1964): 263–68.

———, ed. *Witchcraft and Sorcery: Selected Readings*. Magnolia, MA: Peter Smith, 1971.

Mason, H. J. "Fabula Graecanica: Apuleius and His Greek Sources." In *Oxford Readings in the Roman Novel*, edited by S. J. Harrison, 217–36. Oxford: Oxford University Press, 1999.

Massonneau, E. *La magie dans l'antiquité romaine*. Paris: Libraire du Recueil Sirey, 1934.

Matalene, Carolyn. "Women as Witches." In *Witchcraft, Women, and Society*, edited with introduction by Brian P. Levack, 51–66. Vol. 10 of *Articles on Witchcraft, Magic, and Demonology*. New York: Garland, 1992.

Matthews, John. "Ammianus on Roman Law and Lawyers." In *Cognitio Gestorum: The Historiographic Art of Ammianus Marcellinus*, edited by J. den Boeft, D. den Hengst and H. C. Teitler, 47–57. Amsterdam: Royal Netherlands Academy of Arts and Sciences, 1992.

———. "Religion and Philosophy." In *The Roman Empire of Ammianus*, edited by John Matthews, 425–51. Baltimore, MD: Johns Hopkins University Press, 1989.

———. "Valentinian and Valens: Sex, Magic and Treason." In *The Roman Empire of Ammianus*, edited by John Matthews, 204–31. Baltimore, MD: Johns Hopkins University Press, 1989.

Mauss, Marcel. *A General Theory of Magic*. Translated by Robert Brain. London: Routledge & Kegan Paul, 1972.

McClure, Laura K. Introduction to *Prostitutes and Courtesans in the Ancient World.* Edited by Christopher A. Faraone and Laura K. McClure. Madison: University of Wisconsin Press, 2006.

McDonough, C. M. "Carna, Proca and the Strix on the Kalends of June." *Transactions of the American Philological Association* 127 (1997): 315–44.

McDougall, J. I. "Tacitus and the Portrayal of the Elder Agrippina." *Echos du Monde Classique* 30 (1981): 104–8.

McGinn, Thomas A. J. *The Economy of Prostitution in the Roman World: A Study of Social History and the Brothel.* Ann Arbor: University of Michigan Press, 2004.

McKenzie, John. *Second Isaiah*. Anchor Bible 20. Garden City, NY: Doubleday, 1968.

Meiggs, Russell, and David Lewis. *A Selection of Greek Historical Inscriptions to the End of the Fifth Century B.C.* Oxford: Clarendon, 1989.

Mellor, Roland. *Tacitus*. London: Routledge, 1993.

Merkelbach, Reinhold, and Johannes Stauber. "Die Orakel des Apollon von Klaros," *Epigraphica Anatolica* 27 (1996): 1–53. Reprinted in Reinhold Merkelbach. *Philologica. Ausgewählte Kleine Schriften*, by Reinhold Merkelbach, 155–218. Stuttgart: Teubner, 1997.

———, eds. *Steinepigramme aus dem griechischen Osten*. 5 vols. Stuttgart: Teubner and München: Saur, 1998–2004.

Merlan, Philip. "Plotinus and Magic." *Isis* 44 (1953): 341–48.

Meuli, Karl. *Gesammelte Schriften*. Edited by Thomas Gelzer. Basel: Schwabe, 1975.

Meyer, Marvin W., and Richard Smith, eds. *Ancient Christian Magic: Coptic Texts of Ritual Power*. San Francisco: HarperSanFrancisco, 1994.

Meyer, Marvin W., and Richard Smith, eds. *Ancient Christian Magic: Coptic Texts of Ritual Power*. Princeton, NJ: Princeton University Press, 1994.

Milik, Jozef T., ed. *The Books of Enoch: Aramaic Fragments of Qumran Cave 4*. In collaboration with Matthew Black. Oxford: Clarendon, 1976.

Miller, Patricia Cox. "In Praise of Nonsense." In *Classical Mediterranean Spirituality*, edited by A. H. Armstrong, 481–505. New York: Crossroad, 1986.

Miller, Sarah. "Evil and Fairy Tales: The Witch as Symbol of Evil in Fairy Tales." PhD diss., California Institute of Integral Studies, 1984.

Milnor, Kristina. *Gender, Domesticity, and the Age of Augustus: Inventing Private Life*. Oxford: Oxford University Press, 2005.

Mirecki, Paul, and Marvin Meyer, eds. *Ancient Magic and Ritual Power*. Leiden: Brill, 2001.

———, eds. *Magic and Ritual in the Ancient World*. Vol. 141 of *Religions in the Greco-Roman World*. Leiden: Brill, 2002.

Mitchell, Stephen. *The Ankara District: The Inscriptions of North Galatia*. Vol. 2 of *Regional Epigraphic Catalogues of Asia Minor*. Oxford: B.A.R., 1982.

Mitteilungen aus der Würzburger Papyrussammlung. Edited by U. Wilcken. Berlin: Verlag der Wissenschaften, 1934.

Momigliano, Arnaldo. "The Life of St. Macrina by Gregory of Nyssa." In *The Craft of the Ancient Historian: Essays in Honor of Chester G. Starr*, edited by J. W. Eadie, 443–58. Lanham, MD: University Press of America, 1985.

Mommsen, Theodor, and Paul Krueger, eds. *The Digest of Justinian*. Translated by Alan Watson. Philadelphia: University of Pennsylvania Press, 1985.

Monumenta Asiae Minoris Antiqua. Manchester and London, 1928–1993.

Morales, H. *Vision and Narrative in Achilles Tatius' Leucippe and Clitophon*. Cambridge: Cambridge University Press, 2004.

Morant, Marie-José. "Mains levés, mains supines, à propos d'une base funéraire de Kadyanda (Lycie)." *Ktema* 24 (1999): 289–94.

Morony, Michael G. "Magic and Society in Late Sasanian Iraq." In *Prayer, Magic, and the Stars in the Ancient and Late Antique World*, edited by Scott Noegel, Joel Thomas Walker, and Brannon M. Wheeler. University Park, PA: Pennsylvania State University Press, 2003.

———. "Michael the Syrian as a Source for Economic History." *Hugoye: Journal of Syriac Studies* 3 (2000). Cited August 8, 2010. http://syrcom.cua.edu/Hugoye/Vol3No2/HV3N2Morony.html.

Müller-Kessler, Christa. "A Unique Talmudic Aramaic Incantation Bowl." *Journal of the American Oriental Society* 120 (2000): 159–65.

Müller-Kessler, Christa. *Die Zauberschalentexte in der Hilprecht-Sammlung, Jena, und weitere Nipur-Texte anderer Sammlungen*. Wiesbaden: Harrassowitz Verlag, 2005.

Mulvey, L. "Visual Pleasure and Narrative Cinema," *Screen* 16.3 (1975) 6–18.

Myers, K. Sara. "The Poet and the Procuress: The Lena in Latin Love Elegy." *Journal of Roman Studies* 86 (1996): 1–21.

Myscofski, Carole A. "The Magic of Brazil: Practice and Prohibition in the Early Colonial Period, 1590–1620." *History of Religions* 40, no. 2 (2000): 153–76.

Nabers, Ned. "Lead Tabellae from Morgantina." *American Journal of Archaeology* 70 (1966): 67–68.

———. "Ten Lead Tabellae from Morgantina." *American Journal of Archaeology* 83 (1979): 463–64.

Naether, F., and M. Depauw. *TM Magic*. Cited March 11, 2009. http://www.trismegistos.org/magic/index.php.

Naveh, Joseph, and Shaul Shaked. *Magic Spells and Formulae: Aramaic Incantations of Late Antiquity*. Jerusalem: Magnes, 1993.

Neubauer, Hans-Joachim. *The Rumour: A Cultural History*. Translated by Christian Braun. New York: Free Association Press, 1999.

Neugebauer, Otto, and Henry B. Van Hoesen. *Greek Horoscopes*. Philadelphia: The American Philosophical Society, 1959.

Neusner, Jacob. *The Rabbinic Traditions about the Pharisees before 70*. 3 vols. Leiden: Brill, 1971.

Neusner, Jacob, Ernest S. Frerichs, and Paul V. M.Flesher, eds. *Religion, Science, and Magic: In Concert and in Conflict*. Oxford: Oxford University Press, 1989.

Newall, Venetia, ed. *The Witch Figure: Folklore Essays by a Group of Scholars in England Honoring the 75th Birthday of Katharine M. Briggs*. London: Routledge, 1973.

Newlands, Carole E. "The Metamorphosis of Ovid's Medea." In *Medea: Essays on Medea in Myth, Literature, Philosophy, and Art*, edited by James J. Clauss and Sarah Iles Johnston, 178--208. Princeton, NJ: Princeton University Press, 1997.

Newsom, Carol. "The Development of 1 Enoch 6–19: Cosmology and Judgement." *Catholic Biblical Quarterly* 42 (1980): 310–29.

The Nicene and Post-Nicene Fathers, Series 2. Edited by Philip Schaff and Henry Wace. 14 vols. 1890–1900. Reprint, Peabody, MA: Hendrickson, 1994.

Nickelsburg, George W. E. "Apocalyptic and Myth in 1 Enoch 6–11." *Journal of Biblical Literature* 96 (1977): 383–405.

Nickelsburg, G. W. E. *1 Enoch 1: A Commentary on the Book of 1 Enoch, Chapters 1–36; 81–108*. Minneapolis: Fortress, 2001.

———. "Two Enochic Manuscripts: Unstudied Evidence for Egyptian Christianity." In *Of Scribes and Scrolls: Studies on the Hebrew Bible, Intertestamental Judaism, and Christian Origins Presented to John Strugnell on the Occasion of his Sixtieth Birthday*, edited by H. Attridge, J. Collins, and T. Tobin, 251–60. Lanham, MD: University Press of America, 1990.

Nilsson, Martin P. *Geschichte der griechischen Religion*. 2 vols. 3d ed. Munich: Beck, 1967.

Nixon, L. "The Cults of Demeter and Kore." In *Women in Antiquity: New Assessments*, edited by R. Hawley and B. Levick, 75–96. London: Routledge, 1995.

Nollé, Johannes. *Side im Altertum*. Inschriften griechischer Städte aus Kleinasien 44. Bonn: Habelt, 2001.

Norton, Mary Beth. *In the Devil's Snare: The Salem Witchcraft Crisis of 1692*. New York: Knopf, 2002.

Ogden, Daniel. "Binding Spells: Curse Tablets and Voodoo Dolls in the Greek and Roman Worlds." In *Witchcraft and Magic in Europe: Ancient Greece and Rome*, edited by Bengt Ankarloo and Stuart Clark, 1–90. Philadelphia: University of Pennsylvania Press, 1999.

———. *Magic, Witchcraft, and Ghosts in the Greek and Roman Worlds*. Oxford: Oxford University Press, 2002.

Oliensis, Ellen. "Canidia, Canicula, and the Decorum of Horace's *Epodes*." *Arethusa* 24, no. 1 (1991): 107–35.

Oliver, Kelly. *Reading Kristeva: Unraveling the Double-Bind*. Bloomington: Indiana University Press, 1993.

Olson, D. *Enoch: A New Translation*. North Richland Hills, TX: BIBAL, 2004.

O'Neil, Mary. "Magical Healing, Love Magic and the Inquisition in Late Sixteenth-Century Modena." In *Inquisition and Society in Early Modern Europe*, edited by Stephen Haliczer, 88–114. Totowa, NJ: Barnes & Noble, 1987.

Orlandi, Tito. "A Catechesis Against Apocryphal Texts by Shenoute and the Gnostic Texts of Nag Hammadi." *Harvard Theological Review* 75 (1982): 85–95.

———, ed. *Shenute: Contra Origenistas*. Corpus dei manoscritti copti letterari. Rome: C. I. M., 1985.

Ortega, María Helena Sánchez. "Sorcery and Eroticism in Love Magic." In *Cultural Encounters: The Impact of the Inquisition in Spain and the New World*, edited by Mary Elizabeth Perry and Anne J. Cruz, 58–92. Berkeley: University of California Press, 1991.

Ortner, Sherry B. "Is Female to Male as Nature Is to Culture?" In *Women, Culture, and Society*, edited by Michelle Zimbalist Rosaldo and Louise Lamphere, 67–87. Stanford, CA: Stanford University Press, 1974. Reprint, in *Feminism, the Public and the Private*, edited by Joan B. Landes, 21–44. Oxford: Oxford University Press, 1998.

———. *Making Gender: The Politics and Erotics of Culture*. Boston: Beacon, 1996.

Ovid. *Metamorphoses*. Translated by Frank Justus Miller and G. P. Gould. 3d ed. Vol. 1. Loeb Classical Library. Cambridge, MA: Harvard University Press, 1984.

Pack, Roger. "A Romantic Narrative in Eunapius." *Transactions and Proceedings of the American Philological Association* 83 (1952): 198–204.

Padel, Ruth. "Women: Model for Possession by Greek Daemons." In *Images of Women in Antiquity*, edited by Averil Cameron and Amélie Kuhrt, 3–19. Detroit: Wayne State University Press, 1983.

Pagán, Victoria. *Conspiracy Narratives in Roman History*. Austin: University of Texas Press, 2004.

Pankrust, R. "Historical reflections on the Traditional Ethiopian Pharmacopoeia." *Journal of Ethiopian Pharmaceutical Association* 2 (1976): 29–33.

Papaconstantinou, Arietta. *Le culte des saints en Égypte des Byzantins aux Abbassides. L'apport des inscriptions et des papyrus grecs et coptes*. Le monde byzantin. Paris: CNRS, 2001.

———. "La liturgie stationnale à Oxyrhynchos dans la première moitié du 6e siècle. Réédition et commentaire du POxy XI 1357." *Revue des études byzantines* 54 (1996): 135–59.

Parker, David C. *An Introduction to the New Testament Manuscripts and Their Texts*. Cambridge: Cambridge University Press, 2008.

Parker, Holt. "The Teratogenic Grid." In *Roman Sexualities*, edited by Judith P. Hallett and Marilyn B. Skinner, 47–65. Princeton, NJ: Princeton University Press, 1997.

———. "Why Were The Vestals Virgins?" *American Journal of Philology* 125 (2004): 563–601.

Patterson, Cynthia. "The Case Against Neaira and the Public Ideology of the Athenian Family." In *Athenian Identity and Civic Ideology*, edited by Alan Boegehold and Adele Scafuro, 199–216. Baltimore and London: Johns Hopkins University Press, 1994.

Patout Burns, J. *Cyprian the Bishop*. London: Routledge, 2002.

———. "On Rebaptism: Social Organization in the Third Century Church." *Journal of Early Christian Studies* 1 (1993): 367–403.

Patrologia Graeca. Edited by J.-P. Migne. 162 vols. Paris, 1857–1886.

Peek, Werner. *Grab-Epigramme*. Vol. 1 of *Griechische Vers-Inschriften*. Berlin: Akademie-Verlag, 1955.

Pelling, Christopher. "Tacitus and Germanicus." In *Tacitus and the Tacitean Tradition*, edited by T. J. Luce and A. J. Woodman, 59–85. Princeton, NJ: Princeton University Press, 1993.

Penella, Robert J. *Greek Philosophers and Sophists of the Fourth Century: A Study in Eunapius of Sardis*. Leeds: F. Cairns, 1990.

Percival, Henry R., ed. and trans. *The Seven Ecumenical Councils*. Vol. 14 of *The Nicene and Post-Nicene Fathers*, Series 2. Edited by Philip Schaff and Henry Wace. 14 vols. 1890–1900. Reprint, Peabody, MA: Hendrickson, 1994.

Peters, E. *The Magician, the Witch, and the Law*. Philadelphia: University of Pennsylvania Press, 1978.

Petzl, Georg. "Die Beichtinschriften Westkleinasiens." *Epigraphica Anatolica* 22 (1994): xvii–xviii.

Pfann, S. J. et al., eds. *Qumran cave 4, XXVI, Cryptic Texts and Miscellanea*. Part 1. DJD 36. Oxford: Clarendon, 2000.

Pfuhl, Ernst, and Hans Möbius. *Die ostgriechischen Grabreliefs*. Mainz: Von Zabern, 1979.

Phillips, Charles R. "Nullum Crimen Sine Lege: Socioreligious Sanctions on Magic." In *Magika Hiera: Ancient Greek Magic and Religion*, edited by Christopher A. Faraone and Dirk Obbink, 260–76. New York: Oxford University Press, 1991.

———. "Seek and Go Hide: Literary Source Problems and Graeco-Roman Magic." *Helios* 21, no. 2 (1994): 107–14.

———. "The Sociology of Religious Knowledge in the Roman Empire to AD 284." *Aufstieg und Niedergang der römischen Welt: Geschichte und Kultur Roms im Spiegel der neueren Forschung* 16.3:2677–773. Part 2, *Principat*, 16.3. Edited by H. Temporini and W. Haase. Berlin: Walter de Gruyter, 1986.

Phillips, Oliver. "The Witches' Thessaly." In *Magic and Ritual in the Ancient World*, edited by Paul Mirecki and Marvin Meyer. Vol. 141 of *Religions in the Greco-Roman World*, 378–85. Leiden: Brill, 2002.

Philo. *Supplement I: Questions and Answers on Genesis*. Translated by Ralph Marcus. Loeb Classical Library. Cambridge, MA: Harvard University Press, 1953.

Piovanelli, Pierluigi. "Les origins de l'Apocalypse de Paul reconsidérées." *Apocrypha* 4 (1993): 25–64.

Pollard, Elizabeth. "Magic Accusations against Women in the Greco-Roman World from the First through the Fifth Centuries CE." PhD diss., University of Pennsylvania, 2001.

Pomeroy, Sarah B. *Goddesses, Whores, Wives, and Slaves: Women in Classical Antiquity*. New York: Schocken Books, 1975.

Porphyry. *Letter to Marcella*. Translated by Kathleen Wicker O'Brian. Chicago: Scholar's Press, 1987.

———. "On the Life of Plotinus and the Order of His Books." In *Porphyry on Plotinus. Ennead 1*. Vol. 1 of *Plotinus*, edited by A. H. Armstrong, 1–90. Loeb Classical Library. Cambridge, MA: Harvard University Press, 1966.. "Political Theory in the Senatus Consultum de Cn. Pisone Patre." *American Journal of Philology* 120, no. 1 (1999): 65–88.

———. "Senatus Consultum de Cn. Pisone." *Journal of Roman Archaeology* 11 (1998): 437–57.

———, ed. "The Senatus Consultum de Cn. Pisone Patre." Translated by Cynthia Damon. *American Journal of Philology* 120, no. 1 (1999): 13–42.

Pouilloux, Jean, Paul Roesch, and Jean Marcillet-Jaubert. *Corpus épigraphique*. Salamine de Chypres 13. Paris: Boccard, 1987.

Pourrat, Pierre. *Theology of the Sacraments*. St. Louis, MO: B. Herder, 1910.

Powell, Douglas. "Tertullianists and Cataphrygians." *Vigiliae Christianae* 29, no. 1 (1975): 33–54.

Powis Smith, J. M., William Hayes Ward, and Julius August Bewer. *A Critical and Exegetical Commentary on Micah, Zephaniah, Nahum, Habakkuk, Obadiah and Joel*. International Critical Commentary. 1911. Reprint, Edinburgh: T. & T. Clark, 1985.

Preisendanz, Karl, ed. *Papyri graecae magicae. Die griechischen Zauberpapyri.* 2nd ed. Edited by Albert Henrichs. Stuttgart: Teubner, 1973–1974. [Republished: München: Saur, 2001].

Preisigke, Friedrich. *Namenbuch, enthaltend alle griechischen, lateinischen, ägyptischen, hebräischen . . . Menschennamen.* Heidelberg: Selbstverlag des Herausgebers, 1922.

Preisigke, Friedrich et al., eds. *Sammelbuch griechischer Urkunden aus Aegypten* (SB), vol. 1. Berlin: 1915.

Proclus. *Commentary on Plato's Parmenides.* Edited and translated by Glen Morrow and John M. Dillon. Princeton, NJ: Princeton University Press, 1997.

Prusak, B. P. "Woman: Seductive Siren and Source of Sin? Pseudepigraphal Myth and Christian Origins." In *Religion and Sexism: Images of Woman in the Jewish and Christian Traditions,* edited by R. Radford Ruether, 89–116. New York, 1974.

Przychozki, Gustave. "De commentarii cuiusdam magici vestigia." *Byzantinische Zeitschrift* 22 (1913): 65–71.

Purkiss, Diane. *The Witch in History: Early Modern and Twentieth-Century Representations.* New York: Routledge, 1996.

Rakoczy, Thomas. *Böser Blick. Macht des Auges und Neid der Götter. Eine Untersuchung zur Kraft des bösen Blicks in der griechischen Literatur.* Classica Monacensia 13. Tübingen: Gunter Narr Verlag, 1996.

Ramsay, William R. *The Cities and Bishoprics of Phrygia.* Oxford: Clarendon, 1895.

Rapp, Claudia. "Holy Texts, Holy Men, and Holy Scribes. Aspects of Scriptural Holiness in Late Antiquity." In *The Early Christian Book,* edited by William E. Klingshirn and Linda Safran, 194–222. Washington, DC: Catholic University of America Press, 2007.

Rapsaet-Charlier, M-Th. "Epouses et familles de magistrats dans les provinces romaines aux deux premiers siècles de l'Empire." *Historia* 31 (1982): 56–69.

Reed, Annette Yoshiko. "Beyond Revealed Wisdom and Apocalyptic Epistemology: Early Christian Transformations of Enochic Traditions about Knowledge." In *Early Christian Literature and Intertextuality,* edited by C. A. Evans and H. D. Zacharias, 138–64. London: T&T Clark, 2009.

———. "Enoch in Armenian Apocrypha." In *The Armenian Apocalyptic Tradition: A Comparative Perspective,* edited by K. Bardakjian and S. La Porta, 149–87. Studia in Veteris Testamenti Pseudepigrapha 25. Leiden: Brill, 2014.

———. *Fallen Angels and the History of Judaism and Christianity.* Cambridge: Cambridge University Press, 2005.

———. "From Asael and Šemihazah to Uzzah, Azzah, and Azael: 3 Enoch 5 (§§7–8) and the Jewish Reception-History of 1 Enoch." *Jewish Studies Quarterly* 8 (2001): 1–32.

———. "Heavenly Ascent, Angelic Descent, and the Transmission of Knowledge in 1 Enoch 6–16." In *Heavenly Realms and Earthly Realities in Late Antique Religions,* edited by Ra'anan S. Boustan and Annette Yoshiko Reed, 47–66. Cambridge: Cambridge University Press, 2004.

———. "Reading Augustine and/as Midrash: Genesis 6 in *Genesis Rabbah* and the *City of God*." In *Midrash and Context*, edited by L. Teugels and R. Ulmer, 74–90. Piscataway, NJ: Gorgias, 2007.

———. "The Trickery of the Fallen Angels and the Demonic Mimesis of the Divine: Aetiology and Polemics in the Writings of Justin Martyr." *Journal of Early Christian Studies* 12.2 (2004) 141–71.

Reis, Elizabeth. "Gender and the Meanings of Confessions in Early New England." In *Spellbound: Women and Witchcraft in America*, edited by Elizabeth Reis, 53–74. Wilmington, DE: Scholarly Resources, 1998.

Remus, Harold. "Does Terminology Distinguish Early Christian from Pagan Miracles?" *Journal of Biblical Literature* 101, no. 4 (1982): 531–51.

Retief, François, and Louise Cilliers. "Malaria in Graeco-Roman Times." *Acta Classica* 47 (2004): 127–37.

Rettig, John W., trans. *St. Augustine: Tractates on the Gospel of John 1–10*. Fathers of the Church 78. Washington, DC: Catholic University of America Press, 1988.

Richardson, J. S. "The Senate, the Courts, and the Senatus Consultum de Cn. Pisone Patre." *Classical Quarterly* 47 (1997): 510–18.

Richlin, Amy. "Approaches to the Sources on Adultery at Rome." In *Reflections of Women in Antiquity*, edited by Helene P. Foley, 379–404. New York: Gordon and Breach Science Publishers, 1981.

______. "Carrying Water in a Sieve: Class and the Body in Roman Women's Religion." In *Women and Goddess Traditions*, edited by Karen King, 330–74. Minneapolis: Fortress, 1989.

______. *The Gardens of Priapus: Sexuality and Aggression in Roman Humor*. Rev. ed. Oxford: Oxford University Press, 1992.

______. "Invective Against Women in Roman Satire." *Arethusa* 17 (1984): 67–80.

______. "Zeus and Metis: Foucault, Feminism and the Classics." *Helios* 18, no. 2 (1991): 160–80.

Richter, André. *Virgile, La huitieme Bucolique*. Paris: Société d'édition "Les Belles Lettres," 1967.

Ricl, Marijana. *The Inscriptions of Alexandreia Troas*. Inschriften griechischer Städte Kleinasiens 53. Bonn: Habelt, 1997.

Riedel, W., and Walter E. Crum. *The Canons of Athanasius of Alexandria*. London: Williams and Norgate, 1904. Reprint, Amsterdam: Philo Press, 1973.

Rist, John. "Hypatia." *Phoenix* 19 (1965): 214–25.

Ritner, Robert. "Egyptian Magical Practice under the Roman Empire: The Demotic Spells and their Religion." *Aufstieg und Niedergang der römischen Welt: Geschichte und Kultur Roms im Spiegel der neueren Forschung* 18.5:3333–79. Part 2, *Principat*, 18.5. Edited by H. Temporini and W. Haase. Berlin: Walter de Gruyter, 1995.

———. "The Religious, Social, and Legal Parameters of Traditional Egyptian Magic." In *Ancient Magic and Ritual Power*, edited by Marvin Meyer and Paul Mirecki, 43–60. Leiden: E.J. Brill, 1995.

Rives, James. "Magic in the XII Tables Revisited." *Classical Quarterly* 52 (2002): 270–90.

———. "Magic in Roman Law: the Reconstruction of a Crime." *Classical Antiquity* 22 (2003): 313–39.

Riviere, Joan. "On the Genesis of Psychical Conflict in Earliest Infancy." In *Developments in Psycho-Analysis*, edited by Joan Riviere, with a preface by Ernest Jones. Psychoanalysis Examined and Re-Examined, 37–66. London: Hogarth Press, 1952.

Robert, Louis. *Inscriptions grecques*. Vol. 1 of *Collection Froehner*. Paris: Éditions des Bibliothèques nationales, 1936.

———. *Hellenica*. Vol. 2. Limoges: Bontemps, 1942.

———. "Malédictions funéraires grecques." In *Compte-Rendus de l'Académie des Inscriptions et Belles-Lettres* 1978, 242–89. Reprinted in *Opera Minora Selecta*. Épigraphie et antiquités grecques 5, 697–745. Amsterdam: Hakkert, 1989.

———. *Opera Minora Selecta*. Vol. 7 of *Épigraphie et antiquités grecques*. Amsterdam: Hakkert, 1990.

Robbins, Kevin C. "Magical Emasculation, Popular Anticlericalism, and the Limits of the Reformation in Western France circa 1590." *Journal of Social History* 31, no. 1 (1997): 61–83.

Robeck, Cecil. *Prophecy in Carthage: Perpetua, Tertullian, and Cyprian*. Cleveland, OH: Pilgrim, 1992.

Roesch, Paul. "Une tablette de malédiction de Tébessa." *Bulletin d'archéologie algérienne* 2 (1967–1968): 231–37.

Rogers, Robert S. *Criminal Trials and Criminal Legislation under Tiberius*. Middletown, CT: American Philological Association, 1935.

———. "A Tacitean Pattern in Narrating Treason-Trials." *Transactions of the American Philological Association* 83 (1952): 279–311.

Roper, Lyndal. *Oedipus and the Devil: Witchcraft, Sexuality and Religion in Early Modern Europe*. New York: Routledge, 1994.

Rosenthal, David. *Mishnah Avodah Zarah: Mahadurah Biqortit u-Mavo*. Vol. 1. Jerusalem: Hebrew University, 1980.

Rosen-Zvi, Ishay. "Bilhah the Temptress: The *Testament of Reuben* and the Making of Rabbinic Anthropology." *Jewish Quarterly Review* 96 (2006) 65–94.

———. "Misogyny and its Discontents." *Prooftexts* 25.1–2 (2005) 217–27.

Rotondi, Giovanni. *Leges Publicae Populi Romani*. Milan: Società Editrice Libraria, 1912. Reprint, Hildesheim: Olms, 1966.

Rousselle, Aline. *Porneia: On Desire and the Body in Antiquity*. Translated by Felicia Pheasant. Cambridge, MA: Blackwell, 1988.

Rowlandson, Jane, ed. *Women and Society in Greek and Roman Egypt*. Cambridge: Cambridge University Press, 1998.

Ryberg, Inez Scott. "Tacitus' Art of Innuendo." *Transactions of the American Philological Association* 73 (1942): 383–404.

Saffrey, H.-D. "Neoplatonist Spirituality: II. Iamblichus to Proclus and Damascius." In *Classical Mediterranean Spirituality*, edited by A. H. Armstrong, 250–65. New York: Crossroad, 1989.

Sallares, Robert. *Malaria and Rome: A History of Malaria in Ancient Italy*. Oxford: Oxford University Press, 2002.

Saller, Richard. *Patriarchy, Property and Death in the Roman Family*. Cambridge: Cambridge University Press, 1994.

———. "Symbols of Gender and Status Hierarchies in the Roman Household." In *Women and Slaves in Greco-Roman Culture: Differential Equations*, edited by Sheila Murnaghan and Sandra R. Joshel, 85–91. London: Routledge, 1998.

Santoro L'Hoir, Francesca. "Tacitus and Women's Usurpation of Power." *Classical World* 88, no. 1 (1994): 5–25.

———. *Tragedy, Rhetoric, and the Historiography of Tacitus' Annales*. Ann Arbor: University of Michigan Press, 2006.

Sartre, Maurice. *Les inscriptions grecques et latines de la Syrie*. 13:1. Paris: Librairie Orientaliste Geuthner, 1982.

Satzinger, Helmut, ed. and trans. "The Old Coptic Schmidt Papyrus." *Journal of the American Research Center in Egypt* 12 (1975): 37–50.

———. "Die altkoptischen Texte als Zeugnisse der Beziehungen zwischen Ägyptern und Griechen." In *Graeco-Coptica: Griechen und Kopten im byzantinischen Ägypten*, edited by Peter Nagel, 137–46. Halle: Martin-Luther-Universität, 1984.

Sayar, Mustafa Hamdi. *Perinthos-Herakleia (Marmara Ereğlisi) und Umgebung. Geschichte, Testimonien, griechische und lateinische Inschriften*. Denkschriften der Österreichische Akademie der Wissenschaften. Philosophisch-Historische Klasse. Vol. 269. Vienna: Verlag der Österreichischen Akademie der Wissenschaften, 1998.

Scafuro, Adele C. "Witnessing and False Witnessing: Proving Citizenship and Kin Identity in Fourth-Century Athens." In *Athenian Identity and Civic Ideology*, edited by Alan Boegehold and Adele Scafuro, 156–98. Baltimore and London: Johns Hopkins University Press, 1994.

Scarborough, John. "Pharmacology." In *The Oxford Classical Dictionary*, 3rd ed., edited by Simon Hornblower and Antony Spawforth, 1154–55. New York: Oxford University Press, 1996.

———. "The Pharmacology of Sacred Plants, Herbs, and Roots." In *Magika Hiera: Ancient Greek Magic and Religion*, edited by Christopher A. Faraone and Dirk Obbink, 139–54. New York: Oxford University Press, 1991.

Scarry, Elaine. *The Body in Pain: The Making and Unmaking of the World*. New York: Oxford University Press, 1985.

Schäfer, Peter. *Rivalität zwischen Engeln und Menschen: Untersuchungen zur rabbinischen Engelvorstellung*. Berlin, 1975.

———, ed. *Synopse zur Hekhalot-Literatur*. Tübingen: Mohr/Siebeck, 1981.

Scheid, John. "The Religious Roles of Roman Women." In *A History of Women in the West I: From Ancient Goddesses to Christian Saints*, edited by Pauline Schmitt Pantel, 377–408. Cambridge, MA: Harvard University Press, 1992.

Scheidel, Walter. *Death on the Nile: Disease and the Demography of Roman Egypt*. Leiden: Brill, 2001.

Schlesier, Renate. "Zauber und Neid. Zum Problem des bösen Blicks in der antiken griechischen Tragödie." In *Tradition und Translation. Festschrift für Carsten Colpe*, edited by Christoph Elsas and Hans G. Kippenberg, 96–112. Berlin: Walter de Gruyter, 1994.

Schmidt, Paul Gerhard, ed. *Visio Thurkilli: Relatore, ut Videtur, Radulpho de Coggeshall.* Leipzig: Teubner, 1978.

Schons, Melissa Jane. "Horror and the Characterization of the Witch from Horace to Lucan." PhD diss., University of California at Los Angeles, 1998.

Schultz, Celia. *Women's Religious Activity in the Roman Republic.* Chapel Hill: University of North Carolina Press, 2006.

Sefati, Yitschak, and Jacob Klein. "The Law of the Sorceress (Exodus 22:17[18]) in the Light of Biblical and Mesopotamian Parallels." In *Sefer Moshe: The Moshe Weinfeld Jubilee Volume*, edited by Chaim Cohen, Avi Hurwitz, and Shalom Paul, 171–90. Winona Lake, IN: Eisenbrauns, 2004.

Segal, Alan. "Hellenistic Magic: Some Questions of Definition." In *Studies in Gnosticism and Hellenistic Religions presented to Gilles Quispel on the Occasion of his Sixty-Fifth Birthday*, edited by M. J. Vermaseren, 349–75. Leiden: Brill, 1981.

———. "On the Nature of Magic: Report on a Dialogue between a Historian and a Sociologist." In *The Social World of the First Christians: Essays in Honor of Wayne A. Meeks*, edited by L. Michael White and Larry Yarbrough, 275–92. Minneapolis: Augsburg Fortress, 1995.

Segal, J. B. *Catalogue of the Aramaic and Mandaic Incantation Bowls in the British Museum.* With a contribution by E. C. D. Hunter. London: British Museum Press, 2000.

Seneca. *Tragedies.* Translated by Frank Justus Miller. Vol.1–3. Loeb Classical Library. Cambridge, MA: Harvard University Press, 1987.

Senger, Gerda. *Women and Demons: Cult Healing in Islamic Egypt.* Leiden: Brill, 2003.

Sharpe, James A. "Witches and Persecuting Societies." *Journal of Historical Sociology* 3 (1990): 75–86.

Shatzman, Israel. "Tacitean Rumors." *Latomus* 33, no. 3 (1974): 549–78.

Shaw, Gregory. "Theurgy: Rituals of Unification in the Neoplatonism of Iamblichus." *Traditio* 41 (1985): 1–28.

Sheppard, Anne. "Proclus' Attitude to Theurgy." *Classical Quarterly*, n. s. 31(1982): 212–24.

Shotter, D. C. A. "Tiberius' Part in the Trial of Aemilia Lepida." *Historia* 15 (1966): 312–17.

Sijpesteijn, Pieter J. "Amulet against Fever." *Chronique d'Égypte* 57 (1982): 377–81.

Silverstein, Theodore. "The Vision of St. Paul: New Links and Patterns in the Western Tradition." *Archives d'histoire doctrinale et littéraire du moyen âge* 34 (1959): 199–248.

Silverstein, Theodore, and Anthony Hilhorst, eds. *Apocalypse of Paul: A New Critical Edition of Three Long Latin Versions.* Geneva: Patrick Cramer, 1997.

Skinner, Marilyn B. "*Ego mulier*: The Construction of Male Sexaulity in Catullus." In *Roman Sexualities*, edited by Judith P. Hallett and Marilyn B. Skinner, 129–150. Princeton, NJ: Princeton University Press, 1997.

Smelik, Klaas. "The Witch of Endor, I Samuel 28 in Rabbinic and Christian Exegesis till 800 AD." *Vigiliae christianae* 33, no. 2 (1979): 160–79.

Smith, A. M. *Ptolemy and the Foundations of Ancient Mathematical Optics*. Philadelphia: APS, 1999.

Smith, Jonathan Z. *Drudgery Divine: On the Comparison of Early Christianities and the Religions of Late Antiquity*. Chicago: University of Chicago Press, 1990.

———. "Towards Interpreting Demonic Powers in Hellenistic and Roman Antiquity." *Aufstieg und Niedergang der römischen Welt: Geschichte und Kultur Roms im Spiegel der neueren Forschung* 16.1:425–39. Part 2, *Principat*, 16.1. Edited by H. Temporini and W. Haase. Berlin: Walter de Gruyter, 1978.

Sokoloff, Michael, ed. *The Geniza Fragments of Bereshit Rabba*. Jerusalem: Israel Academy of Sciences and Humanities, 1982.

Solin, Heikki. "Analecta Epigraphica LXVII–LXXVIII." *Arctos* 15 (1981): 101–23.

———. "Analecta Epigraphica CXIII–CXX." *Arctos* 21 (1987): 130–33.

———. "Analecta Epigraphica CXXI–CXXV." *Arctos* 22 (1988): 141–62.

———. *Eine neue Fluchtafel aus Ostia*. Commentationes Humanarum Literarum Societas Scientiarum Fennica 42.3. Helsinki: Helsingfors, 1968.

Soranos D'Éphèse. *Maladies des Femmes, Tomes I–II*. Edited and translated by Paul Burguière, Danielle Gourevitch, and Yves Malinas. Paris: Les Belles Lettres, 1988, 1990.

Sorensen, Eric. *Possession and Exorcism in the New Testament and Early Christianity*. Wissenschaftliche Untersuchungen zum Neuen Testament 157. Tübingen: Mohr/Siebeck, 2002.

Souza, Laura de Mello e. *The Devil and the Land of the Holy Cross: Witchcraft, Slavery, and Popular Religion in Colonial Brazil*. Translated by Diane Grosklaus Whitty. Austin: University of Texas Press, 2003.

Spaeth, Barbette Stanley. *The Roman Goddess Ceres*. Austin: University of Texas Press, 1996.

———. "The Terror That Comes in the Night: The Night Hag and Supernatural Assault in Latin Literature." In *Sub Imagine Somni: Nighttime Phenomena in Greco-Roman Culture*, edited by Emma Scioli and Christine Walde, 231--58. Pisa, Italy: Edizioni ETS, 2010.

Sparks, H. F. D., ed. *Apocryphal Old Testament*. Oxford: Clarendon, 1984.

Staples, Ariadne. *From Good Goddess to Vestal Virgins: Sex and Category in Roman Religion*. London: Routledge, 1998.

Stefanski, Elizabeth, ed. "A Coptic Magical Text," *American Journal of Semitic Languages and Literatures* 56, no. 3 (1939): 305–7.

Stephen, Michele. "Witchcraft, Grief, and the Ambivalences of Emotion." *American Ethnologist* 26 (1999): 711–37.

Stephens, Walter. *Demon Lovers: Witchcraft, Sex, and the Crisis of Belief.* Chicago: University of Chicago Press, 2002.

Stewart, D. E. *The Arrow of Love: Optics, Gender, and Subjectivity in Medieval Love Poetry*. Lewisburg, PA: Bucknell University Press, 2003.

Stewart, Pamela J., and Andrew Strathern, eds. *Witchcraft, Sorcery, Rumors and Gossip*. Cambridge: Cambridge University Press, 2003.

Stone, Michael E. *Armenian Apocrypha Relating to Adam and Eve*. Leiden: Brill, 1996.

——— ed. and trans. *Armenian Apocrypha Relating to the Patriarchs and Prophets*. Jerusalem: Israel Academy of Arts and Sciences, 1982.

———. "Armenian Canon Lists III: The Lists of Mechitar of Ayrivank'." *Harvard Theological Review* 69 (1976): 289–300.

———. *Apocrypha, Pseudepigrapha, and Armenian Studies: Collected Papers*. 2 vols. Leuven, Belgium: Peeters, 2006.

———. "Enoch, Aramaic Levi, and Sectarian Origins." *Journal for the Study of Judaism in the Persian, Hellenistic, and Roman Periods* 19 (1988): 159–70.

———. *Selected Studies in Pseudepigrapha and Apocrypha with Special Reference to the Armenian Tradition*. Leiden: Brill, 1991.

Stone, Michael E., and John Strugnell, eds. *The Books of Elijah Parts 1–2*. Texts and Translations Series 18, Pseudepigrapha Series 8. Missoula, MT: Scholars Press, 1979.

Strack, H. L., and Stemberger, G. *Introduction to the Talmud and Midrash*. Translated by Markus Bockmuehl. Edinburgh: T. & T. Clark, 1991.

Stratton, Kimberly B. "Magic in the Greco-Roman World up to and Including the Republic." In *Cambridge History of Magic and Witchcraft in the West*, edited by David J. Collins. New York: Cambridge University Press, forthcoming.

———. *Naming the Witch: Magic, Ideology, and Stereotype in the Ancient World*. New York: Columbia University Press, 2007.

Stroumsa, Guy. *Another Seed: Studies in Gnostic Mythology*. Leiden: Brill, 1984.

Strubbe, Johan. *ARAI EPITUMBIOI. Imprecations against Desecrators of the Grave in Greek Epitaphs of Asia Minor. A Catalogue*. Inschriften griechischer Städte aus Kleinasien 52. Bonn: Habelt, 1997.

———. *The Inscriptions of Pessinous*. Inschriften griechischer Städte aus Kleinasien 66. Bonn: Habelt, 2005.

Suetonius. *Lives of the Caesars*. Translated by J. C. Rolfe. Vol. 1. Loeb Classical Library. Cambridge, MA: Harvard University Press, 1998.

Suter, David. "Fallen Angel, Fallen Priest: The Problem of Family Purity in 1 Enoch 6–16." *Hebrew Union College Annual* 50 (1979): 115–35.

Swales, J. K., and Hugh McLachlan. "Witchcraft and the Status of Women: A Comment." In *Witchcraft, Women, and Society*. Vol. 10 of *Articles on Witchcraft, Magic, and Demonology*, edited by Brian P. Levack, 40–49. New York: Garland, 1992.

Swenson, R. "Optics, Gender, and the Eighteenth-Century Gaze: Looking at Eliza Haywood's Anti-Pamela." *The Eighteenth-Century: Theory and Interpretation* 51.1–2 (2010): 27–43.

Syme, Ronald. *Augustan Aristocracy*. New York: Oxford University Press, 1986.

———. "Marcus Lepidus, *Capax Imperii*." *Journal of Roman Studies* 45 (1955): 22–33. Reprinted in *Ten Studies in Tacitus*, by Ronald Syme, 30–49. Oxford: Clarendon, 1970.

———. "Princesses and Others in Tacitus." In *Roman Papers*, 1364–75. Oxford: Clarendon Press, 1984.

———. *The Roman Revolution*. London: Oxford University Press, 1939.

———. *Tacitus*. Oxford: Clarendon, 1958.Tacitus. *Annales*. Edited by E. Koestermann. Leipzig: Teubner, 1965.

———. *Histories and Annals*. Translated by J. Jackson. 4 vols. Loeb Classical Library. Cambridge, MA: Harvard University Press, 1931.

Talbert, Richard J. A. *The Senate of Imperial Rome*. Princeton, NJ: Princeton University Press, 1984.

———. "Tacitus and the Senatus Consultum de Cn. Pisone Patre." *American Journal of Philology* 120, no. 1 (1999): 89–97.

Tambiah, Stanley Jeyaraja. "Form and Meaning of Magical Acts: A Point of View." In *Modes of Thought: Essays on Thinking in Western and Non-Western Societies*, edited by R. Horton and Ruth Finnegan, 199–229. London: Faber, 1973.

———. "The Magical Power of Words." *Man* 3 (1986): 171–208.

———. *Magic, Science, and the Scope of Rationality*. Cambridge: Cambridge University Press, 1990.

Tardieu, Michel. *Revue des Études Augustiniennes* 58 (1978).

Tatum, James. "The Tales in Apuleius' Metamorphoses." In *Oxford Readings in the Roman Novel*, edited by S. J. Harrison, 157–94. Oxford: Oxford University Press, 1999.

Tavenner, Eugene. "Canidia and Other Witches." In *Witchcraft in the Ancient World and the Middle Ages*. Vol. 2 of *Articles on Witchcraft, Magic, and Demonology*, edited by Brian P. Levack, 38–39. New York: Garland, 1992.

Theodor, Judah, and Chanoch Albeck, eds. *Midrash Bereshit Rabbah*. 2d ed. 3 vols. Jerusalem: Wahrmann, 1965.

Thomas, Keith. "An Anthropology of Religion and Magic, I." *Journal of Interdisciplinary History* 6 (1975): 91–109.

———. *Religion and the Decline of Magic*. New York: Oxford University Press, 1971.

Thomson, R. W., ed. *Athanasius. Contra gentes and de incarnatione*. Oxford: Clarendon Press, 1971.

Thorndike, Lynn. *A History of Magic and Experimental Science*. 2nd ed. Vol. 1. New York: Macmillan, 1929.

Tischendorf, Constantinus, ed. *Apocalypsis Pauli*. In *Apocalypses Apocryphae*, edited by Constantinus Tischendorf, 34–69. Leipsig: Hermann Mendelssohn, 1866.

Tondriau, Jean L. "Notes ptolémaïques. I: Accusations de magie contre des souverains lagides." *Aegyptus* 28 (1948): 168–77.

Townend, G. B. "The Trial of Aemilia Lepida in AD 20." *Latomus* 21 (1962): 484–93.

Treggiari, Susan. *Roman Marriage*: Iusti Coniuges *from the Time of Cicero to the Time of Ulpian*.. Oxford: Clarendon Press, 1991.

Treu, Ursula, trans. "Christian Sibyllines." In *New Testament Apocrypha*, edited by Edgar Hennecke and Wilhelm Schneemelcher, 2:658–63. English translation edited by R. McL. Wilson. Louisville, KY: Westminster/John Knox Press, 1992.

Trevett, Christine. *Montanism: Gender, Authority and the New Prophecy*. Cambridge: Cambridge University Press, 1996.

———. "Spiritual Authority and the 'Heretical' Woman: Firmilian's Word to the Church at Carthage." In *Portraits of Spiritual Authority: Religious Power in Early Christianity, Byzantium, and the Christian Orient*, edited by Jan Willem Drijvers and John W. Watt, 45–62. Leiden: Brill, 1999.

Trzcionka, Silke. *Magic and the Supernatural in Fourth-Century Syria*. London: Routledge, 2007.

Tupet, Anne-Marie. *La magie dans la poésie latine I: Des origines à la fin du règne d'Auguste*. Paris: Société d'édition "Les Belles Lettres," 1976.

———. "Les pratiques magiques à la mort de Germanicus." In *Mélanges Pierre Wuilleumier*, 345–52. Paris: Gallimard, 1980.

Valler, Shulamit. *Women in Jewish Society in the Talmudic Period* [Hebrew]. Tel Aviv: Ha-Kibuts Ha-Meuhad, 2000.

Van Liefferinge, C. *La théurgie des Oracles chaldaïques à Proclus*. Liège, Belgium: Centre international d'étude de la religion grecque antique, 1999.

VanderKam, James C. "1 Enoch, Enochic Motifs, and Enoch in Early Christian Literature." In *The Jewish Apocalyptic Heritage in Early Christianity*, edited by J. C. Vanderkam and W. A. Adler, 33–101. Assen, Netherlands: VanGorcum & Comp.: 1996.

———. *Enoch and the Growth of an Apocalyptic Tradition*. Washington, DC: Catholic Biblical Association of America, 1984.

Veilleux, Armand, trans. *The Life of Saint Pachomius and His Disciples*. Vol. 1 of *Pachomian Koinonia*. Cistercian Studies Series 45. Kalamazoo, MI: Cistercian Publications Inc., 1980.

Veltri, Giuseppe. "Defining Forbidden Foreign Customs: Some Remarks on the Rabbinic Halakhah of Magic." In *Proceedings of the Eleventh World Congress of Jewish Studies, Div. C, Thought and Literature*, 1:25–32. Jerusalem: World Union of Jewish Studies, 1994.

———. *Magie und Halakha*. Tübingen: Mohr/Siebeck, 1997.

———. "Der Magier im antiken Judentum: von empirisher Wissenschaft zur Theologie." In *Der Magus: seine Ursprünge und seine Geschichte in verschiedenen Kulturen*,edited by Anthony Grafton and Moshe Idel, 147–67. Berlin: Akademie Verlag, 2001.

———. "The 'Other' Physicians: The Amorites of the Rabbis and the Magi of Pliny." *Korot: The Israel Journal of the History of Medicine and Science* 13 (1998–1999): 37–54.

———. "The Rabbis and Pliny the Elder: Jewish and Greco-Roman Attitudes Toward Magic and Empirical Knowledge." *Poetics Today* 19, no. 1 (1998): 63–89.

Vergil. *Eclogues, Georgics, Aeneid*. Translated by H. R. Fairclough. 2 vols. Loeb Classical Library. Cambridge, MA: Harvard University Press, 1916.

Vérilhac, Anne-Marie. *ΡΑΙΔΕΣ ΑΩΡΟΙ: Poésie funéraire*. Athens: Athens Academy Press, 1978.

Versnel, Hendrik S. "Beyond Cursing: The Appeal to Justice in Judicial Prayers." In *Magika Hiera: Ancient Greek Magic and Religion*, edited by Christopher A. Faraone and Dirk Obbink, 60–106. New York: Oxford University Press, 1991.

———. "Destruction, Devotio and Despair in a Situation of Anomy: The Mourning for Germanicus in Triple Perspective." In *Perennitas: Studi in Onore di Angelo Brelich*, 541–618. Rome: Edizioni dell'Ateneo, 1980.

———. "An Essay on Anatomical Curses." In *Ansichten griechischer Rituale: Geburtstags-Symposium für Walter Burkert*, edited by Fritz Graf, 217–67. Stuttgart: Teubner, 1998.

———. "*Kolasai tous hēmas toioutous hēdeōs blepontes*, 'Punish Those Who Rejoice in Our Misery': On Curse Texts and *Schadenfreude*." In *The World of Ancient Magic: Papers from the First International Samson Eitrem Seminar at the Norwegian Institute at Athens, 4–8 May 1997*, edited by David R. Jordan, Hugo Montgomery and Einar Thomassen. Papers from the Norwegian Institute at Athens 4, 125–62. Bergen: Paul Åströms Förlag, 1999.

———. "Religious Mentality in Ancient Prayer." In *Faith, Hope and Worship: Aspects of Religious Mentality in the Ancient World*, 1–64. Leiden: Brill, 1981.

———. "Some Reflections on the Relationship Magic–Religion." *Numen* 38, no. 2 (1991): 177–97.

———. "Writing Mortals and Reading Gods: Appeal to the Gods as a Dual Strategy in Social Control." In *Demokratie, Recht und soziale Kontrolle im klassischen Athen*, edited by David Cohen. Schriften des Historischen Kollegs 49, 68–72. Munich: Oldenbourg, 2002.

Viden, Gunhild. *Women in Roman Literature: Attitudes of Authors under the Early Empire*. Studia Graeca et Latina Gothoburgensia 57. Goteborg, Sweden: Acta Universitatis Gothobugensis, 1993.

Vikan, Gary. "Early Byzantine Pilgrimage *Devotionalia* as Evidence of the Appearance of Pilgrimage Shrines." In *Akten des XII. Internationalen Kongresses für christliche Archäologie: Bonn, 22–28. September, 1991*, edited by Ernst Dassmann and Josef Engemann. Jahrbuch für Antike und Christentum 20, no. 1, 377–88. Münster: Aschendorffsche Verlagsbuchhandlung, 1995.

Voutiras, Emmanuel. *Dionysophontos Gamoi: Marital Life and Magic in Fourth Century Pella*. Amsterdam: Gieben, 1998.

Waelkens, Marc. *Die kleinasiatischen Türsteine. Typologische und epigraphische Untersuchungen der kleinasiatischen Grabreliefs mit Scheintür*. Mainz, Germany: Von Zabern, 1986.

Wahl, Otto, ed. *Apocalypsis Esdrae*. Leiden: Brill, 1977.

Wallace, K. Gilmartin. "Women in Tacitus 1903–86." *Aufstieg und Niedergang der römischen Welt: Geschichte und Kultur Roms im Spiegel der neueren Forschung* 33.5:3556–74. Part 2, *Principat*, 33.5. Edited by H. Temporini and W. Haase. Berlin: Walter de Gruyter, 1991.

Wallis, R. T. *Neoplatonism*. New York: Scribner, 1972.

Walters, Jonathan. "Invading the Roman Body: Manliness and Impenetrability in Roman Thought." In *Roman Sexualities*, edited by Judith P. Hallett and Marilyn B. Skinner, 29–46. Princeton, NJ: Princeton University Press, 1997.

Wandrey, Irina. "Fever and Malaria 'For Real' or as a Magical–Literary Topos." In *Jewish Studies Between the Disciplines (Judaistik zwischen den Disziplinen): Papers in Honor of Peter Schäfer on the Occasion of His 60th Birthday*, edited by Klaus Herrmann, Margarete Schlüter, and Giuseppe Veltri, 257–66. Leiden: Brill, 2003.

Wente, Edward. *Letters from Ancient Egypt*. Atlanta: Scholars Press, 1990.

Wessely, C. "Les plus anciens monuments du christianisme écrits sur papyrus (II)." In Patriologia orientalis 18, 417–20. 1924.

Westermann, Claus. *Isaiah 40–66: A Commentary*. London: SCM, 1969.

Wewers, Gerd, trans. *Hagiga: Festopfer*. Übersetzung des Talmud Yerushalmi II/11. Tübingen: Mohr/Siebeck, 1983.

White, R. J. *The Interpretation of Dreams:* Oneirocritica *by Artemidorus*. Torrance, CA: Original Books, 1990.

Wildfang, Robin Lorsch. *Rome's Vestal Priestesses in the Late Republic and Early Empire*. London: Routledge, 2006.

Wiles, Maurice F. "The Theological Legacy of St. Cyprian." *Journal of Ecclesiastical History* 14 (1963): 139–49.

Wilken, Robert L. *John Chrysostom and the Jews: Rhetoric and Reality in the Late 4th Century*. The Transformation of the Classical Heritage 4. Berkeley: University of California Press, 1983.

Willis, Deborah. *Malevolent Nurture: Witch-Hunting and Maternal Power in Early Modern England*. Ithaca, NY: Cornell University Press, 1995.

Winkler, John J. *The Constraints of Desire: The Anthropology of Sex and Gender in Ancient Greece*. New York: Routledge, 1990.

———. "The Constraints of Desire: Erotic Magical Spells." In *The Constraints of Desire: The Anthropology of Sex and Gender in Ancient Greece*, edited by John J. Winkler, 71–98. New York: Routledge, 1990.

———. "The Constraints of Eros." In *Magika Hiera: Ancient Greek Magic and Religion*, edited by Christopher A. Faraone and Dirk Obbink, 214–43. New York: Oxford University Press, 1991.

Winter, John Garrett. *Life and Letters in the Papyri*. The Jerome Lectures. Ann Arbor: University of Michigan Press, 1933.

Wintermute, O. S. "Jubilees." In *The Old Testament Pseudepigrapha*, edited by James Charlesworth, 2:35–142. Garden City, NY: Doubleday, 1983–1985.

Woodman, Anthony J., and Ronald H. Martin. *The Annals of Tacitus: Book 3, Edited with a Commentary*. Cambridge: Cambridge University Press, 1996.

Wortmann, Dierk. "Neue magische Texte." *Bonner Jahrbücher* 168 (1968): 56–111.

Wright, R. P. "Roman Britain in 1951: I. Sites Explored: II. Inscriptions." *Journal of Roman Studies* 42 (1952): 86–109.

Wypustek, Andrzej. "Magic, Montanism, Perpetua, and the Severan Persecution." *Vigiliae Christianae* 51, no. 3 (1997): 276–97.

Xenophon. *Xenophon: Memorabilia. Oeconomicus. Symposium. Apologia*. Translated by E. C. Marchant. Loeb Classical Library. Cambridge, MA: Harvard University Press, 1923.

Yakobson, Alexander. "The Princess of Inscriptions: Senatus Consultum de Cn. Pisone Patre and the Early Years of Tiberius' Reign." *Scripta Classica Israelica* 17 (1998): 206–24.

Yarnall, Judith. *Transformations of Circe: The History of an Enchantress*. Urbana, IL: University of Illinois Press, 1994.

Yeoman, Louise. "Hunting the Rich Witch in Scotland: High-Status Witchcraft Suspects and Their Persecutors, 1590–1650". *The Scottish Witch-Hunt in Context*, ed. Julian Goodare. Manchester and New York: Manchester University Press, 2002.

Yorke, V. W. "Inscriptions from East Asia Minor." *Journal of Hellenic Studies* 18 (1898): 306–27.

Young, A. "Magic as a 'Quasi-Profession': The Organization of Magic and Magical Healing among Amhara." *Ethnology* 14 (1975): 245–65.

Zeddies, Nicole. *Religio et sacrilegium. Studien zur Inkriminierung von Magie, Häresie und Heidentum (4.–7. Jh.)*. Frankfurt am Main: Peter Lang, 2003.

Ziebarth, Erich. "Der Fluch im griechischen Recht." *Hermes* 30 (1895): 57–70.

Zingerle, Josef. "Heiliges Recht." *Jahreshefte des Österreichischen Archäologischen Institutes in Wien* 32 (1926): 5–72.

Zintzen, C. "Die Wertung von Mystik und Magie in der neuplatonischen Philosophie." *Rheinisches Museum* 108 (1965): 71–100.

Ziv, Abner. *Personality and Sense of Humor*. New York: Springer, 1984.

Citation Index

Subject Index

Printed in the USA
CPSIA information can be obtained
at www.ICGtesting.com
LVHW021352240824
789094LV00002B/114